The Samuel Gompers Papers

THE
Samuel Gompers
PAPERS

VOLUME
12
The Last Years
1922–24

Editors
Peter J. Albert
Grace Palladino

UNIVERSITY OF ILLINOIS PRESS
Urbana, Chicago, and Springfield

Library of Congress Cataloging-in-Publication Data

The Samuel Gompers Papers
   Includes bibliographies and indexes.
   Contents: v. 1. The making of a union leader, 1850–86 — v. 2. The
early years of the American Federation of Labor, 1887–90 — v. 3. Unrest
and depression, 1891–94 — v. 4. A national labor movement takes shape,
1895–98 — v. 5. An expanding movement at the turn of the century,
1898–1902 — v. 6. The American Federation of Labor and the rise of
progressivism, 1902–6 — v. 7. The American Federation of Labor
under siege, 1906–9 — v. 8. Progress and reaction in the age of reform,
1909–13 — v. 9. The American Federation of Labor at the height of
progressivism, 1913–17 — v. 10. The American Federation of Labor and
the Great War, 1917–18 — v. 11. The postwar years, 1918–21 — v. 12. The
last years, 1922–24
   1. Gompers, Samuel, 1850–1924—Archives. 2. Trade-unions—United
States—History—Sources. 3. Labor movement—United States—History—
Sources. I. Gompers, Samuel, 1850–1924.
HD6508.S218   2003
331.88'32'902   84-2469
ISBN-10 0-252-01138-4 (alk. paper : set)
ISBN-13 978-0-252-01138-2 (alk. paper: set)
ISBN-10 0-252-03535-6 (alk. paper: v. 12)
ISBN-13 978-0-252-03535-7 (alk. paper : v. 12)

CONTENTS

INTRODUCTION

Partially blind, diabetic, and heedless of his doctors' advice, Samuel Gompers fully expected to work as hard as he always had. "I am seventy-two years of age," he wrote in January 1922, "and have never even thought of . . . retiring." After all, at this critical moment in AFL history, there was too much work to do. The Federation had lost almost nine hundred thousand members since 1920, President Warren Harding had openly challenged labor's right to strike, and union members were dangerously divided over questions of strategy, politics, and work jurisdiction. Confident that his practical knowledge and wide perspective were too valuable to lose now, the AFL president thought his duty was clear: "I could not stop working if I wanted to."[1]

Few could match Gompers' commitment to trade unionism or his forty-year record of leadership. But whether his long experience was an asset or a liability was a serious question at the time. For as corporations flourished, union shops declined, and nonunion workers dominated the labor market in the 1920s, many wondered whether labor's Grand Old Man had outlived his usefulness. His voluntary principles seemed hopelessly out of date to radicals energized by the Russian Revolution. His aversion to independent politics and an activist state seemed counterproductive to railroad workers inspired by Farmer-Labor party plans for nationalization and economic reform. And his repeated failure to organize the unorganized and generate classwide solidarity seemed downright incompetent to a militant corps of activists who feared he lacked the vision and the political courage necessary to get the job done. In their estimation, Gompers had nothing to offer a rising generation of industrial workers: He was too anti-intellectual to broaden the scope of the movement, too rigid to change with the times, and too determined to maintain control of the AFL, no matter the costs to the working class as a whole.[2]

Hungry for change, many union supporters inside and outside the AFL now looked to William Z. Foster for up-to-date leadership. The embodiment of their vision for change, Foster was a talented organizer whose militant rhetoric and aggressive tactics found widespread support in the labor movement. The forty-one-year-old leader was everything Gompers was not: He embraced Communism and the Red International of Labor Unions, or Profintern (RILU), advocated independent working-class political action, and believed that the AFL would have to function as a strong, centralized organization if it hoped to survive and grow.[3] Whereas Gompers presumed that the great mass of workers would learn the value of solidarity through direct experience, Foster and his supporters favored a more top-down approach: They established the Trade Union Educational League (TUEL) to develop a network of "revolutionary and progressive" unionists, a militant minority that would serve as the "brain and backbone of the organized masses." With amalgamation as its slogan, industrial unionism as its goal, and "boring from within" the established trade unions as its method, the TUEL promised to transform otherwise "timid and muddled" AFL affiliates into "scientifically constructed, class conscious weapons in the revolutionary struggle." "Get off the rocky road of craft unionism," Foster urged his fellow workers, "and enter upon the broad boulevard of departmentalized industrial unionism, the way to social emancipation."[4]

At a time when unemployment and political harassment had ostensibly crippled labor's progress, and the growth of reactionary groups like the Ku Klux Klan promised to make things worse, the TUEL's "Amalgamation or Annihilation" campaign put Gompers' leadership to the test: Who could argue with a plan designed to neutralize jurisdictional battles and unite labor's power once and for all? By March 1922, the Chicago Federation of Labor (FOL) had passed a resolution calling for an AFL conference to merge member unions, and within eighteen months, sixteen international unions, seventeen state federations, and numerous central and local labor bodies had joined the campaign.[5] "The communists have sprung into great prominence in the trade union movement," Foster boasted to the RILU, and the path to the future seemed clear: Amalgamation was "the burning issue of the hour," and Foster the man with a workable plan. "[H]e is a genius in simplifying," his supporters crowed. "He addresses himself to the heart of the problem at hand, and he points the way to success."[6]

But if supporters expected the younger, visionary leader to restructure the Federation, they were soon disappointed. As Gompers had learned over time, there was nothing simple about amalgamation, and anyone familiar with the building trades' ongoing fight to unite their forces knew that amalgamation could not be imposed from above. They also knew that it was not Gompers or the international presidents ("petty despots" in Foster's view) who stood in the way. In the past, rank-and-file workers had vetoed amalgamation plans for a very basic reason: As one labor official put it, they refused to be "traded off to another organization like so much personal property on the say-so of a few men," a situation Gompers had witnessed many times.[7] "We could say, 'You must amalgamate,'" he told a convention of cap makers in 1923. "And suppose the organizations would come back to us and say, 'We will do as we darn please.' What are you going to do about it? Get the militia, get the police, and make them amalgamate?" If history was any guide, Foster's plan for unity promised far more than it could deliver. "The Knights of Labor had the most complete idea of amalgamation that it was ever attempted to put into practice," Gompers noted. "It also had the word 'must' and compulsion and dictatorship as the principle of administration," concepts, he believed, that were as counterproductive in the 1920s as they had been in the 1880s. "People are not made of clay that can be molded into any shape by those who wish to change them," he maintained. "It is human to resent compulsion."[8]

Ultimately, it was this view of human nature, tempered by his long experience in the labor movement, not amalgamation, industrial unionism, or even his "insane hatred for everything radical," as Foster put it, that separated Gompers from his critics: The AFL president genuinely believed that their top-down methods would not work. Where Foster and his followers envisioned an energetic, centralized leadership reshaping the labor movement along revolutionary lines, Gompers saw an acrimonious future of conflict, dual unionism, and disintegration. "To whom are they making this [amalgamation] appeal," Gompers wanted to know. "To the unorganized? Not by any means, but to the organized workers, thus to bring about if possible rivalry, division, antagonism and dis-organization."[9]

Likewise it was Foster's commitment to the Communist party, not his desire for change, or even his challenge to Gompers' leadership, that alarmed the AFL president. Gompers appreciated Foster's passion and abilities—after all, he had trusted him during the war to oversee the all-important steel and packinghouse workers' campaigns. But once Foster allied the TUEL with the Communist movement, the very antithesis of liberty as far as Gompers was concerned, he lost all credibility as a labor leader in Gompers' eyes. "Isn't it a pity," Gompers reportedly asked labor journalist Benjamin Stolberg, "that such an intelligent fellow as Foster should make such an ass of himself?" Foster may have believed that the TUEL was "working in every direction necessary to put life and spirit and power into the trade-union movement," but Gompers perceived just the opposite. "If there be any . . . honest purpose of those who want closer affiliation or even amalgamation," he said, "let them, in the orderly, rational, common sense way, in the unions, talk of it, talk with their fellows. But to organize a clique in each union for its control and mastery, such effort must be exposed to the thinking men and women of the labor movement in America."[10]

A seasoned veteran of ideological warfare by the 1920s, Gompers had no intention of surrendering the Federation to Foster's militant minority: He took every opportunity to impugn Foster's motives, publicize his connection to the Workers' (Communist) Party of America, and censure his supporters' apparent hostility "to every guarantee of freedom which American labor holds fundamental."[11] At this late stage in his life, he was not afraid to play hardball, either, particularly with radical opponents who underestimated him at every turn. Foster and his followers prided themselves on their superior understanding of power and their organizational prowess, but Gompers and the AFL Executive Council were not as impotent or insignificant as their critics presumed. Flexing their organizational muscle, they cut off a monthly subsidy to the Chicago FOL, Foster's main link to AFL unions. They also threatened to revoke the charters of radically inclined central labor bodies, including the Seattle Central Labor Council and the Detroit Federation of Labor, moves that eventually brought these councils back in line. Finally, they put their anti-communist campaign to the test at the AFL's 1923 Portland convention, when an overwhelming majority voted to expel a delegate from Montana's Silver Bow Trades and Labor Council who also carried a Workers' party card. "We have been altogether too tolerant . . . to the men who have openly . . . declared that they are boring from within, for the undermining of the principles and policies upon which the American Federation of Labor is founded," Gompers said. "These men may continue if they will, but they must do so on the outside and not on the inside."[12]

Although critics would blame Gompers' red-baiting for the radicals' decline, by 1923 Foster had already alienated most of his AFL supporters. Embroiled in Communist party politics behind the scenes, he had helped launch the Federated Farmer-Labor party—which had no farmer or labor support to speak of—and in the process had publicly humiliated, and then denounced John Fitzpatrick, his longtime partner in the Chicago FOL. At the same time, bitter factional battles in such unions as the Miners, Carpenters, and Ladies' Garment Workers added credence to Gompers' conviction that Foster was a disrupter at heart with no loyalty to trade unionists and no interest in their everyday struggles. Whatever Foster had hoped to accomplish when he "subordinated trade union progress to communism," as one sympathetic scholar put it, his campaign to revolutionize the trade union movement actually strengthened Gompers' hand. For the rapid rise and fall of TUEL influence in AFL unions, during the years 1922 and 1923, demonstrated that the vast majority of trade unionists had no interest in revolutionary strategies, that militant rhetoric was no substitute for practical gains, and that Gompers and the trade union movement could not be counted out yet.[13] "Differ if you will, upon matters [of] how to make your organization a better fighting machine for the interests of the working people in your industry," Gompers urged AFL members. "Vie with each other to do that, but don't inject anything that is calculated to create bitterness, hostility or division," advice that trade unionists took to heart, at least as far as Foster and the communists were concerned.[14]

No one knew better than Gompers the "shortcomings" and "failures" that dogged the labor movement in the 1920s. But it was not the AFL's structure, he believed, that impeded solidarity and engendered jurisdictional strife. Instead, it was the potent combination of "predatory" employers, "class biased" courts, and hostile legislation.[15] As long as labor still had to fight for the right to organize, strike, and bargain collectively with employers, workers would never feel secure enough to recognize an injury to one as the concern of all or to shoulder the economic burdens that classwide solidarity required. And as long as even skilled workers in good union towns like San Francisco, Chicago, and New York City were battling the open shop, their unions would never give up work without a fight. Gompers took no pride in the fact that too many unions closed their doors to new members or refused to risk union funds on organizing campaigns. But at a time of high unemployment and costly defensive strikes, involving miners, railroad shopmen, textile workers, garment workers, and granite cutters, to name a few, he understood only too well why self-preservation came first.[16]

That being the case, Gompers and the AFL concentrated on changing the immediate political climate during these years. The Conference Committee of Trade Union Legislative Representatives, which had been meeting regularly since the spring of 1921, now monitored thousands of bills introduced into Congress, searching out provisions that affected labor "directly or indirectly" and then lobbying lawmakers accordingly. The AFL also launched a National Non-Partisan Political Campaign Committee in the spring of 1922, participating in primary elections for the very first time, and urging AFL unions to support independent candidates when neither Republican nor Democratic contestants proved friendly. "No freedom-loving citizen should vote for a candidate who [will] not pledge himself to oppose any form of compulsory labor law," the campaign directed. "No justice-loving citizen should vote for a candidate for any office who will not pledge himself to oppose injunctions and contempt proceedings as a substitute for trial by jury."[17]

With the AFL's network of organizers and state and local councils ready to go, the nonpartisan campaign proved effective: Despite a severe lack of funds, it provided voting records, strategic advice, and legislative analysis to thousands of local nonpartisan committees and sent organizers to oversee crucial campaigns in thirteen states, including Minnesota, California, Colorado, and Indiana. Gompers himself delivered addresses in New Orleans, New Jersey, and Connecticut, and frequently met with local committees whenever he traveled on AFL business. "We gave every effort within our power," the Executive Council reported in 1923, and the work had paid off: Twenty-three "friendly" U.S. senators, one hundred seventy "friendly" congressmen, and a number of "friendly" governors were elected, while some deadly "enemies" were soundly defeated.[18] "Labor has no complaint to make against the Sixty-Eighth Congress," the AFL reported in 1924. *"Not one measure opposed by labor was enacted into law in the first session of Congress.*[19] Better yet, one long-standing if controversial political goal, the restriction of immigration (which, Gompers contended, was the key to improving American wage standards), was also achieved that year.

This political victory, alongside labor's militant strike record in 1922, persuaded Gompers that the time was right to make industrial democracy a national priority. Ready to counteract critics who claimed the AFL lacked vision, he now urged the Executive Council to organize a ten-member "Commission of Progress and Co-operation" to meet with industry representatives on a regular basis to develop mutually beneficial industrial policies. By bringing together "the essential productive human elements in industry"—labor, management, engineers, and scientists—Gompers believed the commission would help resolve industrial conflicts, eliminate labor and managerial waste, and make the public more aware of the real culprits behind strikes and lockouts: corporate troublemakers who "seek to operate industry merely in the interests of speculation and profit" and unfair conditions "that make for unrest and for faulty relations in industry." "There must be opportunity for progressive evolution within industry, won by ourselves by our economic power, or else we must deal with revolution," Gompers warned. And it was up to the AFL, he said, to "take an initial step so that voluntarily there shall develop an idea that men and women . . . shall come together and try to devise the ways and means by which agreement can be reached, so that the rights of the men and women engaged in all phases of our industrial and professional life shall be the determining factor, rather than the politicians who know nothing of our problems."[20] Although the

Council ultimately rejected the commission as too expensive and too risky, it did endorse Gompers' basic idea of government-free industrial democracy as "Industry's Manifest Duty."[21]

Around the same time, Gompers was also trying to launch a campaign to organize the unorganized—specifically unorganized women who had previously depended on protective legislation to safeguard their interests. The U.S. Supreme Court had declared Washington, D.C.'s, minimum wage laws for women and girls unconstitutional, potentially threatening the livelihood of more than one million women in twelve states. "Of course there was the child labor decisions and other decisions that were incomprehensive," Gompers noted, "but when the Supreme Court decided that the purchase of labor of women was like going into a butcher shop and buying pigs feet it could not be any worse."[22] Working with Mary Anderson of the Women's Bureau of the Department of Labor and members of the National Women's Trade Union League (NWTUL), Gompers also queried British union leaders on their successful campaigns and surveyed AFL affiliates to learn what role, if any, women played in their industries and their unions. With the groundwork completed by early 1924, and the Women in Industry committee appointed, Gompers also called a series of meetings and conferences to devise political and economic strategies. "There is a woeful waste of power and opportunity in failing to organize the women in industry," he admitted, a problem he chalked up to the fact that male unionists basically ignored their obligations, leaving organizing work to the NWTUL. And that had to change, he insisted, because some 3.5 million working women needed representation. "If each organization acts on its own as done in the past," he said, "we don't get to the heart and soul of it."[23]

It was one thing to launch an organizing campaign, but quite another to get established unions to open their doors to female members. For instance, the Flint Glass Workers politely declined to participate since "we do not have any women in our industry whom our members would be agreeable to admitting." The Barbers were equally uninterested, a position Gompers understood but no longer accepted. "Years ago the labor movement objected to the entrance of women in industry," he wrote to James Shanessy, president of the Barbers' union. "They held, and I was one of them who believed that the proper function of woman was the home and that the man was the natural bread-winner. In the early days I too opposed the acceptance of women to membership in our organization and hoped with other[s] to prevent or at least to check the advent of women in industry." But he gave up when he realized that women were there to stay, and that all workers benefited when women were organized. "I . . . advocated the acceptance of the situation as we found it and to admit women to membership in our organization," and now he urged Shanessy to do the same. His argument broke no new ground—in fact, Gompers encouraged the Barbers to compromise and admit women under the condition that they would not work when they were in an "advanced stage of pregnancy" or during their "periodical condition." But the fact that he personally appealed to Shanessy to support women barbers had good effect: The union voted to accept women members at its 1924 convention.[24]

Perhaps if Gompers had been able to keep up the fight, the organizing campaign might have flourished. But by the time Gompers contacted Shanessy in July 1924, his age and infirmities had finally caught up with him. Gompers' health had been declining since February 1923 when a serious bout of influenza landed him in the hospital. Although he was back on the job in six weeks' time, a trip to the Panama Canal at the end of the year left him exhausted. A few weeks later he came down with a cold that developed into bronchitis, and in early June 1924, when he could no longer walk without assistance, he was hospitalized in New York City with heart failure and uremia.[25]

For the first few weeks only a few trusted colleagues knew about his collapse, so Gompers was able to convalesce quietly. But weak as he was, he managed to follow the Republican convention on the radio and insisted on being kept up to date on pressing AFL matters. Indeed, as soon as he was out of immediate danger, he was anxious to get back to work. "It is easy to say: 'Don't do any work; rest; dismiss work from your mind; relax; play,'" he noted. "But to me that is not rest; that is punishment. And so my physicians decided that work in a reasonably moderate degree shall not be denied me."[26] By the end of June he was up and about, presiding over meetings of the National Non-Partisan Campaign Committee and even addressing the Democratic party's resolutions committee. In an hour-long speech he made it clear that labor would look elsewhere if the party refused to support "unequivocally" progressive measures like labor's right to organize. Back in his hospital room, "his old vigor seemed to return," according to Lucy Robins Lang, who was apparently on the scene. "Soon politicians and labor leaders were crowding into his room, to learn what the Old Man thought about the Democratic convention and about the proposal to unite progressives and labor behind La Follette in a third party. The doctors protested," she added, "but Gompers told them that this was better medicine for him than any they could prescribe."[27]

Of course, that was hardly true, and even Gompers knew it. He could "live another ten years" if he followed doctors' orders, Frank Morrison believed, but Gompers apparently had other plans: Although he was still under the care of a full-time nurse, he spent the last five months of his life boosting Robert La Follette's presidential campaign and defending the AFL's decision to cast a protest vote in the 1924 election—no easy task, given his long-standing opposition to third-party politics. He continued to work on child labor issues and tried to persuade the Executive Council to support the organizing campaign for women. And he kept his longtime secretary, Rosa Lee Guard, busy with dictation and worried that he was jeopardizing his recovery with too much work. When she scolded him for losing his temper during a heated political debate, though, he made his position clear. "He said he fully realized that he was 'burning' himself up" but then told the story of a drunken Irishman who realized too late he had put his last gold piece in the collection plate instead of saving it for the next round. "'It's for the church,'" the Irishman had said; "'to hell with it.'" Then, referring to the exertion that was jeopardizing his health, Gompers added, "'It is for the cause, the cause which is . . . burning me up. To hell with it.'" For better or for worse, he was determined to give whatever he had left to the labor movement.[28]

. . .

Historians would later assess these years as the most conservative and least productive period of Gompers' life, when the AFL president allegedly lost his militant spirit, begged employers to "give unions a break," and "left his people well-nigh bankrupt."[29] But this final volume of *The Samuel Gompers Papers* tells a different story. It begins with the AFL's spirited fight against the open shop and the labor injunction, documents Gompers' continuing battle to expose the abuses of an unregulated economy, and demonstrates that the longtime AFL leader never lost his nerve or his will to fight.

As long as he was physically able, during these years, he traveled wherever he was needed—he regularly visited New England, New York, and the Midwest, for instance, to meet with strikers, resolve jurisdictional conflicts, and address mass meetings. He did not hesitate to challenge the authority of government agencies, like the Railroad Labor Board, or to demand the impeachment of Attorney General Harry Daugherty after he helped cripple the railroad shopmen's strike. And if he was willing to cooperate with corporate leaders like Daniel Willard, president of the Baltimore and Ohio Railroad, he had not joined the opponents' camp. For instance, when an AFL investigator blamed "absentee capitalism" for dismal conditions in the Virgin Islands, Gompers concurred. "I believe also that the industrial interests of the United States should be freed from much of this capitalism here but how are we to accomplish it? I think we are gradually doing it in the way of creating greater power in the industries and in agriculture. To my mind that is the only answer to the development and progress of the universe."[30]

During these years Gompers also worked on a proposed constitutional amendment to deprive the U.S. Supreme Court "of autocratic power" (and allow "unconstitutional" laws to stand if they were passed again in Congress by a two-thirds majority). He supported the Workers' Education Bureau, which developed "study classes" in economics and industrial problems that enrolled 30,000 union members in 1924 and mass education lectures and debates that involved some 300,000 union members that year. He kept in touch with European trade unionists, continued to work with Mexican and Puerto Rican leaders to build up the Pan-American Federation of Labor, and found time to work on his autobiography, which went to press in 1923.[31] Gompers also did his best to keep up with the times, during these years, meeting with Herbert Hoover and others on the issue of hydroelectric power, consulting with social scientists on the value of IQ tests, investigating the possibility of installing a radio broadcast station at AFL headquarters, and even meeting with the leaders of the Young Workers' League, to see what they were all about.[32]

Yet for all his interests and activities, and for all the friends and long-time supporters who bolstered his efforts, these final years of Gompers' life were personally difficult. Almost every week brought news of the passing or the illness of another close friend or associate. And by 1924 his home life and second marriage were also apparently unhappy—in fact, just one day before Gompers set off on his final trip to the AFL convention in El Paso in 1924, he changed his will to ensure that his wife, Gertrude, would only inherit what she was strictly entitled to by law. That was not much, as it turned out: Gompers did not believe in life insurance and left property worth about $30,000 when he died, hardly the riches his critics imagined. But the estate was beside the point, for the revised will also suggested that he was initiating a divorce, although neither his sons, nor anyone else, could shed light on the matter. According to Lucy Robins Lang, who claimed to be Gompers' confidant, Gertrude had closed his home to friends and colleagues and even refused to admit Miss Guard, who often brought work to Gompers at home. As Lang put it, Gompers' first wife, Sophia, had made his home "a fit place for a fighting general who sought temporary repose, but now a man who was old and nearly blind, and whose days were numbered, could not find peace there."[33]

In the end, his true home was the labor movement. And it was with his union brothers and sisters that Gompers spent his final days and enjoyed his final triumphs. Too weak to deliver his opening address to the AFL convention that November, he called upon William Green to do the honors. But it was his voice—and his long experience—that came through loud and clear. Taking the delegates back with him to Pittsburgh in 1881, he recalled the heady days when "a group of labor men with little experience in a national labor movement" set out to build one anyway. "We had to find our problems and devise ways of meeting them," Gompers explained, a practical and frustrating process that had taught him the lessons he was now determined to pass on. "So long as we have held fast to voluntary principles and have been actuated and inspired by the spirit of service," he said, "we have sustained our forward progress. . . . Where we have blundered into trying to force a policy or a decision, even though wise and right, we have impeded, if not interrupted, the realization of our own aims." Building consensus took time and patience, but Gompers knew no better way to hold a diverse work force together—and neither did anyone else at the time. And so he left his friends and family with this charge: "No lasting gain has ever come from compulsion. If we seek to force, we but tear apart that which, united, is invincible."[34]

A few weeks later he traveled to Mexico City to attend the inauguration of President Plutarco Elías Calles, an honor he was determined to enjoy, no matter the consequences. Feted for his years of hard work on behalf of the Mexican Revolution and the Mexican labor movement, he also presided over the convention of the Pan-American Federation of Labor, an organization he had worked hard to build. The effort proved too much, however, and Gompers was rushed back to Texas by train.

When he died in San Antonio, on December 13, the AFL leader was mourned as a national hero. Thousands of citizens from all walks of life formed an honor guard when the train carrying his coffin back to Washington, D.C., passed through their cities. The U.S. Senate memorialized him as an "industrial pioneer." The *New York Times* published his deathbed message to the labor movement. And at his funeral in New York City, Governor Al Smith served as an honorary pallbearer, a mark of just how far Gompers had come from his immigrant days on the Lower East Side. But it was one of his own "boys," Jere Sullivan, secretary-treasurer of the Hotel and Restaurant Employees' union, who captured the spirit that had helped make Gompers the voice of labor in his day. "If ever there was a Square Shooter in this old world," Sullivan wrote, "that man was Samuel Gompers, our late Chief."[35]

ACKNOWLEDGMENTS

As we conclude our work on this final volume of the papers of Samuel Gompers, we wish to acknowledge with deep appreciation the generous financial support we have received from the National Historical Publications and Records Commission (NHPRC) and the National Endowment for the Humanities (NEH). The NHPRC has supported the Gompers Project from the very beginning, and the NEH nearly that long. Without the unwavering commitment of these two agencies and their ongoing financial support of our work, this publication of the Samuel Gompers Papers would not have been possible.

We also wish to acknowledge the support we have received from the AFL-CIO and many international unions. The AFL-CIO and the internationals have opened their archives to us, making available a wealth of documents for our research and publication. In addition, the AFL-CIO, a number of its affiliates, and the George Meany Memorial Archives have been able to give their financial support to the Gompers Project at key times over the years, and this has been a tremendous help to our ongoing work.

We deeply appreciate as well the continuing support we receive from the University of Maryland, College Park. We want to express our gratitude to Richard Price, chair of the Department of History; James F. Harris, dean of the College of Arts and Humanities; Patricia A. Steele and Charles B. Lowry, the present and the former dean of the University of Maryland Libraries; Desider L. Vikor, interim dean of the libraries; to our colleagues in the History Department; and to members of the staff of the University's McKeldin Library, where our principal offices are located. The department, the library, and the university assist the Gompers Project in many important ways, most notably in providing financial support and office space.

In preparing this volume the Gompers Project has turned repeatedly to the collections of the George Meany Memorial Archives, the Library of Congress, the Library of the U.S. Department of Labor, and the National Archives and Records Administration. In addition, the Library of Congress provided us with a research office, which was of great assistance to our work. Beyond the libraries and research institutions located in our immediate vicinity, we received assistance for this volume from, among others, the American Jewish Historical Society, the Chicago History Museum, the Kheel Center for Labor-Management Documentation and Archives at Cornell University, the New York Public Library, and the Wisconsin Historical Society.

Many individuals helped us in our work on this book, and we would like to thank, in particular, Robyn Muncy, Department of History, University of Maryland; Barry Carr, University of California, Berkeley (visiting professor), and Swinburne University of Technology, Melbourne, Australia; Zoe Davis, the U.S. Senate Historical Office, Washington, D.C.; Lynda A. DeLoach, the George Meany Memorial Archives, Silver Spring, Md.; Lesley Martin, the Chicago History Museum; Bunny

Ragnerstam, Malmö, Sweden; Donald A. Ritchie, the U.S. Senate Historical Office, Washington, D.C.; Patrizia Sione, the Kheel Center for Labor-Management Documentation and Archives, Cornell University, Ithaca, N.Y.; and Chris Wilkes, Ruskin College, Oxford University.

Amy Rutenberg transcribed the documents in this volume, and Amy, Kimberly M. Welch, and Jake Kobrick, our three graduate assistants, participated in all aspects of the work involved in creating this volume. We deeply appreciate their commitment to the Gompers Project, and we are indebted to them for the good humor, resourcefulness, and collegiality that they consistently brought to their work. They made this a better book in countless ways. Amy, Katarina Keane, Christina G. Larocco, and Stefan Sotiris Papaioannou helped with proofreading the galley pages.

We are indebted to David Brody, Dorothy Sue Cobble, Melvyn Dubofsky, David Montgomery, and Irwin Yellowitz, members of our board of editorial advisors, for giving this volume a careful reading while still in the manuscript stage and for offering many helpful suggestions and useful criticisms. We appreciate their generous contribution of their valuable time and considered judgment.

We also wish to extend our thanks to the AFL-CIO, to the Gompers family, and to the repositories that hold these documents for giving us permission to publish the materials included in this volume.

And, finally, we wish once again to acknowledge our great debt to our friend and colleague Stuart B. Kaufman, who envisioned and launched the Samuel Gompers Project, brought us together to work with him, and saw the first seven volumes of the Gompers Papers into publication. We owe him a debt of gratitude too great to put into words.

Notes

1. SG to Charles Hastings, Jan. 28, 1922, reel 276, vol. 289, p. 34, SG Letterbooks, DLC; AFL, *Proceedings,* 1922, Report of AFL Executive Council, pp. 24, 56. The AFL's membership dropped from 4,078,740 in 1920 to 3,195,635 in 1922.

2. Robert H. Zieger, *Republicans and Labor, 1919–1929* (Lexington, Ky., 1969), p. 172. For examples of criticism, see Earl R. Beckner, "The Trade Union Educational League and the American Labor Movement," *Journal of Political Economy* 33 (Aug. 1925): 414; David J. Saposs, "After-War A.F. of L. Politics," *American Labor Monthly* 1 (Mar. 1923): 37–44.

3. Bernard Mandel, *Samuel Gompers: A Biography* (Yellow Springs, Ohio, 1963), p. 599; James R. Barrett, *William Z. Foster and the Tragedy of American Radicalism* (Urbana, Ill., 1999), pp. 103–11.

4. William Z. Foster, *The Bankruptcy of the American Labor Movement* (Chicago, 1922), pp. 25, 29; David J. Saposs, "What Lies Back of Foster," *The Nation* (Jan. 17, 1923): 69–70; "The Scare Is Real," translated from the *New Yorker Volkszeitung,* Jan. 19, 1923, Executive Council Records, Vote Books, reel 17,

frames 480–81, *AFL Records; Amalgamation or Annihilation: A Practical Plan of Amalgamation for the Metal Trades* (Chicago, 1922), AFL Microfilm Jurisdiction File, Textile Workers Records, reel 55, frame 2110, *AFL Records.*

5. *Amalgamation or Annihilation;* SG to Charles Stillman, Mar. 2, 1922, reel 277, vol. 290, pp. 328–29, SG Letterbooks, DLC; Mandel, *Samuel Gompers,* p. 511; Philip Taft, *The A.F. of L. in the Time of Gompers* (New York, 1957), p. 454; amalgamation campaign figures from Barrett, *William Z. Foster,* p. 126.

6. Foster is quoted in Barrett, *William Z. Foster,* p. 126; David J. Saposs, "The American Federation of Labor: Growth and Development," *American Labor Monthly* 1 (Oct. 1923): 26; John Huber, "Moods, Personalities, Hopes," *American Labor Monthly* 1 (Sept. 1923): 40–41.

7. For the building trades' difficulty in amalgamating their forces, see Grace Palladino, *Skilled Hands, Strong Spirits: A Century of Building Trades History* (Ithaca, N.Y., 2005), pp. 46–67, 71–72; Foster, *The Bankruptcy of the American Labor Movement,* p. 9; Frank Morrison to Charles Atherton, Jan. 11, 1923, AFL Microfilm National and International Union File, Metal Polishers Records, reel 40, frame 1222, *AFL Records;* E. H. Fljozdal to E. H. FitzGerald, Dec. 21, 1922, AFL Microfilm National and International Union File, Railway Clerks Records, reel 43, frame 2575, *AFL Records.*

8. Gompers was referring to five printers' unions. Address before the Convention of the United Cloth Hat and Cap Makers of North America, May 5, 1923, Files of the Office of the President, Speeches and Writings, reel 118, frames 171–72, *AFL Records;* SG to E. C. Warriner, Nov. 14, 1923, reel 295, vol. 308, p. 151, SG Letterbooks, DLC.

9. Foster, *The Bankruptcy of the American Labor Movement,* p. 8; SG to William Bryan, June 4, 1923, reel 291, vol. 304, p. 331, SG Letterbooks, DLC.

10. Gompers is cited in Gerald Emanuel Stearn, *Gompers* (Englewood Cliffs, N.J., 1971), p. 167; TUEL declaration cited in Saposs, "What Lies Back of Foster," p. 70; SG, Address before Convention of United Cloth Hat and Cap Makers, May 5, 1923.

11. AFL, *Proceedings,* 1923, Report of AFL Executive Council, pp. 37–38; see, for example, SG statement quoted in AFL press release, Apr. 30, 1922, AFL Microfilm Circular and Neostyle File, reel 57, frame 1125, *AFL Records.*

12. David Montgomery, *The Fall of the House of Labor: The Workplace, the State, and American Labor Activism, 1865–1925* (New York, 1987), pp. 433–34; according to SG, William Dunne was not duly elected by the Silver Bow (Mont.) Trades and Labor Council but asked for a credential with the understanding that the council would not finance the trip, AFL, *Proceedings,* 1923, p. 374.

13. Barrett, *William Z. Foster,* pp. 137–39, 142–48, 152–54; Beckner, "The Trade Union Educational League and the American Labor Movement," pp. 428–31, quotation at p. 431.

14. SG, Address before the Convention of the International Ladies' Garment Workers' Union, May 1, 1922, *Report and Proceedings of the Sixteenth Convention of the International Ladies' Garment Workers' Union . . .* (Cleveland, 1922), p. 8.

15. SG to Frank Burch, Nov. 27, 1923, reel 295, vol. 308, p. 731, SG Letterbooks, DLC; AFL, *Proceedings,* 1922, Report of AFL Executive Council, pp. 17, 40.

16. For a discussion of the 1922 strikes see Montgomery, *The Fall of the House of Labor,* pp. 407–9.

17. Executive Council Records, Minutes, Feb. 16, 1923, reel 7, frame 1284,

AFL Records; Taft, *The A.F. of L. in the Time of Gompers,* p. 480; AFL, *Proceedings,* 1923, Report of AFL Executive Council, pp. 48–49, 53, quotation at pp. 48–49.

18. AFL, *Proceedings,* 1923, Report of AFL Executive Council, pp. 50–54, quotation at p. 54; Montgomery, *The Fall of the House of Labor,* p. 435. The Executive Council reported that the 1922 campaign elected 23 friendly senators (18 Democrats and 5 Republicans) and defeated 11 unfriendly ones; 170 congressman elected were either supported by the campaign or their opponents were opposed by the campaign (105 Democrats, 63 Republicans, one Farmer-Labor and one independent), AFL, *Proceedings,* 1923, p. 50.

19. AFL, *Proceedings,* 1924, Report of AFL Executive Council, p. 66. Emphasis in the original.

20. Executive Council Records, Minutes, Sept. 16, 1922, reel 7, frames 1184–87, *AFL Records;* Feb. 19, 1923, ibid., frame 1290.

21. Executive Council Records, Minutes, Feb. 19, 1923, ibid., frame 1290; May 9, 1923, ibid., frames 1323–26; May 11, 1923, ibid., frame 1336. The statement is published in AFL, *Proceedings,* 1923, Report of AFL Executive Council, pp. 31–34.

22. "The Minimum Wage Decision," *Washington Post,* Apr. 10, 1923; AFL, *Proceedings,* 1923, Report of AFL Executive Council, p. 55; Minimum Wage Conference, Minutes, Apr. 25, 1923, Files of the Office of the President, Conferences, reel 122, frame 615, *AFL Records.*

23. "An Excerpt from the Minutes of a Meeting on Organizing Women in Industry," Mar. 9, 1924, below.

24. William Clarke to SG, Apr. 3, 1924, American Flint Glass Workers' Union of North America Records, reel 3, frame 537, *AFL and the Unions;* "To James Shanessy," July 19, 1924, below; SG to Shanessy, Sept. 14, 1924, reel 300, vol. 315, p. 237, SG Letterbooks, DLC.

25. SG to George Wickersham, Mar. 17, 1924, reel 297, vol. 311, p. 529, SG Letterbooks, DLC; R. Lee Guard to Louis LeBosse, Jan. 28, 1925, Files of the Office of the President, General Correspondence, reel 109, frames 154–55, *AFL Records;* W. C. Roberts, Brief Memorandum of the Last Six Months of Samuel Gompers' Life, n.d., Files of the Office of the President, Reference Material, reel 134, frames 441–45, *AFL Records;* "A Memorandum by Lee Rice," Dec. 13, 1924, below.

26. Roberts, Memorandum; Guard to Thomas Rickert, June 28, 1924, reel 299, vol. 314, p. 108, SG Letterbooks, DLC; "To the Executive Council of the AFL," July 8, 1924, below.

27. "Gompers Presents Union Labor Planks," *New York Times,* June 26, 1924; Lucy Robins Lang, *Tomorrow Is Beautiful* (New York, 1948), p. 223.

28. Morrison to W. D. Mahon, n.d. [c. Aug. 27, 1924], AFL Microfilm Jurisdiction File, Street and Electric Railway Employees Records, reel 54, frame 1206, *AFL Records;* R. Lee Guard, Memorandum, Aug. 7, 1924, Files of the Office of the President, General Correspondence, reel 108, frame 104, *AFL Records.*

29. Melvyn Dubofsky, *The State and Labor in Modern America* (Chapel Hill, N.C., 1994), p. 97; Rowland Hill Harvey, *Samuel Gompers, Champion of the Toiling Masses* (New York, 1935; reprint ed., 1975), p. 337; Louis Schultz Reed, *The Labor Philosophy of Samuel Gompers* (New York, 1930; reprint ed., 1966).

30. "Excerpts from the Minutes of a Meeting with Santiago Iglesias," Jan. 25, 1923, below.

31. SG's appointment records reveal a busy schedule during these years (Files of the Office of the President, Appointment Records, reel 137, *AFL Records*); AFL, *Proceedings*, 1924, Report of AFL Executive Council, pp. 39, 60–61.

32. See for example, SG to John Hays Hammond, Jr., Sept. 11, 1923, reel 293, vol. 306, pp. 664–65, SG Letterbooks, DLC; SG to Herbert Hoover, Nov. 5, 1923, ibid., reel 294, vol. 307, p. 674; SG to Hugh Frayne, Apr. 18, 1924, ibid., reel 298, vol. 312, p. 453; "To J. McKeen Cattell," Jan. 9, 1923, below.

33. Lang, *Tomorrow Is Beautiful*, p. 221; William Green to Franklin Webster, Aug. 7, 1925, Files of the Office of the President, General Correspondence, reel 109, frame 400, *AFL Records*; "Gompers in Disagreement with Wife, Will Indicates," *Washington Post*, Dec. 21, 1924; Guard to Charles Jones, Mar. 14, 1925, Files of the Office of the President, General Correspondence, reel 109, frames 254–55, *AFL Records*. See also "The Last Will and Testament of Samuel Gompers," Nov. 8, 1924, below.

34. AFL, *Proceedings*, 1924, pp. 4–5. For SG's address, see "First Day—Monday Morning Session," Nov. 17, 1924, in "Excerpts from Accounts of the 1924 Convention of the AFL in El Paso, Texas," Nov. 17–24, 1924, below.

35. "An Article in the *New York Times*," Dec. 19, 1924, below; "End Comes on Home Soil," *New York Times*, Dec. 14, 1924; Jere Sullivan to Guard, Jan. 24, 1925, Files of the Office of the President, General Correspondence, reel 109, frame 124, *AFL Records*.

SYMBOLS AND ABBREVIATIONS

AFL	American Federation of Labor
ALS	Autograph letter, signed or stamped with signature
DLC	Library of Congress, Washington, D.C.
DNA	National Archives and Records Administration, Washington, D.C.
FOTLU	Federation of Organized Trades and Labor Unions of the United States and Canada
ICHi	Chicago History Museum
IWW	Industrial Workers of the World
KOL	Knights of Labor
MsU	University of Mississippi, Oxford
N	New York State Library, Albany
NIC	Cornell University, Ithaca, N.Y.
NN	New York Public Library, Astor, Lenox, and Tilden Foundations
NNAJHi	American Jewish Historical Society, New York City
PLS and Sr	Printed letter, signed or stamped with signature and with signature representation other than stamp
PLSr	Printed letter, signature representation other than stamp
RG	Record Group
SG	Samuel Gompers
T and ALS	Typed and autograph letter, signed or stamped with signature
TDc	Typed document, copy
TDp	Typed document, letterpress copy
TDS	Typed document, signed or stamped with signature
TDtc	Typed document, transcribed, copy
TLc	Typed letter, copy
TLcS	Typed letter, copy, signed or stamped with signature
TLcSr	Typed letter, copy, signature representation other than stamp
TLp	Typed letter, letterpress copy
TLpS	Typed letter, letterpress copy, signed or stamped with signature
TLS	Typed letter, signed or stamped with signature
TLSr	Typed letter, signature representation other than stamp
TLtcSr	Typed letter, transcribed, copy, signature representation other than stamp

TLtpSr	Typed letter, transcribed, letterpress copy, signature representation other than stamp
TUC	Trades Union Congress of Great Britain
TWcSr	Typed wire (cable or telegram), copy, signature representation other than stamp
TWpSr	Typed wire (cable or telegram), letterpress copy, signature representation other than stamp
TWSr	Typed wire (cable or telegram), signature representation other than stamp
TWtpSr	Typed wire (cable or telegram), transcribed, letterpress copy, signature representation other than stamp

SHORT TITLES

AFL, *Proceedings, 1890*	AFL, *Report of Proceedings of the Tenth Annual Convention of the American Federation of Labor, Held at Detroit, Michigan, December 8, 10, 11, 12, and 13, 1890* (1890?; reprint ed., Bloomington, Ill., 1905)
AFL, *Proceedings, 1893*	AFL, *Report of Proceedings of the Thirteenth Annual Convention of the American Federation of Labor, Held at Chicago, Ill., December 11th to 19th, Inclusive, 1893* (1893?; reprint ed., Bloomington, Ill., 1905)
AFL, *Proceedings, 1895*	AFL, *Report of Proceedings of the Fifteenth Annual Convention of the American Federation of Labor, Held at New York, N.Y., December 9th to 17th, Inclusive, 1895* (1895?; reprint ed., Bloomington, Ill., 1905)
AFL, *Proceedings, 1908*	AFL, *Report of Proceedings of the Twenty-Eighth Annual Convention of the American Federation of Labor, Held at Denver, Colorado, November 9 to 21 Inclusive, 1908* (Washington, D.C., 1908)
AFL, *Proceedings, 1909*	AFL, *Report of Proceedings of the Twenty-Ninth Annual Convention of the American Federation of Labor, Held at Toronto, Ont., Canada, November 8 to 20, Inclusive, 1909* (Washington, D.C., 1909)
AFL, *Proceedings, 1922*	AFL, *Report of Proceedings of the Forty-Second Annual Convention of the American Federation of Labor, Held at Cincinnati, Ohio, June 12 to 24, Inclusive, 1922* (Washington, D.C., 1922)
AFL, *Proceedings, 1923*	AFL, *Report of Proceedings of the Forty-Third Annual Convention of the American Federation of Labor, Held at Portland, Oregon, October 1 to 12, Inclusive, 1923* (Washington, D.C., 1923)
AFL, *Proceedings, 1924*	AFL, *Report of Proceedings of the Forty-Fourth Annual Convention of the American Federation of Labor, Held at El Paso, Texas, November 17 to 25, Inclusive, 1924* (Washington, D.C., 1924)
AFL and the Unions	Dolores E. Janiewski, ed., *The American Federation of Labor and the Unions: National and International Union Records from the Samuel Gompers Era*, microfilm (Sanford, N.C., 1982)

AFL Records	Peter J. Albert and Harold L. Miller, eds., *American Federation of Labor Records: The Samuel Gompers Era,* microfilm (Sanford, N.C., 1979)
AFL Weekly News Letter	*American Federation of Labor Weekly News Letter*
AFL Weekly News Service	*American Federation of Labor Weekly News Service*
FOTLU, *Proceedings,* 1881	FOTLU, *Report of the First Annual Session of the Federation of Organized Trades and Labor Unions of the United States and Canada, . . . December 15, 16, 17 and 18, 1881* (1881?; reprint ed., Bloomington, Ill., 1905)
FOTLU, *Proceedings,* 1884	FOTLU, *Report of the Fourth Annual Session of the Federation of Organized Trades and Labor Unions of the United States and Canada, . . . October 7, 8, 9 and 10, 1884* (1884?; reprint ed., Bloomington, Ill., 1905)
SG Letterbooks	Records of the American Federation of Labor: Samuel Gompers Letterbooks, 1883–1924, Library of Congress, Washington, D.C.
The Samuel Gompers Papers, vol. 1	Stuart B. Kaufman et al., eds., *The Samuel Gompers Papers,* vol. 1, *The Making of a Union Leader, 1850–86* (Urbana, Ill., 1986)
The Samuel Gompers Papers, vol. 2	Stuart B. Kaufman et al., eds., *The Samuel Gompers Papers,* vol. 2, *The Early Years of the American Federation of Labor, 1887–90* (Urbana, Ill., 1987)
The Samuel Gompers Papers, vol. 3	Stuart B. Kaufman et al., eds., *The Samuel Gompers Papers,* vol. 3, *Unrest and Depression, 1891–94* (Urbana, Ill., 1989)
The Samuel Gompers Papers, vol. 4	Stuart B. Kaufman et al., eds., *The Samuel Gompers Papers,* vol. 4, *A National Labor Movement Takes Shape, 1895–98* (Urbana, Ill., 1991)
The Samuel Gompers Papers, vol. 5	Stuart B. Kaufman et al., eds., *The Samuel Gompers Papers,* vol. 5, *An Expanding Movement at the Turn of the Century, 1898–1902* (Urbana, Ill., 1996)
The Samuel Gompers Papers, vol. 6	Stuart B. Kaufman et al., eds., *The Samuel Gompers Papers,* vol. 6, *The American Federation of Labor and the Rise of Progressivism, 1902–6* (Urbana, Ill., 1997)
The Samuel Gompers Papers, vol. 7	Stuart B. Kaufman et al., eds., *The Samuel Gompers Papers,* vol. 7, *The American Federation of Labor under Siege, 1906–9* (Urbana, Ill., 1999)
The Samuel Gompers Papers, vol. 8	Peter J. Albert and Grace Palladino, eds., *The Samuel Gompers Papers,* vol. 8, *Progress and Reaction in the Age of Reform, 1909–13* (Urbana, Ill., 2001)

The Samuel Gompers Papers, vol. 9

Peter J. Albert and Grace Palladino, eds., *The Samuel Gompers Papers,* vol. 9, *The American Federation of Labor at the Height of Progressivism, 1913–17* (Urbana, Ill., 2003)

The Samuel Gompers Papers, vol. 10

Peter J. Albert and Grace Palladino, eds., *The Samuel Gompers Papers,* vol. 10, *The American Federation of Labor and the Great War, 1917–18* (Urbana, Ill., 2007)

The Samuel Gompers Papers, vol. 11

Peter J. Albert and Grace Palladino, eds., *The Samuel Gompers Papers,* vol. 11, *The Postwar Years, 1918–21* (Urbana, Ill., 2009)

CHRONOLOGY

1922	January	United Textile Workers of America strike begins in New England; walkout ends in Lawrence, Mass., in August, in Rhode Island and Lowell, Mass., in September, and in New Hampshire in December
	Mar. 19	Chicago Federation of Labor calls on AFL to create amalgamated industrial unions; SG speaks against the proposal on Apr. 12 in Chicago; AFL Executive Council votes against the measure on May 10
	Apr. 1	Nationwide coal miners' strike begins; bituminous strike ends in August with Cleveland Agreement; anthracite strike ends Sept. 2
	Apr. 1	Nationwide quarry workers' strike begins; ends in most areas by early 1923
	Apr. 1	Nationwide granite cutters' strike begins; ends in most areas by early 1923
	Apr. 21–22	SG testifies before Lockwood Committee
	May 15	U.S. Supreme Court hands down *Bailey* v. *Drexel Furniture Co.* decision, striking down Child Labor Tax Act
	June 1	SG forms Permanent Conference for the Abolition of Child Labor
	June 12–24	AFL convention meets in Cincinnati
	June 22	Herrin Massacre
	July 1	Nationwide railroad shopmen's strike begins; ends on many roads with signing of Baltimore Agreement of Sept. 13; strike officially ends in 1928
	Aug. 20	Authorities raid Chicago headquarters of William Z. Foster's Trade Union Educational League
	Aug. 22	Bridgman Raid
1923	Mar. 7–23	SG hospitalized in New York City with influenza, bronchial pneumonia, and heart congestion; returns to work Apr. 3

	Apr. 9	U.S. Supreme Court hands down *Adkins* v. *Children's Hospital* decision, striking down District of Columbia's minimum wage law for women
	May 9	AFL Executive Council demands affiliated central bodies rescind endorsements of Bolshevism and Soviet government
	July 3–5	Founding convention of Federated Farmer-Labor party meets in Chicago
	Aug. 2	President Warren Harding dies of heart attack; vice-president Calvin Coolidge sworn in as president the next day
	Aug. 13–24	Cigar Makers' International Union of America convention meets in Chicago; SG attends as delegate
	Oct. 1–12	AFL convention meets in Portland, Ore.
	Dec. 4–1924 August	SG attempts to initiate AFL campaign to organize women workers
	Dec. 22	SG presents manuscript of his memoirs to John Macrae of E. P. Dutton and Co.
	Dec. 24–1924 Jan. 17	SG travels to Panama Canal Zone
1924	February–April	SG ill with severe bronchial cold
	June 3–July 8	SG hospitalized in New York City, later convalesces at Brighton Beach, N.Y., and Atlantic City; returns to work Oct. 16
	June 10–12	Republican convention meets in Cleveland
	June 17–19	Farmer-Labor Progressive convention meets in St. Paul, Minn.
	June 24–July 10	Democratic convention meets in New York City; SG presents labor's demands to the platform committee on June 25
	July 4–5	Conference for Progressive Political Action convention meets in Cleveland
	Aug. 2	AFL Executive Council endorses La Follette-Wheeler ticket
	Nov. 17–25	AFL convention meets in El Paso, Tex.
	Dec. 3–9	Pan-American Federation of Labor convention meets in Mexico City
	Dec. 13	SG dies in San Antonio, Tex.
	Dec. 18	SG's funeral held in New York City
	Dec. 19	William Green elected AFL president

Documents

To Edwin Ladd[1]

January 6, 1922.

Hon. E. F. Ladd,
U.S. Senate,
Senate Office Bldg., Washington, D.C.
Sir:

Your letter of January 3 received, and contents noted. You ask a number of questions which I will endeavor to answer seriatim.

1. It is estimated that there are 10,000,000 wage earners in the United States eligible and so situated that they can become members of trade unions. There are many wage earners employed in out-of-the-way places or in occupations that are not readily susceptible of organization. Of the 10,000,000 eligible, 5,500,000 are members of unions, which would be about 55 per cent.

2. (a) The members of unions desire the union shop, for only through collective bargaining can the employes have anything to say concerning their wages, hours and conditions of employment. There is no difference in the desire for the union shop, whether dealing with an association of employers or individual employers.

(b) You probably refer to the railroad brotherhoods when you ask about agreements made for all workmen instead of union men alone. Brotherhoods make the wage scales and those who are not members receive the same wages as the union men. Unorganized secure the benefits without any responsibilities whatever.

(c) This presupposes the union shop. If there is an agreement between employers and employes that all grievances shall be arbitrated, it must of necessity have been made by conferences held by employers and representatives of the unions. Voluntary arbitration has been very successful; compulsory arbitration has been the cause of many strikes. Permit me to refer you to the Kansas arbitration law, or, rather, the Kansas anti-strike law. Men who strike are sent to jail. The Transportation Act of 1920 created a Labor Board to hear all grievances between the railroads and their employes. It was said when passed that the labor clauses in the Transportation Act were simply for the purpose of making it possible to bring about satisfactory agreements. Instead, railroads have been permitted to violate the orders of the Railroad Labor Board with impunity, while the workers when threatening to cease work were charged with conspiring against the government. The railroads are owned by private citizens. The latter most maliciously contend, and others have encouraged the idea, that any opposition raised by the employes against unjust decisions is a fight against the government.

3–4. One hundred per cent of organized labor desire the union shop. It cannot always be obtained, but efforts are continually being made to that end.

5–6. No states have laws requiring the use of the union label. All states have laws permitting the registration of union labels as trade marks. Employers who counterfeit any union label can be punished.

7. No states restrict the use of the union label.

8. The report[2] of the Executive Council to the American Federation of Labor convention in Denver in 1921[3] stated that 1500 strikes had been called during the previous year. Of these, 648 were won, 219 compromised and 633 were still pending. No strikes are ever lost.[4] Even if they are called off the danger of another strike is minimized. Both the employer and the workmen are apt to get together and settle future questions by conferences around a table. Many times employers refuse to deal with the chosen representatives of the employes and strikes follow, but later employers meet with employes and a satisfactory adjustment is made. There are not as many strikes called as one would be led to believe by the agitation against them. Enclosed you will find an article on strikes, in which you will find that there were 60 per cent more days lost in 1919 by illness than by strikes. During the years 1920 and 1921 the strike figures have been greatly reduced. You will find that the loss of time due to strikes is approximately one-half of that due to accidents, and one-third of that due to industrial sickness, and about one-fifth of that due to accidents and sickness.

9. In union shops the wages, hours and working conditions are fixed by agreement with employers; in the non-union shops the employer autocratically fixes the wages, hours and working conditions. The reason he demands the open or non-union shop is to permit him to pay less wages than fair employers. Naturally, as the employes of non-union shops receive less wages and poorer conditions than the employes of union shops the employes of the latter must have received the most benefits.

10. It is not necessary for the state to have a law forbidding or hindering the use of the boycott. The judges make the laws against boycotts.

11. (a and c) More than forty states have workmen's compensation laws, which do away with employers' liability laws. Liability laws guaranteed four defenses for the employer in case of accident to an employe. These were: fellow servant, contributory negligence, waiver of rights, and assumption of risk.

(b) Factory inspection laws are very general among the states.

(d) All states except the following have made 14 years the minimum age at which children can work, but nearly all have exemptions of various kinds:

In Ohio boys under 15 and girls under 16 cannot work, except under certain conditions outside of school hours.

In Maine, Michigan and South Dakota the minimum age is 15 years, while the schools are in session, and 14 years when not.

The minimum age limit in Texas, Montana and California is 15 years, although there are several exemptions.

In Florida the minimum is 14 years in factories and 12 in stores.

In Georgia 14 years for factories, and no age in stores.

In Mississippi 12 for boys and 14 for girls in factories, and no age for stores.

No age limit in New Mexico, Utah or Wyoming.

South Carolina has 14 years in factories, but no age in stores.

(e) Kansas and Colorado have industrial laws. The Kansas law is really an injunction against any cessation of work either before or after the industrial court passes upon a wage controversy. The Colorado law is a compulsory investigation law. No strike can be called until a certain time after an investigation has been made.

(f) Forty-four states have laws governing the maximum number of hours women can work. The hours range from 48 to 60 per week.

(g) About twenty-seven states have mediation and conciliation bureaus.

(h) None of the states has compulsory insurance laws.

(i) Fourteen states have minimum wage laws, also the District of Columbia.

12. According to the Department of Labor the number of strikes from 1916 to 1920, both inclusive, are as follows:[5]

1916,	3,681
1917,	4,324
1918,	3,248
1919,	3,444
1920,	3,109.

During that time the following were the number of lockouts:

1916,	108
1917,	126
1918,	105
1919,	125
1920,	58.

13. (a) Trade unions generally desire a joint trade agreement with all employers in an industry rather than agreements with individual employers. Such agreements create industrial peace in an industry.

(b) All agreements made between employers and employes cover all workmen affected.

(c) All unions are ready at any and all times for mediation, conciliation or voluntary arbitration.

(d) All wage scales are made by collective bargaining. More than 95 per cent of the newspapers of the country bargain with the printing trade unions on all questions relating to wages, hours and conditions of employment.

(e) Practically all unions have rules governing apprentices. In order to protect the boy who wishes to learn the trade the union provides that he must have certain wages and schooling during the term of his apprenticeship. The object of this is to make it obligatory on the employer to teach the boy the trade thoroughly. Fair employers admit the justice of this. Unfair employers who have in mind profits only, desire to take on as many boys as possible in order that they will be assured of greater profits than the fair employer because he can sell his products cheaper. Propagandists against the unions have used the limitation of apprentices as a means of injuring them in the minds of those who know nothing of conditions in industry. The apprenticeship rules of the unions protect the customer of the employer, who otherwise would not obtain as good work because too much of it would be done by apprentices. It is simply a catch phrase for vicious propaganda purposes.

(f) Nearly all unions have accident, sickness and death benefits. A few have old-age benefits. The question of old-age benefits is being considered by nearly all the international unions.

Some of the information you ask for it would be impossible to obtain. Also, some of your questions are difficult to answer because they may not have expressed the idea wished to be conveyed. Nevertheless, if there is anything in these answers that you wish more thoroughly explained and if you will write me, I will be more than pleased to give you the information.

Yours very truly,   Saml Gompers
President,   American Federation of Labor.

TLpS, reel 275, vol. 288, pp. 197–200, SG Letterbooks, DLC.

1. Edwin Freemont Ladd (1859–1925) served as a Non-Partisan Republican senator from North Dakota from 1921 until his death in 1925.

2. AFL, *Proceedings*, 1921, p. 35.

3. The 1921 AFL convention met in Denver, June 13–25.

4. Notwithstanding SG's statement, the AFL Executive Council reported 135 strikes lost during the course of the year (AFL, *Proceedings*, 1921, p. 35).

5. SG's figures for strikes and lockouts are taken from "Strikes and Lockouts in the United States, 1916 to 1920," *Monthly Labor Review* 12 (June 1921): 163. The Bureau

of Labor Statistics later raised its strike count for these years. The new figures were: 1916, 3,789; 1917, 4,450; 1918, 3,353; 1919, 3,630; and 1920, 3,411 ("Strikes and Lockouts in the United States, 1916 to 1928," *Monthly Labor Review* 29 [July 1929]: 133; see also Florence Peterson, "Strikes in the United States, 1880–1936," U.S. Department of Labor *Bulletin* 651 [1937], p. 21).

From Anthony Chlopek[1]

Offices of Anthony J. Chlopek, President
International Longshoremen's Association[2]
Buffalo, N.Y., January 10, 1922.

Subject Matter: Factors in Settling Wage Scales.

Dear Sir and Brother:—

Your favor of December 21st,[3] addressed to our Vice-President Jos. P. Ryan,[4] New York City, has been referred to me for reply, and I have carefully noted contents of same.

Our International organization in settling the wage to be paid our membership, wherever it is possible, takes into consideration the following factors: The proper mode of living, which includes the right of the worker to receive sufficient money to maintain his home properly and rightfully protect and feed his children; to live in a home that is wholesome and sanitary; to permit him to send his children to school properly clothed and fed; to permit the necessary recreation and to lay away a part of his earnings for a "rainy day." These are the principles upon which we endeavor to arrive at a fair wage and as you know, sometimes we are successful and sometimes we are not.

I shall be glad, whenever a representative of Dr. John A. Fitch calls at this office, to give him any and all the information I am able to furnish and you can rest assured I will gladly and willingly cooperate in connection with this matter. If there is anything else I can do to be of service and assistance, please advise.

With best wishes, I am,

Fraternally yours,   Anthony J. Chlopek

P.S. Will be pleased to have a number of additional copies entitled "*Wage.*"[5]

—A. J. C.

TLS, AFL Microfilm Convention File, reel 31, frame 2116, *AFL Records.*

1. Anthony John CHLOPEK was president of the International Longshoremen's Association from 1921 to 1927.

2. The International LONGSHOREMEN'S Association.

3. SG to Joseph Ryan, Dec. 21, 1921, reel 274, vol. 287, pp. 381–82, SG Letterbooks, DLC. The letter related to the AFL Executive Council's study of wage determination, undertaken at the request of the 1921 AFL convention (see *The Samuel Gompers Papers,* vol. 11, pp. 559–60). Research included gathering information on wage rates from each of the AFL's affiliates, and to insure uniformity and accuracy, professors teaching in labor-related fields at universities located near the various union headquarters were asked to send students to collect the data. John Fitch, instructor in industrial relations at the New York School of Social Work at Columbia University, had agreed to handle the research at the Longshoremen's headquarters and to have a student visit the union's offices in Buffalo.

4. Joseph Patrick RYAN served as a vice-president of the Longshoremen from 1919 to 1927.

5. For a typed copy of the article, actually entitled "Wages," see AFL Microfilm Convention File, reel 31, frames 2138–39, *AFL Records.*

From Joseph Ryan

Bethesda Jan 16 1922

[D]ear Sir:—

I am sending you a copy of the individual contract being used by the Moore Drop Forge Co. this copy is the same as the original word for word.

the method this company used to get the men to sign it was to get a bunch of their men that is men that they knew would not refuse to sign it and then the doubtful ones one at a time and no two men in the office where they were asked to sign it were allowed they would tell one that no one had refused to sign it and in order to start to work the next day it would be nesseccary to sign up and no one but signed up men would start to work in the morning when a man refused they would say what are you going to do be a fish and loose your good job and see your family in want as you cant get another job at this time and (smith or Jones) will take your hammer and will be getting the wages you should be bringing home to your family. most all that did sign it would not have done so but for coercion.

I have described this because people say why did they sign it if i[t] is going to injure them.

as the Moore Co is the only Co. at this time that is involved in labor trouble[1] that is being kept before the people they deserve the unpleasant notoriety they are getting from a very hustling chairman of the joint committe Bro Martin[2] and when you go to Springfield[3] he is the man you should get in toutch with to get any information that you may need as he has the whole situation in hand.

Mr Cortharan[4] Sec. of the Mfg. Assocation tried to stop you from com-
ming to Springfield by asking the Mayor[5] to refuse you the use of the
Auditorum but his honor said he would have nothing to do with it.
men were brought into Springfield by misreprentation and when they
found out the true situation refused to go to work and the company
had to pay their Board Bill and transportation costing them hundreds
of Dollars hopeing that your visit will be very succesfull and thanking
you for your consideration I remain

Cincearly   Jos J Ryan

[ENCLOSURE]

APPLICATION FOR EMPLOYMENT.

I apply to Moore Drop Forging Company.
For employment as _____ and if employed, agree that such employ-
ment will be upon the following terms and conditions:
Wages: _____
Hours of Labor, to be arranged as employer may deem expedient, not
Exceeding: _____ Hours in one week.
Overtime: To be optional. For which time and a half will be paid.
Factory conditions are accepted as satisfactory and will not be the sub-
ject of a controversy during my employement, though suggestions for
improvements will be welcomed by employer.
I understand that employement is upon a strictly non-union basis and
I agree that while retained in employement I will not be or become a
member of any trade union. That if I hereafter apply for membership
in any trade union I will at once notify my employer who may there
upon terminate my employment. That upon termination of my employement for any reason I will not in any manner annoy, molest or interfere with the buisness, customers or employees of said company.

Springfield, Mass. _____ 192_

ALS and TDc, AFL Microfilm Convention File, reel 31, frame 1062, *AFL
Records.*

1. In October 1920 the Moore Drop Forging Co. of Springfield, Mass., announced
a 10 percent wage cut. When the unionized workforce at Moore rejected the new pay
scale, the firm initiated a system of separate employment contracts for each individual
worker, with provisions banning union membership and picketing in case of a strike.
Some workmen signed the new contracts when they were presented on Dec. 9, but
others did not, and when those who refused were fired, a strike began. Led by a joint
strike committee, union members held mass meetings and picketed the company in an
effort to force Moore to abandon individual contracts. In January 1921 the firm asked
for a temporary injunction to restrain these activities, but the application was set aside
when the strikers agreed to stop picketing. By August the strike was effectively over.

Given Moore's success with individual contracts, other Springfield employers began using them, and in January 1922 the Springfield Central Labor Union (CLU) started a campaign against the practice. SG spoke at a mass meeting on Jan. 22, and the CLU called for a national boycott against Moore (over half of whose output was used by the Ford Motor Co.), solicited support from local religious leaders, and tried to persuade the company's workers to quit. When Moore asked for an injunction against the CLU, the two sides agreed to submit the case to a special master. Hearings were held in May, and the master's report, favoring Moore, was issued later in the summer. A justice of the Supreme Judicial Court of Massachusetts for Hampden County granted a temporary injunction in September, and in January 1923 the full court made the injunction permanent, ruling that the firm was legally entitled to make individual contracts with its workers and demand that they repudiate union membership (*Moore Drop Forging Co.* v. *McCarthy et al.*, 243 Mass. 554 [1923]).

2. James Martin, a member of International Brotherhood of Blacksmiths, Drop Forgers, and Helpers 570 of Springfield.

3. SG left Washington, D.C., on the afternoon of Jan. 21, 1922, spent the night in New York City, and left for Springfield on the morning of Jan. 22, where he met with local labor leaders and addressed strikers. He returned to Washington that evening.

4. William P. Cotharin (1864–1924), secretary of the Employers' Association of Hampden County, Mass. (1916–24).

5. Edwin F. Leonard (1862–1931), a Republican, served as mayor of Springfield from 1921 to 1924.

To B. M. Jewell[1]

Jan. 19, 1922.

Mr. B. M. Jewell,
President, Railway Employes' Department,
4750 Broadway, Chicago, Illinois.
Dear Sir and Brother:

It is with great gratification that I have received and read your letter of January 7th including the copy of the telegram which you addressed to former President Woodrow Wilson advising him that the National Conference Committee of Divisions one, two and three representing the mechanical shop trades affiliated with the Department and the chief executives of these organizations did at their meeting of even date appropriate the sum of one thousand dollars as a contribution to the Woodrow Wilson Foundation.[2] I am sure that many other organizations affiliated to the American Federation of Labor will make contributions to this fund. I only wish it were possible to have the accurate record of these contributions for it would be an interesting contribution to the history of the part taken by the American Federation of Labor in so fully supporting Mr. Wilson and the League of Nations.

It was my privilege Sunday to participate in the great meeting of the Washington Branch of the National Woodrow Wilson Foundation—a meeting which packed the National Theatre from top to bottom. The enthusiasm was so great that upon motion of some one in the audience the meeting unanimously decided upon adjournment to march in a body to Mr. Wilson's home to pay their tribute of respect. While the last speaker on the program was making his address arrangements were made with the police department for permit and that great audience headed by the band which played at intervals during the program, and with police escort marched to Mr. Wilson's home. The crowd that gathered in front of his home was larger by several thousands than the audience as the marchers were joined by a number of the citizens who fell in with the marching crowd.

Mr. and Mrs. Wilson[3] stood on the porch of his residence and upon request of the chairman of the meeting[4] I spoke for the assembled crowd. It was an impressive occasion and, of course, deeply gratifying to the former president. In my address in the theatre I declared that "Woodrow Wilson is coming back" and judging from the applause that statement brought forth that audience fully shared that belief.

I might add that I am a member of the Advisory Board of the National organization and I am doing and shall continue to do everything that I can to be helpful in making the movement a success.

Reciprocating your kind regards and hoping to hear from you whenever convenient, I am,

Fraternally yours,   Saml Gompers
President   American Federation of Labor.

TLpS, reel 275, vol. 288, pp. 483–84, SG Letterbooks, DLC.

1. Bert Mark Jewell was acting president of the AFL Railway Employes' Department from 1918 to 1922 and president of the organization from 1922 to 1946.

2. Organized in 1921, the Woodrow Wilson Foundation was created to memorialize the former president; Franklin Delano Roosevelt served as chairman of its national committee. The objective of the foundation was to raise $1,000,000 to endow an annual award for distinguished public service.

3. Edith Bolling Galt (1872–1961), who married Woodrow Wilson in 1915.

4. Author and lecturer Charles Edward Russell (1860–1941) chaired the meeting. A former Socialist (see *The Samuel Gompers Papers,* vol. 9, pp. 382–83, n. 4), he served as a member of the U.S. diplomatic mission to Russia in 1917, as a commissioner to Great Britain for the Committee on Public Information in 1918, and as a representative for the public at the President's Industrial Conference in 1919.

Excerpts from the Minutes of a Conference between Herbert Hoover and Samuel Gompers

Jan. 19. 1922.

Mr. Gompers called up Secretary of Commerce, Mr. Hoover over the telephone on the afternoon of January 18 and said to Mr. Hoover that he had one or two matters which he would like very much to present and asked for an interview. Mr. Hoover suggested that evening which was impossible on account of an engagement for dinner with Admiral Kato.[1] Mr. Hoover then set 11 o'clock, January 19th for the conference. Accordingly Mr. Gompers and his secretary, Mr. Oyster, were received by Mr. Hoover in his office at the appointed time.

Mr. Gompers said that there were several matters which he desired to bring to the attention of Secretary Hoover, among them the mining situation and the railroad situation but as these matters were not pressing, he hoped he might be granted the opportunity of presenting them at a later date.

. . .

The real purpose of Mr. Gompers' visit, however, was to present to Secretary Hoover his views on the advisability of the United States Government being represented at the conference in Genoa.[2] He plainly declared that he could not support the United States Government if it should decide to be represented at Genoa and fortified his position with his arguments as presented in the newspaper release of January 12, 1922[3] and the editorial in the February issue of the American Federationist entitled "The Alliance of Reactionary Capital and the Soviets,"[4] both of which are attached hereto.

Mr. Gompers stressed the fact that within the past month two mass gatherings[5] of workers had been held in New York antagonistic to the rational and normal policies and principles of organized labor of America as represented by the American Federation of Labor, and that if the United States recognizes or encourages Bolshevism and the Soviets it would make it all the more difficult, if not entirely futile, for organized labor to longer continue its fight against the propaganda of the Soviet regime in the United States, for if our Government recognizes it, directly or indirectly, that move would certainly be interpreted by the radical element in this country as an approval of Bolshevism and a vindication of their activity which has so far been held in check and controlled by the more intelligent portion of the organized labor movement of America.

Mr. Gompers described his interview with Secretary of State Hughes, at a dinner given by Admiral Baron Kato, of the Japanese Delegation to the Conference on the Limitation of Armaments, at the Shoreham Hotel last night (Jan. 18, 1922). After the dinner, in the presence of General Pershing and Senator Root, Mr. Gompers expressed his views to Secretary Hughes in opposition to any encouragement to or recognition of the Soviet Government of Russia, and especially by accepting the invitation of the Italian Government to participate in what is commonly called an "economic" conference at Genoa. Mr. Hughes thanked Mr. Gompers for presenting his views and said that they were very interesting; Senator Root said, "Mr. Gompers you are right," and later suggested that Mr. Gompers present his views to President Harding.

Secretary Hoover explained that he was practically alone in opposing any and all attempts to aid or encourage the Soviet system of Russia; that he was familiar with the conditions there having spent a great deal of time in that country before 1914 as engineer for large mining interests at a lucrative salary which he gave up to take charge of the Belgian relief work; that he had always differentiated between the Russian people and the Soviet leaders; that the revolution there primarily was an agrarian revolution and the Bolshevists rode into power on the crest of the wave; that the peasants are purely individualists and are now in the throes of a passive revolution declining to produce anything to support the socialistic power emanating from the cities.

He continued by stating that the world is in a terrible mess today, especially Europe on account of the inability of nations to balance their budgets and the source of the difficulty is the French-German impasse. Some of the people in France have put on the German helmet and France is insisting upon more reparation from Germany than Germany is able to pay. This is the root of all the difficulty as the situation in Poland, Chezcho-Slovakia and Hungary could be straightened out for five hundred million dollars which could be loaned by American bankers without action by the government.

Mr. Hoover agreed that Mr. Gompers should present his views on the matter to President Harding, adding that the President's mind was open on the subject but that he was inclined to feel that it was ungracious for the United States at this time to decline an invitation to participate in any conference designed or calculated to better the economic conditions of the world.

The question of Soviet propaganda came up and Mr. Hoover mentioned a Russian relief organization which seemed to be thriving in the Middle West with a number of governors and mayors and which Senator France seemed to be leading.[6] Mr. Hoover's investigation of this relief seemed to be resented and a representative thereof came to Mr. Hoover's office in a rather hostile mood and threatened to "show him up" in the light of opposing their movement to further his own interests in the Russian mines which he owned. During the interview Mr. Hoover obtained the information that his interviewer was working under contract with New York Soviet agents, and in spite of Mr. Hoover's denial of any financial returns from Russian activities since 1914, a circular to the contrary was published by the Russian relief organization in question. It developed during this portion of the interview that under Mr. Hoover's direction Russian relief supplies to the full capacity of Russian ports have been arranged for and that any additional supplies that go into Russia will do so by preventing the importation of the supplies arranged for by Mr. Hoover and already paid for, thus proving how unnecessary and superfluous are the efforts of those relief organizations operating under the auspices and control of Soviet agents.

Mr. Hoover described the present day Soviets as having two wings constantly diverging further and further from each other. On the right Crassin[7] and Lenin and on the left the radicals who would be perfectly willing to reduce the population of Russia to fifty millions in order to carry out their theories; that with a complete repudiation of Bolshevism and Sovietism he would not be adverse to recognizing a representative government in Russia even though it be headed by the individuals now associated with the right wing of the Soviets.

He expressed the opinion that he considered it wise to hold off to determine just what is the purpose of this Genoa Conference, especially as more information is coming in every day. It is known that there are groups in England, France and Italy who are cooperating in the effort to arrange for the exploitation of Russia by Germany as a movement calculated to permit Russia to pay France what she owes her and enable Germany to pay France what she owes her, thereby removing the fundamental obstacle in the way of the economic rehabilitation in Europe.

Mr. Hoover expressed himself as not being sure as to whether or not intrigues of this nature might not find an outlet in the conference at Genoa. He added, however, that he could not consistently vote against the United States being represented in an *economic* conference in Europe, and although the proposed Genoa conference was designated as an "economic" conference, he feared that its scope might be extended to take in the political field, and that the participants would find themselves enmeshed in European politics. His position seemed to be that of "watchful waiting" for definite assurance or evidence as to its exact nature and scope; that he would oppose the acceptance by the United States of an invitation to any conference the agenda of which might indicate the consideration or introduction of political questions; that he could not consistently vote against the participation of the United States in a purely *economic* conference in Europe.

The conference lasted about one hour, and Mr. Gompers expressed himself much pleased with the position of Mr. Hoover, it appearing that there was a complete meeting of the minds on the fundamental principles involved.

TDc, Files of the Office of the President, Conferences, reel 122, frames 35–43, *AFL Records.* Typed notation: "Conference between Samuel Gompers, President, American Federation of Labor and Honorable Herbert Hoover, Secretary, Department of Commerce,—Secretary Hoover's Office, 11 A.M. Jan. 19, 1922."

1. Tomosaburō Katō (1861–1923) served as the Japanese minister of the navy from 1915 to 1922, headed the Japanese delegation to the Washington Naval Conference in 1921, and was the prime minister of Japan from 1922 until his death the next year.

2. Thirty-four nations attended the Genoa conference, called on Jan. 6, 1922, by the Allied Supreme Council to discuss economic and financial questions, including the reconstruction of Central and Eastern Europe. To avoid conveying de facto recognition of the Soviet Union, the United States did not participate in the conference, which met from Apr. 10 to May 19. Instead, Richard Child, the American ambassador to Italy, attended the meetings as an unofficial observer. On Apr. 16, while the Genoa conference was in session, Walther Rathenau and Georgi Chicherin, the foreign ministers of Germany and the Soviet Union, signed the Treaty of Rapallo, by which the two countries established diplomatic relations and agreed to cooperate economically, cancel prewar debts, and drop war claims against each other.

3. For the press release, dated Jan. 12, 1922, see Files of the Office of the President, Speeches and Writings, reel 116, frames 254–55, *AFL Records.* For press coverage of the statement, see, for example, "Oppose Meeting Soviet at Genoa," *New York Times,* Jan. 13, 1922.

4. *American Federationist* 29 (Feb. 1922): 101–5.

5. See *The Samuel Gompers Papers,* vol. 11, p. 550, nn. 4, 7.

6. Joseph Irwin France (1873–1939) served as a Republican senator from Maryland from 1917 to 1923. He spent four weeks in Russia during July 1921, and on his return to the United States emerged as a strong proponent of famine relief and the opening of trade and diplomatic relations with the Soviets.

7. Leonid Borisovich Krasin (1870–1926), a member of the Soviet delegation to the Genoa conference, negotiated the Anglo-Soviet Trade Agreement of 1921 that secured de facto British recognition of the Soviet government. He later served as Soviet ambassador to Great Britain (1922–24, 1925–26) and to France (1924–25).

To Gertrude Gompers[1]

Springfield, Mass. Sunday 1. PM Jan. 22, 1922.

My Beloved Wife:—

Although I may see you before this note will reach you, I can't help. writing a word to you. I am thereby in touch with you I hated to leave you yesterday for many reasons, but particularly that you were to have the first treatment.[2] I should have liked to be with you & to know its reaction last evening & today. It [is] that feeling which prompted me to telephone you so often before I left.

I hope you stood the treatment well and that you will soon receive its fulll benefit. & be cured from that terrible trouble. Wish that I were with you now. The trip so far has been uneventful. The snow is on the ground & is deep. It is cold.

The men [are] waiting waiting for me in another room for the conference. My train left at 7.43 this morning, I had to get up at 6.30 and expecting a dining car on the train only to learn that there was not a thing to eat to be had. Our train was half an hour late so I was hungry

All my good wishes for you & all my love & kisses.

Your Loving Husband   Sam.

Regards to Elsie

ALS, NNAJHi.

1. Gertrude Annersly Gleaves GOMPERS was SG's second wife.
2. It is not known what Mrs. Gompers was being treated for.

To Charles Hastings[1]

Jan. 28, 1922.

Mr. Chas. E. Hastings,
No. 135 East Grand Avenue, Ridgefield Park, N.J.
Dear Sir:

You ask two questions as follows:[2]

(1) At what age should a man retire from active work?

(2) Does retirement, in your opinion, operate beneficially to the man who retires to private life?

(1) I might say with justice that you will have to ask somebody older than I as to what age a man should retire from active work. I am seventy-two years of age and have never even thought of the question of retiring from active work. I never felt better fitted for the work I am doing. Every hour of the day and night while I am awake I am working.

On reaching my seventieth birthday I was asked by the New York World to tell how it felt to be that old. Enclosed you will find my answer.[3]

(2) Men who work continually are more apt to live longer than those who idle away their time. Furthermore, the experience gained by a

man in years of struggle should not be lost to the country no matter in what walk of life he may be. The more active a man has been and the wider his perspective of life the more knowledge he will have gained. Therefore he owes it not only to himself but to those with whom he has traveled down the pathway of life to remain active until he dies. I could not stop working if I wanted to.

Yours very truly,   Saml Gompers
President,   American Federation of Labor.

TLpS, reel 276, vol. 289, p. 34, SG Letterbooks, DLC.

1. Charles Edward Hastings (b. 1878) was a reporter.
2. Hastings to SG, Jan. 24, 1922, Files of the Office of the President, General Correspondence, reel 106, frame 9, *AFL Records*. Hastings was soliciting the opinions of leading men on retirement.
3. For a copy of SG's letter, see *The Samuel Gompers Papers*, vol. 11, p. 246.

An Address before the Conference on Unemployment Insurance at the Annual Meeting of the National Civic Federation in New York City[1]

Hotel Astor, New York. January 31, 1922.

. . .

Samuel Gompers, President of the American Federation of Labor in closing the conference, said:

"I am very much interested in the subject of unemployment and I have my grave apprehensions as to what may result in what is termed unemployment insurance. It means so much and yet the term in itself is meaningless. There has thus far been no employment insurance. It has been payment on account of being unemployed. I hold that any system of so-called unemployment insurance is to recognize unemployment as a permanent condition in our country. I cannot agree, of course, with the idea that the question of employment or unemployment with its periodicity, is influenced by either Venus or Adonis. The question of unemployment is a problem controllable. There is a remedy, if there were now in existence the voluntary methods of employees and employers of workers to deal with the question and take the business of this country into their own hands rather than leaving it to be conducted by the princes of finance to whom Professor Commons has made reference. It is altogether too true that the princes of finance, the banking institutions, are in control of the industries of the country and they have left the hands of the employers. The initiative and the idealism that prompted the men in the business world and, particularly, in railroad construction, maintenance and expansion, have been obliterated from the railroad operation and expansion by this very financial interest which controls railroad presidents, railroad managers, and railroad companies. The railroad business is not conducted in the offices of the railroad presidents and managers but is conducted and directed from Wall Street.

"From Great Britain, I have learned some of the facts which now exist in this so-called unemployment insurance. At the last British Trade Union Congress held at Cardiff in September, 1921,[2] the declaration was made that the so-called unemployment insurance has been a failure; that they cannot now ask for its repeal because of the disarrangement it would cause; but what they want is not unemployment insurance,—they want employment.

"No one can get away from this absolute fact that if we were to have compulsory unemployment insurance, the working people would be subjected to rules and regulations and investigations and supervision of almost every act of their lives. It would open the way—instead of the protection which now every American citizen and every British subject is supposed to hold, that his home, however humble it may be, is his castle—it would open the door to the governmental agents and agencies who would spy and pry into the very innermost recesses of the home life. It would entangle the mass of the working people in a mesh of legalisms and restrictions, to which I am not willing as one American citizen to help to subject the working people of the United States.

"I have said, and I want to repeat it just now, that I doubt [i]f there is any man in all the world who is a more loyal and devoted citizen of the Republic of the United States than I am. Now I [a]m not saying this as a boast, because it is a feeling of reverence and respect and devotion but, loyal as I am to our republic, I would not trust it and its agents to enter the homes of the working people at will.

"The question of involuntary unemployment—there is a question of voluntary unemployment and who is to determine what really constitutes say, a strike or a lockout? A government agent! Well, God save us from that kind of a fellow. Government interpretations, government constructions, government enforcement, government regulations and rules and supervision.

"I know what it means to be unemployed. I am not a professor from a college or a university. The only university from which I have graduated is that of hard knocks. I have been a wage earner at my trade for 26 years and I know whereof I speak, as a workman, as a wage earner, and not only working at my trade but working with my shop mates in several factories and being in close touch all my life with the working conditions and the feelings, the understandings, the intuition, or what not, of men and women who work for wages. The subtleties, the psychology, in the relations of workers to employers, and employers to workers, —the subtlety of it, often. You cannot define it by law or regulation. It is human, it is in that physical, actual, industrial relation which comes from the position of wage earners and the employers, and that which shall come, is the voluntary or involuntary unemployment to be decided by governmental agencies, and evidently enforceable by them.

"I cannot agree that in the industrial life of our country there are forces that are beyond the human control. They cannot be. And I don't know whether I understood quite accurately the statement made by Professor Commons—whom I have known for very many years, and I have enjoyed his friendship, he knows that I have enjoyed our working together. I don't know whether I understood him accurately when he spoke of trade unions, of spreading over the work, or limiting production. I don't know which term, because a little later on he spoke of the unions, of spreading the work, that is, in times of industrial depression, of the union workmen preferring to work shorter hours, or divide the work with those who would be thrown into the streets unemployed. Now, with that latter part, that is, that union workmen are willing to share their employment by reducing the time say one half, or one third, and giving employment to all rather than that any of them should be laid off or discharged, I quite agree. That is true. But if it is intended to convey the idea that the trade union movement of the United States is limiting production, I must express my emphatic dissent. And let me add this on that point. Statistics will prove, and it is common knowledge, that there are no working people either individual or in their collectivity, who produce so much as do the working people of the United States. And I think it comes with bad grace from our own people, when the toilers of our own country are held up to ridicule or to severe censure, that they curtail production, when they have been and are the greatest producers of any working people in the entire world.

"I believe in the voluntary system of trying to provide something for the unemployed worker. I believe that the periodicity which has come upon the industrial life of our country by which these cycles of unemployment come about, are hand made, and, in too great frequency, premeditatedly. If there were as much attention given to the encouragement of our industrial life and its expansion as there is given to curtailing—to shutting down institutions so that there shall be a corner, tending toward the profiteering of manufacturers and financiers, we would have less of this periodical unemployment, much more of general employment, and business prosperity and onward march to a greater and higher civilization.["]

TDp, reel 276, vol. 289, pp. 918–20, SG Letterbooks, DLC. Enclosed in R. Lee Guard to J. Vernon McKenzie, Feb. 16, 1922, p. 917, ibid. Typed notation: "Conference on Unemployment Insurance Annual Meeting The National Civic Federation January 31, 1922, Hotel Astor, New York."

1. The annual meeting of the National Civic Federation was held in New York City, Jan. 30-Feb. 1, 1922.
2. The 1921 conference of the TUC met in Cardiff, Sept. 5–10.

To Edward FitzGerald[1]

Washington, D.C., February 3, 1922.

E. H. Fitzgerald
Second National Bank Bldg., Cincinnati, Ohio.
President Moore[2] of the Canadian Trades and Labor Congress in conference with Secretary Morrison[3] and me here brought to our attention the situation in the labor movement of Canada and the turmoil and confusion which are sure to arise unless definite action is taken by you in reference to the Canadian Brotherhood of Railroad Employes[4] headed by Mr. Mosher[5] *Stop* Mr. Moore called attention to the conference which was held at Chicago recently[6] in which the subject was discussed and at which Mr. Mosher and a number of representative men of international railroad organizations and representatives of your organization participated *Stop* Mr. Moore outlined a tentative agreement which he understands was reached at the Chicago Conference and which has been agreed to by Mr. Mosher for his organization and those he represents and that the entire agreement now is in your hands and if approved by you would clarify the entire situation and make cooperation for the common good possible and positive. President Moore assures Secretary Morrison and me that the officers of the international unions regard the situation as critical and would be in an indefensible position if these negotiations fail *Stop* While we have no warrant or right to interfere with the internal affairs of your organization yet the interests of our movement require that this matter be presented to you as herein set forth.[7]

Samuel Gompers

TWpSr, reel 276, vol. 289, p. 271, SG Letterbooks, DLC.

1. Edward H. FITZGERALD served as grand president of the Brotherhood of Railway and Steamship Clerks, Freight Handlers, Express and Station Employes from 1920 to 1928.

2. Tom MOORE, president of the Trades and Labor Congress of Canada from 1918 to 1935 and from 1939 to 1943.

3. Frank MORRISON served as secretary of the AFL from 1897 to 1935 and as secretary-treasurer of the organization from 1936 to 1939.

4. The Canadian Brotherhood of RAILROAD Employees.

5. Aaron Alexander Roland MOSHER served as president of the Brotherhood of Railroad Employees from 1908 to 1952.

6. At a meeting beginning Feb. 1, 1922, the executive council of the AFL Railway Employes' Department endorsed an amalgamation plan known as the Chicago Platform to bring together the Railway Clerks and the Brotherhood of Railroad Employees.

7. On Sept. 17, 1922, FitzGerald attended a meeting in Montreal to discuss the amalgamation of the two unions, but without result.

From W. D. Mahon[1]

Amalgamated Association of Street & Electric
Railway Employes of America[2]
Detroit, Mich., February 13, 1922.

Dear Sir & Brother:

I write you at this time regarding a temporary injunction that has stood over us for the past couple of years in New York City. It is the Third Avenue Railway Co. seeking a permanent injunction against our organization, setting up the individual contracts, and enjoining us from interfering with them.[3]

The matter came up for discussion at our Board Meeting, which closed Saturday. There was a wide difference of opinion. Mr. Vahey,[4] our attorney, was present, and of course argued from the lawyer's side of it contending that it was an important matter and that we should stand trial on it.

At the outset he seemed to think that we should allow the company to get an injunction against certain of our officers who had been on the ground there and had tried to organize the men at one time after those voluntary contracts had been made with the men. He said we couldn't stop them getting some kind of an injunction but he wanted to try and prevent them from getting it against all of our officers.

I took the position before our Board that that was a foolish thing to do. If the permanent injunction was granted against these men it would also affect all other men, and I took a position that for the last thirty years I have been personally under injunctions in different parts of the country; that I had never, until recent years, ever attempted to answer an injunction or to pay any attention to it, and up to the present time I have never been arrested for refusing to obey them.

I could go back to 1894 when an injunction was granted against me and members of the organization at Toledo, Ohio, by Judge Harmon in the local court.[5] While these injunctions were granted against me and about a hundred and twenty men, as I remember, we built a monument in the street out of the injunctions and set them afire, and said that we wouldn't be influenced or intimidated by such a procedure. A few days after that we secured a settlement of the strike. The temporary injunction was granted and the hearing was set for some weeks away. I presume with the hopes that the strike would be killed before that time. I never went to court nor answered it. We dealt with that company, which was a small company, for some time thereafter until it became consolidated with the other companies.

In St. Louis, Kansas City, and other places, I have been enjoined, so many of them that I have forgotten some of them, but as I have stated, until recent years I have never made any attempt to offset the injunctions. My experience has been that they are never heard of a short time thereafter.

At Indianapolis when Judge Anderson granted his injunction we went into court and then took the case to the Appellate Court and had Anderson reversed,[6] but a short time afterwards, possible a year or two, Anderson granted another injunction along the same lines as the first one,[7] and the lawyers made certain answers to it and then dropped the matter and we have never paid any more attention to it.

Going back to the New York case, I take the position that it would cause our organization thirty or forty thousand dollars to fight this injunction and then in the end they would get one anyhow. I said to our Board and the lawyer, this: That if they had asked me if I knew there were individual contracts, I would say that I supposed there were and that I didn't care if there were individual contracts, as we had fought these kind of contracts ever since we have been an organization, and that we would continue to fight them—that it was a form of slavery and one that I wouldn't be bound by because it was contrary to the constitution of the United States—that I would advise men to organize and break individual contracts wherever they could and I would continue to do so and I would tell any court that asked me.

The lawyer placed the entire case before us and left us. It was Mr. Vahey of Boston. Our Board discussed the matter and did not come to a final conclusion. I think the majority of our Board were practically in favor of saying that they wouldn't spend any more money or fool any longer with this injunction.

However, the Board placed the matter in the hands of the Secretary[8] to draft our position to be forwarded to the lawyer and by him to Court and we are now working on that, and I take this means of asking your advice.

When we discussed this matter before our Board I brought forth Document #65[9] which you had sent me on February 8 and I read it to our Board and it seemed to them that you held practically the same position on this matter that I do, or rather, that I held the position that you had expressed, and which I know you have for years held.

Now I think you are somewhat familiar with this New York case. At first they sought a million dollars or more damages because of our men striking in what they said was in violation of the settlement of 1916. The contract at that time was made with the men and our men did go out on strike, as you know, and continued for a long time. However, the damage end of the matter has been dropped and what they are now seeking is a permanent injunction against us interfering or organizing men that are under private contracts with the company, basing their position on the Hitchman coal case as affecting the mine workers.

I wish you would write me at once upon reading this letter and give me your advice as we are now formulating our position to be placed before our Board and then to be placed, if approved by them, before the lawyer, and as we have no time to lose as the case comes up in the courts in March, I would be pleased if you would answer me immediately upon this matter.[10]

With best wishes, I remain

Fraternally yours,   W D Mahon
International President

TLS, AFL Microfilm National and International Union File, Street and Electric Railway Employees' Records, reel 41, frame 1726, *AFL Records.* Handwritten notation: "Received 6:30 P.M. Feb. 14."

1. William D. Mahon, president of the Amalgamated Association of Street and Electric Railway Employes of America, served as an AFL vice-president from 1917 to 1923 and again from 1936 to 1949.

2. The Amalgamated Association of Street and Electric Railway Employes of America.

3. No sooner had the Street Railway Employees and the Third Avenue Railway Co. settled a strike in August 1916, with a contract securing union recognition and the right to organize, than another walkout began in September as Third Avenue employees joined other streetcar workers in a massive strike against the Interborough Rapid Transit Co. and the New York Railways Co. (see *The Samuel Gompers Papers,* vol. 9, p. 492, n. 1). Union spokesmen justified participation in the new strike by pointing to the firing of workers involved in the August walkout, the organization of a company union to eliminate so-called "outsiders," and the firm's refusal to meet with representatives of the Street Railway Employees. The September 1916 strike was a failure, as was another in 1918 that began when the company laid off some four hundred employees who had

joined the Street Railway Employes. In 1919 the firm was granted a temporary injunction enjoining the union from attempting to organize its workers (*Third Avenue Railway Co.* v. *Patrick J. Shea et al.,* 179 N.Y.S. 43 [1919]). The union considered the injunction illegal but refused to go to the expense of fighting it in court. The injunction was later made permanent.

4. James H. Vahey (1871–1929), a Boston attorney, served as general counsel for the Street and Electric Railway Employes.

5. On Mar. 22, 1894, employees of the Toledo Electric Street Railway Co. went on strike to protest the discharge of four union members. That afternoon Judge Gilbert Harmon (1833–1909), who sat on the Toledo Court of Common Pleas from 1889 to 1895, issued an injunction restraining the strikers from interfering with the operation of the lines. Nevertheless, newspapers reported that the strike continued and that the railway had been brought to a standstill.

6. See *The Samuel Gompers Papers,* vol. 9, pp. 206–7 and p. 208, n. 2.

7. The Indianapolis Traction and Terminal Co. applied for the injunction in November 1918 to prevent a strike by the members of Street Railway Employes' division 645. The union agreed to postpone the strike while Judge Anderson took evidence in the case, but on Dec. 12, while the injunction application was still pending, and against the advice of the local's officers, the men walked off their jobs, demanding a pay raise. Despite the officers' claim that they had not called the strike and that they considered it illegal, Anderson issued the temporary injunction the next day and cited the officers for contempt.

8. Ransom Lincoln Reeves (1860?-1934), a resident of Detroit, was a member of the general executive board of the Street and Electric Railway Employes from 1899 to 1934 and was the longtime editor of the union's journal, *The Motorman and Conductor* (after 1928, *The Motorman, Conductor, and Motor Coach Operator*).

9. This letter to the members of the AFL Executive Council dealt with the growing use of injunctions in labor disputes and concluded: "It should be our object to prevent the issuance of unlawful writs of injunction wherever possible; but where such injunctions are issued, the only course open to the workers is the course laid down in the declarations of our conventions. The unlawful injunction must be regarded by workers as non-existent and their conduct must be such as it would be if no such decree had been issued. The immediate consequences may be inconvenient but the ultimate result will be the retention of our freedom" (SG to the AFL Executive Council, Feb. 8, 1922, Executive Council Records, Vote Books, reel 17, frames 199–202, *AFL Records;* quotation at frame 202).

10. In his reply to Mahon, dated Feb. 15, 1922, SG wrote that "I can see no good results from any present action which the labor movement can take, in defending itself or its members before the courts in these injunction cases. The defences which our attorneys make in these injunctions is the denial of the facts alleged in the injunction applications and in some instances the injunctions are granted with certain modifications, but the injunctions as they are then issued deny the right of the working people to do lawful acts; and so our movement is handcuffed and fettered and incapable of functioning in a normal, rational and lawful and constitutional way. And I say, without any reflection upon the men in the legal profession, but it is a fact beyond peradventure of a doubt that they are afraid to contest the constitutionality of the right to issue the injunction, and I have no hesitancy in stating to you that upon no other ground will the courts ever decide in principle that the injunctions are unconstitutional until the challenge of their constitutionality is made in the preliminary stages of the injunction cases" (reel 276, vol. 289, pp. 729–32, SG Letterbooks, DLC; quotation at p. 731).

To Miner Norton[1]

February 23, 1922.

Hon. Miner G. Norton,
House Office Building, Washington, D.C.
Sir:

Your letter of February 18 received and contents noted.

You state that you are "surprised to hear that the American Federation of Labor would oppose a sales tax for the sole purpose of raising money to pay a bonus for those who were in the service."[2] Is it the sole purpose? The same influences that brought about the repeal of the excess profits taxes and the sur taxes desire to force upon the country a sales tax and they hope to do it by trickery. They know that the people of this country are in favor of a bonus for former service men. They also know that the people are just as unanimously against a consumption sales tax. Therefore it is intended to clinch a consumption sales tax on the people by forcing it through congress on the backs of our former service men and women.

If the bonus with the sales tax is adopted by congress it will be because those opposed to the bonus are so anxious to shift taxation to the masses that they will vote for both. Then the sales tax will be greatly increased and extended until those who believe that the well-to-do should not pay taxes will gain their ends.

In your statement that the sales tax is for the sole purpose of raising money to pay a bonus for those in the service you add:

"while the members of the Federation remained at home and were receiving many times the salary of those who were risking their lives in the defense of the country."

You have overlooked the fact that the profiteers, the men who accumulated vast fortunes during the war and the men whom you are anxious to relieve from paying taxes also remained in this country during the war. They not only received many thousands times the salary of those who offered the supreme sacrifice but they also made profits so high as to be almost inconceivable. And these men did not wear overalls and work with their hands in the making of munitions of war to back up the men in the trenches. They were parasites. Yet your perspective does not reach any further than the man who works for wages and whom you would compel to pay the taxes that those you defend should pay. You even intend that the soldier shall pay his own dues. This is set forth by Representative Lester D. Volk[3] of Greater New York as follows:

"Thus the ex-service man will in a great measure be paying his own bonus.["]

That is the truth in a nut shell. In order to shift the burden from those well able to pay the tax to those already over burdened you would take money out of one of the pockets of a soldier and place it in the other and then pat him on the back and tell him he received the bonus. Many members of Congress are not as much interested in a bonus as they are in grafting a sales tax on the American people.

I am very sorry indeed that you declare yourself in favor of the sales tax. When the housewives of Greater New York feel the effects of the sales tax on the living costs you may then realize how much injury such legislation will do to the masses of our people.

> Respectfully yours,   Saml Gompers
> President,   American Federation of Labor.

TLpS, reel 277, vol. 290, pp. 140–41, SG Letterbooks, DLC.

1. Miner Gibbs Norton (1857–1926), a Cleveland attorney, was a Republican congressman from Ohio (1921–23).

2. Norton was responding to a statement by SG on Feb. 17, 1922, opposing Republican efforts to pass a bonus bill funded by a sales tax. A bonus bill without the sales tax provision was eventually passed by this session of Congress (H.R. 10,874, 67th Cong., 2d sess., introduced on Mar. 13 by Republican congressman Joseph Fordney of Michigan, approved by the House on Sept. 14 and by the Senate on Sept. 15), but President Warren Harding vetoed the measure.

3. Lester David Volk (1884–1962) served as a Republican congressman from New York from 1920 until 1923.

An Editorial in the *American Federationist*

[February 1922]

MINERS AND RAILROADERS

While here and there legislators, energetic but unwise reformers and those who would direct the forces of industries from the watchtowers of intelligentsia-land continue to preach the message of deliverance through governmental compulsion and the mechanism of tribunals, the world of industry itself in some very important particulars is rapidly getting back to first principles and industrial truths. In two great, fundamental industries there is at present a disturbed situation, but in neither of these industries is there any great likelihood of lasting peace, or even the approach to it, except through direct negotiation between the groups involved.

The railroads of the country, in their drive against the workers on the railroads, have secured from the railroad labor board a ruling which removes the penalty for overtime and thus abrogates the eight-hour day. This decision followed a number of others which as a whole form a convincing exhibit to prove the character of the railroad labor board as an institution.

What has happened is that the railroad labor board has accepted (as it was bound to) the philosophy, the analysis and the definition of the employing world as to our economic ills and has made its decisions in accordance.

The situation before the railroad labor board grows more crucial every day. Confidence in it there never was; and such hope as there might have been that the board might at least make an effort to deal fairly, with vision and understanding, has been almost entirely dissipated. The board today stands as a crude, almost brutal, instrumentality, accused of being pro-employer, a link in the anti-union chain, a blind, tottering wreck of an idiotic experiment.

What labor condemned in advance as wrong in principle now stands convicted in practice as worse than wrong because biased—not necessarily by corruption but by natural bent and the force of circumstances—and because it is entirely out of place in the world of economic actualities.

All of this is driving the railroad world back to direct negotiation. Witness the spectacle of the brotherhoods going to Washington instead of to Chicago, going into conference with the executives direct and laying plans for further conferences of a regional character, circumnavigating the railroad labor board's machinery and ignoring its jurisdiction and authority.[1] The railroad employes' organizations are pursuing a course that has been proven to them to be the wisest and the Chicago court of misrule is helpless. Witness the spectacle of the Pennsylvania Railroad enjoining the board from publishing a decision adverse to that railroad—a decision which has not yet seen the light of day, so far as we are informed.[2]

The railroads have sought to use the railroad labor board as a weapon, not as a tribunal, which must always be the case. And either as weapon or tribunal, the thing is a failure, because neither weapon nor tribunal begets voluntary agreement but produces only compulsory compliance, except when organizations are strong enough to resist compulsion.

The railroads have sought and are seeking to drive the shop trades into submission by compelling them to accept abrogation of rules and conditions of work established in railroad practice for years and brought about either through the voluntary action of railroad managements or through negotiation between railroad workers and managements.

The board, which has come to be practically a one-man institution, has decided in favor of abolishing certain important rules and regulations having to do with the shop trades workers. One of these is the rule providing for time and one-half for overtime, the only effective preventive of overtime.

The rules and conditions of work which the board has ordered abolished were established before there was such a thing as a railroad labor board. They were established in the days when employed and employer sat down together to work out their joint problems through negotiation. They were agreed to by the railroads and the workers. They were markers of progress, placing American railroad workers on a higher plane, giving them broader opportunities for citizenship and for self-development as well as more effective service for their employers, because of good will.

The railroad workers now find themselves confronting a situation in which they must look to their economic strength to preserve what a political institution has sought to destroy. This inevitably leads back to direct negotiation. A rehearing may be held, but whatever the course to be pursued, in the background must be the consciousness of reliance on economic strength.

The reason that the railroad situation has reached such a critical stage is because negotiation has been made impossible by the existence of the railroad labor board and in a secondary sense because the board has functioned as a weapon and not as a tribunal. The way to reconstructed railroad relationships lies over the corpse of the railroad labor board and there is no other way.

The railroads may seek to impose unjust conditions upon the workers, board or no board, but without the board the railroads will either have to go into conference and enter into negotiation or answer to the country for their refusal. They can now escape negotiation and blame the governmental court for the results.

In the mining industry there is the same appetite on the part of employers. The mine owners, however, have no tribunal behind which to hide responsibility for their aggression. If the mine owners are arrogant—and they are—they must stand forth in the first person and wear the label to which their conduct entitles them or condemns them as the case may be.

At the present moment the mine owners, swelling with profits reaped from coal prices which have gone beyond all bounds, are seeking to further enrich themselves at the expense of the mine workers. A public that is paying more than war prices for coal while thousands of miners are kept in enforced idleness and thus are forbidden to dig coal, is likely to be fairly accurate in placing the blame for a tie-up of the industry if one comes.

For the mine owners at this time to make demands upon the mine workers is the height of brazen effrontery, the acme of abandoned looting and pillage. Coal prices are sky high and the retail supply is kept on the verge of actual shortage. Meanwhile thousands of miners are kept out of the mines, thus creating a situation in which there is no reserve supply visible to the average person. The coal barons make their own law of supply and demand and they make it just as drastic as possible so far as demand is concerned, worrying not at all about supply except as it is necessary as a basis for the baronial demand for loot.

The president of the United Mine Workers of America[3] has said to the miners and to the country that the miners will not yield. The American labor movement will support the miners in their position, for to yield would be to yield to injustice.

The injustice contemplated by the mine owners is an injustice that is aimed against the miners and the great masses of the coal consumers of the country as well, for it is a double-edged injustice that would drive down wages and maintain inflated profits. There are more than enough idle miners to bring into being an ample and more than ample coal supply and there are more than enough idle cars in which to haul that coal to market. There are more than enough railroad men to maintain and operate those idle cars and there are people who would like the coal and who would like it at a price that would allow the miner a fair wage and the owner a fair profit, but they resent a price that makes every operator a super-Croesus while the miner either goes idle or so nearly so as to make his wage a pittance.

There is one road to justice in both railroad and mine industries. There must be a return to joint negotiation and agreement. The railroads seek to evade it because the railroad labor board offers them the opportunity and the mine owners seek to evade it because they are drunk with what they falsely imagine is power which makes it needless for them either to consult the workers or anyone else and which makes it unnecessary for them to worry about justice.

The American labor movement and the American people will be with the miners if they are forced to defend their rights. If they are forced to fight against bloated, arrogant privilege and profiteering for a fair wage and for the opportunity to go down into the earth to dig coal, may they fight a good fight, for they will be fighting for justice and justice for the miners is the concern of all who love justice.

Two of the great, vital industries have been brought to the verge of turmoil by governmental interference, by injection of the ancient, out-worn idea of compulsion, by arrogant profiteering. It will take the steady, democratic policy of the American trade union movement, put in practice in its full implications to restore those industries to proper functioning and to properly serving the people of our country.

American Federationist 29 (Feb. 1922): 114–16.

1. SG is referring to a meeting of railroad executives and representatives of the railroad brotherhoods, held Jan. 16, 1922, in Washington, D.C. Secretary of Commerce Herbert Hoover arranged the meeting to discuss the feasibility of referring disputes over wages and working conditions to regional conferences of management and labor rather than to the U.S. Railroad Labor Board.

2. In April 1921 the Railroad Labor Board ordered the termination of the U.S. Railroad Administration's wartime provisions on work rules and conditions and directed the various individual railroads to negotiate new provisions with their employees or their employees' representatives. The Pennsylvania Railroad refused to negotiate the new arrangements with union men who represented the majority of its shop craft workers and instead arranged an election of employee representatives that excluded the union. The board ruled the election invalid and ordered a new one, but the railroad refused to comply and obtained an injunction from Judge Kenesaw Mountain Landis to block the board from proceeding further in the matter. Landis's decision was upheld in April 1922 by U.S. district court judge George Page but was reversed in July by the U.S. circuit court of appeals (*U.S. Railroad Labor Board et al.* v. *Pennsylvania Railroad Co.*, 282 F. 701 [1922]). The circuit court ruling overturning the injunction was upheld by the U.S. Supreme Court in February 1923 (*Pennsylvania Railroad Co.* v. *U.S. Railroad Labor Board et al.*, 261 U.S. 72 [1923]).

3. John Llewellyn LEWIS served as acting president of the United MINE Workers of America from 1919 to 1920 and as president of the union from 1920 to 1960.

To David Hanly[1]

March 1, 1922.

Mr. David Hanly,
Chairman, Legislative Committee, Tennessee Federation of Labor,[2]
Nashville, Tennessee.
Dear Sir and Brother:

I note what you say in reference to the protective laws for women. The American Federation of Labor, however, has taken the following position:

"The principle that organization is the most potent means for a shorter work day and for a higher standard of wages applies to women workers equally as to men but the fact must be recognized that the organization of women workers constitutes a separate and more difficult problem. Women do not organize as rapidly or as stably as do men. They are therefore more easily exploited. They certainly are in a greater measure than are men entitled to the concern of society. A fair standard of wages—for all employed in an industry, should be the first consideration in production. None are more entitled than are the women and minors."[3]

It, therefore, devolves on the American Federation of Labor to oppose any amendment to the Constitution of the United States that would take from the women in industry the protection they now have under the laws in the various states.[4] I hope, therefore, that you will do your utmost to defeat such a bill in your legislature.

With best wishes and assuring you of my desire to be helpful in any way within my power, I am,

Fraternally yours, Saml Gompers.
President, American Federation of Labor.

TLpS, reel 277, vol. 290, p. 282, SG Letterbooks, DLC.

1. David Hanly (b. 1875), a member of International Typographical Union 20 of Nashville, was president of the Nashville Trades and Labor Council in 1922 and chairman of the legislative committee of the Tennessee State Federation of Labor (1918–33).

2. The AFL chartered the Tennessee State Federation of Labor in 1902.

3. The passage is taken from the report of the AFL Executive Council to the 1913 AFL convention. See *The Samuel Gompers Papers*, vol. 9, p. 20.

4. SG is referring to the Equal Rights Amendment to the U.S. Constitution, proposed by the National Woman's party. The version of the measure put forward by the party in late 1921 read: "No political, civil or legal disabilities or inequalities on account of sex, or on account of marriage unless applying alike to both sexes, shall exist within the United States or any place subject to their jurisdiction" ("Fixes Equal Rights Amendment Form," *New York Times*, Dec. 12, 1921). The party's 1923 convention adopted a revised version of the amendment which read: "Men and women shall have equal rights throughout the United States and every place subject to its jurisdiction" ("Women Open Fight for Equal Rights," *New York Times*, July 21, 1923). This was introduced in Congress later that year but failed to pass. Submitted to succeeding Congresses, it was finally passed in 1972 but then failed ratification.

To James Davis

March 4, 1922.

Hon. James J. Davis,
Secretary of Labor,
Labor Department, Washington, D.C.
Sir:

I have received a letter[1] from Clovis, New Mexico, in which the following statement occurs:

"I am a railroad machinist and have worked on a good many railroads but find a critical condition existing on the Atcheson, Topeka and Santa Fe Railroad and the Southern Pacific lines. These two railroads have hundreds of Japanese mechanics in their employ besides laborers. They come from parts unknown and are continuously causing dissension among American and Mexican mechanics. There is on an average of twelve to twenty competent American mechanics passing through Clovis each week seeking employment. While the Santa Fe has hired several Americans they have also placed several Japanese shipped in from the South West."

More than a year ago the charge was made in the Immigration Committee of the House that Japanese, Chinese and other foreigners were being smuggled across the Mexican border. The border patrols had been taken off because it was alleged there was no money appropriated for that purpose. Would you kindly let me know what the conditions are at present on the Mexican border? Is there a sufficient patrol to prevent the smuggling of Chinese and Japanese into our country? Is it possible to find out how these Japanese who turn up suddenly in industrial centers in the South West secure admission to the country? While unemployment is so acute it would appear that the greatest effort should be made to prevent smuggling of Orientals. I would also like to know if the appropriations for conducting the Immigration Division are sufficient.

Very respectfully yours,   Saml Gompers
President,   American Federation of Labor.

P.S. It is about the above matter which we shall in part discuss at our forthcoming meeting.[2]

TLpS, reel 277, vol. 290, p. 507, SG Letterbooks, DLC.

1. M. W. Lynch to SG, Feb. 29 [*sic*], 1922. Lynch was an AFL volunteer organizer.
2. SG met with James Davis on Mar. 7, 1922.

To Joseph Miller[1]

March 10, 1922

Mr. Joseph Dana Miller,
c/o Single Tax Review,
New York City, New York.
Dear Sir:

In the February issue of the Single Tax Review there is published a letter by you addressed to me.[2] I really regret that you did not see the wisdom or the amenities between man and man and address the letter to me for consideration and reply but that you deemed it proper to publish the letter in the Review without even doing me the courtesy or giving me the opportunity of seeing it before publication and replying thereto. Perhaps that may be your view of proprieties and depending upon me to get your letter through an indirect source. However, dismissing this from consideration let me make the following observations.

When working at my trade in a factory the Irish World, a New York Weekly, published chapters in each of its issues of Henry George's "Progress and Poverty."[3] These chapters were read aloud each week affording the major part of the discussion among the men. It was due to a few of my friends and myself that the chapters were read and discussed in the "Spirit-and-Light Club"[4] of Brooklyn, New York, of which I was a member. Combined efforts of all were directed in being helpful in having the work "Progress and Poverty" done into a book. Later, we were helpful in having "Progress and Poverty" printed in the Congressional Record.[5] Perhaps these facts might justify my statement that I aided in having Henry George understood.

I aided in the nomination of Henry George in his campaign for mayor of New York and in the campaign in the election.[6] It was he who induced me to buy a bicycle and on our machines we frequently, and particularly on Sunday, took long rides at which most interesting discussions took place and there was established between us a very firm friendship. I have declared and now say that I am a single taxer. I believe the single tax to be the most practical, effective and generally advantageous tax which can be imposed, but you take me to task because in my article on "Abolish Unemployment"[7] I did not declare for the single tax as a remedy for unemployment.

All I need say in reply is that the organized labor movement cannot and will not wait for the establishment of the single tax system to have our unemployed workmen at work.

"While the grass grows, etc." Shakespeare in his time declared that proverb somewhat musty[8] and yet its lesson is as potent today as when the phrase was coined. One of my dear friends for many years a single taxer after reading your letter in the Single Tax Review stated to me "The worst about the single tax is the single taxer." Is it difficult to imagine the type of man he had in mind?

Very truly yours,   Saml Gompers
President   American Federation of Labor.

TLpS, reel 277, vol. 290, pp. 743–44, SG Letterbooks, DLC.

1. Joseph Dana Miller (1864–1939), a longtime associate of Henry George, was

the editor of the *Single Tax Review* (after 1924, *Land and Freedom*) from its founding in 1901 until 1939. In 1917 he edited and published the *Single Tax Year Book: The History, Principles, and Application of the Single Tax Philosophy.*

2. "A Few Words with Samuel Gompers," *Single Tax Review* 22 (Jan.-Feb. 1922): 17–19. SG's reply of Mar. 10, together with Miller's rejoinder, appeared in the following issue ("Mr. Samuel Gompers Replies to Our Criticism," ibid. [Mar.-Apr. 1922]: 42–44).

3. Actually it was *Truth,* a New York City paper edited by Louis Post, that in 1881 undertook the serial publication of *Progress and Poverty.* From the fall of 1881 to the fall of 1882 the *Irish World* published Henry George's regular reports as its correspondent in Ireland.

4. Actually the Spread the Light Club, a public education forum sponsored by KOL Local Assembly 1562 of Brooklyn and established for the purpose of "diffusing knowledge on social and scientific subjects among the masses, to enable them to assert their rights against the universally felt influence of domineering corporations and monopolies" ("Spread the Light," *Brooklyn Eagle,* Dec. 12, 1880). Henry George and John Swinton lectured before the club on Dec. 12, 1880.

5. Actually it was Henry George's *Protection or Free Trade?* not *Progress and Poverty,* that was read—in the spring of 1892—into the *Congressional Record.*

6. For SG's participation in the Henry George campaign of 1886, see *The Samuel Gompers Papers,* vol. 1.

7. "Abolish Unemployment: It Can and Must Be Done; Labor's Remedy," *American Federationist* 29 (Jan. 1922): 13–25.

8. The passage, from Shakespeare's *Hamlet,* act 3, scene 2, reads "Ay, but 'while the grass grows . . . '—the proverb is something musty."

To John Walker[1]

March 10, 1922.

Mr. John H. Walker,
Pres., Illinois State Federation of Labor,
120 South 6th St., Springfield, Ills.
Dear Sir and Brother:

The letter[2] sent you in reference to Representative Shaw[3] was one of the many activities of the Non-Partisan Political Campaign Committee[4] of the American Federation of Labor.

As you know, the American Federation of Labor is well informed as to the records of members of Congress. But it cannot be well informed of the records of candidates for Congress who have never been members of that body. Therefore it has been the practice for the Non-Partisan Political Campaign Committee to work in conjunction with the representatives of labor of the various states and Congressional Districts. As you also know, it is necessary to obtain the sentiment of the representatives of labor in the various states and Congressional Districts as to their knowledge of what is being done to defeat objectionable members of Congress and elect friends of labor and the people.

For these reasons I wrote you, knowing that you were either in touch with the political movements in your state or could very easily secure information that would be useful to the National Non-Partisan Political Campaign Committee. Such letters as that have been written to the officials in the First, Fourteenth, Twentieth and Twenty-third Districts of Illinois.[5] Letters have also been sent to the State Federations in states where primaries will be held within the next two months.[6] Others will follow to other states as the primaries approach. To be effective in any campaign there must be some means of exchanging ideas and advice between the National Non-Partisan Political Campaign Committee and the union officials.

The National Non-Partisan Political Campaign Committee is representing the trade union movement, and is ready at any time to disseminate information as to the legislative activities of Congress. It is keeping itself informed of the members of Congress who should be elected and those who should be defeated. This is being done in an intelligent and as efficient manner as the funds of the organization will permit.

You also suggest that the international unions should each have representatives in Washington working with the Legislative Committee of the American Federation of Labor to take care of the general legislation. There is such an organization now in existence in Washington. It was organized May 2[9], 192[1.] I had previously sent a letter[7] to all the legislative representatives in Washington to meet in the Executive Council Chamber on that date. The meeting organized the "Conference Committee of Trade Union Legislative Representatives in Washington." One of the clauses in the declaration adopted at the first meeting provided that all representatives of labor sent to Washington would automatically become members of the Conference Committee while here if only for a day. At the same time they are given whatever aid is necessary.

Under separate cover I am sending you a copy of the minutes of the various regular and special meetings held since the organization of the Conference Committee. Enclosed you will find a list of the members of the Committee to whom the enclosed circular was sent March 6.[8]

The American Federation of Labor Legislative Committee understands that its duty is to watch all legislation affecting national and international unions, as well as for the masses of the people. As soon as a bill affecting any trade or group of trades is presented in Congress the organizations affected are notified. Besides, during the last four months summaries of the Legislative Committee's reports have been sent to all national and international unions, state and city central bodies and to the [650] colleges in the United States. To this number have been added during the last month the 400 building trades councils. The intention is to gradually grow bigger and bigger until it is hoped every local union in the United States can be reached every month.

Recently two bills were presented in the Rhode Island legislature that were most vicious in their provisions. One provided a penalty of $100 for any trade union that did not incorporate and made the members financially responsible for damages.[9] The other bill prohibited strikes.[10] Under the provisions of the two bills members of trade unions could be sued for damages and the personal and real estate property could be taken to satisfy any judgment. Immediately a letter[11] was written to the State Federation[12] officials, and, to back them up, the 202 trade unions in that state were circularized and urged to fight the bill. Enclosed you will find a copy of the letter sent to the various organizations.[13] March 4 I received a letter[14] from Mr. William J. Guest,[15] President of the Providence Central Labor Union,[16] in which he informed me that the two bills will be permitted to die in committee. The representative who presented them in the House said that he would see that they were killed.

Some weeks ago I wrote a letter to the officials of the New York State Federation of Labor informing them that it was the intention of the enemies of labor to present an anti-strike bill[17] in the legislature. Later on I received information that the bill had been presented[18] and I was requested to appear before the committee having it in charge and enter the protest of labor. The bill was most remarkable in its provisions. It prohibited conferences between employers and employes. They could only write letters to each other in event of a dispute. And in event they could not adjust the dispute it would have to be submitted to the Supreme Court, whose decision would be final. March 1st I appeared before the committee,[19] and according to information that has been given me by members of the legislature and others and the newspapers I believe the bill is effectually killed.

Another feature of our work which has received much commendation and is bringing about remarkable results is the sending of literature to the colleges, universities, high schools and other institutions of learning on legislation that is in force or being proposed. There is great interest in the immigration question, the Kansas Court of Industrial Relations Law, the union and non-union shop and compulsory arbitration. In each letter sent to these institutions of learning is the request that we be notified of the result of the debates. It is surprising to learn of the number of decisions in favor of the debaters who took the side of labor.

These are only a few of the many activities of the National Non-Partisan Political Campaign Committee and the Conference Committee of Legislative Representatives in Washington. It is true that it would be most desirable if every national and international union could have a representative in Washington. But I can say with all sincerity and appreciation that not a measure inimical to labor has been put through the present Congress. On the other hand many bills have been either forced into pigeon holes or defeated in committees. We are now actively engaged in protesting against the extension of the 3 per cent immigration law,[20] and are urging complete restriction for three years except so far as blood relatives are concerned,—and blood relatives are confined to dependent fathers, mothers, wives and minor children. The object of this legislation is to tide over the period of acute unemployment, and then when the law expires on June 30, 1923, immigration will be controlled by the old law which provides for practically no restriction.

What we desire and must have is cooperation of the state and city central bodies in carrying out the non-partisan political campaign and the legislative program. All initiation cannot be expected to originate in Washington. We must work together. We have the machinery,—limited, I regret to say, but most efficient. My greatest desire now is to create enthusiasm in the local unions and central bodies. The deplorable conditions forced upon the workers will undoubtedly awaken them to their duty and I hope before the next election that such interest will be taken in the non-partisan political campaign that we will have opportunity after the election to rejoice as we never did before.

Nevertheless, John, I welcome your letter. After reading it the many things that have been done along the lines suggested by you came to my mind and I could not forego giving you the information. I know you will be as pleased as I am pleased that we are doing good work and getting great results. Any time you feel like writing on any question that will point out a way for better results it will be most gladly received. But I hope the few things here set forth will convince you that your wishes are being carried out.

Before closing it occurs to me that I have overlooked a few important matters that have received the attention of the legislative representatives. They are:

The attempt to scrap the Department of Labor;[21]

The attempt to pass a bill to admit 50,000 Chinese coolies under bond to the Territory of Hawaii;[22]

The legalizing of judicial kidnapping;[23]

The effort to repeal all protective laws for women through an amendment to the Constitution of the United States;[24]

The establishment of a sales tax to shift the burden of taxation from the well-to-do to those least able to bear it.[25]

These are of the greatest importance to labor and the people, and whatever obstacles have been thrown in the way of the passage of such legislation have been initiated by the American Federation of Labor and the Legislative Conference Committee.

With best wishes and assuring you of my desire to be helpful in any way within my power, I am,

Fraternally yours,   Saml Gompers.
President,   American Federation of Labor.

P.S.—I wish you would show this letter to Mr. Victor A. Olander,[26] Mr. John Fitzpatrick[27] and other friends.

S. G.

TLpS, reel 277, vol. 290, pp. 701–4, SG Letterbooks, DLC.

1. John Hunter WALKER served as president of the Illinois State Federation of Labor (FOL) from 1913 to 1919 and again from 1920 to 1930.

2. SG to Walker, Mar. 3, 1922, reel 277, vol. 290, p. 394, SG Letterbooks, DLC.

3. Guy Loren Shaw (1881–1950) served as a Republican congressman from Illinois from 1921 to 1923.

4. The AFL Non-Partisan Political Campaign Committee was created in December 1919. At that time it included members of the Executive Council, presidents and secretaries of the AFL departments, and Sara Conboy, Anna Fitzgerald, John Frey, Anna Neary, and Melinda Scott (see *The Samuel Gompers Papers*, vol. 11, pp. 239–41). The committee was given permanent status by the 1921 AFL convention.

5. SG to George Gilbert and to Abe Wood, both Mar. 6, 1922, reel 277, vol. 290, pp. 503–4, SG Letterbooks, DLC; SG to John Mitchell, to Jacob Herbert, to Roy Stone, to H. C. Sylvester, to George Fritz, and to John Fitzpatrick, all Mar. 9, 1922, ibid., pp. 624–27, 629, 639.

6. SG to J. H. Maurer of the Pennsylvania State FOL, to Thomas Taylor of the Indiana State FOL, to Walker, and to O. R. Hartwig of the Oregon State FOL, all Mar. 7, 1922, reel 277, vol. 290, pp. 568–70, 577, SG Letterbooks, DLC.

7. See SG to Legislative Representatives, May 26, 1921, reel 266, vol. 279, pp. 231–34, SG Letterbooks, DLC.

8. SG to All Trade Union Legislative Representatives in Washington, Mar. 6, 1922, reel 277, vol. 290, pp. 558–59, SG Letterbooks, DLC.

9. H. 539, introduced on Jan. 6, 1922, by representative Fred L. Owen of Providence. It died in committee.

10. H. 540, also introduced by Owen on Jan. 6, 1922. This bill also died in committee.

11. SG to Lawrence Grace, Feb. 17, 1922, reel 276, vol. 289, p. 981, SG Letterbooks, DLC.

12. The AFL chartered the Rhode Island State FOL in 1903.

13. SG to the Secretaries of All Central Bodies and Local Unions in the State of Rhode Island, Feb. 27, 1922, reel 277, vol. 290, pp. 247–48, SG Letterbooks, DLC.

14. William Guest to SG, Mar. 4, 1922. The first page of the letter can be found in the AFL Microfilm Convention File, reel 31, frame 2697, *AFL Records*.

15. William James Guest (1881–1959) served as president of the Providence Central

Federated Union from 1920 to 1922. Business agent and financial secretary of Hotel and Restaurant Employees' International Alliance and Bartenders' International League of America 285 of Providence from 1913 to 1954, he also served as vice-president of the Rhode Island FOL from at least 1918 to 1925, was its president for a short time in early 1926, and was chairman of its legislative committee from 1922 to 1924.

16. The AFL chartered the Providence Central Federated Union in 1908.

17. The legislation, known as the Duell-Miller antistrike bill, was introduced on Feb. 7, 1922, in the New York state senate by Holland Duell of Yonkers and in the assembly by Charles Miller of Genesee County. Authored by the New York State Board of Trade and Transportation, the Duell-Miller bill sought to prevent strikes and lockouts by establishing an industrial relations section of the state supreme court to arbitrate labor disputes. The arbitration panel's decisions were enforceable by court order, and disobedience was to be punishable with contempt proceedings. The legislation did not become law.

18. John O'Hanlon to SG, Feb. 8, 1922.

19. SG left Washington, D.C., for New York City on Feb. 28, 1922, and then went on to Albany. On Mar. 1 he met there with labor representatives, testified before the Joint Labor and Industries Committee of the New York State legislature against the Duell-Miller Industrial Relations bill, and then addressed a mass meeting. (For a transcript of SG's testimony, see Files of the Office of the President, Hearings, reel 125, frames 734–52, *AFL Records;* his remarks were also published in the *American Federationist* 29 [Apr. 1922]: 253–62. For a transcript of his address at the mass meeting, see Files of the Office of the President, Speeches and Writings, reel 116, frames 357–62, *AFL Records.*) SG subsequently went back to New York City, where he spoke on Mar. 4 at an event honoring Meyer London, and he returned to Washington by Mar. 6. (For a transcript of his remarks at the Meyer London event, see Files of the Office of the President, Speeches and Writings, reel 116, frames 374–76, *AFL Records.*)

20. H.J. Res. 268 (67th Cong., 2d sess.), a bill to extend for one year the immigration law of 1921, was introduced on Feb. 14, 1922, by Republican congressman Albert Johnson of Washington. Passing the House on Feb. 20, it was sent to the Senate and referred to the Committee on Immigration. SG wrote members of the committee on Mar. 16, while the bill was under consideration, to urge three other options—complete restriction of immigration except for immediate dependent relatives, indefinite extension of the 1921 law, or a two-year extension (reel 278, vol. 291, pp. 49–68, SG Letterbooks, DLC). On Apr. 15 the Senate approved the two-year extension. The House and the Senate agreed to a final version of the bill in early May, and President Warren Harding signed it into law on May 11 (U.S. *Statutes at Large,* 42: 540).

21. Several bills to create a Department of Public Welfare were introduced in Congress in 1921. SG opposed the measures because many of the Department of Labor's functions would have been transferred to the new department. None of the bills left committee.

22. See *The Samuel Gompers Papers,* vol. 11, p. 484, nn. 1–2.

23. S. 657 (67th Cong., 1st sess.), a bill authorizing judges to issue warrants without a hearing for the extradition from one state to another of defendants under indictment for federal crimes, was introduced by Republican senator Knute Nelson of Minnesota on Apr. 13, 1921. It passed the Senate on June 6 but died in committee in the House of Representatives.

24. The Equal Rights Amendment. See "To David Hanly," Mar. 1, 1922, n. 4, above.

25. Republican congressman Luther Mott of New York introduced an unsuccessful sales tax bill—H.R. 14,956 (66th Cong., 3d sess.)—on Dec. 11, 1920. He reintroduced

the measure on Apr. 11, 1921, as H.R. 2,226 (67th Cong., 1st sess.), which was also unsuccessful, and the next day Republican senator Reed Smoot of Utah introduced a similar bill—S. 202 (67th Cong., 1st sess.)—which failed in the Senate. On May 11 the AFL Executive Council voted to oppose any sales tax bill, and the 1921 AFL convention unanimously passed a similar resolution.

26. Victor A. OLANDER served as secretary-treasurer of the Illinois State FOL from 1914 to 1949.

27. John J. FITZPATRICK was president of the Chicago FOL (1900–1901, 1906–46) and an AFL salaried organizer (1903–23).

To Robert Smith[1]

March 14, 1922.

Mr. R. McD. Smith.
Secretary, Division No. 97, Order of Railway Conductors,
Roodhouse, Illinois.
Dear Sir and Brother:

Your letter of March 10 received and read with interest.

It is gratifying to know that you feel very kindly toward the candidacy of Mr. Henry T. Rainey[2] for Congress.

I am also very glad that you are taking an active interest in the Non-Partisan Political Campaign. But I do not believe your plan will work out successfully. The American Federation of Labor has requested central bodies and local unions to select to Non-Partisan Political Campaign Committees. It does not dictate how these committees shall be constructed. That, I think, is the weak spot in your proposal.

Your suggestion that one Socialist shall be appointed on every committee may cause you great trouble in the future. No one should be a member of such a committee unless he is willing to accept the verdict of the majority. As you may well know a Socialist can not vote for a member of any other party without being expelled from the Socialist Party. You might also know that before a Socialist Party will support a candidate for office, he must sign a blank resignation before his name is allowed on the ticket. If, at any time, after election an official elected under the conditions named should do something not in conformity with the wishes of those who control the Socialist Party, the resignation is presented and the official must give up his office. Therefore, I would suggest that you work through the Non-Partisan Political Committees appointed by the various unions under direction of the American Federation of Labor. If it is not too late, I hope you will change your circular letter to meet the objections I have outlined.

In your postscript you tell of the discussion you had with a yardmaster in which you told him I have "supported and advocated the support of the Democratic Party in 1920." You are not right. I advocated the election of all those who met the requirements of Labor and the people. I supported and voted for Mr. Cox as President and have not regretted that fact. I supported many candidates for Congress on both the Democratic and Republican Party tickets. I am neither a Democrat nor a Republican but a willing supporter of all candidates for office who have been true or by their actions in the past demonstrate that they will be true to Labor and the people.

With best wishes and assuring you of my desire to be helpful in any way within my power, I am,

Fraternally yours,   Saml Gompers
President,   American Federation of Labor.

TLpS, reel 278, vol. 291, pp. 88–89, SG Letterbooks, DLC.

1. Robert McDaniel Smith (b. 1885) served as secretary of Order of Railway Conductors division 97 of Roodhouse, Ill., in 1922 and 1923.

2. Henry T. Rainey, an Illinois Democrat, was reelected to Congress in 1922.

To Oswald Villard

March 24, 1922.

Mr. Oswald Garrison Villard,
Editor, *The Nation,*
20 Vesey Street, New York City
Dear Sir:

There has been forwarded to me from your office by your Publicity Secretary, a copy of The Nation for March 29 together with a letter predicting that I will be interested in the article on "American Labor's Political Strategy—A Failure" by George P. West,[1] who I am informed by the letter, "is a careful student of conditions with labor's welfare very much at heart."

Permit me to say that the writer of the letter from your office is very much in error. Mr. West is rather a forlorn child of the philosophy of despair. I am [un]aware as to where he acquired his tremendous gloom. He was at one time a newspaper reporter. Perhaps the manner in which so often truth is tortured and portrayed in the process of newspaper making warped his vision and depressed his soul beyond recovery.

Perhaps on the other hand it was his experience under the tutelage of some perverts with whom he came in contact in the days of the gentleman's tour across the country with the Commission on Industrial Relations which rendered Mr. West color blind to everything except indigo.

At any rate, of late years his whole existence, at least in a literary way, has been one of tears and sorrow and utter anguish at the unwisdom, fool-hardiness and treachery of everyone in the world except himself and perhaps a few carefully selected "serious thinkers" of similar mental characteristics.

I am exceedingly sorry for Mr. West but I am not much interested in what he has to say. I am interested in the truth always and I am interested always in that which is normal and vigorous. I am interested always in real criticism. There is not time however, nor is there profit in giving time to that which is merely peevish, that which weeps merely for the sake of weeping, that which is eternally lugubrious and melancholy. The assumption of your office that I "may care to comment on his article" is therefore without foundation, for I have been told that "to argue with a man who has lost his reason is like giving medicine to the dead."

In April, 1919, just prior to the convention of the American Federation of Labor, Mr. West wrote an article under the title "Will Labor Lead" which was published in the Nation.[2] In that article Mr. West urged and argued and insisted that it was essential to the existence of the A.F. of L. that I be defeated for the presidency of that organization, and [the] Nation advertised Mr. West's article in nearly every large cap[ital]istic paper in the United States, urging the people to read [the] article which had for its purpose my elimination from leadersh[ip] in our federation. The influence of Mr. West's article may be judged by the fact that I was elected President of the American Feder[ation] of Labor without a dissenting voice or vote.

It may be interesting that the reflections made upon me for failure to do duty to my fellow workers engaged in struggles and giving all the credit for such assistance to Mr. John Fitzpatrick of Chicago was denounced and repudiated by him, and that repudiation and protest were sent to Oswald Garrison Villard, Editor and proprietor of the Nation, but so far [as] I have been able to ascertain, were suppressed by your publication. A copy of Mr. Fitzpatrick's letter to you was sent to me and published in the June 1919 issue of the *American Federationist.*[3]

In that article of Mr. West's there is also a statement that the American Federation of Labor should ally itself with "brains." It is quite evident that Mr. West had his quality of brains in mind; of course the implication is that the American labor movement has not in its ranks men of brains, but must surrender itself to the Wests who have a monopoly of the intelligence, understanding, faithfulness, and "vision." American organized labor declines to surrender its leadership to a so-called "intelligencia"; it is a movement of the workers, for the workers, by the workers.

The latest effusion of Mr. West, published in the March 29th issue of the Nation, advance copy of which has been sent me, is now not [s]o much an attack upon me, but a direct attack upon the American Federation of Labor itself, and again to be published within a few weeks of the forthcoming convention[4] of the American Federation of Labor. Mr. West's latest article discloses his real purpose of his article of 1919. It is a blow aimed not at me either personally or officially, but through me or over me to the heart of the American Federation of Labor itself, and it is a timely attack for Mr. West has joined the money interests in a drive to weaken and destroy our labor movement.

Yours respectfully,   Saml Gompers.
President,   American Federation of Labor.

TLpS, reel 278, vol. 291, pp. 517–18, SG Letterbooks, DLC.

1. *Nation* 114 (Mar. 29, 1922): 366–67.
2. See *The Samuel Gompers Papers*, vol. 11, p. 472, n. 14.
3. John Fitzpatrick's letter to Oswald Garrison Villard was published in Matthew Woll's editorial "Labor Will Lead," *American Federationist* 26 (June 1919): 513–17.
4. The 1922 AFL convention met in Cincinnati, June 12–24.

From Ralph Easley[1]

The National Civic Federation
New York City March 25, 1922.

Confidential:
Dear Sir:

Enclosed are copies of matter describing the Lenin-Foster[2] plan to destroy the American Federation of Labor and the railway brotherhoods preliminary to the establishment of a "Soviet Republic" in this country.[3]

Many ambitious proposals have been put out from time to time by different radical groups for the accomplishment of this purpose; but I think it is safe to say that this is the most scientific and dangerous one yet evolved for their undoing, coming, as it does, directly from Moscow which is instigating revolutionary outbreaks in all parts of the world, the latest in South Africa.[4] That it will not succeed goes without saying but it will undoubtedly make trouble not only for labor but for capital as well.

W. Z. Foster returned recently from a three months' visit to Russia and is alleged to have brought back with him plenty of funds as well as a program. His official organ, the Labor Herald, published at 118 North La Salle Street, Chicago, is an expensive and attractive publication, while the elaborate circularization plan known to be in operation is a costly one. The April number of the Labor Herald will be devoted to plans for promoting their activities in railroad unions.

If the coal strike[5] comes—and it looks now impossible for it to be averted—it will be utilized to the utmost by the Lenin-Foster propagandists.

Additional information from the "inside" will be sent you from time to time.

Very truly yours,   Ralph M. Easley

[ENCLOSURE]
REPRINTED FROM THE LABOR HERALD FOR MARCH, 1922.

A CALL TO ACTION.

Militants! The time has come for action! We must now gird up our loins for a great effort to make a real fighting organization out of the trade union movement. We must now plunge directly into our vital task of amalgamating the many craft unions into a few industrial unions and of inspiring them with genuine proletarian spirit. *The Trade Union Educational League* has launched its nation-wide campaign to organize the militants everywhere to carry on this indispensable work of education and reorganization, a work for which the hard-pressed labor movement now stands in shrieking need. All true trade union rebels are urged to join hands with the League immediately.

The League's task of organizing the militants is a gigantic one, one that will require intelligence, determination, and discipline to accomplish. As things now stand the militants are scattered broadcast through many thousands of local unions, central labor councils, etc., and there is scarcely the faintest trace of communication or co-operation between them. It is an utter chaos. And the only way this chaos can be conquered and the army of militants developed into a unified body capable of exerting great influence in the labor movement is by the rigid application of modern organization methods. Such methods are the very heart of the League's program. It proposes not to attack the problem simultaneously in all its phases—which would be a futile project—but to go at it intensively, section by section. It is going to carry out a series of great national drives, month by month, to organize the militants in one industry after another. When the circuit of the industries is completed—which should be in six or eight months—there will exist a well-defined organization of the militants in every trade union and industrial center in the entire country. Then a general national conference will be held, to map out a complete educational program, to elect League officials, etc. All told, the campaign is one of the most elaborate in labor history, and it must eventually result in making the progressive and radical unionists the determining factor in the labor movement.

The first of these national drives will be directed to establishing local general educational groups of militants of every trade simultaneously in all the important cities and towns everywhere. Once established these local groups, in addition to their other activities, will perform the vital organization work of carrying out the rapidly following later drives to organize the militants in the respective industries. Their first job (the second national drive) will be to organize the railroad educational organization. It will be done, as follows: At a given signal (which will come late in March) the hundreds of local general groups, all over the country will direct their united attention and energy to organizing local educational groups of railroad militants in their respective territories. By this intensive method scores, if not hundreds, of such bodies will come into existence simultaneously in all the principal railroad centers. All these local railroad groups will be put in touch with each other through the general office of the League, and thus the railroad militant organization will take on national scope. It will immediately embark upon a nation-wide campaign to amalgamate the sixteen railroad craft unions into one industrial organization. This educational propaganda will be carried into every local union in the entire industry by the local railroad groups, or rank and file amalgamation committees. For the first time in their history the railroad militants will find themselves in an organized movement to combine their many obsolete craft unions into one modern industrial union. Month by month similar drives will be put on in the other industries—metal, building, clothing, mining, etc.—until finally the educational organization covers every ramification of the trade union structure and the rejuvenating influence of the organized militants makes itself felt throughout the entire labor movement.

With this Call to Action the first phase of the League's organization campaign—the setting up of the local general groups—is initiated. Besides being issued publicly, the Call is also being laid directly before more than 1000 live wire trade unionists in that many cities and towns, with an urgent appeal that they immediately call together groups of militant unionists and get our campaign of dynamic education started among them. Considering the present desperate plight of the trade union movement, the utter failure of its leaders to adopt the indispensable measures of consolidation and inspiriting of the unions, together with the growing understanding of the necessity for organizing the militants in the old unions, it is safe to say that most of the 1000 live wires will respond vigorously to our call. In the first week in March, when the initial meetings of the groups are definitely scheduled to take place everywhere, at least 400 or 500 local branches of *The Trade Union Educational League* will be formed. Thus the organization will be made a positive factor in the labor movement.

Rebel unionists are urged to form such groups everywhere, whether the League national headquarters has corresponded with them directly, or not. Without further ado, they should take serious hold of the situation and organize themselves at once. All groups formed without direct contact with the League's office should immediately select a corresponding secretary and have him write at once for full information on the League and its work. Quick action on their part is necessary if they are to participate in and profit from the League's many rapidly oncoming drives to organize the militants in the various industries.

In organizing the local groups two cardinal principles should always be borne in mind. The first is that all dual union tendencies should be suppressed. The League is flatly opposed to secessionism in the labor movement. Its rock bottom tactical position is that the rebels belong among the organized masses and should stay there at all costs. To avoid every semblance of dualism the League does not permit the collecting of regular dues or per capita tax from members or sympathizing unions. It is financed through donations by its members, sale of literature, etc. The other proposition to remember is that under no circumstances should the groups be confined merely to members of this or that political party or tendency. In England, France, and other countries the organizations of trade union militants are made up of several political factions. They consist of all the honest, active, energetic unionists, regardless of their political beliefs, who oppose the timidity and incompetence of the old bureaucracy, and who are willing to adopt the broad radical measures necessary to make the trade unions into real fighting bodies. And so it must be here. To be effective the League groups will have to include all the natural rebel elements among the trade unions, even though they are not all cut according to one political pattern. Such groups as may fail to take this into consideration—that is, where they restrict their membership along party lines—will automatically condemn themselves to sectarianism and comparative impotency.

Militants! Again we say the time has come for action. For a long, long while we have declared that the supreme goal of the labor movement is to do away with capitalism and to establish a workers' republic. But our efforts, because of our tendency to separate ourselves from the mass into dual unions, have not helped appreciably to this end. Through our dualistic methods the organized masses have been left to stagnate and to flounder about leaderless and at the mercy of a conservative officialdom totally incapable of leading them to emancipation. We must now end this condition, we must assume our proper function as the dynamic, onward-driving element in the trade unions.[6] This we can do efficiently only if we are thoroughly organized throughout the length and breadth of the labor movement—even as the militants in all other countries have long since learned. *The Trade Union Educational League* herewith presents a practical program for bringing about this essential organization. This program represents the most important development in the American labor movement for many years. It constitutes the only means by which the workers of this country can be roused from their mental slumber and lined up definitely and clearly against the capitalists and their abominable profit system. If you are a wide-awake militant; if you really understand modern militant tactics and are not blinded by the impossible theories that have about ruined the American labor movement, you will join hands with the League at once—not next week, or next month, but now, immediately!

GET BUSY! ORGANIZE!

THE TRADE UNION EDUCATIONAL LEAGUE

WM. Z. FOSTER, SECRETARY-TREASURER

118 NORTH LA SALLE STREET, CHICAGO, ILL.

TLS and TDc, George Meany Memorial Archives, Silver Spring, Md.

1. Ralph Montgomery EASLEY served as chairman of the executive council of the National Civic Federation from 1904 to 1939.

2. William Z. FOSTER led AFL organizing campaigns in the packinghouse and steel industries between 1917 and 1919. In 1920 he founded the Trade Union Educational League, and the following year he joined the American Communist party.

3. In addition to "A Call to Action," printed herewith, Easley enclosed an analysis of Soviet-American relations from *Izvestia* and three circulars written by Foster dated Feb. 17, Feb. 25, and Mar. 9, 1922.

4. A reference to the Rand Revolt in South Africa, which began in early January 1922 when white miners struck in protest against a plan to increase the number of black workers in the mines. Violence against white strikebreakers by armed bands of strikers began in late February and by March had spread to include assaults on members of the black community. An unsuccessful general strike was called on Mar. 7, and on Mar. 10 the government declared martial law and began arresting strikers. The strike committee officially called off the strike on Mar. 16. An estimated 230 to 250 people died in the strike.

5. Some six hundred thousand anthracite and bituminous miners struck on Apr.

1, 1922, when their contracts expired. The strike had become inevitable after bituminous operators refused to meet union representatives to negotiate a new wage scale
and anthracite operators called for pay cuts and an end to the dues checkoff. Bituminous miners demanded a five-day week and six-hour day, no pay cuts, and a checkoff;
anthracite miners wanted an eight-hour day, a wage increase, and a dues checkoff. In
July President Warren Harding met in joint conferences with representatives for the
union and the bituminous and the anthracite operators in an effort to end the strike
but without success. Bituminous operators opened their own negotiations with union
representatives, however, and on Aug. 15 several of the operators signed the so-called
Cleveland Agreement, which served as the basis for ending the bituminous strike. It
provided for resumption of mining at wage rates and under conditions in effect prior to
the strike, set Oct. 2 for a conference to begin negotiations on a new contract to go into
effect the following April, and called for a commission to investigate the bituminous
coal industry, with members to be selected by the union and the operators and then
approved by the president. The anthracite strike was settled on Sept. 2 after meetings
between union officials, congressional representatives, and the operators. The agreement called for miners to return to work, operators to extend the old contract another
year, and the creation of a federal commission to investigate the anthracite industry.
Congress subsequently approved legislation, which was signed into law on Sept. 22,
creating the U.S. Coal Commission, its members to be selected by the president, to
investigate the bituminous and anthracite industries.

6. For an elaboration on this point, see the reported remarks of Earl Browder, Foster's representative, speaking before the February 1922 Toronto convention of the
Workers' Party of Canada (report of R. B. Russell, Feb. 17, 1922, enclosed in John Flett
to SG, Mar. 21, 1922, Files of the Office of the President, General Correspondence,
reel 106, frame 271, *AFL Records*).

From John Perry[1]

International Brotherhood of Boilermakers and
Iron Shipbuilders and Helpers of America.[2]
Lodge No. 285
Labor Temple, San Pedro, California. March 28, 1922.

Dear Sir and Brother:—

I wish to inform you that we have a clique of disrupters in San Pedro
using all means possible to obtain the Labor Council Hall for mass
meetings on Russian conditions and labor conditions at large. I find
all of these speakers to be of dual organizations under different names
but always Red! Red! The Council refused the hall to a lady from New
York by the name of Ella Reese Bloor.[3] She claims to have been in Russia and she is going around preaching their doctrine. Now let me tell
you frankly the Council don't want to hear any of them, but the I.L.A.
38–18[4] sees fit to rent our hall for those reds after we refuse it to them.
The I.L.A. here is as red as red can be and stands for all such speakers.
Now they have this dope of W. G. Foster as they can't pass around the
I.W.W. any more with safety and we must block this somewhere and I

thought perhaps you can take it up with the International of the I.L.A. and see if they can't stop it. We have to fight these reds everywhere.

Brother Gompers, I know you will take this up as these birds are working overtime to wreck us and are meeting with more or less success. I, myself, won't let them rest if I can help it. The tricks they are using to get in are surprising. They use all kinds of names to cover up their real identity.

Any and all information from you will be appreciated.

Trusting I have made myself plain, I am, with best wishes,

Fraternally yours,   (Signed) J. B. Perry,
District Organizer,   American Federation of Labor[5]

TLtpSr, reel 278, vol. 291, p. 966, SG Letterbooks, DLC. Typed notation: "*Copy.*" Enclosed in SG to Anthony Chlopek, Apr. 3, 1922, p. 965, ibid.

1. John B. Perry served as president of International Brotherhood of Boiler Makers, Iron Ship Builders, and Helpers of America 285 of San Pedro, Calif., in 1921 and was an AFL district organizer in San Pedro in 1921 and 1922.

2. The International Brotherhood of Boiler Makers, Iron Ship Builders, and Helpers of America.

3. Ella Reeve "Mother" Bloor (1862–1951), born in Staten Island, N.Y., and raised in Bridgeton, N.J., was a veteran of the temperance and woman's suffrage movements. She joined the Socialist Labor party in 1897 and the Socialist party in 1902 and helped organize the Communist Labor party in 1919 and the Workers' (Communist) party in 1922. Bloor (who assumed that name in 1906 when she was working with fellow Socialist Richard Bloor) organized agricultural workers, miners, steelworkers, and garment workers, among others, and she twice served as a delegate to meetings of the Red International of Labor Unions (Profintern) in Moscow. A member of the Communist party's national committee (1932–48), she and her third husband, Andrew Omholt, retired from active party work in 1937.

4. International Longshoremen's Association 38–18 of San Pedro.

5. On Apr. 3, 1922, SG forwarded a copy of Perry's letter to Anthony Chlopek, president of the Longshoremen, and he informed Perry of his action the same day (reel 278, vol. 291, pp. 965–67, SG Letterbooks, DLC).

To Sidney Morse[1]

March 29, 1922

Mr. Sidney Morse,
Executive Secretary, Bureau of Social and Educational Service,
Grand Lodge of Free and Accepted Masons of the State of New
    York,
Masonic Hall, New York, N.Y.
Dear Mr. Morse:—

Your letters of March 17th and March 23rd are duly received in which you enclosed minutes of the last meeting of the National Committee[2] which Mr. Frayne[3] attended as the representative of the American Federation of Labor. You refer particularly to several different points in the minutes and ask an expression from me:

"What is your attitude toward the program, policies and activities suggested by the Interstate Council on Immigrant Education, and what amendments, if any, do you desire to offer? (Minute 7)"

Your attention is called to the fact that a naturalization bill is now before Congress, known as H.R. 10860,[4] which contains very insidious language and has for its purpose not so much the education of the immigrants as it is to place them under surveillance. They must register on arrival in this country and each year thereafter until they shall have become citizens. Until the immigrants become citizens of the United States they are to be under constant surveillance in their homes and employment and as to their political and social activities. Even after they become citizens they can have their citizenship revoked and be imprisoned or deported.

The supporters of the bill declare it is to create "a new federal bureau of recreation to make better and happier all the workers of the country and to absorb more quickly into American life the immigrants of other countries coming to our shores for sanctuary."

The explanation given of the provision that every immigrant must register every year wherever he may be is that it is "not in order to spy upon him but only to be sure of his safety and to educate him."

If it were not a proposed espionage law, would its friends and advocates be so insistent that registration did not mean it was for the purpose of spying upon them?

Public school officials are to be the supervisors of the aliens and anyone who violates the proposed law can be imprisoned and afterwards deported. If they have become naturalized citizens their citizenship can be cancelled and they can be deported. If the immigrants can not satisfy the supervisors as to their behavior, being all it should be, deportation is the penalty.

Do you not believe that after such a system of spying upon immigrants becomes thoroughly enforced that the provisions of the law will be extended to native born citizens of our country? Do you not think it would be a backward step? The advocates of the bill also say "that Uncle Sam does not want to be placed in the attitude of a policeman but of a friend, a true Uncle." Do you not think these repeated denials of any ulterior purposes in the naturalization bill really mean its provisions do provide for those things it is sought to disprove? Is it not just to think that if it were a fair, honest, just measure, really for the good of the immigrants, there would not be so much propaganda to deceive the people as to its purpose?

Under the rule of the Kaiser the people of Germany, natives, or foreigners or visitors, even for one day, were required to register with the police and again have a pass if they wanted to change from their domicile to any other city in Germany or go to any other country. In every country engaged in the recent war a vise was required. When landing in any city or town in the Allied countries it was necessary to be registered and report to be made to the police. That was justifiable during the war time but in times of peace, do you think that should a system of registration be put into operation there would be any insurmountable obstacle to extending it to all—citizens and aliens alike?

"Do you desire to nominate either a representative historian or teacher of history or some person familiar with the subject, identified with your agency, as a member of the special committee on the teaching of American History? (Minute 9)"

The American Federation of Labor has a standing committee on education, the chairman of which is Mr. Matthew Woll,[5] Vice-President of the American Federation of Labor, 6111 Bishop Street, Chicago, Illinois. I suggest Mr. Woll as member of the special committee.

"Do you desire to nominate some person identified with your agency familiar with the subject as a member of the special committee on Naturalization Procedure[?] (Minute 15, Feb. 28)"

I suggest Mr. George L. Berry, President of the International Printing Pressmen's and Assistants' Union of North America,[6] and First Vice-Commander of the American Legion, Pr[essm]en's Home, Tennessee.

"Is there any special project or activity of your organization that you desire to place on the Calendar of the Council and invite the cooperation of other agencies? (Minute 5)"

We will be glad to have the cooperation of the National Council in any other of the activities of the American Federation of Labor to which the Council can give its support and help.

Very truly yours,   Saml Gompers
President,   American Federation of Labor

TLpS, reel 278, vol. 291, pp. 807–9, SG Letterbooks, DLC.

1. Sidney Morse (1874–1939), an author, editor, and publisher, served as executive secretary of the Bureau of Social and Educational Service of the Grand Lodge of Masons of the State of New York from 1921 through 1927.

2. That is, the national committee or governing board of the National American Council, an organization to coordinate the work of patriotic and civic societies that was founded in March 1921. The council's goals included setting standards for Americanization, improving relations with immigrant communities, lobbying at the local, state, and national levels on behalf of funding for education, and preventing duplication of effort and ending waste by patriotic organizations. Hugh Frayne represented the AFL at a meeting of the national committee in New York City on Mar. 13, 1922.

3. Hugh FRAYNE served as an AFL salaried organizer from 1902 until his death in 1934.

4. H.R. 10,860 (67th Cong., 2d sess.) was introduced by Republican congressman Albert Johnson of Washington on Mar. 11, 1922. It died in committee.

5. Matthew WOLL served as president of the International Photo-Engravers' Union of North America from 1906 to 1929 and as a vice-president of the AFL and AFL-CIO from 1919 to 1956.

6. George Leonard BERRY served as president of the International Printing PRESS-MEN's and Assistants' Union of North America from 1907 to 1948.

To W. Carroll Sellars[1]

April 3, 1922.

Mr. Carroll Sellars,
The Pepper Box, Official Publication of Boise High School;
Boise, Idaho.
Dear Sir:

Your letter of March 28 received and contents noted.

You ask what qualifications make a 100 per cent high school girl. Since enlightenment began to create ambitions in the human mind there has always been those who would seek to mold people to their way of thinking. Judges are not always wise in their decisions and I doubt if any one can be found among the judges you have asked to contribute to your symposium who will possess the qualities that they themselves will seek to graft upon the high school girl to make them 100 per cent. The high school is not the place to make the 100 per cent girl. It must be begun with the parents. If the parents are 100 per cent parents their girls will have a better opportunity of reaching the goal wished for by so many. If the father be so employed that he receives an adequate wage, a reasonable work day and is working under favorable conditions the atmosphere of the home will tend to cheerfulness and loyalty. It will tend to maintain the health and bodily vigor of the children. There must be plenty of time for recreation as play is absolutely necessary to build up a healthy mind. If teachers are irritable, easily made so, it will hamper instead of assist in keeping the high school girls cheerful and willing. Children are influenced as adults are influenced by their environments, but more so.

If the home is pleasant and the teachers models of womanhood there will be some reason to believe that the high school girls will conform more to the wishes of those interested in them. If there is unhappiness in the home caused by unemployment, poverty or the continual nagging of parents at their children, there is not much hope for them reaching the 100 per cent stage. Therefore, efforts should be made to make the home happier and to pay adequate wages to the teachers which will make them more effective advisors for the children as a foundation for creating a better environment for them so that when they become high school girls they will be more apt to meet the approval of those who now criticise. If they are in a position to grow up with the proper ideas of life, you will find they will meet the requirements of the sensible, just-minded people who know them.

Very truly yours,
President,   American Federation of Labor.

TLp, reel 279, vol. 292, p. 27, SG Letterbooks, DLC.

1. William Carroll Sellars (1905–92), the son of a railroad switchman, later graduated from Columbia University. He settled in Boise, Idaho, where he became a successful merchant and civic leader.

To John Frey[1]

April 5, 1922

Mr. John P. Frey,
Editor, International Iron Molders' Journal,
Commercial Tribune Building, Cincinnati, Ohio.
Dear Sir and Brother:—

Enclosed you will please find copy of a letter[2] which I have just received from President Thomas F. McMahon of the United Textile Workers' of America[3] who is at present in Lawrence, Massachusetts. You will note the desire he expresses for you to visit Manchester, Lawrence and other cities in that locality. I do hope that you may be able to arrange your affairs to afford you the opportunity of doing so.

As you doubtless know, recently I addressed five or six mass meetings in behalf of the textile workers in Rhode Island, New Hampshire, and Massachusetts.[4] At my request Organizer Frank McCarthy[5] has been giving every possible assistance and with great effect as you will note from President McMahon's letter. I trust you can arrange to undertake this trip. In any event, I have advised President McMahon that I have referred the matter to you and that you will communicate with him direct in regard thereto.[6] I would also appreciate a word from you.[7]

On next Sunday I shall leave [for] Chicago at 3:30 in the afternoon due in Chicago Monday morning at 9:55. I have arranged to address the convention of the Railroad Employes' Department of the American Federation of Labor which opens in Chicago on Monday, April tenth.[8] I have also arranged to hold several very important conferences in that city, one with the presidents and secretaries of all the national and international unions with headquarters in Chicago jointly with the presidents of all the local trade unions, the officers of the Chicago Federation of Labor, the Illinois State Federation of Labor and the A.F. of L. Organizers.[9] In view of the resolution adopted by the Chicago Federation of Labor and reaffirmed at its meeting last Sunday, that is, the resolution declaring for the One Big Union, you can very readily understand that I shall not have smooth sailing in Chicago.[10] From Chicago I shall go to New Haven, Connecticut; Boston, Massachusetts; Newport, Rhode Island and New York City; at all of these points I have engagements to address meetings and hold conferences.[11]

With kind regards and trusting that I may hear from you favorably regarding the above, I am, with best wishes,

Fraternally yours,   Saml Gompers.

President,   American Federation of Labor.

TLpS, reel 279, vol. 292, pp. 170–71, SG Letterbooks, DLC.

1. John Philip FREY served as editor of the *International Molders' Journal* (to 1907, the *Iron Molders' Journal*) from 1903 to 1927.

2. Thomas McMahon to SG, Apr. 3, 1922, AFL Microfilm National and International Union File, United Textile Workers Records, reel 42, frames 2703–4, *AFL Records*.

3. Thomas F. McMAHON served as president of the United TEXTILE Workers of America from 1921 to 1937.

4. SG left Washington, D.C., for New York City on the afternoon of Mar. 11, 1922, and went on to Rhode Island that night. On Mar. 12 he addressed mass meetings in Pawtucket and Providence, R.I., and on Mar. 13 he spoke in Manchester, N.H., and Lowell, Mass. SG returned to Washington on the afternoon of Mar. 14. For transcripts of his addresses, see Files of the Office of the President, Speeches and Writings, reel 116, frames 453–64 (Pawtucket), 465–76 (Providence), 477–90a (Manchester), and 491–504 (Lowell), *AFL Records*.

5. Frank H. McCARTHY served as an AFL salaried organizer from 1903 until his death in 1932.

6. SG to McMahon, Apr. 5, 1922, reel 279, vol. 292, p. 115, SG Letterbooks, DLC.

7. On Apr. 13, 1922, Frey wrote SG that he would be unable to make the trip.

8. The 1922 AFL Railway Employes' Department convention met in Chicago, Apr. 10–22. SG addressed the delegates on Apr. 10.

9. See "Excerpts from the Minutes of a Meeting with Chicago Trade Union Representatives," Apr. 12, 1922, below.

10. On Mar. 19, 1922, by a vote of 113 to 37, the Chicago Federation of Labor (FOL) passed a resolution calling on the AFL "to take the necessary action toward bringing about the required solidarity within the ranks of organized labor, and that as a first step in this direction, the various international unions be called into conferences for the purpose of arranging to amalgamate all the unions in the respective industries into single organizations, each of which shall cover an industry" (J. W. Johnstone et al. to the Delegates of the Chicago Federation of Labor, Mar. 19, 1922, Executive Council Records, Vote Books, reel 17, frame 290, *AFL Records*). On Apr. 2 the Chicago

FOL reiterated its approval of the resolution, which was part of William Z. Foster's "amalgamation or annihilation" campaign. SG spoke against the measure at a meeting of Chicago trade union leaders on Apr. 12 (see "Excerpts from the Minutes of a Meeting with Chicago Trade Union Representatives," Apr. 12, 1922, below). On May 10 the AFL Executive Council voted against calling such conferences, and on May 22 SG notified Chicago FOL secretary E. N. Nockels of the Council's decision (reel 280, vol. 293, p. 344, SG Letterbooks, DLC).

11. SG left Washington, D.C., on Apr. 9, 1922, and arrived in Chicago on Apr. 10, where he addressed the convention of the AFL Railway Employes' Department on Apr. 10, conferred with representatives of the Chicago Building Trades Council on Apr. 11 (see "Excerpts from the Minutes of a Meeting with Representatives of the Chicago Building Trades Council," Apr. 11, 1922, below), and met with trade union leaders on Apr. 12 (see "Excerpts from the Minutes of a Meeting with Chicago Trade Union Representatives," Apr. 12, 1922, below). Then, after a brief stopover in New York City, he addressed the Yale Graduates' Club in New Haven, Conn., on Apr. 15, a labor conference in Boston on Apr. 17, and students and faculty at the Naval War College in Newport, R.I., on Apr. 18 before returning to New York City to testify before the Lockwood Committee on Apr. 21–22 and speak at a Workers' Education Bureau dinner meeting on Apr. 22. He returned to Washington by Apr. 25. For transcripts of his addresses, see Files of the Office of the President, Speeches and Writings, reel 116, frames 655–78 (New Haven), 679–714 (Boston), reel 117, frames 1–22 (Newport), and 69–76 (New York), *AFL Records*. For his Lockwood testimony on Apr. 21–22, see "Excerpts from News Accounts in the *New York Times* of the Testimony of Samuel Gompers before the Lockwood Committee," Apr. 22–23, 1922, below, and Files of the Office of the President, Hearings, reel 125, frames 769–952, *AFL Records*.

Excerpts from the Minutes of a Meeting with Representatives of the Chicago Building Trades Council

Tuesday April 11. 1922.

On March 10, 1922, Mr. Gompers wrote John J. Fitzpatrick,[1] General Organizer, American Federation of Labor, Chicago, Ill., requesting the calling of a conference for Wednesday April 12, 1922, of the Presidents of the local unions in Chicago, the officers of the Chicago Federation of Labor, the Presidents and Secretaries of the National and International Unions located in Chicago, and the organizers of the American Federation of Labor.[2]

On March 29, Mr. Fitzpatrick replied that he would have the meeting arranged as outlined by Mr. Gompers. The call for the meeting, signed by E. N. Nockels, Secretary, Chicago Federation of Labor, dated April 5, was mailed April 6.

Mr. Gompers left Washington April 9 and arrived in Chicago April

10. Shortly after his arrival that morning, a committee consisting of Fred. Mader,[3] President Building Trades Council of Chicago, Dan McCarthy,[4] plumbers, Corey,[5] Engineers, and Bregel,[6] Painters, called upon him at the hotel. The situation in the building trades was discussed and the committee finally requested Mr. Gompers to address a meeting Tuesday afternoon, April 11, of representatives of the different organizations affiliated with the Building Trades Council. Mr. Gompers agreed. . . .

. . .

MEETING OF REPRESENTATIVES
OF THE VARIOUS TRADES AFFILIATED TO THE BUILDING TRADES
COUNCIL OF CHICAGO.

. . .

[Mr. Gompers:] A man might just happen to guess and his guess be right. He might judge by hearing one side; it might just happened that he could reach a conclusion and render a decision that would be right and just, but no man can understand a situation unless he has both sides of the case. Now, having consented to participate in the conference and because there is, I know, division, I feel, unless you think otherwise, that I should preside over this gathering in the endeavor to find out just exactly what exists and what can be done. I am not here to preside and decide but simply to endeavor to bring out the points of difference as between people who represent different points of view, because I feel that no matter who I would select the other side would feel that some one else should have been selected. Probably, I should tell you the story or the fable of the animals in the jungle. They could not decide upon any one to be their leader, the lion was too strong and fierce; the fox was too sly; the serpent was too sneaky etc., and so they finally concluded to select the goose because he had no opinion of his own. Probably that may apply here. At any rate unless there is objection I shall continue to preside over this gathering this afternoon. But if you desire any other course I am perfectly willing to give way. The honors of a presiding officer are not new to me, so I simply suggest to you that we continue in this way. (No objection.)

. . .

Mr. Gompers: First I would like to have the organizations which are represented here this afternoon and the men representing these organizations, so that we might know who we are and what we are doing. Whatever happens to be the situation let it be a free for all and let it be an open statement of fact, just as we think it exists or should exist.

. . .

Mr. Gunther:[7] Perhaps a little further information for the chair will be in order. I will go back a year ago last May. A year ago last May the contractors of the City of Chicago in the building industry decided amongst themselves that they were going to enforce a reduction in wages. An ultimatum was issued to the entire building trades for one dollar per hour. Previous to that we have been receiving $1.25. On the First day of May the majority of the trades refused to accept the cut to one dollar per hour and automatically ceased work—practically every trade in the building industry. After being on the streets for a period of ten days or so, a committee representing the Building Trades Council met in conjunction with a committee representing the Associated Building Construction employers of the City of Chicago with the result that the situation was thoroughly discussed. The result of numerous conferences brought forth the fact that a final agreement [to] enter into arbitration and the selection of an umpire was entered into.[8] At that time after submission of a list of names by both sides, we finally agreed to accept Judge Landis as the umpire, conditioned upon certain facts. These facts were that the carpenters who were not a part of the proceedings would not participate in the arbitration plan, likewise it did not affect the painter. An agreement was entered into whereby the Judge was to be the umpire insofar as the setting of a wage scale. The agreement was very distinct on that particular point. The understanding was in effect that the journeymen and the trades would get together and endeavor to work out a satisfactory agreement among themselves in reference to any disputed points in the trade and what they could not agree upon was to be submitted to the umpire. The matter drifted along to such a point that there was not a trade but had to submit the entire agreement to the umpire. Immediately upon the acceptance of the umpire, work resumed conditionally upon the fact that the men receive $1.25 per hour. The arbitration then proceeded before the judge from approximately June until the 8th or 9th of September when the Judge made his decision. That award as made by the judge carried with it a reduction in wages from $1.25 down to I believe the lowest $0.82 1/2, but it carried with it a material reduction in wages all the way from $1.25 to $0.82 1/2. The only ones who received a flat out and out wage of $1.10 was the brick-layer, the electrician and part of the hoisting engineers. The trades at that time felt that the reduction was too great with the exception of the trades that I have enumerated,—the brick-layers, the iron-worker and the electrician. They continued to work under the terms of the award while the majority of the trades, I dare say 90% of the trades were thoroughly dissatisfied with the conditions of the award and refused to go along with the award as outlined by the umpire. This brought

forth the fact that an alliance had been formed between the journeymen of the city of Chicago and the so-called public-spirited Citizens'
Committee. . . .

The situation today in the City of Chicago is very acute. The Citizens' Committee has got itself thoroughly organized. They have every
industry and every profession in the city thoroughly canvassed for
funds. They have the moral support of the various manufacturers'
associations, banking interests and Chambers of Commerce, in fact
some of the public. Funds are being spent broadcast in advertising by
the Citizens' Committee throughout every city in the United States
asking for non-union men in approximately ten different trades. They
have private watchmen and they have one on every building in town
that they have any of their open-shop men working on. Probably I
am going a little too far for the chair—the Citizens' Committee are
functioning here 100% and making inroads on every trade. The true
situation here is that the reason you have not got a solidified front is
the fact that the moment any trade goes out to support another, the
Citizens' Committee immediately steps in and places them on the
open-shop basis. . . .

. . . This Citizens' Committee is not functioning in the city for the
express purpose of enforcing the Landis award but for the purpose
of forcing an open-shop in the building trades.

Mr. Gompers: Is the resume given by Mr. Gunther just now agreed
in as being correct? Several answers simultaneously: Yes, that is exactly
the situation, Mr. President. . . .

. . .

It is a most difficult thing to express a definite opinion upon the
subject. Of course, you have placed yourselves and your unions in the
position of having accepted a federal judge or a judge of a court to
be an umpire. In your minds you may have had reservations that you
and that he ought not to enter into, but you get an umpire, anyone,
and particularly a judge, and there is a practice in the jurisprudence
of the country, that is you give a judge or a court jurisdiction over a
matter, believe me he will accept it and work under it and extend it and
usurp more. Do you remember the story of a witness who came before
a court and he was asked about a certain quarrel and in an encounter
which ensued and the lawyer asked "How far were these people apart
from each other?" The answer came "At first about seven feet-three
inches and then just about two feet-four inches from each other." The
witness was asked "Well, how is it that you know they were sitting 7 feet
3 inches at first and then 4 [*sic*] feet-4 inches in the second phase?"
"Well," replied the witness, "I thought some damn fool lawyer would
ask me so I measured it." (Laughter)

You are in such a position having agreed as a council to refer this matter to Judge Landis and agreeing to abide by his award. That to the average man a repudiation of it is not fair and it does not appeal to the average citizen who does not know anything about our troubles, does not know our mental reservations and that we are honestly seeking a rightful solution of a problem. Well, these men agreed to arbitration, agreed to Judge Landis being the arbitrator, and they are in honor bound to abide by the award. But it is not as between two men having a dispute about a certain thing, a matter of business, of property claimed, or whether it is just or unjust, or to what extent it may be just or unjust, but here is involved the well-being, the life, the standards of working men and their dependents and their wives and their children and every one of them made a mistake in granting too much power and granting too much in advance without having considered their own situation and the situation of their wives and little ones. People, even workmen, do not give these facts consideration when they themselves are not involved. I can only say this that whatever action is warranted to be taken under the circumstances it ought to be taken by the men and the organizations in the building trades unions as a unit. Accept the award, if you think you can live under it and get along for a while and hold your own, if you think you cannot live under it, if you can't endorse it as a union and take it, and if you cannot accept it, reject it as a united body of workingmen. This way nothing of good is accomplished, nothing of a permanent character, nothing of a comprehensive character. Of course all the charges and counter-charges, all the insinuations of this thing and the other thing, we have got to live, we have got to live that down gentlemen, we cannot prosper, we cannot serve the cause of labor, we cannot serve the men who entrust their interest in our keeping unless we are honest with them and honest in our dealings in every way, for we are fighting for humanity and for the right and fighting to have an influential and commanding voice in industry, and we must, therefore, be better and more honest than those with whom we are contending otherwise we shall lose in the end no matter what we undertake to do. Of course, it is not in my power or jurisdiction and I would not exercise it even if I had the power to render a decision. All I can express after hearing what you have said, and it appeals to me strongly, but I was asked whether I would preside in this conference this afternoon and I immediately said that I would. All that I asked was that it might be a representative gathering of men representing both sides of the problem. I say to you gentlemen that I would suggest that as a result of this meeting today, Tuesday, April 11, you had a preliminary meeting some of you gentlemen, continue meeting, repeat it, see whether you cannot come to some definite and unanimous conclusion as to what you want to do. The interest of the men of labor in your trades demands it, the welfare of the whole labor movement and the cause of freedom, of opportunity for development and progress depend upon your getting together, coming to a conclusion of what you are going to do. I cannot say to you definitely what you should do. That is not within my province but I have the right to say to you, whether it pleases all or not it is not of very much consequence, but the labor movement has given me the votes of respect and confidence and placed me in the position of representing the labor movement of America and I am trying to carry out the spirit of that mandate of the organized workers of America. I am trying to give the best that is in me and all that there is in me in furtherance of that cause. If I were to plead with you, beg of you, and argue with you, I could not do more than this, to impress upon your minds and upon your conduct to continue these conferences for a few days longer and then meet and decide positively, absolutely, the course which you shall pursue affecting every trade and every organization affected by this decision. I want to thank you very much for the courteous manner in which this whole proceeding has been conducted and the respect that has been manifested one toward the other as well as generally toward me and in which I have tried to do my part toward you. I offer the suggestion that you meet not tomorrow, because tomorrow I would like you all to be present at the conference which I have invited. I want to go into the matters and every man bring the matters to me tomorrow as they have been in part presented this afternoon that the labor movement of Chicago like the labor movements of all other sections of our country shall deal with labor affairs rather than with the sun, moon and stars. If there be unity in the labor movement of Chicago then the citizens' committee would not have dared to do what they have done and what they are doing. (Applause)

I do hope that you will be in attendance tomorrow. The very fact that you will be in attendance then if there be anything of unity come out of this conference tomorrow it will strengthen you all as well as the whole labor movement, but decide now that you shall meet again, you, all of you, the electrical local representatives and those other locals which are now engaged in your local primaries and meet day after day until you reach a conclusion. I do not know that I can say any more except to thank you and express my appreciation of your coming together and acting like men, honest men imbued with the great responsibility which had been placed in your keeping by the men who have selected you for the positions you occupy.

. . .

TDc, Files of the Office of the President, Speeches and Writings, reel 116, frames 583, 585, 587, 596–98, 600–601, 605–8, *AFL Records.* Typed notation: "Building Trades Conference, Chicago—Landis Award. President Gompers Presiding and Addressing Conference Tuesday April 11. 1922."

1. SG to John Fitzpatrick, Mar. 10, 1922, John J. Fitzpatrick Papers, ICHi.

2. See "Excerpts from the Minutes of a Meeting with Chicago Trade Union Representatives," Apr. 12, 1922, below.

3. Fred "Frenchy" Mader (b. 1884?), longtime business agent of International Brotherhood of Electrical Workers 381 (Fixture Hangers) of Chicago, served as president of the Chicago Building Trades Council from February to November 1922. Convicted of extortion and conspiracy in 1916, he served at least one year of a three-year sentence in Joliet prison before being pardoned. Mader was found guilty of conspiracy again in 1922, but his conviction was overturned in 1924. Later in 1922 he was tried and acquitted in the murder of two police officers.

4. Daniel Joseph "Duke" McCarthy (b. 1892) was business agent for United Association of Journeymen Plumbers and Steam Fitters of the United States and Canada 130 of Chicago from 1920 to 1931. In 1922 he was charged and acquitted of the murder of two police officers; in 1923 he was charged in the shooting death of a rival labor leader but proved self-defense; and in 1924 he was tried and convicted in a liquor highjacking case, fined, and sentenced to six months in prison.

5. Actually John W. Gorey (b. 1861), a marine steam engineer, who was business agent of International Union of Steam and Operating Engineers 629 of Chicago from 1920 until at least 1929.

6. Actually Joseph A. Briegel (b. 1869), a member of Brotherhood of Painters, Decorators, and Paperhangers of America 830 (Sign, Scene, and Pictorial Painters) of Chicago. He served as secretary of the Joint Publicity Committee of the Building Trades, which held a mass demonstration against the Citizens' Committee on Apr. 29, 1922.

7. William Gunther (1873–1950), a gas fitter, was business agent (1903–31) and secretary (1918–31) of Plumbers' local 250 of Chicago.

8. For the Chicago building trades arbitration case, which was submitted to Judge Kenesaw Mountain Landis, see *The Samuel Gompers Papers*, vol. 11, pp. 496–97, n. 2.

Excerpts from the Minutes of a Meeting with Chicago Trade Union Representatives

New Morrison Hotel. Wednesday April 12, 1922.

. . .

[Mr. Gompers.] . . . No one underestimates the problem and the struggle which the working people of our country and our time are facing. Somehow or other there has grown up in Chicago a spirit which breeds dissension, conflict of views, conflict of plans and of action, estrangement among men so that the great, powerful voice with which organized labor should express the hopes and aspirations as well as the demands of labor is not heard in the same stentorian sounds and bases as of yore. I have some understanding of some of the causes for unity of action in times of industrial activity, or what is usually called industrial prosperity, and if unity of spirit and action is necessary then how much more essential is it that we shall be united in every thought and in every activity in times of depression and unemployment such as now exists. (Applause.)

If any good is to result from my visit here there must be plain speaking among the conferees at this meeting this afternoon. I hope that no one will indulge in any personal criminations or recriminations. Let the enemy of labor have a monopoly on that. Let us talk about what we believe should be done to bring back this powerful labor movement of Chicago so that it may help to stabilize and unite the spirit and action of the toiling masses of your great city and state and of our beloved country.

. . .

Mr. W. Z. Foster. Mr. Chairman and brothers and sisters I arrived rather late at the meeting. I happened to be in another meeting and I was informed that there was quite considerable talk being leveled against me and some of the things that I advocated and I thought it was my duty to come over here and interject a few words into this discussion. My personality has been dragged into this assembly and sort of wiped up the floor with it more or less but I am not going to say anything about that. It is easy to use personalities when you have got no better argument. (Applause.) . . .

. . .

Now as to the resolution,[1] itself, it calls for amalgamation of the various organizations into unions, each of which will cover an industry. Now what is . . . so startling and alarming about that kind of a proposition? . . . [A]re we, in proposing a resolution of this character, making such a radical departure? Has not the Mine Workers gone into the American Federation of Labor, year after year, along with the Brewery Workers[2] and other organizations and tried to get the American Federation of Labor to go on record for industrial unionism and if they can petition the American Federation of Labor to do that, why can't we, in the Chicago Federation of Labor, why can't we ask? . . .

. . .

. . . Consider the big basic industries. The printers with at least fifty percent of the men organized in a industry have gone on record for an industrial union in their industry.[3] The Lumber Workers, in their industry have gone on record to that effect.[4] The miners have had an industrial union for years. The Steel Workers,[5] they also have claimed jurisdiction over all the workers in the steel industry and they are emphasizing that fact in all the literature that has been sent out. The Textile workers are claiming jurisdiction over all the workers in their industry and if I went over the constitutions we would probably find others. What is there in this resolution so startling? The only thing that is startling in my judgment of it is that it is a sort of a recognition of a movement that is developing and it is coming. I want to tell you right here and now—about ten years ago the machinists' organizations[6] adopted a slogan "Amalgamation or annihilation." The Machinists raised the banner of amalgamation in the metal trades. They stand for an industrial union in the metal trades but with the on-coming of the war that slogan was dropped in abeyance but it is being raised again and why? Simply because economic conditions are hard. Unemployment is pressing down upon us in all states and we have simply got to amalgamate our organization or we will go down in defeat. . . .

This is not a One Big Union resolution. It only calls for one union in each industry and that is not One Big Union. You are going to have one union in each industry before long or else no unions at all and when you get them, do you think you are going to stop there? Then you will take your next step into what you call "The One Big Union." . . . [B]ut this resolution does not provide anything of that kind. This is a very conservative resolution. . . .

. . .

[Mr. Gompers.] I was in hopes that in this conference we might have all shades of opinion expressed, but converging to one point and that is how we can help each other. At least the one point has not been missed, the thought that I expressed yesterday and that is for sessions of the men in the Building Trades. Men who are divided and stand on opposite sides of the streets making faces at each other and barking at each other are not likely to get into a common compact of action. Get together! Discuss your proposals, your views and the only hope that you can unite is by conference, the only hope and not by standing apart. I am looking forward to your doing that, men in the Building Trades, and I am looking forward to you men in the other trades to work upon that same principle and if nothing comes out of this conference or the one of yesterday than the culmination of that desirable suggestion, I think we should feel pretty well gratified.

I cannot forego, however, consideration of some of the matters which have been presented here this afternoon. There is a difference of opinion among the advocates of the resolution adopted by the Chicago Federation of Labor. . . . My own opinion is that in essence and in fact and in intent it is one big union. (Applause.) One union—of course, I do not suppose that anyone has lost his reason to such a degree as to believe that there can be one union of all industries, not even the fly-by-night, most intense advocate of one big union idea, advocates one union for all trades and industries. What they have declared and what they insist upon is one union in the industry, and that is the proposal which the Chicago Federation of Labor resolution contains,—one union in one industry.

. . .

. . . If you read copies of this sheet[7] since it has been published, it is the selection of some person [or] two in each locality or union to correspond with them, to correspond with that office, to gather some men who may be radical, dissatisfied, discontent,—to get them at the meeting—it is not necessary to mention names, it is not necessary to pay any dues. All send in subscriptions for this mongrel sheet, and these men in these localities they are not to have a vote or voice. They are not to have anything to determine, all they have to do is to pay, all they have to do is to obey orders. Why never in the history of industry or in any other era that I know of or has ever come under my attention has there been such a self-appointed and self anointed autocrat to determine and dictate what shall be done. The Trade Union Educational League! What have they to educate upon? What philosophy is presented? . . . He[8] has been to Russia recently and judging from his own statement no man was treated better than he was by Lenin and Trotsky and the Soviets and in spite of the fact that he was treated so wonderfully well in the few weeks that he was there he lost thirty pounds of his flesh. I am not gathering this out of my own imagination I am quoting Mr. Foster's own words and he comes from Russia where he has been hand and glove with the Soviets and if you read this new discovery that shocked you, you will find that it is not even industrial unionism which he advocates but it is dictatorship of the new proletariat and the dictator being William Z. Foster . . . not trade unionism, but sovietism, and the reformation which came to him after leaving the I.W.W. if it ever came to him was dissipated and he returned to his red blanket of sovietism and bolshevikism.

Now I am just so much of a labor man, just 100 per cent. I am a trade unionist from the ground up, inward and outward, every way you can measure me or gage me, I am 100 per cent trade unionist and in the United States of America my trade unionism means 100 per cent Americanism. (Applause.) I do not want either by my willingness or without my protest permitting the wool being pulled over the eyes of America's workers. That is what it is. It is not the mere resolution adopted. I do not know whether you remember the story but I will take advantage of your patience to tell it. A drummer[9] went out on the road every now and then of course to attend to his business and when he returned and presented his travelling account he always had placed there a new suit, or a new pair of trousers and his employer said to him "You must cut that out. I won't have you buying your clothes, trousers and all that sort of thing and placing it in your expense account." So he said alright and on his return from the next trip he presented his bill for expenses and his employer, after looking it over carefully, in response to the drummer's question, said that it was alright, that he did not see any item for a suit of clothes or trousers in the bill. The drummer left the office and said to his friends "the boss did not see it in there but the cost of the trousers and suit was in there just the same," and so it is in the resolution, and so it is in the resolution and that which is back of it and it is nothing more or less than propaganda of radical revolution to overthrow the Government of the United States and as Lenin said a condition precedent to accomplishing that must be the destruction of the American Federation of Labor. (Applause.)

I won't accept any challenge for a debate from Mr. Foster. Probably he would not do me the honor of offering that challenge but this I say I will submit to any committee of three trade unionists grounded in their trade unionism to have him submit his philosophy upon that subject and my plain statement of fact of the trade union position and let you decide whether my analysis and my criticism of his proposal because it is his proposal and I charge him with being the drafter of that resolution. He wants to fool the working people of Chicago [who are] unsatisfied, dissatisfied. You are justified in being dissatisfied and unsatisfied. Surely there is not anything in our present day life that could make us satisfied or content. But in this battle no one is more ready to fight for Labor than I am. But in this pretentious industrial organization it should be in solid bounds of the union and wherever trade unions shall be they should be as distinct as the billows and yet in our Federation as one as the ocean. I have read this thing and the article which was given—published in this April issue ["]Amalgamation or Annihilation." I wonder whether the wish was not father to the thought. Speaking of amalgamation or annihilation, I wonder how amalgamation could be brought about even if all agreed. In the meantime it means annihilation. But does it, does it? Have the working people in the United States in their labor movement not encountered greater contests, bitter strife and endured more sacrifice than now? They have not been annihilated. In 1881 there were about 45,000 workmen organized in the United States and Canada and we grew and grew and grew. You could not find more than a little bit of a spark in any one town or city but a few unions and we have organized nearly 6,000,000. We have rece[d]ed a bi[t] now and then but we never go back to the conditions from which we have emerged— never. (Applause.)

. . .

TDc, Files of the Office of the President, Speeches and Writings, reel 116, frames 610, 612–13, 615, 617–21, 631–32, 638–40, *AFL Records.* Typed notation: "Conference Representative Labor Men of Chicago, President Gompers Presiding and Addressing Conference. Wednesday April 12, 1922, Cameo Room, New Morrison Hotel."

1. See "To John Frey," Apr. 5, 1922, n. 10, above.

2. The International Union of United BREWERY, Flour, Cereal, and Soft Drink Workers of America.

3. The International TYPOGRAPHICAL Union's 1921 convention approved a resolution calling for amalgamation of all unions in the printing industry. The union's 1922 convention, however, reversed this decision.

4. A reference to the International Union of TIMBERWORKERS, which amalgamated in 1918 with the International SHINGLE Weavers' Union of America. The *Timberworkers' Bulletin* described the union as "an *Industrial Organization*. All workers in the Timber Industry are eligible for membership. . . . There are no *Craft* lines drawn" (May 20, 1921).

5. The Amalgamated Association of IRON, Steel, and Tin Workers.

6. The International Association of MACHINISTS.

7. A reference to William Z. Foster's journal, the *Labor Herald*.

8. Foster.

9. A traveling salesman.

From Martha Ford[1]

Washington, D.C., April 20, 1922.

Samuel Gompers,
Continental Hotel, New York City.
Following telegram just received from G. W. Perkins.[2]
"OBU rejected yesterday, convention of railway employes department."[3]

M. R. Ford.

TWpSr, reel 279, vol. 292, p. 434, SG Letterbooks, DLC.

1. Martha R. Ford (1891–1974) was a stenographer for the AFL from 1913 until at least 1956. She was born in New Jersey and moved to Washington, D.C., in 1913 when her father, Cornelius Ford, was appointed Public Printer of the United States.

2. George William PERKINS, the president of the Cigar Makers' International Union of America from 1891 to 1926.

3. Over forty resolutions calling for amalgamation of the various railroad unions into a single organization were referred to the Committee on Laws at the 1922 convention of the AFL Railway Employes' Department. A majority of the committee recommended non-concurrence, but a minority proposed that affiliates should submit the question to their members and that a special convention should be called to work out an amalgamation program if a majority of railroad workers voted in favor of the proposition. After almost a full day of debate on Apr. 18, the convention voted in favor of the majority report, which rejected the amalgamation resolutions.

From William Z. Foster

Wm. Z. Foster, Secretary-Treasurer
Trade Union Educational League
Chicago, Ill. April 20, 1922.

Dear Sir and Brother:—

At a meeting on April 11th, in the Hotel Morrison, Chicago, which was attended by several hundred local union presidents and other trade union officials, you issued me a challenge which I must accept.[1] During the meeting an A.F. of L. Organizer[2] made a virulent attack upon the proposition of amalgamation of the unions by industry, as outlined in the resolution recently adopted by the Chicago Federation of Labor.[3] In reply thereto, I offered to debate the question with him on any trade union platform in this city. He made no response. But later on, when you took the floor, you expressed some surprise that I had not done you "the honor" of challenging you, and you also added that you would be willing to have a committee appointed, consisting of three reputable trade unionists, to which both you and I might submit our respective views regarding the general question of industrial unionism versus craft unionism.

Considering your high office in the movement, I would not have been presumptuous enough to have so challenged you to such a debate, but seeing that it is your own proposition, I herewith accept your offer, and am holding myself in readiness to present my arguments to the proposed committee as soon as it is selected. The personnel of the committee, and the manner of its selection, I am willing to leave entirely in your hands.[4]

My contention is that craft unionism is obsolete. The old type of organization, based upon trade lines, can no longer cope successfully with Organized Capital. To fit modern conditions, our unions must be based upon the lines of industry, rather than upon those of craft. The necessary industrial unionism will be arrived at, not through the founding of ideal dual unions, but by amalgamating the old organizations. Already the trade unions, by federations and other get-together devices, have made much progress in the direction of industrial unionism. I hold that this tendency should be consciously encouraged; we should not simply blunder along blindly. The thing that must be done is to boldly proclaim our inevitable goal of one union for each industry, and to adopt every practical means that will tend to get us there at the earliest date.

Awaiting your pleasure, I am,

Fraternally yours,   Wm. Z. Foster

TLS, George Meany Memorial Archives, Silver Spring, Md.

1. Actually Apr. 12, 1922. See "Excerpts from the Minutes of a Meeting with Chicago Trade Union Representatives," Apr. 12, 1922, above.

2. Oscar Fred NELSON, a vice-president of the Chicago Federation of Labor from 1910 to 1935.

3. See "To John Frey," Apr. 5, 1922, n. 10, above.

4. SG apparently made no reply to this letter.

Excerpts from News Accounts in the *New York Times* of the Testimony of Samuel Gompers before the Lockwood Committee[1]

[April 22, 1922]

"GOD SAVE LABOR FROM THE COURTS," EXCLAIMS GOMPERS

Bitter opposition to any legislative grant of power to the courts in cases where great financial losses were being sustained by the public and innocent contractors due to jurisdictional quarrels between labor unions, was voiced yesterday before the Lockwood committee by Samuel Gompers, President of the American Federation of Labor.

Under the examination of Samuel Untermyer, who brought out that work on the $30,000,000 Hell Gate power house of the New York Edison Company, at East River and 134th Street, has been held up for six months because of a jurisdictional fight between the plumbers and the steamfitters and that no power existed in the Plumbers' Union or the A.F. of L. to compel the plumbers on the job to accept the decision of their international union, Mr. Gompers maintained that, although the plumbing contractor was ruined, the condition was "one of the risks of industry."[2]

Referring to the ruined plumbing contractor, Mr. Untermyer asked, "Don't you think that in such a case the courts should have the right to give him redress?"

"The courts cannot give him any redress," replied Mr. Gompers. He explained that the courts could not compel men to perform any specific duty other than in prison. He said he believed in remedying the situation only by voluntary effort, and admitted that six months' voluntary effort had not accomplished anything. He admitted, also, that the plumbers on the job could defy the orders of their local union, the international union and the A.F. of L., and in reply to all questions aimed to ascertain what good the union organizations were if their rulings could be defied, Mr. Gompers stuck to his contention that the labor movement was "voluntary, after all."

"God Save Labor from the Courts."

"God save labor from the courts," was the keynote of Mr. Gompers's testimony. He declared that as between litigants who were equal before the courts they were fair and impartial, but that in matters between employers and labor the courts were "most unfair." He referred to the Carnegie Foundation's report on "Justice to the Poor"[3] and some writings by Chief Justice Taft and Elihu Root, and a book, "Mental Overstrain," by Stimson,[4] in support of his assertions.

Mr. Gompers said that expelling a man from a union, if effective, was really a form of "capital punishment" and prevented him from earning a livelihood, but he was absolutely opposed to giving the courts the right of review of cases where men had been expelled from unions. . . .

Mr. Gompers approved of the limitation of the number of apprentices in the various trades on the ground that such action was necessary in order to prevent the trades from being overwhelmed by apprentices so that living and wage standards might be beaten down by the employers. Mr. Untermyer maintained that the purpose of the arbitrary limitation of apprentices was to bar the coming generations from obtaining work and to force the employers to accept the demands of the workers.

"I'd hate like the mischief to submit this question to the courts," declared Mr. Gompers, when asked if he would favor the courts having the right of review of the number of apprentices in the trades. His suggestion was to remedy the situation "by the voluntary movement of labor. . . ."

There were several lively interchanges between the witness and Mr. Untermyer, and when the audience, which consisted largely of trade unionists, applauded their leader's remarks, Acting Chairman McWhinney[5] threatened to clear the Aldermanic Chamber if there was any further demonstration.

Limitation of Union Membership

Asked whether he would justify the limitation of the number of members in labor unions, Mr. Gompers said as a matter of principle he disapproved of limitation, but as a matter of practice he justified it, explaining that as a matter of right, the men who fought for unions for years felt they were entitled to jobs before those who had failed to make sacrifices for the unions. He said he did not excuse the practice of limiting membership and would not admit that he was condemning it, but insisted he was merely criticising it.

"You are criticising it in a condemnatory but mild spirit?" he was asked.

Mr. Gompers straightened up in his chair, leaned forward and said slowly: "I am the mildest mannered man that ever cut throat or scuttled ship." After saying that he favored taking away from the unions the right of expelling members and condemning the imposition of exorbitant fines that amounted to expulsion, Mr. Gompers made his remark concerning labor and the courts.

"You have no faith in the courts?" asked Mr. Untermyer.

"Very little," replied the witness.

Q.—I am sorry, Mr. Gompers. A.—I am not.

Q.—You are not sorry that you have no faith in the courts? A.—It is the fault of the courts.

The labor leader maintained he was not prejudiced against the courts. A long argument on the courts followed, and Mr. Gompers asserted that it was a matter of fact, not opinion, that legislation enacted in the interests of working people had been modified or declared invalid by the courts.

A FLING AT THE BAR.

Q.—You are not a lawyer? A.—I hope not.

Q.—You think you have got a better job? A.—No, it satisfies my conscience better.

Q.—Mr. Gompers, I am glad to say that I have a better opinion of labor leaders than you have of lawyers. A.—I think that is true.

The remedy advocated by the witness for expulsion for Unions on insufficient grounds was "the growth of intelligence among the men and women in the labor movement" which, he said, "cured many an ill and wrong."

Pressed for a direct reply to the question as to whether he would permit any kind of court review on expulsion Mr. Gompers said he would not, admitting he would "allow that injustice to remain unredressed until the enlightenment of the labor movement has reached the stage at which expulsion would no longer exist."

"As a seer and a philosopher, can you give us any idea of how long that is likely to be?" he was asked.

"Well," said Mr. Gompers, drawling out his words as he contemplated the top of Mr. Untermyer's head, "probably the first of January, 1923 if it doesn't rain."

The audience laughed. Mr. Untermyer said he failed to see the application of the answer. "And so do I of the question," commented the witness. "I would rather allow it to continue or to support its continuance than to submit a question of this character to the courts," he added. His reason was that the courts were "still dominated by the old concept of master and servant." He would not give his assent or approval "to any measure that would increase the power of the courts in any matter affecting the organization of the working people of our country or our State."

Q.—No matter how grave might be the injustice that was sought to be corrected? A.—Rather bear the injustice we have than to fly to others we know not of.[6]

Q.—And those others are the courts of the land? A.—Yes, in so far as labor is concerned, so far as the poor are concerned, yes, sir.

SEES COURTS "NEARLY" CLOSED TO POOR.

Q.—You believe that the courts are closed to the poor, don't you? A.—Very nearly so, and when it comes to the relations between employer and the workers it is shut tight and on the outside to keep the workmen in.

Mr. Gompers would not admit Mr. Untermyer's characterization of his remark as being "revolutionary doctrine." He said that the provisions of the Clayton act were being used against labor and that recently a Supreme Court Justice declared that it was the duty of the courts to stand by capital.[7]

Mr. Untermyer agreed with the witness when he said a man who served a term in prison should be permitted to rejoin his union. If the right of admission to a union were exercised wantonly and arbitrarily for the purpose of limiting membership, Mr. Gompers said, he would place the right of review only within the labor movement.

In defense of the limitation of apprentices he said: "We are not living under normal conditions when men can exercise their natural attributes and abilities and find compensation and rewards coming from fair dealing among men, in the modern industrial life of our country there are organizations and corporations and trusts on the one hand and the workingmen on the other, and if the workingmen did not do any normal thing to protect their interests they would be poltroons and unworthy of the name of men and citizens. We have to protect ourselves against the exploitation and relentless antagonism of men."

Q.—And one of your ways of doing that is to curtail the opportunities for the sons of your own members to engage in the trades in which their fathers are engaged in? A.—I do not think that is the proper inference or proper deduction.

After Mr. Gompers expressed the opinion that organized society has no understanding of the affairs of labor, Mr. Untermyer turned to the committee and said that his examination of Mr. Gompers was for the purpose of having the committee and the Legislature know all the reasons that could be advanced "why there should be a certain amount of regulation over the affairs of these unions."

Turning to Mr. Gompers, he asked: "Do I understand you correctly on that subject to say that you would, apart from the ranks of labor itself, allow no review of any acts of these unions, however autocratic, unjust or detrimental they might be to the public interest?"

"I think they are not detrimental to the public interest," answered Mr. Gompers.

Tie-Up of $30,000,000 Power House.

In order to prove that the questions under discussion some times were detrimental to the public interest, Mr. Untermyer went into the case of the $30,000,000 power house under construction for the Edison Co.

The witness said that in cases of dispute between unions it was not right that the employer should be made to bear the burden and the loss and said it was "regrettable." It was possible, he said, that unions "cannot sometimes enforce their decisions" and he was asked if he did not think it "scandalous" that a contractor should be ruined because of a jurisdictional dispute.

"Greatly regrettable," said Mr. Gompers mildly, "but as to being scandalous, no."

The witness opposed any power inside or outside the unions which could compel men to do anything. He said there was no power vested in the voluntary labor organizations, either the national, international unions or the federation, which has power to say to any body of men "You have got to do anything." The alternative to such power, he said, was that if men failed to do what they were ordered they would have to go to jail.

Gompers Admits Lack of Power.

The labor leader said it would be impossible for him to order the international union of plumbers to expel the plumbers who quit work on the power house job and to give the contractor permission to get other plumbers to do the work.

"The President of the American Federation of Labor would have no more power or right to give any such direction to the President of the United Association of Plumbers and Gas Fitters than he would have to give a direction to the President of the United States," he declared.

Q.—You are perfectly helpless. A.—I am not. I can advise.

Mr. Gompers said that the big jurisdictional fight which is now on was one between the carpenters and sheet metal workers.[8]

"So there are plenty of other suffering contractors?" asked Mr. Untermyer.

"Honestly, my heart goes out in sympathy for the contractors," said the witness sarcastically.

"And for the public?"

"I have as much concern for the public as any other man I know."

Asked why he should not sympathize with the innocent contractors suffering an injury for which they were not responsible the witness declared that "here and there one suffers, but I think for an unconscionable group they take the cake."

He thought it was fair that union men should keep at work pending the settlement of jurisdictional disputes, but said this condition had not yet come to pass.

. . .

New York Times, Apr. 22, 1922.

1. For a transcript of SG's testimony before the Lockwood Committee on Apr. 21, 1922, see Files of the Office of the President, Hearings, reel 125, frames 769–841, *AFL Records;* for his testimony on Apr. 22, see ibid., frames 842–952; and for his testimony on May 4, see ibid., reel 126, frames 1–134.

2. The Hell Gate power station, said to be the largest electric power plant in the country and one of the largest in the world, was officially opened in March 1922. While the plant was under construction, a jurisdictional dispute arose between plumbers and steamfitters affiliated with the United Association of Journeymen PLUMBERS and Steam Fitters of the United States and Canada, when members of the steamfitters' local began laying water pipe, work claimed by the plumbers. John Coefield, president of the international, ruled in favor of the plumbers, but the steamfitters ignored the ruling and continued to install the pipe. The plumbers' local then struck the job, demanding they be allowed to rip out the pipe and reinstall it themselves. The strike by the plumbers held up completion of the power plant for months. The plumbing contractor referred to here was Patrick F. Kenny (1876–1941).

3. The report *Justice and the Poor: A Study of the Present Denial of Justice to the Poor and of the Agencies Making More Equal Their Position before the Law, with Particular Reference to Legal Aid Work in the United States* was written by Reginald Heber Smith and issued in 1919 by the Carnegie Foundation for the Advancement of Teaching. It outlined the inequities poor people encountered as a result of delays, costs, and fees when they sought redress through the court system and stated: "The administration of American justice is not impartial; the rich and the poor do not stand on an equality before the law; the traditional method of providing justice has operated to close the doors of the courts to

the poor, and has caused a gross denial of justice in all parts of the country to millions of persons" ("Says Poor Can't Get Justice in Courts," *New York Times,* Oct. 22, 1919).

4. That is, *Moral Overstrain* by George William Alger. See *The Samuel Gompers Papers,* vol. 8, p. 493, n. 20.

5. Thomas A. McWhinney (1864–1933), vice-chairman of the Lockwood Committee and a Republican member of the New York state assembly (1915–23).

6. The line is from the soliloquy "To be, or not to be" in Shakespeare's *Hamlet,* act 3, scene 1: "Who would these fardels bear,/ To grunt and sweat under a weary life,/ But that the dread of something after death,/ The undiscovered country from whose bourn/ No traveller returns, puzzles the will,/ And makes us rather bear those ills we have/ Than fly to others that we know not of?"

7. Reference to a remark made by Justice James Cornell Van Siclen of the New York Supreme Court. See *The Samuel Gompers Papers,* vol. 11, p. 458, n. 5.

8. See *The Samuel Gompers Papers,* vol. 8, p. 151, n. 8.

[April 23, 1922]

GOMPERS ADMITS LABOR UNION ABUSES; OFFERS NO REMEDY

For three and a half hours yesterday Samuel Untermyer tried to convince President Samuel Gompers of the American Federation of Labor that the failure of labor to clean house was forcing the Lockwood Committee to consider measures for the regulation of unions and that although unions (the plumbers particularly) had promised faithfully to eliminate abuses, such action had either not been taken or when taken had been rescinded when the unions felt the Lockwood Committee was about to wind up its deliberations.

Mr. Gompers denounced as unjustifiable and wrong many of the abuses in the unions but when asked for a remedy short of regulation by the courts he counselled "patience," saying "the world was not made in a day." He said he would rather see union men go without redress for vicious and oppressive wrongs committed against them by their comrades than to permit the injured men redress through the courts. Regrettable as many union practices were, Mr. Gompers said he would not have the Legislature "interfere."

Even though officers of unions stole the funds Mr. Gompers would not have the Legislature compel unions to install accounting systems. He expressed the opinion that the Legislature should not "interfere" in any way with the unions.

Mr. Gompers said frankly that he had no other remedy to suggest for industrial evils, and declared that it must be recognized that the labor movement was a struggle of workers for improvement of their condition—"a rough struggle," he said, "of the masses to find their way out."

Justifies "Snowballing" Strikes.[1]

Mr. Untermyer took up the recent "snowballing" strikes, and showed that plasterers and bricklayers working under an agreed wage scale of $10 were exacting up to $16 a day. Mr. Gompers justified acceptance of the higher wages by the workers on the ground that they should take anything "offered" by the employers in improved wages and working conditions. While the unions should try to control the presentation of demands by groups of employes, he confessed this could not control it, "because you must remember you are dealing with human beings who are benefiting by the competition of contractors."

To the question of what good a contract was if it was not enforced by labor as well as by employers, the veteran labor leader replied that "time develops discipline," but Mr. Untermyer quickly interjected the remark: "What good does it do for the contractor to philosophize to the effect that while he cannot enforce his contract, time will remedy things so that some other fellow can enforce his?"

Toward the conclusion of his testimony President Gompers declared emphatically that the evils of the unions had their origin in the struggle of the working men to "right the wrongs that the employers have imposed upon the men."

All abuses in labor unions, he asserted, had their origin "in the corruption and tyranny of the builders and contractors." The origin of bribery in the building trades, he added, lay with those Chicago building contractors who corrupted Sam Parks, "an honest iron worker earning $2, $3 or $4 a day, and made a business agent and laying before him two, three, four and five $100 bills—a poor devil who never saw a $10 bill in his life."

Q.—So you think Parks was not responsible but the other fellow was?
A.—I think Parks was responsible for his acts, but I know the origin of his downfall.

His Opinion of Brindell.

Q.—Is that true of Brindell? A.—I think so.
Q.—You do? A.—Yes, sir.
Q.—You think it was not Brindell's own corrupt soul, but it was the corruption that was forced upon him, do you? A.—Not necessarily; the system grew up.

In reply to questions Mr. Gompers said he did not know that Brindell in the eleven months he presided over the Building Trades Council reaped about $1,000,000 in graft or that within thirty days after he came into power Brindell began to blackmail builders.

"Don't you know that he forced this tribute from builders and that they didn't go to him and voluntarily pay it to him?" asked Mr. Untermyer.

"That may be very true," replied the witness. "I say the system grew up and he learned of it very quickly."

"He was the inventor of it?"

"No."

Mr. Gompers challenged Mr. Untermyer to draw a statute that would "bind the activities of organized labor" by embodying in it the reforms and methods of regulation suggested by the counsel for the committee. Labor could not be put into a straightjacket, he said. Mr. Untermyer said he hoped to confront Mr. Gompers with such a regulatory statute and to get his approval of it.

Mr. Untermyer pointed out that the Plumbers' Union and other unions accepted the nineteen points for reform suggested by the Lockwood committee, but that recently the plumbers rescinded their resolution of acceptance.[2] Under the circumstances, he wanted the witness to say what was left to the committee to do but to recommend legislation looking to the regulation of unions so that there would be some power to enforce promises made by unions.

Mr. Gompers said that such things would be regulated by the unions. Mr. Untermyer argued that the unions were doing nothing.

"What else is left for the committee to suggest?" he asked.

"The recognition of the fact that this is a struggle, a struggle of the working people of our State and of our country for improved conditions," replied the witness.

Mr. Untermyer pointed to the struggle of others to give the people housing accommodations and to get away from the "despotic and unjustifiable union regulations." Mr. Gompers repeated his desire for recognition of the fact that the masses were trying "to find their way out," a remark that was greeted by Mr. Untermyer as merely "a figure of speech."

"Patience" Gompers's Remedy.

"To have patience and to bear with the ills we have rather than to fly to others we know not of,"[3] was Mr. Gompers's reason for opposing legal regulation of trade unions.

Mr. Gompers approved the regulation of trade combinations and associations because they dealt in material products and could fix prices. While admitting that abuses of labor unions also affected the public, he opposed regulation, because unions were voluntary organizations of human beings, not for the personal profit of the members, but for the improvement of their condition.

The witness admitted it would be a breach of contract if, in the face of a $9 scale of wages for plasterers, the employers, because of business depression, tried to reduce the scale to $8. But it would not be equally a breach of contract on the part of the union if its members took advantage of activity in the trade to get $10 or $12 in the face of its contract to work for $9.

Although he considered the contract to receive $8 and to pay it a mutual one between contractor and worker, Mr. Gompers was of the opinion that if more money were "offered" the men they would be justified legally in accepting the increase.

"The contract is based upon a minimum wage and not a maximum one," he said in support of his contention. Mr. Untermyer intimated he could hardly believe an employer would make such a contract.

OPPOSED TO "FIXED WAGES."

Q.—Now, how is it possible for any one to get into the building business and expect to succeed without stability in wages? Don't you see it is absolutely essential to any legitimate building that there should be stability in wages? A.—Approximate stability in wages, yes; fixed wages, no.

Mr. Gompers said he saw no reason for absolute stability in wages in order to get the best results in cheap homes for the masses. He reiterated his belief in "approximately stable but not fixed wages," and Mr. Untermyer wanted to know how he could determine how far to go in reaching "approximate stability."

The witness maintained that the men had not demanded increases, but that they receive more money because of the competition among contractors for men. Asked whether he thought the union should permit the practice to continue, the witness said, "I think that it should not be stopped." He believed that even when the bricklayers contracted to take $14 a day in wages they should accept $14 or "anything the employers will offer in improved wages and living conditions."

Q.—Suppose there is a depression in building, should unions permit the men to work below the agreed rate of wages as fixed by contract? A.—Not if they can help it.

They sometimes tried to prevent such occurrences by disciplining the men who accepted lower wages, he added.

HIS VIEWS ON DISCIPLINE.

Q.—If they discipline men for breaking the scale below the fixed rate, why should they not discipline them for breaking the scale above the fixed rate? A.—Because that is a development of human aspiration, to get more out of life.

Q.—Isn't it also a denial of human aspirations, when there is not enough work going around and a man has a wife and family to support that he takes the best wages that he can below the fixed wage; isn't that the same aspiration? A.—No, sir; that is tearing down the standards of life of the wives and children of all the others, as well as his own.

Mr. Gompers denied that permitting men to accept wages higher than the agreed scale would paralyze the industry.

Mr. Untermyer pointed to several recent cases where demands above the agreed scale were made by workers. One was on the job of Matthews and Link, constructing six houses at Jackson Street and Eighteenth Avenue, Long Island City. The bricklayers receiving $10 demanded $12. The owner was forced to pay in order to go on with the contract. On the job of Valento building a house on Fifth Avenue, Astoria, bricklayers receiving the scale of $10 asked for and received $13.

In some cases, according to Mr. Untermyer, plasterers in Brooklyn and Queens exacted $14 and $16 a day.

"Don't you think there ought to be a stop to that sort of thing?" asked Mr. Untermyer.

"No."

Mr. Gompers added that the unions should endeavor to control it, adding: "I think that they cannot control it, nor can any other agency control it."

"If that is so, what is the use of a contract with the employers?" asked Mr. Untermyer. "Why should the employers make a contract with labor unions if the labor unions cannot stabilize it?"

Admits Contract Can't Be Stabilized.

"They cannot," replied the witness. "Nor can the contractors, nor can the State or the Government enforce or stop anything of that kind. It is the historic fact that all attempts to fix wages have proved futile, and in the attempt to impose his fixation of wages there has been absolute brutality, tyranny, injustice and slavery enforced throughout."

Q.—Can you imagine any greater brutality than to get a contractor who may have everything that he has involved in a construction work getting into a contract on a fixed scale of wages, and then when he is in the middle of the contract, under obligations to other people, raising wages on him so that he will probably go bankrupt. A.—I do not think that is right.

Mr. Gompers would not accede to the reasonableness of the proposition that, while a worker might sue an employer for failure to pay wages agreed to by contract, employers should have the right to sue workers for failure to supply services at wages agreed on. He said there should be no remedy by law but that the remedy should be in the organized labor movement, which was constantly growing and improving.

The witness was willing to go far enough along Mr. Untermyer's road to say the unions should have a by-law preventing men from taking higher wages than called for in agreements and should have the power to discipline men who broke the by-laws, but he still maintained that the employer should not be able to go to court to have the excess wages returned to him.

"How will he get it?" asked Mr. Untermyer.

"The best he can," said Mr. Gompers.

"The best is nothing, isn't it?"

"That may be true in the cases of a few and then it is wrong," said the labor leader.

The attention of the witness was called to the recent consent decree entered into in the Federal court by several unions of bricklayers and plasterers in which the union promised to give up certain rules held by the authorities to be illegal.[4] Mr. Gompers declared angrily that the decree had been forced on the unions by duress and under threats, and this was denied by Mr. Untermyer.

Mr. Untermyer then read a long list of abuses in the trades unions, many of which were disapproved by the witness. The abuses were exposed by the Lockwood Committee.

Mr. Gompers disapproved of fines as high as $1,000 imposed on union men, and said that it was "unwarranted" for plasterers to fine employers for non-attendance at union meetings. He did not think that it should be insisted on that foremen should be members of unions, and said that there was no justification for plasterers smashing molds so that they could not be employed by contractors on other jobs.

The witness said one cure for labor's ills, which has been urged by his executive council, by conventions of the federation and in publications of labor was "a greater consideration in decent conduct among men."

Q.—And while you have been engaged in this moral uplift among your men, are you aware that these practices, most of them are of recent origin, many of them since 1919, and that they have been steadily growing? A.—I know there have been some of them in vogue in recent times.

Q.—It is not bearing very good fruit, this uplift campaign, is it? A.— Yes, it is.

REBELLIOUS UNION CITED.

Mr. Untermyer went on to explain that every attempt had been made by employers to have conditions remedied, that in one case

John P. Donlin,[5] President of the Building Trades Department of the Federation and the higher officers of the bricklayers' union agreed with the contractors and architects in charge of the construction of the Ambassador Hotel, but that, despite this, the plasterers' union would not rescind action deemed unwarranted.[6] Mr. Untermyer went into some detail in explaining this case, which created considerable comment when first exposed by the Lockwood committee. Mr. Gompers was incredulous of the facts, and said, frankly, that he did not believe them. Mr. Untermyer reminded him that he was quoting from the report of the Lockwood committee.

Counsel took up the report that members of the lathers' union in Chicago were fined $20 if they attended a baseball game by any team under the jurisdiction of Judge K. M. Landis, whose recent arbitration award in the Chicago building trades was objected to by some unions.

Mr. Gompers declared that the lathers had adopted no such resolution, but admitted that Germans and Danes in the building trades had been fined for working on St. Patrick's Day. The latter procedure he said was "wrong and ludicrous."

When the witness said again that he would leave the correction of labor ills to the unions Mr. Untermyer accused him of wishing to have the abuses abated "by nobody except the people who are practicing them for their own profit and their own aggrandizement."

. . .

New York Times, Apr. 23, 1922.

1. A reference to attempts by building trades workers to raise wages despite contracts with employers stipulating wage rates. Workers would walk off a job, citing a grievance, and return only after wages were raised. At that point, other workers would walk off, causing a "snowball" effect that eventually raised wages overall.

2. Reference to a list of demands made by the Lockwood Committee requiring specific changes in union by-laws and practices. New York City building trades unions agreed to the proposals at a meeting on Jan. 4, 1922, between Samuel Untermyer and union representatives. Local 463 of the United Association of Journeymen Plumbers and Steam Fitters of the United States and Canada—the largest plumbers' local in the city, with a membership of some four thousand—subsequently repudiated the agreement.

3. See "'God Save Labor from the Courts,' Exclaims Gompers," Apr. 22, 1922, n. 6, above.

4. Threatened with federal prosecution for ostensible violations of the Sherman Act, representatives of the Bricklayers', Masons', and Plasterers' International Union of America negotiated a consent decree with U.S. Attorney William Hayward agreeing to refrain from various practices prohibited by the law. The decree was signed on Feb. 24, 1922, and entered in the U.S. district court in New York City on Feb. 28 (*U.S. v. Bricklayers', Masons', and Plasterers' International Union*).

5. John H. DONLIN served as president of the AFL Building Trades Department from 1916 to 1924.

6. According to Untermyer, Jack Pearl, business agent for Plasterers' local 60 of New York City, had demanded that a wall be ripped out during construction of the Ambassador Hotel in Manhattan because he did not care for the color. Untermyer also

charged that one hundred forty-five insulated mantles had been discarded because the union did not approve the installation method. Michael Colleran, president of the local, disputed the allegations.

To William Green[1]

June 3, 1922.

Mr. William Green,
Secretary, United Mine Workers of America,
1102–8 Merchants Bank Bldg., Indianapolis, Indiana.
Dear Sir and Brother:

At a meeting held in the Executive Council Chamber of the American Federation of Labor Building, Washington, D.C., a "Permanent Conference for the Abolition of Child Labor" was formed.[2] There were present nearly sixty representative men and women who have been engaged and are now interested in the preservation of child life by the abolition of child labor. A general discussion ensued and the declaration was made that the conference shall have as its primary purpose the abolition of child labor from the United States, its territories and possessions. The officers selected were:

Samuel Gompers, Chairman
Mrs. Florence Kelley,[3] Vice-Chairman
Miss Matilda Lindsay,[4] Secretary

The chairman was authorized and directed to appoint a committee of ten or more whose mission shall be to prepare for submission to a subsequent meeting of this conference, both a constitutional amendment and the best form of law it finds itself capable of submitting.[5]

I have the honor to extend to you an invitation to become a member of the committee above named and I trust that we may have the benefit of your attendance, advice and co-operation when a meeting of the committee shall be called.

In the meantime may I request that you will give some further consideration to the entire project and how in your judgment the situation may be met by legislation, federal or state, or by proposing a constitutional amendment.

Trusting that I may hear from you at your early convenience, and that it may be your acceptance as a member of the committee,[6] I have the honor to remain

Very truly yours,   Saml Gompers
President,   American Federation of Labor.

TLpS, reel 280, vol. 293, p. 713, SG Letterbooks, DLC.

1. William GREEN served as secretary-treasurer of the United Mine Workers of America from 1913 to 1924. In 1914 he became a member of the AFL Executive Council and, after SG's death in December 1924, he became AFL president, an office he held until his death.

2. SG formed the Permanent Conference for the Abolition of Child Labor after the U.S. Supreme Court ruled the Child Labor Tax Act unconstitutional (*Bailey* v. *Drexel Furniture Co.*, 259 U.S. 20 [1922]; see *The Samuel Gompers Papers*, vol. 11, p. 514, n. 2). The court announced its decision on May 15, 1922; the meeting SG refers to was held June 1. The child labor committee met at AFL headquarters, proceeded to the House Office Building to meet with the House Committee on the Judiciary, and then reconvened at the AFL building. SG told the Judiciary Committee: "It is my judgment, as the result of many years of activity, thought, and study, that any industry which can not succeed in the United States unless the young and innocent children shall be employed in it, should not exist, and the sooner that industry is thrown out of the body politic and economic the better it will be for all of us" (U.S. Congress, House, *Child Labor: Hearing before the Committee on the Judiciary . . . on H.J. Res. 327*, 67th Cong., 2d sess., 1922, p. 2).

Invited to attend the June 1 meeting were members of the AFL Executive Council, officers of AFL Departments, the editor of the *Weekly News Letter,* representatives of the Information and Publicity Service, Legislative Committee, and Research Department, and delegates from international affiliates, railroad brotherhoods, and central bodies. Also invited to the June 1 meeting or a subsequent conference on July 17 were Samuel McCune Lindsay of Columbia University, Methodist bishop William McDowell, Rev. John Ryan of the Catholic University of America, and Rabbi Stephen Wise, as well as representatives of the American Association for Labor Legislation, the American Association of University Women, the Federal Council of Churches of Christ in America, the General Federation of Women's Clubs, the National Board of Farm Organizations, the National Catholic Welfare Council, the National Child Labor Committee, the National Congress of Mothers and Parent-Teachers Associations, the National Council of Catholic Women, the National Council of Jewish Women, the National Council of Women, the National Organization for Public Health Nursing, the National Women's Relief Society, the National Women's Trade Union League, the Public Education and Child Labor Association of Pennsylvania, the YMCA and the YWCA, and the Children's Bureau and the Women's Bureau of the Department of Labor.

3. Florence KELLEY, a prominent reformer, was secretary of the National Consumers' League and served on the boards of directors of the New York State and the National Child Labor Committees.

4. Martha Matilda Lindsay (1892–1959), a member of National Federation of Federal Employees 105 of Washington, D.C., served on the staff of the national union's legislative department (1920–22) and served the National Women's Trade Union League as organizer (1922–24, 1928–31) and executive board member (1924–32). A graduate of the Bryn Mawr Summer School for Women in Industry in 1922, she later served as the school's assistant director (1924–25) and executive secretary (1926–27). Lindsay was an organizer for the Federation of Federal Employees from 1932 until at least 1954 and at the time of her death was serving as director of the union's research department.

5. For the constitutional amendment prepared by the committee, authorizing Congress and the states to restrict or prohibit the labor of individuals under the age of eighteen, see AFL, *Proceedings*, 1923, p. 34. The amendment was presented in the Senate on July 26, 1922, by Illinois Republican Joseph McCormick as S.J. Res. 232 (67th Cong., 2d sess.) and in the House of Representatives on Dec. 11 by Ohio Re-

publican Israel Foster as H.J. Res. 407 (67th Cong., 4th sess.). SG and other members of the committee testified on behalf of the measure on Jan. 10 and Feb. 22, 1923, but Congress adjourned without acting upon it. (For SG's testimony, see U.S. Congress, Senate, *Child-Labor Amendment to the Constitution: Hearings before a Subcommittee of the Committee on the Judiciary . . . on . . . S.J. Res. 232 . . .* , 67th Cong., 4th sess., 1923; Files of the Office of the President, Hearings, reel 126, frame 136, *AFL Records.*) Another AFL-supported constitutional amendment to prohibit child labor was introduced in the House of Representatives by Foster on Feb. 13, 1924 (H.J. Res. 184, 68th Cong., 1st sess.). It was approved by the House on Apr. 26 and by the Senate on June 2 but failed ratification.

6. Green accepted the appointment.

From Joanna Snowden-Porter[1]

Chicago, Illinois, June 5th, 1922.

Sir:—

It is gratifying to note that immediate constructive measures are on foot to protect the child welfare of America.

It is my pleasure, personally and as president of the Northwestern Federation of Colored Women's Clubs[2] to congratulate you on being in the forfront in this matter as you were in the matter of opening the doors of labor to all workers, in unions.

No group of people in America can be more intensely interested in the matter of Child Labor as our children are peculiarly affected.

For this reason I write to ask that a Colored woman be named as one of the Committee which has to do with investigative and provisional measures tending to the absolute abolition of Child Labor in the United States.

As president of this Federation and an Officer of the National Association of Colored Women,[3] I am sure that I voice the sentiments of those great bodies of Americans working for the uplift of all humanity.

I shall be glad to be of any service in this matter and close, trusting for serious consideration and an early reply.[4]

Yours for service to humanity.
President.

TLc, RG 102, Records of the Children's Bureau, DNA.

1. Joanna C. Snowden-Porter (née Hudlin; 1864–1941), a clerk in the Cook County Recorder's Office, served for many years as president of the Northwestern Federation of Colored Women's Clubs and from 1026 to 1030 was an organizer for the National Association of Colored Women.

2. The Northwestern Federation of Colored Women's Clubs was organized in Chicago in 1915 to unite black women's clubs in midwestern and western states,

promote better religious, social, and civic conditions, and protest against harmful legislation.

3. The National Association of Colored Women was founded in 1896 with the merger of the National Federation of Afro-American Women and the National League of Colored Women. A federation of state and local organizations, the federation worked to improve living and educational standards for women and children, secure civil and political rights, and promote interracial understanding.

4. Snowden-Porter was apparently not added to the committee.

A Statement by Samuel Gompers

June 12, 1922

It is no exaggeration to say that the country was shocked when the Supreme Court declared the child labor law unconstitutional.[1] The fact that Congress had sought to prevent child labor by means of a law imposing a tax on the products of child labor when carried in interstate commerce in no measure lessened the force of the blow.

The great fact that stood out in the public mind was that the Congress of the United States had released the children of our country from the factories, the mills and the shops and the Supreme Court had sent them back to work.

In deciding the case the Supreme Court had recourse to all of the niceties and technicalities of the law. The people in contemplating the decision saw only the essential facts.

The Supreme Court dealt with the problem in the most approved, legalistic manner. It brought to the case the erudition of our most noted institutions of learning. It decided that in view of various precedents, provisions and stipulations the law enacted by Congress was unconstitutional and therefore void.

The people in examining the decision of the Supreme Court saw only the fact that children who had been taken out of factories must now go back to the factories, to the detriment of their health, to the neglect of their education and to the future weakening of the fiber of our civilization.

The fact that the Supreme Court said in effect that it regretted the necessity for such a decision in no way diminished popular resentment against the decision and in no way increased popular admiration for the intellectual ability of the Supreme Court.

It is more than strange that a Supreme Court, which can wend its way through the difficult paths which have led up to the acknowledgment of the futility of what Roosevelt called "trust busting" and which finally evolved "the rule of reason,"[2] as a haven of safety for corporations should be able to find no way through which the children might be protected in their escape from bondage.

If there were a Congress in Washington possessed of even a moderate sense of public duty, devoted [in] even a moderate degree to the cause of progress and of human well-being, this action of the Supreme Court would have precipitated a furor among Congressmen and we should have long since heard of plans for another effort to liberate the children. It will be remembered that this is the second case in which the Supreme Court has nullified an act of Congress to liberate the children.

Congress accepts the blow casually, as a matter of little or no moment. Congress nowadays does many strange things. This is·only one of many instances but it is not the least of them.

We live in a trying time. Officialdom seems unable or unwilling to hear the voice which comes bearing the message of human needs, of human desires. There is a great complacency in high places. There is a great misunderstanding. This must be changed and rectified for the simple reason that the people of the United States will not long tolerate the hideous evil of child labor. We tolerate many strange things in our democracy but this goes beyond the point of tolerance. It is an anachronism too glaring for our time and the social conscience which has been built up through decade after decade of protest and enlightenment.

The Congress of the United States must find a way to liberate and protect the children. If Congress does not appreciate this fact it must be brought by insistent public demand to a proper realization of the necessity for action.

The Supreme Court by its decision did not close the case. The case can never be closed until the childhood of America is guaranteed its freedom.

TDp, reel 280, vol. 293, pp. 836–38, SG Letterbooks, DLC. Typed notation: "Written for the Philadelphia Public Ledger. By Samuel Gompers."

1. See "To William Green," June 3, 1922, n. 2, above.
2. The doctrine, enunciated by the U.S. Supreme Court in *Standard Oil Co. of New Jersey* v. *U.S.* (221 U.S. 1 [1911]), held that the Sherman Antitrust Act should be interpreted in the light of reason and that, construed in this way, the law prohibited only unreasonable combinations or contracts in restraint of interstate commerce.

Excerpts from News Accounts of the 1922 Convention of the AFL in Cincinnati

[June 16, 1922]

MINERS' STRIKE INDORSED BY FEDERATION OF LABOR; RAIL WALKOUT[1] UNOPPOSED

Devoting its entire morning session to the consideration of business, the American Federation of Labor, holding its forty-second annual convention at the Freeman Avenue Armory, yesterday, went on record as indorsing the miners' strike[2] and approved a resolution recommending that all international unions change their constitutions so as to permit the transfer of the member of one organization to another organization without payment of initiation fees.[3]

The vote on the indorsement of the coal strike was unanimous.

Loud cheers from all parts of the hall greeted the announcement by B. M. Jewell, President of the Railway Employees' Department of the federation, that the rail union chiefs would not interfere to stop a railroad strike.

A resolution introduced by E. H. Fitzgerald, Cincinnati, President of the Amalgamated Railway Clerks and Freight Handlers of America,[4] providing for the amalgamation of unions into single organizations, each covering an industry, was voted down.[5] The plan met its death in a report of the Organization Committee, which recommended the rejection because the plan was said to be "already in effect through various departments of the American Federation of Labor."

. . .

Commercial Tribune (Cincinnati), June 16, 1922.

1. In April 1921 the U.S. Railroad Labor Board approved wide-ranging pay cuts for railroad workers, ended wartime work rule provisions, including overtime for Sundays and holidays, and authorized railroads to negotiate new work rules with their employees. When the board approved further pay cuts in May and June 1922, some four hundred thousand machinists, blacksmiths, carmen, boilermakers, electricians, and sheet metal workers walked off their jobs on July 1. With 90 percent of the shop craft workers on strike, carriers were initially forced to curtail service, since locomotives could not be maintained or repaired. But on July 3 the board declared that shop craft unions no longer represented railroad employees, since their striking members were no longer actually working for the railroads, asserted that replacement workers had a moral and a legal right to take the place of strikers, and urged railroads to form new workers' organizations. Railroad executives responded by stripping seniority rights from striking shopmen and hiring strikebreakers.

President Warren Harding proposed a settlement that would have preserved both the wage cuts and the shopmen's seniority rights as long as both sides agreed to abide by the Railroad Labor Board's decisions in the future, but neither the shopmen nor railroad executives would agree to these terms. Harding then proposed that strikers return to work and submit seniority questions to the board, but the shopmen rejected this as well. On Sept. 1 Attorney General Harry Daugherty obtained a temporary restraining order from James Wilkerson, U.S. district court judge for Northern Illinois, barring striking shopmen or any officers of their unions, of the AFL Railway Employes' Department, or of some 120 system federations from interfering with railroad operations. On Sept. 23 Wilkerson rejected a defense motion to dismiss the order (*U.S. v. Railway Employees' Department of American Federation of Labor et al.*, 283 F. 479 [1922]), which he then reissued as an injunction with nationwide force.

Meanwhile, Railway Employes' Department president B. M. Jewell was meeting with Seaboard Air Line Railway president S. Davies Warfield and Baltimore and Ohio Railroad president Daniel Willard to create a framework for settlements with individual railroads. On Sept. 13, unable to finance the strike any longer, the shopmen's strike committee accepted the terms of the so-called Baltimore Agreement negotiated by Jewell, Warfield, and Willard, authorizing settlements restoring full seniority to strikers and establishing labor-management committees to resolve other issues. Although 74 railroads made individual settlements by month's end and 225,000 shopmen had their seniority restored, 130 railroads refused to accept the terms of the Baltimore Agreement, and 175,000 shopmen ultimately lost their seniority. The strike continued on some roads into 1923 but finally collapsed in 1924; it was officially terminated in 1928.

2. On June 15, 1922, W. D. Mahon proposed that the AFL endorse the strike of the United Mine Workers of America. His motion was passed unanimously.

3. Resolution 9, introduced on June 13, 1922, by Harry Fox of the Wyoming State Federation of Labor, called for affiliated national and international unions to allow the members of other affiliates to transfer in without paying new initiation fees. On June 15 the Committee on Organization recommended against adopting the resolution on the grounds that affiliates had complete autonomy in matters of membership, but the convention passed the resolution over the committee's recommendation.

4. The Brotherhood of RAILWAY and Steamship Clerks, Freight Handlers, Express and Station Employes.

5. Resolution 29, introduced on June 13, 1922, by delegates of the Railway Clerks, proposed that the AFL call a conference of affiliated national and international unions in order to create an amalgamated union in each industry. Resolution 30, introduced the same day by Herman Defrem of AFL Bookkeepers', Stenographers', and Accountants' Union 12,646 of New York City, made a similar proposal. On June 15 the Committee on Organization recommended against adopting the resolution on the grounds that the policy was already being implemented by the various AFL departments. The convention concurred in the committee's recommendation.

[June 17, 1922]

. . .

A resolution providing for a universal union label[1] was defeated by a vote of the convention as savoring too much of the "one big union" idea rejected so decidedly during the first part of the convention. Matthew Woll,[2] a Vice President of the American Federation of Labor, opposed passage of the resolution and intimated that it originated with those who had fostered the single union plan and were still hopeful of seeing their plans consummated. He urged rejection of the resolution "to end the whole question for all time." G. F. Mikel,[3] an Arkansas delegate, presented the universal label resolution and spoke in support of the idea.

. . .

Commercial Tribune (Cincinnati), June 17, 1922.

1. Resolution 10, introduced on June 13, 1922, by Harry Fox of the Wyoming State Federation of Labor (FOL), and Resolution 37, introduced the same day by George Mikel of the Arkansas State FOL, called for the AFL to endorse a standard label design for affiliates to use on all their products and shop cards. Acting on the recommendation of the Committee on Labels, the convention voted down the resolutions on June 16.

2. Matthew Woll represented the International Photo-Engravers' Union of North America.

3. George Elmer Mikel (1869–1949), a member of United Mine Workers of America 1810 of Jenny Lind, Ark., represented the Arkansas State FOL.

[June 18, 1922]

. . .

"STRICT AUTONOMY" UPHELD.

For the third time the advocates of a policy departing from the classic position of the A.F. of L. plan of ["]strict autonomy" for the trade unions experienced a defeat yesterday in the convention. The Law Committee reported adversely on a number of resolutions, the purpose of which was amendment of the constitution providing that affiliated internationals must compel their locals to join state and city central bodies.[1]

Max Hayes,[2] Cleveland, delegate of the Typographical Union, led the advocates for the resolution. He said he was not committed to the exact form of the resolution and had expected the committee to report an adequate substitute. Many state and central bodies had little more [than] a "paper existence," so weak are they, he said. State and city central bodies were capable of great things, but the burden of their maintenance was upon a few unions, he declared.

Chairman Daniel Tobin, Indianapolis, Teamsters,[3] and Treasurer of the Federation, said the committee was in favor of the spirit of the resolution. He said he well knew the benefits of state and central bodies. The constitution now provided, he said, that the Federation could instruct internationals when it learned of non-affiliating local organizations, but it cannot compel. Splendid results, he declared, have resulted. The report of the committee was adopted by a vote of 171 to 55.

A few minutes afterwards the advocates of industrial unionism suffered a blow in the adoption of the report of the Law Committee adverse to a resolution that sought to amend the constitution so that in the event of a strike of one craft members of other crafts would not work for the employer against whom the one craft was striking.[4]

ANOTHER REPORT SUSTAINED.

The committee was also sustained in its report that when an international does not admit women the Executive Council should seek to arrive at an understanding with the internationals in the granting of direct Federal charters to unions of women.[5]

. . .

Cincinnati Enquirer, June 18, 1922.

1. On June 13, 1922, eleven resolutions—5, 11, 12, 13, 15, 17, 34, 39, 42, 45, and 48—were proposed that would have required national and international affiliates to compel their locals to join their respective central labor bodies. On June 17 the Committee on Laws recommended non-concurrence, and the convention endorsed the committee's recommendation.

2. Max Sebastian HAYES served as the editor of the *Cleveland Citizen* from 1894 to 1939.

3. Daniel Joseph TOBIN, of the International Brotherhood of TEAMSTERS, Chauffeurs, Stablemen, and Helpers of America, served as president of the union from 1907 to 1952 and as treasurer of the AFL from 1918 to 1928.

4. A reference to Resolution 50, introduced on June 13, 1922, by James Legassie of the Berlin, N.H., Central Labor Union. The resolution criticized unions for allowing members to continue working for employers against whom other unions were striking and advocated revising the AFL constitution to delete the recognition of strict trade autonomy. On June 17 the Committee on Representation in Central Bodies advised non-concurrence, and the convention endorsed the committee's recommendation.

5. Resolution 112, introduced on June 13, 1922, by Luther Steward of the National Federation of Federal Employees, called for the AFL to issue charters directly to groups of women denied membership in national or international unions. The Committee on Laws amended the resolution to restate the declaration of the 1921 AFL convention encouraging affiliates to admit women and to require the Executive Council to negotiate the matter with the unions involved before issuing such federal charters. The amended resolution was adopted unanimously on June 17.

Cincinnati, June 20.—[1922]

. . .

AIMED AT KU KLUX KLAN.

While not specifically mentioning the Ku Klux Klan, the convention adopted a declaration aimed at that organization, which said "It is not conducive to government by law and the maintenance of peaceful and safe conditions in the community to have members of any organization parade the streets so disguised that their identity cannot be discovered, when such disguises are adopted for the purpose of inspiring the thought or belief that the disguised individuals represent an invisible government."[1]

In refusing to report favorable a resolution condemning the Ku Klux Klan introduced by the Central Labor Union of Berlin, N.H.,[2] the resolution committee said the federation "should not assume to endorse or condemn any organization, fraternity or association of American citizens, unless the purpose of such organization is to organize for the purpose of interfering with the rights, opportunities and liberties of wage earners."

. . .

Other resolutions adopted called upon Governor Stephens of California for an "unconditional pardon" for Tom Mooney and Warren Billings, labor leaders, now serving life sentences in connection with the San Francisco Flag Day bomb explosion plot;[3]

Demanded a new trial for Nicola Sacco and Barthelomeo Vanzetti, communists, sentenced to death at Dedham, Mass., for murder.[4]

. . .

SEEK FREEDOM OF POLITICAL PRISONERS.

Urged the Executive Council to keep up its efforts to obtain the freedom of all the so-called political prisoners in this country.[5]

. . .

INSIST ON BACKING LEWIS.

Anti-administration elements in the convention decline to accept as final the announcement by John L. Lewis, President of the United Mine Workers, that he would not be a candidate for the presidency of the federation in opposition to the re-election of Samuel Gompers.

The Lewis boom, which started late last night, was going full blast today, although the miners' chief held aloof from any active participation in the campaigning, declaring he was "absolutely not a candidate."

. . .

New York Times, June 21, 1922.

1. Resolution 71, introduced on June 13, 1922, by James Legassie of the Berlin, N.H., Central Labor Union, called for the AFL to condemn the Ku Klux Klan. On June 20 the Committee on Resolutions recommended amending the resolution to avoid explicit mention of the Klan but stating that any secret organization whose members paraded disguised in the streets and sought to give the impression they constituted a secret government usurped the power of legitimate authority, encouraged mob action, and threatened the rule of law. The amended resolution was adopted unanimously.

2. The AFL chartered the Berlin Central Labor Union in 1903.

3. Two resolutions on this issue were presented to the convention on June 13, 1922—

Resolution 20, introduced by John Clay of the Chicago Federation of Labor, which called for "a complete and unconditional pardon" for Thomas Mooney and Warren Billings, and Resolution 51, introduced by the delegates of the International Molders' Union of North America, which called on the governor of California to "immediately issue a pardon" to the men (AFL, *Proceedings*, 1922, pp. 186, 198). On June 20 the Committee on Resolutions recommended adoption of Resolution 51, and the convention unanimously endorsed its recommendation.

4. Two resolutions introduced on June 13, 1922, called for a new trial in the Sacco-Vanzetti case—Resolution 53, presented by William Doherty and Henry Abrahams of the Boston Central Labor Union and John Frey of the Molders, and Resolution 54, presented by Luigi Antonini of the International Ladies' Garment Workers' Union. The Committee on Resolutions recommended adoption of Resolution 53, which provided more detail on the injustice of the case, and it was adopted unanimously on June 20.

5. Two resolutions calling for the release of political prisoners were introduced on June 13, 1922—Resolution 76, introduced by the delegates of the Ladies' Garment Workers, and Resolution 98, introduced by delegates of the International Association of Machinists. Neither resolution was adopted. Instead, on June 20, the convention endorsed the AFL Executive Council's report on the matter that recounted the Council's efforts on behalf of political prisoners since the 1920 AFL convention and reported that of the 1,484 prisoners convicted under the espionage law, only 45 remained behind bars.

Cincinatti, Ohio, June 21.—[1922]

LABOR URGES VETO ON SUPREME COURT

Four amendments to the Constitution of the United States and repeal of the Sherman Anti-Trust law were recommended to the convention of the American Federation of Labor today as a means of depriving the Federal Courts of "the despotic powers which they have assumed, and to make our Government in a full measure a government of the people, for the people, and by the people."

The proposal submitted by the Special Committee on Court Decisions urged that labor enlist the aid of all "fair-minded and liberty-loving" citizens in a campaign for the adoption of Constitutional amendments providing for prohibition of child labor, specific exemption from legislative or judicial limitation of the right of labor to organize, to deal collectively, or to boycott, establishment of a Congressional veto over decisions of the United States Supreme Court and "easier amendment of the United States Constitution," the method not being specified.

The program of the committee which is expected to be finally approved by the convention tomorrow, recommended that Congress be urged to enact legislation making more definite certain sections of the Clayton law which, the committee said, was "manifestly ignored or over-ridden by the Court." Recommendation was also made that the Federation Executive Council be authorized to establish a legal defense bureau.[1]

In urging repeal of the Anti-Trust law the committee, which was composed of America's foremost labor leaders, declared that, through "judicial misinterpretation and perversion," this law had been "repeatedly and mainly invoked to deprive the toiling masses of their natural and normal rights."

. . .

Tells of "Judicial Oligarchy."

"A judicial oligarchy is threatening to set itself up above the elected legislators and above the people themselves," said the committee's report. "Profiting by the unsettled industrial conditions of the country and the political apathy of the people which have followed upon the conclusion of the World War, the forces of privilege and reaction have embarked upon a concerted and determined campaign to deprive the citizens of their Constitutional liberties, to break down the standards of life which the American workers have laboriously built up in generations of suffering and struggle, and to emasculate or destroy their most effective weapon of resistance and defense—the labor unions.

"Side by side with the implacable anti-union drive conducted by powerful organizations of employers throughout the country, who exercise their own unquestioned right to organize and yet brazenly deny their employes the same right, the unblushing subservience of many public officials to the dictates of big business and their undisguised contempt for the interests of the workers, the courts of the country, and particularly the Supreme Court of the United States, have within recent years undertaken to deprive American labor of the fundamental rights and liberties which heretofore have been accepted as deeply and organically ingrained in our system of jurisprudence.

"What confronts the workers of America is not one of several casual court decisions favoring the interests of property as against the human rights of labor, but a series of adjudications of the highest tribunal of the land, successively destroying a basic right or cherished acquisition of organized labor, each forming a link in a fateful chain consciously designed to enslave the workers of America."

Complains of Usurped Authority.

The committee cited several decisions against labor rendered in the last five years,[2] and said:

"This despotic exercise of a usurped power by nine men, or a bare majority of them, over the lives and liberties of millions of men, women and children is intolerable. With the immortal Lincoln we believe that 'the people of these United States are the masters of both Congress and courts, not to overthrow the Constitution, but to overthrow the men who pervert the Constitution.'

"We are determined to preserve our rights as workers, citizens and freemen, and we call upon all fair-minded and liberty-loving citizens to unite with us in a determined effort to deprive the courts of the despotic powers which they have assumed, and to make our Government in full measure a government of the people, for the people and by the people."

To this end the committee presented its recommendation for amendments to the Constitution of the United States, and added:

"Your committee further recommends that in conjunction with the campaign for the adoption of the suggested constitutional amendments, Congress be urged to enact:

"A child labor law which will overcome the objections raised by the United States Supreme Court to the laws heretofore passed by Congress and nullified by the Court.

"A law which will make more definite and effective the intention of Congress in enacting Sections 6, 19 and 20 of the Clayton act, which was manifestly ignored or overridden by the court.

"A law repealing the Sherman anti-trust law, which was intended by Congress to prevent illegal combinations in restraint of trade, commonly known as 'trusts,' but through judicial misinterpretation and perversion has been repeatedly and mainly invoked to deprive the toiling masses of their natural and normal rights."

. . .

New York Times, June 22, 1922.

1. On June 22, 1922, the convention endorsed the establishment of a legal defense bureau to collate "all laws and judicial decisions on the rights of labor" and "enlist the voluntary assistance and co-operation of lawyers friendly to the cause of labor, and experienced in industrial litigation" (AFL, *Proceedings,* 1922, p. 398). Acting on this authorization, the Executive Council subsequently created the AFL Legal Information Bureau under the direction of Matthew Woll, which collected information about cases pertinent to labor and disseminated it to affiliated organizations. Industrial relations lawyers also volunteered advice under its aegis, although they did not provide legal counsel.

2. The six cases mentioned in the report of the committee were *American Steel Foundries* v. *Tri-City Central Trades Council et al.,* 257 U.S. 184 (1921; see *The Samuel Gompers Papers,* vol. 10, p. 253, n. 3); *Hitchman Coal and Coke Co.* v. *Mitchell et al.,* 245 U.S. 229 (1917; see *The Samuel Gompers Papers,* vol. 10, p. 287, n. 1); *United Mine Workers of America et al.* v. *Coronado Coal Co. et al.,* 259 U.S. 344 (1922; see *The Samuel Gompers Papers,* vol. 10, p. 323, n. 3); *Duplex Printing Press Co.* v. *Deering et al.,* 254 U.S. 443 (1921; see *The Samuel Gompers Papers,* vol. 11, p. 408, n. 2); *Bailey* v. *Drexel Furniture Co.,* 259 U.S. 20 (1922; see *The Samuel Gompers Papers,* vol. 11, p. 514, n. 2); and *Truax et al.* v. *Corrigan et al.,* 257 U.S. 312 (1921).

The *Truax* case involved a dispute that arose in 1916 between the owners of a Bisbee, Ariz., restaurant and a number of their employees who were members of Hotel and Restaurant Employees' International Alliance and Bartenders' International League of America 380 (Cooks and Waiters). When the dispute resulted in a strike and a boycott, William Truax, representing the restaurant, brought suit in the Superior Court for Cochise County asking for an injunction against the union (*Truax et al.* v. *Bisbee Local No. 380, Cooks' and Waiters' Union et al.*, 19 Ariz. 379 [1918]). The union filed a demurrer on the grounds that the strike and boycott were protected by an Arizona law allowing peaceful picketing and prohibiting courts from issuing such injunctions (Arizona, Rev. Laws of 1913, par. 1464). The Superior Court sustained the union and dismissed the complaint, a judgment affirmed by the Supreme Court of Arizona (*Truax et al.* v. *Corrigan et al.*, 20 Ariz. 7 [1918]). The case reached the U.S. Supreme Court on appeal in April 1920, and on Dec. 19, 1921, it reversed the lower court and remanded the case, ruling the Arizona law abridged the due process and equal protection clauses of the Fourteenth Amendment.

[June 23, 1922]

LET VETO CURB SUPREME COURT, UNIONS DEMAND

After consuming most of the morning session in debate, the American Federation of Labor yesterday adopted the report of the special committee appointed to formulate the federation's policy regarding recent decisions of the United States Supreme Court considered inimical to the trades union movement.

. . .

Max Hayes of Cleveland, representing the International Typographical Union, cast the only dissenting vote against acceptance of the special committee's report. He asserted the proposals in the report were cowardly and totally inadequate to cope with the crisis faced by organized labor throughout the country.

. . .

Mr. Hayes, attacking the report, declared that it was typical of the reactionary group which so long had controlled the federation.

"Even if we were assured that the amendments would be adopted, it would take years to get them written into the law of the land," Mr. Hayes said, "and in the meantime what is to become of us?

"I tell you that the trades union movement faces a struggle for its very existence. It is a poor time to procrastinate and await developments. Nothing will develop so long as the American Federation of Labor maintains an attitude of apathy.

"What I propose is a labor political party that will seat men in Congress whose interests are primarily with the laboring classes. The present Congress never will pass any legislation of benefit to the workers for the simple reason that the ranks of the present Congress are filled with men who are not toilers.

"I have been trying to get the federation to institute such a party all during the twenty-three years I have been a delegate to its conventions. The only result I have obtained is the title 'radical' and the reputation of being the leader of a revolutionary element."

Matthew Woll, Secretary of the special committee, then took the floor in answer to Mr. Hayes's criticisms.

"The special committee has been criticized for ultra-conservatism," Mr. Woll said, "and I think it opportune that I say a few words in its defense.

"In the first place, the committee has been confronted with the most serious problem that ever has confronted organized labor. It decided under the circumstances that it would be best to proceed in a cautious manner.

"That is why the report contains no definite plan of action regarding the method to be used in obtaining adoption of the four proposed amendments other than to recommend that labor co-operate with all bodies of citizens who see in the recent decisions of the courts a blow at human liberties.

"However, I would not have you think that the committee did not consider any plans of action. Quite the contrary. The committee considered many, some of which were presented by its members and some by others.

"One of the courses suggested was to seek to evade the action of the courts and another was to defy the judicial, the legislative and the administrative powers of the country to go as far as they like, warning them that too much infringement on the rights of the workers would scatter the seeds of revolution and raise aloft the red flag of rebellion.

"In the final analysis, however, your committee decided upon the course which it has outlined in its report. Such a course will take years to develop, it is true, but we believe that such a course, based on law, is the only course for the federation to pursue."

At the conclusion of Mr. Woll's address Samuel Gompers, President of the federation, asked if the convention were ready to vote on the report. Several delegates expressed their desire to speak, but Mr. Gompers said he thought the matter had been sufficiently discussed.

He asked for a standing vote on the question of ending the debate. One hundred and sixty-seven delegates voted that the discussion end and sixty-two delegates that the discussion continue.

When the report itself was submitted Mr. Hayes was the only one voting against it.

. . .

Commercial Tribune (Cincinnati), June 23, 1922.

Cincinnati, Ohio, June 23.—[1922]

GOMPERS, ELECTED, FIGHTS SOVIET MOVE

Samuel Gompers was re-elected without opposition today as President of the American Federation of Labor,[1] making his forty-first election, and immediately faced one of the hardest fights of his career to prevent a declaration for recognition of the Russian Soviet Government.[2]

The radical element demanded that organized labor reverse its position and when the convention was suddenly adjourned late today through a coup of the administration supporters, the veteran labor chief, who has consistently denounced the Soviet régime for the past four years, was faced with the possibility of defeat, as the United Mine Workers, a number of the railroad organizations, and the Machinists' Union, announced that they were a unit back of the move for recognition of the Soviet Government by the United States.

Administration forces were active tonight in rounding up their supporters, who were apparently being outnumbered by the radicals and progressives, led by William Z. Foster, former steel strike leader. Foster and William Dunn,[3] former I.W.W. leader and now connected with the Workers' Party of America, have been here for several days aiding the campaign to reverse the position of American labor on Bolshevism.

. . .

MINORITY REPORT STARTS FIGHT.

The fight on the Russian question was precipitated by a minority report of the International Relations Committee brought in by Max S. Hayes of Cleveland, delegate of the Typographical Union, and Timothy Healy[4] of New York, President of the Stationary Firemen and Oilers Union, which demanded "that the Government of the United States recognize the existing Russian Government and take immediate steps to restore facilities for communication and commerce."

The majority report, to which was attached the name of President Gompers, contained what was declared by labor leaders to be "American labor's strongest indictment of the Soviet autocracy in Russia."

. . .

PREFERS SOVIET TO WALL STREET.

Arthur Keep of the Tailors' Union[5] denounced the majority report as an "insult to the intelligence of the convention" for condemning the Soviets, which were infinitely to be preferred, he said, to the Soviet of Wall Street. He compared Lenin and Trotzky to the American revolutionary leaders, declaring that all great countries had been "born in revolution."

Declaring that the Soviets had the "right to the good-will and backing of the American Federation of Labor," Mr. Healy ridiculed the argument that the Russian leaders were out to destroy the American labor movement.

He called it "bugaboo" to injure the Russian cause. He held up a leaflet advertising a Foster meeting to be held here, and added: "I don't believe Bill Foster is out to destroy the American Federation of Labor. If he is, I wish him luck."

. . .

"As for the Soviet Government," said Mr. Gompers, "we might as well recognize a Government of savages. I doubt if there is any one who has manifested more sympathy for the Russian people than the one who addresses you. Never in the history of the world has a Government used such domination of governmental power and brutal dictatorship. Brutal, domineering, it has not received the consent of the Russian people—they have no voice."

Gompers closed his appeal by urging that if the delegates had sufficient confidence to elect him President they should also have confidence in what he was saying and stand by his declarations.

. . .

When President Gompers ended his address nearly a dozen delegates were clamoring for the floor, but they were rapped down by James Duncan,[6] Vice President, who was in the chair. The administration delegates began calling for a halt in the debate and by a vote of 124 to 82 carried their point.

. . .

New York Times, June 24, 1922.

1. Together with SG, the officers elected by the convention to serve during the following year were James Duncan, Joseph Valentine, Frank Duffy, William Green, W. D. Mahon, Thomas Rickert, Jacob Fischer, and Matthew Woll, first through eighth vice-presidents; Frank Morrison, secretary; and Daniel Tobin, treasurer.

2. Three resolutions dealing with the Soviet Union were introduced on June 13, 1922. Resolution 25, introduced by Herman Defrem of AFL Bookkeepers', Stenographers', and Accountants' Union 12,646 of New York City, and Resolution 28, introduced by delegates of the Brotherhood of Railway and Steamship Clerks, Freight Handlers, Express and Station Employes, called for the United States to recognize the Soviet government and negotiate a trade agreement with the Soviets. Resolution 84, introduced by Charles Baine, Jere Sullivan, Thomas McMahon, Sara Conboy, and John Voll, opposed recognition because of the brutal tyranny of the Soviet regime and its stated goal of destroying the American labor movement. The three resolutions were debated on June 23–24 after the Committee on Foreign Relations, in a lengthy report, recommended adoption of Resolution 84 (see AFL, *Proceedings,* 1922, pp. 420–37, 457–65). The convention ultimately adopted Resolution 84.

3. William (variously Willis) Francis Dunne (1887–1953) was editor of the *Worker.* Born in Missouri, he grew up in Minnesota, by 1907 had gone to Montana, and by 1912 was in Vancouver, where he was business agent for International Brotherhood of Electrical Workers 213 (1913–14) and district organizer for that international union (1915). Returning to Butte, Mont., he was a leader of the 1917 strike against the Anaconda Mining Co., was elected to the legislature in 1918 on the Non-Partisan League ticket, and served as editor of the *Butte Bulletin* (1918–21, 1922–24?). Dunne was convicted in

1919 in a Montana state court for violating the state's sedition act with an editorial in the *Bulletin,* but his conviction was overturned in 1920 by the Montana Supreme Court (*State* v. *Dunn* [*sic*], 57 Mont. 591 [1920]). From 1922 to 1934 he served on the central executive committees of the Workers' Party of America, Workers' (Communist) Party of America, and Communist Party of the United States of America (Communist Party USA). In August 1922 Dunne was arrested in the Bridgman raid (see "From George Perkins," Aug. 26, 1922, n. 3, below), and in 1923, because of his party connections, he was unseated as the delegate to the AFL convention from the Silver Bow (Mont.) Trades and Labor Council. (See "Dunne Defies A.F. of L. to Expel Him," Oct. 8, 1923, in "Excerpts from Accounts of the 1923 Convention of the AFL in Portland, Ore.," Oct. 8–12, 1923, below.) From 1924 to 1927 he served as coeditor of the *Daily Worker.* In 1934 Dunne was dropped from his party leadership position and in 1946 was expelled from the Communist party.

4. Timothy HEALY, of the International Brotherhood of FIREMEN and Oilers, served as president of the union from 1903 to 1927.

5. The Journeymen TAILORS' Union of America.

6. James DUNCAN served as president of the Granite Cutters' International Association of America (1912–23) and as an AFL vice-president (1895–1928).

Cincinnati, Ohio, June 24.—[1922]

LABOR ROUTS REDS FOR FOURTH TIME

The American Federation of Labor adjourned its forty-second annual convention here today after administering what was declared by its President, Samuel Gompers, a "complete and crushing defeat to the apologists and propagandists for the Bolshevist autocracy."

The radical and "progressive" elements in the convention were routed in their fight for recognition of the Russian Soviet. The delegates by a large majority backed President Gompers in his denunciation of the Lenin-Trotzky régime, and for the fourth time declared against recognition of the Soviets.

Gompers won his victory in a tumultuous session, marked by fiery oratory and a scattering attack upon the communist movement in this country and its attempt to destroy the American labor movement. When the division was finally called to determine whether the dispute should go to a roll-call, it was found that the railway and miners' unions had left the field and only the Gompers adherents and a handful of radicals were in the auditorium.

. . .

New York Times, June 25, 1922.

From J. A. H. Hopkins

New York NY Jun 23 1922

Saml. Gompers
Cincinnati Ohio
The ferocious and inhuman atrocities perpetrated in Illinois[1] demand your unqualified condemnation whatever the provocation and whoever was responsible Labor will suffer irreparable injury unless you immediately take official action and guarantee to punish the offenders I speak as one whose sympathy and friendship for labor is unquestionable.

J. A. H. Hopkins
Executive Chairman of the Committee of 48[2]

TWcSr, United Mine Workers of America Records, reel 3, frame 1011, *AFL and the Unions.* Typed notation: "*Copy.*" Handwritten notations: "For Mr Lewis"[3] and "No answer has been made by Mr Gompers."[4]

1. Despite the coal strike that began Apr. 1, 1922, the United Mine Workers of America allowed the Southern Illinois Coal Co. to continue operations short of actually mining coal at its strip mine near Herrin, Ill. In June, however, breaking an agreement with the union that it would go no further than clearing underbrush and stripping surface dirt, the company imported members of an independent steam shovel workers' union from Chicago to work the mine, hired armed guards to protect them, and began mining coal. Col. Samuel Nase Hunter of the state militia attempted to persuade the company to desist, but to no avail, and United Mine Workers' president John L. Lewis further exacerbated tensions when he called the steam shovel operators "common strikebreakers" and their union "an outlaw organization" ("Text of Telegram from Miners' President Which Preceded Bloodshed at Illinois Mine," *New York Times,* June 23, 1922). On June 21, after mine guards shot and killed two men who had gone to the mine to protest, a crowd of strikers and sympathizers numbering more than a thousand attacked the mine and, after an all-night gun battle, forced forty-seven strikebreakers and mine guards to surrender. As the captives marched back to Herrin, they were attacked by strikers and their sympathizers, and twenty prisoners were killed, including mine superintendent Claude Kline McDowell. A grand jury issued over four hundred indictments, charging seventy-seven persons with counts of murder, conspiracy, assault, and rioting. Only eleven men were actually brought to trial, and they were all acquitted. The other indictments were eventually dropped.

2. The Committee of Forty-eight, a group founded and chaired by John Appleton Haven Hopkins (see *The Samuel Gompers Papers,* vol. 10, p. 161, n. 5), sought to create a Liberal party in the United States and called for public ownership of transportation systems, public control of natural resources, and rigorous protection of the rights of free speech and peaceful assembly.

3. SG passed this telegram on to John L. Lewis at the AFL convention in Cincinnati. For Lewis's acknowledgment, see Lewis to SG, June 26, 1922, United Mine Workers of America Records, reel 3, frame 1011, *AFL and the Unions.*

4. The *Washington Post* quoted this comment by SG about the Herrin incident: "I regret, yes, resent, the resort to violence in the Herrin strike. The strike of the miners

is on such a high plane of principle that it must depend on solidarity of action, but it need not and it ought not, to fall upon physical force" ("The Herrin Atrocity," *Washington Post*, June 24, 1922).

To Charles Evans Hughes

July 1, 1922.

Honorable Charles E. Hughes,
Secretary Department of State,
Washington, D.C.
Sir:

Acting under instructions of the Cincinnati convention of the American Federation of Labor, June 12–24, 1922, I am transmitting to you herewith copies of Resolutions Nos. 31 & 103, adopted by the convention, in which the United States government is urged to grant its official recognition to the Mexican Government of which Honorable Alvaro Obregon is President.[1]

In view of the recent incidents in Mexico as reported by the daily press—the kidnapping of a number of American citizens,[2]—as they took place after the Cincinnati convention had acted on the enclosed resolutions, I consider it appropriate and timely to say that these incidents in no wise change the position of the American Federation of Labor on the question of recognition of the Mexican Government. Quite the contrary, our position is strengthened, for it is easy to see the hand in these incidents of the political enemies of the Obregon Government. As long as recognition is denied to the Mexican Government, its political enemies who happily are very few in number and of no nation wide importance, will feel encouraged and emboldened in their reprehensible attempts to create trouble and embarrassment for the Obregon Government.

Therefore it is hoped that in the interests of peaceful and harmonious relations between the United States and Mexico the official recognition of our government will be extended to the present government of the Republic of Mexico, without any further unnecessary delay.[3]

I am, Sir,

Respectfully yours,   Saml Gompers
President,   American Federation of Labor.

TLpS, reel 281, vol. 294, p. 188, SG Letterbooks, DLC.

1. Resolutions 31 and 103 called for the United States to recognize the government of Alvaro Obregón.

2. A. Bruce Bielaski, former chief of the Bureau of Investigation of the Department of Justice and now president of Richmond Levering and Co., a firm with Mexican oil holdings, was kidnapped on June 25, 1922, near Cuernavaca, Mexico. He escaped four days later. Between June 27 and July 1, outlaw groups led by Eusebio Gorozave and Manuel Larraga seized several American-owned oil fields and held them for ransom along with their employees, a number of whom were Americans. All were quickly freed, although the wife of one American worker was killed.

3. Undersecretary of State William Phillips acknowledged SG's letter on July 13, 1922. The United States recognized the Obregón government on Aug. 31, 1923.

To Bert Miller

July 6, 1922.

Mr. Bert Miller,
720 North Geary St., Oklahoma City, Oklahoma.
Dear Sir and Brother:

Your letter of July 2 received and read with regret.

Your suggestion as to the "One Big Union" was made undoubtedly without a thorough study of the subject. Permit me to call your attention to the action of the American Federation of Labor Convention held in Cincinnati June 14–24, 1922 on the question you propose as follows:[1]

"The A.F. of L. believes it advisable to direct attention to certain facts relative to the trade union movement. In one respect it differs from all other movements of men organized for the purpose of righting their wrongs, securing their rights, protecting their welfare and advancing their interests.

"The trade union movement was not founded as a result of any definite, preconceived industrial, economic, social or political theory. It was born of sheer necessity and developed through the lessons it was compelled to learn in the stern school of practical affairs. Its policies and methods were forged white hot upon the unyielding anvil of experience. Its development has been directed by applying the principles and the methods of democracy.

"The American Federation of Labor from the beginning has held that each group of organized wage-earners should be left free and unhampered to develop and apply that form of organization which was most advantageous to them in working out their own problems. From the beginning it has favored amalgamation between organizations when the majority of these organizations believed such amalgamation to be advantageous. The A.F. of L. has on many occasions given its kindly assistance in bringing about such amalgamations. Firmly in accord with the principles and methods of democracy, the A.F. of L. has opposed the spirit or methods of dictatorship, within or without the trade union movement.

"We believe that only through voluntary association, through voluntary cooperation and federation, can the American workingmen successfully and effectively work out their industrial problems.

"Twenty-one years ago the policy of the American Federation of Labor towards its affiliated organizations, their jurisdiction, their right to self-government, their freedom to develop and apply such form of organization as seemed most advantageous to them was adopted."

The Scranton convention in 1901[2] adopted the following:[3]

"We hold that the interests of the trade union movement will be promoted by closely allied and subdivided crafts giving consideration to amalgamation, and to the organization of district and national trade councils to which should be referred questions in dispute, and which should be adjusted within allied crafts' lines."

The Labor movement has grown like a language. As words are created because of their need so will changes be made in the Labor movement. But any assault on the principles on which trade unions are founded will be to the detriment instead of to their benefit.

With best wishes and assuring you of my desire to be helpful in any way within my power, I am,

Fraternally yours,   Saml Gompers
President,   American Federation of Labor.

TLpS, reel 281, vol. 294, pp. 279–80, SG Letterbooks, DLC.

1. SG is quoting from a report to the convention by the Committee on Resolutions, which was unanimously approved on June 20, 1922 (AFL, *Proceedings*, 1922, pp. 337–38).

2. The 1901 AFL convention met in Scranton, Pa., Dec. 5–14.

3. For the full text of the resolution, see *The Samuel Gompers Papers*, vol. 5, pp. 443–44.

Excerpts from the Minutes of a Meeting on the Railroad Situation[1]

Thursday, July 13, 1922.

. . .

Mr. Gompers: I have asked that a conference might be held this morning of some of the active labor men located in Washington just to review the situation as labor is affected by it and to at least exchange our views upon the situation and try to decide what can best be done to help those engaged in the struggle. . . .

Now the miners' conflict—we may have possibly less to say about it. . . . I refer to the fact that the miners are conducting their own movement and while they are asking for financial assistance I doubt that they are asking any other kind of assistance but in the railway shop organizations we are, have been and are now and will be expected to give co-operation in their fight. It has taken on another phase, and that is that every word that could be construed in the Esch-Cummins Act, commonly known as the Transportation Act is being strained and stretched and power assumed by the United States Railway Labor Board, their functions, their duties, their responsibilities, their powers are all being warped to exercise the power that even the fathers and framers of the act never intended and so declared.[2] Since then it has received, the action of the Railway Labor Board has received, the support of the President of the United States. That has his open support by the issuance of a proclamation which appeared in the newspapers yesterday morning under date of July 11. . . .[3]

I feel that we are in the midst of a crisis in the labor movement of the United States. It has been in the making since the war and it has been taken up by the financial, industrial and commercial interests of the country and it is now supported to the fullest by the political powers governing the United States and it has for its purpose not only the reduction of wages but the destruction of the effective labor organizations of the United States—the trade union movement.

On several occasions when anything arose that I deemed worthy of your consideration and mine, I have taken upon myself the liberty of inviting you to a conference and I have done so this morning so we may take up the matter, and I trust that, while we are all busy men, and I do not think that there is any one more so than I am, but the subject is such an important one, and its potentialities so far reaching, that I think that any time that we can spare will not be wasted. Now, I would like very much to hear a general discussion of the entire situation. . . .

Conlon,[4] Machinists. The thing is an open shop proposition, pure and simple. . . . There is a vicious circle that is dominating the railroad policy of the country. Attabury,[5] Loree[6] and two or three more on the Penn. Railroad. The railroad executives throughout the country would be glad to have this thing ironed out and settled up but this circle controlled by the House of Morgan holds them and they cannot move except as a unit. . . . They seem to sense our weak point and that is the difficulty of financing it. Our main hope lies in a short, quick struggle and in having a sufficient number of grievances to enlist the attention of every railroad man throughout the country, or else suffer in silence. This was our first venture of this kind and as a consequence we are fearful of it because we have not had the experience of a nation wide strike in the railroad industry up to this time. The railroad executives also sense the fact that if they can hold public opinion in their favor for two or three months by their propaganda that they may wear us out and have the newspapers poison public opinion. We will have to do something to offset that. . . .

. . .

. . . If we lose we are [real]ly killed on the railroads from this time on, and that means of course, that six organizations are pretty badly crippled because one-half of the entire machinists' unions are working on the railroads, about 125,000 men pay tax dues to the railway department, and the boilermakers, blacksmiths run about the same ratio. The electricians, there are not so many of them. The chances are if we can not get our central bodies aroused to build up in their localities a healthier public opinion than exists at the present time, due to the fact that they are unable to reach the public through the newspapers and the labor papers, they are possibly going to put the screws on us that are going to be our undoing. . . .[7]

. . .

[Mr. Noonan:][8] . . . The request now of the Department is for something that will be of material assistance. The reason for the request is apparent. Consider the situation as it exists today as affecting the shopcraftsmen affiliated with the American Federation of Labor. They are on strike all over the United States. Other organizations affiliated with the A.F. of L. who were affected adversely in about equal ratio and some of them in greater ratio than the shopmen employed by the railroads are not on strike today, and are unlikely to be on strike in the near future. That condition gives the railroad managers everywhere with their publicity bureau the right to point out to organized labor and its friends throughout the country that this is not a movement which the labor movement of the country, the American Federation of Labor is behind. If they were behind it these other organizations affiliated with the A.F. of L. would be out and that propaganda is being used and it is going to hurt. They point out to them that the shopcrafts are only a small portion of the men and they minimize the extent of the strike, and say, "We are not being crippled very much, the clerks are out in just a few places, a few Maintenance of Way men quit, the signalmen are on the job and they are all part of the American Federation of Labor. Does not that prove to you that the A.F. of L. is not in sympathy and is not behind this movement?["] This is not an argument as to whether it is right or wrong, but it has its effect and a very great effect. . . . We feel that something should be said to the labor movement of the country at this time and the friends of the labor movement throughout the country saying that the American Federation of Labor is in sympathy with the move taken by the men, that it recognizes that their cause is just and that the men have cause for the step they took and we believe that should come from the American Federation of Labor. . . . Now, that is the crux of the request, that is the kernel in the nut just at this time. What we want is something to go out quick to offset the propaganda that is being spread around. . . .

. . .

. . . We do not care what words you put into it but what we want is the meat of the thing,—that we recognize the injustice that has been done by this board, this board, a board set up to be a board of mediation and to make decisions that are not binding but which they hope to put into force have now twisted the situation into a strike against the Government instead of a strike against the railroads. It is a strike against the railroads pure and simple. . . . The big fact is that the strike is a legal one and considered a just one by the American Federation of Labor and that the A.F. of L. does approve of the strike. That is the big thing we want. . . . We should meet the propaganda of the employers by a pronouncement of some authoritative source within the A.F. of L. as to the wrongs that have been forced on these men by the Railroad Labor Board and the recognition of the strike and the justice of the causes of the strike. . . . [9]

. . .

Mr. Gompers: I think that you have thrown a great deal of light on the situation, in fact, the suggestion which you make appeals strongly to me. . . . I have gone to the front and taken every opportunity of standing by the men and the organizations on strike. When the Labor Board issued its pronouncement of declaring striking organizations outlawed I think I made the case as strong as I was capable of making it.[10] I may say too, that there was an editorial[11] appearing in the New York Times . . . in which they stigmatized two others, Jewell and Lewis and myself particularly as falsifiers for stating that these unions were outlawed by the Board, and I wrote a letter[12] . . . answering that situation and saying that if there was any liar it was the New York Times. . . . Probably that will appear tomorrow.[13] But in the meantime I took cognizance of the President's proclamation. I have not read this morning's papers, but the New York Times has what purports to be my statement upon that, but that is not in full.[14]

. . .

I may say this: I am perfectly willing not only willing but anxious to be helpful in doing everything that I can do and I shall of course communicate[15] with the Executive Council at once immediately after the adjournment of our conference so that I may get some authority of the Executive Council to give forth some pronouncement[16] in the name of the Executive Council or by the Council. . . .

. . .

TDc, AFL Microfilm Convention File, reel 31, frames 2705, 2707–9, *AFL Records.* Typed notation: "R.R. Situation."

1. Participants at the meeting included SG, Frank Morrison, and Matthew Woll, representatives from the AFL Metal Trades, Mining, and Publicity departments, from the AFL Legislative Committee and the *AFL Weekly News Service,* and from nine AFL affiliates.

2. On July 3, 1922, the U.S. Railroad Labor Board ruled that since most members of the railway shop craft unions had gone on strike, that is, left the employment of the railways, these organizations could no longer represent the interests of workers who remained on the job or were hired to replace the strikers. It called on non-striking workers to form new organizations in place of the old unions. SG issued a statement that evening condemning the board's action as "utterly Bolshevist in character and . . . too ridiculous and fatuous to be accepted as permanent American Government policy. By this astounding ruling the board undertakes to disband unions at will and to command at will that new organizations be formed. This no Government agency can do, because trade unions are voluntary organizations of the workers, formed in response to their demand, to serve their needs and to respond to their democratically expressed will and desire. The action of the board is exactly a replica of the action of the Communists in turning the unions into Government-controlled agencies for the carrying out of the orders of the State" ("Ban Put on Shopmen; Gompers Decries It," *New York Times,* July 4, 1922).

3. On July 11, 1922, President Warren Harding issued a proclamation recognizing the U.S. Railroad Labor Board as a legally constituted government agency empowered with the authority to adjust disputes between railroad operators and employees, supporting the right of workers who accepted the terms of the board's decisions to take the place of strikers who did not, and calling on "all persons to refrain from all interference with the lawful efforts to maintain interstate transportation and the carrying of the United States mails" ("President's Proclamation Forbids Interference with Transportation," *New York Times,* July 12, 1922).

4. Peter J. Conlon (1869–1931) served as a vice-president of the International Association of Machinists from 1901 to 1916 and again from 1921 to 1931 and was an organizer for the union from 1916 to 1921. He was a member of Machinists' local 174 of Alexandria, Va.

5. William Wallace Atterbury (1866–1935) served as a vice-president of the Pennsylvania Railroad from 1909 to 1925, with a leave of absence from 1917 to 1919 to serve as director-general of transportation for the American Expeditionary Forces in France. Returning to the Pennsylvania Railroad after the war, he served as the company's president from 1925 to 1935.

6. Leonor Fresnel Loree (1858–1940) was president of the Delaware and Hudson Railroad (1907–38) and chairman of both the executive committee (1906–36) and the board of directors (1909–36) of the Kansas City Southern Railway.

7. On July 1, 1922, the day the strike began, SG wired B. M. Jewell: "On this most momentous day in the struggles of the railroad workers the impression prevails here

that the public has no adequate knowledge of the grievances suffered by the workers *Stop* Only those who have kept careful account of developments are fully informed and able to form intelligent opinion *Stop* Can you not arrange to present to the newspapers a concise statement of facts setting forth issues involved and to repeat this on every possible occasion *Stop* Rest assured I shall be glad to do all in my power to assist and shall appreciate any suggestion from you or the officers of affiliated organizations" (AFL Microfilm Convention File, reel 31, frame 2705, *AFL Records*). On July 5 Jewell replied that he hoped to have the statement ready in a day or two (ibid., frame 2706).

8. James Patrick NOONAN was president of the International Brotherhood of Electrical Workers.

9. After he spoke, Noonan submitted a memo listing the shopmen's complaints: "Railroad Labor Board took away Conditions from the Men that they Secured by Negotiations with management Direct And have Been in Existence for 20 Years. Overtime pay for Sunday work. Adequate pay for men Called for Extra Work outside of Regular hours. Seniority Rights Enjoyed by the Workers for Years passed. Reduction of Pay in 1921 Below that neccessary to maintain a proper American standard of Living. Additional Reduction of Pay while the trend of the Cost of Living is upward" (AFL Microfilm Convention File, reel 31, frame 2708, *AFL Records*).

10. A reference to SG's statement of July 3, 1922, which was published the next day in the *New York Times* in the article "Ban Put on Shopmen" (see n. 2, above).

11. "Truth and Labor Leaders," *New York Times,* July 8, 1922.

12. SG to the Editor of the New York Times, July 11, 1922, reel 281, vol. 294, pp. 412–14, SG Letterbooks, DLC.

13. "Grave and Gay. Mr. Gompers Is Alternatively Indignant and Humorous," *New York Times,* July 14, 1922.

14. For news coverage of SG's statement, see "Gompers Criticises the Proclamation," *New York Times,* July 13, 1922. For a copy of the entire statement, dated July 12, for release July 13, see Files of the Office of the President, Speeches and Writings, reel 117, frames 270–75, *AFL Records*.

15. See SG to James Duncan et al., July 13, 1922, Executive Council Records, Vote Books, reel 17, frame 301, *AFL Records*.

16. For a copy of the statement, see "A Circular," July 18, 1922, below. See also "Excerpts from the Minutes of a Conference with Newspaper Reporters," July 14, 1922, below.

Excerpts from the Minutes of a Conference with Newspaper Reporters

July 14, 1922.

Mr. Gompers: I want to thank you gentlemen for responding to my invitation to come here. There are a few things upon my mind that I want to express to you. . . .

The general public have been led to believe that the men on strike, the men leaving their positions and non-union workmen engaged in these industries who joined the strikers have violated the law of the land, that they have violated the provisions of the Transportation Act and therefore placed themselves in defiance of the Government and that the fight that they are making, i.e., the withholding of their labor is a fight against the government, a fight upon the government, when, as a matter of fact there is not the slightest basis or foundation for such a thought or such a statement. . . .

. . .

. . . The limitation of the power of the board is that if any party has violated a decision or an award of the Railway Labor Board, it may, after a hearing, declare that such a violation has occurred, and there ends the limit of the power of the Labor Board. And what violation there was was a refusal on the part of the men whose case was before the Board to abide by the decision reducing their wages. They were perfectly well within their lawful right to refuse to abide by that decision. Under the law they had no such legal power to leave the service of the companies before the Board would have the opportunity of hearing and deciding or awarding according to their own best judgment, but after the award and after the decision of the Board, it was within the right of the employes to refuse to abide by that decision and it was no violation of law nor a violation of the Esch-Cummins Law, and yet the whole impress[ion] that is conveyed to the general public is that these men have violated law. The controversy is not between the Government and the employes or the unions engaged in this present contest. It is between the railroad managements and the employes, and it is quite easy for them—the railroad managements—to shunt off the idea and place the Government in front as if the Government itself is the one assaulted or attacked by these railroad organizations rather than a protest against the reduction of wages from which the railroad managers are the beneficiaries. . . .

. . .

. . . No one questions the right and the duty of the government of our country and the government of the states to uphold the law, to prevent lawlessness, but this question is not involved in the present struggle. It is the question of these men on strike within their lawful right to protest against a wholesale reduction in wages that cuts to the very bone. The railway labor board in its decision has reduced the wages of thousands upon thousands of men below eight hundred dollars a year when working regularly every day, a wage that does not afford the opportunity of anything like a living for a man and his family. That fact should be brought home to the mind of every man and woman in our country—that the Board has slashed wages to the bone and below the standard of possible decent living or anything approaching American citizenship and standards. . . .

. . .

Question: Are the railroads disregarding the Transportation Act in ignoring the decisions of the Railway Labor Board?

Mr. Gompers: 92 railroads have violated 104 decisions of the Railway Labor Board and the Executives and the Boards of Directors have not been declared outlaws. They have simply gone along and defied the Board.

. . .

. . . The Railway Labor Board . . . has undertaken to outlaw the bona fide organizations of the working people themselves and encourage strikebreakers, whether those who remained at work or those who may be hired, to form organizations, organizations of strikebreakers. Either one way or another they urge that these strikebreakers shall form new organizations for the purpose of taking their part before the Railway Labor Board. . . . The railroad Labor Board is a governmental agency and it has placed itself in the position of being a strikebreaking agency.

Question: Is there any resolution parallel to the one which you have just spoken of outlawing the unions, i.e., any resolution with reference to the railroad management which parallels that in any way? Has the Railway Labor Board in any way ever refused to meet with any railroads that ever violated any decision?

Mr. Gompers: No, Sir. There has been no such action taken. In fact, one of the rail roads has gotten an injunction from a Federal Court enjoining the Railway Labor Board from interference.[1]

. . .

Now, I want to say this to you gentlemen, if there could be—I am expressing my judgment and making no authoritative statement, but I firmly believe that if the railroad executives and the representatives of the railroad organizations were to meet and discuss this situation among themselves, that they could reach an adjustment of this present strike. The railroad act, proclaimed before the award as being the instrument by which strikes on the railroads will be prevented, has been demonstrated to be an absolute fallacy. Just as pointed out by the railroad men and by my associates and by myself before the committees having this legislation under consideration, you cannot prevent strikes by law. . . . Now every man, every labor man of experience has done his level best and speaking for myself, I in my long life, and I hope that I may say service to my country, to my fellow citizens and particularly to my fellow workers, I have aided to some extent in prevent[ing] or averting or avoiding strikes whenever it was possible to do so, but there comes a condition in life and work when men are wholly unsatisfied and dissatisfied and resentful of existing conditions of wages, of hours of labor and conditions of employment, of relations between employers and employes and they demand a change, they demand improvement, call it if you will that they have aspirations for something better or protest against deterioration in their standards. . . . The civil war was fought for the abolition of human slavery, the 13th amendment to the Constitution was adopted to constitutionally prohibit human slavery, involuntary servitude. If the Government, in the use of its power, with all its power, judicial, military, naval, police power and all, shall strike at this very fundamental and take away the right of the man to own himself, that men may not stop work, you go beyond that, that men are violating law when they stop work, from that moment the emancipation proclamation of Lincoln, the 13th amendment to the Constitution of the United States are annulled at once. Do you think the working people of America, the great masses of the people, the liberty loving people of our country who are not workers, that they will submit to such a condition of affairs? They will find a way in which their rights as men, as workers will be recognized and maintained. There has not been and is not now in existence in all our country or in all the world such an agency of conservatism as the unions of labor on the railroads and in all other services. The labor movements of any other country. In what position are they? In one form or another they have their hands upon the throats of their governments, strangling them or forcing them into conditions where they do not care to go. Our country has never had and has not now a more loyal citizenship and a greater support for rational and natural develop[ment] and the maintenance of order and prosperity and progress than the labor movement of America and . . . concentrating . . . the power of government against the men of labor of America . . . [is] doing the greatest injury to the republic and the cause for which the republic in its essence stands.

I may say this to you that the American Federation of Labor stands whole-heartedly behind the men engaged in this strike. There is not a man belonging to any union in the American labor movement who would do one thing but in absolute accord with the right of the men in this strike to maintain themselves and their families to win this strike. Everything within the law will be done, is being done and will be done to help the men win against this unfair action on the part of the Railway Labor Board.

· · ·

TDc, AFL Microfilm Convention File, reel 31, frames 2701–4, *AFL Records.* Typed notations: "Conference between President Gompers and a Group of About Twenty Five Washington Newspaper Correspondents and Reporters on the Strike of the Railroad Shop Crafts, July 14, 1922, Executive Council Chamber, A.F. of L. Building, Washington, D.C." and "Newspaper Conference, July 14, 1922, Executive Council Chamber, A.F. of L. Building, Washington, D.C."

1. See "An Editorial in the *American Federationist*," February 1922, n. 2, above.

To Jerome Jones[1]

July 15, 1922.

Mr. Jerome Jones,
Organizer, American Federation of Labor,
513 Pettis Bldg., Atlanta, Georgia.
Dear Sir and Brother:

Your letter of the 12th instant is received and I have noted carefully what you say relative to the necessity for organizing the colored employes in the railway shops and that it has been suggested to you that they should be organized into Federal Labor Unions.

For a long period of time we have been making a special effort to organize the colored freight handlers, porters, coach cleaners, etc., and by referring to our list of affiliated organizations you will note that we now have about 95 unions of these colored workers.

The last three or four conventions of the American Federation of Labor have given much consideration and discussion to this general subject matter. By referring to the proceedings of the Cincinnati convention, Resolutions 87–88–89–90–91, you will note that the President of the American Federation of Labor, representing the colored workers' organizations is to have a conference with the President of the Brotherhood of Railway Clerks for the purpose of bringing about an adjustment of the grievances set forth in the several resolutions on the several railroad systems named in the resolutions. I have not yet had the opportunity of arranging for this conference but as soon as other conditions will permit I expect to do so.[2] In the meantime, there is no reason why the colored helpers in the different railway centers throughout the south should not be organized either into local unions directly affiliated with the American Federation of Labor, or where the national unions whose jurisdiction is involved will admit them, to organize them into local unions to become chartered by the national or international unions having jurisdiction. In any event, as a matter of strength to and protection of the organized white railway workers, the colored railway workers should be helped and encouraged to organize.

Hoping to hear from you further and with kind regards, I am

Fraternally yours,   Saml Gompers
President,   American Federation of Labor.

TLpS, reel 281, vol. 294, pp. 524–25, SG Letterbooks, DLC.

1. Jerome JONES was a salaried AFL organizer and, from 1898 to 1940, the editor of the *Journal of Labor* in Atlanta.

2. On July 31, 1922, SG wrote Edward FitzGerald, president of the Brotherhood of Railway and Steamship Clerks, Freight Handlers, Express and Station Employes, to arrange a meeting (AFL Microfilm Convention File, reel 31, frame 2435, *AFL Records*). FitzGerald delegated the task to James Forrester, the Railway Clerks' national legislative counsel, whose office was located in the AFL headquarters building. There is no evidence in SG's appointment records, however, to indicate that he met with Forrester to discuss the matter.

From James Kline[1]

Headquarters,
International Brotherhood of Blacksmiths,
Drop Forgers and Helpers[2]
Chicago. July 15, 1922.

Dear Sir and Brother:—

The Chicago papers report you as saying that the United States Railroad Labor Board, as an agency of the Government, is rather a strike-breaking agency, and that it became so when it adopted the resolution out-lawing the union.[3] I want to congratulate you for making that statement, if true. You also say that the Board is not trying to outlaw the railroads which have ignored the Board's decision etc. That is also a frank and truthful statement that will carry weight. Your observation on the question of violence is another well directed thrust at the imperialistic tendencies and military inclination of our Government.

Uncle Sam, you have a pretty good eyesight and you usually hit the mark and every time you get a chance, repeat it.

I am, yours very truly and fraternally,

With best wishes,   J W Kline
General President.

TLS, Samuel Gompers Scrapbooks, NN.

1. James Waller KLINE, of the International Brotherhood of Blacksmiths, Drop Forgers, and Helpers, served as president of the union from 1905 to 1926.
2. International Brotherhood of BLACKSMITHS, Drop Forgers, and Helpers.
3. Kline is referring to statements appearing in the press that were made by SG at a news conference held the day before. (See "Excerpts from the Minutes of a Conference with Newspaper Reporters," July 14, 1922, above.)

A Circular

Washington, D.C. July 18. 1922.

Greetings:

(We convey to you herewith a resolution adopted by the Executive Council setting forth the facts in relation to the strike of the railroad shop crafts and an appeal to the workers and the people generally of our country to support in every proper and lawful manner the men engaged in that struggle, to the end that justice may prevail. We ask that you bring this resolution and proclamation to the attention of all labor in your community and that you secure for it the widest possible publicity.)

Whereas, There is misrepresentation of the cause of the railroad workers now on strike against the nation's most powerful combination of financial and economic strength; be it

Resolved, By the Executive Council of the American Federation of Labor, speaking for and in the name of the American Federation of Labor, that the following *proclamations of facts* be issued to the workers and to the people of our country generally:

The workers engaged in the present struggle are in no sense engaged in a conflict against the government of the United States and we denounce most vigorously the efforts that have been made to make it appear as if the government is being attacked.

The workers have ceased work because the Railroad Labor Board has made an award in response to a plea by the railroads putting into effect terms and conditions of employment sought by the railroads and which the workers are unable to accept.

The stoppage of work can be ended at any moment through joint negotiation between the railroad managements and the workers and there is nothing to prevent the railroads from adopting this course at any moment. The Transportation Act specifically provides that both parties to an industrial dispute may come together for the purpose of reaching an agreement without giving the slightest consideration to the Railroad Labor Board or any of its decisions affecting conditions of work and wages for services performed.

The conduct of railroad managements is the result of Wall Street control of the railroads. The great majority of railroad executives would long since have come to an amicable agreement with the workers were it not for the fact that the association of railroad executives is absolutely dominated by a small minority representing the great allied financial interests of Wall Street. It is a fact that more than 100 railroad directorships are controlled by a group of about twenty-five of the most powerful financial magnates in Wall Street and that this same concentrated power extends in like manner into practically every industrial field in the country. Boards of directors of various New York banks control 270 directorships of ninety-three Class 1 railroads.

The following statement of facts is agreed upon by the railroad unions, by the American Federation of Labor, and by nearly every authority that has made adequate investigation of the subject:

1. The control of the transportation system of the country, including nearly every important system today centers in New York City and the main lines of policy for the industry are determined on a national basis by a comparatively small group of New York banks.

2. This group of New York banks is closely knit together into a single unit through a maze of interlocking directorates and leadership in this combine has been maintained through credit control by the House of Morgan.

3. This control extends not only to the various railroad systems but also to the chief industries of the country which furnish the railroads with fuel, material for maintenance of way and equipment, new equipment and other supplies.

4. Certain members of this financial group are primarily railway directors and they constitute what might be termed the railway department or committee of this unified financial combination.

5. Thomas DeWitt Cuyler[1] and W. W. Atterbury (of the Pennsylvania Railroad, handmaiden of the United States Steel), and L. F. Loree (president of the Delaware and Hudson Railroad), who are at present leading the attack upon the organized employes of the road, both before the country and the Railroad Labor Board, are members of this railway committee of the combine.

6. The spread of control of this New York railway department extends to every section of the country, thereby accounting for the fact that the present policies are being followed on a national basis.

By various devices and largely by virtue of the government guarantee following the return of the railroads to their owners after the Armistice millions upon millions of dollars have been taken by the railroads from the United States Treasury. The findings of the Interstate Commerce Commission and of the Railroad Labor Board clearly indicate the accuracy of the statement that approximately two billion dollars a year are wasted by mismanagement, by improper financing and by useless duplication of effort. This enormous wastage thus far has been covered by drafts upon the Treasury of the United States.

The decision at this time to reduce the wages of the workers is an effort to take from their pockets the enormous sums hitherto provided by the government to cover the cost of railroad waste, extravagance and high financing.

We repeat and emphasize the declaration of the American Federation of Labor in convention in Cincinnati last month as follows:

It is of immediate importance that the rights of the railroad workers to cease work, whenever the pressure becomes too great and whenever they deem themselves justified in so doing must be fully protected. It is well enough to urge the needs of continued transportation facilities in the interests of the general public but it can not be in the interest of the general public to continue further and further the enslavement of free workers under the devious methods employed by the railroads, to earn dividends and profits for a few at the sacrifice of the very existence of the railroad workers.

We point to the fact that the railroads in practically every case have completely ignored decisions which they considered contrary to their interests and we state specifically that ninety-two railroads in 104 cases have thus ignored the awards of the board. We repeat that in none of these cases has there been the slightest effort on the part of the government to coerce railroad managements into acceptance of displeasing awards. On the contrary, in one of the most notable cases involving the award against the Pennsylvania Railroad, that railroad obtained an injunction which prevented the Railroad Labor Board from enforcing or even publishing the decision.[2] The government by its silence has been a party to the conduct of the railroads in ignoring the awards of the Railroad Labor Board and it must thus stand convicted not only of inconsistency but of bad faith in its present tremendous effort to coerce the railroad workers into an acceptance of an award that is bitterly unjust and that violates every tradition of American fairness and justice.

On July 3, the Railroad Labor Board adopted a resolution, which it has since neither rescinded nor modified, declaring that the recognized national organizations of railway employes who have suspended work have ceased to represent those classes of employes and calling upon non-union men employed by the carriers to form organizations which would be recognized by the Railroad Labor Board. This attempt to sanctify and purify strike breakers and strike breaking can be construed as nothing less than an effort on the part of the government to assist the railroads and their Wall Street owners in breaking the strike and thereby destroying the standards of wages and conditions which have in many cases existed on practically all railroads for a period of thirty years or more.

We construe that action on the part of the Railroad Labor Board as an effort to assist the general movement of Bourbon employers and reactionary financial interests throughout the country to destroy the voluntary organizations of the workers and to open the door for the re-establishment of an industrial autocracy in which the workers would be helpless and in which they would be in virtue of bondage to the masters of the industrial world.

We construe the presidential proclamation issued on July 11, as of the same character and we call attention to the fact that the proclamation, while citing a single phase of railroad violation of the Labor Board's awards, placed emphasis upon the stoppage of work by the workers, sought to create the impression that the workers were acting unlawfully, and called for action everywhere to curb this alleged unlawful conduct of the workers, but called for no action to alter the conduct of railroad managements.

We call attention to the abject failure of the Railroad Labor Board and to every other court or tribunal established by law to make strikes either unlawful or impossible and we call attention to the position which Labor has maintained from the outset to the effect that these courts and tribunals are undemocratic, that they destroy the peaceful and constructive processes of negotiation and joint agreement, and that they lead only to disturbance of industry replacing negotiation with litigation.

The fact that any organizations affiliated with the American Federation of Labor have not participated in the strike up to this time in no way lessens the justice of the cause for which all other affiliated unions are striking. Indeed the effort by the Railroad Labor Board to placate these organizations is at once an admission and confession that the Railroad Labor Board has erred in its decision and that it has now stooped to the position of trying to divide the ranks of the organized wage earners and is attempting to create friction and strife among the wage earners.

Let there be no mistake. This is a strike against the Wall Street interests and their hirelings, the managers who control the railroads of the land and not against the United States Government. The Railroad Labor Board is not a judicial, executive or legislative branch of the government. It is purely an advisory and recommendatory body and the public has had no choice in the selection of the personnel nor has the public any control over any of its members.

We call upon working people everywhere and upon all Americans who love justice to sustain the cause of the railroad workers who have ceased work as their only remaining method of protest against an injustice which must rank as one of the most reprehensible which any American industrial or political institution has ever sought to impose.

No workman, whether a member of a union or not, will, if he is possessed of true American manhood, engage in any work formerly done by men now on strike.

No man now on strike, will, if he is true to the cause, conduct himself in any but a law-abiding manner.

The cause for which the workers are contending is worthy of every just and proper effort that can be put forth in its behalf.

Let there be a determination and a solidarity which shall at the same time bring victory in the present struggle and serve notice upon reactionary employers and financial interests everywhere that there is to be no return to autocratic, despotic methods in American industrial life.

Fraternally, Saml Gompers. President.
Attest: Frank Morrison Secretary.
James Duncan, First Vice-President.
Joseph F. Valentine,[3] Second Vice-President.
Frank Duffy,[4] Third Vice-President.
William Green, Fourth Vice-President.
W. D. Mahon, Fifth Vice-President.
T. A. Rickert,[5] Sixth Vice-President.
Jacob Fischer,[6] Seventh Vice-President.
Matthew Woll, Eighth Vice-President.
Daniel J. Tobin, Treasurer.
Executive Council American Federation of Labor.

PLS and Sr, AFL Railway Employees' Department Papers, Labor-Management Documentation Center, NIC.

1. Thomas DeWitt Cuyler (1854-Nov. 2, 1922) was a member of the board of directors of the Pennsylvania Railroad from 1899 until his death and chairman of the Association of Railway Executives from 1918 until his death.

2. See "An Editorial in the *American Federationist*," February 1922, n. 2, above.

3. Joseph F. VALENTINE, president of the International Molders' Union of North America, served as a vice-president of the AFL from 1906 to 1924.

4. Frank DUFFY, secretary of the United Brotherhood of Carpenters and Joiners of America (1903–48), served as an AFL vice-president from 1914 to 1939.

5. Thomas Alfred RICKERT, president of the United Garment Workers of America (1904–41), served as an AFL vice-president from 1918 to 1941.

6. Jacob FISCHER, secretary-treasurer of the Journeymen Barbers' International Union of America (1904–29), served as an AFL vice-president from 1918 to 1929.

To James Kline

July 18, 1922.

Mr. J. W. Kline,
President, International Brotherhood of Blacksmiths, Drop Forgers
and Helpers,
2922 Washington Boulevard, Chicago, Illinois.
Dear Sir and Brother:

Your letter of the 15th instant[1] is received and contents noted. I am gratified to know that the statement I recently gave to the press on the railroad situation meets fully with your commendation. I have been and am now giving and shall continue to give every possible assistance in my power to the railroad men in their fight. I have kept in close touch by long distance telephone, telegraph, and mail with President Jewell and have sent him from day to day copies of the press statements issued by the undersigned and also through the publicity service of the A.F. of L. and I have had conferences here with the representatives of the shop crafts who are in this city. Yesterday, by authority of the Executive Council, I issued a statement in the name of the Executive Council, copy of which is enclosed herein.[2] The article to which you refer in your letter was the result of a two-hour conference I had with twenty-five newspaper men of this city in my office last Saturday.[3] I talked to them straight from the shoulder and then submitted myself to any questions they desired to ask. I found them all friendly and sympathetic and you can rest assured that I took full advantage of the opportunity.

Earnestly hoping and believing in the ultimate success of the railway shop men and repeating my assurance of continuing to do everything within my power to be helpful, I am,

Yours fraternally,   Saml Gompers
President   American Federation of Labor.

TLpS, reel 281, vol. 294, p. 545, SG Letterbooks, DLC.

1. "From James Kline," July 15, 1922, above.
2. For a copy of the statement as SG gave it to the press on July 17, 1922, see Executive Council Records, Vote Books, reel 17, frames 319–22, *AFL Records*. For the document as it was published the next day in the form of a circular, with an introduction and five additional paragraphs not included in the original version, see "A Circular," July 18, 1922, above.
3. The press conference was actually held on Friday. See "Excerpts from the Minutes of a Conference with Newspaper Reporters," July 14, 1922, above.

From Yoshio Nishimura[1]

Helper, Utah. July 22, 1922.

Sir:

While I am assisting in organizing Utah Coal field since the strike declared, I have in hand many reports from the Japanese workers in railroad circle to the effect that though they are on strike aiding A.F. of L., they are not allowed to join the union and also there is vague fear of unemployment after the strike is over. The reason is on October 28th, 1919 the shop crafts union proposed to 17 carriers to exclude Japanese and it resulted those on employ may stay but the Companies would not employ those who once out of employ and also new Japanese who seek job in shop would be rejected. According to the agreement between shop unions and carriers their fear has its ground. They have no place to stand at present as well as future. Aside this question, all carriers of Western States are inviting new Japanese as strike breaker with lots of sweet words and many went in various shops already while those who continuing services are getting promotion. To my demand to keep off shop, these people answer that they are not permitted to join union therefore they are obliged to side of Capitalist, who welcomes them and not Labor who reject. Though the answer does not touch the bottom rock of labor spirit, yet for ordinary laborers it may furnish some ground of excuse. To exclude Japanese workers, shop crafts union must have taken the matter very seriously and there must be good reasons to do so, but driving them to scab gang and to let them fight against, is not least wise policy of union in general, I presume. The powerful organization of broad standing needs no fear in swallowing and digesting them. Capital is more democratic in getting their men and kicked away race, creed, political and trade prejudices long ago; the fact was proved here that 18 years ago all genuine American miners were driven out of Utah coal mines and in their places foreigners put in. If they can make more money, capitalist will willingly move their plants to the heat of China depriving thousands American workers from their dear jobs. Why labor cast away their solemn swear on the *Principle of Labor* and adhere to prejudices? Up to this year the American Labor did not wake up in politically so the vote in shop had little weight in 1919 and moreover young intelligent Japanese fastly taking place of old Japanese immigrants who, even in Japan, are not good material of social evolution. Back in 1907 Japanese admitted to the United Mine Workers of America and they were proved to be good union men with clean record behind them. We wish you will have consideration on this subject and confer with the president of each craft in shop.[2]

Submitting this case,

Respectfully yours,   Yoshio Nishimura
Secretary,   Japanese Labor Fraternity
Member,   The U.M.W. of A.

TLtpSr, reel 282, vol. 295, p. 95, SG Letterbooks, DLC. Typed notation: "*Copy.*" Enclosed in SG to William Green, Aug. 1, 1922, ibid., p. 94.

1. Yoshio Nishimura (b. 1882) was an organizer in Utah for the United Mine Workers of America.

2. On Aug. 1, 1922, SG forwarded a copy of Nishimura's letter to William Green, requesting his advice (reel 282, vol. 295, p. 94, SG Letterbooks, DLC). For a similar letter, see Nishimura to B. M. Jewell, July 10, 1922, AFL Railway Employees' Dept. Papers, NIC.

From Clemente Nicasio Idar

El Paso, Texas, July 27, 1922.

Dear Sir and Brother:

Beginning July 2, date of my arrival in this city, I have been in touch by correspondence and telegraph with different labor organizations and officials of the Federal government in Mexico. The strikers here have seen the effect of all my efforts. We are getting great cooperation from Mr. Calles.[1] He ordered a train load of strike-breakers who were about to cross the Rio Grande at Laredo returned to their homes, in view of the fact that he was apprised that the men were going to work at the Denison, Texas railroad shop. Quite a difference in the attitude of Calles and that of our government.

We are sending bulletins and telegraphic information to different parts of Mexico every day. Mexican Consular officials in this country and city officials at Juarez are helping us very effectively.

I respectfully request you to please bear the above information in mind as a time may come when you have will have an opportunity to express, officially, your appreciation.

The financial distress of the strikers down here is beginning to hurt a little, but I do not believe any of them will go back. This is a very important geographical point and we are endeavoring to keep it tightly closed against imported strike-breakers. If I did not do anything else but work against the importation of labor, that in itself would be quite a contribution of the American Federation of Labor to the success of the strike. I have been sending out bulletins, printing matter in the Spanish language, addressing public and executive meetings of strikers with very little expense to the Federation. I have also helped to raise funds for the Finance Committee. I may be lacking in modesty, but nevertheless, I feel that the men are satisfied with my services.

God grant that the strike may soon close with victory to the men. They all feel somewhat disappointed over the fact that other railroad organizations have not walked out.

With best wishes, I remain,

Fraternally yours, (Signed) C. N. Idar
organizer

TLtpSr, reel 282, vol. 295, pp. 9–10, SG Letterbooks, DLC. Typed notation: "*Copy.*" Enclosed in SG to B. M. Jewell, July 31, 1922, ibid., p. 8.

1. Plutarco Elías Calles (1877–1945) served as governor of Sonora (1917–19) and held various cabinet posts under Venustiano Carranza and Alvaro Obregón including minister of the Secretariat of Industry and Commerce (1919–20), minister of the Secretariat of War and Navy (1920), and minister of the Secretariat of Government (1920–23). He served as president of Mexico from 1924 to 1928 and was subsequently again minister of the Secretariat of War and Navy (1929, 1931–32) and minister of the Secretariat of the Treasury and Public Credit (1933). He was a founder of the Partido Nacional Revolucionario (National Revolutionary party) in 1929.

An Editorial by Victor Berger[1]

[August 5, 1922]

Skinning a skunk is disagreeable business, but at times it has got to be done—because it is the only way to get his pelt.

Discussing Sammy Gompers is just as disagreeable, but sometimes his antics compel us to take off his hide.

And we are told that Sammy wants to come to Wisconsin to make speeches for Robert M. La Follette—in reality to help his own prestige, which has gone down to the freezing point even among the most stupid, since Sam sold out the steel strike.

Nobody seems to know whether J. Pierpont Morgan or E. H. Gary—who dislike La Follette and want to see him defeated—or Sammy's incredible vanity is at the bottom of Sam's proposal.

The fact is—that the last time Sam honored Milwaukee with his presence and his whisky-breath—was during the preparedness campaign for the war to make the world safe for democracy.[2]

Sam, as everybody knows, was more of a war fiend—than Pierpont Morgan himself. Besides helping his trust friends and the American profiteers, he also received special honors from the King of England for saving the ruling class of Great Britain.

Sam came here upon the invitation of the City Club. H. C. Campbell[3] of The Journal—who seemingly had charge of the propaganda in Milwaukee for our entry into the World War—engineered the Gompers meeting.

The Milwaukee Journal had a three-column cut on its first page— and many columns on its second page in praise of Sam. The entire capitalist press of the city outdid itself to boost the meeting. All the fakirs and hold-ups of the Building Trades Council sat on the platform.

A band was playing martial and paytriotic airs. The Association of Commerce, the City Club, the Manufacturers' Association, the American Security League, the Loyalty Legion and the Rotary Club were there in full force. Flags were there galore—but the hall was not a quarter full.

The working people were not there. The Leader—already an "outlawed paper"—because it was opposed to the criminal war—was indifferent. And the working people were not there.

And in 1920, Sam Gompers and all his pals and mercenaries of the A.F.L. worked day and night to rehabilitate Woodrow Wilson—and the Democratic party—by electing James Cox president.

The issue to no small extent was the World War.

Woodrow Wilson and the Democratic party suffered the worst defeat in the history of the country, although they had the unanimous—the "unstinted"—and the "unlimited" support—of Sam and his American Fakiration.

Now the war is the big issue in this fall election in Wisconsin. The reactionaries in their stupidity—a reactionary must always be an ass— have made it so.

The Milwaukee Journal editorially declared this fall election to be "a referendum on the war." And Henry C. Campbell unfailingly accompanies La Follette to all his meetings—like a louse follows the soldier to the trenches.

Does anybody in his right senses believe that a speech by Sammy Gompers in this election can add a single vote to the majority for Robert M. La Follette?

Any speech by Sam, the war fiend? Sam comes here for one purpose only. He wants to claim afterwards that he elected La Follette.

The re-election of Bob by a vote of about 3 to 1 is a foregone conclusion. But if Sam Gompers comes to Wisconsin to make speeches for Bob—Sam may lose Mr. La Follette from 10,000 to 20,000 votes. Such is the "popularity" of Sam among radical farmers, radical workingmen, small business men and German-Americans generally in Wisconsin, that Sam might put a doubt into their minds whether the Senator is on the right track after all—by simply indorsing La Follette.

That, of course, is the purpose of Wall Street in sending Sam to Wisconsin.

If Morgan, Gary and others must have their way and Sam must speak in Milwaukee in order to vindicate the right of free speech, which Sam helped to undo—we warn him not to go near any steel workers, railroad workers or radical farmers.

Let Sam speak to the Association of Commerce—its members eulogized him because he helped them to make untold profits. Let him speak to the City Club—it dined and wined him when he came to speak for the war. Let him address the Rotary Club or the Security League—or even to the American Legion.

Sam might be kicked into the Menomonee river, where it is the smelliest, however—if he should dare to address Socialist workmen in Milwaukee.

The days are over when Sam was furnished "secret service men" as a bodyguard by the national administration—just as The Journal was furnished secret service men against the "German plotters" that didn't exist. Sam would have to hire his own private detectives—and charge them up to expenses.

Well, Wall Street would pay the bill, of course, but why should Sam take the chances?

Milwaukee Leader, Aug. 5, 1922.

1. Victor Luitpold BERGER was editor of the *Milwaukee Leader* (1911–29) and a member of the national executive committee of the Socialist Party of America (1901–23). From 1923 to 1929 he served as a Socialist congressman from Wisconsin.

2. For SG's trip to Milwaukee in December 1915, see *The Samuel Gompers Papers,* vol. 9, pp. 353–54 and p. 355, nn. 1–3.

3. Henry Colin Campbell (1862–1923) was assistant editor of the *Milwaukee Journal* and president of the City Club of Milwaukee.

To Reuben Fink[1]

Aug. 8, 1922.

Mr. Reuben Fink
280 Broadway, New York, N.Y.
Dear Sir:
Your letter of July 31st received and contents noted.

The questions you asked me are not difficult to answer.

First, you ask how I can reconcile my attitude against immigration with the fact that I am an immigrant myself. If a friend invites me into his home, does that give me the privilege of taking all my friends with me? He might not object to one or two, but I might want to secure the same friendly reception for a dozen or more that I receive myself.

Because I was an immigrant does not give me the right either morally or selfishly to demand that the doors of the United States should be opened to all who desire to enter. Being an immigrant does not give me the right to demand that the United States shall be flooded with foreigners to the detriment of those who were born here and gave their efforts and sometimes their lives to making this the greatest country on earth. Being a member of the Jewish race does not give me the right to break down the standards in this country any more than if I were an Irishman, an Englishman, a Scotchman, an Australian, an Italian or a Russian.

Did it ever occur to you that there are millions of square miles of vacant fertile lands in South Africa, South America, and Australia that would support all and every immigrant who desired to leave his home in the eastern hemisphere to better his conditions? The Americans, aided by naturalized citizens, have builded this glorious nation. My coming to the United States was at a time when the country needed men and women and children who could either work or fight for freedom and unity and not as now when millions of workers in America are in enforced idleness.

The sentiment of the American Federation of Labor against unrestricted immigration is that which animates the great mass of our people. Those who would flood the country and break down the labor market are those who desire to reduce wages to the lowest possible point. They are the same people who are opposed to education because they believe it creates desires in the human breast for advancement.

The opposition to unrestricted immigration is not an individual opposition, but is universal among those who work for wages. I am sorry that you do not realize that feature of the deep feeling against immigration. It is self-preservation.

You cannot but know that if immigration were not restricted, America would no longer be the land of promise for the oppressed of other nations. America has her unemployed and her oppressed. Because I was permitted to come to this country does not give me the right selfishly to insist that all other foreigners should be allowed to come.

A few days ago I celebrated my fifty-ninth anniversary as an American. I am American in thought, in word and in deed. And as long as

I am permitted to live neither race, creed, color nor nationality will control my actions as to anything that I believe is right, not only for America, but for the peoples of the whole world. Might I not call your attention to the fact that unrestricted immigration is not only injurious to the people now in the United States, but that it is a great wrong to those who are induced to come now, for the state of unemployment would be to the disadvantage of both.

This letter is written in as friendly a spirit as you expressed. I hope you will consider what I have said, and then I would like to hear from you again.

Yours very truly,   Saml Gompers
President,   American Federation of Labor.

TLpS, reel 282, vol. 295, pp. 366–67, SG Letterbooks, DLC.

1. In 1921 and 1922 Reuben Fink (1889–1961; b. Finkelstein) served as associate manager and then manager of *Die Zeit* (The Jewish Times), official organ of the Jewish Workers' Alliance and the Poale-Zion (Workers for Zion) Party of America. He subsequently went into the insurance business.

From Thomas Conboy

Omaha, Nebr. August 14, 1922

Dear Sir & Bro:—

William Z. Foster, following his deportation from Denver, Colo.,[1] after being detained one night in jail, arrived in Omaha on time to fill his engagement to deliver his address "The Crises in the Labor Movement."

His audience numbered 175 people, made up of Socialists, Communists and a few workers from other organizations. Admission fee of 25 cents was charged. When through speaking, the chairman asked his audience for a voluntary contribution owing to insufficient funds taken in at the door to pay Mr. Foster's expenses. He was required to pay $25.00 for the hall and war tax on the admissions.

I am informing you of some of the statements he made.

The American Labor Movement, the most backward movement in the World.

American Labor Movement has no program. Other countries are determined to abolish Capitalism as their program.

American Labor Movement not intelligently led. Employers have no respect for workers because we are not thoroughly organized.

We are suffering from intellectual paralysis.

American Labor Movement on the retreat.

Criticised our political efforts by supporting our friends and punishing our enemies.

Other countries don't believe we have a labor movement—the mention of Gompers name is Nuf Ced.

We must change from Craft Unionism to Industrial Unionism.

Germany has an industrial Metal Trades Union from the Jewelry Workers to Battleship Builders, numbering 800,000 members.

Made comparison of Germany with 7000000 members to America, including Canada, with 3,500000, and not half the population.

He was heckeled to explain why the Germans received such low wages when they were so well organized. He attributed the cause that the money was being confiscated by the Allies. He was told that goods before the war were sold always in this country lower than what the workers received for wages plus overhead in this country.

National officers are opposed to Industrial Unionism—afraid of losing their positions if amalgamation would come.

Gompers don't believe in industrial unionism.

When Gompers desires to send a message to railroad bodies, he sends the little crown prince Woll of the Photo engravers.[2]

Its up to the workers to make Gompers believe in industrial unionism.

When the question of industrial unionism was before the A.F. of L. convention at Cincinnati, not a man in the American Labor Movement had the intelligence or courage to discuss one word on industrial unionism. They voted to reaffirm the Scranton resolution.[3]

Industrial unionism cannot be accomplished by secession or dual movements. We must take up the industrial or the Amalgamation question within our craft organization.

President Gompers sent Paul J Smith, Manning[4] and Hays[5] of the Typographical Union to Minnesota State Convention to defeat Amalgamation but they adopted it unanimously.[6]

He closed by saying the shop crafts were going to win their strike.

I am enclosing clippings. Foster stopped at the Editors home. I suppose that Foster wrote this statement.

Fraternally yours,   T. J. Conboy

TLS, Files of the Office of the President, General Correspondence, reel 106, frames 499–501, *AFL Records*.

1. William Z. Foster was on a speaking tour on behalf of the Trade Union Educational League. On Aug. 6, 1922, he arrived in Denver from Salt Lake City and was arrested in his hotel room by state Rangers, taken by car to Brighton, Colo., and jailed overnight. The next day he was taken to Greeley, Colo., and then Cheyenne, Wyo., and from there Wyoming authorities took him to the Nebraska state line near Torrington,

Wyo., where they put him out of the car and warned him not to return. According to Adj. Gen. Patrick Hamrock, who supervised the Denver kidnapping, Foster was a dangerous radical who was forcibly ejected to prevent disorder in the state. For his part, Foster took a train into Nebraska from Torrington and continued his speaking tour.

2. The International PHOTO-ENGRAVERS' Union of North America.

3. See *The Samuel Gompers Papers*, vol. 5, pp. 443–44.

4. John J. MANNING, secretary-treasurer of the AFL Union Label Trades Department from 1917 to 1934.

5. John W. HAYS, secretary-treasurer of the International Typographical Union from 1909 to 1928 and president of the AFL Union Label Trades Department from 1916 to 1928.

6. The 1922 convention of the Minnesota State Federation of Labor, which met in Crookston, July 17–19, unanimously adopted a resolution recognizing the need for "the organization of unions along industrial lines, having full jurisdiction over all crafts employed in any industry" and calling on the officers of the federation to promote "discussion and education amongst the rank and file" to bring this about (*Proceedings of the Fortieth Convention of the Minnesota State Federation of Labor Held at Crookston, July 17–19, 1922* [St. Paul, 1922], p. 49).

To the Executive Council of the AFL

Washington, D.C. August 15, 1922.

Document No. 4

Executive Council, American Federation of Labor.

Colleagues:

Enclosed you will please find copy of a letter[1] which I received this morning from Mr. B. M. Jewell, president of the Railway Employes Department of the A.F. of L. On behalf of the railway shopmen's organizations he makes application to the American Federation of Labor for the issuance of an appeal for voluntary financial assistance.

After the receipt of the letter today I had a long conference with the men representing the unions of shop crafts whose members are on strike.[2] We went into the situation very fully. I called their attention to the circular appeal[3] for financial assistance which upon authority of the Cincinnati convention was sent out to all organized labor immediately after the adjournment of the convention, asking for aid for the Textile Workers,[4] the Quarry Workers[5] and the Granite Cutters,[6] and that thus far a little more than $5,000. had been received from that appeal and distributed pro rata to the three organizations according to their respective memberships. I also called their attention to the fact that the International Typographical Union had spent several million dollars in support of its members in the fight for the 44-hour week; that the whole membership of the Miners had been involved in a tremendous strike for some months; and that in view of the existing conditions and circumstances little response could be expected to such an appeal, but that I would place the matter before the Executive Council with my recommendation that the issuance of the appeal be authorized.

Mr. Jewell and his colleagues stated that they fully understood the situation; that they did not anticipate any appreciable financial returns to such an appeal but that they desired it issued because of its moral effect so that their representatives when addressing meetings or when in personal conversation or conference they could point to the appeal issued by the Executive Council as further evidence of the full support and help of the American Federation of Labor and in this way not only silence criticism but hearten the men.

Based upon my conference with Mr. Jewell and his colleagues, my judgment is that the appeal should be issued.

The members of the Executive Council will please return their vote by telegraph upon the following:

Shall an appeal be issued for voluntary financial assistance for the striking railway shopmen?[7]

Fraternally yours,   Saml Gompers.
President   American Federation of Labor.

TLcS, Executive Council Records, Vote Books, reel 17, frames 353–54, *AFL Records.*

1. B. M. Jewell to SG, Aug. 14, 1922, Executive Council Records, Vote Books, reel 17, frames 354–56, *AFL Records.*

2. On the afternoon of Aug. 15, 1922, SG met with Jewell; James Kline, president of the International Brotherhood of Blacksmiths, Drop Forgers, and Helpers; Martin Ryan, president of the Brotherhood of Railway Carmen of America; and Joseph Franklin, president of the International Brotherhood of Boiler Makers, Iron Ship Builders, and Helpers of America.

3. SG to All Organized Labor, July 3, 1922, United Brotherhood of Carpenters and Joiners of America Records, reel 2, frame 779, *AFL and the Unions.*

4. When New England textile manufacturers announced a 20 percent pay cut in January 1922, following a reduction of over 20 percent already implemented in December 1920, the United Textile Workers of America authorized a strike at any mills making the cutback. Outside Massachusetts, where they were prohibited from doing so, employers also raised hours from forty-eight to fifty-four per week. By early February some fifteen thousand Rhode Island workers were out, and by mid-month the strike had spread to Connecticut, Maine, Massachusetts, and New Hampshire. The largely unorganized workers in Lawrence, Mass., joined the strike toward the end of March after the wage reduction was announced there, bringing the number of strikers to eighty-five thousand and making this the largest textile strike in New England history. The walkout ended in Lawrence in August and in Lowell, Mass., in September after mill owners agreed to restore the old wage rates. The strike also ended in September in Rhode Island, when mill owners went back to the old wages and hours, although the Amalgamated Textile Workers of America accepted the fifty-four hour week in the Pawtuxet Valley. Wages were also restored in New Hampshire, where the strike was

called off in December, but the fifty-four-hour week remained in force in most mills there.

5. The QUARRY Workers' International Union of North America was resisting a nationwide campaign by employers to reduce wages and impose the open shop. The employers' campaign began in New England in May 1921, when quarrymen received notice of a pay cut. The union refused to accept the wage reduction, and on July 1 many New England quarry workers went on strike. Employers in California began instituting the open shop toward the end of the summer, and by September quarrymen in San Francisco and Los Angeles were on strike as well, and by October union quarrymen throughout California were locked out. Employers' associations east of the Mississippi jointly declared an open shop in early 1922 and demanded a 20 percent pay cut as well, so when contracts there expired on Apr. 1 quarrymen in the eastern half of the country joined what had become a national strike. By year's end most Quarry Workers' locals had negotiated new contracts with employers, retaining union conditions but compromising on wages. The California strike and lockout continued into 1923.

6. The GRANITE Cutters' International Association of America was also resisting a nationwide open shop campaign. The struggle began in California when granite manufacturers began a lockout on June 1, 1921, and indicated they would not negotiate new union contracts. Union granite cutters walked off their jobs on Aug. 1 when their contracts expired, and granite manufacturers responded by declaring an open shop. In September New England granite manufacturers' associations gave notice they would demand a 20 percent pay cut in any new agreements, and union granite cutters in the region stopped work when contracts expired on Apr. 1, 1922. As the strike spread, granite manufacturers' associations across the country declared an open shop. Many employers did not agree with the open shop demand, however, and began signing new contracts with Granite Cutters' locals on a firm-by-firm basis. Granite manufacturers in Quincy, Mass., and Barre, Vt., led the way in July with contracts restoring a $1 hourly wage, a forty-four-hour week, and union working conditions. By early 1923 most firms in the eastern part of the country, excepting a few in Georgia, North Carolina, and Vermont, had made similar agreements. The strike and lockout continued in California, however.

7. The AFL Executive Council endorsed Jewell's request. For the circular, SG to All Organized Labor, Aug. 19, 1922, see Executive Council Records, Vote Books, reel 17, frame 359, *AFL Records*.

To Ernest Bailey

Aug. 18, 1922.

Mr. Ernest Bailey,
Recording Secretary, Freight Handlers' Union #17545,[1]
1804 Ivy Ave., Newport News, Virginia.
Dear Sir and Brother:

Your communication of August 11th received in regard to the subject of the opposition of members of your local who have not responded to the strike call issued by the Brotherhood of Railway Clerks. In the instance of the issuance of charters by the American Federation of

Labor to the Colored Freight Handlers I will state, that these employes come under the jurisdiction of the Brotherhood of Railway Clerks, the issuance of the charters by the A.F. of L. is temporary arrangement pending the time when the colored workers will be admitted by the Brotherhood of Railway Clerks. Notwithstanding the fact that charters are issued direct by the A.F. of L. it is the understanding that these local unions will govern themselves in accordance with the policy and procedure of the Brotherhood of Railway Clerks in all subjects affecting the conditions of labor in their crafts.

The American Federation of Labor has no authority to order any affiliated organization on strike. The members determine these questions for themselves. But while this is a fact, the colored freight handlers should govern themselves in accordance with the policy of their trade as determined by the Brotherhood of Railway Clerks the same as though they were operating under charter from that body and should not pursue any policy that will tend to thwart the efforts of the clerks to establish fair and just conditions of employment for all members.

The members of your local who have been in continuous good standing in your local for one year and upon whom per capita tax has been paid to this office are entitled to strike benefits.

With best wishes, I am,

Fraternally yours,   Saml Gompers
President   American Federation of Labor.

TLpS, reel 282, vol. 295, pp. 655–56, SG Letterbooks, DLC.

1. AFL Freight Handlers' Union 17,545 of Newport News, Va., was chartered in 1921.

From W. T. Sherman

District Organizer A.F. of L.
President of Cooks & Waiters Local #142.
El Dorado, Ark, 8-23-[19]22.

Dear Sir and Brother:

An instance came up here yesterday that I think worthy of report. The pumps on Rock Island R.R. are getting in very bad shape, therefore making it difficult to furnish engines with water. The R.R. people made arrangements with Lane & Bowlen, deep water well contractors, to repair their pumps, although the National deep water well people had put down the wells and furnished pumps. Yesterday the Lane & Bowlen people sent a car with supplies and three men here to fix the pumps. Before unloading their tools they took a squint at the wells. Noting they were National Wells, the men thought something wrong. They hunted up the Labor Temple and conferred with the strikers. Finding they would be doing work that belongs to the shop crafts they delivered these words to the assembled strikers, "Men, we do not belong to any union, but we will never fix those pumps. We never have scabbed and damned if we ever will." The men gave them a rising vote of thanks and the three men left the hall.

I was going to report this last night, but waited to make sure they were on the level. And they were, for they left at 9:30 last night.

Here is another thing that developed. The R.I. road has one well that has never failed, and the pump is in fine condition; yet, all enginemen have orders to take water from that particular well "only on emergency." One would naturally infer that the management was doing that in order to further the impression that it was difficult to have engine water, thereby laying a greater blame on the strikers.

There are 270 men affected here by the strike. They meet at 2 P.M. every day except Sunday. Everything orderly. The cooks and waiters, plumbers, painters, carpenters, bakers, m.p. operators, printers, and barbers have donated liberally. Eighty-nine per cent of the merchants have voluntarily contributed from $5.00 to $25.00 cash, and told the men "stick to it, boys, we will go broke with you." I would very much appreciate any and all data you can send me.[1]

　　　　　　　　　　Yours fraternally　　(Signed) W. T. Sherman

(Business conditions good.)

TLtpSr, reel 282, vol. 295, p. 867, SG Letterbooks, DLC. Typed notation: "Copy." Enclosed in R. Lee Guard to B. M. Jewell, Aug. 26, 1922, ibid., p. 866.

　　1. On Aug. 26, 1922, R. Lee Guard forwarded a copy of W. T. Sherman's letter to B. M. Jewell, president of the AFL Railway Employes' Department (reel 282, vol. 295, p. 866, SG Letterbooks, DLC).

From George Perkins

Headquarters
Cigar Makers' International Union of America[1]
Chicago, Ill. August 26, 1922.

Dear Sir:

You have undoubtedly read of the raid made on William Z. Foster's office here in Chicago[2] and of the arrest of about thirty so-called radicals who were supposed to be holding a convention in the woods near St. Joseph, Michigan.[3]

I notice among those arrested, and I suppose a follower and adherent of William Z. Foster, is one Cabel Harrison.[4] I remember that in the Bailin confession,[5] copy of which you have in your office, he says that Cabel Harrison and Charles Winfield[6] sold out Union 527 Chicago in their arbitration of the difficulties that they had with the LaKirby Cigar Company.[7] Cabel was one of the arbitrators and if ever a union got the worst of arbitration it was in that case. I have the original signed copy of the arbitrators' award.

I am sending you this merely for your information. It may come in handy sometime.

Yours fraternally,   G. W. Perkins
Int'l. President.

TLS, AFL Microfilm National and International Union File, Cigar Makers' Records, reel 36, frame 2036, *AFL Records*.

1. The CIGAR Makers' International Union of America.

2. Authorities in Illinois raided the Trade Union Educational League's Chicago headquarters on the night of Aug. 20, 1922, confiscating correspondence and other papers belonging to William Z. Foster. They acted on the pretext that strike-related sabotage, said to have been encouraged by Foster, had caused a fatal train wreck in Gary, Ind., earlier that day, but later admitted finding no evidence that Foster had advocated violence in connection with the railroad strike.

3. On Aug. 22, 1922, federal agents and state police raided Forest House, a resort near Bridgman, Mich., just south of St. Joseph, where a Communist party convention was being held. They arrested fifteen of the radicals, but most were able to make their escape, including Foster, who was seized in Chicago on Aug. 23, extradited to Michigan on Sept. 12, and then released after posting bail. Thirty-two of those who had been at the convention were eventually tracked down and arrested. Their supporters, including Roger Baldwin and Eugene Debs, organized a national campaign to raise money for their defense, and Frank Walsh agreed to take Foster's case. His trial, Mar. 12-Apr. 4, 1923, ended in a deadlocked jury. Charles Ruthenberg, the next Bridgman defendant, was tried Apr. 16-May 2 and convicted of advocating criminal syndicalism, sentenced to three to five years in prison, and fined $5,000. Ruthenberg was jailed briefly after the Michigan Supreme Court turned down his appeal for a stay of sentence pending an application for rehearing the case, but was released on bail pending his appeal to the U.S. Supreme Court. He died before further rulings were made in his case. Foster was never retried, and no other Bridgman defendants went to trial.

4. Cabel Harrison (b. 1879), subsequently identified as a member of International Association of Machinists' local 113 of Chicago, served as executive secretary and as national organizer for the Workers' Party of America in 1922. He was the Socialist Labor party's candidate for vice-president of the United States in 1916 and had served as an IWW organizer (1919) and as general secretary of the American Labor Alliance (1921), whose objective was to create a workers' republic in the United States.

5. A lengthy deposition made in November 1920 by Albert Balanoff or Balanow (alias Albert Bailin; b. 1895?), that recounted his career from 1917 to 1920 as a double-agent for the U.S. Department of Justice and the William J. Burns and G. H. Thiel detective

agencies, among others, infiltrating left-wing groups, acting as an agent provocateur to foment radicalism and labor unrest, and writing false reports that exaggerated the potential threat from these organizations. (For a copy of the confession, see AFL Microfilm National and International Union File, Cigar Makers Records, reel 36, frames 1748–60, *AFL Records*). George Perkins sent SG a copy of the document in May 1921.

6. Charles W. Winfield (b. 1880) worked in cigar shops in Peoria and Chicago before serving as secretary of Cigar Makers' Progressive local 527 of Chicago in 1916 and 1917. Apparently he was also employed as a company spy. He was expelled from the international union in 1918.

7. Difficulties between the Cigar Makers and the La Kurba Cigar Co. in Chicago apparently dated from as early as 1914. The company moved some of its operations to Benton Harbor, Mich., in 1916 to get around the union, but in 1917 the Cigar Makers declared a boycott on the firm. Later that year Winfield announced that the conflict had been settled through arbitration, but the union struck the Benton Harbor plant again in 1918. La Kurba responded by moving again, this time to Evansville, Ind.

Excerpts from an Article in the *New York Times*

Washington, Sept. 1.—[1922]

OUTRAGEOUS, SAYS GOMPERS

The threat of a general strike was organized labor's reply today to the action of the Chicago Federal Court in granting Attorney General Daugherty's request for a temporary restraining order against the striking railway shop craft unions from interfering with the operation of the railroads.[1]

In the course of a bitter attack upon the court order, denouncing it as illegal and provocative of Bolshevism, Samuel Gompers, President of the American Federation of Labor, said that the matter of recommending a general strike would be taken up Sept. 9 by the Executive Council of the Federation.[2]

"No one knows what may happen," Mr. Gompers declared, "but it is my duty to bring to the attention of the Executive Council the proposition of a general strike because of the widespread insistence upon such a course."

Neither Mr. Gompers nor the Executive Council has the power to call out all the members of organized labor, but its recommendations would have a far-reaching effect upon the action taken by the various trade unions composing the American Federation of Labor. Mr. Gompers declined to say whether he would make such a recommendation. Although the heads of organized labor are plainly in a resentful and even defiant mood against the Federal Government's request for what is probably one of the most sweeping injunctions ever framed in a labor dispute, it is exceedingly doubtful that all of the 2,000,000 and more members of organized labor could be brought out on a strike of sympathy with the railway shop crafts. For one thing there are 500,000 bituminous miners who have just returned to work after a strike of nearly five months' duration. It is believed unlikely that they would place in jeopardy the points they have gained by quitting work once more.

Gompers Predicts Defiance.

Mr. Gompers denounced the court action as a violation of constitutional rights and a reversion to slavery, and all but predicted outright that the enjoined heads of the shopcrafts would defy the court's order. He said that the annual convention of the American Federation of Labor for years had passed a resolution authorizing its members to ignore injunctions when they were deemed invasions of constitutional rights and liberties of labor.

. . .

. . ."Every man must follow his own bent of judgment and convictions. The American Federation of Labor has no mandatory powers, but I think I know the calibre of the men involved. They are intelligent, patriotic Americans, and are not likely to surrender their constitutional rights at the behest of a court that undertakes to interfere with those rights."

The labor chief read from Sections 6, 19 and 20 of the Clayton Anti-Trust act, passed early in the Wilson Administration, and declared the Chicago court order to be in direct violation of this law.

. . .

Denies Any Conspiracy.

"The word 'conspiracy' used in the injunction," he continued, "is one of those legalistic terms injected to confuse the situation. There has been no conspiracy on the part of the shopmen. They merely counselled to prevent invasion of their rights and reduction of their wages. If it were not so tragic, it would be farcical to say that 500,000 men had entered into a conspiracy."

Mr. Gompers said that the provision in the injunction restraining labor leaders from giving interviews to the newspapers encouraging men to leave employ of the railroads was "entirely new." He asserted that the restraining of union funds was a new procedure for the Federal courts.

"The last word has not been heard from the brotherhoods, and no one knows what effect the injunctions will have on other railway workers," Mr. Gompers said, discussing the provision in the court order forbidding communication between the strikers.

"The Government through its attorney general has stirred up a hornet's nest when it might have placated the men and found a solution to the situation.

"I do not wish to appear facetious but I note radio is about the only means of communication [not] restrained in the injunction. I wonder if the ether of the air is to be enjoined by the Court."

Referring to the restraining clause against taunting, Mr. Gompers observed: "It may be a new crime to taunt. However, I never heard of it being a violation of the law. If men cannot call the strikebreakers 'scabs,' possibly they may be permitted to call them industrial angels.

"This injunction is most outrageous and is a process for the manufacture of radicalism and Bolshevism. It is indeed strange that in a republic founded on the principle of freedom and justice and a recognition of the rights of man that the political party of Lincoln, Phillips, Beecher and Garrison, under whose leadership slavery was abolished, should now be engaged in a movement of restoration of compulsory labor. I belong to no political party, and I therefore do not speak as a partisan, but the whole procedure bears out Thomas Jefferson's warning of usurpation of power by the courts. And in this case it has been spurred on by the Government of the United States."

Mr. Gompers declared that President Harding would have Congress make strikes unlawful.[3]

CALLS IT WORSE THAN LAW ASKED.

"But Congress has refused to pass such a law," he said, "and now the Attorney General goes into the courts and asks for an injunction more far-reaching than any law. You ask me what I think the attitude of the Harding Administration is toward labor. I do not know, but I recall that Mr. Harding has declared his intention of getting back to normalcy. Maybe he wanted to go back several centuries."

Mr. Gompers said that on the night before the conference report on the Esch-Cummins Transportation act was submitted to Congress he read at a meeting of labor leaders and members of both houses of Congress a telegram sent by a railroad lobbyist to a railroad executive. This message, he said, pointed out the difference between an anti-strike clause then contained in the bill and the conference report. The railway executive was advised that the conference report was preferable from the railroad viewpoint, as the injunction method could be followed under it, while the anti-strike clause called for trial by jury, and convictions of labor leaders by juries were declared to be difficult.

"Here we see it," exclaimed Mr. Gompers. "The railroad executives required no lawyer to bring this case. United States Attorney General Daugherty became the attorney of the railroads. Surely the Attorney General would not have made application for this injunction without the approval of the Government. I noticed in the newspapers of today it was emphatically declared that the shopmen's strike would collapse on or before Sept. 15. If that is so confidently predicted, why has it been necessary to enjoin the men? As a matter of fact, this injunction is a confession that the strike is to be successful in securing the rights to which the men are entitled. It is an injunction in which all the powers are brought into play to coerce the men to surrender their rights and interests, when not a move was made against the railroad carriers in 104 cases on ninety-two roads in which they violated orders of the Railroad Labor Board.

"If any unlawful acts have been committed by the shopmen, they can be apprehended, indicted, tried, convicted and punished. All that they have done is to stop work, and nothing else. They are not interfering with the operation of the railroads but they have declined to work under conditions offered. If they are compelled to work, then they are not free men."

Mr. Gompers struck back at what he said was General Daugherty's reference to him as "more malicious than untruthful."

RESENTS ATTACK BY DAUGHERTY.

"That is a foul aspersion of me," Mr. Gompers exclaimed heatedly. "I will stake my reputation for veracity even against Mr. Daugherty's. He has declared himself to be an open-shopper, but after both he and I are dead organized labor will live.

"Mr. Daugherty says that the injunction was not intended to be a blow against unionism. I wonder if it was not his guilty conscience that led him to say that. Up to that moment no one had accused him. Like Hamlet's mother, 'Methinks he doth protest too much.' [4]

"I do not know who is guilty of acts of sabotage on the railroads but it was most unjust and unwarranted to accuse the strikers. The railroad companies employ private detectives, gunmen and agents provocateurs who might be as well responsible for these acts as the strikers."

. . .

Strong pressure has been brought upon him to call a general strike, Mr. Gompers said. He explained that he has not this power, nor has the executive counsel of the American Federation of Labor, which will convene Sept. 9 for a regular meeting called last June.

"I have been praised to the skies and damned to hell by persons on both sides of the question who believe I have the power to call a general strike. By letters, telegrams, resolutions of labor locals, newspaper clippings and circulars, I have been urged to take such a course."

Asked what advice he had given in reply to these demands Mr. Gompers replied:

"I would prefer to keep my replies to myself at this time. Perhaps when the strike is over in a month or two it might be well to give them out. Never before in my memory has there been such a demand for a general strike."

New York Times, Sept. 2, 1922.

1. See "Text of the Rail Strike Injunction Defining the Acts Now Restrained," *New York Times,* Sept. 2, 1922.

2. The AFL Executive Council met Sept. 9–16, 1922, in Atlantic City. It voted 6–3 not to call a general strike but denounced the railway injunction and called for mass meetings on Oct. 1 to show support for the strikers, protest the injunction, and call for the impeachment of Attorney General Harry Daugherty and Judge James Wilkerson. For the Council's statements, see Executive Council Records, Minutes, reel 7, frames 1150–51, 1188, *AFL Records.*

3. SG is referring to President Warren Harding's address to Congress on Aug. 18, 1922, which called, among other things, for a mechanism to enforce the decisions of the U.S. Railroad Labor Board. No legislation was passed to implement Harding's proposal.

4. The line in Shakespeare's *Hamlet,* act 3, scene 2, reads: "The lady protests too much, methinks."

To Jan Oudegeest[1]

Washington, D.C. September 16, 1922.

Mr. J. Oudegeest,
Secretary, International Federation of Trade Unions,
61 Vonderstraat, Amsterdam, Holland.
Dear Sir and Brother:

Your letter of June 7th[2] to which we are now replying was written just prior to the assembling of our annual convention and was received during the course of that convention. We deemed it wise to await the action of the convention before making answer. Since the adjournment of the convention our domestic industrial situation has imposed upon us so many duties that we have found it impossible to make reply until now.

Your letter indicates that you and the other officers of the International Federation of Trade Unions feel that your course has been fully justified and your policies thoroughly sustained by the action of the congress held in Rome.[3] This attitude on your part seems to make it more difficult than ever to arrive at an understanding.

You inform us that the full report of your activities was adopted unanimously and "without any noteworthy criticism," and you continue to say that "we now have the positive assurance that the policy hitherto pursued entirely conforms to the views of all our affiliated organizations." This can mean only that those points to which the American Federation of Labor has raised objection have been sustained by all of your affiliated organizations and we are forced to the conclusion that your affiliated organizations do not desire any change in that policy so as to meet the views of the American Federation of Labor.

We are compelled to make clear to you the fact that the American Federation of Labor did not raise points of objection for the sake of creating argument nor did it raise points of objection with the intention of later abandoning those points. The American Federation of Labor is willing to discuss the points at issue and to undertake to reach an agreement in a conciliatory spirit but it is not willing to make the sacrifice of principle which would be involved if we were to follow the course indicated by your communication.

Permit us to say that the convention of the American Federation of Labor, which was in session when your communication arrived, by an overwhelming majority reaffirmed the action of the previous two conventions and sustained the actions of its officers in connection with the international movement. We are under instructions to continue our effort to find a way to bring about affiliation with the International Federation of Trade Unions, but we are also under instructions to adhere to the principles which we have laid down in that connection.

Notwithstanding the fact that you say in your letter that the International "is doing its very utmost to prevent any misunderstanding in order that the American Federation of Labor shall no longer remain outside the ranks of the International Federation of Trade Unions" your previous statements as to the action of the congress in Rome make it clear that no deviation from your former course is intended.

We must state to you as plainly as we can and with the frankness which the situation demands, that affiliation on the part of the American Federation of Labor is out of the question unless and until the objections which it has raised are considered and met satisfactorily by the International Federation of Trade Unions. That has been explained so many times that it seems to us almost unnecessary that it should be set forth again but we feel that it is our duty to you to be sure that there is no room left for doubt as to our position. It is an absolute necessity that the autonomy of the American Federation of Labor be completely safeguarded and it is a necessity that the American Federation of Labor be free from the possibility of being committed by the International Federation of Trade Unions to policies and principles to which it cannot give assent.

It is furthermore essential that the questions of dues be considered and that there be an arrangement which will materially lessen the obligation which the International Federation of Trade Unions seeks to impose and that there also be an understanding as to the unit of currency which is to serve as the measure for the payment of dues by all countries.

It is our point of view now as it has been from the first that these conditions may be the subject of discussion but they cannot be abandoned on our part or ignored on your part.

In addition let us assure you that your letter of September 29, 1921,[4] has been read and discussed several times and the formula which you suggest therein[5] has been given thorough attention in our conferences and in our communications to you. We can only repeat in this connection that we cannot consent to any invasion of the autonomy and self-determination of the American labor movement.

We shall be glad to have from you your interpretation of the position of the International Federation of Trade Unions as to whether, in view of the action of the congress of Rome and the action of our convention in Cincinnati, in June 1922 there is open for adoption any course which will make possible affiliation of the American Federation of Labor to the International Federation of Trade Unions. In the event that you find some course possible of adoption we shall be glad to know in what manner the International Federation of Trade Unions will find it possible to consider the points raised by the American Federation of Labor and in what definite manner the International Federation of Trade Unions can give assurances to the American Federation of Labor in respect to those points.[6]

Fraternally yours,

Executive Council,   American Federation of Labor.

_____ President

TLp, reel 283, vol. 296, pp. 360–61, SG Letterbooks, DLC.

1. Jan OUDEGEEST served as secretary of the International Federation of Trade Unions (IFTU) from 1919 to 1927.

2. Oudegeest to SG, June 7, 1922, AFL Microfilm Convention File, reel 31, frame 2590, *AFL Records*.

3. The second congress of the IFTU met in Rome, Apr. 20–26, 1922.

4. Oudegeest to SG, Sept. 29, 1921, AFL Microfilm Convention File, reel 31, frame 2590, *AFL Records*.

5. Oudegeest suggested that SG clearly outline the barriers to the AFL's affiliation

with the IFTU and that representatives of the two organizations then meet in conference to reach a compromise.

6. On Oct. 17, 1922, Oudegeest again asked SG for specific proposals for the AFL's affiliation and suggested that the two men meet at the IFTU's upcoming conference at The Hague in December (AFL Microfilm Convention File, reel 31, frame 2593, *AFL Records*). In a letter of Nov. 25, SG rejected the idea of a face-to-face meeting and insisted that the two sides negotiate matters through correspondence (ibid.).

Excerpts from the Minutes of a Meeting of the Executive Council of the AFL

Saturday, September 16, 1922.

MORNING SESSION.

. . .

President Gompers submitted the following document:

RESOLUTION.

Whereas, The great conspiracy of reactionary business and high finance to destroy the organizations of the workers has been effectively brought to a stand-still, with its more important moves checked through

(a) the triumphant victory for the miners;

(b) the vindication of joint direct negotiations and victory for the railroad workers, now partially gained and wholly assured;

(c) the magnificent victory for the Textile Workers;

(d) the wage restoration on the part of the United States Steel Corporation and twenty-six other steel and related corporations;

(e) the assurance that the coming congress will contain sufficient intelligent and progressive members to prevent the enactment of reactionary, laborcrushing legislation; and

Whereas, The paramount requirement of all Americans is for a harmonious conduct of industry on the most equitable and the most productive basis which it is now possible to contemplate because of the passing of the militant movement of reaction, be it

Resolved, That the Executive Council of the American Federation of Labor speaking in the name of the organized workers and for the unorganized workers of our country, contemplating with deep satisfaction the victorious efforts of the workers to retain standards of living necessary to American progress, though relaxing no vigilance where vigilance is necessary, believes it opportune to suggest proposals for progressive, constructive effort in the future to the end that every advantage be taken of so much of our effort as may be released from militant defense of progress already gained; and that, in the interests of a better America, a richer life for all, a greater basis for material, mental and spiritual well-being, we propose as follows:

That a Commission of Progress and Co-operation be and is hereby authorized, to be appointed by the President of the American Federation of Labor, by and with the consent of the Executive Council, consisting of ten members who shall be selected from among American trade unionists.

That this commission shall have for its objects the following:

(a) To seek out more effective methods of cooperation between the essential productive human elements in industry—Labor, Management, Engineers, and Scientific organizations.

(b) To seek and so far as possible formulate methods of eliminating waste in industry, that which is due to faulty human relations as well as that which is due to faulty handling of material.

(c) To find and make public the influences which hamper industry, which seek to operate industry merely in the interests of speculation and profit.

(d) To find the facts in relation to all things that make for unrest and for faulty relations in industry and to make public those facts.

(e) To undertake such investigating and educational work as may be found best calculated to enlighten our citizenship as to reasons for the failure to operate our national industrial plants to capacity and to endeavor to bring that operation to capacity.

(f) To endeavor to bring about appointment of similar special commissions by organized management, by Engineering, Technical and Scientific organizations and to seek to promote a cooperative relationship between the Trade Union Commission and such other commissions as have been here indicated.

And be it further

Resolved: That our purpose in taking this action is to promote production with justice, to enhance the value of human effort, to realize to the highest for all of the masses of our people on the good will and the energy and initiative of our people, and finally to inspire all Americans with the trade union ideal of service, the highest ideal that can be implanted in our industrial life. Because we have resisted unwarranted encroachment, because we have stood fast against a tremendous effort to crush our organizations, and to restore autocracy in industry because the industrial sky is now clearing, with the autocrats, the exploiters, the backward looking and the ignorant defeated in their unpatriotic purposes, we feel it now possible to turn our eyes toward the future for the improvement of our whole industrial fabric and all that it means to the life of our people.

It was moved that the document be considered seriatim. This motion was lost by a vote of three in favor to five against. It was moved and seconded to adopt the document as read.

President Gompers requested to withdraw the words "most able" before "American trade unionists."

President Gompers: Technical societies were dominated by Taylor and Emerson[1] who brought into prominence for a period of years the so-called scientific management based upon the stop watch system. To all that we are opposed, the American Federation of Labor deserves the honor of having practically destroyed the so-called stop watch system and prevented its being advocated by the Engineers. It was through our position that the system gained no further headway in the industrial countries of Europe. We stopped it so far as governmental activities in industry are concerned; we checked it, and in addition we have converted the most influential engineers of our country against that system, because it failed to take into consideration the human equation in industry. Our opposition indicated the fallacies of the system and pointed the way to sound methods.

It has been my pleasure to have conferences with the leading industrial engineers of our country. I had the honor of an invitation which I accepted, to deliver an address before the annual conference of the American Association of Mechanical Engineers held in the Engineers' Building in New York City.[2] I delivered my address. It was a prepared paper. The speakers following who were the leading engineers, agreed entirely with the position of the American Federation of Labor which I expressed there in regard to the old time system which left out the human equation in industry. Every speaker on that occasion followed with the endorsement of my position. Later the Federated American Engineering Societies adopted a program outlining a position far in advance of the old time Taylor and Emerson system of so-called scientific management and in opposition to the fundamentals of the old school of thought. That is now the dominating association of engineers and their position on this issue is the position of the American Federation of Labor.

The first undertaking of the F.A.E.S. was a study of Waste in Industry, carried out by a committee of fifteen appointed by Herbert Hoover, then president of the organization.[3] After determining various wastes in a number of the more important industries, the committee allocated responsibility as follows: over 50 percent of waste in industry is due to management, 25 percent or less is due to labor, and the other 25 percent is outside elements, largely management in other industries.

In the President's Unemployment Conference I was a member of the Committee on Manufactures. Mrs. Sara Conboy[4] served with me. On that committee were some of the largest manufacturers in America. I proposed that the committee recommend to the Conference as a basic step in stabilizing employment, that management assume responsibility for the industrial waste allocated to it by the engineers, and that labor assume its due responsibility and develop plans for eliminating the causes of waste—all for the great advantage of the business and the people of America. The manufacturers on the committee rejected my proposal because it attributed to them over 50 percent of waste in industry. They were unwilling to admit that or have it officially recorded against their management.

I submitted an additional suggestion so that the records of management efficiency might be more readily available: uniform cost accounting and publicity for production records. This I pointed out was the only alternate to state regulation and control. This also was rejected by the employer members of my committee.

There must be opportunity for progressive evolution within industry, won by ourselves by our economic power, or else we must deal with revolution. The constructive method is based upon cooperation to work out better methods, followed by intelligent acceptance of results through mutual agreements. There has been long in my mind a thought that there ought to be annual or biennial gatherings of representatives of international unions of the same industrial group with the employers in that group for the consideration and determination for some period of time as to conditions in the industry, not including wages, except as the demands of the workers for improvement in their conditions. That has developed in my mind into something broader. We have always declared, and it has been a deep-seated conviction with us, that the worst feature of political government is its efforts to deal with economic and social problems. Constitutional government of any country, whether monarchical, whether imperial, even of our Republic, was inaugurated with the movement in Great Britain which resulted in Magna Charta where there was wrung from an unwilling monarch the establishment of an agency for defining and maintaining rights political, rights of the people, with the people, the subjects, which were denied theretofore. That was secured. It was the emancipation of the British people from that old concept that the King could do no wrong, that the people had no rights other than what the government conceded to them.

The democratic concept of government is that it is not the government that concedes rights to the people but that the people concede powers to the government. The participation of the people in the affairs of the government was followed by processes which are not necessary here to enumerate, of the colonies in America which developed into the assertion of the political rights of the people. The severance from the mother country was necessary, self-expression, self-determination, self-government and all of them you will find in the political affairs of the people of the country, and this was necessary. The great war was to destroy for all time any attempt for European domination of autocracy or political autocracy, and all these things are natural developments in the history of the human family, and that in my judgment has been pretty well established now.

I have had in mind in my long years of life and experience the hope and yearning for the time that I could express what I have in mind. I think you know that no man has fought harder against socialist philosophy and sophistry than I have. Everyone has done his share and I think I have a right to say that no one has done more to fight that theory and I think I have been and am as insistently opposed to company unions, shop unions and all that sort of thing.

Since the Republic has been established in Germany, since the war and opportunities of the war, there has grown up a system which I ought to relate. There has been created and developed into the best form up to the present time a Chamber, called I think, the Economic Congress of Germany. They have no power to inaugurate legislation but they have the power and the right to discuss in all its forms their economic condition and relations and they have the power to recommend laws which ought to be enacted in the interest of industrial and commercial life of the people.

The Reichstag being purely a political body is exceedingly jealous of this body, in which organized labor is represented with employers, business men, a few scientists, the profession of law, medicine, surgery. The Reichstag of Germany is exceedingly jealous of that new constitutional body for in that body must be discussed all of the economic and sociological problems and the Reichstag is forbidden to discuss these things before they have had the consideration of this national Economic Chamber. The discussions in this Chamber are so broad and comprehensive that when the subjects recommended by that body reach the Reichstag any discussion in the Reichstag discloses that the subject has been thrashed out ably by the best minds of the working people, scientific and professional men, and that there is nothing new for the Reichstag to bring into it. The Reichstag of Germany has lost its prestige. The members of the Reichstag are elected by districts regardless of any knowledge or interest in industrial or commercial affairs and this Chamber is made up of the representatives of the working people and the other groups. In other words, it is an attempt to bring about a further development of the rights of the Fourth Estate, industry, commerce, by people who know and who are interested. There come to me reports from Germany—I have two correspondents[5] who are unknown to each other but I think they are most able men, who are competent to deal with the subjects of industry and commerce in that country—and they inform me that it has brought new relations, new progress, new thoughts.

The Republic of Germany has been organized now for about four years and they have no preconceived notions as to legendary obstacles which stand in the way of their determining what they want to do. Our Republic, in existence now nearly one hundred and fifty years, has had its constitution and its constitution is the political constitution of the United States. Because of their starting with the experience of other nations, ours included, they have started upon a new line, a line in which the knowledge of industrial and commercial conditions is the dominating influence of the German people.

I fancy that we will agree that although this is the greatest Republic on the face of the earth, that conditions must necessarily take some change so that the industrial affairs of our country and our people will receive greater consideration at the hands of those who are in authority to speak for the people. I have in mind that at least the working people of the United States organized in the movement which leads in industrial affairs and ought to lead in industrial affairs, shall take an initial step so that voluntarily there shall develop an idea that men and women most intensely and vitally interested shall come together and try to devise the ways and means by which agreement can be reached, so that the rights of the men and women engaged in all phases of our industrial and professional life shall be the determining factor, rather than the politicians who know nothing of our problems.

I shall help in cooperating in the idea and the work so that voluntarily we shall come to the position where cooperation may be secured. I am under the impression that the creation of such a commission as recommended in the resolution will be one of the great contributory causes for the progress and the triumph of American life and of the Republic.

I submit this resolution as a way to the accomplishment of this industrial cooperation. As to the details that is nothing. If you think the number is too large, why reduce it. We shall always be independent and able to break away.

President Gompers stated that he felt the action of the representatives of the organized workers of the railroads, the action of President Lewis of the Mine Workers in declining to arbitrate and declining governmental agencies to determine conditions of the Miners, was a splendid strategic course, a breaking away from governmental agencies imposing themselves upon labor of which they know nothing.

An amendment was offered to the motion that because of the importance of the subject requiring further consideration at the hands of the Executive Council that consideration of the subject be deferred until our next meeting.

Adopted.[6]

. . .

TDc, Executive Council Records, Minutes, reel 7, frames 1184–87, *AFL Records.*

1. Harrington Emerson (1853–1931), a leading proponent of efficiency in the workplace, argued that efficient production could emerge naturally and organically with good leadership, flexible organization, standardized tools, and interdependence and cooperation among workers. He was the author of *Twelve Principles of Efficiency* (1913), and in 1921 he served on Herbert Hoover's Committee on Elimination of Waste in Industry.

2. A reference to SG's address at the fortieth anniversary meeting of the American Society of Mechanical Engineers in New York City, Nov. 5, 1920 (see Files of the Office of the President, Speeches and Writings, reel 115, frames 273–77, *AFL Records*).

3. The report, *Waste in Industry,* was published in 1921 by the Committee on Elimination of Waste in Industry of the Federated American Engineering Societies. The federation was founded in November 1920.

4. Sara Agnes McLaughlin CONBOY served as secretary-treasurer of the United Textile Workers of America from 1915 to 1928.

5. William English Walling and L. Krause, a resident of Leipzig, whose articles appeared in the *American Federationist.*

6. The AFL Executive Council discussed the proposal at its subsequent meetings until SG, lacking unanimous support for the measure, finally withdrew it in May 1923.

To B. M. Jewell

Sept. 19, 1922.

Mr. B. M. Jewell,
President, Railway Employes Department, A.F. of L.,
Riviera Bldg., 4750 Broadway, Chicago, Illinois.

Dear Sir and Brother:

Of course you have been exceedingly busy, but more than likely you have seen in the newspapers the declaration of the Executive Council of the American Federation of Labor which was made in connection with the Railway Shopmen's strike, and the injunction and the impeachment proceedings[1] against Attorney-General Daugherty.

Acting upon the directions of the Executive Council I prepared and had printed yesterday and put in the mails, a circular to all organized labor.[2] Enclosed you will find a copy. I also telegraphed to our legislative committee to put in appearance last Saturday before the Judiciary Committee when a hearing was had on the impeachment proceedings and our committee submitted a statement that we desired to have the opportunity of appearing before the committee for a hearing either on my own account or by counsel.[3] Notice was taken of it and an order entered for my hearing today. However, yesterday the committee decided to defer consideration of the hearings until after the elections, that is, early in December.[4]

You know that there were several resolutions passed by a number of organizations calling upon me to issue a call for a general strike and also calling upon the Executive Council to order a general strike. Of course you know that no such power or right is vested in the E.C. or myself. You and your associates exercised your best judgment in not making such a request or suggestion. However, the Executive Council took such cognizance of the situation as was necessary and adopted the following declaration:

"The Executive Council declared that neither it nor any officer of the American Federation of Labor has either the right or power to call or advise a general strike."

I may say that the circulars and the appeal have been sent broadcast throughout the organized labor movement of America.

With the best of good wishes and hopes for success, I am

Fraternally yours, Saml Gompers.
President, American Federation of Labor.

TLpS, reel 283, vol. 296, pp. 457–58, SG Letterbooks, DLC.

1. On Sept. 11, 1922, Republican congressman Oscar Keller of Minnesota presented a list of charges against Attorney General Harry Daugherty in the House of Representatives, accusing him of failing to prosecute antitrust violations, recommending release from prison of several men convicted of infractions of the Sherman Act, and infringing on freedoms of press, speech, and assembly with the injunction against the railroad shopmen. The House Committee on the Judiciary took testimony from Dec. 12 to 21, and on Jan. 9, 1923, recommended dismissing the charges because of lack of evidence. On Jan. 25 the House approved the committee's report.

2. "To All Organized Labor," Sept. 18, 1922, Executive Council Records, Vote Books, reel 17, frame 370, *AFL Records*.

3. On Sept. 16, 1922, AFL Legislative Committee member Edward McGrady appeared before the House Committee on the Judiciary to ask that the AFL be heard in the Daugherty impeachment case.

4. When the Judiciary Committee met on Sept. 16, 1922, Keller was unprepared to

present evidence and asked for time to prepare his case. The hearings resumed when Congress met in December, and SG testified on Dec. 13. For SG's testimony, see U.S. Congress, House, *Charges of Hon. Oscar E. Keller against the Attorney General of the United States. Hearings before the Committee on the Judiciary, House of Representatives . . . on H.Res. 425,* 67th Cong., 3d and 4th sess., 1922, pp. 171–77.

To Jerome Jones

Sept. 25, 1922

Mr. Jerome Jones,
Organizer, American Federation of Labor,
321 Austell Building, Atlanta, Georgia.
Dear Sir and Brother:—
Continuing my letter to you of September thirteenth,[1] I beg to advise you that I am in receipt of a letter from President B. M. Jewell of the Railway Employes Department of the American Federation of Labor in which he says:—
"Your letter of the 13th inst.,[2] relative to Organizer Jerome Jones' letter to you about the colored workers in the railroad service, has been duly received and noted. In reply want to advise that the Blacksmiths take the colored helpers into their organization by giving them an auxiliary local. The Carmen's[3] organization take the colored helpers into an auxiliary or local of their own. The Boilermakers do not take the colored helpers in their organization, but claim the right to legislate for the colored helpers on any matter pertaining to work that the Boilermakers claim jurisdiction over. The Sheet Metal Workers,[4] Electricians[5] and Machinists do not take the colored helpers into their organizations."
With kind regards and hoping to hear from you whenever convenient, I am,

Fraternally yours,   Saml Gompers
President,   American Federation of Labor.

TLpS, reel 283, vol. 296, p. 696, SG Letterbooks, DLC.

1. SG to Jerome Jones, Sept. 13, 1922, reel 283, vol. 296, p. 291, SG Letterbooks, DLC.
2. SG to B. M. Jewell, Sept. 13, 1922, reel 283, vol. 296, p. 290, SG Letterbooks, DLC.
3. The Brotherhood of Railway Carmen of America.
4. The Amalgamated Sheet Metal Workers' International Alliance.
5. The International Brotherhood of Electrical Workers.

To William Rubin

Sept. 25, 1922.

Mr. W. B. Rubin,
First National Bank Building, Milwaukee, Wisconsin.
Dear Sir and Brother:

Your telegram of August 24th[1] referring to my proposed visit to Wisconsin to help in the success of Senator LaFollette in the primaries could not be answered at that time for reasons which you will understand.

I was willing to go to Wisconsin,—anxious to go, and try to help in the success of Senator LaFollette's re-election; as evidence of it I had organizer Paul J. Smith go into Wisconsin and he has done such work as to meet with the entire approval of organized labor. I wrote to our organizer to confer with the representative labor men of Wisconsin as to the time and cities where I could speak.[2] He had the conference, and in that conference they committed an unpardonable blunder; they sent a man to consult with Victor Berger, the man who bears me greater enmity than any other man I know, and supposedly in confidence, asked his advice as to my coming to Wisconsin to speak for Senator LaFollette's re-election.

Instead of regarding this matter confidentially, he did, as under the circumstances I knew he would, that is, he wrote and published an editorial, vitriolic and vicious, against me and against the American Federation of Labor, and stated that if I came to Wisconsin to speak it would simply defeat Senator LaFollette's re-election.[3]

The only deduction is that if I went to Wisconsin and it should happen that Senator LaFollette was defeated, Berger and his gang would attribute the defeat to me; that if LaFollette be elected he would assert that I made no contribution to that result.

It is not a question of Berger's influence or the influence of his paper. I care little for that. But it is quite true that if one throws mud often enough in the minds of the people, some of it will stick.

While it is true that Senator LaFollette's re-election in November is absolutely certain there should not be one iota of let-up in an aggressive campaign to that end.

During the primary campaign not only did I assign Organizer Paul J. Smith to aid in every possible way in Senator La Follette's campaign for the nomination or organized labor's campaign for the nomination of Senator La Follette, but I was in constant touch with organized labor of the state and it may be interesting for you to know that I received a

splendid telegram from Senator La Follette expressing his appreciation and gratitude for the services which I rendered to him in that
campaign.

With best wishes and assuring you of my desire to be helpful in any
way within my power, I am

Fraternally yours,   Saml Gompers
President,   American Federation of Labor.

TLpS, reel 283, vol. 296, pp. 787–88, SG Letterbooks, DLC.

1. William Rubin to SG, Aug. 24, 1922, William B. Rubin Papers, WHi.
2. SG to Paul Smith, Aug. 1, 1922, reel 282, vol. 295, p. 38, SG Letterbooks, DLC.
3. See "An Editorial by Victor Berger," Aug. 5, 1922, above.

From John L. Lewis

John L. Lewis, President
United Mine Workers of America
Indianapolis, Indiana
Leland Hotel, Springfield, Illinois, September 30, 1922.

Dear Sir and Brother: ·

Permit me to acknowledge receipt of your letter of September 18th[1]
with respect to the employment of Mr. James Lord,[2] former President
of the Mining Department, as a salaried organizer of the American
Federation of Labor.

You are, of course, aware that Mr. Lord esteems himself to be not
only a personal enemy of mine but one who is entirely out of accord
with the policies of the United Mine Workers of America. Notwithstanding this fact, while I was in attendance at the Cincinnati convention of the American Federation of Labor I learned that plans were
afoot to provide Mr. Lord with an appointment on the official staff
of the Federation, and that this was to be done at the meeting of the
Executive Council which would follow the adjournment of the convention.[3] I was, therefore, not surprised when Secretary Green later
informed me of the action of the Council in authorizing the employment of Mr. Lord under the guise of a temporary appointment. Secretary Green told me then, as you now advise, that the appointment
was for a period of three months only, after which time I was to be
permitted as President of the United Mine Workers to express my approval or disapproval of the action. I advised Secretary Green then,
as I now advise you, that I resented such action. I recognize of course
that it was impossible for the Council to consult me on the question

at that time, because of the possible danger of my refusing to endorse Mr. Lord, which would have wrecked the plans as then prepared. I am now called upon after Mr. Lord has been in service for three months or more, has moved his family to the Pacific Coast at a great expense, and has given eminent satisfaction, as you suggest, to approve or disapprove his employment.

I have no desire to embarrass Mr. Lord in any material way. Did I possess such desire, I would have recommended to the Executive Board of the United Mine Workers the withdrawal of our union from the Mining Department several years ago, because as a matter of fact the Mining Department under the Presidency of Mr. Lord was of no constructive value and the tax paid into it by the United Mine Workers represented a sheer waste of funds. By the same token, I do not now have any desire to ruthlessly separate Mr. Lord from a lucrative position which has been secured for him, despite the fact that he had not received the endorsement of his own organization. I prefer to give him ample time to recoup himself for the extraordinary expense to which he has been put in transferring his lares and penates[4] to the state of California. At the same time I am hopeful that the day will come within the not far distant future when the Executive Council of the American Federation of Labor will refrain from following out its seemingly consistent policy of appointing members of the United Mine Workers who are avowed enemies of the President thereof and in public opposition to its proclaimed policies.[5]

I do not herein venture to make any request of yourself or of the Executive Council. It has been brought home to me through rather painful experience that a request of myself as President of the International Union, or a request of the Executive Board of the United Mine Workers of America, does not weigh very heavily with the members of the Executive Council. If, however, conditions were more nearly what they should be, I would ask that no further appointments be made by the President of the American Federation of Labor of any members of the United Mine Workers unless such individuals are endorsed by the President of the International Executive Board. In the event that at any time there is opportunity for the employment of members of the United Mine Workers on the official staff of the Federation, I assure you that we have in our ranks a large list of eligibles eminently capable and loyal to their union whom we would be glad to recommend for your consideration.

Very truly yours,　　(signed) John L. Lewis,
President.

TLtcSr, Executive Council Records, Vote Books, reel 17, frames 400–401, *AFL Records*. Typed notation: "*Copy.*"

1. SG to John L. Lewis, Sept. 18, 1922, reel 283, vol. 296, p. 362, SG Letterbooks, DLC.

2. James LORD was president of the AFL Mining Department from 1914 to 1922 and treasurer of the Pan-American Federation of Labor from 1918 to 1924.

3. The AFL Executive Council met in Cincinnati, following the convention, on June 25, 1922.

4. Roman household gods. As used here, the phrase refers to household possessions.

5. SG did not extend Lord's three-month appointment as a salaried AFL organizer.

An Excerpt from the Minutes of a Meeting between Attorneys for the Railroad Shopmen and Representatives of the AFL, Affiliated Unions, and the Railroad Brotherhoods[1]

October 2, 1922

. . .

Attorney Mulholland[2] explained the reason for the attorneys being in Washington. He said that he had made arrangements in Chicago to meet Attorney General Daugherty for the purpose of expediting the hearing on the injunction issued by Judge Wilkerson[3] so that an appeal could be made to the Supreme Court. He said that Judge Wilkerson was favorable. When the attorneys of the shopmen reached the Attorney General's office they found no one present to meet them. Assistant Attorney General Beck[4] with whom they managed to secure an interview, said he could not do anything; that he would inform the attorney general of their presence in the city and would report to them the next morning whether a meeting for the purpose indicated could be held. He said that the attorneys for the unions did not want to go up to the Supreme Court on an interlocutory decree. They could only go to the court of appeals where the case might be heard on its merits. He said that the attorney general made the date for the meeting referred to. He was not only not there but left no word. He added: "The Attorney General knew we were here. He telegraphed Mr. Richberg's[5] office that he would meet him at 4 P.M. October 8. Not only was he not there but no one else."

Attorney Mulholland then went on further to explain the case. He said that, first, they could try it on its merits. Second, to cross examine the witnesses who had made depositions and thus widen the scope of the hearings. He charged bad faith on the part of the Attorney General. "We were to ask this be heard immediately by Judge Wilkerson."

Attorney Richberg told of being called up by Attorney Untermyer, whom he met in the Blackstone Hotel in Chicago. He said: "Attorney Untermyer said it was important to get a decree from the United States Supreme Court. He suggested that we get the Attorney General to stipulate that the affidavits obtained by the government should be accepted as depositions without cross examination or reply. Then let the court enter final decision so it would go immediately to the Supreme Court. Untermyer said he was well acquainted with Assistant Attorney General Beck and he could bring it up."

He then went on to say that Judge Wilkerson had passed on the affidavits and if Attorney Untermyer's suggestion failed it would simply mean that the Supreme Court would uphold Judge Wilkerson by finding the defendants guilty of a criminal conspiracy on the ground that the strikers could not do lawful acts to carry out unlawful conspiracies. He said he felt that a determined effort was being made to place the shopmen in a fight for their constitutional rights. This would sacrifice the most important defense to the charge of a conspiracy to do an unlawful act. He added: "We desire to see Mr. Daugherty in order to urge that the case be left to three judges and go from the three judges to the Supreme Court. The veiled threat was made to go to a final hearing and take evidence all over the country."

President Gompers then spoke of the Coronada case. He said: "It is not difficult to imagine that the Supreme Court will go to any lengths to approve of the decisions of Judge Wilkerson. I expressed myself to Mr. Jewell in a telegram[6] in which I urged that the shopmen challenge the jurisdiction of the court and rest on that. Or, to ignore the injunction entirely."

Attorney Richberg said that when the argument was made that the court had no jurisdiction the court took it under advisement and did not decide until the final day when he issued the injunction. The judge in his first decision had ruled out certain affidavits. Attorney Richberg continued: "We considered whether we should withdraw before the court had decided, but felt that it would leave a bad impression on the public because we felt organized Labor could not flout the court."

President Gompers interjected: "If you had remained passive during all the proceedings, holding in reserve all other objections until the decision was made would that not have been effective?"

Attorney Richter[7] replied: "When the order was under consideration we refused to suggest any form of order and contended that the proceedings were illegal."

"The court held" said Mulholland "that notwithstanding the claims of the defense the injunction would lie."

Mr. Richberg—The court refused to declare the strike an unlawful conspiracy from the start. It was what occurred after the strike that was claimed to be an unlawful conspiracy.

Mr. Gompers—You cannot afford to bring the case to the Supreme Court on affidavits unchallenged and unanswered. As the illegal act of issuing the injunction would not be up for consideration then all would devolve upon the court proceedings. The Court of Appeals in Illinois is made up of men of broad vision who have thrown injunctions out of court. They are Judges Alscheuler, Baker[8] and Evans.[9] I do not know what the time and expense would be but is it not worth a thought to take an appeal to that court of appeals?

Mr. Richberg—If the Attorney General cites the case as a public measure it would go to those three judges. If the Attorney General has to take the record, digest it and print two million words, the delay will be a matter of weeks. The Attorney General is blocking our request.

Mr. Mulholland—If we get a hearing before Judge Wilkerson we can go direct to the Supreme Court, but if we go to the Court of Appeals it will end there if the decision is against us. I am in favor of going before Judge Wilkerson and demand a hearing. It can be made such a gigantic affair that it would be impossible to hear it. Affidavits were presented in bunches of hundreds and the great bulk of them were made against persons unknown. It will be impossible to bring in either the persons who made the affidavits or those charged with illegal acts. The case would fade away if called.

Mr. Gompers—I cannot advise what you should do but I agree with you that you cannot go to the Supreme Court on these depositions. The Supreme Court has held picketing to be lawful.

Mr. Mulholland—Yes, but not in carrying out a conspiracy.

Mr. Richberg—We have told the men to go ahead in an orderly way in carrying on the strike. If they call us into court we will be ready for them.

Mr. Gompers—The time will come when going to jail will be a badge of honor.

Mr. Richberg—If they are sent to jail now it will be a badge of honor. The object is to break the strike but it is going on.

Mr. Gompers—When the working people feel the necessity of protesting they will strike, injunction or no injunction. The Executive Council of the American Federation of Labor at its last session decided we should press proceedings of the impeachment against Attorney General Daugherty and Judge Wilkerson if his decision is with the Attorney General. The Attorney General is in so bad with other matters that he may be driven from office by public opinion.[10] I intend to invite a conference[11] of attorneys and representatives of the American Federation of Labor to go over this matter and see what can be done. Also to consider some means of relief. I do not want any group of individuals to act independently of the American Federation of Labor. We should all be united.

Mr. Mulholland—I would hate to hear that we had not acted in accord with the American Federation of Labor. You cannot pussyfoot this situation. My thought was to scrap the whole process and go to jail. My idea was to get rid of the injunction. If the decision is against the shopmen, the 400,000 should immediately go forth with the determination to do all things lawful.

Mr. Easby-Smith[12]—I will help to get the Attorney General out. I did help in having Federal Judge Wright[13] removed from office.

Mr. Richberg—The injunction order has not been served on any one yet.

Mr. Mulholland said that they would see Assistant Attorney General Beck again the following morning and would let President Gompers know the result of the conference.

The meeting then broke up.

TDc, AFL Microfilm Convention File, reel 32, frame 1354, *AFL Records.* Typed notation: "Conference Held October 2, 1922 between the Attorneys for the Railroad Organizations and Representatives of the American Federation of Labor and Affiliated Organizations to Consider the Injunction Secured by Atty. General Daugherty from Judge Wilkerson."

1. The meeting was attended by SG, his secretary Guy Oyster, and Frank Morrison, attorneys for the shopmen, and representatives from the AFL Legislative Committee, Building Trades, Metal Trades, Union Label Trades, and Publicity departments, the railroad brotherhoods, and several unions.

2. Frank Mulholland.

3. James Herbert Wilkerson (1869–1948) served as a U.S. district court judge for the Northern District of Illinois from 1922 until his death in 1948.

4. James Beck.

5. Donald Randall Richberg (1881–1960), a Chicago attorney who served as chief counsel for the railway and shop craft unions in the injunction case, was later counsel for the Railway Labor Executives' Association (1926–33) and for the National Recovery Administration (1933–35).

6. Probably SG to B. M. Jewell, Sept. 2, 1922, reel 283, vol. 296, pp. 111–13, SG Letterbooks, DLC.

7. This should read Richberg, not Richter.

8. Francis Elisha Baker (1860–1924) served as a judge on the U.S. Court of Appeals for the Seventh Circuit from 1902 until his death in 1924.

9. Evan Alfred Evans (1876–1948) served as a judge on the U.S. Court of Appeals for the Seventh Circuit from 1916 until his death in 1948.

10. SG is referring to the widespread criticism of Attorney General Harry Daugherty for his failure to prosecute corruption cases involving war contracts.

11. The conference was held on Nov. 20, 1922.

12. James Stanislaus Easby-Smith (1870–1948) was a Washington, D.C., attorney.

13. For the investigation of Daniel Wright on the grounds of official misconduct and moral turpitude, and his subsequent resignation, see *The Samuel Gompers Papers*, vol. 9, p. 106, n. 6.

From Fannia Cohn

Educational Department of the
International Ladies' Garment Workers' Union[1]
New York October 10, 1922.

My dear President Gompers:

Since my return from Europe, I have been hoping that I might be able to see you and relate to you my experiences as a delegate of the Workers' Education Bureau[2] to the First International Conference on Workers' Education.[3] But as I am very busy preparing the educational activities of our International Union, I feel that it will probably take some time before I will be able to see you. And, on the advice of your secretary,[4] I am writing this letter to you.

It is needless to say that Europe is ruined. Everybody realizes now that there is no "victor" and that all sides lost in this terrible calamity of 1914–18. Everywhere one notices exhaustion, indifference and despair. There is hardly any display of energy. The middle classes, who were always a great factor in European civilization, admit moral and financial bankruptcy. They lack a leadership with vision. At present, the leaders in power are persons who care nothing for the future of Europe,—not even for the future of their own capitalist class,—and concern themselves only with the immediate interest of groups. It prevents them even from forming an international policy. It seems as if Europe expects a miracle, a supreme man who will come and make over their house and prevent its complete collapse. Many of the representatives of the middle class admitted that the Trade Unions and the Socialist Organizations are the ones that show the greatest promise of vigor and vitality. If only they could join forces for united action, their power is unlimited. It seems as if the ruling classes of Europe will be forced voluntarily to "abdicate" their reign and give way to the workers.

Everywhere in Europe I heard complaints against America. In Germany they tell you that if it had not been for President Wilson's 14 points, the battle would have been fought on the Rhineland and with

different results. That now America has left them to the discretion
of the French, their historical enemy. In the Allied countries there
are complaints too. They say that America came into the war [at] the
last minute, forced a peace upon them and then deserted ruined Europe, unwilling to take part in the reconstruction of these devastated
countries.

The more progressive elements and the Labor Movement think that
if America suggested to the Reparation Commission the cancellation
of the war debts, provided all the nations disarm, together with a plan
for the re-organization of Europe on a peaceful basis, there will be a
possibility for forward action. If the governments, however, did not
agree to such a plan there would be a popular demand on the part of
the masses for it and then the governments would not dare to resist.

So many with whom I discussed the European situation were of the
opinion that the only hope of Europe is America and especially, the
American Labor Movement. And it seems to me that organized Labor
of America has a chance to perform a historic deed by making a study
of the European situation, there on the spot especially as affecting
Labor, and suggesting a constructive plan.

I wish to say that as a delegate of the Workers' Educational Movement
of America, I tried to acquaint the thirty-six delegates, representing
eleven countries and twenty-three educational activities under workers' auspices, with the problems and aims of the American organized
Labor Movement in the best way I knew how.

I still hope to have a chance to see you and tell you more about what
I saw, heard, observed and experienced during my trip in Europe.

With best personal wishes and kindest greetings,

Sincerely and Fraternally,   Fannia M. Cohn.

TLS, AFL Microfilm National and International Union File, Ladies' Garment
Workers Records, reel 37, frame 2750, *AFL Records.*

1. The International LADIES' Garment Workers' Union.

2. The Workers' Education Bureau of America was organized in 1921 to extend educational opportunities to trade unionists. Headquartered in New York City, it coordi-
nated labor education programs, undertook research, and beginning in 1923 published
a monthly newsletter and a series of pamphlets known as "The Workers' Bookshelf."
In 1922 the AFL Executive Council agreed to cooperate with the bureau and to appoint three members of its executive board, and by 1924 a majority of AFL affiliates
were connected with it. The AFL absorbed the bureau in 1950 as a department of the
Federation and in 1951 officially renamed it the AFL Department of Education.

3. The first International Conference on Workers' Education was held at Uccle, a
suburb of Brussels, Aug. 10–17, 1922.

4. Rosa Lee GUARD, SG's private secretary.

To B. M. Jewell

October 20, 1922

Mr. B. M. Jewell,
President, Railway Employes Department of the A.F. of L.,
4750 Broadway, Riviera Building, Chicago, Illinois.
Dear Sir and Brother:—

This morning I returned from New Orleans[1] where, by direction of the Cincinnati convention of the A.F. of L., I delivered an address to the convention of the American Legion[2] and I also addressed a labor conference in that city. Several days before my departure for New Orleans, I asked for some information regarding the condition of the strike and the situation respecting the injunction proceedings and I received, through the courtesy of Brother Scott,[3] Special Bulletin dated September 30th, 1922[4] and Special Circular dated October 2, 1922.[5] Both documents were read with the keenest interest. They contained the information which I sought.

I am writing to you upon a declaration contained in the Special Bulletin relative to the injunction. Without here discussing any other feature of the injunction sought by Attorney-General Daugherty and issued by Judge Wilkerson, I desire to call your especial attention to the following quotation from your bulletin:

"The Railway Employes Department and their organizations have no objection to any injunction prohibiting unlawful acts."

Of course, no self respecting trade unionist, or other citizen can either justify or excuse the commission of unlawful acts on the part of anyone. On the contrary, such acts must not only be disapproved but frowned down upon and prevented by every means within our power. But, I submit to your consideration this fact, that such an official declaration as above quoted from your bulletin justifies the issuance of any of the injunctions and particularly the injunction issued against the striking railway shopmen. The fact that certain acts are held to be unlawful is to say that there are laws upon the statute books forbidding the performance of such acts and, if there be such laws upon the statute books, as there are, then these unlawful acts should be presented to a grand jury for investigation and if the acts are found to be unlawful, an indictment may be found, the person or persons guilty of the unlawful acts apprehended, placed upon trial before a court and a jury of their peers, and an opportunity given to the defendant or defendants charged with the commission of the unlawful acts, placed face to face with his or their accusers and the innocence or guilt of the defendant or defendants determined by a jury. This procedure is the ordinary course of law, based upon the fundamental guarantees of the constitution of the United States and of the several states. In other words, there is adequate remedy in the law against the commission of unlawful acts and if there be an adequate remedy at law, it is inconceivable how you can, in an official bulletin of the Department, over which you preside, include a declaration that "the Railway Employes' Department and their organizations have no objection to any injunction prohibiting unlawful acts, which was the position of the employes, as stated to the court from the beginning."

Since this has been the position of your department in the injunction proceedings from the beginning, no wonder that the injunction proceedings were against you.

In the letter I addressed to you under date of September 2nd,[6] I endeavored to impress upon the minds of your attorneys the keeping in mind and presenting of the principles involved. At the conference which several labor men and I had the pleasure of having with the attorneys when they were in Washington,[7] the above feature to which I am calling your attention was not disclosed.

It seems to me a duty which I owe to you and to the labor movement, in the cause of justice and freedom, that I must submit the above to your very serious consideration and to the serious consideration of your associates as well as your counsel.

Both you, Secretary Scott and others, who have communicated with me by mail, telegram, or orally, have done me the honor of saying that I have rendered some service to you and their cause in this great struggle and I feel not only warranted, but I feel it a compelling duty to submit the above to you and your associates and counsel, for further consideration.

Assuring you of my earnest desire to be further helpful in any way within my power, and with best wishes, I am,

Fraternally yours, Saml Gompers
President, American Federation of Labor.

TLpS, reel 284, vol. 297, pp. 590–91, SG Letterbooks, DLC.

1. SG left Washington, D.C., on the evening of Oct. 14, 1922, met briefly with organizer Jerome Jones in Atlanta on Oct. 15, and arrived in New Orleans on Oct. 16, where he addressed the convention of the American Legion, met with local labor representatives, and had a conference with Judge Kenesaw Mountain Landis. He met again with Jones in Atlanta on Oct. 19 and had returned to AFL headquarters by the morning of Oct. 20.

2. The 1922 American Legion convention met in New Orleans, Oct. 16–20; SG addressed the convention on Oct. 17. For a transcript of his remarks, see Files of the Office of the President, Speeches and Writings, reel 117, frames 620–31, *AFL Records*.

3. John SCOTT, secretary-treasurer of the AFL Railway Employes' Department from 1912 to 1926.

4. That is, the AFL Railway Employes' Department's "Special Bulletin" of Sept. 30, 1922. For a copy of the document, see Executive Council Records, Vote Books, reel 17, frames 407–9, *AFL Records*.

5. That is, the AFL Railway Employes' Department's "Special Circular," Oct. 2, 1922. For a copy of the document, see Executive Council Records, Vote Books, reel 17, frames 409–11, *AFL Records*.

6. SG to B. M. Jewell, Sept. 2, 1922, reel 283, vol. 296, pp. 111–13, SG Letterbooks, DLC.

7. See "An Excerpt from the Minutes of a Meeting between Attorneys for the Railroad Shopmen and Representatives of the AFL, Affiliated Unions, and the Railroad Brotherhoods," Oct. 2, 1922, above.

To Frank Bohn

October 28, 1922.

Mr. Frank Bohn,
362 Riverside Drive, New York, N.Y.
Dear Mr. Bohn:

Your letter reached me Wednesday, just before I left for Indianapolis.[1] I read it with the deepest interest and I am deeply appreciative of the keeness of your feeling as regards the political situation. So that you may understand that we have not been unresponsive to the needs and the demands of the situation, I want to tell you briefly some of the things we have been trying to do, trying to the best of our ability with the very limited means with which to conduct any campaign.

The American Federation of Labor has not labored under any delusions as to the reactionary policies governing the present administration which includes congress and the supreme court.

In December 1922, by authority and direction of the Executive Council, circular letters[2] were sent to all state federations and city central bodies warning the wage earners of the country of the reactionary forces that were guiding legislation. All organizations were urged to appoint legislative committees to keep a record of the votes on measures of interest to labor of members of their respective state legislatures. These committees were advised that during the present campaign they could become non-partisan political campaign committees to further the interests of Labor and the people. They were also informed that the records of all members of congress in their respective states or districts would be sent them when the campaign opened.

March 8 last, circular letters[3] were sent to all state federations of labor and city central bodies in which it was urged that all municipal and state non-partisan political campaign committees should become more active than ever before. They were advised to hold mass meetings and to confer with farmer and other organizations of liberty loving people for the purpose of acting in harmony on election day.

April 4 another circular[4] was addressed to all organizations of labor informing them that it was vital to the protection of Labor's interest and welfare that a vigorous campaign be conducted to place in the national congress and the state legislatures men who, without regard to party affiliation, would serve the dictates of justice and not the autocratic domination of the exploiting interests. This was followed by a circular[5] being sent to all organizations of Labor on May 1 calling attention to the fact that every energy should be used in the primaries to nominate members of congress and the state legislatures who believed in progress and even-handed justice. Encouraging reports were received from many of these committees.

On July 29, a special circular[6] was sent to nearly 40,000 non-partisan political campaign committees outlining what should be done to make the campaign a success and in which they were urged to give as wide publicity as possible to the following principles:

"No freedom loving citizen should vote for any candidate who will not pledge himself to oppose any form of compulsory labor law;

"No justice loving citizen should vote for any candidate for any office who will not pledge himself to oppose injunctions and contempt proceedings as a substitute for trial by jury;

"No freedom loving citizen should vote for any candidate who will not pledge himself to vote for legislation abolishing child labor."

This agitation began to show encouraging results. Up to August 14 eighteen states had held their primaries and the outcome in the main were most encouraging for the cause of Labor and the people.

August 14 and 24 additional circulars were sent to organizers of the American Federation of Labor and of its various departments. These directed the organizers to visit the various central bodies and local unions and inform them of the dangers ahead if the wage earners were not awakened.

During September the individual records of every member of the United States Senate and House of Representatives was brought down to date and sent to all central bodies and the nearly 40,000 local unions in the respective states and districts.[7] A circular was prepared for each state which was also sent to all central bodies and local unions. This circular pointed out the legislation which reaction had prepared for passage in the coming session of congress. It also called especial attention to the attitude toward Labor of certain members of the Senate.[8]

During the primary campaigns organizers were sent into North Dakota, Minnesota, Wisconsin and other states to help nominate those who would help restore congress to the people. At the present time 2,183 organizers of the American Federation of Labor are at work in every state urging the election of those who it is believed will be true to the people and the defeat of those who have proved their unworthiness.

The Publicity Department of the American Federation of Labor also has been very active in sending out vast quantities of literature containing information that would be of value to those who are earnestly seeking the truth about the candidates and the issues they represent. I cannot too warmly commend the work it has accomplished.

You will forgive me if, in order to give you the information you desire, I say a few words about my own activities. Of course, such a campaign must be directed along the proper lines. Besides my part in outlining what should be done I have visited many cities in the past year, held many conferences with representatives of Labor and discussed what would be the best to do to defeat reaction.

I have made a number of addresses, among them one in New Orleans before the American Legion convention. I found the delegates to that convention very receptive and felt very much elated over the warmth and enthusiasm shown for the hopes and aspirations of Labor.

Before the election I expect to make several speeches, especially in New York City and New Haven, Connecticut.[9] At the same time I have written numerous articles for the *American Federationist* bearing upon the political situation and the necessity for the people to safeguard their interests by being sure to vote only for those who, by their past record, would faithfully carry out the wishes of the people.

Many public statements have been issued by me through the press, the last entitled "*The Bugle Call,*" a copy of which you will find enclosed. It will be republished in the November issue of the *American Federationist.*[10]

In order that you may see the kind of literature that has been sent to the various organizations, I am also enclosing a number of circulars.

Besides the work done at the headquarters all members of the Executive Council have been very active in pressing upon the attention of the people the issues at stake. Nine members of the Executive Council are executives of international unions and are located in various parts of the country. Their work during the campaign has been invaluable. The organizers of their respective organizations have also given as much of their time as possible to the spreading of knowledge among the voters.

You know that the past few years has been very strenuous, especially the last, for Labor. What has been done in the non-partisan political agitation has been in addition to the usual work necessary for the economic advancement of the wage earners. This has been unusually heavy.

What you say about the almost total disappearance of the third party movement is true. It is because of this fact I hope and believe with all my being that the pendulum will swing from reaction and toward progress. It cannot be possible that the people are asleep to the wrongs being perpetrated or that they will be so remiss in this most crucial time to remain away from the polls, or, if they go to the polls, vote against their own interests.

I am very glad you wrote the letter you did. After reading my answer you will see that what you have suggested has already been done, but not to the extent we wished owing to conditions beyond our control as previously stated.

Rest assured that I am not unmindful of the effect on the 1924 campaign the result of the present elections will have. It will determine whether reaction will be in the saddle or that the progressive people of our country will turn the ship of state again toward progress.

Yours very respectfully, Saml Gompers
President, American Federation of Labor.

TLpS, reel 284, vol. 297, pp. 827–30, SG Letterbooks, DLC.

1. SG left Washington, D.C., for Indianapolis on the afternoon of Oct. 25, 1922. When he arrived there the next morning, he met with Jacob Fischer, Thomas Rickert, and Daniel Tobin in an attempt to mediate a dispute between the United Brotherhood of Carpenters and Joiners of America, the Amalgamated Sheet Metal Workers' International Alliance, and the AFL Building Trades Department. He left Indianapolis on Oct. 27 and arrived back in Washington the following afternoon.

2. Actually 1921. See SG to All Organized Labor, Dec. 29, 1921, printed in AFL, *Proceedings*, 1922, p. 79.

3. SG, Frank Morrison, and James O'Connell to All State Federations of Labor and City Central Bodies, Mar. 8, 1922, printed in AFL, *Proceedings*, 1922, pp. 80–81.

4. SG, Morrison, and O'Connell to All Organized Labor—Greetings, Apr. 4, 1922, printed in AFL, *Proceedings*, 1922, pp. 81–82.

5. SG, Morrison, and O'Connell to All Organized Labor, Greetings, May 1, 1922, reel 280, vol. 293, p. 329, SG Letterbooks, DLC.

6. A copy of the circular from SG, Morrison, and O'Connell to All Labor Non-Partisan Political Campaign Committees, July 29, 1922, can be found in the Minneapolis Central Labor Union Papers, MnHi.

7. Copies of two examples of this circular, SG, Morrison, and O'Connell to the Secretaries of All Organizations of Labor in the Third Congressional District of Kansas and SG, Morrison, and O'Connell to All Secretaries o[f] Organizations of Labor in Minnesota, both dated Sept. 28, 1922, can be found at the George Meany Memorial Archives, Silver Spring, Md.

8. Copies of two examples of this circular, SG, Morrison, and O'Connell to All Secretaries of Organizations of Labor in Illinois, Sept. 28, 1922, and SG, Morrison, and O'Connell to All Secretaries of Organizations of Labor in Maryland, Oct. 7, 1922, can be found at the George Meany Memorial Archives, Silver Spring, Md.

9. SG left Washington, D.C., on Nov. 4, 1922, for Newark, N.J., to address a non-partisan political meeting in the city that evening and a midnight rally in Jersey City. Then, after a brief stopover in New York City on Nov. 5, he went on to New Haven, Conn., where he addressed another non-partisan political meeting that evening. He returned to New York the next day and was back at AFL headquarters by Nov. 8. For transcripts of his remarks in Newark, Jersey City, and New Haven, see Files of the Office of the President, Speeches and Writings, reel 117, frames 655–69, 649–54, 670–82, *AFL Records.*

10. "A Bugle Call to Duty," *American Federationist* 29 (Nov. 1922): 809–13.

To Peter Snyder[1]

October 30, 1922.

Mr. P. F. Snyder,
Clerk, House of Representatives—Committee on Immigration,
Washington, D.C.
Dear Sir:

Your letter of October 28 received and read with much surprise.

Although clerk of the Immigration Committee of the House apparently you have not kept abreast of the times sufficiently to learn of the propaganda being spread that has for its purpose the amending of the immigration bill in the interest of big corporations. In an interview published in the New York Times July 23,[2] Representative Siegel[3] said there was a movement in progress to amend the 3 per cent immigration law to 2 per cent. In fact there is every reason to believe that such a bill[4] will be introduced in congress immediately after the opening of the next session.

Representative Siegel, according to his interview, is very much concerned over the proposed change. His condemnation was so emphatic that Representative Rossdale[5] had it placed in the Congressional Record of September 20.[6] The "Iron Age" in its issue of September 21 attacks the literacy test.[7] It says:

"A literacy test is required which from the standpoint of the good of the country is a farce."

Then the "Iron Age" insists that many able-bodied immigrants are excluded and therefore commends the psychological test which has been proposed by a number of different people all apparently working together in distributing propaganda on that subject. The evidence so far shows that there will be a bill[8] presented in congress to amend the immigration law in the interest of those who desire to flood the Labor market of this country in order to break down wages. You take objection to that statement in the report of the Legislative Committee of the American Federation of Labor and printed in the October issue of the *American Federationist.*[9] You say:

"Reference in your article to control of wages of unskilled labor and your attempt to connect the question of wage scales with the immigration problem, are distortions of fact and innuendoes unworthy of note, perhaps, except for the fact that their implications are most unjust and inexact."

For your information permit me to state that that statement was based on charges made by Representative Albert Johnson of Washington, Chairman of the Committee on Immigration. On September 22 he made the following statement on the floor of the House of Representatives:

"I have before me various letters and printed statements of large employers and big bankers protesting restriction. In a recent pamphlet the National City Bank of New York City, and it ought to know, attributes the recent increase in the wages of common labor in the steel industry to the three per cent law. Similarly the president of the R. H. Johnson Co., of Wayne, Pa., writes that the percentage law, unless repealed, will necessitate a 'further increase of 50 cents to $1 a day.' Propaganda to break down restriction and open up the alien floodgates has been launched by big employers and importers of foreign cheap labor. The drive is on and is increasing. Members of congress are being besieged with letters from factory districts and labor centers picturing a shortage of common labor and demanding foreign labor's importation in order to hold down the wages of unskilled workers. Common labor receives from $500 to $600 a year in the basic industries. As official investigation has shown and the writer of the above letter states, labor in these industries is practically all foreign."

Evidently you have not read the speech of Representative Johnson or you would not have so scathingly criticised a statement made by the Legislative Committee that was based on the charges made by the Chairman of the Immigration Committee, Mr. Johnson.

Labor believes that any attempt to open the immigration law for amendment will permit those who are opposed to any limitation to so change it that America will be flooded with hordes of immigrants. There are many members of congress who have the real interest of our beloved country at heart and will not vote for laws that will be detrimental to the people. There are a number of reactionary members who in their zeal to carry out the wishes of the vested interests will so manipulate consideration of the bill that the big interests that care nothing for the people will secure everything they desire. Labor sees danger in amending the bill at the present time and wonders why there is such haste. The only explanation seems to be that it is the intention to amend the bill not for the protection of Labor but for the protection of the big corporations who want to pay lower wages.

So far as concerns your threat to publish your letter in a certain eventuality,[10] let me answer that you need not wait until that provided you have the fairness to publish my reply at the same time.

Very truly yours,   Saml Gompers
President,   American Federation of Labor.

TLpS, reel 285, vol. 298, pp. 18–20, SG Letterbooks, DLC.

1. Peter Frederick Snyder (1889–1963), a Washington, D.C., attorney, served as secretary to congressman Albert Johnson from 1914 to 1929 and as clerk of the House Committee on Immigration and Naturalization from 1919 to 1929.

2. The interview was actually published in the *Washington Times* of July 23, 1922.

3. Isaac Siegel (1880–1947) served as a Republican congressman from New York from 1915 to 1923.

4. A number of bills were introduced in the next session of congress with this provision.

5. Albert Berger Rossdale (1878–1968) served as a Republican congressman from New York from 1921 to 1923.

6. Siegel's *Washington Times* interview was actually published in the *Congressional Record* on Aug. 23, 1922 (67th Cong., 2d sess., vol. 62, pt. 11, pp. 11,722–23).

7. Acheson Smith, "Scarcity of Common Labor in Industry," *Iron Age*, Sept. 21, 1922, pp. 717–18, quotation at p. 718.

8. For a discussion of the various bills before Congress designed to relax the current restrictions on immigration, see "Immigration" (pp. 180–81), in "Report of the Legislative Committee," *American Federationist* 30 (Feb. 1923): 179–82.

9. "Immigration" (pp. 782–83), in "Report of Legislative Committee," *American Federationist* 29 (Oct. 1922): 778–84.

10. For Snyder's response to SG of Nov. 4, 1922, see AFL Microfilm Convention File, reel 32, frame 1278, *AFL Records*. Snyder wrote that no good purpose would be served by publishing his letter.

From Samuel Untermyer

New York, N.Y. November 11, 1922.

Dear Mr. Gompers:

Thanks for your letter of the 4th instant[1] particularly for thinking of me in connection with Mr. Frey's book entitled, "The Labor Injunction," which has just reached here. It was very good of you to have Mr. Frey send me a copy of his book. I have written to him expressing my appreciation.

My interest in the impeachment of Attorney General Daugherty has not diminished with the lapse of time. I wrote yesterday to Mr.

Manly,[2] to ascertain what was being done toward preparing the case. In my judgment no headway can be made based upon the issuance of the injunction, but upon other grounds far more substantial on which the prosecution should be pressed. The decision of the Illinois Court has relieved Mr. Daugherty of the responsibility for the issuing of that injunction and has placed the responsibility upon the Court. I can conceive of no theory on which progress can be made with that branch of the case, although the decisions, in my judgment, are utterly unsound and well nigh monstrous, from the point of view of the legal—especially the sweeping drag net form of the injunction.

With kind regards, believe me

Very truly yours,   (Signed) Sam'l. Untermyer.

TLtcSr, Executive Council Records, Minutes, reel 7, frame 1223, *AFL Records.*

1. SG to Samuel Untermyer, Nov. 4, 1922, reel 285, vol. 298, p. 113, SG Letterbooks, DLC.

2. Basil Manly.

To John Frey

November 27, 1922.

Mr. John P. Frey,
Editor, International Molders' Journal,
Commercial Tribune Building, Cincinnati, Ohio.
Dear Sir and Brother:

The question of intelligence tests is becoming more and more important in the industrial world. Tests of this character are being introduced in a great many places of employment. It is necessary that our movement be prepared either to cooperate intelligently in the development of this new trend in applied psychology or that it be prepared to combat its extension.

Until the time of the world war practically no use had been made of the so-called intelligence test in industry. For the most part experiments had been confined to the educational world for the purpose of building up a basis of practice. Almost at the outset of the war, however, psychologists came to the War Department and with the cooperation of the War Department developed a series of tests[1] which were applied in four of the national army cantonments. This sweeping introduction of the intelligence test has naturally given a great impetus to its introduction in industry. We are now confronted with a situation which makes it necessary to give immediate attention to the question in order that we may know its weaknesses, its value, if it has value, and its dangers to the welfare of the workers, if there are such dangers.

I have concluded to ask a number of trade unionists to give particular thought and study to the subject and to let me have their carefully considered opinions. A volume on psychological examining in the United States army, prepared under the direction of the National Academy of Sciences and published by the Government Printing Office, contains the entire detailed history of the work done in the army.[2] In this volume will be found the tests used in the army and the steps by which those tests were developed. This is the most complete record in existence and will convey a better idea of the psychological intelligence test than any other volume with which I am familiar.

I am sending you by mail today a copy of this volume and I ask that you give it your most careful study. You will understand that only the most carefully considered opinion, based upon real study, will be of value. Our conclusions must be unassailable. I am looking to you, and to a few others to whom I am writing a similar letter,[3] to be of great assistance in searching out the truth in relation to this very important question. I may find it possible in the near future to send you additional information which will be of interest and which will be helpful to you. Meanwhile it will be a sufficient task on your time and patience to study carefully the volume which is being sent you by this mail.

If in the course of your consideration of the subject there are suggestions you would care to offer or any matters at all that you would care to discuss I shall be glad to hear from you and to give you what assistance may be possible.

I should appreciate deeply your service which will, I assure you, be of much value to our movement.

Fraternally yours,   Saml Gompers
President,   American Federation of Labor.

TLpS, reel 285, vol. 298, pp. 608–9, SG Letterbooks, DLC.

1. A reference to the intelligence tests developed for the Army during World War I by a team of psychologists under the direction of Robert Mearns Yerkes (1876–1956). The tests were of two types, a standard Alpha test for those who were literate and a Beta test consisting of symbols and pictures designed for those who were illiterate or foreign-born and had little skill in the English language. By the end of the war the tests had been given to over 1.7 million recruits in some thirty-five Army cantonments.

2. Yerkes, ed., *Psychological Examining in the United States Army,* Memoirs of the National Academy of Sciences, vol. 15 (Washington, D.C., 1921).

3. For similar letters, see SG to William Clarke, Nov. 27, 1922, reel 285, vol. 298, pp. 610–11, SG Letterbooks, DLC; SG to Spencer Miller, Nov. 28, 1922, ibid., pp. 647–48; SG to A. F. Anderson, Nov. 28, 1922, ibid., pp. 649–50; SG to Andrew Furuseth, Nov. 28, 1922, ibid., pp. 651–52; and SG to A. J. Berres, Nov. 28, 1922, ibid., pp. 653–54.

To Edward Bates

November 29, 1922.

Mr. Edward A. Bates,
Secretary-Treasurer, The New York State Federation of Labor,
Room 14—Jones Building, Utica, New York.
Dear Sir and Brother:

Your letter of November 16 received and read with interest.

The result of the elections[1] in New York State should bring joy and courage to every wage earner who had begun to believe that reaction could not be unhorsed. With such a magnificent leader as former Governor Smith the result was not unexpected. It is a sweeping victory, one that will long be remembered by those who went down in defeat because they advocated measures inimical to the interests of not only labor but of the mass of the people.

Your kind references to the success of the conference I called in New York[2] and which led to such an outcome are highly appreciated. During the last few years there has arisen in public life a new idea of what constitutes loyalty to the people. Instead of loyalty to the people it has been loyalty to the privileged few. The un-American campaign of the unfair employers of the so-called open shop has as you say received a blow.

The defeat of Governor Allen's candidate[3] for Governor in Kansas was a distinct warning to those who favor compulsory labor that the people are opposed to such legislation. The defeat of Senator Sutherland[4] in West Virginia was notice to him that the people will not calmly stand by and permit him to appoint as a federal judge a man who is not in sympathy with the rights of the people.[5] Mr. Beveridge[6] wanted to relieve the well-to-do from taxation and place the burden upon those least able to bear it through a sales tax. He received emphatic notice that his methods of taxation were not acceptable. Senator Poindexter[7] endeavored by a trick to foist compulsory labor legislation on the railroad employes and his constituents recalled him from the United States Senate.

Senator Kellogg[8] who introduced a bill[9] in Congress to give jurisdiction to the federal courts of the police powers of the states where aliens were involved caused his downfall. Senator Pomerene[10] had the idea that if he attacked Labor it would help in his election. But he also went down in defeat. Senator Frelinghuysen[11] who bore the distinction of being the only member of Congress who had a 100 per cent legislative record against labor was repudiated by the citizens of his state by an enormous majority. The non-partisan policy of the

American Federation of Labor has brought about these results. It also was helpful in the return to the Senate of Senator LaFollette by an enormous majority.

The election of Smith W. Brookhart[12] of Iowa, Henrik Shipstead of Minnesota, Lynn J. Frazier[13] of North Dakota, Hiram Johnson of California, William H. King[14] of Utah, John B. Kendrick[15] of Wyoming, Key Pittman[16] of Nevada and Andreius A. Jones[17] of New Mexico as senators besides 156 members of the House of Representatives through the non-partisan political policy of the American Federation of Labor gives us much to be thankful for.

The success of the non-partisan policy was because of the absence, except in a few instances, of a third party. Third parties always draw votes from friends of Labor.

Permit me to congratulate you and your associates for the most practical campaign you carried on. I was very much impressed with it early in the year when you began preparations for the primaries. You organized non-partisan committees in every county. In compliance with your request to send a letter to the officials of national and international unions requesting them to write their local unions urging them to join in the non-partisan movement brought good results. I read the literature you sent out very carefully and was pleased at the method used in arousing the wage earners and all other liberty-loving people to take an interest in the campaign. It is to be hoped that the result of the recent elections will sink so deeply into the wage earners of New York state that they will repeat their efforts in coming campaigns with as great a solidarity as that just closed.

With best wishes and assuring you of my desire to be helpful in any way within my power, I am,

Fraternally yours,   Saml Gompers
President,   American Federation of Labor.

P.S. Later I will send you report made by the A.F. of L. National Non-Partisan Campaign Committee.[18] I think you will find it interesting.

S. G.

TLpS, reel 285, vol. 298, p. 802, SG Letterbooks, DLC.

1. The Democratic party won significant victories in New York in 1922. William Calder (1869–1945), a Republican senator from New York from 1917 to 1923, lost his seat to Democrat Royal Copeland (1868–1938), who served as senator from 1923 until his death in 1938. The Democrats also swept all major state offices, including the governorship, won by Alfred E. Smith, took control of the state senate, and picked up seats in the assembly.

2. Probably a reference to an Oct. 5, 1922, meeting of the Central Trades and Labor Council of Greater New York at which SG spoke on the issues facing labor in

the upcoming election. For a transcript of his remarks, see Files of the Office of the President, Speeches and Writings, reel 117, frames 595–611, *AFL Records*.

3. William Yost Morgan (1865–1932), Republican lieutenant-governor of Kansas from 1915 to 1919, lost the Kansas gubernatorial election of 1922 to Democrat Jonathan McMillan Davis (1871–1943), who served as governor from 1923 to 1925.

4. Howard Sutherland (1865–1950), a Republican senator from West Virginia from 1917 to 1923, lost the seat in 1922 to Democrat Matthew Mansfield Neely (1874–1958), who served as senator from 1923 to 1929, 1931 to 1941, and 1949 until his death in 1958.

5. A reference to George Warwick McClintic (1866–1942), who was appointed in 1921 as a U.S. district court judge for the Southern District of West Virginia and who served in that post until his death in 1942. He issued a number of injunctions against striking miners in his district in the spring of 1922.

6. A reference to Albert Jeremiah Beveridge (1862–1927), a Republican senator from Indiana from 1899 to 1911, who was unsuccessful in bids for the governorship (1912) and reelection to the Senate (1914, 1922). In 1920 he received the Pulitzer Prize for his four-volume biography, *The Life of John Marshall.*

7. Miles Poindexter, a Republican senator from Washington from 1911 to 1923, lost the seat in 1922 to Democrat Clarence Cleveland Dill (1884–1978), who served as senator from 1923 to 1935.

8. Frank Billings Kellogg (1856–1937), a Republican senator from Minnesota from 1917 to 1923, lost the seat in 1922 to Henrik Shipstead (1881–1960). Kellogg later served as secretary of state (1925–29); in 1928 he sponsored the Kellogg-Briand Peace Pact, for which he was awarded the Nobel Peace Prize the next year. Shipstead served in the Senate until 1947—until 1941 as a member of the Farmer-Labor party and thereafter as a Republican.

9. S. 1943 (67th Cong., 1st sess.), introduced by Kellogg on June 2, 1921, authorized federal courts to assume jurisdiction in state-level suits against resident aliens when the cases involved possible violation of treaty obligations. Critics of the measure maintained that it was intended to block cases against Japanese landowners in California, which were legal under state law but which contravened treaty provisions. The bill died in committee after hearings in August 1922.

10. Atlee Pomerene, a Democratic senator from Ohio from 1911 to 1923, lost the seat in 1922 to Republican Simeon Davidson Fess (1861–1936). Fess served as senator from 1923 to 1935.

11. Joseph Sherman Frelinghuysen (1869–1948), a Republican senator from New Jersey from 1917 to 1923, lost the seat in 1922 to Democrat Edward Irving Edwards (1863–1931). Edwards served as senator from 1923 to 1929.

12. Smith Wildman Brookhart (1869–1944) served as a Republican senator from Iowa from 1922 to 1926 and from 1927 to 1933.

13. Lynn Joseph Frazier (1874–1947) served as a Republican senator from North Dakota from 1923 to 1941. He had served as governor of the state from 1917 to 1921.

14. William Henry King (1863–1949) served as a Democratic senator from Utah from 1917 to 1941. He had served as a Utah congressman from 1897 to 1899 and again from 1900 to 1901.

15. John Benjamin Kendrick (1857–1933) served as a Democratic senator from Wyoming from 1917 until his death in 1933. He had served as governor of the state from 1915 to 1917.

16. Key Pittman (1872–1940) served as a Democratic senator from Nevada from 1913 until his death in 1940.

17. Andrieus Aristieus Jones (1862–1927) served as a Democratic senator from New Mexico from 1917 until his death in 1927.

18. *Non-Partisan Successes: Report of the Activities of the Non-Partisan Political Campaign Committee of the American Federation of Labor in the Primaries and Elections of 1922* ([Washington, D.C., 1922]).

To Gilman Parker[1]

Washington, D.C., Dec. 27—[1922]

Mr. Gilman Parker,
New York Tribune,
New York City.

The program declared for by the communists in New York conference[2] was a surprise only to those who have been inclined to believe communism an innocent pastime but also to those who have failed to observe what has been taking place[3] *Stop* The New York conference made clear to all observers the direct line between Moscow and subversive propaganda in the United States. What should now be made clear is the relation between various groups in the United States, not all using the communist label, but all interlocking, all [p]reaching the same thing and all operating under instructions from the headquarters [in] Moscow where the greatest existing autocracy has its life and being *Stop* There are only thirty thousand enrolled communists. More than one hundred million Americans are not communists. They can be fooled and overcome only if they neglect to think and neglect to live their belief in democracy *Stop* The greatest menace of the New York communist program is not in that program, but in the indifference of Americans *Stop* The American Federation of Labor has from the first understood and denounced the Russian communist idea *Stop Labor* has not been fooled *Stop* The communists seek to destroy the American Federation of Labor as an essential, necessary precedent to destruction of our republic and the official communist declarations have repeatedly made this clear *Stop* Americans can best stop the spread of communist propaganda by recognizing the effectiveness, the democracy and the scientific foundation of our trade unions which stand as the first line of defense against communist dictatorship *Stop* This I have said repeatedly *Stop* The communists are not attacking congress, legislatures, corporations or employers; they are attacking trade unions *Stop* If they can destroy trade unions they can do what they like with the rest of society, as they have done in Russia where there are no more bona fide trade unions *Stop* The communist propaganda now stands more in the open than formerly, but their secrets have long been open books to labor *Stop* Labor will continue its fight for the preservation and the extension of democracy, because it understands democracy and needs democracy *Stop* Those who now fight trade unions fight the battle for communism, for the dictatorship of Leninism, which means absolutism under which all, including workers, must be servile subjects of a monarch, no matter what his title *Stop* The more than one hundred millions of Americans who are not communists can preserve American institutions, but they had best look to their facts, for it is well that none be deceived by the insidious and treacherous propaganda which is spread so generously by so many who are not communists at all, including many of our indolent newspapers.

Samuel Gompers.

TWtpSr, reel 286, vol. 299, pp. 965–67, SG Letterbooks, DLC.

1. Gilman Moncure Parker (1891–1932) was a reporter for the *New York Tribune*, specializing in labor news.

2. The Workers' Party of America held its second national conference in New York City, Dec. 24–26, 1922. The conference adopted a program that endorsed the leadership of the Communist International, creation of a Soviet-style government in the United States, dictatorship of the proletariat, and amalgamation of trade unions to unite them in a revolutionary mass workers' struggle against capitalism.

3. SG was reacting to the *New York Tribune*'s characterization of the program adopted by the recent convention of the Workers' Party of America: "In both text and spirit the principles and declarations presented in the program are the most revolutionary declared for by any organization in this country for many years" ("U.S. Soviet Is Demanded by Reds Here," Dec. 26, 1922). SG's reply was published in the paper the following day ("Labor at War with U.S. Reds, Says Gompers," *New York Tribune*, Dec. 28, 1922).

To George Anderson[1]

January 3, 1923.

Mr. George Anderson,
109 N. Knox St., Princeton, Illinois.
Dear Sir:

Your letter of December 29 received and contents noted.

You ask for information on the question "Resolved: That the federal government should own and operate all the coal mines in the United States."

The American Federation of Labor never has made any declaration upon this subject. Government ownership of coal mines, however, would eliminate collective bargaining and leave to the government the power of controlling the destinies of the workers. It would mean that not only the prices but the wages paid the miners would be fixed by the government.

> Very truly yours,   Saml Gompers
> President,   American Federation of Labor.

TLpS, reel 287, vol. 300, p. 87, SG Letterbooks, DLC.

1. George M. Anderson, the son of a Princeton, Ill., teamster, was about fifteen years old.

To Newton Baker[1]

Washington, D.C., Jan. [3], 192[3].[2]

Hon. Newton D. Baker,
President, Cleveland Chamber of Commerce,
Cleveland, Ohio.
Dear Mr. Baker:

I have been much interested in your letter of November 23d, pursuing the question of the union and non-union shop. I am interested in the reasons which you set forth for your belief in the "open shop." I am not ready to agree, in the absence of proof, with your optimism in regard to the number of truly open shops in Cleveland. But that is rather beside the point.

I think that in all of your argument for the open shop, an argument which, it seems to me, is largely ethical, or perhaps I had better say, is largely an argument based on what appears to you to be ideals, you have overlooked the most important considerations of all; you have neglected entirely to take into account those things which I should expect you to first take into account.

The formation of unions is the expression on the part of the workers of a feeling which seems to me to be close kindred of the feeling which possessed the men who first battled against the control of political institutions by a few and the exclusion from political expression of the many. If there is any truth at all in democracy, if democracy has any real justification, it is as thoroughly justified in our industrial life as it ever was in our political life.

I am sure it must occur to you that our relationships in industry are fully as important in our life today as our relationships in the realm of political affairs. Decisions which are made and conditions which are confronted in industry are of infinitely greater moment to thousands upon thousands of people than are all the political decisions and conditions in the country. Justification for democratic practices and the consideration of democratic rights in industry, it seems to me, is most emphatically equal to the justification for those same things in political life. If this is true, there can be absolutely no justification for employers to believe that they ought to be the sole judges of the manner in which those democratic rights are to be exercised, or even of what are those democratic rights. The moment the first principle is accepted the whole structure of employer superiority and domination has got to disappear. The problem must then be looked at as one in which the workers have a voice, not under somebody else's terms and under somebody else's restrictions, but on terms of equality.

Beyond doubt the principle which I have set up, if carried to its logical conclusion, would carry much beyond that for which workers contend at present. That surely can not be used as an argument against that for which the workers now contend. It speaks rather for the moderation of American labor and its desire to function constructively, without doing anything to risk the structure in which I am sure we must all live for a considerable period yet to come.

I have no wish to say that every shop must be a union shop regardless of what may be the wishes of the workers themselves, but I do say that if it is the expressed wish of the workers to have a union and to have a union shop, that then there can be no denial of that wish without an exercise of power on the part of the employer, which of itself must be construed as a repudiation of democratic methods and of democracy itself.

You are no doubt aware that only a small proportion of the strikes of American workers are for the establishment of union shops, or for the recognition of the union. Labor has fought much more vigorously and with much greater tenacity of purpose for the establishment of proper working conditions, proper wages and reasonable hours of labor. American labor will, however, never cease to contend for the right to organize and for the right to carry organization to its logical conclusion, which means the union shop and a working relationship between the organizations of the workers and the employers. There is something so fundamentally American in this idea that I can never believe that those Americans who argue against it are so arguing out of anything except a mistaken understanding.

It is yet to be satisfactorily explained how there can be any expression in modern industry which will give voice to the viewpoint of the workers, unless there is organization and unless that organization is of a type formulated by the workers themselves without any obligation whatever to employers. The open shop, if it is truly open, means that union men and non-union men may work in that shop. If there is no trade agreement there is likely to be no machinery by which workers can approach the employer with regularity through channels which the employer is bound to respect and will respect. Moreover, even if the union workers have established channels of connection through their union organization, the non-union workers are left as voiceless, floating units in the industry, without any adequate means of either expressing themselves or protecting themselves. They are much like the residents of the District of Columbia in our political life, who are voiceless because they are not possessed of the form of political government which finds expression in the union of the states.

If, in a shop which is open to the extent that there is no objection to the workers becoming members of unions, all workers in the shop elect to join unions, then it is clearly logical, unless we are to deny the principles of democracy, that the workers so organized in a union have the right to function as such. This means they have the right to establish joint relations with the employer and to reach agreement with the employer upon terms and conditions under which they will give service. It is quite in keeping with the principles of democratic conduct that they should agree with the employer that in order to prevent destruction of standards through the introduction in the plant of a majority of non-union workers, none be employed except those who belong to the union, or those who within a reasonable length of time are willing to become members.

You express a belief in the open shop and it is my contention that if you believe in the open shop, meaning a shop in which union men are not forbidden to work, you must as a consequence grant the right of workers to organize and to establish a union shop. It is my conviction that you can not be hostile to the union shop without also being hostile to the really open shop. I have no doubt, of course, as to the sincerity of your belief in the idea of the open shop, but I can not refrain from saying that I think you do not follow your own beliefs to their logical conclusion. You do not think the problem through and you furnish merely a half way application of principles, which you believe in to be right.

So far as the open shop is concerned, it is of the greatest importance to remember that it is not a matter of what your conception, or my conception, may be in that respect. It is not a matter of what you think the open shop is, or of what I think it is. The important fact is that employers and employers' associations that have declared for the "open shop" have in practice under that declaration discriminated against the employment of union workers. Whatever the "open shop" may be in theory and whatever may be your opinion of it, the fact of what it has been and of what it is in practice is what counts, and it is by the practice that the workers are bound to form their opinions. The fact is that in the competitive industrial struggle, employers strive to impose upon workers such terms as they have the power to impose. Wherever possible they seek to drive with each worker the hardest possible bargain. On the other hand, the workers aspire to and strive to achieve better conditions of work and life, not only in the place of employment, but in the whole realm of sociological, political and spiritual existence.

In your letter to me you say: "The declaration of labor policy of the Chamber (of Commerce) sanctions representative negotiations—a form of collective bargaining." I find you saying further that the Chamber rejects "as prejudicial to the public interest, arbitrary power alike of employer over employe and employe over employer." Presumably this is the reason for sanctioning only "a form of collective bargaining." What you do not say, but what must appear as the fact to anyone who carefully examines the question, is that this is the exercise of autocratic power on the part of the employers of Cleveland, expressing themselves through the Chamber of Commerce. They sanction "a form of collective bargaining" which is not collective bargaining, which retains to the employers the absolute control of wages and working conditions and which permits the workers to have no effective voice whatever in determining the terms and conditions under which they are to give service in the industries of Cleveland. It looks very much as if the Cleveland Chamber of Commerce had felt it necessary to consider something in the way of shadow to public opinion and that in considering the shadow it had been very careful not to consider any of the substance.

You are apparently convinced that unions mean industrial strife. You are, of course, not alone in holding that belief. Here again you are, I am afraid, thinking half way th[r]ough and leaving many things out of account. You speak of the "war theory" and you appear to hold that it is the theory upon which labor operates. You want something to "believe and preach as better than war." In response to that desire I offer you the trade-union movement, not as you believe it to be, but as it is with all of its progressive, constructive possibilities and desires.

I might easily enough turn your own argument against the organizations of employers and say that I am opposed to them because I am opposed to the "war theory" and because such organizations are mainly responsible for industrial strife. I am not going to make any such argument, because I am not going to accuse even the most reactionary organization of employers of evil without full acknowledgment of the good things achieved by organizations of employers and of the immense possibilities for future contributions to human welfare by such organizations. Without organization civilization as we have it today would be an impossibility. The trade union offers to employers the opportunity for cooperative relationships through which there may be developed the greatest possible degree of service and through which there may be brought into being the greatest possible degree of justice to all.

You seem greatly disturbed because I do not agree with your point of view in regard to what you term a public interest in labor controversies. I will not say that it is yours, but it is a rather general assumption that this public interest, so-called, would somehow operate to prevent strikes, or at least to compel workers to return to work when they have struck. There is, of course a widespread interest in the results of relations between workers and employers and this depends always upon the nature of the commodity produced. There is a much wider interest, for example, in a coal strike than there would be in a strike against a local plant making heavy machinery. This by no means indicates any public right to step into a controversy with a command that workers shape their conduct to suit orders which may be issued either by a governmental tribunal, or any other form of expression of outside force.

American labor has no desire to disregard public welfare, but, on the contrary has every regard to promote and serve the public welfare. American labor, however, will never admit a public right to enforce involuntary servitude because that principle is wrong and because if it is ever admitted to even the smallest degree, it will by the same token be admitted in its fullest implications. It should not be necessary to have to say to you that the minute America begins to travel that road, America begins to undo every democratic principle for which the republic has stood and upon which it was founded.

I do not wish you to feel that labor is uninterested in the public welfare, or that it has a desire to disregard intelligent public opinion. The stress which you lay upon the interest of the public is justified and is thoroughly shared, not only by myself, but by the labor movement. The public welfare and a decent regard for the public interest and for the expressions of public opinion must have great influence in shaping the direction of any movement. The Standard Dictionary defines the public as the people collectively, or in general as a body locally, or in the state, or in the nation. I am bound to ask you where you can find in the action of the "public" any effective determination to take the gyves from the wrists of the toilers, to take women out of the mill and men, women, and children out of the sweatshops, or to shorten the hours of toil of the burden bearers, where that action did not have its initiative and inspiration in the protests and struggles and sacrifices of the labor movement itself. Sometimes, it is true, the "public" is for a brief period inconvenienced by rupture of the relations between employers and workers, but we customarily find that before that rupture "the public" had given no thought and taken no action of constructive, beneficent character to remedy the wrongs imposed upon men and women of toil. The strike of the miners in the anthracite coal regions did more to take the breaker boys out of the mines than anything else; the strike of the miners of this year did more to halt the "open shop" drive and the drive for wage reductions than all those who composed "the public," but who so frequently fail to take account of the facts of life.

Your abhorence of industrial war is shared not only by those whose positions are similar to your own, but by the workers themselves. I think the workers understand much better than anyone else the cost of industrial war. They pay the full price. They experience what you observe. Does it not occur to you that there must be something of importance to induce them to undergo experiences which you abhor merely as an observer? Labor will cease to engage in contests with employers as soon as labor finds it possible to induce employers to conduct the affairs of industry on a higher plane. Labor is ever eager to substitute negotiation for contest.

In 1776 the American colonies engaged in a war with England. They did not expect to remain forever at war with England, but they were determined to remain at war until a certain definite object had been gained and until certain principles had been established beyond question. That having been done, the war ceased. Since 1812 we have had no war with England and we do not expect to have any. This is not because we believe less firmly than did our forefathers in 1776 in the principles that were then at stake, but it is because England does not question those principles as she then did. In that war it is quite likely that a great many neutral nations were inconvenienced, but some of them were able to see the principles involved and some of them were able to find ways to render effective support in the struggle to establish those principles.

I am deeply touched by your eloquent portrayal of the horrors and wastage of war. Having been a most pronounced and active pacifist until the breaking out of the world war I feel all that you feel and all that you abhor in the wars of peoples and nations; and yet feeling as you do, were you not among the foremost in waging war upon those who would take the life and soul out of free democratic institutions and who would if triumphant in their unholy cause have turned civilization backward? That war transformed me from an ultra-pacifist to one willing to fight and sacrifice with my fellow countrymen in defense of the principle of living our own lives and working out our own destiny; and if there be a mad-man nation still, large or small, which will attempt to repeat that monumental crime I hope that the generations, perhaps yet unborn, of our self-governing civilized nations, may throw themselves with equal vigor in the battle to maintain the fundamental principles of freedom, justice and humanity.

Before the United States entered the world war I said to a gathering of members of my family that if any one of my sons or their sons failed to respond to the needs of our republic that I would disown him as not of my blood,[3] but they kept the faith and they and I have met the obligation both in blood and treasure.

It is a vivid picture which you have drawn and I join you in the feeling of horror against war, but I ask you whether the world even now is safe from the struggles which have been going on and which are likely to go on, particularly in the nations, some large and more small, which are scheming, planning and preparing to emerge as conquerors of the world.

During the Washington Limitation of Armament Conference when we were all approaching a plan for the destruction of dreadnaughts and other major warships, a friend of mine facetiously said: "I have seen as interesting and bloody pugilistic contests with bantam weights as with heavy-weight fighting men."

Who knows now which form the international conquest will take in the future? One day, some day, when the world of men shall have reached a higher state of civilization and humanity, there may be comity and peace, when the causes of war shall have been removed, and no one more than you, and may I say I, fervently hope and work—dedicate myself to service to that end, but in the meantime I believe with the declaration of the American Federation of Labor—we favor universal disarmament by general agreement.

The analogy which you make between international wars and the relations of employers with employes, in my judgment is misapplied.

From slavery to serfdom, peonage, to the modern worker in the struggle of thousands of years, the historically developed labor movement of modern times has for its purpose not only the improvement of wages, hours, and conditions of employment, but the attainment and maintenance of all the industrial, political and social rights to which the toiling masses of our republic are entitled, when democracy in industry shall supplant autocracy in industry, and employers, entrepreneurs and the workers, giving intelligent and effective industrial service, shall stand as industrial equals.

The much misunderstood labor movement has done much to foster education and uproot ignorance; to shorten hours of toil and lengthen life; raise wages and increase independence and decrease dependence; develop manhood and balk tyranny; establish fraternity and discourage selfishness; reduce prejudice and induce liberality; enlarge society and eliminate classes; create rights and abolish wrongs; lighten toil and brighten man; cheer the home and fireside and make the world better. Can you imagine any service in the accomplishment of these high ideals to which non-union workers and the "open shop" have contributed or are likely to contribute anything?

I do not like war and I do not like strikes, but I am unwilling to oppose all wars and for the same reason I am unwilling to say that strikes are wrong. Both are right and necessary and should be used when the cause of justice can be retained in no other way. This is not an expression of disregard for the interests of the great masses of our people. It is, on the contrary, an expression of the highest regard for them. If you are inclined to question this, I ask you to consider what would be the status of the masses of our people one year hence if today all unions were to be wiped out of existence and resistance to injustice in industry was rendered impossible. The public interest should be, and in the long run I think is, primarily in justice. I am unwilling to believe that the public, if it is informed, is willing to inflict injustice even at the price of temporary inconvenience.

You speak in the closing paragraphs of your letter of having too few years left to hope to see any progress made "by merely continuing and intensifying the old class struggle" and you propose to use your influence to "emphasize the public interest" and in the "creation of another atmosphere and another spirit." I do not think American labor is engaged in a class struggle and I do not think American labor believes it is engaged in a class struggle, because in our country we have no such thing and I hope never will have. We are engaged in a struggle for common justice and for principles which are applicable to all alike. American labor wants no "working class domination," but it does want a development of the social order in which unrestrained exploitation of the workers by great financial powers and by great combinations of employers, will be impossible. It is continually seeking to create in the industrial world "another atmosphere and another spirit" which shall be one of helpful cooperation, mutual understanding and democratic expression on the part of all factors in industry. If this is not service in the public interest, then I entirely mistake what is public interest and what constitutes constructive progress.

You are right in stating that perhaps capital is but "the stored up products of labor available for further production," but you are again in error when you make the analogy of making a vessel for use. Neither capital nor labor, that is the workers, are static. When the toilers receive a larger share of the product of that toil it not only materially and morally improves their own conditions but has a like effect upon all the masses of workers. One improvement in the conditions of wage workers is but a forerunner for the improvements of all others and then again it must not be left out of calculation that with every material improvement in the conditions of the masses of the workers there is let loose upon the world greater improvements and inventions in machinery, power, tools, making production of wealth upon a greater scale.

I can not fail to take account of your statement that "the typical worker has the pride of a craftsman in the product of his hands." This is an excellent statement of a truth and I regret very much that you should have surrounded it with so many statements that are entirely out of harmony with that expression. May I first ask you, in modern industry when each individual worker performs one infinitesimal part of the whole thousands and thousands of times each day, what joy or "pride of the craftsman" can he have "in the product of his hands?"

You continue to say that if thoughtful persons "keep on saying to employers and employes that the best labor relation to be adopted by them to accomplish these respective fundamental desires is one of incessant conflict, they are likely to take our word for it and spend a large part of their strength and time getting ready for battle and fighting battles." Underlying this there is, of course, the assumption that trade unions and the union shop imply a condition of strife and battle. I regard this, and experience proves it, a wholly wrong assumption, because on the contrary trade unions are organizations of peace and functioning in joint relation with employers are tremendous agencies for industrial harmony, for human well-being, and also for increased production.

Workers do, as you say, want "to make money under as favorable conditions of employment as to hours, continuity, sanitary conditions and comfort as possible." Because of this it is impossible for them to want strife. What they most want is peace, but what they insist on is peace with as much justice and fair dealing as can be secured. There is no greater punishment that can be visited upon workers than lack of continuity in industry and the continuity is broken by the action of workers only where the provocation is beyond all bearing. When continuity of operation is broken under such circumstances, it surely can not be said that labor is eager for battle for the sake of battle. It must be said in fairness that labor is willing to sacrifice for the sake of justice.

If I may return for a moment to your war analogy, having in mind your statement of a growing opinion to the effect that "there is no such thing as a successful war," I might say that there is no such thing as an unsuccessful protest against injustice. Every protest against injustice is in some measure a success. If that were not the case, the toilers would long since have become discouraged and the struggle to achieve justice would not have the vigor and the spirit it has today and it would not have to its credit the victories of which we are all so proud.

I ask you to give careful consideration to this letter and to see whether I have not conveyed to you some additional understanding of our principles, our policies and our hopes. I appreciate very much your whole attitude in this discussion and I trust that you will have the kindness to write me again.

Very truly yours,   Samuel Gompers,
President,   American Federation of Labor.

PLSr, *Correspondence between Mr. Newton D. Baker, President of the Cleveland Chamber of Commerce, and Mr. Samuel Gompers, President of the American Federation of Labor* (Washington, D.C., 1923), pp. 24–31.

1. This is the last in a series of letters between SG and Newton Baker on the open shop movement published by the AFL in February 1923 as *Correspondence between Mr. Newton D. Baker, President of the Cleveland Chamber of Commerce, and Mr. Samuel Gompers, President of the American Federation of Labor.* The other letters included three from SG (dated Aug. 19, Oct. 2, and Oct. 15) and three from Baker (dated Aug. 24, Sept. 28, and Nov. 23).

2. Misdated in *Correspondence between Baker and Gompers* as Jan. 13, 1922.

3. For an earlier reference to the incident, see *The Samuel Gompers Papers*, vol. 10, p. 203.

An Excerpt from the Minutes
of a Meeting between Representatives of the AFL[1]
and Officers of the Democratic National
Committee[2]

January 6, 1923

. . .

President Gompers said he desired to talk to the gentlemen present on a matter of very great importance. He said that the Democratic Party was the party of the people, the protesting party, but that it had been drifting away from its moorings so that it was difficult to tell the difference between some of the leaders of the party in congress and other places and republicans. He said that Labor was a protesting group of American citizens and that it desired to join any party that would be true to its principles. He said that if the Democratic Party would come out as a true progressive party, a party for the people, a party that would protest against any injustice and wrong that labor would be only too willing to join forces with it. He said that he believed that in certain districts in the United States union men should be endorsed by the Democrats not only for members of the legislature but for members of the federal congress. Then Labor and the Democrats could work together for the election of true, progressive, protesting legislators.

Rep. Rouse[3] and Rep. Hull[4] both said that if the same meeting had been held the same time last year there would have been a great many more successes in the Congressional elections of last Fall. The question of leadership of Democrats in the House was then considered.

It was understood that Rep. Garrett of Tennessee and Representative Garner[5] of Texas were the candidates, both of whom are unfriendly to Labor.

Mr. Rouse said that he favored Mr. Hull for that position but the latter said that would be impossible because of his position as chairman of the National Democratic Committee.[6]

President Gompers laid great stress on what he meant by cooperation which he said could not be carried out unless the Democratic Party became a real protesting party.

The meeting adjourned with the understanding that other meetings would be held in the future. The conference was most satisfactory to all concerned. It was the unanimous verdict that the conference was a long step in the right direction and that the results would be of benefit to not only the Democratic Party and Labor but to the people of the entire country.

. . .

TDc, Files of the Office of the President, Conferences, reel 122, frames 322–23, *AFL Records.* Typed notations: "*Copy*" and "Conference Held in Office of Pres. Gompers January 6, 1923 at 2:00 P.M."

1. The AFL representatives were SG, Frank Morrison, James O'Connell, Chester Wright, Edgar Wallace, Edward McGrady, and W. C. Roberts.

2. The representatives of the Democratic National Committee were Cordell Hull, Arthur Rouse, and H. K. Hempstead.

3. Arthur Blythe Rouse (1874–1956) served as a Democratic congressman from Kentucky from 1911 to 1927.

4. Cordell Hull (1871–1955) served as a Democratic congressman from Tennessee from 1907 to 1921 and from 1923 to 1931. He then served briefly as a Democratic senator from the state (1931–33) but resigned to become secretary of state, a post he held from 1933 to 1944.

5. John Nance Garner (1868–1967) served as a Democratic congressman from Texas from 1903 to 1933 and as vice-president of the United States from 1933 to 1941.

6. Hull served as chairman of the Democratic National Committee from 1921 to 1924.

To J. McKeen Cattell[1]

January 9, 1923.

Mr. J. McKeen Cattell,
President, Psychological Corporation,
2617 Grand Central Terminal. New York City.
Dear Mr. Cattell:

Copies of your report[2] of the announcement arrived today and I desire to thank you for your kindness in sending them to me.

It is my opinion that in refusing to consider an appropriation from the Rockefeller Foundation and the Carnegie corporation you took very high ground. This I am exceedingly glad to learn.

It seems to me that your attitude toward the whole subject of psychological tests is most admirable. I am, for my part, very much in the inquiring stage but even my rather superficial inquiry thus far indicates the wisdom and caution of your viewpoint expressed in your statement that "we simply do not know to what extent our present pencil and paper tests measure native ability or what are the best tests for intelligence."

I am glad to note your position in relation to the bill introduced by Representative Cable of Ohio which would require use of the army tests in accepting or rejecting immigrants.[3] For our part we are not ready to accept any such test as a basis for judging prospective immigrants and I believe we may take that position without in the least implying a criticism of the tests themselves. The fact is, however, I believe, that we haven't sufficient proof of the suitability of the tests for such work and in any event we are not ready to agree to the letting down of the bars which would undoubtedly follow such a departure in our immigration policy.

Of course I heartily agree with your thought that the whole question of investigation as to how to determine fitness in immigration would be better done if done under the auspices of the trade unions than under the auspices of Mr. Gary.

Mr. Gary has great abilities but they do not lie in the direction of finding, expounding or begetting human welfare. His world is distinctly a material world in which humanity is a means to a material end.

Trade unions, however, cannot do all things. Some things they have not the means to do and some things they do not yet wish to undertake because it is not yet sure that they are the right things to undertake. The trade unions are, as you know, willing to give thought to all things which may lead to human progress and willing to give effort in so far as that is possible.

If you will permit me, in conclusion I should like to say that I have found your correspondence particularly interesting and I think exceptionally valuable for the reason partly that you seem not at all inclined to overrate the possibilities of your profession; and this, I must say, is an attribute which I find is not universal.

I shall hope to have from you from time to time further information and if you feel so inclined such suggestions as may occur to you.

Sincerely yours,   Saml Gompers
President,   American Federation of Labor.

TLpS, reel 287, vol. 300, pp. 468–69, SG Letterbooks, DLC.

1. James McKeen Cattell (1860–1944), formerly a professor of psychology at the University of Pennsylvania (1888–91) and at Columbia University (1891–1917), was founder and president of the Psychological Corporation in New York City. The organization sought to perfect the application of intelligence and aptitude testing to candidates for positions in business. Cattell was also a founder of the American Psychological Association and the American Association of University Professors.

2. SG had written Cattell to inquire about the use of intelligence tests in industry (SG to Cattell, Dec. 20, 1922, reel 286, vol. 299, p. 769, SG Letterbooks, DLC). For SG's inquiries to others in the field about the use of intelligence tests in business and education, dated Dec. 15 and 20, 1922, see ibid., pp. 527–29, 767–69, and 771–77.

3. H. Res. 476 (67th Cong., 4th sess.), introduced on Dec. 30, 1922, by Republican congressman John Levi Cable of Ohio (1884–1971), called on the secretary of labor and the surgeon general to issue a report on the possible use of intelligence tests as a method for screening immigrants. The measure died in committee. Cable served as a Republican congressman from Ohio from 1921 to 1925 and again from 1929 to 1933.

To John Walker

January 9, 1923.

Mr. J. H. Walker,
President, Illinois State Federation of Labor,
728 Illinois Mine Workers Building, Springfield, Ill.
Dear Sir and Brother:

Your letter of December 28 received and read with interest.

In my letter of November 18[1] in reply to yours of December 11 I had no intention of conveying to you in any way the idea that I thought you had criticized the action of the A.F. of L. National Non-Partisan Political Campaign Committee in issuing the report[2] on its activities for the year 1922. I simply wished to answer the point you advanced that when we pointed out our successes we laid ourselves open to blame for those things we had not done. This you believe spurs "our enemies to increase their efforts." I do not take that view of it. Members of congress are influenced more or less by Labor's enemies only when they believe it would not injure their political fortunes.

The result of the recent elections has given the members of congress who have followed the practice of accepting advice from our enemies considerable of a jolt. For instance, Representative Steenerson[3] of Minnesota has repeatedly contended that he did not care for the Labor vote as there was no Labor vote in his district. Since returning to Washington he makes no secret of the fact that he was defeated through the influence of Labor. There are quite a number of such cases. It has had a moral effect on members of even this reactionary congress. There is one fact established by the Report of the National Non-Partisan Political Campaign Committee of the A.F. of L. and that is that when there is no third party in the field the non-partisan political campaign of Labor has surer chance of success.

I much regret that we do not have same viewpoint, as you say: "I believe that we should have a Labor political organization."

A certain m[ember o]f [congress in] Il[linois proposed to a] member of the A.F. of L. Legislative Committee that a Labor Party be started in his district in order that he be assured of election. He was very emphatically informed that the American Federation of Labor would not countenance such a proposition. That Representative was defeated in the election.

There is no doubt that you carried out the policy which you outlined to me in the Fall of 1921 and that it was successful has been proved by the results. If there had been a strong "Labor political organization" during that campaign, however, it would have been very difficult for you to have swung it as you did to the non-partisan policy. Yet you favor a permanent "Labor Political organization" that will be strong and influential enough to enable the workers "to use their votes most effectively in their own interests."

The fact is that there was really no Labor-Farmer Party in existence in 1922 outside of isolated localities. In Washington where it showed the greatest strength it was badly defeated. In Illinois the vote was so small it was only incidentally mentioned in the official result. How much better would it have been if Labor in Washington had supported former Representative Dill for Senator instead of by their action making it possible for Senator Poindexter to be elected. During his term as a member of congress Mr. Dill's legislative record on measures of interest to Labor was 100 per cent.

The votes of the progressive forward looking citizenship of our country cannot succeed in the election of public officials unless they are united. Where a third party is in existence all its members cannot be influenced to vote just the way its leaders may desire.

The most convincing arguments against a "Labor political organization" is your statement that the same men who represent Labor in the making of agreements with employers usually lead in the political campaign. If there is a partisan labor party in existence between elections some of those labor officials who take part are likely to sacrifice the economic movement for the political movement.

You also state that "if the officials of those organizations are not a part of the 'labor political organization' it usually means disaffection, division and weakness." Therefore when you have a partisan labor party you are between the upper and the nether mill stone. That being the case, why create an organization that will cause so much dissatisfaction which ever way the labor officials act?

Third parties have never been successful in the history of American politics. The efforts wasted in such movements would have radically changed conditions in this country if they had been directed along non-partisan lines. So far as the farmers are concerned they wi[ll] not vote for a third party. They will vote for labor, however, in support of one of the old party tickets, as was the case in Oklahoma.[4] There must be much agitation and a better understanding between Labor and the farmers before the latter will unite with the wage earners in a third party political movement. During the last campaign great headway was made in this respect. We found that the farmers were willing to vote for friends of Labor on either dominant party ticket but would refuse to vote for a candidate on a third party ticket.

The American Federation of Labor has conducted a campaign among the farmers for years that is beginning to show results. It is hoped that nothing will interfere with this encouraging situation.

I feel very deeply on this matter. Whenever a partisan labor party did not intervene we generally have been successful in elections. The progress of the labor movement in its political activities has been hampered much. Along the pathway it has struggled can be found the wrecks of many labor parties none of which did any good for the labor movement.

I am sending you, under separate cover, copies of pamphlets entitled "Should a Political Labor Party Be Formed,"[5] and "Forty Years of Action."[6] After you have read them I would like to know whether it has changed your convictions. If our convictions are antagonistic to those of the labor movement do you think we should continue to defend them?

You and I are simply individuals in a tremendous human movement for the advancement of humanity. The great mass of our people believe in the non-partisan political policy. Therefore, in all seriousness I hope I can convince you that a labor party political organization is a detriment and not a benefit to our economic movement. Like yourself you know my make up is of your type, strong in conviction but tolerant in opposing views, with the absence of feeling of hostility or bitterness to anyone no matter what differences of opinion may exist.

To return for a moment to the original cause of our correspondence. I feel that when the report of the Executive Committee of the American Federation of Labor National Non-Partisan Political Campaign Committee was prepared it did service to the cause of Labor and justice and was of advantage to all the people of our country.

With best wishes and assuring you of my desire to be helpful in any way within my power, I am,

Fraternally yours,   Saml Gompers.
President,   American Federation of Labor.

TLpS, reel 287, vol. 300, pp. 368–70, SG Letterbooks, DLC.

1. Actually, the letter was dated Dec. 18, 1922 (SG to J. H. Walker, reel 286, vol. 299, pp. 835–36, SG Letterbooks, DLC).

2. See "To Edward Bates," Nov. 29, 1922, n. 18, above.

3. Halvor Steenerson (1852–1926) served as a Republican congressman from Minnesota from 1903 to 1923.

4. Members of Oklahoma's short-lived Farmer-Labor Reconstruction League endorsed Democratic candidate John C. Walton in that state's 1922 gubernatorial election, leading to his victory in a bitterly contested campaign.

5. *Should a Political Labor Party Be Formed? An Address by Samuel Gompers, President of the American Federation of Labor, to a Labor Conference Held at New York City, December 9, 1918* (n.p., n.d.). See *The Samuel Gompers Papers,* vol. 11, pp. 8–16.

6. *Forty Years of Action: Non-Partisan Political Policy, American Federation of Labor* (Washington, D.C., 1920).

To John Walker

Jan. 12, 1923.

Mr. J. H. Walker,
President, Illinois State Federation of Labor.
728 Illinois Mine Workers' Building, Springfield, Ill.
Dear Sir and Brother:

I am glad to hear your interesting views following the visit of Albert Thomas[1] to Springfield and Chicago.[2] It is gratifying to know that the representatives of labor acquitted themselves well on this occasion.

I agree entirely with you that it is humiliating that our country should be entirely aloof from that work so valuable, in which other nations are participating with such good effect. I am confident, however, that this intolerable condition must soon come to an end and that our country will demand that America assume its rightful duties and responsibilities in the affairs of the world. It is particularly desirable that we assist in the work of the International Labor Organization which, as you say, was the fruit of American inspiration. I appreciate very much your kindness in sending me copies of the correspondence between Mr. Thomas and yourself.

Mr. Thomas has been here since and including Monday, January eighth and I had an hour's conference with him in this office that afternoon. Then that evening he and his staff were given a dinner by the Secretary of Labor, the officers of the Labor Department being the other hosts. On Tuesday evening he was given a dinner by the Civitan Club of Washington, at which a number of labor men were present including the undersigned, and on Wednesday evening I gave M. Thomas and his staff a dinner at which there were about eighty representative labor men and women and, in addition, a few persons prominent in the progressive, constructive work. Yesterday afternoon Director Thomas was in my office from three o'clock until after five and Vice-President Matthew Woll, Secretary Frank Morrison, our legislative committee and several others participated. It was a splendid interchange of views and I am sure that M. Thomas was very much gratified. We expect to meet each other again before his departure from Washington on Tuesday. He sails from New York for Europe on the Steamship Olympic on January 20th.

Altogether I shared Mr. Thomas' view when he expressed his gratification of the results of his visit and conferences in the various cities to which he traveled in his brief stay in the United States. He is specially appreciative of the fact that I have been able to bring him into contact with the labor men such as you, Mr. Woll, Mr. Perkins and Mr. Fitzpatrick and others of approximately equal standing in the other cities of the country where he visited.

With kindest regards, and best wishes, I am,

Fraternally yours,   Saml Gompers
President   American Federation of Labor.

TLpS, reel 287, vol. 300, pp. 473–74, SG Letterbooks, DLC.

1. Albert Aristide Thomas served as director-general of the International Labor Organization from its founding in 1919 until his death in 1932.

2. Between Dec. 12, 1922, and Jan. 20, 1923, Thomas visited a number of cities in Canada and the United States, including Ottawa, Montreal, Quebec, Toronto, New York City, Chicago, Springfield, Detroit, Boston, and Washington, D.C. He addressed the Mid-Day Luncheon Club in Springfield, Ill., on Dec. 26, and in Chicago the next

day he addressed the opening session of the American Association for Labor Legislation and the City Club of Chicago.

To Harry Fox[1]

January 22, 1923.

Mr. Harry W. Fox,
President, Wyoming State Federation of Labor,[2]
Mine Workers Bldg., P.O. Drawer 892, Cheyenne, Wyoming.
Dear Sir and Brother:—

I am delighted to know that the Wyoming State Federation of Labor is taking the initiative in promoting educational work among the unions of your state. The subjects that you have in mind are especially important. I think the best way that I can help you is to get you in touch with the Executive Secretary[3] of the Workers' Education Bureau.

The Committee on Education of the Federation has just completed negotiations with that Bureau which resulted in a satisfactory agreement for cooperation between the Federation and the Bureau. Under the agreement the Bureau becomes responsible for executive and administrative work in the educational field. It has been preparing various lists of text books that will be helpful to labor unions wishing to undertake specific educational work. By writing to Spencer Miller, Jr., Executive Secretary, Workers' Education Bureau, 465 West 23d Street, New York City, you can get definite suggestions.

One of the best short volumes on economics that I know is by Henry Clay.[4] Another general book that is very interesting is "The Acquisitive Society" by Tawney.[5] A small volume of unusual importance is "American Individualism" by Herbert Hoover.[6] However, for information on text books to be used in reading classes I think you would do much better to consult with Mr. Miller who is in charge of that specific activity.

With kind regards and hoping to hear from you whenever convenient, I am

Fraternally yours,   Saml Gompers.
President,   American Federation of Labor.

TLpS, reel 287, vol. 300, pp. 853–54, SG Letterbooks, DLC.

1. Harry W. Fox, a member of Hotel and Restaurant Employees' International Alliance and Bartenders' International League of America 337 (Culinary Workers) of Cheyenne, Wyo., was president of the Wyoming State Federation of Labor from 1916 to 1924.

2. The Wyoming State Federation of Labor was organized in 1909 and affiliated with the AFL the same year.

3. Spencer Miller, Jr. (1891–1968), an educator trained in engineering and law, served as director of the Workers' Education Bureau from 1921 to 1942.

4. Henry Clay, *Economics: An Introduction for the General Reader* (London, 1916). Clay (1883–1954), a British economist who wrote on industrial matters for the *New York Evening Post* from 1919 to 1921, later founded the National Institute of Economic and Social Research (1938). He served as chairman of the Institute's council from 1940 to 1949 and as the Institute's president from 1949 to 1952.

5. Richard Henry Tawney, *The Acquisitive Society* (New York, 1920). Tawney (1880–1962), a noted British economic historian, was a founder of the Economic History Society (1926) and coeditor of its journal, the *Economic History Review* (1927–34). He served as president of the Workers' Educational Association from 1928 to 1943.

6. Herbert Hoover published the book in 1922.

To the Editor of the *Washington Post*

January 24, 1923.

To the editor,
Washington Post,
Washington, D.C.
Sir:

I am writing to call your attention to a situation the seriousness of which I think you will readily admit. It would be much more to the point, however, if the seriousness of the situation were made manifest by its news treatment. I have reference of course to what has been transpiring at Harrison, Arkansas and in the vicinity of that place along the line of the Missouri and North Arkansas Railway.[1]

I am writing this letter to you, not for publication, but as a personal communication intended specifically to call your attention to what appears to me to be an unwarrantable newspaper neglect of a situation involving the safety and the liberties of large numbers of persons and involving the complete breakdown of civil government over a considerable area. It may be that I am poorly informed in the matter of news values and that I am over-estimating the importance of the situation in Arkansas but I am convinced nevertheless that the general newspaper treatment of the Arkansas case has been neglectful and warrants a challenge to the newspaper world generally.

It has not been more than four or five days since the first news came from Arkansas to the effect that a man had been hanged by a mob.[2] At that time it was practically impossible to get complete accounts from the scene of mob activities because the mob so completely controlled the means of communication and had so thoroughly intimidated all persons who might be inclined to convey information. So far as I am aware, the first detailed accounts came from refugees who had succeeded in getting away from Harrison to points of safety.

Yesterday morning, comparatively meager dispatches to various newspapers made known the fact that a legislative inquiry was under way. This morning, so far as the newspapers are concerned, that inquiry has been all but forgotten.

I ask you to bear in mind these facts:

1. One man was lynched because he would not admit a mob to his house. When the mob threatened to dynamite his house he surrendered rather than see his wife and children blown up. He was not accused of having committed any crime or any wrong.

2. Municipal officers in a number of communities were either compelled to do the mob's bidding or resign from office. In at least one community the municipal officers resigned and turned the government over to the mob.[3]

3. Working people were compelled either to swear allegiance to the mob "committee" and to the Missouri and North Arkansas Railway or leave their homes and their communities. The constitution means nothing to a mob.

4. It appears to be established that a number of persons suffered physical injury at the hands of the mob.

5. Large numbers of persons, including women and children, were compelled to flee for safety over the hills, deserting their homes and leaving such possessions as they might have.

6. It is indicated clearly that the mob was controlled by "a committee" of ten or twelve and that this "committee" was inspired either by the Missouri and North Arkansas Railway or by its friends.

7. It is indicated clearly that cars were furnished by the railroad for transportation of the mob from point to point.

These, briefly, are the facts as they appear to be at this moment. It has been alleged that workers formerly employed by the Missouri and North Arkansas Railway and now on strike were responsible for the burning of some railroad bridges. Thus far this has been mere allegation and there has not been produced, so far as I am aware, the slightest scintilla of evidence to prove that such is the case.

If railroad property has been destroyed it is the duty of civil government in the state of Arkansas and in the communities in that state to find and punish the guilty persons. If those guilty persons are union men all good union men will be glad to see the law vindicated and enforced. If, on the other hand the guilty persons happened to be provocative agents the law should be enforced with equal energy and speed.

As another alternative it will doubtless occur to many that fires have been known to occur without a criminal intent on the part of anyone.

Let me compare the Arkansas situation, which apparently is considered of little news value and little public interest, with the situation existing for example in Louisiana. In Louisiana where the Ku Klux Klan is under fire there have been two horrible murders.[4] A few other persons have been deported but the number of deportees is small and I believe in most cases they have been allowed to return. The civil government virtually ceased to function in one community. In Arkansas there was but one murder while in Louisiana there were two, and these two were most revolting in the hideous cruelty that was practiced. The total amount of violence and the total surrender of civil authority has been greater in Arkansas, however, than in Louisiana. The number of persons subjected to mob rule has been many times greater in Arkansas.

In Louisiana mob vengeance apparently was directed against certain individuals because of individual enmities. In Arkansas mob violence was directed particularly against a large group of persons and not because of any individual enmity but because of the affiliation of those persons. In short, the mob violence in Arkansas was directed against union men who refused to accept the employment terms offered by a railroad.

In Louisiana the state government took charge of the situation and restored orderly procedure. The state government has put into the field all of its resources in an effort to apprehend and punish the criminals.

What is much more to the point in this discussion is that in the Louisiana case the newspapers of the country have displayed great energy and have reported events in the most minute detail to the extent of columns upon columns each day. Regardless of what actually may have been the state of public interest the newspapers have compelled a public interest and have kept it alive and active from day to day. This is to the great credit of the newspapers.

In the Arkansas case almost the contrary has been true. For a day or two fairly adequate stories were published, although they were far from complete in most cases. No effort has been made to follow up the initial stories or to develop information concerning the details of what took place or what influences were back of the mob movement. Practically every newspaper that I have examined this morning, and I have examined most of the leading newspapers, contents itself with publishing a small portion of a statement which I issued yesterday[5] and contains nothing at all from Arkansas. It seems to me that such a situation warrants some self-examination on the part of newspaper editors and that they really ought to make some explanation to the public. I don't know by what news standards Arkansas could be permitted to vanish so quickly and so completely from the columns of our newspapers.

Let me make another comparison. During the strike of the coal miners a terrible massacre took place at Herrin, Illinois.[6] A large number of persons were killed. In this community also civil government apparently broke down but in this case the newspapers were alert not merely to the extent of publishing every possible detail connected with the crime but to the extent of seeking to fix the responsibility for the crime. Not only did the newspapers continue day after day to publish long accounts of what took place in Herrin and of what was alleged to have taken place in Herrin but the Chamber of Commerce of Chicago took it upon itself to raise a fund to finance the prosecution of those accused of the crime by the grand jury in Herrin.

It is true of course that the first three persons killed in Herrin were union men[7] who were shot by armed guards employed by mine owners and that but little has appeared in the newspapers about this particular phase of what took place; but I am willing to let that pass in the present discussion. I am willing also to forego discussion of the fact that the union men placed on trial, and who were apparently believed guilty by most of the newspapers, have been acquitted by a jury under a lawfully constituted court of justice.[8] What I wish mainly to point out is the great energy displayed by the newspapers in publishing every word which it was possible to get from Herrin. There is clearly no such energy in the case of Arkansas. On the contrary, there is no energy at all.

The inference must necessarily be that it is no cause for excitement and no matter of great public interest when a railroad or its friends assume to administer "law" and in the interest of their particular kind of "law" commit murder and assault and overthrow civil government and drive peaceful citizens and their families into distant communities.

It has been indicated that the mob kept newspaper correspondents under surveillance and censored their dispatches; but usually, I believe, newspapers look upon such conduct as a challenge to redoubled efforts. It is a defiance which in the face of newspaper determination seldom accomplishes its object.

I have set forth the facts as far as I have been able to learn them and I have given you my views at some length because I believe the situation to be important and because I believe that the newspapers have been negligent in a matter in which they should feel a public responsibility and a public trust. I do not wish to convey the thought that I am a carping critic because I do not often indulge in criticisms of this kind. I do believe firmly, however, that the present case is an exceptional illustration of a frequently observed one-sided news judgment and it is for that reason that I am calling it to your attention.

I am not writing this letter for publication but I have no objection of course if its contents are made known.[9] It is intended primarily however for yourself and if you think that my own judgment is in error, and if you care to reply, conveying to me your point of view, I shall be happy to have such a reply.[10]

Very truly yours,   Saml Gompers
President,   American Federation of Labor.

TLpS, reel 287, vol. 300, pp. 900–903, SG Letterbooks, DLC.

1. On Feb. 27, 1921, a strike began on the Missouri and North Arkansas Railroad in protest against a 20 percent wage cut. The railroad, which ran some 365 miles between Joplin, Mo., and Helena, Ark., and had its headquarters at Harrison, Ark., continued operating for a time with strikebreakers but had to suspend service at the end of July. When management again employed strikebreakers to resume service in May 1922, repeated vandalism damaged railroad property and hampered operations. Finally, after seven bridges were burned and another dynamited between Jan. 9 and Jan. 12, 1923, Missouri and North Arkansas general manager James Murray issued a statement on Jan. 13, accusing the strikers of sabotage and warning local citizens that it was up to them to protect railroad property if they wanted service to continue. In response, a mass meeting, organized by the railroad and the Farmers' Bank of Harrison, was held in Harrison on Jan. 16 and attended by an estimated one thousand local citizens determined to end the strike and expel the strikers. Calling themselves the "Committee of 1,000," participants at the meeting rounded up strikers and sympathizers for questioning by a twelve-member citizens' court and demanded that they either renounce the strike or leave the area. The circuit court and a grand jury in Harrison cooperated with this citizens' court and used its evidence to bring in thirty-six indictments, leading to the arrest of a number of strikers. Two, under duress, pleaded guilty to arson and were sentenced to prison terms. Other citizens' courts were set up in Eureka Springs, Heber Springs, and Leslie, Ark. The strike officially ended on Dec. 21, 1923, when Frank Mulholland, attorney for the strikers, signed an agreement with the prosecuting attorney and the judge of the circuit court that quashed the indictments and released the two strikers sent to jail.

2. Edward Charles Gregor (1870?-1923), financial secretary of International Association of Machinists 301 of Harrison, refused to cooperate with the mob and, according to one account, would not leave his house until told it would be dynamited if he did not surrender. He reluctantly complied and was marched off to jail; later that night he was hanged from a railroad bridge. Gregor was not involved with the strike and had been working in Branson, Mo., since September 1922, only returning to Harrison at Christmas time to visit his family.

3. The citizens' court of Harrison demanded the resignations of the mayor and board of aldermen. Although the mayor initially refused to comply, he eventually did so, as did three aldermen and the local sheriff, who had deputized fifty marshals to protect local citizens.

4. On Aug. 24, 1922, Klansmen from the northern Louisiana town of Bastrop kidnapped five men from the neighboring town of Mer Rouge, torturing and then murdering two of them and flogging two others. The murdered men, F. Watt Daniel and Thomas Richards, were outspoken opponents of the Ku Klux Klan. The incident touched off further violence between Mer Rouge and Bastrop, leading Louisiana governor John Parker to declare martial law in the area and bring in the Louisiana National Guard. Two grand juries heard evidence in the case but refused to issue indictments, and no one was ever brought to trial for the murders.

5. For SG's press statement of Jan. 23, 1923, see Files of the Office of the President, Speeches and Writings, reel 118, frame 38, *AFL Records.*

6. See "From J. A. H. Hopkins," June 23, 1922, n. 1, above.

7. According to press reports, two union miners, George (variously Jorgy or Jordy) Henderson and Joseph Petkewicz (variously Pitcavitz or Pitchiewicz), were shot and killed when they went to the Herrin mine to protest. A third, James Morris, was also shot and subsequently died of his wounds.

8. Eleven men were put on trial; all were acquitted.

9. The *Washington Post* did not publish SG's letter, but it did print extracts from his press statement. See "Gompers Seeks State Curb of Harrison Mob," *Washington Post,* Jan. 24, 1923.

10. On Jan. 24, 1923, SG sent similar letters to the *Baltimore Sun,* the *New York Times,* the *New York Tribune,* the *New York World,* the *Philadelphia Public Ledger,* and the *Washington Herald* (reel 287, vol. 300, pp. 904–7, 909–28, SG Letterbooks, DLC). When S. M. Reynolds, managing editor of the *Baltimore Sun,* replied he had been unable to publish fuller reports because nothing more had been furnished by the news services, SG wrote the Associated Press, United Press, and the International News Service on Jan. 31 and Feb. 2 to ask to review their coverage (ibid., reel 288, vol. 301, pp. 205–6, 262–65). Associated Press agreed to allow William English Walling to review their press files and sent a reporter to Arkansas, and United Press sent SG a complete set of their clippings on the incident. For SG's reports on the matter to the AFL Executive Council, dated Feb. 16 and 17, see Executive Council Records, Minutes, reel 7, frames 1293–94, 1311–12, *AFL Records.*

Excerpts from the Minutes of a Meeting with Santiago Iglesias[1]

Thursday, January 25, 1923.

. . .

Secretary Morrison read the report submitted by Mr. Iglesias dated December 16, 1922, on his visit to the Virgin Islands.[2] After reporting in detail on conditions in the islands Mr. Iglesias stated the following conclusions:

"In view of the deplorable colonial conditions herewith stated the doctrine to be embodied by Congressional Legislation that may be granted for the new government of the Virgin Islands should contain among others, the following principles:

"First:—That economic independence from absentee capitalism is essential to the welfare of the Virgin Islands.

"Second:—That industrial power should be a public trust and for the public interest.

"Third:—That public utilities should be constructed, owned and operated by bonafide residents.

"Fourth:—That the taxing power should be used to advance the public good by encouraging enterprises and home industries breaking down monopoly by the diffusion of wealth.

"Fifth:—That the gradual municipalization of the soil is a just and practical method of dealing with the land monopoly problem. The principles of the Homestead Law[3] of Porto Rico should be a model to institute its form of protection to provide land and homes to the people of the Virgin Islands.

"Sixth:—That the right and duty to work is a clear corollary from the right to life, liberty and the pursuit of happiness.

"Seventh:—The banking and credit should not be left to absentee private manipulation, speculation and monopolies, but controlled by the Government of the Virgin Islands in the interest of all."

In connection with the first principle above, Mr. Gompers questioned Mr. Iglesias to the manner in which the recommendation is to be brought about and Mr. Iglesias said he could not offer any remedy, but the evil, the ill is there.

Mr. Gompers: I believe also that the industrial interests of the United States should be freed from much of this capitalism here but how are we to accomplish it? I think we are gradually doing it in the way of creating greater power in the industries and in agriculture. To my mind that is the only answer to the development and progress of the universe. I think it applies to the Virgin Islands as well as it does to Porto Rico, to the United States, to England, France, Germany and all other countries of the world.

Mr. Iglesias: The great difference is that these little islands have no different industries. They have the capitalists living in Paris or in Denmark or in Wall Street, and they pay no attention to what is going on. The conditions of that people are worse than any other continental nations.

Mr. Gompers said of course, and it was because conditions were so bad that Mr. Iglesias was sent to investigate. But you say "economic independence from absentee capitalism is essential to the welfare of the Virgin Islands." As a matter of fact the industries of the United States are controlled really either by formerly British capitalism, now by the capitalism in the United States and I don't know so far as labor is concerned that one is better than another. It is the same for us here in a big land in which there is a diversity of products and soil and industry and commerce, while over there there is practically just one thing, in that island far away. We have still maintained the Federal governmental control over our possessions including Porto Rico and if that is so there must be general laws governing all of them whether it be the mainland or the possessions. That is the difficulty, instead of granting absolute control, self-government. There will be very little opportunity for self-development. That is the thing to which I wanted an answer.

In connection with the second recommendation, Mr. Iglesias explained that there really is an industry there. The harbor of St. Thomas is now in the hands of the Danish government, that would have to be taken by the government. It is industry because they give oil and coal and repair machinery for the steamers going and coming. That port has been for years just as it is a free port and that constitutes the industry of St. Thomas.

The third recommendation was along the same line, Mr. Iglesias explained, the Danish living in Denmark collect the money from the Virgin Islands and do nothing for the people, pay no taxes.

The fourth recommendation would mean that the land now paying no taxes should be taxed for the welfare of the Island so that the foreign owners of the land would have to pay taxes or go.

Mr. Wright[4] referred to the third suggestion and said that even in the United States, public utilities are owned by New York capital, for instance that public utilities in a city in Illinois are owned by New York capital, and there is no law that could be passed in the United States that could stop that. Mr. Gompers said that as a matter of fact for every new enterprise they float an issue of bonds or securities.

Mr. Iglesias: As I have said before, these islands are isolated pieces of land where the inhabitants cannot go anywhere; they must remain there, they cannot go away; these islands are not states. They are governed by the congress of the United States, the authority of congress. I have been reading something of what the United States is doing in Alaska to develop Alaska. The federal government has already through congressional legislation put a great many millions of dollars to develop Alaska. Now why cannot these colonial isolated islands be controlled in the proper way when they need so very few millions of dollars in comparison with the work that is being done in Alaska.

On recommendation No. 5 Mr. Iglesias explained that they have in Porto Rico a law where they grant five acres of land to a bona fide agricultural family and they build a little house for themselves and have possession of the land. They can work in an industry and at the same time develop their land until they can become self-supporting. They do not want to go to the hills to work but they have to go to work in order to have some rights.

Mr. Gompers asked if the people of the Virgin Islands speak English, and Mr. Iglesias said yes, they do, and that their school attendance is about 80%.

Mr. Gompers asked what is their state of mental ability for self-government. Mr. Iglesias said they are not entirely ready for self-government.

Mr. Gompers: You think then that there should be set up a government something like that which obtains in Porto Rico.

Mr. Iglesias: Yes, I think that will be good, I think that they will be content if they could get just the same suggestion that the Secretary of the Navy[5] made in the letter to Judge Towner,[6] to get the three islands to go together and instead of two colonial councils that they have one, a legislature and give the right to vote to all the citizens.

Mr. Gompers: They have not yet American Citizenship. They are in the same position now that the Porto Rican people were prior to the granting of citizenship to them.

Mr. Iglesias: Exactly.

. . .

Mr. Gompers asked whether the affairs of the Virgin Islands come under the jurisdiction of the Bureau of Insular Affairs. Mr. Iglesias said no, General MacIntyre[7] has nothing to do with it. Mr. Roosevelt[8] is the man in charge. It comes under the Navy Department. Mr. Gompers then said but the political affairs of the islands come under the jurisdiction of the Committee on Insular Affairs of both houses of congress and Mr. Iglesias agreed with him.

Mr. Gompers: What do you think of trying to get the Committee on Insular Affairs to meet for the purpose of having this case brought to them by the American Federation of Labor.

Mr. Iglesias: It would be all right. In another letter[9] I have suggested to you, President Gompers that you have a talk with Mr. Roosevelt about this matter to know what the position of the federal government is in regard to that. They know that something has to be done.

Mr. Gompers: Probably that can be done next week but the thing I have in mind is whether to present that to Secretary Roosevelt or to present it to the committee on Insular Affairs. Which do you think is most practical?

Mr. Iglesias: The first thing to do is to have an interview with Mr. Roosevelt because I am sure that Mr. Roosevelt will become a partisan in your action. He will like to know that you are going to take an interest in it and with the suggestion made by the secretary of the Navy in regard to political organization I think that the people will be content for the time being. . . .

Mr. Gompers promised to try to get a conference with the secretary of the Navy during the coming week[10] and during the early part of the coming week I want you to remind me of that.

. . .

The question of Porto Rican agricultural workers was taken up. Mr. Gompers explained that there is no question but that if the applications for strikes were endorsed it will affect all the agricultural workers' unions in Porto Rico, that they will all want to go out and be supported financially; that if there are a couple of thousand men on strike, in about two weeks the funds will be all gone.

Mr. Iglesias said that he has been delaying these things for the last three years. . . .

. . .

Mr. Gompers: I don't want to escape everything. What do you think if I sent them a cablegram saying that the American Federation of Labor will aid financially to the extent of its ability?

Mr. Iglesias: That will be a great thing. Sure, it will be a great help.

Mr. Morrison asked if they do not win in six weeks what is the chance.

Mr. Iglesias: I assure you that the Federation organizers will not let a single cent be lost for a cessation of work without being sure something is going to be got in a reasonable time. A strike of agricultural workers that goes over six weeks is liable to be lost entirely. We do not let them go back to work, but of course these poor people cannot sustain themselves, they go out and they are liable to win because everybody goes out.

It was decided to frame a telegram in accordance with Mr. Gompers' suggestion that the American Federation of Labor will aid financially to the extent of his ability.

TDc, Files of the Office of the President, Conferences, reel 122, frames 378–83, 385, 387–88, *AFL Records*. Typed notation: "Conference in President Gompers' office, President Gompers, Secretary Morrison, Santiago Iglesias, Chester Wright and W. C. Roberts participating."

1. Santiago IGLESIAS Pantín served as president of the Federación Libre de los Trabajadores de Puerto Rico (Free Federation of the Workers of Puerto Rico) from 1900 to 1933 and was the AFL salaried organizer for Puerto Rico and Cuba from 1901 to 1933. Meeting with Iglesias were SG, Frank Morrison, W. C. Roberts, and Chester Wright.

2. Iglesias to SG, Dec. 16, 1922, reel 288, vol. 301, pp. 281–88, SG Letterbooks, DLC.

3. Reference to a statute passed in 1917 by the Legislative Assembly of Puerto Rico, and then revised in 1921, providing for the construction of urban housing for laborers and artisans and the distribution of small farms to the rural poor on a lease-to-own basis.

4. Chester Maynard WRIGHT, director of the AFL Information and Publicity Service (1920 to at least 1925), assistant editor of the *American Federationist* (1922 to at least 1925), and English-language secretary of the Pan-American Federation of Labor (1919–27).

5. Edwin Denby (1870–1929) served as secretary of the navy from 1921 until he resigned in 1924 because of the Teapot Dome scandal. He had previously served as a Republican congressman from Michigan (1905–11).

6. Horace Mann Towner (1855–1937), an Iowa judge from 1890 to 1911, served as a Republican congressman from that state from 1911 to 1923 and as governor of Puerto Rico from 1923 to 1929.

7. Maj. Gen. Frank McIntyre (1865–1944) served as chief of the Bureau of Insular Affairs from 1912 to 1918 and again from 1920 to 1929.

8. Theodore Roosevelt, Jr. (1887–1944), son of President Theodore Roosevelt and a decorated veteran of both world wars, served as assistant secretary of the navy from 1921 to 1924. He later served as governor of Puerto Rico (1929–32) and as governor-general of the Philippines (1932–33).

9. Iglesias to SG, Dec. 21, 1922, reel 288, vol. 301, pp. 279–80, SG Letterbooks, DLC.

10. SG, Iglesias, and Roberts met with Roosevelt on Jan. 31, 1923. For an account of the meeting, see Files of the Office of the President, Conferences, reel 122, frames 429–30, *AFL Records.*

Excerpts from the Minutes of a Meeting of the Executive Council of the AFL[1]

Monday, February 19, 1923.

AFTERNOON SESSION.

. . .

Robert Fechner[2] and P. J. Conlon, representing the international Association of Machinists appeared before the Executive Council. Both gentlemen addressed the Council upon two requests, one in behalf of securing the assistance of the Council in the effort that is being made to get the Governors of some of the eastern states in a conference with the railroad executives in an effort to bring about a settlement of the shop crafts' strike,[3] and the other for publicity in the interests of the strike. They referred to the fact that the strike of the shopmen is referred to by the newspapers as a dead issue. They assured the Council that it is not over by any means. The shop crafts are still on strike on fifty-five of what are known as major trunk lines. The men can go to work tomorrow morning on one condition, that is, that they surrender their cards in unions affiliated to the American Federation of Labor. The labor press does not refer to the strike except the strike of last Summer. The central bodies should be advised of the strike and the number of lines on strike. The men laid aside the issues of the restraining of their rights and restraining of rules. The question they are now contending for is one not of their own making, one that they did not vote for but one raised by the railroad managers, that of surrendering union membership. They expressed the hope that the Executive Council could give them some relief by even having the labor press publish the facts in connection with the shop crafts' strike and the truth with reference to the shortage of coal which is due to the shortage of cars to move the coal.

President Gompers advised the two representatives that the members of the Council would want to do anything we possibly can. He suggested that they prepare something as a memorandum for them to act upon, both in the matter of appealing to the Governors and in the matter of publicity desired, and put it in such shape as the Executive Council can act upon.

. . .

Tuesday, February 20, 1923.

AFTERNOON SESSION.

. . .

Pursuant to the request of the Executive Council, Messrs. Fechner and Conlon submitted resolutions embodying the requests which they had stated orally to the Executive Council, which were taken up and acted upon in the following order:

Whereas, On July 1, 1922, The Railway Shop Crafts of the United States ceased work to resist reductions in wage rates and loss of overtime rules by order of the United States Railroad Labor Board that to them seemed unwarranted and unjust, and

Whereas, On July 28, President Harding requested them to lay the cause for which the Shop Crafts went on strike in abeyance to be considered at a later date on his assurance that he would arrange for the men to peaceably resume work, and

Whereas, The Shop Crafts complied with this request, but the railroads shamefully repudiated its promise and set up instead another issue than that which originally caused the strike, thereby, inaugurating a general lockout from said date, and

Whereas, Since August 1, 1922, the Federated Shop Crafts have been locked out by [the] American Railroad Executives' Association, controlled by a vicious minority, representing powerful New York Banking interests, and

Whereas, On September 13, 1922, due to financial reasons, the Policy

Committee of the Shop Crafts decided to relinquish some of the men to resume work under what was known as the Willard-Jewell-Warfield[4] Agreement. This arrangement settled the controversy on 137 railroads, affecting less than 50 per cent of the 475,000 men originally involved, and,

Whereas, Since September 13, 1922, the press of our country has been painfully silent on all matters affecting the Shopmen's lockout and when compelled to refer to it always using the past tense, and

Whereas, Notwithstanding the above change in policy, there are still locked out over 200,000 shopmen, contending against 52 major trunk lines and 53 short lines since July 1, 1922, and

Whereas, The issue created by the American Railroad Executives on August 1, 1922, as the terms these strikers can again be reinstated in the service of their various companies is that they be employed as individuals and agree to become a member of the Company's Union and foreswear allegiance to their former associations and relinquish all the rights they formerly held by reason of their continuity in service, and

Whereas, It has been brought to our attention that the Labor Press and Central Bodies have seemed to accept the Shopmen's controversy as a closed incident.

Therefore Be It Resolved, That the Executive Council of the American Federation of Labor in session assembled hereby assure the railroad shop crafts of our unstinted support, and compliment them upon the effective resistance they have put up in their fight for the past eight months, and

Be It Further Resolved, That the President and Secretary of the American Federation of Labor be hereby instructed to issue a circular letter to all Central Bodies and Officers of the American Federation of Labor calling to their attention the fact that the Shopmen are still locked out, and be it

Further Resolved, That the Labor Press be called upon to give the Shopmen's Lockout due publicity to the end that the campaign of silence instituted by the American Railroad Executives' Association to keep the American public uninformed through the daily press may be overcome, and

Be It Finally Resolved, That the Weekly News Letter of the American Federation of Labor from week to week keep the Labor Press of the country informed as to the progress of the Shopmen's Lockout.[5]

It was decided that the request as set forth in this document be complied with by the Executive Council.

Whereas, We are informed on reliable authority that by reason of the Federated Shopmen's strike and consequent lockout the motive power of ninety per cent of the roads which are continuing the lockout is less than forty per cent efficient, and

Whereas, As a result of this break-down in motive power embargoes of all kinds are now arbitrarily placed by the railroads on all classes of freight except perishable goods, and

Whereas, Owing to the recent cold weather and epidemic of La Grippe in New York, Pennsylvania, New Jersey and the New England States there has been a demand for coal that has exhausted the local supply on hand and extra stocks cannot be obtained although there are thousands of cars loaded with coal within a few hours of these markets, and

Whereas, The apparent cause of the inability of the people to obtain coal is because railroads which are continuing to keep their employes locked out have not been able to keep their motive power in condition to meet the normal requirements, and

Whereas, These conditions have been brought to the attention of Administrative officers, both Federal and State, and no relief measures have been taken,

Therefore Be It Resolved That the Executive Council of the A.F. of L. in session assembled do hereby condemn our Administrative officials who will allow such a condition to continue, especially when they have exerted themselves to such extremes to see that commerce was not interrupted by the Federated Shopmen in the matter of their pursuing peaceful picket duty.

Be It Further Resolved, that the President and Secretary of the A.F. of L. be instructed to cooperate with the movement now in motion in the States of New York, New Jersey and Pennsylvania—set in motion by the labor forces of these states—demanding that the Governors of these states confer with a view of finding some solution of the present deplorable situation now prevalent in these states by reason of the attitude of certain railroad executives who desire to crush Union labor on their respective railroads, and

Be It Finally Resolved, that the officers of the American Federation of Labor do everything within their power to hasten the end of the present unwarranted lockout of the railroad employes.

It was decided that the Executive Council authorizes and directs that every effort be made for the purpose of bringing about a conference of the Governors of the several states particularly in interest in the coal shortage situation and for the purpose of bringing about an adjustment between the railroad shop crafts and the railroad executives.

. . .

TDc, Executive Council Records, Minutes, reel 7, frames 1293, 1295, 1298–1300, *AFL Records.*

1. The AFL Executive Council met in Washington, D.C., Feb. 14–20, 1923.

2. Robert Fechner (1876–1939) was a member of the general executive board of the International Association of Machinists from 1914 to 1916 and again from 1918 until his death. A longtime member of Machinists' local 23 of Savannah, he had also served as secretary-treasurer of the Georgia State Federation of Labor (1910–16). In 1925 he was named a vice-president of the Machinists, a position he held until 1933 when he took a leave of absence to accept an appointment as director of the Civilian Conservation Corps.

3. On Feb. 28, 1923, SG wrote Gifford Pinchot, George Silzer, and Alfred E. Smith—the governors of Pennsylvania, New Jersey, and New York—asking for a conference with them to help settle the railroad shopmen's strike (reel 289, vol. 302, pp. 33, 38–39, SG Letterbooks, DLC). Pinchot responded positively, but Silzer and Smith declined on the grounds that the matter fell under federal, not state, jurisdiction (ibid., pp. 264–65, 418; see also Pinchot to Silzer, Mar. 3, 1923, Alfred E. Smith Papers, N).

4. Solomon Davies Warfield (1863–1927), a banker and businessman, was president of the Seaboard Air Line Railway Co. and organizer and president of the National Association of Owners of Railroad Securities. For the negotiation of the agreement by Warfield, Daniel Willard, and B. M. Jewell, see "Miners' Strike Indorsed by Federation of Labor; Rail Walkout Unopposed," June 16, 1922, n. 1, in "Excerpts from News Accounts of the 1922 Convention of the AFL in Cincinnati," June 16–24, 1922, above.

5. See, for example, "Rail Shop Employes Are Resisting Modern Feudalists," *AFL Weekly News Service,* Mar. 17, 1923; "Railroads That Enforce Shop Lockout," ibid., Mar. 24; and "Railroads' Lockout Policy Is Costly; Vast Sums Spent; Public Pays Bill," ibid., Mar. 31.

To H. F. Gordon

February 21, 1923.

Mr. H. F. Gordon,
Secretary-Treasurer, New Orleans Typographical Union No. 17,
642 Commercial Place, New Orleans, La.
Dear Sir and Brother:

Your letter of February 8 received and read with interest.

The feeling is fast growing in our country that the Volstead Act has created criminals instead of reducing their number. Among the most persistent opponents for the modification of the Volstead Act so that wholesome beer can be manufactured and sold are the bootleggers, undertakers, dope dealers and wood alcohol manufacturers. Could you let me know the general opinion of the people of your city on this question?

With best wishes and assuring you of my desire to be helpful in any way within my power, I am,

Fraternally yours, Saml Gompers
President, American Federation of Labor.

TLpS, reel 288, vol. 301, p. 810, SG Letterbooks, DLC.

Samuel Gompers en route to Portland, Ore., Sept. 25, 1923, to
attend the AFL convention. (Photography Collection, Miriam
and Ira D. Wallach Division of Art, Prints, and Photographs,
New York Public Library, Astor, Lenox, and Tilden Foundations)

SG receiving his 1924 Red Cross button from Beverly Moffett, daughter of Rear Admiral William Moffett, chief of the Naval Aeronautics Bureau. (George Meany Memorial Archives)

SG and his second wife, Gertrude Annersly Gleaves Gompers. (Library of Congress)

SG testifying before the House Judiciary Committee to
advocate manufacture and sale of 2.75 percent beer and wine,
Apr. 21, 1924. (Library of Congress)

SG meeting with Robert La Follette Sr., Sept. 19, 1924. Seated, left to right, La Follette, SG, and Matthew Woll. Standing, left to right, William Collins, John Coughlin, Robert La Follette Jr., W. C. Roberts, Hugh Frayne, and Chester Wright. (Library of Congress)

SG and AFL headquarters staff cheer the arrival of Mexican president-elect Plutarco Elías Calles in Washington, D.C., Oct. 31, 1924. W. C. Roberts is standing front row center; Florence Thorne is standing at far right. (George Meany Memorial Archives)

SG relaxing during his visit to Panama, January 1924.
(George Meany Memorial Archives)

SG presiding over a meeting of the Pan-American Federation of Labor,
Mexico City, Dec. 6, 1924. James Duncan is seated to the right of SG; Chester
Wright is seated at far left. (Photography Collection, Miriam and Ira D.
Wallach Division of Art, Prints, and Photographs, New York Public
Library, Astor, Lenox, and Tilden Foundations)

SG on his arrival in Mexico City, Nov. 30, 1924. (Photography Collection, Miriam and Ira D. Wallach Division of Art, Prints, and Photographs, New York Public Library, Astor, Lenox, and Tilden Foundations)

Frank Morrison and William Green, Dec. 30, 1924.
(Library of Congress)

A San Francisco iron worker at the hour of SG's funeral, Dec. 18, 1924. (Photography Collection, Miriam and Ira D. Wallach Division of Art, Prints, and Photographs, New York Public Library, Astor, Lenox, and Tilden Foundations)

To James Roberts

February 21, 1923.

Mr. J. H. Roberts,
Secretary, Central Labor Union,[1]
211 Spring St., Charleston, S.C.
Dear Sir and Brother:

Permit me to thank you for your letter of February 16 enclosing resolutions you adopted in condemnation of Mr. William A. Sunday[2] for his attacks on labor.

You must remember that Mr. Sunday is not attacking me personally. He is attacking the American Federation of Labor and its 4,000,000 members. He is simply using my name to hide his real motive. Only a short time ago he delivered an address in which he maliciously misrepresented labor and came out openly for the non-union shop. The expenses of Mr. Sunday's work is carried on by contributions from people who take him seriously. The sudden injection of himself into the industrial field by upholding unfair employers is evidence that contributions from that source have influenced his declarations. It would not be proper for me to ask any newspaper to publish your resolutions. That should be done by you. However, I thank the Charleston Central Labor Union for its expressions of confidence and support.

With best wishes and assuring you of my desire to be helpful in any way within my power, I am,

Fraternally yours, Saml Gompers
President, American Federation of Labor.

TLpS, reel 288, vol. 301, p. 812, SG Letterbooks, DLC.

1. The AFL chartered the Central Labor Union of Charleston (S.C.) and Vicinity in 1912.

2. William Ashley "Billy" Sunday (1862–1935), ordained in 1903 after a short career in professional baseball (1883–91) and work in the Y.M.C.A., was a flamboyant evangelistic preacher, known for his revivalist style, his fundamentalist theology, and his opposition to alcohol, liberal religion, immigrants, and radicals.

To Matthew Woll

Feb. 23, 1923.

Mr. Matthew Woll,
Director A.F. of L. Legal Information Bureau,
Room 701, 166 West Washington St., Chicago, Ill.
Dear Sir and Brother:

In conformity with the promise I made to you when you were at headquarters on Wednesday, February 21, I am herewith sending you the following documents:

Draft of "An Act Concerning Labor Organizations" submitted by attorney Jackson H. Ralston, January 24, 1923.[1]

The criticisms thereon by Professor Francis B. Sayre[2] of the Law School of Harvard University, February 13, 1923.

The suggested draft of the constitutional amendment on the Veto Power of the Supreme Court by Hon. Meyer London submitted February 6, 1923.[3]

The suggested draft of constitutional amendment on the Rights of Labor Unions by Morris Hillquit.[4]

Further communication from Mr. Ralston, Feb. 17, 1923.

Copy of action from A.F. of L. Convention, Cincinnati 1922 authorizing the above.[5]

Copies of bills of H.J. Res. 457[6] and S.J. Res. 232[7] for constitutional amendment prohibiting and regulating Child Labor.

As you were advised when you were at headquarters, the Senate Committee on the Judiciary had favorably reported to the Senate our Child Labor amendment. Yesterday, I appeared before the House Judiciary Committee in support of our Child Labor Amendment.[8] Before I left the Capitol to go to the station to take the train for New York,[9] I was advised that the House Committee had reported the amendment favorably to the House. We will leave no effort untried to secure the enactment of this legislation before the adjournment of the present Congress.

Fraternally yours,   Saml Gompers
President   American Federation of Labor.

P.S. I might add that the review of the Veto Power of the Supreme Court by Meyer London will be published in the March issue of the *American Federationist*.[10]

S. G.

TLpS, reel 288, vol. 301, pp. 868–69, SG Letterbooks, DLC.

1. See SG to Ralston, Feb. 10, 1923, reel 288, vol. 301, pp. 501–2, SG Letterbooks, DLC.

2. Francis Bowes Sayre (1885–1972) was a member of the faculty of the Harvard Law School from 1917 to 1934. He later served as assistant secretary of state (1933–39).

3. The text of Meyer London's draft amendment read: "Should the Supreme Court declare any law to be in conflict with the Constitution, the re-enactment of such law by two thirds of both Houses, with the approval or over the veto of the President, shall establish the constitutional validity of the law, and of every part thereof, as [of] the date of its original enactment, and the validity of such law shall not thereafter be called into question by any court" (SG to Ralston, Feb. 10, 1923, reel 288, vol. 301, pp. 501–2, SG Letterbooks, DLC; quotation at p. 501).

4. Morris HILLQUIT was a member of the national executive committee of the Socialist Party of America and counsel to the International Ladies' Garment Workers' Union. He submitted his draft of the amendment to SG on Feb. 19, 1923. (See SG to Hillquit, Feb. 23, 1923, reel 288, vol. 301, p. 863, SG Letterbooks, DLC.)

5. See "Labor Urges Veto on Supreme Court" and "Let Veto Curb Supreme Court, Unions Demand," June 21 and 23, 1922, in "Excerpts from News Accounts of the 1922 Convention of the AFL in Cincinnati," June 16–24, 1922, above.

6. Actually H.J. Res. 407. See "To William Green," June 3, 1922, n. 5, above.

7. See "To William Green," June 3, 1922, n. 5, above.

8. Files of the Office of the President, Hearings, reel 126, frame 136, *AFL Records.*

9. SG left Washington, D.C., on Feb. 22, 1923, for a series of conferences in New York City. He had returned to AFL headquarters in Washington by Feb. 26.

10. "The Veto Power of the Supreme Court," *American Federationist* 30 (Mar. 1923): 224–31.

To John Leary, Jr.[1]

Washington, D.C., February 26, 1923.

Mr. John J. Leary, Jr.,
The World,
New York City.

We ought to enter the Hague tribunal[2] *Stop* I can see no chance for an argument against such a step *Stop* I am for going into it now, as suggested in the president's message to congress[3] *Stop* That we must for the time being remain out of the League of Nations seems necessary, because of a necessity imposed by the fortunes of politics and the obduracy of some of our best minds *Stop* But rather than not enter the court at all let us enter as we may and as soon as possible *Stop* It is to be hoped that those who have been called irreconcilables will not be irreconcilable to this modicum of reason and justice.

Samuel Gompers

TWtpSr, reel 288, vol. 301, p. 920, SG Letterbooks, DLC.

1. John Joseph Leary, Jr. (1874–1944), reported on labor and the economy for the *New York World.* He worked for the paper from 1919 to 1931, gaining national prominence for his reports on the Leo Frank lynching in 1915 (see *The Samuel Gompers Papers,* vol. 9, pp. 278–79, n. 2), his coverage of the 1919 coal strike (for which he received a Pulitzer Prize in 1920), his exposé on conditions among the miners in West Virginia (see *The Samuel Gompers Papers,* vol. 11, pp. 295 and 297, n. 6), and his reporting on the Sacco-Vanzetti case. He subsequently worked as a public relations representative for various AFL building trades unions.

2. While the United States was never officially a member of the Permanent Court of International Justice, also known as the World Court, which was established at The Hague under the Covenant of the League of Nations, American judges served on the Court from its inception in 1922 until 1942. These included John Bassett Moore (1922–28), Charles Evans Hughes (1928–30), Frank B. Kellogg (1930–35), and Manley Ottmer Hudson (1936–42).

3. On Feb. 24, 1923, President Warren Harding sent a message to the Senate urging it to approve full American participation in the World Court.

A Memorandum of a Conference with James Davis[1]

February 28, 1923

Secretary Davis began the conference by saying that he was making an effort to educate alien labor and was much surprised to know that labor was opposed to it. He told of conditions in Pittsburg and other steel districts where "bohunks" and "padrones" received as high as $1000 to $1500 a week from the foreigners at work in the steel mills. They also received pay from the steel companies and had been known to call strikes to force the payment of tribute to them the "bohunks." He told how difficult it was to educate foreigners as to the meaning of America.

President Gompers pointed out that the remedy for illiteracy among the foreigners was organization. He told how the needle trades for years used yiddish in their meetings and that through the influences of the trade union movement they were now using nothing but English. The brewery workers who are mostly Germans and at one time used German in their meetings had changed to English. The musicians had the same experience. President Gompers said it was the education obtained in the trade union movement that had brought about the education of those who spoke a foreign language.

President Gompers then brought up the coolie labor bill[2] in the House and expressed most earnestly a protest against it. He said that if the sugar planters of Hawaii wanted to Americanize the Islands they could not do it by bringing in Chinese coolies under bond. He said that the Executive Council had directed him to ask the Secretary of Labor for a report made by a commission sent by the Secretary to Hawaii to investigate labor conditions.[3]

The Secretary said that by direction of Secretary of State Hughes the report could not be given to the public but that he would ask the Secretary if a copy could be secured for President Gompers. He said the object in suppressing the report was because it would raise racial antagonism, which the Secretary of State desired to avoid.

President Gompers told the Secretary of an appeal being made by the Filipino Labor Union of Hawaii to the public to explain why they were asking for an increase in wages. He said that undoubtedly the object of the coolie bill being presented at this time was to make the government a strike breaking agency.

Secretary Davis made no verbal reply but shook his head as if in doubt. He then called up Chairman Johnson of the Immigration Committee of the House and asked him whether he had done anything in the Near East matter. Mr. Johnson apparently told him that the Walsh[4] bill[5] was then under consideration.

Secretary Davis said that Representative Mondell[6] had called up to find out if he thought it wise to give a rule to consider the immigration bill submitted by the Immigration Committee (H.R. 14273[7] by Johnson). The Secretary said that he had told Representative Mondell that he was not prepared to give a definite answer. He said that he was making a survey of the relative question and it would be astonishing when completed. For that reason he did not care to pass upon the question of giving a rule for the bill.

President Gompers continued to explain the dangers to the United States in the coolie bill and stated that when the request of admission by Hawaii to the United States was under discussion the sugar planters agreed to accept the laws pertaining to labor in force in the United States.

Secretary Davis said that he was sending two members of the Commission who went to Hawaii to Louisiana fields to investigate the sugar industry (the Hawaiian Commission said that there was no shortage of labor in the sugar or pineapple industries but there was in the rice fields and that only Chinese could do that kind of work. They have rice fields in Louisiana).

At this juncture the Secretary turned to the question of registration of aliens. He told how ships would bring in large numbers of sailors and that many of them would leave the ships and remain in this country; that 40,000 Chinese had been smuggled into the United States in the last few years as well as many thousands of Japs. The price paid the smugglers was from $500 up. He said that there were at least 100,000 aliens smuggled into the United States in the past year that had no legal right here. He said that he favored the registration of every alien so they would know where they were and at the same time compel them to learn to speak English, read and write and the principles upon which our country is founded. He knew of workers in the Jones and Laughlin Steel Works in Pittsburg who had been there for thirty years and still could not speak English.

In conclusion he said "what I would like is to have labor with me. I am going out on the Chatauqua Circuit this year and I intend to advocate registration and compulsory education of aliens.[8] I am in favor of compulsory education of children. An alien who could not read or write or speak english is a child and should be compelled to learn. Therefore, I am for compulsory education of the alien. I will tell my audiences that Mr. Gary is opposed to the registration of aliens. I do not also want to say that the A.F. of L. is opposed to the registration of aliens and their education. The bill in congress does not compel the alien to become naturalized. It simply compels him to become educated."

President Gompers then said that it was a matter that would require consideration and that he would take it up in a day or two with his associates and give an answer. He admitted that all that Secretary Davis had said about the failure of our government and our people to educate aliens was true but that he did not believe that the Secretary's remedy would accomplish what he thought it would.

The meeting then broke up with the understanding that President Gompers would take the matter under consideration.

TDc, Files of the Office of the President, Conferences, reel 122, frames 570–72, *AFL Records.* Typed notation: "Immigration and Coolie Labor. Conference Held in the Office of Secretary of Labor James J. Davis, February 28, 1923 at 2:30 P.M."

1. Participants in the conference with Secretary of Labor James Davis were SG, Frank Morrison, and AFL Legislative Committee members E. F. McGrady, W. C. Roberts, and Edgar Wallace.

2. H.J. Res. 171 (67th Cong., 1st sess.). See *The Samuel Gompers Papers,* vol. 11, p. 484, n. 2.

3. Members of the commission, appointed by Davis in November 1922, included Hywell Davies, commissioner of conciliation for the U.S. Department of Labor; John Donlin, president of the AFL Building Trades Department; Otto Hartwig, president of the Oregon State Federation of Labor; Fred Keightly, secretary of the Amalgamated Association of Iron, Steel, and Tin Workers; and Lucius Sheppard, president of the Order of Railway Conductors of America. The commission submitted its report to the secretary in January 1923.

4. David Ignatius Walsh (1872–1947) served as a Democratic senator from Massachusetts from 1919 to 1925 and from 1926 to 1947. He had previously served as governor of the state (1914–15).

5. S.J. Res. 252 (67th Cong., 4th sess.), to admit refugees, primarily Armenians, from Asia Minor into the United States, was introduced by Walsh on Dec. 5, 1922. The bill died in committee, and no such legislation was passed during this session of Congress.

6. Frank Wheeler Mondell (1860–1939) served as a Republican congressman from Wyoming from 1895 to 1897 and from 1899 to 1923.

7. Republican congressman Albert Johnson of Washington introduced H.R. 14,273 (67th Cong., 4th sess.) on Feb. 9, 1923. The bill died in committee.

8. For subsequently proposed legislation calling for the registration and education of immigrants, see "Excerpts from the Minutes of a Meeting of the Trade Union Legislative Conference Committee," Nov. 13, 1923, below.

To Robert Fechner

March 2, 1923.

Mr. Robert Fechner,
Member, General Executive Board,
International Association of Machinists,
708 Machinists Bldg., Washington, D.C.
Dear Sir and Brother:

Your letter of January 23 received and contents noted.

Evidently you did not carefully read my statement regarding unemployment. I did not say that I believed "unemployment can be completely eliminated." I said that our legislators "should endeavor to enact laws that would prevent acute unemployment." Acute unemployment means when great numbers of workers are idle because of business depression. Business depressions are manufactured maliciously. They can be prevented so that there would not be such serious periods of unemployment.

You refer to my statement that the American Federation of Labor expects the national, city and local governments to adopt measures necessary to prevent unemployment. You state that very little has yet been done along that line. If unemployment insurance were established it would prove the greatest obstacle to anything ever being done to cure excessive unemployment. You are misinformed of the benefits of great reclamation projects as what you term "common labor" only is employed. Wherever great dams have been constructed to irrigate desert lands it has required mechanics of many trades in the work. Wheel barrows are needed, shovels, powder, dynamite, stone cutters, cement workers and a long list of other workmen. When the lands are irrigated and become fruitful towns are built. This would require building trades of all kinds and they would have to make purchases of the necessaries of life which would give men in the clothing, food and other industries employment. The purchases of those employed in building the dam, building the towns and making the machinery to cultivate the land would extend into many trades. You may not have thought of this in that manner. Besides these projects pay for themselves and at the same time advance the welfare of the people of our country. Public works do not enter into competition with private industries. Instead they stimulate private industry. Railroads are built over the reclaimed lands giving employment to many after completion.

Your suggestion that employers "should provide for the sustenance of the laid off employes" is subject to criticism. A bill[1] was introduced in the Wisconsin Legislature providing that employes laid off should receive $1.50 a day while idle if over eighteen years of age and $.75 a day for those of sixteen and eighteen years of age. The question of when an employe is unemployed or not is contained in the following clause:

"When an employe has lost employment through his own fault or voluntarily leaves his employment without reasonable cause he shall be disqualified in receiving unemployment compensation."

If an employer sought to reduce wages and his employes ceased work they would not be unemployed. A state agent would determine who was unemployed. He could say: "There is work for you and so long as you can get work you are not entitled to payment for non-employment."

Another objection to this measure was that it required every employe in the state to carry a certificate card or book known as a "service card." This is to be surrendered to a deputy of the Industrial Commission upon entering an employment district under the jurisdiction of a different state employment agency. This card would be kept in the employment agency as long as the employe was in the service of employers in their jurisdiction. This would create an espionage system as objectionable as that in Germany before the war. Agents of the state would be empowered to go into the homes and lives of the workers as spies. We already have enough spies and detectives entering into the lives and workshops of the toilers. While the bill provided that the burden of paying the unemployed should rest on the employers, the latter were permitted to secure insurance from private insurance companies. These companies would undoubtedly create a spy system also. While the private insurance companies would use every means to defeat the purposes of the law if enacted.

Don't you think that English experience with so-called "unemployment insurance" is enough of a warning to us of its evil influences. I would rather that our people shall be safeguarded from the "dole" handed out to them; that they shall work out a solution of a problem which has its cause in human mismanagement, ignorance, negligence, unwillingness to think and act (and if necessary sacrifice) to end a curse upon life and progress, civilization and humanity.

In 1908 the American Federation of Labor declared:

"In our country there must not be permitted to grow up or to be maintained a permanent army of unemployed."[2]

I hope you will consider this matter again after reading this letter. The attitude of the American Federation of Labor is based on the principle that the securing of employment is more advantageous to the interest of the country that any form of compensation paid unemployed workmen. We must endeavor to create employment instead of an army of unemployed pensioners.

With best wishes and assuring you of my desire to be helpful in any way within my power, I am,

Fraternally yours,   Saml Gompers
President,   American Federation of Labor.

TLpS, reel 289, vol. 302, pp. 130–32, SG Letterbooks, DLC.

1. Wisconsin Republican state senator Henry Huber introduced a compulsory unemployment compensation bill in the state senate in 1921, but it was defeated on a close vote. When he introduced the measure again in 1923, it was again narrowly defeated. The legislation would have required employers to absorb the full cost of unemployment compensation through the payment of premiums to a mutual insurance company, and it made no provision for those not working because of strikes or lockouts.

2. AFL, *Proceedings*, 1908, p. 9.

To Ralph Noe[1]

March 2, 1923.

Mr. Ralph Noe,
Beaufort, North Carolina.
Dear Sir:

Your letter of February 26 received and contents noted.

You refer to a statement made by Senator Underwood as follows:

"The by-laws of many of these labor organizations proclaim that no man can work in certain shops unless he belongs to a particular organization and works according to that organization. If labor has the privilege and the right to deny to other labor the unrestricted right to toil and earn its daily wage, does it lie in their mouths to say that the Congress is taking away from them an inherent right that belongs to them when the Congress says, 'you can work only under certain limitations,' Congress speaking for the whole people of the United States."

The senator has resorted to sophistry to prove the case.

Permit me to refer you to page 8 of the pamphlet entitled "The Union Shop and Its Antithesis"[2] which says:

"Wages in union shops are higher than in non-union shops. The hours of work are less and the working conditions are more desirable. These are gained through the workers dealing with the employer collectively. Each member contributes a small sum to carry on the work of the union. Why should a non-unionist be permitted to enjoy the benefits gained without paying his share of the cost of securing them? It is a fundamental principle that those who are the beneficiaries of organization should share in the responsibilities and obligations involved in the achievements."

Agreements are made between the employers and the unions of which their employes are members for adequate wages and desirable conditions of employment. This indicates that the employers prefer to employ union men as the best workmen join unions. The Senator seems to believe that this takes away some inherent right from a non-union man. That is merely subterfuge when he says that because unions make agreements with employers to employ only its members that this takes away an inherent right of some worker not a member of a union. If an employer wishes to build a factory he makes a contract with some builder to the detriment of all other builders.

If it were correct in the case of unions making contracts with employers it would also be true of the same employer giving the contract for the erecting of a building.

If the false logic of the senator were correct Congress would be justified in enacting a law saying "you can give out contracts only under certain limitations."

What the Senator approves of, however, is a round about way to destroy the right of collective bargaining between employers and employes. No one denies the right of a man to work when and where he pleases if he can get a job. There is no inherent right to a job. This was clearly demonstrated a year or so ago when nearly 6,000,000 wage earners in the United States were idle and they were made idle maliciously. The Federal Reserve Board carried on a campaign to deflate labor and the farmers. Deflation always brings unemployment. I have not seen or heard of any criticism from Senator Underwood in regard to the action of the Federal Reserve Board.

The wage earners were forced to organize trade unions in order to protect themselves from the autocratic acts of employers. They are a necessity. But since the beginning of time there has been an incessant war against labor. Since the art of printing was discovered labor has had to suffer from misrepresentation. Members of Congress in order to bolster up some scheme to attack labor resort t[o] what Mr. Gladstone called "glittering generalities."[3] Platitudes a[nd] sophistries are their weapons to deceive the uninformed. But Senator Underwood's statement is so far fetched and so impracticable that it cannot be possible any intelligent person will be led astray by [i]t.

Very truly yours,   Saml Gompers
President,   American Federation of Labor

TLpS, reel 289, vol. 302, pp. 127–28, SG Letterbooks, DLC.

1. Ralph W. Noe (b. 1906).
2. *The Union Shop and Its Antithesis* (Washington, D.C., 1920).
3. The phrase is generally attributed to Franklin J. Dickman, who used it to describe a lecture by Rufus Choate ("We fear that the glittering generalities of the speaker have left an impression more delightful than permanent," *Providence Journal*, Dec. 14, 1849). It was later used in a reference to Choate by Ralph Waldo Emerson.

To Frank Hering[1]

March 3, 1923.

Mr. Frank E. Hering,
Chairman, Old Age Pension Commission of the Grand Aerie,
Fraternal Order of Eagles,
South Bend, Indiana.
Dear Sir:

In reference to our conference yesterday in my office[2] permit me to say that the American Federation of Labor is in favor of the principle of old age pensions.

For a number of years an investigation has been in progress by committees appointed by the American Federation of Labor to determine the best method of securing such legislation whether through the states or the federal congress.

In 1909 the Toronto convention indorsed[3] an old age pension bill[4] introduced in Congress by Representative William B. Wilson,[5] formerly Secretary of the United Mine Workers of America. It provided for a method of meeting constitutional requirements.

The Cincinnati convention held June 12–24, 1922, reaffirmed the action of the Toronto convention.[6] It also directed that if it was found impractical to secure the enactment of an old age pension law through federal legislation that the same ends might be attained through state legislation.

Reports that I am organizing opposition to old age pension bills introduced in various state legislatures are without foundation in fact and are absolutely false.

Very truly yours,   Saml Gompers.
President,   American Federation of Labor.

TLpS, reel 289, vol. 302, p. 129, SG Letterbooks, DLC.

1. Frank Earl Hering (1874–1943), past national president of the Fraternal Order of Eagles (1909–10, 1911–12), was chairman of the Eagles' Old Age Pension Commission and managing editor of the *Eagle Magazine*.

2. For notes of the meeting, see Files of the Office of the President, Conferences, reel 122, frame 579, *AFL Records*. Hering asked SG for a statement regarding the AFL's position on pensions that he could publish in the *Eagle Magazine*.

3. The 1909 AFL convention, which met in Toronto, Nov. 8–20, endorsed the concept of pensions for "poor and needy" older workers and called for passage of pension legislation by the U.S. Congress and the Canadian Parliament (AFL, *Proceedings*, 1909, pp. 330–31, quotation at p. 330; see also *The Samuel Gompers Papers*, vol. 8, p. 413).

4. On Dec. 14, 1909, Democratic congressman William B. Wilson of Pennsylvania introduced H.R. 14,494 (61st Cong., 2d sess.), which called for the creation of an Old-Age Home Guard of the U.S. Army, made up of citizens over the age of sixty-five who were to be paid army pensions on a quarterly basis. The bill was designed to circumvent questions about the constitutionality of federally sponsored old-age pensions. It died in committee.

5. William Bauchop Wilson, secretary-treasurer of the United Mine Workers of America from 1900 to 1908, served as a Democratic congressman from Pennsylvania from 1907 to 1913 and as secretary of labor from 1913 to 1921.

6. The 1922 AFL convention reaffirmed the decision of the 1909 convention, on the grounds that Wilson's strategy was still constitutionally sound and practically feasible (see AFL, *Proceedings*, 1922, pp. 141–44, 360).

R. Lee Guard to Matthew Woll

Washington, D.C. March 10, 1923.

Matthew Woll, care Frank Cox,
468 B. Nicolet Street, Montreal, Quebec Canada.
Telegram received. President Gompers seriously ill[1] but is reported some better this morning. Secretary Morrison is sending telegram and letter to Executive Council.[2] In view of President Gompers' illness can you not come to headquarters earlier than your contemplated trip March eighteen?

R. Lee Guard.

TWpSr, reel 289, vol. 302, p. 300, SG Letterbooks, DLC.

1. SG became critically ill in March 1923 while in New York City, where he had gone to discuss state and national affairs with a variety of political figures. On Mar. 7, what had initially appeared to be a bad cold was diagnosed as influenza and bronchial pneumonia, along with congestion of the heart, and after consulting Dr. Gustav Fisch, SG entered Lenox Hill Hospital in Manhattan. There, on Mar. 9, he began to show signs of kidney failure; he responded to treatment, however, and by Mar. 12 he was out of danger. SG remained at Lenox Hill under the care of Fisch and Dr. Evan Evans until his release on Mar. 23; then he went to Atlantic City to continue his recuperation. He returned to AFL headquarters in Washington, D.C., on Apr. 3, but his doctors warned him against any exertion until he had completely recovered.

2. On Mar. 10, 1923, Frank Morrison sent two telegrams to the members of the AFL Executive Council (Morrison to James Duncan, Mar. 10, 1923, vol. 530, pp. 175–76, 186–87, Frank Morrison Letterbooks, George Meany Memorial Library, Silver Spring, Md.).

Henry Streifler to Frank Morrison

Office General Organizer
American Federation of Labor
Buffalo, N.Y. March 12th, 1923.

Mr. Frank Morrison,
Secretary, A.F. of L.,
Washington, D.C.
Dear Sir and Brother:—

Replying to yours of March 3rd,[1] in which was enclosed a copy of a letter[2] sent to you by General Secretary-Treasurer Greenstein,[3] of the Jewelry Workers International Union,[4] and which referred to certain matters at Buffalo, N.Y., I desire to state that for some time past there has been waged a factional war in our Local movement between the so-called Reds or Radical members and what might be termed the Trades Unionists, whose forces are from the Building Trades Crafts and Printing Trades, and it is true that the meetings of the Central Labor Council,[5] since the 1st of the present year have been somewhat noisey and, at times, out of order, particularly the one which was held a few weeks ago of which the correspondent of the Jewelry Workers speaks. Although I was not present I heard it commented upon in a very unfavorable manner by some of the Delegates who are classed as Conservative members and who made an oath that at the next meeting of the Central Body the Trades Unionists would rally their forces together and impress the radical crowd with their determination to rule the Council in a sane way. This [was] done in a very neat way at the meeting held Thursday, March 8th, 1923, when the forces of Law and Order gave warning to the advocates of one big union and self styled Progressives, that the majority must and shall rule.

The cause for all this rumpus and disorder is due to the fact that Mr. W. Z. Foster, of the Workmens Educational League, and other representatives of this and other radical groups, have been holding many meetings in this City and the advice which their followers have received was to the effect that many of the International and National Unions should amalgamate and ultimately to bring about the One Big Union. Then, too, the Trades Unionists, especially the Building Trades, were luke warm in their attendance at the meetings of the Central Body, which gave the radical group the chance which they desired and they tried to put across some of their rough tactics which, of course, aroused the other fellow and his side asserted their power and influence that they possess. This I believe they will do providing their delegates will be present at the meetings of the Central Body.

The line up i[s] very peculiar, for there are in with this so-called Radical faction, Local Unions whose International Unions have always resisted successfully their members whose views differ very materially from the Trades Union Policy of the A.F. of L. This is another case of "When the Cat is away, the Mice will Play," for our Trades Union fellows allowed their interest in the Local Movement to lag, with the usual result.

The correspondent[6] of the Jewelry Workers hails from Toronto, Canada, where, I understand, the Reds, as he terms them, are in control and are of the more noise making variety than they are in Buffalo, and I am quite sure he has, at times, been called upon to withstand the insults and criticisms heaped at those who, like myself, defended the Trades Union Policy of the A.F. of L.

One of the leaders of this so-called Red Crowd, is none other than Organizer Murphy,[7] of the Amalgamated Iron and Steel Workers, the one who criticised me on a few occasions, especially during the Steel Strike and when I blocked his effort to kidnap the Horse Nail Makers L.U., #17490 A.F. of L.,[8] he lodged another complaint for my action in upholding Trades Unionism in this City. I would not be surprised if he and the others associated with him upon the Local Organization Committee will soon charge me with being inactive and out of tune with their world wide programme.

Relative to what was stated about the management of the contemplated Labor Temple being taken care of in a haphazard way, the truth of the matter is that it was under the control of a part of the element referred to as the Red Crowd, but is now in safe hands and more progress has been made in the past three months than was had in the last three years.

Much more could be written upon the situation in Buffalo as it exists today. However, I feel as if I, a Representative of the A.F. of L., should not give offense to any local Union whose International or National Organization is a part of our movement.

Trusting that this will give you the information you desire, and with kind regards and best wishes, I remain,

Yours fraternally, Henry Streifler
Organizer, A.F. of L.

TLS, AFL Microfilm National and International Union File, Jewelry Workers Records, reel 38, frame 2639, *AFL Records*.

1. Frank Morrison to Henry Streifler, Mar. 3, 1923, AFL Microfilm National and International Union File, Jewelry Workers Records, reel 38, frame 2639, *AFL Records*.

2. Abraham Greenstein to Morrison, Mar. 1, 1923, AFL Microfilm National and International Union File, Jewelry Workers Records, reel 38, frames 2638–39, *AFL Records*.

3. Abraham GREENSTEIN served as secretary-treasurer of the International Jewelry Workers' Union from 1916 to 1923.

4. The International JEWELRY Workers' Union.

5. The AFL chartered the Central Labor Council of Buffalo and Vicinity in 1913.

6. Greenstein's letter to Morrison of Mar. 1, 1923, quoted a report received from a Jewelry Workers' organizer in Buffalo but did not identify the man.

7. Joseph F. Murphy, an organizer for the Amalgamated Association of Iron, Steel, and Tin Workers and secretary of Iron, Steel, and Tin Workers' Progressive Lodge 17 of Buffalo.

8. The AFL chartered Horse Nail Makers' Union 17,490 of Buffalo in 1920. The Iron, Steel, and Tin Workers subsequently claimed jurisdiction over the union, and in late 1922 Murphy appeared at a meeting of the local to urge its affiliation with his union. Streifler, who was also at the meeting, cautioned the local to contact SG or Morrison before changing affiliation. The local voted not to affiliate with the Iron, Steel, and Tin Workers, and the international abandoned its claim to jurisdiction.

To the Executive Council of the AFL

New York City, March 23, 1923.

To the Members of the Executive Council,
American Federation of Labor.
Dear Friends:—

Advices have reached me that Secretary Morrison has kept the members of the Executive Council advised as to the progress of my illness and improvement while in the hospital.

It is impossible for me to attempt to describe all that through which I passed. It seemed that you would be pleased to have a word direct from me now that the most crucial time has passed. It is Friday afternoon and I expect to be discharged from the Lenox Hill Hospital before the close of the day, very much "chastened." I expect to go somewhere for a few days to gather strength, and then proceed to Washington and be at my desk for the performance of the duties devolving upon me, to do my level best in furtherance of our great cause.[1]

Appreciating more than I can find words to say the kind expressions of the members of the Executive Council toward me, and assuring you that I am yours for the cause and in the service, I am,

Yours fraternally　Samuel Gompers
President　American Federation of Labor

p.s. I have authorized Miss Holden,[2] in the New York office of the A.F. of L., to type my name to this letter instead of my signing it.

S. G.

TLcSr, United Brotherhood of Carpenters and Joiners of America Records, reel 2, frame 337, *AFL and the Unions.*

1. After his release from the hospital on Mar. 23, 1923, SG went to Atlantic City to continue his recuperation. He returned to AFL headquarters in Washington, D.C., on Apr. 3.

2. Henrietta Holden (b. 1882) was a secretary in the AFL's New York City office.

An Excerpt from an Interview with Samuel Gompers

[April 4, 1923]

. . .

The materialism of the Labour Movement has never appealed to me. It is the idealism of the Labour movement which has been the inspiration of my life. It has not been alone to put another piece of meat on the workingman's table; it has not been alone to raise his wages and to shorten his hours; it has not been even alone to improve his housing conditions; nor to better his educational facilities; nor even to give him access to realms of Art and Science from which he has been too long debarred. No; what I have striven to gain for the workers of America, and, so far as I could of the world, is that brighter and better and happier day, for which you[1] with me have been working. My endeavor has ever been to enable the worker to attain to the complete human ideal.

TDc, Executive Council Records, Vote Books, reel 17, frame 579, *AFL Records.*

1. SG was speaking with British socialist and pacifist Francis Herbert Stead, who was on a speaking tour in the United States.

To John Walker

Washington, D.C., Apr. 9, 1923.

Mr. J. H. Walker,
728 Illinois Mine Workers Bldg., Springfield, Ill.
Telegram received stop Pensions paid by international unions follow stop Bricklayers[1] five dollars week and five dollars week to widows of pensioners stop Bridge and Structural Iron Workers[2] twenty dollars month stop Granite Cutters members over fifty two years old ten dollars month six months in year stop Paving Cutters[3] exempt members over sixty years from dues stop Quarry Workers fifty dollars to sixty year old members and exempt from dues stop Railway Employes eight hundred dollars to twenty year members stop Typographical Union eight dollars week to members over sixty years old or twenty year members totally disabled stop These are all the records we have stop To give the dues paid it would require going into long detail stop However payments for these benefits are very low.

Samuel Gompers

TWpSr, reel 289, vol. 302, p. 928, SG Letterbooks, DLC.

1. The BRICKLAYERS', Masons', and Plasterers' International Union of America.
2. The International Association of BRIDGE, Structural, and Ornamental Iron Workers.
3. The International PAVING Cutters' Union of the United States of America and Canada.

To James A. Duncan

April 10, 1923

Mr. James A. Duncan,
Secretary, Central Labor Council of Seattle and Vicinity,
Labor Temple, Seattle, Washington.
Dear Sir and Brother:
The Executive Council of the American Federation of Labor at its last meeting had before it complaints made against the Seattle Central Labor Union by several affiliated national and international unions speaking in behalf of their respective local unions in Seattle,[1] that the central body of Seattle devotes more time in support of and to efforts to secure the recognition of Soviet Russia and the independence of India than it does to the affairs connected with the trade union move-

ment which seeks to protect and promote the rights and interests of the working people of Seattle and of the whole country;

That despite the declarations of conventions of the A.F. of L. the central body declares for the recognition by the United States government of the Soviet government of Russia;

That the officers of the A.F. of L., of the national and international unions and of the Washington State Federation of Labor are repeatedly unjustly and unwarrantably attacked and denounced;

That communications from the A.F. of L. are treated with indifference and contempt;

That the central body refuses to cooperate with the Washington State Federation of Labor and has on occasions openly defied that body;

That the Seattle central body not only ignored the Non-Partisan Political program of the A.F. of L. as carried on under directions of the convention of the A.F. of L. but worked in direct opposition to that program;

That the policy pursued by the Seattle Central Labor Union has greatly impeded the progressive development of the labor movement of Seattle by needlessly arousing and antagonizing groups of citizens who would otherwise be favorably disposed toward the labor movement.

By authority and direction of the Executive Council these various complaints were referred to the official representative of the A.F. of L. in that section, Organizer C. O. Young,[2] for investigation and report to this office. His investigation has been made and his report submitted and considered by the Executive Council at its recent meeting. Stated briefly Organizer Young's report sets forth:

That the complaints made as above enumerated are substantially correct; that Seattle Central Labor Union ignores communications from and defies the American Federation of Labor, its policies and its laws; that the Seattle central body admits the full affiliation of delegates from local unions suspended by affiliated national or international unions or the A.F. of L., as well as delegates from independent unions; that the efforts of those who control and direct the policy of the Seattle Central Labor Union are directed along lines the object of which is to mould the Seattle labor movement to conform to the policies and principles enunciated by Soviet Russia; that the Seattle central body in violation of the constitution of the American Federation of Labor admits the full affiliation and representation of unaffiliated local unions; that the Seattle Central Labor Union is actively opposed to the Non-Partisan Political program of the A.F. of L.; that the Seattle central body received with favor the report of H. N. Wells that the A.F. of L. should affiliate with the "Red Internationale," the report being printed in the Union Record, the controlling power of which is the Seattle Central Labor Union; that the Seattle Central Labor Union furnished credentials to a person to attend the Red Trade Union Internationale.[3]

The Executive Council very carefully considered the above complaints and the report of Organizer Young. The Executive Council directed that the Seattle Central Labor Union should be advised, as I now advise you, that within a reasonable period, that is, two months from the date of this communication, the Seattle central body shall formally and officially advise the president of the A.F. of L. that the above causes of complaint and protest shall be eliminated by the refutation of these actions and by giving the assurance that the central body for the future pledges its fealty and loyalty to the constitution, and to the laws and policies of the A.F. of L.

It is sincerely hoped that the central body will without delay comply with these instructions and directions of the Executive Council. Failure on the part of your central body to comply with these directions and instructions within the time designated will compel the Executive Council to enforce the law of the A.F. of L. by the revocation of the charter of the central body.

It is earnestly desired that by the prompt compliance of your central body with the above that this procedure may be avoided.

Copies[4] of this communication have been mailed to William Short,[5] President of the Washington State Federation of Labor and to Organizer C. O. Young, the special representative of the American Federation of Labor in that district.

Fraternally yours,
By Order of the Executive Council,
American Federation of Labor,
Saml Gompers.   President.

TLpS, reel 289, vol. 302, pp. 988–90, SG Letterbooks, DLC.

1. On Feb. 15, 1923, the AFL Executive Council considered complaints from John Coefield, president of the United Association of Journeymen Plumbers and Steam Fitters of the United States and Canada, and Edward McGivern, president of the Bricklayers', Masons', and Plasterers' International Union of America, as well as the report of AFL organizer C. O. Young.

2. Charles O. YOUNG served as a salaried AFL organizer from 1904 until his retirement around 1933.

3. See *The Samuel Gompers Papers*, vol. 11, p. 487 and p. 488, nn. 1–2.

4. SG to William Short, Apr. 10, 1923, reel 289, vol. 302, p. 985, SG Letterbooks, DLC, and SG to C. O. Young, Apr. 10, 1923, ibid., p. 984.

5. William Mackie SHORT served as president of the Washington State Federation of Labor from 1918 to 1927.

To Matthew Woll, John Frey, and George Perkins

April 12, 1923.

Mr. Matthew Woll,
Mr. John P. Frey,
Mr. George W. Perkins,
American Federation of Labor Committee on Education.
Dear Sirs and Brothers:

From an authentic and friendly source I received a copy of the application dated February 3, 1923, which you, together with the officers of the Workers' Education Bureau, made to the American Fund for Public Service, Inc.,[1] asking the trustees thereof to make an appropriation of $100,000 to the work of the Workers' Education Bureau.

I also have a copy of the reply made by Roger Baldwin[2] under date of March 26, in the name of the trustees of the Fund, declining to make the donation requested, giving his reasons and the reasons of the trustees of the corporation for its refusal.

I can not begin to tell you how surprised I was upon reading the correspondence, and I feel that had you known the calibre and character of the activities of the board of trustees of that Fund you would not have joined in the application for a donation at their hands.

I felt it my duty to give out a public statement regarding the action of the trustees of the Fund,[3] to disclose to the public the real purposes to which that Fund is being devoted and to tear away the mask of hypocrisy and deceit to which the trustees of the Fund are resorting in order to keep the public from knowing the real purpose to which the Fund is being and is to be utilized. In the statement I have given out (and which is expected to be published in tomorrow, Friday morning's newspapers) I predicate the application which you and the officers of the Workers' Education Bureau made on the desire really to disclose to you and to them the real purpose of the trustees of the Fund.

Perhaps the newspapers may not carry the full story and some may give a garbled account while others may entirely suppress it. Therefore in order that you may know what I have prepared and issued, enclosed you will please find a copy as presented to the newspaper representatives and agencies.

I am of the opinion that the ground upon which I have predicated the application as set forth in the statement should be maintained as being the most dignified and most practical way out of the peculiar situation created by the application having been made to the trustees of the Fund.

I am sending a copy of the statement to Mr. Spencer Miller, Secretary of the Workers' Education Bureau, but without any comment I believe that you gentlemen should convey to him the suggestion contained herein and as more amply set forth in the statement enclosed.

Fraternally yours,   Saml Gompers
President   American Federation of Labor.

TLpS, reel 290, vol. 303, pp. 7–8, SG Letterbooks, DLC.

1. The American Fund for Public Service, also known as the Garland Fund because it was subsidized by an $800,000 gift from Charles Garland, loaned money and gave outright grants to organizations involved in social and economic reform.

2. Roger Nash Baldwin (1884–1981) was founder and director of both the National Civil Liberties Bureau (1917–18, 1919–20) and its successor, the American Civil Liberties Union (1920–50). He also served as a trustee of the Garland Fund.

3. Press release for publication in newspapers Apr. 13, 1923, Executive Council Records, Vote Books, reel 17, frames 537–40, *AFL Records;* "Gompers Charges Garland's $800,000 Helps Revolution," *New York Times,* Apr. 13. SG's statement contended that the Fund's organizers and trustees had "red" sympathies, and that their real but unspoken objective was the support of radical organizations. The Workers' Education Bureau, he claimed, had applied for an endowment of $100,000 from the Fund simply to demonstrate its revolutionary goals.

To Lester Markel[1]

April 13, 1923.

Mr. Lester Markel,
Sunday Editor, The New York Times,
New York City.
Dear Mr. Markel:

The following is my comment in reply to your letter of April 6:

It is impossible to know what issues the politicians may seek to develop for the 1924 campaign; but so far as the people are concerned there are many issues already developed which are of paramount importance.

More important than any single specific issue is the general question of whether the policy of government is to be a big business policy or a people's policy.

The tendency at present is in favor of big business and I am of the opinion that many politicians sadly underestimate the resentment against this which is felt by the masses of our people. Recent decisions of the Supreme Court, for example, have shown this tendency in the minimum wage for women case,[2] in the child labor case, in the Coronado case and in other cases.

I do not see how the issue thus created can be avoided by politicians. Neither do I see how there can be an escape from the consequences of such things as the shameful Teapot Dome oil scandal[3] and the iniquitous ship subsidy bill.[4] I am convinced also that our attitude toward the rest of the world will be striking a vital issue in the next campaign. I am convinced also that on that issue there will be a sounder, more constructive judgment than was rendered in the last campaign.

Many thus will enter into the next campaign as issues but all of these things will be summed up in the one great question of whether government is to serve the people or what has become popularly known as "the interests."

Very truly yours, Saml Gompers
President, American Federation of Labor.

TLpS, reel 290, vol. 303, p. 74, SG Letterbooks, DLC.

1. Lester Markel (1894–1977) served as Sunday editor of the *New York Times* from 1923 to 1965.

2. In 1918 Congress passed a minimum wage law for the District of Columbia, empowering the city's commissioners to appoint a board with the authority to fix minimum wages for women working in the District. The Children's Hospital of D.C., which employed women at wages below those mandated by the board, sued the board on the grounds that its minimum wage standards violated the right to freedom of contract. In November 1922 the Court of Appeals of the District of Columbia declared the minimum wage law unconstitutional on freedom of contract grounds (*Children's Hospital of D.C. v. Adkins et al.*, 284 F. 613 [1922]), a decision upheld by the U.S. Supreme Court on Apr. 9, 1923 (*Adkins et al. v. Children's Hospital of D.C.*, 261 U.S. 525 [1923]).

3. The Teapot Dome scandal involved Secretary of the Interior Albert B. Fall's acceptance of large gifts and interest-free loans in 1921 in exchange for secret leases to drilling rights on naval oil reserve lands—those at Teapot Dome, Wyo., to Harry F. Sinclair and those at Elk Hills and Buena Vista Hills, Calif., to Edward L. Doheny. In 1922 the Senate authorized Democratic senator Thomas J. Walsh of Montana to investigate these transactions, and the Walsh hearings in late 1923 and early 1924 led to Fall's conviction for accepting bribes. Doheny and Sinclair were tried for bribery but acquitted, although Sinclair was eventually convicted of contempt of the Senate and contempt of court.

4. Ship subsidy bills were introduced concurrently in the Senate and House on Feb. 28, 1922, by Republican senator Wesley Jones of Washington and Republican congressman William Greene of Massachusetts (S. 3217 and H.R. 10,644, 67th Cong., 2d sess.). Between Apr. 4 and May 19 the House and Senate conducted joint hearings on the legislation, and Greene introduced a revised version of the bill on June 14 (H.R. 12,021, 67th Cong., 2d sess.) and yet another on Nov. 20 (H.R. 12,817, 67th Cong., 3d sess.). All the bills called for the federal government to subsidize private companies in purchasing government-owned merchant vessels or building and operating new ones. In return, the privately owned merchant marine would be required to carry government freight and mail and transport American troops and officials without charge, as well as provide passage for one-half of all immigrants coming to the United States. H.R. 12,817 passed the House on Nov. 29 but failed in the Senate.

To the Executive Council of the AFL

Washington, D.C. April 20, 1923.

Document No. 85.
Executive Council, American Federation of Labor.
Colleagues:

By document No. 76[1] under date of March 3, 1923, I sent to the members of the Executive Council copy of a circular[2] I had gotten out, the printing of which was borne from the funds which I was able to influence a number of the executive boards of the national and international unions to contribute for a special fund for the A.F. of L. Information and Publicity Service. The circular was published and sent to people and groups of people in sore need of labor information which we have heretofore altogether too meagerly presented to them.

Enclosed you will find copy of an additional circular.[3] I think the information which it contains as to the makeup and functioning of the A.F. of L. will supply a long felt want.

If the members of the Executive Council have in mind a half dozen persons to whom you would like to have the enclosed circular sent and you will furnish me with their names and addresses, I shall be very glad to send it to them.

The Executive Council will please bear in mind that by action of our meeting in February, the Council will again meet at headquarters at two o'clock, Tuesday afternoon, May 8.[4]

Sincerely hoping that every member will be in attendance and anticipating the pleasure of our meeting, I am

Fraternally yours,   Saml Gompers.
President   American Federation of Labor.

TLcS, Executive Council Records, Vote Books, reel 17, frame 570, *AFL Records.*

1. Executive Council Records, Vote Books, reel 17, frame 512, *AFL Records.*
2. "Labor Information," Feb. 26, 1923, Executive Council Records, Vote Books, reel 17, frames 512–14, *AFL Records.*
3. "Labor Information," Apr. 18, 1923, Executive Council Records, Vote Books, reel 17, frames 570–72, *AFL Records.*
4. The AFL Executive Council met in Washington, D.C., May 8–15, 1923.

To Eugene Young[1]

April 20, 1923.

Mr. E. J. Young,
News Editor, The World,
New York City.
Dear Sir:

Of course it is unthinkable that the American public should continue to allow the expressed will of the people to be nullified by five to four decisions of the Supreme Court, or for that matter by majority decisions of the Supreme Court. I am unable to see a cure for the evil in requiring two-thirds decisions.

It is quite conceivable that two-thirds of the wrong kind of a Supreme Court would give us just as many bad decisions as we have at present. The child labor decision and the minimum wage decision would be no more palatable if they had been concurred in by one or two more justices.

We must have a remedy and therefore let us have an effective remedy. In its last convention at Cincinnati in June, 1922, the American Federation of Labor recorded itself emphatically in favor of giving Congress the power to veto a decision of the Supreme Court.[2] By this means, any law declared unconstitutional by the Supreme Court could be reenacted by Congress and thereafter the Supreme Court would have no authority to declare the act unconstitutional.

The American Federation of Labor believes that a constitutional amendment carrying such a provision as that would restore representative government in accordance with the original intentions of the framers of our Constitution.

Proposals to require seven to two, six to three, or even unanimous decisions by the Supreme Court would be at best only half-way palliatives.

Let us not trifle with the evil. Let us apply a full-fledged cure and achieve at the same time a restoration of representative government.

Very truly yours,　Saml Gompers.
President,　American Federation of Labor.

TLpS, reel 290, vol. 303, p. 245, SG Letterbooks, DLC.

1. Eugene Jared Young (1874–1939) was an editor for the *New York World* from 1912 to 1931.

2. See "Labor Urges Veto on Supreme Court" and "Let Veto Curb Supreme Court, Unions Demand," June 21 and 23, 1922, in "Excerpts from News Accounts of the 1922 Convention of the AFL in Cincinnati," June 16–24, 1922, above.

To Albert Thomas

April 21, 1923.

M. Albert Thomas,
Director, International Labour Office,
Geneva, Switzerland.
My dear M. Thomas:

There has just come to my attention the Bibliography of Industrial and Labor Questions in Soviet Russia,[1] published by your office. I have examined it with some care and I am moved to write you in that connection.

It is quite evident to me that this Bibliography is entirely in harmony with some other matters which I have felt it necessary to criticise in former communications with you. It is particularly because of this similarity that I feel I ought to write you in the present instance.

Careful study of the Bibliography convinces me that the emphasis is all on the side of the pro-Soviet publications and reports. Reports as friendly to the Soviets as that of the British labor delegation to Russia in 1920 are described at length and in language well calculated to impress the reader. It is even set forth that this delegation upon its return expressed valuable and interesting opinions, even though it made no considerable addition to the known facts in the case. On the other hand, the report of Arthur Crispien,[2] which may fairly be said to be one of the most important reports made by European observers, is dismissed without any description whatever in the briefest possible manner.

Such observers as H. N. Brailsford,[3] Louise Bryant,[4] Alexander Kolontai,[5] George Lansbury,[6] Arthur Ransome,[7] Mrs. Philip Snowden, and others, are given the benefit of special emphasis in the Bibliography while I can find no emphasis whatever placed on valuable reports and documents presenting the other side of the question.

This is a matter of importance to American labor regardless of how labor elsewhere may feel about it.

I dislike to place myself in the role of critic of a work such as this and I should not permit myself to indulge in this criticism if it were not for the fact that in certain other connections the viewpoint of American labor has been practically set at naught by the International Labour Office. Manifestly, occurrences such as this will not create the enthusiasm of the rank and file of our American labor movement for participation in the International Labour organization.

In your office it may be considered that the Bibliography is a minor matter toward which to direct criticism. Perhaps in a way that is so, but what impresses me is the fact that the work done in preparing the Bibliography must represent a certain trend of mind in the International Labor Office.

I am convinced, on the showing made in the Bibliography that the trend of mind there indicated is a pro-Soviet trend of mind. Of course a bibliography ought not to be pro any thing. But much more important than that, I can not understand why there should be any sympathy in the International Labour Office for the outrageous dictatorship in Moscow.

I wish you to believe that I am writing this letter in no unfriendly spirit. I am trying to call your attention, however, to a matter which is of some interest to us. I shall be pleased as always to have the benefit of your observations.[8]

With assurance of my very best wishes, I am

Sincerely yours, Saml Gompers.
President, American Federation of Labor.

P.S. In the above, I momentarily omitted to call attention to the report of the Commission of the League of Nations upon the conditions practiced and the mal-administration of the affairs of Russia, by the so-called Soviet Government.[9]

S. G.

TLpS, reel 290, vol. 303, pp. 251–52, SG Letterbooks, DLC.

1. *Bibliography of Industrial and Labour Questions in Soviet Russia* (Geneva, 1922).

2. Artur Crispien (1875–1946) served as president of the German Independent Social Democratic party from 1919 to 1920 and was an Independent Social Democratic and then a Social Democratic member of the Reichstag from 1920 to 1933. He fled Germany in 1933; his German citizenship was revoked in 1937.

3. Henry Noel Brailsford (1873–1958), a British journalist and author, was an active supporter of liberation movements around the world. He was one of the first Western journalists to visit Russia after the Revolution and from 1922 to 1926 was the editor of the *New Leader,* the journal of the British Independent Labour party. Brailsford was the author of *The Russian Workers' Republic* (1921).

4. Louise Bryant (1885–1936), an American journalist and the wife of John Reed, traveled to Russia with Reed in 1917 and subsequently wrote *Six Red Months in Russia: An Observer's Account of Russia before and during the Proletarian Dictatorship* (1918). She remained in Russia as a journalist after Reed's death and was one of the first Western reporters to travel in eastern Russia in the 1920s.

5. Actually Aleksandra Mikhailovna Kollontai (1872–1952). She served variously as People's Commissar for Social Welfare (1917–18), head of the Women's Section of the Central Committee (1920), and secretary of the International Women's Secretariat of the Comintern (1921–22) and then served as Soviet ambassador to Norway (1923–25, 1927–30), Mexico (1926–27), and Sweden (1930–45).

6. George Lansbury (1859–1940), a British socialist and pacifist, was editor of the *Daily Herald,* a British labor paper (1913–22), and subsequently editor of *Lansbury's Labour Weekly* (1925–27). He served in the House of Commons as a member of the

Labour party (1910–12, 1922–40) and was the First Commissioner of Works (1929–31) in the government of Ramsay MacDonald.

7. Arthur Michell Ransome (1884–1967), a British journalist and later the author of children's books, served in Russia from 1915 to 1919 as a foreign correspondent for the *Daily News* (London). From 1919 to 1930 he wrote for the *Manchester Guardian,* reporting on Russia, Egypt, and China. Expelled from Russia in 1919 by the Soviet government, he escaped to Estonia with Leon Trotsky's secretary, Evgenia Petrovna Shelepina, whom he later married. He was the author of *Six Weeks in Russia in 1919* (1919) and *The Crisis in Russia* (1921). In 2002 it was discovered that Ransome was actually serving in Russia as a British secret agent, working for MI6, and filed regular reports from Russia with the British intelligence service.

8. Albert Thomas sent two letters in reply (not found) with a "detailed explanation" of the bibliography, which SG acknowledged on July 28, 1923. SG expressed satisfaction at Thomas's assurance that the bibliography was prepared by "an ardent opponent of the Bolshevik regime" and acknowledged that its completion in early 1921 necessarily circumscribed the titles it could include (reel 292, vol. 305, pp. 660–62, SG Letterbooks, DLC; quotations at p. 660).

9. League of Nations, *Report on Economic Conditions in Russia with Special Reference to Famine of 1921–1922 and Agriculture* (Geneva, 1922). For discussion of the report, see William English Walling, "The League of Nations and Soviet Responsibility for the Russian Famine," *American Federationist* 30 (Apr. 1923): 297–302.

From the Central Labor Council
of Seattle and Vicinity

Central Labor Council of Seattle and Vicinity.
Affiliated with American Federation of Labor,
Reorganized May, 1905
Seattle Wash., April 21, 1923.

Dear Sir and Brother:

Your letter of April 10th 1923,[1] addressed to this Council by order of the Executive Council of the American Federation of Labor was read before this body at it's regular meeting April 18th and in reply we are directed by this Council to say that it is astounded to learn that any person or persons should be guilty of such a gross misstatement of facts as would cause your honorable Council to contemplate the action indicated by your letter.

We have no criticism to offer against the officers of National or International Unions who registered the complaints or against the Executive Council which, evidently believing that it was acting upon reliable information from sources in which it had confidence, did the thing which nine delegates out of every ten in this Council would probably have done if placed in your position under like circumstances. We might, however, feel a little aggrieved that we were not given the courtesy of an opportunity to present our position to you before action was taken, but in view of the confidence you undoubtedly had in the sources of your information even this failure can be understood.

In answering your letter we will endeavor to be very frank and state, as clearly as we are capable of, the conditions as they exist in this locality; but at the outset, regardless of our traducers statements, we declare that we are, and always have been, loyal to the American Federation of Labor and we trust that we shall convince you of this fact.

In this field, where the International Timber Workers' Union has just had to relinquish it's charter on account of it's inability to withstand the inroads made by the I.W.W. and the L.L.L.L.,[2] where time after time advocates of One Big Union and other secessionary movements have made strong and determined appeals to and attacks upon us, this Council has stood solid and kept the banner of the American Federation of Labor ever flung to the breeze, and in so doing has merited the unqualified appreciation and support of the officers of the American Federation of Labor and affiliated organizations. This appreciation and support we expect to continue to merit and receive.

In the conduct of this Council's business we have had both harmonious and stormy sessions, just as other labor bodies have had including conventions of the American Federation of Labor, but any differences which have arisen over issues before us have, almost without exception, been thrashed out on the basis of what contenders on each side conceived to be for the best interests of labor.

Through the gross and malicious exaggerations contained in reports to you we feel that you have been outrageously imposed upon by people in this locality responsible for them and we cheerfully avail ourselves of this opportunity of presenting the naked truth regarding the situation which is the subject of your letter.

In paragraphs one and nine you refer to complaints that this Council "devotes more time in support of and to efforts to secure the recognition of Soviet Russia and the independence of India than it does to the affairs of the trade union movement" and "that the efforts of those who direct and control the policy of the Seattle Central Labor Union are directed along lines, the object of which is to mould the Seattle labor movement to conform to the policies and principles enunciated by Soviet Russia." These statements are positively ridiculous. It is difficult for any delegate to recall a time when a discussion of Russian or Indian affairs has occupied more than fifteen minutes of time at any of this Council's sessions, excepting the occasions of listening to the report of Hulet M. Wells or a short address by Mr. Wadia[3] while stopping here on his way home to India. The only other occasions upon which these questions come up for discussion at all are when communications are received upon these subjects and which come to us at very infrequent intervals.

On the Russian situation we have never pronounced ourselves as favorable to establishing a Soviet form of Government here, nor have we ever sought to "mould the Seattle labor movement to conform to the policies and principles enunciated by Soviet Russia," but we do believe that a government which recognized and had no compunctions about doing business with the governments of the Czars need have no scruples about recognizing the present government of Russia. Indeed, we believe that such a course would be distinctly beneficial to the interests of the workers of Russia and the United States alike and we have no hesitancy in stating that we have so pronounced ourselves in line with these convictions on several occasions.

We did believe that the American Federation of Labor could quite properly be represented at the Trade Union Congress at Moscow and we probably so notified you at that time. We did authorize Hulet M. Wells, former President of this Council, to represent this body at the Moscow conference, solely as an observer. This action was repeated last year in the case of Miss Anna Louise Strong[4] who was formerly connected with the "Union Record" as Special Feature Editor. She went to Russia as a representative of the Society of Friends, herself the daughter of a prominent Congregational minister[5] of this city. When the American Relief Association took over the work of the Quakers, Miss Strong remained in Russia as a correspondent for a number of the leading publications of this country. She has transmitted her report to us and it was simply referred to the Union Record in line with our desire to secure and give publicity to truthful information on all matters of interests, especially to labor.

With regard to India; in conformity with the action of the American Federation of Labor we have registered our protest against any attempt to deport certain Hindus to, what appeared to be, sure death upon their arrival in India, and we have also gone on record against the persecutions of non-co-operationists in that unhappy land. We do not feel that there was anything improper about this action from a trade union standpoint, particularly in view of the lengths that A.F. of L. conventions have gone in behalf of Ireland, and in regard to which we offer no criticism.

In connection with the Council's action upon political matters, it would seem impossible to pursue a course that would produce complete harmony and this Council adopted the policy it thought would conserve the best interests of labor. When we followed the non-partisan policy, the criticism was made that too much time was consumed discussing political matters on the floor of the Council. The Council later endorsed the Farmer-Labor Party program when the state labor movement endorsed it, and we referred political questions pertaining to the state and nation to that body thus removing them from the floor of the Council and leaving more time for strictly union business.

The constitution of this Council provides that all union business must be transacted before any other matters can be taken up and that "Reports of Sections and Delegates" must take place at nine o'clock if not reached in the regular order of business before that time. Discussion on questions before the house is limited to five minutes for each delegate desiring the floor and adjournment is mandatory at 11 P.M. unless extended for a given time by a four-fifths vote and which has only been done in one instance for thirty minutes. This goes about as far as is possible to assure a square deal to all and makes it extremely difficult to slip anything over, even on a small minority of delegates.

We certainly thought, and think yet, that we have a right to adopt policies such as judgment indicates will conserve the best interests of the trade unions of this section, even though those policies may not be entirely in line with the policies of our national body as we recognize the extreme difficulty of establishing policies such as will apply equally well North, South, East and West and under varying conditions.

In this position we probably share our impressions with many other labor bodies. For instance, when Brother Frank Morrison was returning home from Portland, Ore. just before Christmas,[6] at a few hours' notice, we got up a luncheon in his honor and a very representative gathering listened attentively to him outline the position of the American Federation of Labor on various problems. On that occasion he pointed out that the A.F. of L. could not declare for a producers' political party until labor bodies in various sections and localities have built up such a movement and he indicated that when this is accomplished, the American Federation of Labor will naturally and gladly conform to the new policy desired by the membership and give it all the encouragement and support within it's power. In support of this position the United Mine Workers' Cleveland convention[7] went on record for a producers' political party, and International Officers of some of the largest unions affiliated with the American Federation of Labor, reflecting the sentiment of their membership, urge independent political action by the producers and a policy toward Russia not in keeping with that of the A.F. of L. conventions.

The question naturally occurs to us that if a central council is to be punished for such honest differences as to best policy for a given locality, what measure of discipline will be meted out to other affiliated organizations whose officers take such positions and urge central bodies to do likewise? Surely our views must be shared by many in this great movement for we cannot conceive of their knowingly and wilfully violating the laws of the American Federation of Labor any more than we would do so ourselves.

In connection with the State Federation of Labor, we realize the importance of this body and the necessity of increasing it's efficiency and influence in the interests of labor's cause but we have never understood that central bodies were subordinate to state federations. We have always been affiliated with the State Federation of Labor and have sought to exercise our rights as an affiliated organization. We have no quarrel with that body and we venture to suggest that any apparent lack of harmony in our relations can be traced to one individual who also has the same difficulty with the Tacoma, Everett[8] and other central bodies as with the Seattle Council. All we ask of this official of the State Federation is that courtesy and respect be met with courtesy and respect and square dealing with square dealing. Our sessions may have been complained of to you by the President of that body but if Organizer C. O. Young will but tell you all he knows of the last State Federation of Labor Convention,[9] we will gladly have you compare the dignity and transactions of this body with that and take our chances on your findings. It should be enough to indicate that we are not entirely at fault when other central bodies in the state experience that same difficulty in working harmoniously and wholeheartedly with the same official of the State Federation.

As to disrespect being shown communications from the A.F. of L. and International Unions, such a charge is entirely unwarranted. This Council, like others, is made up of many different types of delegates and it cannot be held responsible for the act of some delegate who might make an uncalled for remark entirely unsupported by other delegates. Such an incident might easily occur at an A.F. of L. convention and probably would be dealt with by the presiding officer exactly as our presiding officer would deal with it. The proceedings of this Council are open at all times for inspection by your representatives and an examination of them together with the ever-courteous line of correspondence which has passed between the offices of the A.F. of L. and this Council will readily disprove any such charge as you refer to.

With regard to the seating of delegates of suspended unions or unions unaffiliated with the A.F. of L., out of ninety-five unions affiliated with this Council there are three only which can possibly be classed under this head: Blacksmiths' Local #211.;[10] Shipyard Laborers;[11] and the Lady Barbers.[12] Blacksmiths' Local #211. is also affiliated with the State Federation. This case has been very carefully examined by an unbiased committee from this Council which reports that Local #211. has been persecuted by President Kline for acting in strict conformity with the laws of the International in submitting matters pertaining to finances to affiliated unions. The truth of the findings of our committee is being borne out more strongly each day and to unseat this local will mean the stirring up of a hornets' nest unnecessarily, as the local has given it's word that it will wait patiently for vindication until the situation works itself out unless an aggressive attitude is assumed against it, in which case it will have no alternative except to carry it's fight to other affiliated unions.

With this case we have pursued a course which in our judgment would conserve the best interests of the Blacksmiths' International and the labor movement generally. However, if you order this Local unseated, it will be unseated, and of course, responsibility for the consequences will be removed from our shoulders. We have done our best.

The Shipyard Laborers' Local is a wartime legacy. After unsuccessfully endeavoring to secure a charter from the Carpenters[13] and later the Laborers,[14] a charter was issued to it by the Riggers and Stevedores' International.[15] This group functioned efficiently and in full co-operation with the general labor movement. To this day there has been no official demand for their unseating and we understand that they are ready and willing and anxious to accept a charter from any proper source in the A.F. of L. As you must well know, there is an organization in this locality which would welcome the unseating of this union and if accomplished would use every influence to win it's membership to swell it's own and would also take all the propaganda value in it for it's use against the American Federation of Labor. With regard to this case we await your specific instructions which will be followed to the letter. The only suggestion we would venture to offer is that whatever is done, sufficient time be allowed to place them where you determine they properly belong so as to run no risk of alienating their good will.

Last, is the case of the Lady Barbers. For years these women sought organization and we were the objects of criticism and ridicule when we proclaimed that the A.F. of L. was big and broad enough to embrace all wage earners and were asked "why don't you organize the Lady Barbers?"

In 1918 we undertook the task and had a remarkable and gratifying response from these women workers. We sent forty of their names to the Barbers' International[16] and requested that a charter be issued. We were told that they did not issue charters to women and that they were not eligible to membership. We then made application to Secretary Morrison for a Federal charter only to be referred back to the Barbers' International. We made a second application to the Barbers' International thinking that an understanding had been reached but we were met with the same reply as before. We then made the second appeal for a Federal charter, only to get turned down and to stand humiliated before these women workers.

Finally, in a fit of despair and unable to longer deny their appeal for a union, we organized them 100% strong and notified the Barbers' International that they were now a union and that whenever it indicated it's willingness to take them in they were ready to come. To this day they have maintained their organization, worked harmoniously with Barbers' Local Union #195 of this city, maintaining prices and conditions and have been an everlasting credit to the trade union movement. We understand that the American Federation of Labor is quite properly on record to the effect that whenever an International Union fails to grant a charter or to organize workers because of color, sex or like objection to them, the A.F. of L. will issue a Federal charter.

We, herewith now submit the application of the Lady Barbers for a charter within the jurisdiction of the American Federation of Labor and sincerely hope and trust that it will be issued. If further difficulty arises over the issuance of a charter to the Lady Barbers we shall abide by whatever decision the Executive Council may see fit to make, but of course will reserve the right to carry the case to the floor of the A.F. of L. convention if necessary in the event that such decision is not satisfactory.[17]

As to groups of citizens which it is claimed have been needlessly antagonized by this Council, this statement, as you will readily agree is extremely vague and is therefore impossible of intelligent reply. We know of no such groups except those organized for the express purpose of destroying the American Federation of Labor. If you will insist upon your informants being specific in their charges and state the groups it is claimed have been thus antagonized, we will assure you a full, frank and truthful statement regarding each case referred to.

We can hardly be expected to answer generalities although we have not attempted to sidestep any of the points raised in your letter. We feel however that we are entitled to a bill of particulars setting forth every specific occasion upon which any violations of the laws of the American Federation of Labor have been committed by this Council. Further, we respectfully request that in case your Council contemplates further action upon, what we believe you will now agree to be ridiculous charges against this body, that the Seattle Central Labor Council be given a day in court and afforded a full opportunity to be heard before any decision is handed down.

We ask this, not because we hold any fears for the future of the workers of this section, or for their ability to meet a given situation, or that we would have any hesitancy in placing our case before organized labor generally throughout the country; but we ask it in the name of justice, in the interests of the future welfare of the American Federation of Labor, particularly in this section, and because we repeat again, we feel that you have been outrageously imposed upon through the intrigue of one or two individuals in this community who, in reporting to you, withheld important facts such as would have painted a very different picture.

For instance, did they tell you of the wording of this Council's obligation, which every delegate is compelled to repeat aloud before being seated? We quote it for your information:

OBLIGATION.

"I _____ pledge my word and honor that I will faithfully and truly represent the organization which has sent me here as a delegate, and I will abide by the constitution and by-laws and rules of order of the Central Labor Council of Seattle and Vicinity.

["]I further renounce any and all allegiance that I may now have to any labor organization whose work or objects in any manner conflict with the American Federation of Labor, and I will not join any such organization as long as I am a delegate to this Council, but will strive at all times for the upbuilding of the American Federation of Labor."

A central labor council which has gone so far to protect and upbuild the American Federation of Labor, particularly under the conditions and circumstances peculiar to this section of the country, in place of condemnation, is worthy the highest commendation, and given the facts, we are confident of receiving it at the hands of the Executive Council.

We would welcome and cherish visits of unbiased investigators representing the American Federation of Labor who would examine carefully the problems with which we are dealing and report to you upon our methods of handling them.

The action of this Central Labor Council at it's last meeting should serve as a distinct rebuke and most effective answer to all our slanderers. This reply to your letter of April 10th was read and after a cool and calm debate punctuated with expressions of indignation, was adopted unanimously with a good attendance present. This action in itself should cause your honorable body to ask the natural question "who and where are the complainants?"

Assuring you that this Council is unswervingly loyal to the American Federation of Labor and that it will remain so as long as it is accorded just and square treatment, and awaiting with confidence the outcome of your deliberations, we are

Yours fraternally,
Central Labor Council of Seattle and Vicinity,
By it's Special Committee
Bert Swain,[18]   Delegate, Engineers' Local #843.
T. H. Wagner,[19]   Delegate, Musicians' Local #76.

Alice M. Lord,[20]   Delegate, Waitresses' Local #240.
C. W. Doyle,   Business Representative, C.L.C.
J. E. Phillips,[21]   President, C.L.C.
James A. Duncan,   Secretary, C.L.C.

TLtcSr, Executive Council Records, Vote Books, reel 18, frames 25–28, *AFL Records.*

1. "To James A. Duncan," Apr. 10, 1923, above.

2. That is, the Loyal Legion of Loggers and Lumbermen.

3. Probably B. P. Wadia, a textile workers' organizer in Madras, India. He founded the Madras Labor Union in 1918.

4. Anna Louise Strong (1885–1970), a journalist and lecturer, went to Russia in 1921 to report on the famine but then settled there and continued to live primarily in that country until 1949. In 1930 she founded the *Moscow Daily News,* the first English-language newspaper in the Soviet Union. In 1949 she was arrested and expelled from Russia as an alleged American spy, and she spent much of the remainder of her life living and writing in China.

5. Sidney Dix Strong (1860–1938) was a Congregational minister and a pacifist.

6. Frank Morrison traveled to Portland, Ore., in December 1922 to make arrangements for the upcoming AFL convention there (see "James Barrett to Frank Morrison," May 8, 1923, n. 3, below). He then went on to Seattle, where he spoke at a luncheon attended by labor representatives.

7. A resolution adopted by the 1919 convention of the United Mine Workers of America, which met in Cleveland, Sept. 9–23. See *The Samuel Gompers Papers,* vol. 11, p. 269, n. 3.

8. The AFL chartered the Everett (Wash.) Trades Council in 1912.

9. The 1922 convention of the Washington State Federation of Labor, which met in Bremerton, July 10–14.

10. The International Brotherhood of Blacksmiths, Drop Forgers, and Helpers expelled local 211 of Seattle in March 1922 after the local attacked the international union for its use of funds and then apparently launched a referendum calling for amalgamation.

11. Shipyard Laborers, Riggers, and Fasteners 38 A-2 of Seattle.

12. Lady Barbers 1 of Seattle.

13. The United Brotherhood of CARPENTERS and Joiners of America.

14. The International HOD Carriers', Building and Common Laborers' Union of America.

15. That is, the International Longshoremen's Association.

16. The Journeymen BARBERS' International Union of America.

17. For discussion of this issue at the 1923 AFL convention, see "Ninth Day—Wednesday Morning Session," Oct. 10, 1923, in "Excerpts from Accounts of the 1923 Convention of the AFL in Portland, Ore.," Oct. 8–12, 1923, below.

18. Albert "Bert" Swain (1887–1950) was secretary of International Union of Steam and Operating Engineers 843 of Seattle from 1921 until his death. He also served as secretary of Steam and Operating Engineers' local 40 of Seattle (1916–19), secretary of the Seattle Metal Trades Council (1918–22), and manager of the Seattle Labor Temple Association (1919–50), and at the time of his death was director of the Washington State Labor News.

19. Theodore H. Wagner (b. 1860), a member of American Federation of Musicians 76 of Seattle.

20. Alice M. Lord (1876–1940) was a founder of Hotel and Restaurant Employees' International Alliance and Bartenders' International League of America 240 (Waitresses) of Seattle and served for many years as the local's secretary (1906–31) and president (1935–40). She was instrumental in the passage of eight-hour legislation for women in Washington state.

21. James E. Phillips (b. 1882?) was a member of Brotherhood of Painters, Decorators, and Paperhangers of America 300 of Seattle.

To John Fitzpatrick

April 25, 1923.

Mr. John J. Fitzpatrick,
President, Chicago Federation of Labor,
166 West Washington Street, Chicago, Illinois.
Dear Sir and Brother:

You are fully aware of the nation-wide campaign against organized labor which has been waged since the signing of the Armistice and of the unexampled extent of unemployment which prevailed for a considerable period. These circumstances occasioned considerable financial stress for a number of our affiliated organizations, through the requirement to finance struggles against the onslaught of antagonistic employers and by the curtailment of income on account of the large number of unemployed members. This condition has been reflected in the income of the American Federation of Labor which necessarily fluctuates with the prosperity or financial reverses of its constituent bodies.

The Executive Council has been confronted with the necessity of curtailing the expenses of the American Federation of Labor in order to keep them within the income. As a result of this necessity organizers receiving salary from the American Federation of Labor, with the exception of yourself and Organizer Frayne, were furloughed twice in alternating periods of four weeks each.

In acting upon this subject the Executive Council has had under consideration the arrangement with the Chicago Federation of Labor for the payment of one-half of the expenses for the maintenance of the headquarters and for the organizer. This is the only instance in which such arrangement exists. It is the practice of the American Federation of Labor in appointing organizers to place them under full pay and they to be solely under the direction of the officers of the American Federation of Labor. In a few instances, to extend special assistance to a local movement where the situation warranted the action and where the Central Body had not the funds to finance a campaign, the Executive Council has assisted the Central Body by defraying part or all of the salary of a special organizer; in each instance this has been temporary assistance and discontinued upon the expiration of the time designated by the Executive Council. These special organizers have worked under the direction of the Central Body they were appointed to assist.

In the arrangement with the Chicago Federation of Labor the organizer is subject to the demands of the work as carried on by the Chicago Federation of Labor, as well as the calls which are made upon his services by the officers of the American Federation of Labor. The funds of the American Federation of Labor are limited and in order that they may be disbursed to the best possible advantage in carrying on the work of the A.F. of L., those who receive salary from the American Federation of Labor should be subject solely to the direction of the officers of the American Federation of Labor, both as to the character of the work to be done as well as to the field of the organizers' activities. This condition cannot exist where half the expenses are borne by a Central Body, for it is only reasonable under such an arrangement that a Central Body and its various activities should have equally the assistance of the services of the organizer, as well as be able to in part define his duties.

Having all the above in mind and after the fullest consideration, the Executive Council, at the meeting held at headquarters, February 14–24, 1923, took the following action:

The Executive Council directs that the partial payment of the rental of the office of the Chicago Federation of Labor will be discontinued after the expiration of the present lease, if there be a lease.

It was moved and seconded that the President notify John Fitzpatrick that the American Federation of Labor will discontinue paying half of the organizer's expenses and half of the other expenses of the Chicago Federation of Labor after June 1, 1923.

Carried.

It had been my intention to bring this action to your attention in person. I made engagements which would have taken me to Chicago but I developed a serious illness while on a business trip to New York by reason of which I was obliged to cancel the engagements I had made for the subsequent period. This will account for the delay in communicating the action of the Executive Council.

You will note that the discontinuance of the partial payment of the rental of the offices for the headquarters of the Chicago Federation of Labor is contingent upon the expiration of the lease, if a lease exists. You will, therefore, kindly advise me if the offices are now rented under a lease and if so when it expires in order that we may have definite information as to when this part of the decision of the Executive Council shall take effect, and so that I may be in a position to report to the Executive Council at its meeting which begins May 6th.

Hoping to hear from you at your convenience[1] and with best wishes, I am,

Yours fraternally, Saml Gompers.
President American Federation of Labor.

TLpS, reel 290, vol. 303, pp. 364–67, SG Letterbooks, DLC.

1. John Fitzpatrick replied that he regretted losing the funds but believed the Chicago Federation of Labor could meet its expenses without the AFL's support. For a summary of his letter, see the AFL Executive Council minutes of May 9, 1923, Executive Council Records, Minutes, reel 7, frame 1322, *AFL Records.*

Excerpts from the Minutes of a Conference on the Minimum Wage[1]

April 26, 1923

. . .

President Gompers called attention to the reduction in wages being made by the employers of Washington since the Supreme Court held that the minimum wage law for women and minors was unconstitutional. . . .

"Already I am informed that a number of employers have reduced wages from 30 to 50 per cent. Where wages have not been reduced a scheme has been devised to base wages on the amount of sales. This would compel employes to secure more customers. Old employes have been discharged and new employes taken on at a low rate. A conference[2] has been called by the Women's Trade Union League for May 14–15 to consider the present situation. But we can talk of that later when we have decided what we can do to begin an organization campaign of the women of Washington.

"I am not certain that anything can be done by legislation and not until December anyway because Congress will not meet until that time. In the meantime the intent of the employers to reduce present standards will continue if not halted by the organization of the employes. In my opinion with the influence of the trade union movement, and with the full cooperation of all other sympathetic organizations, we can get to cooperate with us, we can do something. We cannot expect to restore wages now. But if we make emphatic protest against the course being pursued the employers may be influenced to restore the wages taken away or at least stop any further reduction in wages. We should let them know that if they continue they will lose the patronage of the workers of Washington. The 1922 strikes stopped wage reductions. If an organization move to help the women is inaugurated I feel we can do much good. I believe all here will be glad to cooperate in this move. The officers of the A.F. of L. will be glad to help even temporarily by having one or two organizers present. This will be subject to the approval of the Executive Council."

. . .

Mr. Coulter[3] of the Retail Clerks . . . said:

"The only salvation is for the women to organize and present agreements that will end the present wage cuts and discharges by someone who does not happen to feel well. Until the employes had gone to work in the mornings they never knew whether they still held their jobs. The girls are afraid to protest against reductions as they think they cannot get work anywhere else. Girls getting $16.50 a week are told business is bad but as they are good employes they will be gotten jobs in some other store. When they go to the other stores they are told that because of the recommendation given they will be put to work but cannot be paid more than $10 or $12 a week."

Miss McNally[4] insisted that there must be an organization drive at the head of which should be someone responsible.

Mr. Gompers then said:

"I wonder whether we can not formulate something as an expression of this conference upon certain phases of this subject, something,— let me think aloud what I have in mind to suggest:

"That this conference of women and men trade unionists of the city of Washington in emphatic protest against the reductions of wages imposed upon women and girls wage earners of the District of Columbia, whether by direct reduction or subterfuges having the same purpose, insist upon the restoration of cuts in wages of women and girls already made;

"That the conference pledges its cooperation in the movement to organize the women wage earners of the District of Columbia in bona fide unions to protect and promote the rights and interests and to establish the best possible relations with employers and business houses;

"That the conference urges upon women wage earners to organize into such unions;

"That the American Federation of Labor, the Washington Central Labor Union, the Women's Trade Union League and all other organizations of wage earners will cooperate with the movement to hold a conference in the city of Washington on May 14 and 15 for the further and fuller consideration of such action as may be deemed wise and practicable to maintain or improve the standards of life and work of women wage earners, and call upon the enlightened American public opinion and the sympathy of the residents of the City of Washington for their full cooperation and support in this effort to prevent the deterioration of the standards of the women workers of the District; and

"That we call upon the employers in the District of Columbia to maintain at least the rates of wages provided under the minimum wage law even though the law has been annulled by the Supreme Court of the United States."

On motion of Mr. Morrison, the suggestion of Mr. Gompers was adopted unanimously.

There was much discussion by Miss Smith,[5] Mr. Rosamund,[6] Mrs. Forrester,[7] Mr. O'Connell,[8] Mr. Hushing[9] and others present on various phases of the matter. It was believed by Miss Smith that the denials of business men that any reductions had been made would be accepted by the uninformed as true.

Mr. Morrison said the meeting was called to plan an organization campaign. That as the retail clerks expected to have organizers in Washington after May 7 that those present could cooperate and keep up the fight for at least a year.

Mr. Gompers thought to have some kind of a permanent organization formed to meet weekly and with a committee to take charge of the campaign between meetings. He said the American Federation of Labor would do its full share.

Miss Smith said there were 18 or 20,000 women in gainful employment in Washington. 7,000 of these were in stores, 3,000 in hotels and restaurants, 1,200 in laundries, 1,000 in the printing trades and the remainder in other occupations, including telephone operators. She told of a girl getting $3 in a candy factory.

Mr. Gompers called attention to the fact that there were many stenographers and assistants in the offices of professional men and that he had received several communications telling of the deplorable conditions under which bank clerks work. If an organization campaign is kept up he said there could be no question of the outcome.

Miss McNally then moved that the conference be made the "Permanent Conference for the Protection of the Rights and Interests of Women Wage Earners." This was carried.

On motion of Miss McNally the conference agreed to meet regularly every Thursday morning at 11 A.M. and to meet at such other times as may be necessary.

On motion of Miss McNally the Chairman was instructed to appoint an Executive Committee to take charge of the campaign between meetings. The following were appointed on the committee:

Mr. Frank Morrison,
Miss Ethel Smith,
Mrs. Rose Forrester,
Mr. Newton A. James[10]
Mr. C. C. Coulter

Mr. Richardson[11] said that statistics should be gathered so that the proper kind of a publicity campaign could be carried on.

Miss Smith suggested that the unions should be requested to instruct their members to gather all information they could on wage reductions and report it to the Executive Committee.

. . .

TDc, AFL Microfilm Convention File, reel 32, frames 1459–60, *AFL Records.* Typed notation: "Minimum Wage. Conference held in the Executive Council Chamber, A.F. of L. Building, Thursday, April 26, 1923, at 11 A.M."

1. Participants at the meeting included SG, Frank Morrison, and James O'Connell as well as members of the AFL Legislative Committee and representatives of the AFL Union Label Trades Department, the Washington, D.C., Central Labor Union, the Washington Union Label League, the National Women's Trade Union League, and eight AFL affiliates.

2. The National Women's Trade Union League conference, which was held in Washington, D.C., actually met on May 15–16, 1923. Presided over by SG and Maude Schwartz of the League, the conference urged women to organize to safeguard wage standards and working conditions and created a three-person committee to study possible constitutional amendments to restrict the power of the Supreme Court, guarantee the rights of labor, and authorize Congress and the states to enact minimum wage legislation.

3. Clarence Castrow COULTER was the business representative for Retail CLERKS' International Protective Association 262 of Washington, D.C., and a vice-president of the international union.

4. Gertrude Marie McNALLY, vice-president (1919–25) of the National Federation of Federal Employees.

5. Ethel Smith.

6. Charles L. ROSEMUND, president (1920–42) of the International Federation of Technical Engineers', Architects', and Draftsmen's Unions.

7. Rose Yates Forrester.

8. James O'CONNELL, president of the AFL Metal Trades Department (1911–34).

9. William Collins Hushing (1883–1966), a member of the Pattern Makers' League of North America, was the legislative representative in Washington, D.C., for the unions located in the Canal Zone. He later served as an AFL salaried organizer (1928–32) and as a member of the Legislative Committee of the AFL (1932–55) and AFL-CIO (1955–56).

10. Newton A. JAMES, a vice-president (1922–33) of the Maryland State and District of Columbia Federation of Labor.

11. George James RICHARDSON served as secretary-treasurer of the International Association of Fire Fighters from 1920 to 1956.

To B. M. Jewell

Washington, D.C., May 2, 1923.

Mr. B. M. Jewell,
Riviera Bldg., 4750 Broadway, Chicago, Illinois.

Newspapers publish report of withdrawal of counsel from the court proceedings to contest making permanent the temporary injunction obtained by the government in the railway shopmen's strike. It is further stated that the withdrawal of the counsel was upon a letter to them by you upon authority of your executive board. Your letter is not published in the newspaper. Will you do me the kindness to let me have a copy of that letter at your earliest possible convenience.[1] Thank you in advance. Best wishes.

Samuel Gompers.

TWpSr, reel 290, vol. 303, p. 503, SG Letterbooks, DLC.

1. For a copy of the letter—B. M. Jewell et al. to Donald Richberg, Frank Mulholland, and James Easby-Smith—dated Apr. 30, 1923, see Executive Council Records, Minutes, reel 7, frames 1356–58, *AFL Records*.

To John Stevens[1]

May 4, 1923.

Mr. John Stevens,
191 Fourth St., Meriden, Connecticut.
Dear Sir:

Your letter of May 2 received and contents noted.

You ask for information on the subject that "a recent decision of the United States Supreme Court on the minimum wage deserves support." There is no moral affirmative side to this question.

The decision of the Supreme Court places the labor of women in the same category as a link of sausage, a pound of liver, or a gallon of kerosene. The Supreme Court says labor is a commodity, that it can be bartered and sold over the counter. The court wiped out the inequality of sex and placed women on the same basis as men because it said that the Nineteenth Amendment granting them suffrage eliminated this inequality. Then again the court held that an employer did not have to pay an adequate wage or even a living wage to a woman employe for it said:

"The moral requirement implicit in every contract of employment, namely, that the amount to be paid and the service to be rendered shall bear to each other some relation of just equivalence, is completely ignored. The necessities of the employe are alone considered and these arise outside of the employment, are the same when there is no employment, and as great in one occupation as in another. Certainly the employer by paying a fair equivalent for the service rendered, though not sufficient to support the employee has neither caused nor contributed to her poverty. On the contrary, to the extent of what he pays he has relieved it."

Then, women can be sold like any other commodity for the labor of women cannot be separated from themselves. The court said:

"In principle there can be no difference between the case of selling labor and the case of selling goods. If one goes to the butcher, the baker or grocer to buy food he is morally entitled to obtain the worth of his money but he is not entitled to more."

Enclosed you will find copy of an article entitled "Labor is Not a Commodity."[2]

The only redress for women workers now is a constitutional amendment giving Congress power to enact minimum wage laws or to organize into trade unions and through their economic power obtain adequate wages. The decision has aroused the women of the country and a great campaign has been launched to organize them for their protection.

As soon as the decision was made the employers in Washington began reducing the wages of employes from 20 to 50 per cent. They discharged old and tried employes and took on new employes at lower wages. Some of those discharged would be sent to other employers who would employ them at a reduced rate.

The cost of living in Washington is generally higher than in any city in the United States according to the Bureau of Labor Statistics of the Department of Labor. During the war, when the wages of government employes were raised the same men who are now discharging their employes would raise prices so that they would receive the benefit from increased wages given the government employes.

In 1913 the following was adopted by the American Federation of Labor convention:[3]

"Women do not organize as readily or as stably as men. They are therefore more easily exploited. They certainly are in a greater measure than are men entitled to the concern of society. A fair standard of wages, a living wage for all employed in industry should be the first consideration in production. None are more entitled to that standard than are the women and minors. An industry which denies to all its workers and particularly to its women and minors who are toilers a living wage is unfit and should not be permitted to exist."

The decision of the Supreme Court declaring unconstitutional the child labor act was by a vote of five to four. The vote on the minimum wage question was five to three. One of the justices[4] did not take part because his daughter[5] was employed by the Minimum Wage Commission and because he had advocated the minimum wage before he had become a member of the Supreme Court. This decision was practically five to four. Therefore one man decided the two questions. It means that he knows more about law and right and common sense than congress, the President of the United States and the Legislatures of many states.

In its minimum wage decision the court violates its own rule as will be seen by the following quotation from that opinion:

"This court, by an unbroken line of decisions from Chief Justice Marshall to the present time, has steadily adhered to the rule that every possible presumption is in favor of the validity of an act of Congress until overcome beyond rational doubt."

If four men out of nine believe the minimum wage law constitutional does that not imply a rational doubt. This is a most dangerous menace to the liberties of our people especially when the Supreme Court has two members who were repudiated by the people. Justice Taft was overwhelmingly defeated for President of the United States and Justice Sutherland met defeat in his candidacy for re-election as senator from Utah. Nevertheless they are permitted to make decisions that are inimical to the advancement of the people of our country.

The American Federation of Labor in order to prevent such decisions is advocating an amendment to the Constitution of the United States to provide that when Congress repasses a law that has been declared unconstitutional by the Supreme Court that it will be the law of the land.

Very truly yours,   Saml Gompers.
President,   American Federation of Labor.

TLpS, reel 290, vol. 303, pp. 1011–13, SG Letterbooks, DLC.

1. John Stevens, the son of a Meriden, Conn., insurance salesman, was about fifteen years old.

2. *American Federationist* 21 (Oct. 1914): 866–67.

3. See *The Samuel Gompers Papers,* vol. 9, p. 20.

4. Justice Louis Brandeis.

5. Elizabeth Brandeis (1896–1984) served from 1919 to 1923 as assistant secretary and then as secretary of the District of Columbia Minimum Wage Board. She later married Paul Raushenbush, son of Social Gospel theologian Walter Rauschenbusch, and taught in the Department of Economics at the University of Wisconsin (1928–67).

James Barrett[1] to Frank Morrison

Managing Editor
The Charlotte Herald
Charlotte N.C. May 8, 1923.

Mr. Frank Morrison,
Sec'y., American Federation of Labor,
Washington, D.C.
Dear Mr. Morrison:—

Not having heard from you I have been wondering if you received the papers I mailed to your home address containing the beautiful essay written by Mrs. Morrison.

We are in the midst of one of the most titanic struggles here now that the South's industries have ever known. Natural prejudice that exists here against the organization of labor, a heritage handed down from the slave owners of past history, combined with the bigotry of the new rich,—with that mixture given to the situation by the coming of the Northern and Eastern capitalists to the Southland—pr[oduces] a problem [whi]ch calls for all that there is in the hearts of the men and women of labor to solve. Added to this, is the advent upon the scene of activity of James Tansey[2] of the amalgamated union. He is being dined and wined by the manufacturers and no doubt, will be used in their scheme to organize craft unions among the textile workers for the purpose of destroying the solidarity of this great big group of workers. Then to, this heathenish, middle-age policy of the employers owning not only the mill but the community as well, and every house in which the workers live—even the store buildings that the merchant occupies in which he sells merchandise to the workers, gives to the employers absolute control over the human being—the man and woman who works in his mill, not only while at work but in their homes as well. If the worker displeases the employer, the employer's power does not stop with that of discharging the employee, but is immediately followed with the issuance of orders for that worker to get out of the place which he and his family had been calling their home, and if a merchant expresses any sympathy whatever for the worker, he to is notified to vacate the store building which he has rented from the Lord and Master—the owner of the Cotton Mill.

Frank, I am really disturbed about the conditions here. It does not seem possible that intelligent men will continue to push a group of people further, and still further, toward the edge of the precipice. It is a trait of human nature, as old as the world itself, to fight back when the edge of the precipice becomes visible to the naked eye of him who is being pushed toward it. The battle is going to break here e're long, and nothing less than the strong support of Almighty God can enable the leaders to hold in check the fighting Southern blood when it does finally become thoroughly aroused.

I wish t[hat] you could come down here and deliver that address that you delivered in the Northwest[3] and also touch upon Tansey's gang and his amalgamation. I believe it would help us considerably.

Eatough and Miss Kelleher[4] are doing splendid work here now and the textile organization is having a gradual and steady growth. The other crafts are picking up slowly and despite all the obstacles thrown in the way, the movement as a whole is making some progress. It is the textile industry that I am concerned in just now, because I know their thoughts, their feelings and that they have reached about the limit of their endurance.

Of course, you are constantly engaged but yet I know of no work that you could do which [would give] a greater benefit to the labor movement than to pay us a vi[sit to this] section.[5]

With best wishes, I am

Your friend,   James F. Barrett

TLS, AFL Microfilm National and International Union File, United Textile Workers Records, reel 42, frame 2717, *AFL Records.*

1. James Festus BARRETT served as managing editor of the *Charlotte Herald* from 1923 until 1925.

2. James TANSEY was the longtime president of the American Federation of Textile Operatives, established by a seceding faction of the United Textile Workers of America.

3. Frank Morrison spoke in Portland, Ore., while making arrangements for the 1923 AFL convention to be held there. He said that while the AFL favored the amalgamation of related trades, it refused to force unions to combine and left the matter to affiliates to decide for themselves.

4. Mary J. Kelleher (b. 1882) was an organizer for the United Textile Workers of America (1912–28). From 1914 to 1920 she had also served as a salaried AFL organizer.

5. Morrison apparently did not make the trip.

The Executive Council of the AFL to James A. Duncan

May 14, 1923

Mr. James A. Duncan,
Secretary, Central Labor Council of Seattle and Vicinity,
Labor Temple, Seattle, Washington.
Dear Sir and Brother:

I am directed by the Executive Council to reply to the letter addressed to me under date of April 21,[1] signed by yourself and members of a special committee.

The Executive Council has given careful consideration to your communication. It also has had before it a further report from Organizer C. O. Young, together with certain other information and documents.

The Council was impressed by the fact that while your letter expressed the surprise of the Seattle Central Labor Council at the complaints made, your communication contained admissions that in each case the charge was accurate. In view of the admissions contained in your reply it seems unnecessary to make any further reference to evidence from other sources.

It is admitted that communications from the American Federation of Labor have been referred to auxiliary bodies for consideration and action; that your central body has in affiliation local organizations not affiliated to international unions within the American Federation of Labor and not directly affiliated to the American Federation of Labor; that your central body endorsed the soviet dictatorship in Russia; that it has given its friendship to the I.W.W. and its endorsement to the communist doctrine.

The Executive Council feels it necessary to require that the Seattle Central Labor Council take action in accordance with the following stipulations:

First: That the Seattle Central Labor Council must give this Executive Council definite and tangible assurance of its purpose to be loyal to the American Federation of Labor, to abide by the decisions of the A.F. of L. conventions and to conduct itself in all matters in accord with the laws and principles of the A.F. of L. and the policies declared by it.

Second: That the Seattle Central Labor Council repudiate the I.W.W. and all similar movements.

Third: That the Seattle Central Labor Council repudiate its approval of the soviet dictatorship and the principle of communism.

Fourth: That the Seattle Central Labor Council must not in future issue credentials of any kind accrediting any person either as delegate or "observer" to any congress, convention, or gathering, of the Red labor internationale, the Communist internationale or any other body hostile to the American Federation of Labor.

Fifth: That the Seattle Central Labor Council dissociate organizations which are not affiliated to bona fide international unions or to the American Federation of Labor direct.

Sixth: That communications from the American Federation of Labor must be read before the Seattle Central Labor Council and acted upon by that body and not referred to any auxilliary body, however remote or close may be the relationship between the Central Labor Council and that auxilliary body.

The Executive Council is not of the opinion that further action is required at this time, but it is deemed fair to say to your central labor council that this Executive Council intends to observe the conduct of your body and requires that evidence be furnished to show that the conditions herein set forth have been complied with.

In setting forth the six requirements the Executive Council has been mindful only of the best interests of the working people and of the law and the constitution of the American Federation of Labor. It has set forth requirements that must be observed if the law, the constitution and the decisions of our conventions are to be observed. Manifestly they must be observed by all alike and it is our duty to require observance wherever it is found that observance is lacking.

The Executive Council had before it the letter from the special committee of your council in which certain specific admissions were made; and it also had before it certain matter relating to the celebration of May Day in Seattle. Among other things the council had before it certain leaflets or circulars issued in promoting the May Day celebration. These purported to be issued and the celebration projected under "auspices of joint committee of Seattle labor organizations endorsed by Seattle Central Labor Council." It is apparent that the speakers selected were strong I.W.W. sympathizers, but most striking of all was the appearance on the reverse side of some of these circulars of the I.W.W. emblem and its sabotage motto, "take it easy." It was set forth that this celebration was for "the release of class-war prisoners."

We shall pass over the obvious effort of your letter to dissemble. We find therein the admissions that are pertinent to the discussion and to the charges made. We are gratified at your stated intention to observe the laws, the constitution and the principles of the American Federation of Labor and the decisions of its conventions. We feel that we may expect action to follow in the wake of promise and we look for that action with hope, because of our great desire for unity and solidarity in the labor movement.

Because of our concern for the unity of our movement and for the best interests of the working people, and because of our concern for the dignity of the laws, the constitution and the decisions of the conventions, we shall observe with care the course of the Seattle Central Labor Council and we will be pleased to have an early assurance that compliance with the requirements herein contained has been established and will be maintained.[2]

With all earnest good wishes for the success, permanency and the great work yet before the Central Body in furtherance of the rights, interests and welfare of the toilers not only of Seattle, but of the great state of Washington and of our beloved Republic, we are,

Fraternally yours,

Executive Council   American Federation of Labor

Saml Gompers   President.

TLpS, reel 290, vol. 303, pp. 766–69, SG Letterbooks, DLC.

1. "From the Central Labor Council of Seattle and Vicinity," Apr. 21, 1923, above.

2. For the reply to this letter, see "The Central Labor Council of Seattle and Vicinity to the Executive Council of the AFL," June 6, 1923, below.

To Charles Evans Hughes

Washington, D.C., May 17, 1923.

Honorable Charles Evans Hughes,
Secretary of State,
Washington, D.C.
Sir:

Newspapers report that one Samuel Semprevivo, born in Italy, but claiming to have lived in the United States twenty years and to have been in the American army during the late war, has just returned to America after a six months' absence in Italy, bearing credentials as an organizer for the Fascisti movement, assigned to the territory of Louisiana, Alabama, Texas, Arkansas, Georgia, Florida, North Carolina and South Carolina.[1]

Mr. Semprevivo's credentials are reported to have been issued by the "political secretary in charge of the office for Canada and America." It is his announced purpose, according to the report which I have seen (New York Evening Post, May 12), to educate Italians in America "particularly in regard to Fiume and Zara and the other cities that Italy has conquered" and to "make them think of Italy in terms of Mussolini[2] and what he stands for, rather than in terms of the bolshevists and anarchists who had control of the country before Mussolini overthrew them."

These Fascisti organizations in America are to report to Rome, according to this Fascisti organizer.

American labor regards the Fascisti propaganda as being opposed to democratic institutions. There is little difference in principle between Fascism and bolshevism. Propaganda cannot be stopped entirely, but what I do have in mind is to protest against the organization of groups in America which either approximately or in fact admit allegiance to a foreign state.

I have no feeling of assurance that any preventive measures can be applied, but it is at least possible to make our protest against this violation of American hospitality and freedom—a violation which is none the less repugnant if it is merely a violation in spirit and not actually in fact.

To retention of an admiration for the culture of the homelands of our foreign born none will raise objection, but it must outrage the sense of patriotism of every true American to find foreign emissaries in our midst organizing foreign born residents for the purpose of "educating" them to support a foreign government and its policies. This would be repugnant in any case, but it is particularly so when that foreign government happens to be under control of a practical dictatorship.

We quite well understand the circumstances which brought that dictatorship into being. But whether it was a choice between bolshevism and Fascism or not, our objection is, I feel, entirely valid. We have consistently voiced our opposition to the teachings of bolshevism and we have waged effective war against its brutal, destructive, autocratic doctrines. We make slight differentiation between autocracies and we are impelled by our loyalty to democracy to make protest against this new intrusion upon the hospitality of our free soil.[3]

Very truly yours,　　Saml Gompers.
President,　　American Federation of Labor.

TLS, RG 59, General Records of the Department of State, DNA.

1. Samuel Semprevivo (variously Sempre; 1892–1961) served as a sergeant in the U.S. Army from February 1916 to February 1918. Born in Zara, he immigrated to the United States and lived in New Orleans before the war; he later moved to the Bronx, where he ran an export-import business. He had arrived in New York City on May 7, 1923, on the S.S. *Conte Rosso,* sailing from Genoa.

2. Benito Amilcare Andrea Mussolini (1883–1945), founder of the Fasci di Combattimento (Fighting Bands or Fighting Leagues; 1919) and the Partito Nazionale Fascista (the Italian Fascist party; 1921), was subsequently prime minister and then dictator of Italy (1922–43). After his overthrow in 1943, he was installed by the Nazis as the titular head of a Fascist regime created in German-occupied northern Italy. He was captured by partisans on Apr. 27, 1945, and shot the next day.

3. Undersecretary of State William Phillips acknowledged SG's letter on May 19, 1923 (AFL Microfilm Convention File, reel 32, frame 1777, *AFL Records*).

From William Short

Pres. Executive Council
Washington State Federation of Labor
Seattle, Wash., May 18, 1923.

Dear friend Sam:

I have been waiting to hear from you relative to action you propose to take in connection with the Central Labor Council here, but haven't had a word from you as yet.

I ran across day before yesterday, something that I know will be of interest to you. I had heard something about it prior to that time, and finally got my hands on copies of the documents in question which consist of a proposal to turn over control of the Seattle Union Record to a committee designated by George Vanderveer,[1] head of the legal bureau of the Seattle Central Labor Council, and general counsel for the I.W.W.

It seems that some time ago the American Fund for Public Service, which is the Garland Fund of New York, made through Mr. Vanderveer a loan of $5000 to the Seattle Union Record. You will see from the documents,[2] copy of which I herewith enclose to you, that the condition on which the money was loaned was that not only a mortgage to be given them on two intertype machines but that they be given a contract giving them supervisory authority over the paper's policies and operations. And that the editorial policy of the paper is to be governed as the interests of the Fund may seem to require.

One of the reasons why this thing was being attempted to be put through was due to the fear that the charter of the Council might be lifted and that the 51,000 shares of stock in the paper, which practically control it, owned by the Council would not revert into the hands of the American Federation of Labor but would continue in the control of the reds, independent of the A.F. of L. No bones are made by the red element as to this being their purpose, and you will note in the resolution prepared by Mr. Vanderveer that the present trustees of the Council, and not their successors in office, are to continue to exercise control over the paper.

This proposal was recommended by the Board of Trustees of the Union Record, a week ago, to the trustees of the Seattle Central Labor Council. Kindly note that both the letter and resolution in connection therewith are prepared by Mr. Vanderveer. The trustees would have voted to recommend it to the Council last Wednesday night, and the Council would have adopted it without question, had it not been for the threat made by Mr. Robt Hesketh,[3] delegate from the Cooks and Assistants Union,[4] and a trustee of the Council, and who is also an International Vice-President of the Culinary Workers,[5] to the effect that if the trustees recommended it to the Council and the Council adopted it that it would insure the lifting of the charter and that the four culinary workers locals of the city would immediately withdraw from the Council.

They then decided not to take any action on the proposal last week, but it will undoubtedly again come up in some other camouflaged form at a later date, as the board of control of the Union Record has already approved it and the machinery is in motion to put it over, either direct in the form in which I am enclosing or later in some other form that will serve the same purpose. The reading of the enclosed documents will very clearly reveal the purpose sought to be served and its relation to their pretended loyalty to the A.F. of L.

The proposal, in substance, is to turn over the control and direction of this paper to a bunch of long-haired, crack-brained Socialists in New York in return for a loan of $5000 and subordinate entirely the A.F. of L. Unions of Seattle and the rest of the State that have invested at least $200,000 in actual money in stock in the paper.

I regret that Brother Hesketh put any opposition in their way, as I think if they had been permitted to go ahead and do it it would have awakened the sleeping A.F. of L. trades unionists of this city more effectively than anything I know of, as several of our good big substantial local unions have several thousand dollars invested in the paper. In fact, it was the $3000 that is invested in the paper by Brother Hesketh's own local that prompted his vigorous stand against the proposals. However, this doesn't detract any from the vicious purpose they were seeking to serve and which will undoubtedly be served at some later date in some other form.

I was sure that you would be interested in reading the document and in having a copy of it in your possession for your files.

Kindly let me know at your convenience what course the A.F. of L. plans to pursue in connection with the Central Council of this City.[6]

Accept my kindest good wishes, as ever,

Your sincere friend,   (S) W. M. Short.

N.B. The reason for designating the *present* trustees of the Central Labor Council *and not their successors* is because a majority of the present trustees are tied up with the red crowd and subservient to Mr. Vanderveer, while a change in the control of the Council would also bring a change in the control of the paper and put it under the control of the A.F. of L. trades unionists; hence the move to safeguard the control of this propaganda organ.

W. M. S.

TLtcSr, Executive Council Records, Vote Books, reel 18, frame 4, *AFL Records.* Typed notation: "*Copy.*" Enclosed in SG to AFL Executive Council, May 28, 1923, ibid., frame 1.

1. George Francis Vanderveer (1875–1942) served as chief counsel (1921–27) for the legal bureaus of the Seattle, Tacoma, and Everett, Wash., central labor bodies. From 1917 to 1920 he had served as the principal attorney for the IWW.

2. For copies of the documents, see Executive Council Records, Vote Books, reel 18, frames 5–6, *AFL Records.*

3. Robert Bruce HESKETH was a Seattle city councilman and a vice-president of the Hotel and Restaurant Employees' International Alliance and Bartenders' International League of America.

4. Hotel and Restaurant Employees' local 33 (Cooks and Assistants) of Seattle.

5. That is, the HOTEL and Restaurant Employees' International Alliance and Bartenders' International League of America.

6. SG wired William Short on May 25, 1923, to ask what action the Seattle Central Labor Council had taken regarding the loan and the transfer of *Seattle Union Record* stock (Executive Council Records, Vote Books, reel 18, frame 7, *AFL Records*). Short and C. O. Young wired in reply that the Council had approved the proposal in order to keep the paper from coming under AFL control, and they asked SG to revoke the Council's charter immediately (ibid., frames 7–8).

To William Gerber[1]

May 31, 1923.

Mr. William Gerber,
308 Grand Central Station, Memphis, Tenn.
Dear Sir:

Your letter of May 28 received and contents noted.

In compliance with your request for material to be used in a debate on the question that immigration should be prohibited for a period of 20 years I am sending under separate cover a copy of the *American Federationist* for November, 1922,[2] and for June, 1923. On page 489 of the latter is an editorial[3] that will give you the information you request.

One thing to be considered in discussing immigration is that the greater the number of immigrants the less American the United States becomes. During the war it was found that the average mentality of the men entering the United States army was that of a 13 year old boy.

This is a most astounding fact. The American Federation of Labor believes that the foreigners now in this country should be assimilated before others are permitted to come except from such countries as Great Britain, France, Germany and Scandinavia. The illiteracy and low mentality of our own people, of those born in this country cannot be overcome unless we raise the standard of knowledge among the foreigners. America must be kept American. Those who would flood the country with hordes of immigrants from southeastern Europe care no more for America then do the Hottentots. Their desires are governed by greed. We hear much of movements to Americanize our people but this cannot be done any easier than water can be purified that is continually being contaminated.

Recently Mr. Elbert H. Gary, Chairman of the Board of Directors of the United States Steel Corporation, denounced immigration conditions as the worst that ever happened to this country economically. Secretary Davis of the Department of Labor in a letter[4] to President Harding stated:

"It is unnecessary to point out the evil of throwing open the gates at a time of prosperity in order to flood the country with workers and non-workers whose very presence would serve to bring prosperity to an end. It is a short sighted policy to secure cheap labor through immigration."

Very truly yours,   Saml Gompers
President,   American Federation of Labor.

TLpS, reel 291, vol. 304, pp. 446–47, SG Letterbooks, DLC.

1. William E. Gerber, the son of a Memphis dry goods merchant, was about fifteen years old.

2. The November 1922 issue of the *American Federationist* included an article by Oliver Hoyem entitled "Immigration and America's Safety" (29:818–27).

3. "Immigration? Utilize First What We Have," *American Federationist* 30 (June 1923): 489–93.

4. That is, a report presented at a cabinet meeting held on Apr. 17, 1923, by Secretary of Labor James Davis. For excerpts of the report, see "Harding Convinced of Labor Shortage," *New York Times*, Apr. 18, 1923.

To William Hays[1]

June 1, 1923.

Mr. Will H. Hays,
Director, Moving Picture Industry,
New York City, New York.
Dear Sir:

The wonderful growth of the motion picture industry has caused many people with axes to grind to scheme how they can use it for their own personal gain. For many years the American Federation of Labor has supported every movement having for its purpose the protection of the motion picture industry from fanatical legislation that would hamper its progress. During that time the only request made has been that in the making of pictures labor should not be misrepresented or placed in any light contrary to facts. The American Federation of Labor believes not in license but in the greatest freedom of speech, press, assembly and motion pictures. It also believes that propaganda of any kind launched with the view of discrediting the trade unions and their officials should not be given publicity by the motion picture industry.

Recently I received a copy of a letter[2] sent to the members of the National Founders Association by William H. Barr,[3] as President, in which he proposes to use the moving picture industry in a campaign of that organization to destroy the trade unions. He states that it is proposed to create a three million dollar foundation, the stock to be offered particularly to the men engaged in industry. Not only is the foundation to be a channel for the dissemination of anti-labor motion pictures, but is to be a commercial proposition, paying 8 per cent to preferred stock holders. Mr. Barr proposes "that the industrial relationship of the United States shall furnish a part of the initial capital funds of this organization." He proposes that pictures will be made to be shown in homes, industrial plants, schools and churches. He does not believe society is furnished the proper teaching by the church, which he states has become old fashioned. He hypocritically declares that "the strong men of the country must face their duty to the future. They must provide intellectual guidance along sound lines."

Before the armistice, while our boys were offering the supreme sacrifice to maintain the political democracy of not only our own country but of the world, the same influence that is seeking to launch this anti-labor motion picture foundation began the spreading of propaganda to establish industrial autocracy in our beloved Republic. They declared for the so-called "open shop" and traitorously designated it the "American-shop." For nearly four years they kept up a persistent organizing campaign to induce every employer in the country to join with them, but it may be said to the honor of the great mass of employers of the United States they refused to join in such an un-American cause.

But having control of all avenues of publicity to which labor was not admitted they endeavored to poison the minds of the just-minded citizens of the land. But their schemes failed, the people found out that the cry of the "American shop" was simply a shield behind which to hide their desire to destroy the organizations of labor in order that wages might be cut to the bone, hours of labor increased and thereby take the spirit out of the hearts and souls of the workers.

Having failed to gain their un-American ends through the printed word, they are now seeking to use your great industry in the last effort to carry our their schemes.

I am impelled to write you on this subject because of the insidious propaganda that is being woven into motion pictures against labor. This question was discussed by the A.F. of L. in its convention[4] and by the Executive Council at its recent meeting.[5] A thorough discussion brought out many instances of evidently inspired motion picture propaganda and the opinion was expressed that a report[6] condemning this misrepresentation should be included in the report of the Executive Council to the next convention[7] this fall of the American Federation of Labor.

Much has appeared in the newspapers during the past year or so of the desire of the motion picture industry to create a better sentiment among the people. Motion pictures have been made in the interests of this campaign. Therefore, it is my hope, and that is the purpose for which I am writing today, that not only will the insidious misrepresentations of Labor be frowned down upon but that this new scheme of propaganda by the enemies of Labor will not find favor with any motion picture producer. The pictures which the National Founders Association would produce would not be true to life. Far from it. They would be based on the theory that the wage earners constitute a lower order of citizenship than employers and big business and that repressive measures should be taken to keep them there.

May I hope that this grave injustice to the greater mass of your patrons will be discontinued and that a more sympathetic treatment of the hopes and aspirations of Labor be given in the future so that a report upon the subject may be made by my associates of the Executive Council to our forthcoming convention.

With kind regards and hoping for an early reply, I am,

Cordially yours,   Saml Gompers.

President,   American Federation of Labor.

TLpS, reel 291, vol. 304, pp. 248–49, SG Letterbooks, DLC.

1. William Harrison Hays (1879–1954) served as president of the Motion Picture Producers and Distributors of America from 1922 to 1945. He had served as postmaster general of the United States from 1921 to 1922.

2. William Barr to the Members of the National Founders' Association (Weekly Letter No. 272), Apr. 10, 1923, reel 291, vol. 304, pp. 540–44, SG Letterbooks, DLC.

3. William Henry Barr (1874–1944) served as president of the National Founders' Association (1917–28?) and the American Pictures Corporation (1925).

4. See AFL, *Proceedings*, 1922, pp. 138–41, 360.

5. The AFL Executive Council discussed the matter at its meeting on May 15, 1923. (See Executive Council Records, Minutes, reel 7, frames 1351–52, *AFL Records*.)

6. At its August 1923 meeting in New York City, the Executive Council voted 5–3 to drop the issue of motion pictures from its report to the upcoming AFL convention in Portland, Ore. SG voted against the motion.

7. The 1923 convention of the AFL met in Portland, Ore., Oct. 1–12.

To Harry Ward[1] and Roger Baldwin

June 1, 1923.

Dr. Harry F. Ward, Chairman,
Mr. Roger N. Baldwin, Director,
American Civil Liberties Union,
100 Fifth Avenue, New York City.
Gentlemen:

Your letter of May 24 denies that the American Civil Liberties Union is a vehicle for pro-soviet propaganda.

It is quite possible that from your point of view your contention is correct. Permit me to say, however, that as we see the situation your contention is not correct.

I have not the slightest intention of entering into a debate with you as to the conduct, or the merits or demerits of the American Civil Liberties Union.

But of this there is no doubt: The Organization has been a source of comfort and strength to the communist propaganda in the United States and by the character of its operations it has aided the communist propaganda.

Your service, if it may be so called, has been mainly to organizations frankly engaged in communist propaganda, or else so strongly inclined toward it as to bring them within the category of organizations, movements and factions opposed to the bona fide, democratic American labor movement.

[I]f you choose to rest your case upon technicalities we do not; and studying your operations from the broad viewpoint of general policy and general activity, we assert again without qualification that we regard the whole influence of the so-called American Civil Liberties Union as pro-soviet in character. Its efforts to invade the labor press in behalf of communists and other red and pink organizations and individuals have been of little avail, but they have been stamped indelibly with the character of your general policy and your general activities.

I know of no case in which you have consulted the officers of the American Federation of Labor as to the course to be pursued in connection with what you are pleased to call labor cases. But I do know that in one important case your organization interfered against the expressed wish of the trade union involved. I am informed by the editor[2] of the United Mine Workers' Journal that the United Mine Workers asked that your organization keep out of West Virginia; but that you persisted in holding a meeting in spite of this request—a meeting which may have established free speech for lawyers, but not for mine workers.[3]

There are times when the cause of free speech needs legitimate defense. Free speech, when really assailed, calls forth the sacrifice and effort of all believers in freedom and democracy. It is impossible to find the evidence that your organization serves merely in that role for that purpose.

Whether or not you are in agreement with the philosophy of communism is not a matter that requires debate here; nor are your present professions in that respect of much interest to me.

The use which the trustees of the "Garland Fund," of which you, Mr. Baldwin, are one, as already pointed out elsewhere, have made of the energies and the finances of that Fund in efforts in favor of communism and sovietism, is well supported by other activities in the same direction which are being disclosed. The use of such funds to control and hold under duress the pro-soviet editorial utterances of some labor or semi-labor publications adds interest to the entire matter and to your activities in general.[4]

Your letter to me is signed by Dr. Harry F. Ward and Mr. Roger Baldwin and both of you gentlemen have long records which portray your sentiments, inclinations and policies quite effectively. And I am certain that the communists will not say either of you has done communism or its propaganda in America any disservice.

Very truly yours,   Saml Gompers.
President,   American Federation of Labor.

TLpS, reel 291, vol. 304, pp. 235–36, SG Letterbooks, DLC.

1. Harry Frederick Ward (1873–1966), Methodist minister and social critic, was general secretary of the Methodist Federation for Social Service (1911–44) and a member of the faculty of Union Theological Seminary in New York City (1918–41). He served as chairman of the board of the American Civil Liberties Union from 1920 to 1940.

2. Ellis Searles (1866–1945), a former reporter for the *Indianapolis News,* was editor of the *United Mine Workers' Journal* from 1918 to 1940.

3. The United Mine Workers of America had sought an injunction in the U.S. district court for the southern district of West Virginia to prevent Sheriff Don Chafin of Logan County and his deputies, or the Logan Coal Operators' Association and its seventy-four member companies, from interfering with the constitutional rights of union members to assemble, speak freely, and organize. On Feb. 17, 1923, the case was dismissed on the grounds that it was a state matter and federal courts had no jurisdiction (*United Mine Workers of America, Dist. No. 17, et al.* v. *Chafin et al.,* 286 F. 959 [1923]). On Mar. 4 the American Civil Liberties Union held a free-speech meeting in Logan County to call attention to the issue, with Arthur Garfield Hays, the Rev. Henry Huntington, and the Rev. John Ryan as speakers.

4. See "From William Short," May 18, 1923, above.

To Jere Sullivan[1]

June 4, 1923.

Mr. Jere L. Sullivan,
Secretary-Treasurer, Hotel and Restaurant Employes
 International Alliance,
528–530 Walnut St., Cincinnati, Ohio.
Dear Sir and Brother:

In reply to the inquiry contained in your letter of June 2nd, permit me to advise you that inasmuch as the Chinaman you mention in your letter is a natural born citizen of the United States, he is eligible to membership in a union affiliated to the American Federation of Labor.

With best wishes, I am

Fraternally yours,   Saml Gompers
President,   American Federation of Labor.

TLpS, reel 291, vol. 304, p. 333, SG Letterbooks, DLC.

1. Jere L. SULLIVAN served as secretary-treasurer of the Hotel and Restaurant Employees' International Alliance and Bartenders' International League of America from 1899 to 1928.

The Central Labor Council of
Seattle and Vicinity to the
Executive Council of the AFL

Central Labor Council of Seattle and Vicinity
Affiliated with American Federation of Labor.
Seattle, Washington. June 6th, 1923.

Executive Council, American Federation of Labor,
Mr. Samuel Gompers, President,
A.F. of L. Bldg., Washington, D.C.
Dear Sirs and Brothers:

Replying to yours of May 14th,[1] we desire to express our profound regrets and surprise that at the outset of your letter you should commit so gross an error as to state that our letter of April 21st[2] "contained admissions that in each case the charge (set forth in your letter of April 10th)[3] was accurate."

We further deeply deplore the fact that the text of your misleading letter of May 14th was given to the press on May 9th, ten days before your communication was delivered to this Council, and later was published in full through the instrumentality of your office, causing irreparable damage to this Central Labor Council.[4]

In an effort to protect this Council from further injury and to give readers an opportunity to learn both sides, we have determined to give full publicity to all the correspondence which has passed between us relative to this matter, concurrently with the delivery of this letter to your office.[5]

In addition to dealing further with the subject matter of your letter of April 10th and our reply of April 21st, your letter of May 14th refers to a May-day celebration in Seattle in which the I.W.W. finally figured somewhat conspicuously and in which you infer this Council played a prominent part.

The facts which any fair-minded person, interested in learning them, could have ascertained are as follows:

The local Metal Trades' Council sent resolutions to this Central Labor Council urging endorsement of proposals to celebrate May 1st as International Labor Day and setting forth the program indicated by you. The matter was referred to our Resolutions Committee which, in its report, recommended that all reference to International Labor Day be stricken as this Council does not recognize May 1st as such, and that the resolutions then be adopted as amended in this manner. The committee's report which was in strict conformity with American

Federation of Labor principles and policies, was adopted and that was the sum total of this Council's activities in connection with any Mayday celebration.

There has been no effort or desire, on our part, to dissemble.

This Council acted in good faith and is in no way responsible for any false interpretation or improper publicity given its action.

Regarding your six stipulations, we shall take them up in consecutive order, except that we shall deal with the first one last, as its interpretation probably presents the only differences between us.

"Second: That the Seattle Central Labor Council repudiate the I.W.W. and all similar movements."

We have never countenanced any form of secessionary or dual organization to the A.F. of L. and as we have always classed the I.W.W. as such, we have nothing to repudiate.

"Third: That the Seattle Central Labor Council repudiate its approval of the soviet dictatorship and the principle of communism."

This council has never given its approval to a soviet dictatorship or to the principle of communism, and therefore has nothing to repudiate.

"Fourth: That the Seattle Central Labor Council must not in future issue credentials of any kind accrediting any person either as a delegate or "observer" to any congress, convention, or gathering, of the Red labor internationale, the Communist internationale or any other body hostile to the American Federation of Labor."

This Council has never knowingly granted credentials to any person as a delegate or "observer" to any organization known to be hostile to the American Federation of Labor, and will not. Further we shall be glad to have for our guidance any information that [you][6] will furnish relative to such organizations, together with evidences of their hostility.

"Fifth: That the Seattle Central Labor Council dissociate organizations which are not affiliated to bona fide international unions or to the American Federation of Labor direct."

With regard to these cases, Blacksmiths' Local #211., Shipyard Laborers' Local #38-A2., and Lady Barbers' Local #1., we asked you for specific instructions as to the particular course we should pursue with each and you failed to furnish them to us, therefore we desire to advise you that we have dealt with them in the following manner:

In the case of the Blacksmiths: in spite of the fact that they hold a court injunction preventing their International from taking their charter without first complying with that union's laws, and which injunction might be interpreted to prevent our action, we have unseated their delegates. This we understand to be your instructions to us.

The Shipyard Laborers, whose former International, (the Riggers and Stevedores, or I.L.A.) we understand, was instructed to relinquish jurisdiction over this local, have formally withdrawn their delegates from this Council pending the results of their efforts to become chartered by some other international. We sincerely trust that means will be found to save this membership to the American Federation of Labor.

In the case of the Lady Barbers, it is with feelings mingled with shame and humiliation that we have, with great reluctance, notified this splendid organization of women wage workers and loyal trade unionists that, orders of the Executive Council of the American Federation of Labor, whose flag we have ever fought to defend as the emblem of freedom through organization, we must dissociate them from this Central Labor Council and cast them into the slough of despond with others unorganized. Surely with the Journeymen Barbers' International Union disclaiming jurisdiction over women workers, this order of the Executive Council is unwarranted and without justification. In order that a proper solution might yet be applied to this case, we respectfully request that you reconsider this action of yours which, if persisted in, will cast such odium upon our movement as will not soon be overcome; and further, that you grant a federal charter to the Seattle Lady Barbers' Union pending further action by the Journeymen Barbers' International Union. In case you decide you are without authority, (which we think the constitution gives you) we trust you will join us in our efforts to secure proper action by the A.F. of L. convention, at Portland, Ore. next October, to see that a place is provided in our movement for these Lady Barbers, in keeping with true A.F. of L. principles which call for the organization of all wage workers regardless of *sex*.

"Sixth: That communications from the American Federation of Labor must be read before the Seattle Central Labor Council and acted upon by that body and not referred to any auxiliary body, however remote or close may be the relationship between the Central Labor Council and that auxiliary body."

Communications from the American Federation of Labor, whether from officers, departments, or committees thereof, will be read and acted upon by this Council as [is][7] its custom to do, and will not be referred to any auxiliary body.

"First: That the Seattle Central Labor Council must give this Executive Council definite and tangible assurance of its purpose to be loyal to the American Federation of Labor, to abide by the decisions of the A.F. of L. conventions and to conduct itself in all matters in accord with the laws and principles of the A.F. of L. and the policies declared by it."

It is our contention that we are not violating any law of the American Federation of Labor, and that we are adhering religiously to its principles as set forth in the preamble of its constitution as follows:—

"A struggle is going on in all the nations of the civilized World between the oppressors and the oppressed of all countries, a struggle between the capitalist and the laborer, which grows in intensity from year to year, and will work disastrous results to the toiling millions if they are not combined for mutual protection and benefit."

With absolute agreement between us upon all matters touching the laws and principles of the American Federation of Labor, it is inconceivable that any very serious difficulty should arise over matters of policy to be pursued in given localities for the purpose of advancing those principles, as there is always room for honest differences upon questions of policy, and such honest differences must be tolerated if the democratic spirit with which our organization was born, is to survive.

For instance, on the question of political policy.

A committee from the American Federation of Labor, headed by President Gompers, attended the last national convention of the Republican Party and sought to have embodied in the Republican platform, Labor's Bill of Rights and other provisions in the interests of wage workers.

Reporting to the A.F. of L. convention at Montreal in 1920 the result of its efforts, the committee said in part:—

"The platform declaration as adopted proposes an industrial enslavement and an abrogation of rights as precious as life itself.———

["]The heritage left to the Republican Party by Abraham Lincoln, the great liberator, is abandoned in a platform which embraces every opportunity to strengthen the concept of repression and coercion of the working people." (see page #332 A.F. of L. proceedings for 1920)

Later, a similar committee, headed by President Gompers, presented labor's demands at the Democrats' convention at San Francisco, and received little, if any, more consideration.

In view of this hopeless situation, and recognizing the truth as set forth in the preamble of the A.F. of L. constitution that "a struggle is going on in all nations of the civilized World between the oppressors and the oppressed of all countries, a struggle between the capitalist and the laborer," the Seattle labor movement, in fact the Washington State labor movement, believing that there is no more sense in attempting to line up capitalist and laborer in the same political organization than in the same industrial organization as would recognize the truth embodied in those cardinal principles enunciated in the preamble of the constitution of the American Federation of Labor.

The only political organization which embodies these principles and the full demands of the A.F. of L. in its platform is the Farmer-Labor Party. Therefore the whole Washington State labor movement backed it in 1920, and this Council is still on record as supporting it.

Regarding your policy of opposition to recognition by the United States government of the present government of Russia, we cannot honestly and conscientiously support it, and so, in common with many of the best minds and greatest patriots of our nation, we beg to differ with you. Therefore, we urge the recognition of the present government of Russia by the United States government, and the reopening of trade relations with that great nation.

Another policy adopted by you, which if forced upon us would split our movement wide open, is that which demands the repeal of prohibition legislation. You probably will recall the vigorous protests received by you at the Atlantic City convention,[8] from the biggest Washington State Federation of Labor convention[9] ever held, and from the Seattle Central Labor Council condemning your action on the liquor question.[10]

These should indicate to you the utter futility, the lack of wisdom, and the extreme danger in attempting to compel conformity to all policies adopted, when every law and principle of the American Federation of Labor is being observed and only the matter of policy stands between us and complete harmony.

Another point involved in any attempt to fasten exact policies upon central councils arises over the question as to which shall govern when policies of the A.F. of L. and of affiliated International Unions are in conflict. Common sense surely demands that both give considerable latitude to Central Councils in these matters so long as the laws and principles of the American Federation of Labor are held inviolate.

Sincerely trusting that we have made our position clear and that out of this exchange of correspondence will come a better understanding which will be highly beneficial to all parties concerned and make for the advancement of our cause, we are

Yours for Tolerance, Unity and Progress,

Central Labor Council of Seattle and Vicinity
By it's Special Committee
Bert Swain   Delegate, Engineers' Local #843.
T. H. Wagner,   Delegate, and President,
Musicians' Local #76.

Alice M. Lord   Delegate, and Bus. Rep.
Waitresses Local #240.
C. W. Dayly   Business Representative C.L.C.
J. E. Phillips,   President, C.L.C.
James A. Duncan,   Secretary, C.L.C.

Endorsed by the Central Labor Council of Seattle and Vicinity, June 6th 1923.

TLcSr, Executive Council Records, Vote Books, reel 18, frames 18–20, *AFL Records.* Typed notation: "*Copy.*"

1. "The Executive Council of the AFL to James A. Duncan," May 14, 1923, above.

2. "From the Central Labor Council of Seattle and Vicinity," Apr. 21, 1923, above.

3. "To James A. Duncan," Apr. 10, 1923, above.

4. The AFL Executive Council discussed the Seattle situation at its meeting on May 9, 1923, instructing SG to draft a reply to the Apr. 21 letter from the Seattle Central Labor Council (CLC) and enumerating the major points to be covered in his letter. SG presented a draft to the Council on May 14, which approved his letter without change. What the Council actually released to the press on May 9 was a statement demanding that central bodies rescind any endorsements of Bolshevism or the Soviet government, stop referring official AFL communications to committees on political action, and follow AFL "policies and principles" in their future conduct (See, for example, "Seattle Unions Get Ultimatum to Reject Reds," *Seattle Times,* May 10, 1923, "A.F. of L. Sends Ultimatum to Seattle Labor," *Seattle Post-Intelligencer,* May 10, 1923, and "Orders Union Labor to Boycott Soviet," *New York Times,* May 10, 1923).

5. On June 13, 1923, the Seattle CLC published its correspondence with the AFL Executive Council as a pamphlet entitled *Statement of the Seattle Central Labor Council Relative to Its Controversy with the Executive Council of the American Federation of Labor* ([Seattle, 1923]), and it began sending copies of the publication to state federations of labor and city central bodies throughout the country.

6. The text in brackets is supplied from the copy of the letter printed in *Statement of the Seattle Central Labor Council* (Executive Council Records, Vote Books, reel 18, frame 49, *AFL Records*).

7. The text in brackets is supplied from the copy of the letter printed in *Statement of the Seattle Central Labor Council* (Executive Council Records, Vote Books, reel 18, frame 49, *AFL Records*).

8. The 1919 AFL convention met in Atlantic City, June 9–23. On June 11 the convention endorsed by an overwhelming vote the partial repeal of prohibition, and on June 14 many of the delegates went to Washington, D.C., to demonstrate in support of the repeal. (See *The Samuel Gompers Papers,* vol. 11, pp. 79–81 and p. 81, nn. 1, 5.)

9. The 1919 convention of the Washington State Federation of Labor, meeting in Bellingham, June 16–21, adopted a resolution stating that "we the Washington State Federation of Labor . . . do denounce, condemn and repudiate the action of the American Federation of Labor" in opposing the Prohibition amendment (*Proceedings of the Eighteenth Annual Convention of the Washington State Federation of Labor* . . . [n.p., n.d.], p. 130).

10. On June 10, 1919, delegate James A. Duncan introduced a resolution at the AFL convention, adopted by the Seattle CLC on May 28, protesting against the repeal of Prohibition laws and urging organized labor to assist in their enforcement. The convention voted against adopting the resolution.

From William Short

W. M. Short, President.
Executive Council
Washington State Federation of Labor
Seattle, Washington, June 7, 1923.

Dear friend Sam:

I am herewith enclosing you press clippings from the four Seattle papers dealing with last night's meeting of the Seattle Central Labor Council, at which their letter of reply[1] to the American Federation of Labor was considered and endorsed. I of course, have not seen a copy of their letter, but understand it deals at length with the question of light wines and beer as a "smoke screen" to avoid the real issues.[2]

The vote of "71 to 19" is not a representative vote, of course, as a large portion of the delegates voting for it would not be sent to any new council that is formed, as many of the local unions just allow anybody to go and listen to the rabble in the Central Labor Council due to the fact that they long ago grew tired of listening to the kind of stuff that is pulled at the meetings.

Kindly note also that despite the fact that they had drummed up all their friends for the meeting, that there were only ninety votes cast whereas there used to be from two hundred to two hundred fifty delegates attend the Council meetings. I understand that there are approximately ninety-five locals affiliated with the Council.

It is amusing to read some of the tactics employed by them to try and avoid the responsibility of their actions, notably the statement in the morning paper (The Post-Intelligencer) where they deny the charge that they participated in the I.W.W. Day celebration but admit they endorsed a request that they do so from the Metal Trades Council of Seattle. This is on a par with their position that they have not endorsed the Soviet dictatorship, but have merely demanded recognition of it and the establishment of trade relations.

All of the real fellows in the movement in the City anticipate the lifting of the charter by the A.F. of L. and are prepared to proceed with the work of re-organizing the Council on a strictly A.F. of L. basis, and unless the charter is lifted and a reorganization brought about things are going to be left in a bad way here, as many of the local unions will undoubtedly withdraw and refuse to support the Council, while the Reds will feel elated at having hoodwinked the A.F. of L. (as they will put it) and be greatly encouraged to proceed with their program. No matter what pledges might be made by the Seattle Central Labor Council, as at present constituted, it cannot be and will not be loyal to the A.F. of L. but will continue to be an eye-sore and source of disruption to the ligitimate A.F. of L. trades union movement of both this City and State, and I frankly am hopeful that the decision will be to lift the charter and reorganize the Council under such stipulations as will guarantee it being maintained under loyal A.F. of L. control.

If such a course should be decided upon by the A.F. of L. I would be glad to be delegated to assist either C. O. Young or whomever is designated by you to direct the work of reorganization, as I know this situation thoroughly and intimately and believe I know just what is needed to be done in order to clean it up. Our State Federation Convention meets the 9th of July, at Bellingham,[3] but I could give some assistance in the work, if such a course is decided upon, both before and after the Convention. The A.F. of L. trades unionists of this City have rallied around me every time their support has been needed in any fight that I have been involved in, and I can probably do as much as any man in the movement towards rallying them together and solidifying them in the new Council.

I am enclosing you herewith the returns on our State Federation referendum election of officers, which were tabulated at headquarters last Saturday.[4] I had no opposition myself and the entire Executive Board and Tellers elected are my slate. Kindly note that James A. Duncan was even defeated for Teller in the State Federation election, which will give you an indication of just how high he stands with the rank and file of the labor movement of this state as well as with its leaders and officers. It is the most humiliating defeat he has yet sustained, and has made him the laughing stock of the labor movement of this city in the last few days. With the exception of Miss Lord, the other two Tellers elected are practically unknown in the state and it was purely a case of voting for anyone other than Duncan.

Kindly let me know as early as possible what decision you make or contemplate, as a large number of the boys here, together with myself and Dad Young, are on edge to know what course is to be pursued.[5]

With kindest regards,

Very sincerely yours,   Signed W. M. Short.

TLcSr, Executive Council Records, Vote Books, reel 18, frame 21, *AFL Records*.

1. "The Central Labor Council of Seattle and Vicinity to the Executive Council of the AFL," June 6, 1923, above.

2. William Short subsequently reported to SG that in an interview with the *Seattle Star* published on June 12, 1923, James A. Duncan said: "We are conforming to every letter of the law but it is impossible for us to endorse every whim of policy and quirk of Gompers personal beliefs. . . . For instance there is the liquor question. Gompers is

for light wines and beer. This Council is strongly dry and favors rigid enforcement of Prohibition law. This Council would rather be destroyed than recede from its stand on the liquor question" (Short to SG, June 13, 1923, Executive Council Records, Vote Books, reel 18, frame 23, *AFL Records*).

3. The 1923 convention of the Washington State Federation of Labor met in Bellingham, July 9–12.

4. For the tabulation, see Executive Council Records, Vote Books, reel 18, frame 22, *AFL Records*.

5. At its Aug. 27-Sept. 1, 1923, meeting, the AFL Executive Council decided to postpone a decision on the Seattle Central Labor Council (CLC) until all parties involved could meet in person. The Executive Council met with representatives of the CLC, *Seattle Union Record* editor Harry Ault, William Short, C. O. Young, and others on Sept. 29 and 30 in Portland, Ore., and then drafted a list of demands that SG presented to CLC representatives on Oct. 1. (See "To Charles Doyle," Oct. 1, 1923, and "The Minutes of a Conference in Portland, Ore.," Oct. 1, 1923, below.)

From C. O. Young

C. O. Young
General Organizer A.F. of L. for U.S. and Canada.
Seattle, Washington, June 10, 1923.

Dear Sir and Brother:

In connection with the Seattle situation, I am enclosing some clippings which for most part will be self explanatory.

You will note particularly the one dealing with an altercation between President Short of the State Federation of Labor and Texas Phillips, President of the Seattle Central Labor Council.[1] While the article is not the whole truth, it gives an idea of what occurred.

The man Doyle, mentioned in the article as saying that [if] I came to the Building Trades Council on last Friday evening he would throw me out, is the local district organizer of the A.F. of L., so he says, and because I did not consult him in my investigations of the conduct of the Central Body as directed by you, he said I had done him a great wrong and was "Cutting the ground from under my feet," and for which he was going to do me bodily harm. The first thing that started Doyle in his antagonism of me, was when you ordered me to investigate the conduct of the Seattle Bookkeepers, Stenographers, Typewriters and Assistants Union[2] some time ago. He took issue with me in that work and has insistantly since that time, told many that he would "Get" me.

I suppose that he had made up his mind to do the "getting" on last Friday evening at the Building Trades Council, where I had been invited by the officers of that organization. While President Short and Phillips were fighting, Doyle came over to me and told me that I was going to get it next and that he was going to whip me before I left the hall. I am sure that he thought that Phillips was getting the best of Short and that would lend encouragement to those favorable to he and Phillips, and that he would conclude the victorious onslaught by giving me a licking. But his surmise that Phillips would whip Short was far from the mark, as the Scotchman made Mr. Phillips say, "Enough" in fairly short order. The only thing that hindered Short in doing it sooner was the fact that Phillips with his over two hundred pounds did the hanging on or hugging act. After this was over, and though there was much talk, Doyle did not attempt to assault me. However, Phillips or some one else got hold of James Duncan and others and brought a mob of fellows up to the hall, but by good management further fighting was avoided.

Doyle, as perhaps you know is the Business Agent of the Seattle Central Labor Council and has always lined up with Duncan in anything he promoted. Doyle made the statement when I was investigating and straightening out the Bookkeepers, Stenographers, Typewriters and Assistants' Union, that if his interpretation as to the jurisdiction covered in their charter was not complied with, he would never organize another union for the A.F. of L., and that he would see to it that no one else did. I suppose you will think this letter trivial, but I have it off my mind and that helps some.

Yours fraternally,   (S) C. O. Young

TLcSr, Executive Council Records, Vote Books, reel 18, frame 38, *AFL Records.* Typed notation: "*Copy.*"

1. For a transcribed copy of the article, "State and City Labor Chiefs in Fist Fight; Short and Phillips Stage Fierce Battle in Seattle Headquarters; Soviet Issue, Ultimatum of Gompers Cause Clash," *Seattle Daily Times,* June 10, 1923, see Executive Council Records, Vote Books, reel 18, frames 36–37, *AFL Records.*

2. AFL Stenographers', Typewriters', Bookkeepers', and Assistants' Union 16,304 of Seattle, chartered in 1918.

Excerpts from the Minutes
of a Meeting with Representatives of the
Young Workers' League of America[1]

Morrison Hotel, Chicago,[2] Illinois, June 18 [1923]

. . .

In answer to questions Mr. Abern[3] said he was not a member of the office workers' union[4] but had made application. He is not working at the present time.

Mr. Krumbein[5] said he was working.

Mrs. Gomez[6] was not working.

Mr. Albright[7] said he was not working.

Mr. Abern said that the League had held a meeting in the Workers' Lyceum at Hirsch Boulevard and that delegates from thirty cities were present. The proceedings were not yet printed but a copy would be furnished President Gompers when they were.

Mr. Abern then read the constitution of the Young Workers League in America which contained the following section:

"Section 2. Its purpose shall be to organize and educate the young of the working class to understand their true position in capitalist society, to work for abolition of capitalism and the establishment of a Soviet Republic (Republic of Workers Councils) (a government functioning through a dictatorship of the proletariat—as the first step towards the establishment of an International Classless Society, free from all political and economic slavery)—Communism."

President Gompers asked how it happened that the letter written him was printed in the "Worker" before he received it.

Mr. Abern said that it had been sent June 1 and was not printed in the "Worker" until later. He said that the League was desirous of having the A.F. of L. cooperate with the organizing of "young proletariats between the ages of 14 and 30."

President Gompers pointed out that the unions provide that workers shall be eighteen years before they join unions. He said that the purpose was to give those under eighteen the opportunity of securing an education. He added:

"You say 14 years; we say 18. Yours is that youngsters go into industry; we want them in the schools."

Abern denied any idea of a dual organization.

President Gompers then gave the history of the efforts of the American Labor Movement to prohibit child labor, that laws had been secured but had been declared unconstitutional but that the trade unions had succeeded in abolishing child labor in many industries, especially the mining, textile, cigar making and needle trades.

Mr. Abern demonstrated that he knew little of the labor movement as he said that the A.F. of L. was conducted on money paid in by the central labor bodies.

President Gompers told of the efforts to secure a child labor amendment to the United States constitution.

President Gompers said that there were 28,000,000 people eligible for organization into trade unions. He said the organization of adults is of primary importance and that the organization of children was supplemental. There are now 5,500,000 organized. He added:

"We have organizers paid out of the pennies of the workers. In some trades there are ten or fifteen. There are now 2200 holding commissions as volunteer organizers of the A.F. of L. You speak of service. Each national and international union has its own official journal, so have city central bodies. The A.F. of L. prints the American Federationist and a weekly news service for labor and reform publications. Then there is an International Labor News Service. I do not know whether you regard yourself as having greater knowledge and vision than the men and women in the trade union movement. . . . What is the goal of labor? It is to be freed from any domination whatever. What is your goal? Is it the establishment of the soviet government under the dictation of the proletariat?"

Mr. Abern—That is the goal.

Mr. Gompers—There is no such thing as a goal in the struggle of life. We are not dealing with the Einstein theory.[8] The goal is to do the thing right ahead. First things first. Make today better than yesterday. Tomorrow, a better day than has gone before. In your effort to gain favor you assume the position of the dog and the bone.[9]

Mr. Abern—Have you not a woman's secretariat?

Mr. Gompers—No.

Mr. Abern said that the idea the League had was that the A.F. of L. should send out literature through its means of publicity for the purpose of organizing the young workers, and asked President Gompers to consider the proposition.

Mr. Gompers—I am not going to ignore it.

Mr. Abern—We want to keep in touch with President Gompers.

The meeting adjourned at 11:30 o'clock.

. . .

TDc, Files of the Office of the President, Conferences, reel 122, frames 723–24, 729, *AFL Records.* Typed notation: "Young Workers League of America. Conference held by President Gompers in Morrison Hotel, Chicago, Illinois, Monday, June 18 at 11 A.M. with . . . representatives of the Young Workers League of America."

1. The Young Workers' League of America was officially organized in Brooklyn in May 1922 as the legal counterpart of the underground Young Communist League. After the two organizations merged in 1926, the Workers' League was renamed the Young Workers' Communist League of America. Its name was changed again in 1929 to the Communist Youth League of the United States of America, and in 1931 to the Young Communist League of the United States. The organization was dissolved in 1943.

2. SG was in Chicago as part of a larger trip, which also included a stop in New York City. He left Washington, D.C., on the afternoon of June 16, 1923, and arrived the following morning in Chicago, where he attended a number of meetings over the next few days. He met with representatives of the Young Workers' League in response to a letter from Martin Abern dated June 1, asking for AFL approval of the organization. (See SG to Abern, June 14, 1923, reel 291, vol. 304, p. 585, SG Letterbooks, DLC.) SG left Chicago the evening of June 22 for further meetings in New York and returned to

AFL headquarters in Washington on June 25. For the minutes of several of these meetings, see Files of the Office of the President, Conferences, reel 122, frames 723–64, *AFL Records;* for transcripts of several of SG's addresses during the trip, see ibid., Speeches and Writings, reel 118, frames 234a-49.

3. Martin Abern (born Abramowitz; 1898–1949) was born in Romania and immigrated to the United States with his family at the age of four. During World War I he refused to cooperate with the draft, was expelled from the University of Minnesota, and was sent to prison. The secretary of labor issued a warrant for his deportation, but it was stayed pending appeal and then apparently dropped (*U.S. ex rel. Abern v. Wallis*, 268 F. 413 [1920]). At one time a member of the IWW, Abern served as secretary of the Workers' Party of Minnesota (1920–21), secretary of the Young Workers' League of America (1922), and member of the central executive committee of the Workers' Party of America (after 1925, the Workers' [Communist] Party of America; 1923–28). Expelled from the party for Trotskyism in 1928, he helped organize the Communist League of America (1929), the Socialist Workers' party (1938), and another Workers' party (1940).

4. AFL Stenographers' and Typists' Association 12,755 of Chicago was chartered in 1909. It apparently changed its name to AFL Office Employes' Association 12,755 in 1913.

5. Charles Krumbein (1889–1947), a member of United Association of Journeymen Plumbers and Steam Fitters of the United States and Canada 597 of Chicago (the Steam Fitters' Protective Association), was a founding member of the Communist Labor Party of America in 1919. In 1920 he was convicted in Cook County Criminal Court for conspiracy to overthrow the government and sentenced to a year in the county jail; he was pardoned after serving a day of his sentence. In 1930 Krumbein was arrested in Great Britain for use of a false passport and sentenced to six months in jail; after serving three months of his term he was deported to Russia. In 1931 he went to Shanghai to work with the Profintern's Pan-Pacific Trade Union Secretariat, but by 1932 he had returned to the United States and was secretary of the Communist party's New York State branch. Arrested in 1934 for using a false passport and sentenced in 1935 to a term in federal prison, Krumbein was released in 1936 for good behavior. From 1938 until his death in 1947 he was treasurer of the Communist Party of the United States of America.

6. Natalie Gomez was a nineteen-year-old Chicago office worker.

7. Albion D. Albright (1898–1987) was a Chicago barber.

8. Albert Einstein (1879–1955), who proposed the theory of relativity.

9. A reference to Aesop's fable about a dog with a bone crossing a footbridge over a stream. Seeing his reflection, he dropped the real bone in his mouth in an attempt to seize the reflected bone carried by his image in the water.

An Excerpt from the Minutes
of a Meeting with Representatives of
Affiliated Unions in the Steel Industry

Great Northern Hotel, Chicago, June 20, 1923

They were meeting to arrange for a[n] organization campaign in the steel industry. M. F. Tighe,[1] President of the Amalgamated Association of Iron, Steel and Tin Workers who presided gave this information to President Gompers as to the action taken by the conference:

"We are facing a very serious situation in the steel industry. We have decided to start a campaign in certain localities where steel plants are located. The organizers will be instructed to keep constantly in view that organization work must be carried out along the lines prescribed by the A.F. of L. No 'Isms will be permitted. Neither will anyone be allowed to discuss strikes like in the last organization campaign. It is to be an educational campaign and under no condition will strike sentiment be permitted."

President Gompers was then asked to address the committee which he did in part as follows:

"I want to assure you that your meeting and the outline of your plans by Chairman Tighe gives me additional cause for gratification. I think you know how enthusiastically I entered into the campaign when we undertook to organize the steel industry in 1918.[2] You know what happened. The organization scheme went on in a haphazard manner; not for the improvement of the workers in the steel industry but for another purpose. I remember all the conferences that were held and there was one man[3] whose name I will not mention who continually raised the question of strike and I asked him point blank 'do you mean that the whole meaning of your movement is to organize a strike' and he answered 'That is what I mean.' I told him I never ran away from a strike but I did not believe in calling a losing strike. I took up the matter with the Secretary of Labor in an effort to bring about a satisfactory conclusion. When this man went before the Senate Committee he turned yellow.[4] He was asked a question which he said he would not answer if the newspaper men were not sent out of the room where the hearing was held. I told him to talk, talk, talk. But he would not. After that there was a bad taste in the mouths of the participants in the labor movement. After the strike in the steel industry was ended the money left in the treasury was turned over to you to be used at an opportune moment in carrying on another organization movement in the steel industry.[5] I recently had a conference with a big official and Gary's name came up. I made the statement that there never was a more deceitful statement than that made by Gary on the twelve hour day.[6] The reasons given by Gary were that (1) to change [to] the eight-hour day was impractical; (2) that if adopted prices would be increased 15 per cent and (3) that the people would not pay the increase. What more malicious argument could be sent out to farmers against the eight-hour day than to declare it would cost fifteen per cent more to make the change. One of the parties said: 'When I read that statement I put a little different meaning to it. Gary is a lawyer and lawyers like to use legal expressions.' I said 'yes' but would the farmers think [o]f Gary being a lawyer when they read his statement. In your organization campaign I doubt if the same difficulty will be met as before. If we make a mistake we learn. Therefore a haphazard style of organization will not be permitted again."

President Gompers then told of the organization of wage earners in organized industries especially the miners. He said from 1873 to 1897 they were disorganized, demoralized, impoverished, degraded. Their condition seemed hopeless but they did organize, they went through the struggle and the sacrifices until finally they removed such grievances as the company store, and the company burial grounds. A miner's baby was brought into the world by company doctors, when he married it was by a company minister, when he was buried it was in a company cemetery by a company undertaker. There is no such term in our vocabulary that wage earners are unorganized. I am much encouraged in what you have done and I will give you all the help I can.

President Noonan of the International Electrical Workers Union said that Mr. Gary had helped the committee by his statement regarding the twelve hour day. The organization work could be carried on independent of central bodies. He added:

"We propose to tell the people that the steel industry worked men twelve hours. They did not do that to slaves or the black man who was held in bondage. It will be made the big issue, a moral issue. During the last campaign some of the organizers were discredited in central bodies. In this campaign no one will be given credentials without a thorough understanding of his capabilities and his loyalty to the A.F. of L. policies. I would like to ask if you, Mr. Gompers, will give organizer's credentials if they are recommended to you by this committee."

Mr. Gompers—"Yes."

Then, said Mr. Noonan: "We would like the A.F. of L. to instruct all central bodies to render all assistance they can to our organizers. During the last strike charges of aliens and un-American labor men were made against the strikers. We want to eliminate that. We are glad that you are with us and will help us to take advantage of Mr. Gary's break."

Mr. Gompers then explained how the authority to issue organizer's credentials had grown up. He had seen it a valuable way to have volunteers in the various cities working in the interest of building up the labor movement. He added:

"If you will through your Executive Council recommend three men as organizers I will issue credentials. As to your request to request central bodies to aid the organizers I will do that. Anything that you can think of to suggest to me that will help just ask me.[7] You should write for organizer's commissions however. I will join you in conferences at any time. If there is any way in which I can help just call it to my attention."[8]

. . .

TDc, Files of the Office of the President, Conferences, reel 122, frames 745–47, *AFL Records.* Typed notation: "Steel Industry Committee. Conference held at the Great Northern Hotel, Chicago, June 20, 1923 at 4 P.M. with representatives of 16 organizations of the Metal Trades."

1. Michael Francis TIGHE served as president of the Amalgamated Association of Iron, Steel, and Tin Workers from 1918 to 1936.

2. See *The Samuel Gompers Papers,* vol. 10, pp. 477–80, 500–502.

3. William Z. Foster.

4. Foster testified before the Senate Committee on Education and Labor on Oct. 3, 1919, during its investigation of the recent steel strike. He was evasive when committee members demanded to know if he still believed in the revolutionary ideas espoused in his earlier writings, initially refusing to answer such questions on the grounds that his answers would be misrepresented by the reporters who were present. Although he eventually said he repudiated these publications, he was equivocal when asked about specific statements he had made in them.

5. See *The Samuel Gompers Papers,* vol. 11, p. 365, n. 5.

6. Responding to a May 1922 request from President Warren Harding, Elbert Gary, chairman of the U.S. Steel Corporation, had formed a committee to investigate the feasibility of eliminating the twelve-hour day in steel mills. The committee's report, presented by Gary on May 25, 1923, at the annual meeting of the American Iron and Steel Institute, rejected abolishing the twelve-hour day on the grounds that workers wanted the higher wages they earned by working longer hours, labor shortages would make filling new shifts difficult, and shorter hours would lead to increases in consumer costs.

7. The 1923 AFL convention passed a resolution pledging the Federation's support of the organizing effort, and on Apr. 6, 1924, SG addressed a mass meeting in Bethlehem, Pa., encouraging steel workers there to organize. For a transcript of SG's remarks, see Files of the Office of the President, Speeches and Writings, reel 118, frames 833–36, *AFL Records.*

8. The organizing campaign was unsuccessful, and in January 1925 its managing committee (the Executive Council of National and International Organizations for Organizing the Steel Industry) voted to wrap up its affairs and turn all remaining funds ($3,530.38) over to the Iron, Steel, and Tin Workers. For Tighe's report on the matter, see "Final Financial Statement of the Executive Council of National and International Organizations for Organizing the Steel Industry," Mar. 15, 1925, AFL Microfilm National and International Union File, Iron, Steel, and Tin Workers Records, reel 38, frame 2466, *AFL Records.*

An Excerpt from the Minutes of a Meeting with John Fitzpatrick and Senator William Roberts[1]

Morrison Hotel, Chicago, June 22, [1923]

Senator Roberts said he had been sent north by prominent citizens of the south to see if something could not be done to stop the negro exodus. He told President Gompers that labor could not trust them and they would be a detriment to the unions if taken in. He said that this country was on the verge of a cotton famine and that prices would be at least twice as high. Labor he said could have nothing as important to consider as the negro exodus. In answer Mr. Gompers said:

"This exodus of the negro of the south creates a very great and grave problem. I could see that coming the last third of the century. Whether we like it or not negro ownership as such is gone. The 14th and 15th amendments, no matter what we thought of them, are part of the Constitution. Negroes are now equal with the white man. In the Spanish and last war the negroes were drafted and taught self-assertiveness and independence. I am telling you as a southern man that insofar as it is physically possible for employers in the south they have kept the negro down. If you conceded anything it was to keep them there. During and after the war under leadership of misleaders the negroes left and are leaving the south. While they got $30 a month in the south they are getting $1.50, $2 and $3 a day in the north as laborers. I have found in the north as well as in the south that where negroes have had the opportunity to organize they remain loyal. We send organizers to the south and instead of being permitted to talk to the negroes on ~~racial~~ rational lines our organizers have been mistreated and driven out of towns."

Mr. Fitzpatrick: "I have just been told of a man who had a rope put around his neck and told never to come back to the south."

Mr. Gompers: "If we get no chance to deal with the negroes we can do nothing for them. I do not think the exodus can be stopped but it can be checked. Employers and planters should decide to give them more liberal treatment. We can help. If the negro is homogeneous to any place it is in the south. We are engaged in a struggle harder than in the south. We have secured no improvements without sacrifices and we do not intend to permit our standards to be degraded by immigration. Progress and civilization go on. No one can hold them back. Who in Europe will take the place of the negroes?"

Senator Roberts: "Italians are coming in."

Mr. Fitzpatrick:—"And Mexicans."

Mr. Gompers: "Mexicans are undependable. You cannot expect the Irish, English or Scandinavians to immigrate to the south. Those who come from the south of Italy you will find will not be constructive. They would be destructive. My concept is that the one remedy is to keep the negro in the south in better treatment. They got through their limited brain the $150 a month paid in the north but have no idea what it costs to live."

Senator Robinson [*sic*] said that the negroes were leaving the south just like blackbirds. On his plantation he had 80 families and every man between 18 and 25 had left. After reaching the north the negro would write back home that he was getting $5 a day. This was going like wildfire in the south and was instrumental in encouraging exodus.

Mr. Gompers then suggested that a number of representative men of the south should hold a conference, this conference to be called at a time when some representatives of labor can attend. He asked the Senator to keep in touch with him and not launch a plan that would disintegrate both the whites and blacks. He said he was willing to attend a conference of representative men of the south and suggested that it be held in North Carolina.[2] Senator Roberts appeared pleased with the suggestion and said he would keep in touch with President Gompers.

. . .

TDc, Files of the Office of the President, Conferences, reel 122, frames 758–59, *AFL Records.* Typed notation: "Negro Exodus from the South. Conference held in the Morrison Hotel, Chicago, June 22, at 2 P.M., with Senator Roberts of Mississippi on the exodus of negroes from the South. John Fitzpatrick, President of the Chicago Federation of Labor, made arrangements for the conference and was present."

1. William Beauregard Roberts (1861–1940) was a Mississippi state senator.
2. There is no evidence SG attended such a conference.

To James Knollin[1]

June 30, 1923.

Mr. J. C. Knollin,
Editor, "Orchard and Farm,"
Examiner Building, 1111 South Broadway, Los Angeles, Calif.
Dear Sir:

Your letter of June 23 received and contents noted.

You submit a neostyle circular sent out by the Citizens Alliance of Ramsay and Dakota counties Minnesota, which gives a statement published in the New York Herald by Graham F. Blandy.[2] You ask me what are my views on the subject contained in the circular.

First, I would like to inform you of the campaign being made by the Citizens Alliance to establish autocracy in industry. At the present time, in Minnesota, the Citizens Alliance is endeavoring to destroy the trade unions by calling their leaders communists. The object is to place a stigma upon labor in order that the unions can be disrupted. At the bottom of the circular of the Citizens Alliance is the slogan:

"Patronize the 'open shop.'"

The Alliance, in sending you the circular, believes that you will print it and thereby secure customers for unfair employers of labor to the detriment of fair employers of labor and you will pay just as much, if not more, for what you buy from the unfair employers as from the fair employers. I do not know who Mr. Blandy is or whether there is such a man in existence but it is only necessary to mention two of the statements he makes.

He says it takes 63 1/2 dozen of eggs to pay a plasterer for one day of eight hours work. At 35¢ a dozen this would be $22.23 a day for the plasterer which is untrue. The highest wage scale in the United States for plasterers is $14.00 a day just secured by them in St. Louis. In other cities the wages are from $10 to $12 a day. He says it takes 17 1/2 bushels of corn to pay a bricklayer one day. The price of July corn in Chicago today was $.87 7/8 a bushel and 17 1/2 bushels would be worth $15.47. The highest wage scale in the United States for brick-layers is $12 paid in New York City. They had been paying $10 a day. When you understand that men in the building trades average only six or seven months a year even under present conditions you will readily realize that $10 or $12 a day is not an exorbitant wage. Building was declared non-essential and there was very little work done by building trades workmen during the war. The cantonments built by the government were not plastered and only one brick building was built by the government during the war. This meant that the plasterers and bricklayers had to find other work. They went into the munition plants and other occupations where they found they could work 300 days a year and have a pay envelope every Saturday. Then when the building industry began to boom many of these building trades' workmen refused to return to their old trades. They remained in the factories at less pay because they had steady work. Then we must not forget that for more than two years, more than 5,000,000 wage earners in the United States were unemployed. Whatever funds they had saved were spent in supporting themselves and those dependent upon them. Millions of them were deeply in debt when business conditions began to pick up. All that unemployment was caused by the scheme to deflate the farmer. The wages had to be taken away from the wage earner. You know what happened to the farmer.

Much has been said about the strikes of the miners, shopmen, printers and other trades during the past year or more but had those strikes not been called wages would have been reduced and there would not have been such prosperity in our country as at present. Those strikes were called to prevent wage reductions and they succeeded. But just here I would like to point out to you that the miners, after a five months strike against a 20 per cent wage reduction returned to work at the same wages they had received the previous year. Still the price of coal increased from 25 to 50 per cent, although it did not cost a penny more to mine than in the year 1921. If the wage earner does not earn enough he has no purchasing power. If he earns adequate wages to permit him to live in reasonable comfort he can consume farm products according to what he receives.

June 20, 1923, on the invitation of the promoters of the Wheat Conference in Chicago, I delivered an address to the farmers who took part. Enclosed you will find a copy of that address.[3]

The great trouble with the farmer is that he does not realize that organizations like the Citizens Alliance are trying to drive a wedge between Labor and the farmers, not in the interest of the farmers but in the interest of the members of the Citizens Alliance and all those who believe in autocracy in industry. If the Citizens Alliance had its way wages would be cut to the bone. If low wages, long work days and unbearable working conditions made a country great China would be the greatest commercially and financially in the world. If the farmer could only understand that American standards were built up through the force of the trade union movement they would begin to understand what is best for the farmer. Is there any farmer in the United States who would be willing to go to China to make a living on a farm? Let them consider this question. Let it sink in and after they have thoroughly absorbed the truth in what I have said let them join hands with labor to continue to raise American standards not only for the benefit of labor but for themselves.

The copy of the circular of Graham F. Blandy of the Citizen's Alliance is enclosed.

Very truly yours,   Saml Gompers
President,   American Federation of Labor.

TLpS, reel 291, vol. 304, pp. 984–86, SG Letterbooks, DLC.

1. James C. Knollin (1893–1960) served as editor of *Orchard and Farm* from around 1920 to 1923.

2. Graham Furber Blandy (1868–1926) was a New York City stockbroker.

3. SG addressed the National Wheat Conference in Chicago on June 20, 1923. For a transcript of the speech, see Files of the Office of the President, Speeches and Writings, reel 118, frames 235–42, 247–49, *AFL Records*.

To Charles Evans Hughes

Washington, D.C., July 9, 1923.

Honorable Charles Evans Hughes,
Secretary of State,
Washington, D.C.
Sir:

I should be grateful to you for an expression of your views concerning what seems to me an important phase of the American position regarding the Russian soviet power.

We are confronted frequently with the statement that economic conditions in Russia are improving, that the soviet authority is proving stable, that Russian agriculture is recovering and that the American government, because of these and other similar matters, should extend recognition to the soviets.

Of course much that is reported by returning travelers is misinformation gathered during closely supervised tours, but I am not at the moment discussing the truth or falsity of reports as to Russian economic conditions. What I have in mind is that it might serve some purpose if those who are standing for American principles and for the American concept of right and justice and democracy could be given clearly to understand that the backbone of the whole situation regarding Russia is the denial to the people of Russia of any opportunity to pass judgment on their own affairs or to say by whom or in what manner they shall be governed.

It has been the consistent contention of the American Federation of Labor that the soviet power cannot be recognized because it is an autocracy forced upon the people of Russia without their consent and against their will and maintained in the same manner.

I find that Mr. Bullard,[1] then chief of the Division of Russian Affairs of the Department of State, appearing before the House Committee on Foreign Affairs of the Sixty-sixth Congress, Third Session, and discussing House Resolution 635,[2] said:

"The State Department is very energetically opposed, and necessarily, to the present people in control of Russia because they believe they are a tyrannical minority imposing themselves on a reluctant people."[3]

This has been repeatedly stated to be the belief of the government of the United States, although it should be said, as you doubtless would agree, that the personnel of the present tyranny is not the point of objection; the point of objection is the tyranny itself and a change of personnel would be of no significance, so long as the tyranny remains.

While the position stated by Mr. Bullard has been put forth by the Department of State on various occasions, the statement of that fundamental policy has usually been as a portion of a statement containing other provisions, so that the essential has been more or less involved with other and less vital matters.

It has for a long time seemed to me that we should understand that this is the vital principle, the very essence of our whole point of view regarding Russia; and that other matters are secondary and of minor importance.

I have stated many times that so far as my viewpoint is concerned, I am not able to see where good crops, or an improving economic condition, or any one of a number of things, including an acknowledgment of Russia's financial obligations, could change the American position regarding recognition, as long as the principle of tyranny remains. It has been urged that the so-called New Economic Policy,[4] modifying the practice of communism, removed some of the objection to recognition, but we have held that any policy that was changed one way by edict could as well be changed another way by edict—and we are opposed to the whole autocratic principle under which people are governed by fiat, edict and military command.

The definition of the policy of the Department of State, as read into the record of the hearing on House Resolution 635, seems to me to put the whole question on the proper basis; to put it, indeed, upon the only sound basis. I am unable to see any other tenable basis upon which a democracy could take a position that could be maintained with consistency. There is involved here an unchanging position upon which, if I see the matter rightly, we are bound to hold without abatement, because of our very faith in democracy and because of our determination that freedom is the heritage of every human being, the denial of which we cannot look upon anywhere with complacency.

I shall be deeply obliged to you if you will inform me whether I have correctly interpreted the views of democratic America as expressed officially for our people by the Department of State.[5] It will be a reassurance of great value if we may all understand clearly that the denial of freedom to the Russian people is the keystone of our position in relation to the question of recognition. To the wage earners of the United States the present tyranny in Russia is a thing despicable and intolerable in practice and beyond consideration in principle; and any thought that the United States might under any circumstance extend official recognition, even in a modified form, to such a villainous despotism is repugnant.

I am, sir,

Yours respectfully,   Saml Gompers.
President,   American Federation of Labor.

TLS, RG 59, General Records of the Department of State, DNA.

1. Arthur Bullard (1879–1929) served in the Russian Division of the Department of State from 1919 to 1921 and was chief of the division from November 1920 to March 1921.

2. H. Res. 635 (66th Cong., 3d sess.), requesting information on conditions in Russia from the secretary of state, was introduced by Republican congressman Frederick Dallinger of Massachusetts on Jan. 6, 1921. The House Committee on Foreign Affairs accordingly held hearings on Russia between Jan. 27 and Mar. 1, taking testimony from a number of witnesses including Bullard and three other State Department officials.

3. Bullard testified before the House Committee on Foreign Affairs, Feb. 9–11, 1921.

4. The New Economic Policy, introduced by Vladimir Lenin at the Tenth Party Congress in 1921, represented a major if temporary shift away from the policies of centralization and nationalization implemented by the Bolsheviks. The new policy allowed for private ownership and management of light industry, agriculture, and the retail trade, the granting of concessions to foreign investors, and stabilization of the currency; the Soviet state kept control of heavy industry, transportation, and banking. The New Economic Policy was abandoned later in the decade, and state control of industry, agriculture, and commerce was reimposed.

5. "From Charles Evans Hughes," July 19, 1923, below.

To A. Philip Randolph[1]

July 17, 1923.

Mr. A. Philip Randolph,
The Messenger Publishing Company,
2305 Seventh Ave., New York, N.Y.
Dear Sir:

In compliance with your request I am very glad to enclose to you herein an article for publication in your September issue. I would appreciate it if you will send me marked "personal" copies of that issue containing my article.

Very truly yours,   Saml Gompers.
President,   American Federation of Labor.

[ENCLOSURE]

FOR THE MESSENGER PUBLISHING CO.

2305 7TH AVE., NEW YORK, N.Y.
BY
SAMUEL GOMPERS
PRESIDENT OF THE AMERICAN FEDERATION OF LABOR.

With the Negro becoming a more and more important factor in the industrial life of the nation, it is of increasing importance that he be organized in trade unions, not only for his own benefit but for the benefit of all labor as well.

If the Negro is not organized, he will tend to hamper the onward march of his white brothers and be an influence in holding back the improvement of the condition of American toilers in every state. In the past, the Negro was only too frequently been used by the employers to break strikes and to beat down wages in our industrial centers. The Negro could not have been used in this way if he had been organized and infused with the point of view of the working people of the United States. Hence the vital importance of pushing organization work among the Negro workers of all trades and industries.

The American Federation of Labor is doing its best to advance organization work among the Negro and it seeks the help of all forward looking men and women in this task. The Federation is striving in every way to live up to the purpose repeatedly declared at its conventions, that of organizing all wage earners without regard to class, race, religion, sex or politics.

As I have pointed out before, Labor Day is the real Emancipation day for the Negro, for it signalizes the dignity of labor and the organization of the working people, with their consequent ability to win freedom and happiness for themselves. As the Negro forms strong labor organizations, he will more and more win a real emancipation for himself and take his rightful place in the ranks of those who do the world's useful work.

TLpS and TDp, reel 292, vol. 305, pp. 286–87, SG Letterbooks, DLC.

1. Asa Philip RANDOLPH served as coeditor of the *Messenger* from 1917 to 1928.

From Charles Evans Hughes

The Secretary of State
Washington July 19, 1923.

My dear Mr. Gompers:

I have your letter of the ninth instant[1] with respect to the grounds upon which the recognition of the present regime in Russia has been withheld.

You refer with just emphasis to the tyrannical exercise of power by this regime. The seizure of control by a minority in Russia came as a grievous disappointment to American democratic thought which had enthusiastically acclaimed the end of the despotism of the Czars and the entrance of free Russia into the family of democratic nations. Subsequent events were even more disturbing. The right of free speech and other civil liberties were denied. Even the advocacy of those rights which are usually considered to constitute the foundation of freedom was declared to be counter-revolutionary and punishable by death. Every form of political opposition was ruthlessly exterminated. There followed the deliberate destruction of the economic life of the country. Attacks were made not only upon property in its so-called capitalistic form, but recourse was had also to the requisitioning of labor. All voluntary organizations of workers were brought to an end. To unionize or strike was followed by the severest penalties. When labor retaliated by passive resistance, workmen were impressed into a huge labor army. The practical effect of this program was to plunge Russia once more into medievalism. Politically there was a ruthless despotism and economically the situation was equally disastrous.

It is true that, under the pressure of the calamitous consequences, the governing group in Russia has yielded certain concessions. The so-called new economic policy permitted a partial return to economic freedom. The termination of forcible requisitions of grain has induced the peasantry to endeavor to build up production once more and favorable weather conditions have combined to increase the agricultural output. How far the reported exports of Russian grain are justified by the general economy of the country is at least an open question. Manufacturing industry has to a great extent disappeared. The suffrage, so far as it may be exercised, continues to be limited to certain classes and even among them the votes of some categories count more than the votes of others. A new constitution has just now been promulgated providing in effect for the continuance of the regime of the 1917 coup d'etat under a new title. The Constitution, it is understood, contains no bill of rights, and the civil liberties of the people remain insecure.

There is no press except the press controlled by the regime, and the censorship is far-reaching and stringent. Labor is understood to be still at the mercy of the State. While membership in official unions is no longer obligatory, workmen may not organize or participate in voluntary unions.

The fundamentals of the Russian situation are pretty generally understood in the United States and have made a profound impression upon the thought of our people. We are constantly made aware of this in the Department of State by the various ways in which public opinion makes itself felt in the seat of government. We learn of the hope of America that Russia should have the opportunity of free political expression and that she should be enabled to restore her economic life and regain prosperity and once more to take her place among the nations on the basis of mutual helpfulness and respect. There can be no question of the sincere friendliness of the American people toward the Russian people. And there is for this very reason a strong desire that nothing should be done to place the seal of approval on the tyrannical measures that have been adopted in Russia or to take any action which might retard the gradual reassertion of the Russian people of their right to live in freedom.

To the Department of State, charged with the conduct of our foreign relations, in accordance with the accepted principles of international intercourse, the problem presents itself necessarily in somewhat less general terms. We are not concerned with the question of the legitimacy of a government as judged by former European standards. We recognize the right of revolution and we do not attempt to determine the internal concerns of other States. The following words of Thomas Jefferson, in 1793, express a fundamental principle: "We surely cannot deny to any nation that right whereon our own Government is founded,—that everyone may govern itself according to whatever form it pleases, and change these forms at its own will; and that it may transact its business with foreign nations through whatever organ it thinks proper, whether king, convention, assembly, committee, president or anything else it may choose. The will of the nation is the only thing essential to be regarded."[2] It was undoubtedly this principle which was invoked by the representative of the Department of State, in the statement which you quote as having been made in February, 1921, before the House Committee on Foreign Affairs on the consideration of House Resolution 635, 66th Congress, 3d Session. It must be borne in mind, however, that while this Government has laid stress upon the value of expressed popular approval in determining whether a new government should be recognized, it has never insisted that the will of the people of a foreign State may not be manifested by long continued acquiescence in a regime actually functioning as a government. When there is a question as to the will of the nation it has generally been regarded as a wise precaution to give sufficient time to enable a new regime to prove its stability and the apparent acquiescence of the people in the exercise of the authority it has assumed. The application of these familiar principles, in dealing with foreign States, is not in derogation of the democratic ideals cherished by our people, and constitutes no justification of tyranny in any form, but proceeds upon a consideration of the importance of international intercourse and upon the established American principle of non-intervention in the internal concerns of other peoples.

But while a foreign regime may have securely established itself through the exercise of control and the submission of the people to, or their acquiescence in, its exercise of authority, there still remain other questions to be considered. Recognition is an invitation to intercourse. It is accompanied on the part of the new government by the clearly implied or express promise to fulfill the obligations of intercourse. These obligations include, among other things, the protection of the persons and property of the citizens of one country lawfully pursuing their business in the territory of the other and abstention from hostile propaganda by one country in the territory of the other. In the case of the existing regime in Russia, there has not only been the tyrannical procedure to which you refer, and which has caused the question of the submission or acquiescence of the Russian people to remain an open one, but also a repudiation of the obligations inherent in international intercourse and a defiance of the principles upon which alone it can be conducted.

The persons of our citizens in Russia are for the moment free from harm. No assurance exists, however, against a repetition of the arbitrary detentions which some of them have suffered in the past. The situation with respect to property is even more palpable. The obligations of Russia to the taxpayers of the United States remain repudiated. The many American citizens who have suffered directly or indirectly by the confiscation of American property in Russia remain without the prospect of indemnification. We have had recent evidence, moreover, that the policy of confiscation is by no means at an end. The effective jurisdiction of Moscow was recently extended to Vladivostok and soon thereafter Moscow directed the carrying out in that city of confiscatory measures such as we saw in Western Russia during 1917 and 1918.

What is most serious is that there is conclusive evidence that those in control at Moscow have not given up their original purpose of destroying existing governments wherever they can do so throughout the world. Their efforts in this direction have recently been lessened in intensity only by the reduction of the cash resources at their disposal. You are well aware from the experiences of the American Federation of Labor of this aspect of the situation which must be kept constantly in view. I had occasion to refer to it last March in addressing the Women's Committee for the Recognition of Russia.[3] It is worth while to repeat the quotations which I then gave from utterances of the leaders of the Bolshevik Government on the subject of world revolution, as the authenticity of these has not been denied by their authors. Last November Zinoviev said, "The eternal in the Russian revolution is the fact that it is the beginning of the world revolution."[4] Lenin, before the last Congress of the Third Internationale, last fall, said that "the revolutionists of all countries must learn the organization, the planning, the method and the substance of revolutionary work." "Then, I am convinced," he said, "the outlook of the world revolution will not be good but excellent."[5] And Trotsky, addressing the Fifth Congress of the Russian Communist Youths[6] at Moscow last October,—not two years ago but last October,—said this: "That means, comrades, that revolution is coming in Europe as well as in America, systematically, step by step, stubbornly and with gnashing of teeth in both camps. It will be long protracted, cruel and sanguinary."

The only suggestion that I have seen in answer to this portrayal of a fixed policy is that these statements express the views of the individuals in control of the Moscow regime rather than of the regime itself. We are unable, however, to find any reason for separating the regime, and its purpose from those who animate it, and control it, and direct it so as to further their aims.

While this spirit of destruction at home and abroad remains unaltered the question of recognition by our Government of the authorities at Moscow cannot be determined by mere economic considerations or by the establishment in some degree of a more prosperous condition, which of course we should be glad to note, or simply by a consideration of the probable stability of the regime in question. There cannot be intercourse among nations any more than among individuals except upon a general assumption of good faith. We would welcome convincing evidence of a desire of the Russian authorities to observe the fundamental conditions of international intercourse and the abandonment by them of the persistent attempts to subvert the institutions of democracy as maintained in this country and in others. It may confidently be added that respect by the Moscow regime for the liberties of other peoples will most likely be accompanied by appropriate respect for the essential rights and liberties of the Russian people themselves. The sentiment of our people is not deemed to be favorable to the acceptance into political fellowship of this regime so long as it denies the essential basis of intercourse and cherishes, as an ultimate and definite aim, the destruction of the free institutions which we have laboriously built up, containing as they do the necessary assurances of the freedom of labor upon which our prosperity must depend.

I am, my dear Mr. Gompers,

Very sincerely yours,   Charles E. Hughes

TLS, AFL Microfilm Convention File, reel 31, frames 2290–91, *AFL Records.*

1. "To Charles Evans Hughes," July 9, 1923, above.

2. The quotation is from Thomas Jefferson's letter of Dec. 30, 1792, to Gouverneur Morris (Julian P. Boyd et al., eds., *The Papers of Thomas Jefferson*, 31 vols. to date [Princeton, 1950-], 24: 800–801).

3. On Mar. 21, 1923, Hughes addressed a delegation of some forty members of the Women's Committee for Recognition of Russia, an organization formed in 1921 by the Women's International League for Peace and Freedom. For the text of his remarks, published in a press release issued on Mar. 21 by the State Department, see *Papers Relating to the Foreign Relations of the United States, 1923,* 2 vols. (Washington, D.C., 1938), 2:755–58.

4. Grigory Zinoviev, "A Five-Years' Lesson," *Die Rote Fahne,* Nov. 7, 1922.

5. The fourth congress of the Communist International met in 1922 in Petrograd (Nov. 5–8) and Moscow (Nov. 9-Dec. 5). Vladimir Lenin delivered his report to the meeting on Nov. 13.

6. That is, the Fifth All-Russian Congress of the Russian Communist Youth League.

To Frank Farrington

July 27, 1923.

Mr. Frank Farrington,
President, Illinois District, United Mine Workers of America,
Farmers' Bank Building, Springfield, Ill.
Dear Sir and Brother:—

Information reaches me of a character of which I am taking cognizance [in] respect to elements at work to disrupt the labor movement of the country and concentrating for the time being all their efforts upon the labor movement of Illinois. Recent events in Chicago in connection with the invitation issued by the "Farmer Labor Party" and its outcome, is perhaps well known to you, or should be.[1] What the Sovietized agencies of Moscow have so cleverly and devilishly done at the Chicago conference is no doubt being attempted insofar as the trade union movement of Illinois is concerned.

[Mr.] Matthew Woll, who came here from Chicago last week informed me that there is some apprehension among the right thinking trade unionists in Chicago and in Illinois regarding a possible grave situation that may confront [th]e Illinois labor movement unless an immediate interest is aroused to the dangers ahead and proper steps taken to meet all possible contingencies. It is said that the Moscow agents are very active among the miners of Illinois and that they are seeking to round up every destructionist to go to the coming convention[2] of the Illinois State Federation of Labor for the purpose of having that convention endorse the fake resolution on "amalgamation" and to take favorable action toward this newly Sovietized Federated Farmer [Lab]or political movement.[3] While a similar resolution was defeated at the Illinois State Federation of Labor convention a year ago,[4] these propagandists of [So]vie[t] Russia are encouraged by their achievement at the recent farmer labor party conference and are making every possible effort to control this coming convention of the Illinois State Federation of Labor in some way or other.

Desirous of helping in every possible way to counteract this situation Secretary Morrison and I have talked the matter over and have assigned organizers Emmett Flood[5] and Paul J. Smith to devote their time to the work in Illinois for we deem it of the utmost importance in the interest of the working people of Illinois and the trade union movement of the state that every opportunity be utilized to rally the various unions and central bodies [of] Illinois so that they will be represented by their full quota of delegates at the forthcoming annual convention of the Illinois State Federation of Labor and that these delegates be true and tried trade unionists and devoted to the cause of the bona fide labor movement of the state and of the c[ountr]y.

Organizer Paul J. Smith has been at headquarters for the past few days and [wi]ll meet Secretary Victor A. Olander at his office on Saturday, August fourth or Monday, August sixth. I also advised President Mahon of the Str[eet] Railwaymen and President Tobin of the Teamsters of the situation in Illinois[6] and requested their cooperation and help through their Illinois [local] unions. I am now bring[ing] the matter especially to your attention, not b[ut] that I am sure you are conv[ersant] with the situation in Illinois but so t[ha]t you may be fully informed as to what we are endeavoring to do to be helpful in cooperation with the officers of the Illinois State Federation [of] Labor and with the Illinois miners, the teamsters, the street rail[wayme]n and others.

With kind regards, I am,

Fraternally yours,   Saml Gompers
President,   American Federation of Labor.

TLpS, reel 292, vol. 305, pp. 522–23, SG Letterbooks, DLC.

1. In response to a call from the Farmer-Labor party (FLP), an estimated six hundred to eight hundred delegates from the FLP and various minority political parties, labor bodies, and other organizations met in Chicago, July 3–5, 1923, with the goal of hammering out a common political program for the 1924 elections. Although delegates from the Workers' Party of America had to win a floor fight in order to participate, they and their supporters soon dominated the meeting and won support for a platform that launched the Federated Farmer-Labor party (FFLP). The new party, which called among other things for nationalization of public utilities and greater farmer and worker control of management, broke any remaining ties between progressive trade unionists and the Workers' party. John Fitzpatrick condemned what he called a Russian dictatorship over the new party, John Brophy of the United Mine Workers of America notified the FLP convention that his organization would not cooperate, and a majority of the FLP delegates refused to join the FFLP. By the time of the 1924 elections, the Workers' party had withdrawn its support of the FFLP, and the new party was no longer functioning.

2. The 1923 convention of the Illinois State Federation of Labor (FOL) met in Decatur, Sept. 10–15.

3. The 1923 convention defeated two resolutions that called for the Illinois State FOL to arrange conferences to bring about the amalgamation of unions in the same industry into single, industry-wide organizations. It referred back to its sponsors another resolution that called on the AFL to advocate the creation of a political party made up of trade unionists, farmers, and members of other bodies in harmony with the organized labor movement.

4. The 1922 convention of the Illinois State FOL met in Rockford, Oct. 16–21. SG is referring to a resolution that called on the AFL to hold conferences of international affiliates in order to amalgamate those in the same industry. The resolution was defeated.

5. Emmet T. FLOOD served as an AFL salaried organizer from 1904 to 1925.

6. SG to W. D. Mahon, July 16, 1923, reel 292, vol. 305, pp. 309–10, SG Letterbooks, DLC, and SG to Daniel Tobin, July 20, 1923, ibid., pp. 356–57.

A Memorandum by Samuel Gompers

August 6, 1923.

Conforming to the engagement made with President Coolidge last Saturday afternoon,[1] Secretary Morrison and I had conference with him at his temporary office in the New Willard Hotel.[2] Mr. Butler,[3] a personal friend of the President was present.

I presented to the President in a formal letter[4] the declaration of the labor conference[5] held in the office of the American Federation of Labor Friday August 3rd and which was published in the New York Times and the Washington Evening Star and other newspapers.[6] A copy of that letter is attached hereto. The President expressed his gratification and appreciation of the offer of support as well as of the condolence and sympathy to Mrs. Harding.[7]

The President asked me what in my mind were the pressing questions of the day. I answered that I preferred not to discuss the political situation because it would be most inappropriate at this time. I referred to the propaganda now going on to throw wide open the ports of our country to a tremendously larger immigration; that I had recently made a special investigation regarding industrial conditions and find that in every field of industry there is a larger production of material things than at any time in the history of our country, which proved conclusively that there is no necessity for this proposed largely increased immigration; that we are all endeavoring to more thoroughly Americanize the foreign language people in the United States and certainly the influx of large numbers of other alien peoples would postpone for an indefinite period anything like the Americanization of all; that there is now altogether too much of a conglomeration rather than an assimilation, so that from the viewpoint of industry, for industrial needs as well as for the spread of Americanism we ought to have a considerable longer period of time before any largely increased immigration should be allowed.

The President said that he had some definite views upon that subject and that he entertained no dissent from the thought I had expressed. Mr. Butler reminded me that he was a member with me upon the committee of Manufactures in the Unemployment Conference of 1921 and I then called to the President's attention the fact that as a member of that committee I proposed that inasmuch as the Committee of Industrial Engineers had definitely determined that the waste in industry, properly allocated, was 50% to management, 25% to Labor and the other 25% indefinite, that the employers at the conference should assume the responsibility for the elimination of the 50% and that labor would pledge itself to do its level best for the elimination of its 25%; that the proposal was rejected by the employers at the conference, and facetiously I said "Evidently the other members of the committee were the obstinate jurors." The remark caused the President to give a faint smile.

I said that the workers were fairly well employed, that the shadow on the horizon was the failure of the mine operators and the mine workers' representatives to reach an agreement in the anthracite coal regions. He asked me whether negotiations had been broken off; I informed him that they were for the present, although I had no definite information whether they will be resumed in the near future and incidentally I suggested whether it might not be well at some time convenient to him for a conference to be held with President Lewis. He said that while he had no objection, he would prefer that the operators and miners would agree without any governmental interference, to which I replied that I was in entire sympathy with that view. He said that he believed in high wages for that would mean a greater degree of prosperity. He said "And yet, of course, it is necessary that employers should have a profit upon their investment and their enterprise." I said that on that point there is no difference of opinion, that as a matter of fact it is the basis for my action all my life.

I remarked that it was not my intention to be impertinent by putting the question as to whether or not he intended to call a special session of Congress, my only reason for reference to it being that I must leave Washington on Saturday, August 11th and go to Chicago[8] and that I will be there two weeks on an important mission as delegate to the Cigarmakers' International Union convention[9] as well as officer of that organization; and that on August 27th I would be at a meeting of the Executive Council of the American Federation of Labor in New York,[10] and that whether a special session will be called or no session held until the regular meeting in December, I would like to have an opportunity of meeting with him and conferring with him upon specific matters in which labor is vitally interested. In reply he said "I now have no intention of calling a special session; I do not now see the necessity of calling it although my mind is not closed upon the subject and it may develop that I shall deem it my duty to call a special session but I repeat at this time it is rather vague and uncertain in my mind."

We discussed a number of topics of more or less interest. I told the President that on Saturday when I left him, newspaper men were anxious to get from me the subjects which the President and I discussed and I informed him that as was my custom whenever I had any conference with the President, I have always referred the newspaper men to the President rather than give any statement to them. He replied that no doubt I would be questioned upon my leaving him and he said that I might tell them what had transpired between us. He again expressed his great pleasure at the call of Secretary Morrison and me; that he was not going to say definitely when we could see him but suggested that after the Executive Council should meet and policies have been outlined, that then I should communicate with him and he will be glad to see me any time he can. He said, "I do not pretend to say that I have approached these subjects with any economic knowledge, but I do think that the basis of high wages to labor with reasonable profits to employers, is the basis of our prosperity." He expressed his appreciation of the work which I have done in support of our Republic.

TDc, AFL Microfilm Convention File, reel 32, frame 1318, *AFL Records*.

1. SG and Frank Morrison met briefly with President Calvin Coolidge at the New

Willard Hotel on Saturday, Aug. 4, 1923, and arranged to have a formal conference on Monday, Aug. 6.

2. With the death of President Warren Harding on Aug. 2, 1923, Coolidge returned to Washington, D.C., from Vermont and from Aug. 3–21, when he moved into the White House, had a temporary office at the Willard Hotel.

3. William Morgan Butler (1861–1937), Coolidge's campaign manager in 1924, served as a Republican senator from Massachusetts from 1924 to 1926, filling the vacancy caused by the death of Henry Cabot Lodge.

4. SG to Coolidge, Aug. 6, 1923, reel 292, vol. 305, pp. 787–88, SG Letterbooks, DLC.

5. Some thirty-five labor representatives met at AFL headquarters on Aug. 3, 1923, to draft a declaration expressing sorrow and condolence on the death of President Warren Harding and offering support and cooperation to the new administration. For minutes of the meeting, see Files of the Office of the President, Conferences, reel 123, frames 5–10, *AFL Records.*

6. "Express Sorrow of Nation's Labor," *New York Times,* Aug. 4, 1923; "D.C. Labor Bodies Voice Deep Loss," *Washington Star,* Aug. 4, 1923.

7. Florence Mabel Kling Harding (1860–1924).

8. On the afternoon of Aug. 11, 1923, SG left Washington, D.C., for Chicago, where from Aug. 14–24 he held a number of conferences and served as a delegate to the convention of the Cigar Makers' International Union of America. He visited Milwaukee briefly on the evening of Aug. 23, where he addressed the convention of the International Photo-Engravers' Union of North America (for a transcript of his remarks, see Files of the Office of the President, Speeches and Writings, reel 118, frames 363–84, *AFL Records*). He left Chicago on Aug. 25 for New York City, where he attended conferences and from Aug. 27-Sept. 1 attended meetings of the AFL Executive Council. He delivered a Labor Day address at Fort Hamilton in Brooklyn on Sept. 3 (for a transcript of his remarks, see ibid., frames 398–401), then left New York on Sept. 5, stopping briefly in Philadelphia and returning to AFL headquarters by Sept. 6. For transcripts of other speeches by SG while on this trip, see ibid., frames 341–62, 386–89; for minutes of several of SG's meetings, see ibid., Conferences, reel 123, frames 29–41.

9. The Cigar Makers' union held its 1923 convention in Chicago, Aug. 13–24.

10. The AFL Executive Council met in New York City, Aug. 27-Sept. 1, 1923.

To John Hickey[1]

August 9, 1923.

Mr. John H. Hickey,
Organizer, American Federation of Labor,
1225 West Fourth St., Wilmington, Delaware.
Dear Sir and Brother:

In continuation of my letter of July 31st[2] regarding organizing the colored firemen or fire builders employed on the Pennsylvania Railroad, permit me to advise that I have just received a letter from President Timothy Healy of the International Brotherhood of Firemen and Oilers, in which he says:

"I beg to call to your attention the fact that the Shop crafts and our organization are still on strike on the Pennsylvania Railroad. However, I am writing Brother Hickey, suggesting to him to see the local officers of the Shop Crafts and if they believe it good policy to organize these men, I have no objection to them being organized and chart[er]ed by our Brotherhood. They come under the jurisdiction of our Organization. I would certainly object to these men being organized directly by the American Federation of Labor. The American Federation of Labor can not give any protection whatsoever to men employed on the railroads in this country. It is only the organizations of their crafts that can legislate for men on the railroads according to provisions of the Transportation Act of 1920."

In proceeding with the work of organizing the workers above referred to, you will please be guided by the jurisdiction claims of the Brotherhood of Firemen and Oilers, and if you succeed in organizing these men, application for charter must be made direct to the Brotherhood of Firemen and Oilers. President Healy has no doubt communicated with you in connection with this matter.

With best wishes and hoping to hear from you whenever convenient, I am

Fraternally yours, Saml Gompers.
President, American Federation of Labor.

TLpS, reel 292, vol. 305, p. 875, SG Letterbooks, DLC.

1. John H. Hickey (b. 1878?) was an AFL volunteer organizer living in Wilmington, Del. He was a carpenter by trade.
2. SG to Hickey, July 31, 1923, reel 292, vol. 305, p. 628, SG Letterbooks, DLC.

To Mazaire Jolin[1]

August 9, 1923.

Mr. Nazaire Jolin,
Secretary-Treasurer, Central Labor Union of Waltham, Newton,
    Watertown and Vicinity,[2]
99 South St., Waltham, Mass.
Dear Sir and Brother:

Your letter of August 4 addressed to Secretary Morrison has been referred to me for answer.

The report you made of the policies and methods of the Chamber of Commerce of Waltham is most gratifying. Your conference with the representatives of the Chamber of Commerce is a good stroke of policy.

The request of the Chamber for either the central body or individual union men to join should be favorably considered. Joining the Chamber of Commerce does not commit you to any policy that is detrimental to the interests of the labor movement. It gives you an opportunity to oppose any proposition that would endanger the interests of the labor movement. You may not know it but it is true nevertheless that I am a member of the United States Chamber of Commerce by direction of the Executive Council. However, if you do not feel inclined to join as an organization it might be well to let some of your officers do so as the relations now according to your report are very friendly. Membership in the Chamber of Commerce would place you in a position to maintain those friendly relations.

Thanking you for the extended report and with best wishes, I am,

Fraternally yours, Saml Gompers.
President, American Federation of Labor.

TLpS, reel 292, vol. 305, p. 866, SG Letterbooks, DLC.

1. Mazaire (variously Mazire) Jolin (b. 1879), a Waltham, Mass., metal polisher, served as secretary-treasurer of the Central Labor Union of Waltham, Watertown, Newton, and Vicinity in 1922 and 1923.

2. The Central Labor Union of Waltham, Watertown, Newton, and Vicinity was chartered in 1917.

To John Moffitt[1]

August 10, 1923

Mr. John Moffet,
c/o Max Andur,
232 N. 9th, Philadelphia, Pa.
Dear Mr. Moffet:—

Our mutual friend, John Manning, Secretary-Treasurer of the Union Label Trades Department of the American Federation of Labor conveyed to me your message for citations on Picketing. Many states have dealt with the question of picketing with the result that about one-third of them condemn it in any form while the others recognize peaceful picketing. Of course, in peaceful picketing it all comes down as to what in the courts' opinion shall be construed peaceful. Then there is the Massachusetts rule, so called. In Massachusetts the Courts have the power to determine whether or not a strike is lawful or not. In lawful strikes peaceful picketing is allowed. The following references allow picketing in some form or another.

American Steel Foundries vs. The Tri-City Central Trades Council,[2] hold that a trade union may post a single picket at each gate to an industrial plant to advise and persuade. (42 Sup. Ct. 72).

Trade Union Publishing Company vs. Milwaukee Typographical Union No. 23.[3] Pickets limited to one at each gate. (Vol. 4, Page 19, Law and Labor).

Segenfeld vs. Friedman.[4] (New York Law Journal, Jan. 19, 1922). The right to picket was asserted.

Keuffel & Esser vs. International Association of Machinists.[5] (New Jersey Court of Errors and Appeals). Picketing is to be judged by the conduct of the pickets.

American Lithographic Co. vs. Castro.[6] (New York Law Journal May 3, 1922.) Picketing was considered and strictly limited.

Drake vs. Perry.[7] (Supreme Judicial Court Essex County, N.J.). The court states that "If the strike is legal, then I say you have a right peaceably to picket for the exclusive purpose of preventing others from entering into the employ of the petitioner in competition with the defendants." But refused to allow interference with the customers.

In *Corns vs. Pattern Makers' Association of Toledo.*[8] (Courts of Common Pleas, Lucas County, Ohio). Pickets abusing their rights were enjoined from all picketing.

The Milton Ochs Company vs. Clothing Workers.[9] (Superior Court of Cincinnati, Ohio), pickets were limited to secure peaceful picketing.

The Ice Delivery Company of Spokane vs. Local No. 690 of Teamsters[10] (Superior Court, Spokane, Wash.) picketing was limited to two pickets.

Jaeckel vs. Kaufman[11] (New York Supreme Court, New York County), the court said, "It is well settled that labor organizations may by lawful means secure adequate compensation for their services, fair hours of labor and that picketing, while lawful if peaceably conducted, will, however, not be permitted when its purpose is to affect interference with anothers' business."

Greenfield vs. Central Labor Council[12] (192 Pac. 783, Ore.) Picketing in support of a strike resulting in a breach of a trade agreement by the employer is lawful within the terms of the Oregon anti-strike law.

Several courts also hold that when the strike is over to all intents and purposes and the employer has replaced all the strikers with a permanent force picketing is then illegal.

These cases may all be found in Volumes 2 and 4 of Law and Labor.

In *Swift and Company vs. United States,*[13] (196 U.S. 375, 396, 401) it is said that "we equally are bound by the first principles of justice not to sanction a decree so vague as to put the whole conduct of the defendants' business at the peril of a summons for contempt. We cannot issue a general injunction against all possible breaches of the law.["]

Gray vs. Building Trades Council[14] (91 Minn. 171). An injunction which enjoined the defendants from notifying customers or prospective customers that plaintiffs are unfair was modified.

Trusting that this conveys to you the information you desire and with kind regards, I am,

Fraternally yours,   Saml Gompers.
President,   American Federation of Labor.

TLpS, reel 292, vol. 305, pp. 907–8, SG Letterbooks, DLC.

1. John A. Moffitt, former president of the United Hatters of North America, was now serving as a commissioner of conciliation for the U.S. Department of Labor.

2. See *The Samuel Gompers Papers*, vol. 10, p. 253, n. 3.

3. *Trade Press Publishing Co. et al. v. Milwaukee Typographical Union No. 23 et al.*, 180 Wis. 449 (1923).

4. *Segenfeld and Kalin v. Friedman*, 193 N.Y.S. 128 (1922).

5. *Keuffel and Esser v. International Association of Machinists*, 93 N.J. Eq. 429 (1922).

6. The case was decided in 1922. For an excerpt of the decision, see *Law and Labor* 4 (June 1922): 165–66.

7. The case was decided in 1919 by the Supreme Judicial Court (Trial Branch) of Massachusetts for Essex County. For an excerpt of the decision, see *Law and Labor* 2 (Jan. 1920): 9.

8. The case was decided in 1920. For an excerpt of the decision, see *Law and Labor* 2 (July 1920): 182.

9. The case, *Milton Ochs Co. v. Amalgamated Clothing Workers of America*, was decided in 1920. For an excerpt of the decision, see *Law and Labor* 2 (Aug. 1920): 205.

10. The case was decided in 1920. For an excerpt of the decision, see *Law and Labor* 2 (Sept. 1920): 220–21.

11. *Jaeckel et al. v. Kaufman et al.*, 187 N.Y.S. 889 (1920).

12. SG is referring to *Greenfield v. Central Labor Council*, 104 Ore. 236, 192 P. 783 (1920). See also *Greenfield v. Central Labor Council*, 104 Ore. 236, 207 P. 168 (1922).

13. *Swift and Co. v. U.S.*, 196 U.S. 375 (1905).

14. *Gray et al. v. Building Trades Council et al.*, 91 Minn. 171 (1903).

An Article in the *American Federationist*

[August 14, 1923]

ACCEPT THE MACHINE—ORGANIZE THE WORKERS

I feel a very deep interest in the question before the convention at the present time.[1] Lest I might forget it, I can not allow this moment to pass without taking cognizance of the statement made by Delegate Rhine[2]—let well enough alone. If that was the policy of the labor movement in general we would be where the working people of the United States were fifty years ago. The fact of the matter is we can not let well enough alone, it won't let us alone.

It is true that for quite a number of years I haven't worked at the trade of cigar making, but I did work at the bench for a period of 26 years of my life, and during all that time I was a hand workman, and for the last 20 years of working at the trade I worked at the Spanish system[3] of cigar making. My personal pride in the trade is really very great.

I remember working in one of the large shops in New York City, and when we were fairly well organized as trade unionism was then understood, the question of molds was before the union. In the old Turner Hall in Orchard Street, New York, the members divided as to those who would favor a strike against the molds and those who would favor molds. And I remember going with a crowd of the boys who voted to strike against the introduction of the molds if an attempt was made to introduce them. And I remember the time when, as a result of that vote, Conrad Kuhn,[4] president of that organization, came to our shop and said, as he did to other shops: "This shop is on strike," and not a mother's son of us remained in the shop a minute after. We struck, and it was a hard struggle; we lost and the molds were introduced.

I am free to say that from that time there came some light to my mind, and I realized then for the first time that it was absolutely futile for workmen to protest against or go on strike against the introduction of a new machine, a new device or a new tool.

In the old time when the cotton spinning jenny was introduced and the machine put into the textile plants the men in the industry, outraged at seeing their trade taken away from them, a trade they had to serve several years to acquire, destroyed the machine. Was the machine destroyed? Yes, but was the idea destroyed? No. The blue prints were in existence for that machine, and in any event the scheme and the plan was in the mind of someone who had burned the midnight oil. The machines in the textile industry became universal in every modern country.

The conditions of the textile workers are not what they ought to be by any means, but were the conditions of old, when the men worked by hand, better than those that now prevail? By no means. The hours of labor were from sun up to sun down, and as soon as artificial light was discovered the men and women and children worked from early morning until late at night, until organization took place among them and reduced their hours of labor from sixteen to twelve, to ten, to nine, and in many instances to eight, and their whole condition has improved.

The change in the constitution to which several of the delegates have referred antedates the Cleveland convention by many years. I was a delegate to the first Cleveland convention[5] and there I had 42 votes, more than all the other delegates to that convention combined. I never used that power of voting in that convention, not on one question; it seemed to me that if I could not influence the delegates to accept what I believed, and still am convinced of, I would not overwhelm them by the power of the vote I had a right to cast. It was after a three days' struggle in that convention a resolution was adopted that the local union would have a right to recognize and organize the bunch breakers and rollers.[6] I was a hand worker and working at my trade.

Let me disclose what might otherwise be a confidential matter. You know that all fines imposed by local unions upon members must be approved by the Executive Board. I tell you now right frankly that whenever there was an application for the imposition of a fine upon a member of the union because of the introduction of the mold system and rolling up, I voted against the imposition of the fine. I felt, as I feel now, that there has come into our trade a change with which we are compelled to reckon.

Delegate Hilfers[7] referred to the glass bottle blowers. He gave a graphic description of what occurred. That organization has dwindled, but in addition it has made every automatic bottle blowing machine operator, every man who operates one of those machines a mortal enemy of the organization.

President Perkins adds at this time to my remark, and I want to incorporate it as my own, giving him credit for his statement, that they will not come into the union now.

The water carriers of Egypt protested when pipe lines were being laid to carry water to some central parts of the cities because it did away with their trade of carrying water. The rickshaw runners of China raised a revolution because horses were put to wagons to carry people. In some of our cities hack drivers protested against the erection of railroad stations near the cities because it took away their jobs.

Some years ago I had occasion to travel in the southern states, and there I saw in the middle of the rivers colored men who were dredging with buckets and long poles. They were getting 20 and 30 cents a day. Wherever men are cheap no machinery is used in industry or any other way. It is only when men are dear and wages are high that machinery is brought in.

The Typographical Union has been mentioned. I had the great pleasure of having the opportunity to meet with the late William B.

Prescott,[8] then president of the International Typographical Union; his office and the office of the American Federation of Labor were in the same building, the DeSoto Block, Indianapolis, Indiana, and I talked to him on this question. With his courageous spirit he went before the people and pleaded with them to recognize the Mergenthaler machine, and instead of what would have occurred, that girls running typewriting machines to operate the Mergenthaler typesetting machine, it was the printer that was given a chance to learn the trade over again. What has been the result? Wages higher in the printing trades, hours of labor lower, the eight-hour day prevailing in the industry, and on the newspapers the 44-hour week, and the International Typographical Union, to secure the 44-hour week for the printers in the book and job trade has expended more than $15,000,000. And it has more members and more money in its treasury than before the strike took place.

The garment workers sewed with the needle, and then there was a riot and a revolt when the sewing machine came in. There are now many tailors who do nothing but make fine clothes by hand sewing. But what has happened to the men in the garment industry? Working, instead of in the old-time sweatshop, in sanitary factories, working not more than eight hours a day, working not more than 44 hours a week, and a better organization than ever obtained in their history.

The miners of old worked with the pick and shovel, and they were slaves in the mines. From miserable conditions, slavish conditions, electrical power has been employed and the men are earning more wages, working shorter hours, not because they opposed the machine, but because they accepted it.

The shoe workers, the old cobblers that made shoes before the time of many of you, worked long hours and for a mere pittance. The modern shoe industry requires about 64 operations, 64 different people to do certain parts of it before the shoe is completed.

I don't want anyone to infer from what I have said that I am content with the conditions those men enjoy. There isn't anything in this world or beyond it that I do not want for the workers of America to have. I have gone through many of the struggles of the cigar makers of our country. In 1864, I first became a member of the international union, and then but 14 years of age. I have not joined the union many times, I only joined it once, but I stuck. I have always believed it was our imperative duty, a duty which we can not shirk, to organize every wage earner, I do not care at what he works. Every man or woman who works for wages should be organized; it is not only his right but his duty to become a member of a union to protect him from the exploitation of the employers. I also hold as an equally positive duty and obligation that no union has the moral right to deny or close its doors to any man or woman who works in the industry.

I want to ask you men and women in this convention what are you going to do? I know that there may be several men who have charged the American Federation of Labor as such to be against what they are pleased to call industrial unionism or the one big union, and I venture to say that when they come to consider this proposition outside of our international union then they are industrialists; but when there is a proposal to open our doors and go into the highways and byways and organize these men and women against whom literally we are closing our doors, it is opposed.

I ask any delegate in this convention whether he knows of any trade where the union has recognized the machine or improved tool where the conditions of the working people were made worse. It is not in the order of nature and of things. The better we organize the more thoroughly will we be in a position to defend, not only that which we have, but to move onward and forward for the things which ought to be ours and which we can obtain.

I can see no danger to the men in the industry in New England. I am proud of being a member of an international union of which they have shown themselves to be such valiant fighters. I am proud of the record of our international union and of our local unions, even the smallest of them. Something in this convention struck me with great force. Look through your roll call of delegates and you will find there are more delegates here representing two, three or four local unions than at any time in the history of our international union. And why? Because the trade has left these small places and they have little memberships. And so a thousand miles away from each other they have been required to combine and send a delegate. Is it not a lesson for us? Are we to go on and let well enough alone? This is not well enough, it is bad enough, and in the name of all that is good and right and in the interest of our members and our wonderful international organization let us see things as they are and deal with them, open the door wide of our international union so that every man and woman will be a member. Let us come to them with the invitation to come into our organization. What we have at the present time is a great tribute to what we have built, but the time has come to change.

I don't know whether it will ever be my privilege to again attend a convention of the Cigar Makers' International Union. I have no misgivings, I have no false notions. I have worked all my life, and so long as life shall remain in me I shall work, and work, and work in this great movement to which I have devoted every ounce of my energy. I want to continue, and will continue, whether in office or in the ranks, so long as there is a breath of life in my body and until the end.

I repeat, it is exceedingly doubtful that I shall ever have the pleasure of being at another convention of the Cigar Makers' International Union of America. I have been a delegate at every convention from and including the Rochester convention of 1877,[9] a record of 46 years. I repeat, I don't again expect to be at a convention of the international union, but whether I shall or shall not, I propose that while I am here I shall give expression to the best thought of which I am capable, and the best advice that my life and experience has given to me to share with you for the good of the men and women of our industry, so that you may resume the great part which we have heretofore played in this most wonderful movement, the American Federation of Labor.

American Federationist 30 (Sept. 1923): 718–21. Printed note: "Discussion August 14, 1923, in the convention of the Cigarmakers' International Union (Chicago) on an amendment of the constitution which provided for removing all obstacles to the organization of all wage workers in the cigarmaking industry.—S. G."

1. The matter under discussion was an amendment to section 61 of the constitution of the Cigar Makers' International Union of America, introduced at the union's 1923 convention by the Committee on Constitution. It called for elimination of a provision that read, "It shall be optional with local unions to permit the introduction of the roller and bunch breaking system under their respective jurisdictions, wherever this system does not exist at the present time" (*Constitution of the Cigar Makers' International Union of America. Amended and Adopted at the Cleveland Convention, April, 1920* [n.p., n.d.]). The convention adopted the amendment on Aug. 16.

2. Jacob Rhine represented Cigar Makers' local 90 of New York City. He served as secretary of the local from 1910 to 1924.

3. So-called Spanish cigars, including Clear Havanas, were produced by hand, usually using tobacco grown in Cuba. By the 1880s most of the "Spanish" trade had moved from New York to Florida, although some large New York factories retained "Spanish Departments," and some "Spanish" cigars continued to be made in small factories.

4. Conrad Kuhn (variously Kuhne; 1838?-84?), born in Bavaria, was president of Cigar Makers' local 90 during the late 1860s and early 1870s; the union had roughly a thousand members at this time. During the same period he also served as president of the Deutsche Arbeiter Union (German Workingmen's Association), a federation of German-speaking trade unions in New York City, and as a vice-president of the National Labor Union. Kuhn left the cigarmaking trade in 1872 or 1873.

5. The Cigar Makers' 1881 convention met in Cleveland, Sept. 20–23. The union held a second convention in the city in 1920, Apr. 12–28.

6. Actually, the issue was debated at the Cigar Makers' 1880 convention, which met in Chicago, Sept. 21–26. See *The Samuel Gompers Papers*, vol. 7, p. 308, n. 3.

7. Henry F. HILFERS was secretary of Cigar Makers' local 138 of Newark (1897–1927), of the Essex (N.J.) Trades Council (1907–29), and of the New Jersey State Federation of Labor (1909–26). Hilfers also served as an AFL salaried organizer in 1912 and from 1917 to at least 1924.

8. William Blair PRESCOTT served as president of the International Typographical Union from 1891 to 1898.

9. The Cigar Makers held its 1877 convention in Rochester, N.Y., Aug. 30–Sept. 2.

To James Wolfe[1]

September 5, 1923.

Mr. James H. Wolfe,
1002 Boston Building, Salt Lake City, Utah.
Dear Sir:

It is usually impossible to convince pro-bolsheviks, parlor reds and a certain type of liberals that much that today travels under the name of liberalism and progressivism is not genuinely so at all. Your second letter convinces me that no matter how much I might write I could not change your mind about the organizations to which you have reference in your correspondence and I am much too busy to attempt the impossible.

There is not an organization named in the articles in *Labor Information* to which you have referred that is not and has not been actively friendly to the soviet cause. Not only have they been actively friendly to that cause but they have been actively hostile to the American Federation of Labor in that they have lost few opportunities if any to preach to American workers the superiority of some other doctrine and the alleged reactionary character of American labor organizations.

I presume that no evidence that I could lay before you would convince you that the American Civil Liberties Union is much more interested in what might be termed dramatizing the class conflict than it is in any genuine effort to safeguard free speech. The activities of this organization in West Virginia were undertaken in defiance of the wishes of the labor organization most concerned and resulted only in demonstrating that there is in West Virginia free speech for lawyers and preachers.[2]

Much the same might be said regarding the organization's activities in Pennsylvania.[3] The leading spirits in the American Civil Liberties Union were active in connection with members of the Workers' Party and other revolutionary organizations in promoting during the last mine strike a so-called relief committee which conducted an organized revolutionary propaganda under cover of alleged relief work.[4]

So far as the American trade union movement is concerned the sooner the American Civil Liberties Union closes its doors the more secure we will feel as to the genuine safety of free speech and freedom of the press.

The record of the Fellowship of Reconciliation[5] goes back to the days of the World War when that organization was engaged in an effort to promote terms of peace which could have benefited only the country which was then our principal antagonist.

The National Council for the Prevention of War was organized under another name[6] following the call of President Harding for the international conference on the limitation of armament.[7] It was organized in direct opposition to the General Committee for the Limitation of Armament, the call for the formation of which was issued by the American Federation of Labor.[8] Whatever may be the beliefs of those organizations which are affiliated to the National Council for the Prevention of War, the officers of the Council itself have done far more to promote the cause of pacifism than to promote genuine efforts for the prevention of war.

I shall not go further because I am convinced it is useless. I can assure you that we understand thoroughly the problem with which we have to deal. We do not mistake its seriousness and neither do we mistake the importance of the fact that the pro-sovietists and parlor bolsheviks have captured so large a section of American intellectual life, a fact which leads me to wonder whether it was after all really intellectual.

You expressed the opinion that the attitude of the officials of the American Federation of Labor is becoming more and more unpopular with the membership of American trade unions. Permit me to say in that respect that the officers are carrying out the declared policy of the American Federation of Labor as expressed in conventions and that the American Federation of Labor can change its policy at any future convention. I assure you, however, that the policy, whether it is to be continued as it is or whether it is to be changed, will be the policy of the wage earners of the United States and not the policy of their "friends," from some of whom at least may the good Lord deliver them.

Very truly yours,   Saml Gompers
President,   American Federation of Labor.

TLpS, reel 293, vol. 306, pp. 546–47, SG Letterbooks, DLC.

1. James H. Wolfe (b. 1885?) was a Salt Lake City attorney.

2. See "To Harry Ward and Roger Baldwin," June 1, 1923, above.

3. SG is referring here to information contained in the fourth of a six-part United Mine Workers of America exposé on communist activities in the American labor movement (see "Dunne Defies A.F. of L. to Expel Him," Oct. 8, 1923, n. 5, in "Excerpts from Accounts of the 1923 Convention of the AFL in Portland, Ore.," Oct. 8–12, 1923, below; see also "Say 'Relief Funds' Keep Reds Going," *New York Times,* Sept. 13, 1923). SG had seen advance proofs of all six articles before he wrote this letter to Wolfe, and

noted that he read them "with the deepest interest and satisfaction" (Ellis Searles to SG, Sept. 4, 1923, quotation from SG to Searles, Sept. 6, 1923, both in AFL Microfilm National and International Union File, United Mine Workers Records, reel 40, frame 1454, *AFL Records*).

4. The American Civil Liberties Union maintained that its efforts in Pennsylvania during the 1922 miners' strike had focused on guaranteeing the free exercise of speech and assembly, and that it had worked closely with local and district officers of the United Mine Workers. The United Mine Workers dismissed these claims, charging it had only been concerned with keeping communist agitators out of jail and helping them "bore from within."

5. The Fellowship of Reconciliation was founded in Cambridge, England, in 1914. An American branch of the organization was established in 1915, and an international body with that name was founded in 1920. The Fellowship's basic principles included opposition to war and the use of love and non-violence to resolve conflicts.

6. The organization was founded in 1921 as the National Council for Limitation of Armaments and changed its name in 1922 to the National Council for Prevention of War. It acted as a clearinghouse for national peace organizations, coordinating efforts to reduce armaments and settle international disputes through law and negotiation.

7. The International Conference on Limitation of Armaments, which met in Washington, D.C., from Nov. 12, 1921, to Feb. 6, 1922. (See *The Samuel Gompers Papers*, vol. 11, p. 524, n. 2.)

8. The General Committee on Limitation of Armaments. (See *The Samuel Gompers Papers*, vol. 11, p. 548, n. 3.)

To the Executive Council of the AFL

Washington, D.C., September 10, 1923

Document No. 115.
Executive Council American Federation of Labor.
Colleagues:—

Enclosed is a copy of a document which I regard of paramount importance. It is a letter issued by John Fitzpatrick and Ed. Nockles, President and Secretary of the Chicago Federation of Labor, addressed to "Organized Labor, International Unions, State Federations and City Central Bodies." It is a declaration of loyalty to the American Federation of Labor and a repudiation of all agencies and particularly the so-called "Trade Union Educational League" of which the American agent of the Moscow Soviet is the head.

I have just received from Secretary Olander of the Illinois State Federation of Labor a galley proof of the letter (of which the enclosed is a copy) stating that it will appear in the Weekly Newsletter of that body and that it will appear in the official journal of the Chicago Federation of Labor, "The New Majority" in the issue of tomorrow, Tuesday, September 11th.

While in Chicago in attendance upon the Cigarmakers' convention and doing all kinds of work for our Federation I arranged a conference, first with Secretary Olander[1] and later with him, John Fitzpatrick, Ed Nockles and myself.[2] Vice-President Woll and President Perkins of the Cigarmakers' International Union also participated in the last named conference. The whole situation in Chicago and Illinois and their relation to the American Federation of Labor was gone over in every detail. A splendid spirit was developed and in all essentials the proposed declarations were discussed with the result that the enclosed letter has been sent forth and published as above stated.

I feel confident that the members of the Executive Council share my exaltation in this present splendid declaration and situation. It brings about renewed cooperation and revived mutual respect and confidence and augurs well for our future unity and solidarity. I earnestly hope each member of the E.C. will, if necessary, steal the time to carefully read and re-read the letter with all that it implies.

Anticipating the pleasure of our early meeting and hoping for a harmonious and successful convention at Portland, I am,

Fraternally yours,   Saml Gompers.
President,   American Federation of Labor.

P.S. Enclosed you will also please find copy of a telegram[3] which I have just sent to Mr. John L. Lewis.

S. G.

[ENCLOSURES]

NEWSLETTER ONE.

President John Fitzpatrick and Secretary Edward N. Nockels of the Chicago Federation of Labor have addressed an open letter to state federations of labor, city central bodies and local unions in which they point out that the Chicago Federation of Labor and its officers are not responsible for propaganda circulars and other literature reflecting unfavorably upon the American Federation of Labor which have been circulated in various quarters. The letter is as follows:

To Organized Labor, State Federations of Labor,
City Central Bodies and Local Unions.
Greetings:
During the recent past, circulars, apparently designed to create the impression that the Chicago Federation of Labor is promoting a so-called "amalgamation" scheme, have been received by various organizations. In some instances an effort is being made to create the impression that the Chicago Federation of Labor is not in harmony with the

trade union movement as represented by the American Federation of Labor and its affiliated national and international unions, state federations of labor, city central bodies and local unions. We believe it our duty, therefore, to inform you that the Chicago Federation of Labor is not responsible for the circulars referred [to] and has not authorized the use of its name in connection therewith.

In order that you may be fully advised concerning our attitude regarding the so-called "amalgamation" resolution, or "program," we submit the following frank statement of facts: Nearly a year and a half ago, at one of the regular meetings of the Chicago Federation of Labor, March 19, 1922, a resolution was adopted referring to attacks being made upon the trade union movement by reactionary interests and requesting the American Federation of Labor to call a conference of national and international unions to consider the question of amalgamation. It was our position then, as it is now, that the question can only be finally determined by the American Federation of Labor. The resolution was accordingly sent to President Gompers and was given consideration by the Executive council of the American Federation of Labor. The Executive council decided against the conference proposal, pointing out that the time for the annual convention was then near at hand. The Chicago Federation of Labor took no further action.

At the Cincinnati convention of the American Federation of Labor in June, 1922, resolutions similar to that which had been adopted in Chicago were introduced and referred to the committee on organization which committee recommended non-concurrence for the reason that the "subject matter," that is to say the means of a closer co-operation and affiliation, "is already in effect through the various departments of the American Federation of Labor." The recommendations of the committee were adopted by the convention.[4] There the matter ended, so far as we are concerned.

In the meantime, however, a controversy had arisen as to the meaning and purpose of the original resolution. The Chicago Federation of Labor, as we understand its action, had purposed merely to present the question for discussion and final determination by the American Federation of Labor. Much to our surprise and chagrin, it was insisted, in some quarters, that by its action the Chicago Federation of Labor had undertaken to pass final judgment upon a matter which could only be determined by the American Federation of Labor and its affiliated national and international unions and that, since the American Federation of Labor convention did not forthwith adopt the resolution, we therefore must necessarily be in opposition to all the principles and policies of the parent body under whose charter we operate. That, of course, is sheer nonsense.

Here is the whole matter in a nut shell: The Chicago Federation of Labor requested the American Federation of Labor to consider the subject matter of a resolution. This the American Federation of Labor did, first at a meeting of the executive council and finally at the Cincinnati convention. Thereupon the whole matter was closed, having been passed upon by the parent body.

We regard it as extremely unfortunate that the name of the Chicago Federation of Labor continues to be used by individuals and organizations, over which we have no control, in such a way as to create the impression that our central body continues to urge its adoption by local unions and central bodies and state Federations notwithstanding the action of the Cincinnati convention. We repeat, with emphasis, that the Chicago Federation of Labor is not responsible for the action of such individuals and organizations.

One of the leading errors in recent circulars on this subject is the claim that the resolution of the Chicago Federation of Labor was defeated at the annual convention of the Illinois State Federation of Labor held in October, 1922, thus giving the impression that there is lack of harmony between the Chicago Federation of Labor and the Illinois State Federation of Labor. The truth is that the so-called "amalgamation" resolution which was defeated in the convention of the Illinois State Federation of Labor was not introduced by any representative of the Chicago Federation of Labor. We repeat again, that when the Cincinnati convention of the American Federation of Labor took place in June, 1922, the matter was brought to a close in so far as we were concerned and since then no officer or other accredited representative of the Chicago Federation of Labor has suggested its further discussion. We resent the implication that we are in any way antagonistic to the American Federation of Labor or to President Samuel Gompers.

The best interests of our movement unquestionably demand the promotion of harmony and good will throughout its various sections. We have work enough ahead to combat the vicious assaults upon our movement and we have neither time nor the energy to spare for useless quarreling and bickering within our ranks. Internal dissension can only serve to divide us. Thus do the enemies of labor desire to have us divided.

NEWSLETTER TWO.

The development of closer affiliation, mutual aid and co-operation within the trade union movement, depends entirely upon the degree to which we can promote harmony, good will, loyalty, tolerance and the confidence that comes only from mutual respect. Willingness to apply the principles of mutual aid can not be brought about by compulsion. It can come only through a free will offering in which all of whom take part act voluntarily. The substance is in the spirit developed and not in the forms, which are mere shadows.

Yours fraternally,

John Fitzpatrick, President.
E. N. Nockels, Secretary.
Chicago Federation of Labor.

P.S. It is necessary to add that the Chicago Federation of Labor is not connected in any way either directly or through any of its officials with the so-called "Trade Union Educational League."

TLS, TDtc, TLtcSr, Executive Council Records, Vote Books, reel 18, frames 87–89, *AFL Records*.

1. SG met with Victor Olander on Aug. 14, 1923. For a summary of the conference, see Files of the Office of the President, Conferences, reel 123, frame 33, *AFL Records*.

2. SG met in executive session with Olander, John Fitzpatrick, Edward Nockels, George Perkins, and Matthew Woll on Aug. 19, 1923.

3. The telegram congratulated John L. Lewis on resolution of the 1923 anthracite strike (SG to Lewis, Sept. 10, 1923, Executive Council Records, Vote Books, reel 18, frame 89, *AFL Records*). The strike, which involved some 160,000 miners, had begun Sept. 1 and was settled Sept. 8, with the mediation of Pennsylvania governor Gifford Pinchot. The new contract ran for two years and provided for an eight-hour workday, a 10-percent wage increase, and union recognition.

4. See "To Bert Miller," July 6, 1922, above.

From Joseph Dehan

N.Y. Sept 10–1923

My dear Chief:—

After spending six days in different parts of Brooklyn during the past two weeks I am pleased that I have been successful in securing the only picture ever taken of Mr. Laurel[1] and the only one in existence that the family know of. I received same from his daughter Mrs. G. Walters[2] 2412 Ralph St. Ridgewood Brooklyn. I sent same to you to day under seperate cover registered. The lady on the picture is Mrs. Laurel. Same was taken fifteen years ago in the garden of their home in Jersey. I promised faithfully that *you* would return the original directly to her. and that if you had it reproduced I would ask of you if possible to send her an extra copy or two. Mrs Walters told me she would never leave the picture out of her possession as other members of the family tried often to get it. I told her why you wanted it, but she at first refused, saying that the members of the union treated her father disgracefully and shamefully. After she finished her story I promised I would write you of the facts and told her how very much grieved I know you would be. This is what she said. About seven years ago Mr Laurel was struck by an Auto from which accident he never recovered and was never able to leave his bed at the hospital or at home. During all that time not a member of the union visited him and not one was there at his funeral. Almost daily during his illness in those seven years he would say another day gone and not a pal of the union here. I did all I could for them now they don't care to visit me. This so preyed on his mind that he lost his reason and never reganied same. and passed away Feb. 26–1921[3] at the age of 79

Since then all the members of the family have been embittered towards all members of the union. I know I tried and think I was successful in soothing matters over although I did not excuese the members for their actions. and when I finished speaking of you she was willing and did loan me the picture for you, especially when I told her why you wanted it. She then asked me if you would have a book sent to her when published. I said I would write you of her request and also that I felt she would receive a word from you regarding all these matters I agreed to inform you of.[4] Chief pardon me for writing you all of this but I promised I would. I do hope Chief you and yours are well. With best wishes

Sincerely   Joe.

Enclosed please find cartoon & editorial Did you see the Governor[5] since?

ALS, Files of the Office of the President, General Correspondence, reel 107, frames 348–50, *AFL Records*.

1. Carl Malcolm Ferdinand LAURELL, SG's mentor during the 1870s.

2. It is not clear which of Laurell's daughters this refers to. He had at least four: Emma (b. 1877?), Clara (b. 1882), Sophia (b. 1888), and Margaret (b. 1890).

3. Actually, Laurell died on Feb. 26, 1922.

4. See "To Mrs. G. Walters," Sept. 14, 1923, below.

5. Probably a reference to New York governor Alfred E. Smith. According to SG's appointment records, SG was the toastmaster at a dinner given for Smith on Aug. 30, 1923. In his reply to Joseph Dehan, SG indicated that he had not subsequently met with the governor (see SG to Dehan, Sept. 14, 1923, reel 293, vol. 306, p. 882, SG Letterbooks, DLC).

To Donald Richberg

Washington, D.C., Sept. 13, 1923.

Mr. Donald R. Richberg,
Attorney at Law,
London Guarantee & Accident Bldg., 360 No. Michigan Ave.,
   Chicago, Ill.
Dear Sir:

During a conference November 20, 1922, held in the Executive Council Chamber, A.F. of L. Bldg., to consider matters of interest to Labor two questions arose of great importance, but owing to the limited time at the disposal of those present nothing definite was done.

The subjects referred to were the growing menace of the injunction in labor disputes and the lack of a clear definition of what labor has a legal right to do in industrial disputes.

It was suggested that these questions should be submitted to the various attorneys present with the request that they each prepare a statement as to the best wording to be used in bills to be presented in congress to limit the use of the injunction in labor disputes and in defining the legal rights of wage earners in labor disputes. In conformity with the action of that conference I submitted these questions to a number of attorneys for their consideration.

Sunday, September 9, 1923, Mr. Jackson H. Ralston, Attorney for the American Federation of Labor, and Mr. Francis B. Sayre, professor of Law of Harvard College, submitted two bills which they after much thought had agreed upon covering the questions stated above. It was decided that copies of these proposed bills should be sent to all those attorneys taking part in the conference of November 20, 1922, and to such others as would be willing to be helpful in approving or pointing out any changes or additions that might be necessary to make them more effective and more certain to pass muster before the Supreme Court of the United States. To that end I am enclosing copies of the proposed bills and sincerely trust that you will be willing to give us your advice on these most important questions.[1]

Both Professor Sayre and Mr. Ralston have expressed the positive conviction that in order to secure the relief labor seeks it is necessary to divide the measure into two bills rather than to have it in one bill, so that each measure would be definite and less subject to misinterpretation by the courts.

When the bills are presented in congress we want them to be Supreme Court proof and we know of no way in which that can be done except to submit them to those who we believe are most competent to pass upon them. Whatever changes or conditions you or the other attorneys to whom the bills have been submitted for consideration may suggest will be referred to the Executive Council of the American Federation of Labor for the purpose of completing the preparation of the measures before presenting them to congress for action.

If it were not for the sincere sympathy you have shown in matters pertaining to labor and your recognized ability I would hesitate before encroaching upon your generosity to analyze the two bills. I feel, however, that after those to whom they have been submitted have passed judgment upon them that we can without fear of future action by the Supreme Court, urge their passage by Congress.

I wish, therefore, to thank you sincerely in advance for whatever advice you will kindly give, knowing full well that it will be greatly appreciated by the organized wage earners of the United States.

Very truly yours, Saml Gompers
President, American Federation of Labor.

TLS, Donald Randall Richberg Papers, ICHi.

1. For copies of similar letters, see reel 293, vol. 306, pp. 792–99, 802–23, SG Letterbooks, DLC. For copies of the enclosures, see "An Act Concerning the Granting of Injunctions," AFL Microfilm Convention File, reel 32, frame 1360, *AFL Records,* and "An Act Concerning Labor Organizations," ibid., frames 1360–61. There is no evidence that the AFL submitted these bills to Congress.

To Mrs. G. Walters

Sept. 14, 1923

Mrs. G. Walters,
2412 Ralph Street, Ridgewood, Brooklyn, N.Y.
My dear Mrs. Walters:

Mr. Joseph Dehan has been so kind as to call on you in my behalf and you have been good enough to lend him, for me, what I am sure is one of your most treasured possessions, that is the picture of Mr. and Mrs. Laurel.[1] I appreciate more than I can express to you your kindness in entrusting the picture to me.

I am going to take it to a photographer here in this city who does wonderful reproduction work with old photographs and if he succeeds in reproducing it, I shall not only return the original to you but also a copy of the reproduction.

I have been working on my memoirs for the past four or five years and no story that I write of the early struggles of the labor movement, in which we participated, would be complete or would be fair and just without full tribute being paid to your father, and that is what I have tried to do. When the book shall have been published and you have the opportunity of reading it, I think you will be satisfied with the way I have dealt with the memory of your father.

Mr. Dehan wrote me quite comprehensively of his interview with you and of what you told him regarding the last years of your father's life. What he wrote me has caused me great grief. I am sure that if the union members in New York, who were aware of the history of the early years of the labor movement and the work of your father for the movement, had known of the condition of his health and where he lived that they would have gone to him and would have given him the comfort of their presence and comradeship during the closing years of his life.

Next week I shall have to leave Washington for the Pacific coast[2] and I will not be able to return for six weeks or more. By the time I get back I hope to be able to return the photograph to you, together with one of the reproductions.[3]

Again thanking you for your kindness and with sincere good wishes, I am

Very truly yours,
President, American Federation of Labor.

TLp, reel 293, vol. 306, pp. 877–78, SG Letterbooks, DLC.

1. Louisa Laurell (b. 1855?).

2. SG left Washington, D.C., on the afternoon of Sept. 21, 1923, and arrived in Portland, Ore., on Sept. 27 after making brief stops for meetings in Chicago, Minneapolis, and Seattle. In Portland he presided over meetings of the AFL Executive Council (Sept. 29-Oct. 2, Oct. 12–13) and the AFL convention (Oct. 1–12), addressed conventions of the AFL trades departments (Sept. 27–28), and delivered several addresses over the radio (Oct. 5 and 10). On Oct. 7 he took a day trip to Astoria, Ore., to address a mass meeting (for a transcript of his remarks, see Files of the Office of the President, Speeches and Writings, reel 118, frames 535–38, *AFL Records*). On Oct. 15 he left Portland for San Francisco, where he addressed an American Legion convention on Oct. 18 (for a transcript, see ibid., frames 591–97). He went on to Los Angeles by boat on Oct. 19 and left there by train for El Paso, Tex., on Oct. 24, arriving on Oct. 25. There, he met with representatives of the Mexican and the Pan-American Federations of Labor on Oct. 26 and 27, traveling to Ciudad Juárez, Mexico, with the delegation on the second day. He left El Paso on Oct. 29 and arrived back in Washington on Nov. 1, after making brief stops to attend meetings in Kansas City, Kans., and St. Louis, Mo. For transcripts of additional speeches given on the trip, see ibid., frames 472–79, 489–513, 517–34, 540–42, 553–64, 569–90, 600–18, 624–32. For minutes of some of the conferences, see ibid., Conferences, reel 123, frames 86–95, 97–99, 101, 103–14, 116–18.

3. SG to Mrs. G. Walters, Sept. 21, 1923, reel 294, vol. 307, p. 18, SG Letterbooks, DLC.

An Excerpt from the Minutes
of a Meeting with Selma Maximon[1] and
Harry Lang on the Sacco-Vanzetti Case

Saturday, Sept. 15, 1923

. . .

Mrs. Maximon set forth the situation in the Sacco-Vanzetti case. She said that a hearing would be held October 1 by the court to decide whether there should be a retrial of the case. They had very many witnesses. For instance, Mr. Hamilton, expert who testified that the bullet which killed the victim did not fit Vanzetti's revolver.[2] Then there were a number of witnesses who had testified on both sides who are absolutely unreliable and their testimony should be ruled out. Other very important features had been discovered that would redound to the benefit of Sacco-Vanzetti but the most trouble was the lack of funds. Mrs. Maximon requested that President Gompers issue a letter to the National and International unions urging that they contribute to the cause of Sacco-Vanzetti.

Mr. Gompers said that all the unions were impoverished and that he did not know where he could turn to raise a dollar. He said, however, that he was to have a conference this morning with a friend with whom he would discuss the question and that afterward he would see Mrs. Maximom again.

After Mrs. Maximon had left President Gompers took up the matter with Mr. Harry Lang. He asked that Mr. Lang have a talk with Mrs. Maximom. This they did retiring to the Executive Council room.

On their return to President Gompers Mr. Lang said that he had agreed to print an article in the "Foreword"[3] appealing for funds for the defense of the two men. Mr. Gompers said that he could use his name as being in sympathy with the movement.

Mr. Lang also said that he would see Mr. Sigman[4] of the Ladies Garment Workers to talk to President Gompers at Portland for the purpose of getting officials of national and international unions interested in the matter.

Mrs. Maximon thanked Mr. Gompers for the aid he had given and she said that his approval would be of inestimable value to the cause.

TDc, Files of the Office of the President, Conferences, reel 123, frame 61, *AFL Records.* Typed notation: "Sacco-Vanzetti Case. Conference held in the Office of President Gompers, Saturday, Sept. 15, 1923, at 11 o'clock."

1. Selma Cohen Maximon (1893–1966) identified herself as field secretary of the Sacco-Vanzetti Defense Committee.

2. Albert Hine Hamilton (1859–1938), a firearms expert from Auburn, N.Y., provided ballistics testimony that the Sacco-Vanzetti defense included in an April 1923 motion for a new trial.

3. That is, the *Jewish Daily Forward,* a New York City Yiddish-language daily newspaper (variously *Forverts* or *Vorwärts*).

4. Morris Solomon Sigman served as president of the International Ladies' Garment Workers' Union from 1923 to 1928.

To John Macrae

Oct. [Sept.] 21, 1923.[1]

Mr. John Macrae,
Dutton & Company 681 Fifth Avenue, New York, N.Y.
My dear Mr. Macrae:

Indicative of that which is yet to come, I take pleasure in enclosing to you herein the foreword for my book

SIX DECADES OF LIFE AND LABOR
AN AUTOBIOGRAPHY
BY
SAMUEL GOMPERS

I hope you will like it.

Last Sunday being alone in my office I wrote it in longhand and had it typed, as per enclosed.

I know you will be interested in my statement that about one-third of the manuscript for the book is in final form.[2]

I regret very much that I shall not be able to give much attention to the remainder of the work for awhile, by reason of the fact that this afternoon I shall be on my way to Portland, Oregon, to attend the convention of the American Federation of Labor. If I can do anything on the work in the meantime I shall do so but of this I am not quite sure.

With kindest regards, I am

Very truly yours,
President, American Federation of Labor.

TLc, Files of the Office of the President, General Correspondence, reel 107, frame 384, *AFL Records.*

1. This copy of SG's letter is misdated. It was actually written on Sept. 21, 1923, the day he left for the AFL convention in Portland, Ore.

2. For details on the preparation of SG's memoirs, see *The Samuel Gompers Papers*, vol. 11, pp. 68, 117–18, and 522–23. SG was finally able to deliver the completed manuscript to John Macrae of E. P. Dutton and Co. in December 1923 (see "To Matthew Woll," Dec. 17, 1923, and "To John Macrae," Dec. 24, 1923, below). The book was not published, however, until February 1925, after SG had died. Florence Thorne, who had helped him research the book, wrote the summary of SG's last year that was included as an appendix to the autobiography.

The Minutes of a Conference in Portland, Ore.

Portland, Oregon, October 1, 1923.

President Gompers had called in representatives of the two factions of the Central Labor Council in Seattle to present to them a letter[1] agreed upon by the Executive Council of the American Federation of Labor in which the decision of the Council as to the future of the Seattle Central Labor Council was outlined.

The first to call upon President Gompers were James A. Duncan, Charles Doyle and Mr. Pearl,[2] representing the Central Labor Council.

President Gompers handed them the letter prepared by the Executive Council and left them alone to read it. When President Gompers returned to the room he spoke to the representatives of the Seattle Central Labor Council as follows:

"I say to you as a trade unionist man to man, that the Executive Council does not want to do the slightest thing to injure any local union or central labor body. An army corps must move as fast and no faster than the slowest group. Each group has its own particular sphere. If each group does as it pleases, the worst that could come to it would be an order to move. So with the labor movement. Each group has its duty in the labor movement. Central labor bodies have full autonomy in their own field.

"I want to say to you this; you are not in affluent circumstances, you are property poor. The question with you is how to keep up. But if you had all the money necessary to keep up and more, not a jot of it would we want. I do not know what your idea of my attitude in the hearing was, but things were said that were an aspersion on my character. I was accused of being under capitalist and military rule. I have always tried to eliminate myself from any consideration while acting as a judge. What is in the document I have handed you is the unanimous declaration of the Executive Council. There is not one paragraph in it that was animated by a vindictive spirit. The last two paragraphs express the sentiment of the Executive Council. The other we regarded as a duty.

"If anyone thinks I am satisfied with the conditions as they are, they are sadly mistaken. Anyone who has striven as hard as I have, knows what has been achieved; but counted in the rhythm of time there is no labor movement comparable with the American labor movement. Distance lends enchantment to the view when we consider the labor movements of other countries, but I am willing to match our movement as to solidarity and effectiveness with any other movement in the world. I say to you gentlemen whom I know very well, except I do not know Mr. Pearl very well, but I know Doyle and Duncan, and I know that the services they have given,—I cannot say whether it is a lack of understanding or they are misguided or in the exaggeration of their sentimentality, that has brought about the present situation. The Executive Council is satisfied more than ever since the hearing, of the necessity of the action taken. I know Billy Short has in his make up the militant. As men I think you have both done each other an injustice. I think you should not question Billy Short's honesty. If it is a question of the best interests of the labor movement you can work together. I do not give a damn what you say about me. I think if I had given whatever ability and energy I have to something else I could have done as well financially. I never had anything, never expect anything more, and am probably getting more than my deserts.

"I worked for years without a salary. I worked a number of years for $1,000 each year and could do nothing else; my salary gradually rose to $3,000 and every time it has been raised since that I have protested. I believe in the philosophy of my grandfather,[3] which was that if the Good Lord will save me from poverty, I would save myself from riches. I have told them that if they increased my salary I would 'blow' it in."

President Gompers then referred to how he had obtained what little he had. This was from the frugality of his wife[4] and from his daughter[5] who earned considerable money before her death in the musical world. What they had left behind he still had. He said that he had no insurance except that which will be paid upon his death by the Cigarmakers' International Union. He ended:

"If when I am gone I leave a great pile of money, any one will be justified in questioning my honesty. I want you to know that I have borne many scars of battle. My honesty has been put in the balance, but I can not help it. I say this as one man to you men, if you believe it.

"Let me hope that you can get together and work together; not fight against each other."

During Mr. Gompers talk Mr. Short came in and listened to what he was saying. Later on Vice-President Martin F. Ryan[6] and Organizer Young came in. At the conclusion of Mr. Gompers' speech Mr. Duncan started to say "I think we are nearer together than we thought—" but President Gompers refused to listen to any further talk on the matter under the circumstances. As the Seattle Central Labor Council representatives were leaving the Room, Secretary Doyle said to President Gompers, "I intend to do what I can to bring about harmony, but I will not be dominated."

After they had left President Gompers gave a copy of the letter to President Short of the State Federation of Labor and to Organizer Young. They then left the room.

TDc, Files of the Office of the President, Conferences, reel 123, frames 97–99, *AFL Records.* Typed notation: "Conference held in Room 509, Multnomah Hotel, Portland, Oregon."

1. "To Charles Doyle," Oct. 1, 1923, below.
2. Philip J. Pearl (b. 1888) was the secretary of Journeymen Barbers' International Union of America 195 of Seattle.
3. Samuel Moses GOMPERS.
4. Sophia Julian GOMPERS.
5. Sadie Julian (variously Julia) GOMPERS.
6. Martin Francis RYAN, president of the Brotherhood of Railway Carmen of America (1909–35), served as an AFL vice-president from May 1923 until 1928.

To Charles Doyle

Multnomah Hotel, Portland, Ore., October 1, 1923

Mr. C. W. Doyle,
Secretary, Seattle Central Labor Council,
Portland, Oregon.
Dear Sir and Brother:—

The Executive Council of the American Federation of Labor at its two days session at Portland, Oregon,[1] having under consideration the subject of the relations between the Seattle Central Labor Council and the American Federation of Labor, had before it the three representatives of the Seattle Central Labor Council—James A. Duncan, C. U. Doyle and Philip Pearl; E. B. Ault, Managing Editor of the Seattle Union Record; Wm. H. Short, President, and Mr. Ballinger,[2] Vice-President of the Washington State Federation of Labor; C. O. Young, Organizer of the American Federation of Labor and Mr. Bailey,[3] Business Agent of the Pattern Makers' Union of Seattle, when the entire subject of the revocation of the charter of the Seattle Central Labor Council was considered. All parties were fully heard on both sides of the question and the official minutes of the meetings of the Seattle Central Labor Council for the past three years were examined.

The testimony of the representatives of the Seattle Central Labor Council and the official minutes of the meetings of that body substantiated the complaints made against that organization, that it has inaugurated and carried out policies in defiance of the declarations and decisions of the American Federation of Labor, the parent body. After due deliberation and pursuant to the laws of the American Federation of Labor and the requirements of the charter issued to the Seattle Central Labor Council the Executive Council reached the following decision:

1. That the Seattle Central Labor Council is required to confine its activities within the locality of Seattle;

2. That the Seattle Central Labor Council must recognize and is required to sustain the jurisdiction of the Washington State Federation of Labor;

3. The Seattle Central Labor Council must at all times recognize and maintain the supreme authority of the national and international trade unions within the trade and industrial jurisdiction as recognized by the American Federation of Labor.

4. That the Seattle Central Labor Council must at all times recognize, support and maintain the laws, principles and policies of the American Federation of Labor in all national and international relations and policies and shall disavow any action taken by it, which directly or indirectly conflicts with or evades its unquestioned support of the laws, principles and policies of the American Federation of Labor as contained in the instructions conveyed by the Executive Council of the American Federation of Labor to the Seattle Central Labor Council in the communication dated May fourteenth, 1923.[4]

5. That unless the Seattle Central Labor Council shall on or before thirty days from the date of this action officially inform the President of the American Federation of Labor at the headquarters at Washington, D.C., that the Central Labor Council of Seattle has agreed to the above decision, the charter of the Central Labor Council shall automatically stand revoked.[5]

The Executive Council of the American Federation of Labor, in reaching the above conclusion, has the sole purpose of adjusting the differences existing between the Seattle Central Labor Council and the American Federation of Labor and to restore harmony and cooperation within the labor movement of Seattle with that of [the] American labor movement. There is always guaranteed to organizations affiliated to the American Federation of Labor the right of changing any of its laws, its principles or its policies but this must be done in an orderly manner—a manner provided by the rules and procedure of the

American Federation of Labor in whose conventions the freest forum prevails and whose whole manner of conduct is the most democratic of any general labor movement in the whole world.

It is the earnest hope of the Executive Council that the decisions and conclusions above set forth shall meet with prompt and hearty support of the Seattle Central Labor Council and the rank and file of the organized trade union movement of your city.

By Order of the Executive Council of the
American Federation of Labor.
(Signed) Samuel Gompers.
President.

TLcSr, reel 294, vol. 307, pp. 250–51, SG Letterbooks, DLC.

1. That is, Sept. 29–30, 1923.

2. John Napoleon Belanger (b. 1888) was the business agent for United Association of Journeymen Plumbers and Steam Fitters of the United States and Canada 473 of Seattle (Steam Fitters and Helpers; 1921–25) and a vice-president of the Washington State Federation of Labor (1923–25).

3. William B. Bailey (b. 1866?) served as business manager and financial secretary of the Pattern Makers' League of North America's Seattle local from 1922 to 1931. From 1923 to 1931 he also served as the local's recording secretary.

4. "The Executive Council of the AFL to James A. Duncan," May 14, 1923, above.

5. The Seattle Central Labor Council voted full acceptance of these terms at its meeting on Oct. 10, 1923 (see Charles Doyle et al. to SG, Oct. 19, 1923, and Doyle to SG, Oct. 27, 1923, Executive Council Records, Vote Books, reel 18, frames 115–16, *AFL Records*). The AFL Executive Council subsequently authorized SG to present similar terms to the Detroit Federation of Labor, the Silver Bow Trades and Labor Council of Butte, Mont., and the Tacoma (Wash.) Central Labor Union (see "An Excerpt from the Minutes of a Meeting of the Executive Council of the AFL," Oct. 13, 1923, n. 1, below).

From Paul Smith

Hotel Hibbing, Hibbing, Minn. Oct. 2nd 1923

Mr Samuel Gompers
President A.F. of L.
Portland, Oregon.
Dear Sir and Brother:—

I thought you would be interested in Knowing that Delegates Emmie[1] of St Paul and William Dunn of Butte Mont. are attending the Convention in Portland without any expense to the organizations they represent. They secured the Credentials by reason of the fact that they would go to the Convention at their own expense.

Mr A Bordson[2] of the Mine Mill and Smelter Men from Great

Falls Mont. informed me about Bill Dunn, and while in St Paul I learned about Emmie being a delegate without cost to St Paul Trades Assembly

Assuring You of my Kind regards I remain

Yours Fraternally   Paul J. Smith

ALS, AFL Microfilm Convention File, reel 33, frame 1042, *AFL Records.*

1. Julius Frederick (later Frank) Emme (1879–1935), a member of International Association of Machinists 459 of St. Paul, was the delegate to the convention from the St. Paul Trades and Labor Assembly (TLA). He ran unsuccessfully for mayor of St. Paul on the Socialist ticket (1916 and 1918) and for Congress on the Farmer-Labor party ticket (1924). In 1925 Emme was expelled from the St. Paul TLA and the Minnesota State Federation of Labor because of his communist connections. He was reinstated after he left the party, and he later served as secretary of the Minnesota Industrial Commission (1930–35).

2. Alfred B. Bordsen (b. 1878) was a member of International Union of Mine, Mill, and Smelter Workers 16 of Great Falls, Mont., and from 1916 through at least 1926 was also a member of the international union's executive board.

Excerpts from Accounts of the 1923 Convention of the AFL in Portland, Ore.

[October 8, 1923]

DUNNE DEFIES A.F. OF L. TO EXPEL HIM

Confronted with expulsion from the convention of the A.F. of L. because of his admitted sympathy with the communist principles as promulgated by the Third Internationale at Moscow, William F. Dunne of Butte, today challenged the delegates to revoke his credentials in a scathing arraignment of the officials of the federation.

The reply of Dunne to charges made by William Green, secretary of the United Mine Workers, and Phillip Murray,[1] delegate of the same organization, was characterized by the bitterness of its attack upon the leaders of organized labor from President Samuel Gompers down.

Adjournment was taken at 12:30 o'clock before putting the question of expelling Dunne to a vote.[2]

COMES FROM BUTTE

Dunne, editor of the Butte Bulletin and a director of the Workers Party of America, is a delegate from the Silver Bow, Mont., Central Labor council[3] and a member of the electrical workers' union.

Much of the fire of the conservative element of the convention was provoked by his Sunday night address at the Women's club building,[4] although his record as a champion of the communist program has been known for several years.

"I doubt if you can find a lower standard of knowledge of the history of the working classes and economic struggle of the workers anywhere than among the international officers of this convention," Dunne told his accusers, whom he charged with seeking to preserve the fragments of the A.F. of L. in order to keep their positions "paying $5000 to $15,000 a year."

Blames Gompers.

"President Gompers, himself head and shoulders intellectually above the rest of the delegation, is most responsible," said Dunne. "He does not want intellectual leadership among the officials and he has succeeded in depriving you of it."

Roars of derisive laughter from the delegates greeted this remark.

"He knows you all," Dunne continued. "He plays upon you like a violinist plays upon the strings of his violin; and if my judgment is correct, he despises you all. He despises you as these newspaper men in the press box despise you. You, who live upon publicity and whose doings and plans for this convention have been published weeks in advance."

The motion to unseat Dunne was made by Murray of the United Mine Workers after Secretary Green had read articles from the Butte Bulletin and reports from the coal mining regions of Pennsylvania, intended to show that Dunne had opposed the work of the mine workers in organizing coal miners during the strike of 1922.

. . .

Efforts of other delegates to gain the floor failed when Gompers recognized Dunne.

As the defendant before the court of labor arose to speak a volley of applause roared from the gallery, partially filled with sympathizers. Dunne was halted by Gompers, who warned the visitors that any "approval or disapproval of the proceedings of the convention" would result in the galleries being cleared.

Dunne Opens Defense

"I realize fully the underlying motives back of this move," said Dunne, "but when I said and wrote that officials of this organization were more interested in their positions than in the spread of the union labor movement, I told the truth and you know it, and you cannot deny it. You strut and swank about the convention hall as if you had the capitalist class by the throats, yet I have heard only reports of union charters being revoked and nothing of new bodies or groups being brought into the organization."

The sharpest clash centered around the charge of Dunne that John L. Lewis, president of the United Mine Workers, had delivered members of his organization "into the hands of the hangmen."

Asked by Green to reaffirm or deny this charge, Dunne cited the publication in "publicity matter sponsored by the United Mine Workers," after a recent mine shooting, the statement that "80 communists, now working in the mines, were responsible for the murder."[5]

SPEAKS AS COMMUNIST

"As a communist," Dunne told the delegates with a dramatic pause, "I believe that trade unions must strive for political power. If you say to me I am against constitutional measures, I ask you, if after you have exhausted all constitutional means and the workers still starve by millions in the streets, what then?"

"It will not help the labor movement to expel me. No matter what you do I will continue to fight the battle along my lines. I have always felt that a distinction should be made between the high salaried officials of labor and the workers."

"It has been, and still is, my opinion that progress in the labor movement is made in spite of the officials rather than because of them."

. . .

BRANDED AS TRAITOR

Green branded Dunne as a traitor, because "he parades under the cloak of trades unionism" and seeks to destroy "the movement of which he professes to be a part."

After reading an editorial from a recent issue of the Chicago Tribune, Green asked the convention if it could, without being previously informed, tell whether the article is from Dunne's Butte Bulletin or from the Tribune. The editorial attacked the United Mine Workers.[6]

"I must congratulate President Lewis of the Mine Workers," said Green, "for being so active that he has drawn the fire of both this capitalistic sheet at Chicago and the communist sheet at Butte."

In conclusion, Green cited the ejection of Lucifer from heaven as precedent for the action which he urged upon the convention in expelling Dunne from the floor.

"I am glad," said Dunne, when he made his reply, "that the speaker has seen fit to cite the Biblical reference as a precedent. It gives the matter a religious atmosphere quite in keeping with the heresy-hunting activities of the officialdom of the A.F. of L."[7]

. . .

Oregon Journal (Portland), Oct. 8, 1923.

1. Philip MURRAY served as a vice-president of the United Mine Workers of America from 1920 to 1942.

2. The roll call vote on unseating William Dunne was taken on the afternoon of Oct. 8, 1923. The official convention proceedings give the vote as 27,837 in favor, 108 opposed, and 643 not voting (AFL, *Proceedings,* 1923, pp. 258–59).

3. The AFL chartered the Silver Bow Trades and Labor Council of Butte, Mont., in 1910.

4. Dunne addressed the Portland Woman's Club on Oct. 7, 1923.

5. In September 1923 the United Mine Workers furnished a series of six articles to the daily press outlining what the union viewed as communist efforts to take control of the American labor movement. The third article, which dealt with the 1922 miners' strike, claimed that a group of eighty-six communists—sixty-seven of them members of the party's local chapter in Herrin, Ill., and the rest of them outside agents brought in from Chicago especially for the purpose—had been responsible for inciting the massacre at Herrin. "This revolting, inexcusable crime was fomented, promoted and caused solely by Communists," the article reported. "It was a carefully planned affair, schemed with all the diabolic cruelty and disregard for law that characterizes the Communist movement" ("Lays Herrin Riot to 86 Alien Reds," *New York Times,* Sept. 12, 1923). The United Mine Workers subsequently published the articles as *Attempts by the Communists to Seize the American Labor Movement* (Indianapolis, 1923).

6. "The 'One Big Union' Menace to Unionism," *Chicago Tribune,* Oct. 2, 1923.

7. For a transcript of the discussion, including the remarks of Murray and William Green, see AFL Microfilm Convention File, reel 33, frames 1043–52, *AFL Records.*

Portland, Ore., October 8, 1923.

. . .

SEVENTH DAY—MONDAY AFTERNOON SESSION

. . .

EVOLUTION IN THE TRADE UNION MOVEMENT

Under this caption, pages 37–39, the Executive Council sets out clearly and convincingly the historic developments and processes of organization that have been taking place in the organized labor world of America and the policy pursued by the American Federation of Labor thereto. Because resolutions Nos. 32, 44 and 54[1] all deal with this subject of form and method of organization, your committee has considered as one all these proposals relating to a so-called "amalgamation of craft unions" into arbitrarily alleged industrial unions. Though they may slightly vary in verbiage, the intent and purpose, if not the motives underlying, are quite the same.

All these resolutions carry with them the imputation that the American Federation of Labor is confined to "craft" unions and that it uncompromisingly resents recognition of any organization that resembles or approximates an industrial form. An examination of the roster of the affiliated organizations of the American Federation of Labor disproves that false imputation and stigmatizes those who would advance such untruths either as being ignorant or deliberate frauds.

Again, these so-called "amalgamation" proposals carry with them the implication that affiliated "crafts" unions cannot co-operate, federate or amalgamate because of some fancied power of resistance alleged to be exercised by the American Federation of Labor. Again, an examination of the records of the American Federation of Labor brands such an implication as false and untrue. In view of this assertion your committee commends a careful reading of the Executive Council's report on this subject.

It is not, however, so much the false implications and imputations involved in these so-called "amalgamation" resolutions that should move us to renewed vigor and drastic action as it is the motives of the prime movers who are continually urging these proposals upon the councils of labor. Demonstrative proof is overwhelming that those who are constantly at work dividing the organized workers on abstract discussions of forms of organization and spreading the poison of suspicion against the officers of trade unions have never been loyal trade unionists and have always antagonized the trade union movement. In addition, the self-acclaimed "amalgamationists" are not bent on amalgamation, but upon the disruption and destruction of the organized labor movement of America. In this they serve well the employers who would again assume complete mastery over the destinies of the wage earners.

The purpose and aim of these destructionists, as well as their standing within our communities, is no less savory than that of private detectives who would sell the soul of their fellow man for the jingle of gold. In the religious world such men are excommunicated. In the political world such men are ostracized from society, if not treated more severely through the operation of laws relating to treason. In the industrial world, we have tolerated them altogether too freely.

These sinister agents, propagandists and destructionists of a foreign foe to our American institutions, should be singled out wherever found and the light of day be thrown upon their nefarious work. Likewise, employers, frenzied in their blindness for wealth and gold, and who, for the moment, find encouragement and hope and give passive if not active support to this and similar movements which seek to distract attention and divide labor's forces, may well hesitate. They should realize that to destroy the evolutionary processes of progress, advancement and application of the ideals of democracy and of the golden rule in all relations of mankind is but to hasten revolutionary tendencies with all that these great social revulsions impress so tragically upon humankind.

. . .

The report of the committee was adopted by unanimous vote.

. . .

AFL, *Proceedings,* 1923, pp. 247, 258, 266–68.

1. The three resolutions were introduced on Oct. 2, 1923. Resolution 32, introduced by J. J. Riley of the Pennsylvania State Federation of Labor, called for a conference at which national and international affiliates would arrange for the amalgamation of the unions in their respective industries. Resolution 44, introduced by William Dunne of the Trades and Labor Council of Butte, Mont., called for the convention to endorse industrial organization and for the AFL Executive Council to work out an amalgamation plan for the various unions, to be submitted at the 1924 AFL convention, and to urge national and international affiliates to undertake an extensive educational campaign on the benefits of industrial unionism. Resolution 54, introduced by G. A. Von Schriltz of the Central Labor Council of Seattle and Vicinity, also called for the convention to endorse amalgamation. The Committee on Resolutions recommended non-concurrence, and its recommendation was endorsed unanimously.

[October 9, 1923]

THIRD PARTY TURNED DOWN BY A.F. OF L.

Organized labor, as represented by the A.F. of L. convention, today refused to lend its support to the formation of a third political party, to be formed through a union of labor and the farmer organizations of the country.

By a decisive vote, cast after debate had been summarily cut off while proponents of the farm-labor party plan were shouting vainly for permission to speak, four resolutions of similar import were defeated in line with the adverse recommendations of the resolutions committee.[1]

The vote, as unofficially tabulated, was 1816 favoring the labor party out of a possible 27,946, the figures representing the force represented by the delegates.[2]

Policy Justified

Three of the four resolutions dealing with the formation of a political party were dismissed by the committee with brief consideration.

The fourth, sponsored by D. A. McVey[3] of the Chicago Federation of Labor, was opposed by the committee, which recommended that the trade union movement concentrate its strength upon securing remedial legislation through extension of the economic and industrial influence rather than invading the field of political action.

"The policy and practice of the A.F. of L." said the committee, "to be partisan to principles and not to be partisan to political parties has been fully justified by experience."

Socialist Speaks

Max Hayes of Cleveland, delegate from the Typographical union and one-time candidate for vice president on the Socialist ticket, was the only speaker that got the floor in behalf of the labor party resolution.

Hayes, after claiming that the question involved in the resolution was whether "we shall remain on our knees before the political parties now existing, begging for crumbs of legislation that drop from the table," drew the fire of Matthew Woll,[4] secretary of the resolutions committee and spokesman for the administration, by charging that the committee had "dragged the red herring of Fosterism, bolshevism and communism across the trail of these resolutions."

READS TELEGRAM

In reply Woll countered with the assertion that the "isms" referred to had drawn this on themselves by sponsoring the resolutions referred to and read a telegram from the secretary of the Illinois State Federation of Labor, taken Sunday, against the third party resolution, was reported.[5]

The resolution around which most discussion centered today was the resolution sponsored by McVey of this organization.

In the midst of the discussion, [with] Vice-President Duffy[6] in the chair, to permit President Gompers to speak on the question, the previous question was called and debate cut off.

While at least three delegates shouted for recognition at the same time, the question was put and announcement made that the motion to adopt the committee's report had carried. A roll call was demanded, and in response to a protest from the floor of the convention President Gompers announced that hereafter speakers would be limited to 10 minutes, in conformity with the rules, in order that both sides of the debate might be presented.

. . .

Oregon Journal (Portland), Oct. 9, 1923.

1. Resolution 9, introduced by E. G. Hall of the Minnesota Federation of Labor (FOL), called for the AFL to remove any constitutional provisions preventing AFL participation in the formation of an independent political party of farmers and workers. Resolution 24, introduced by the delegates of the Amalgamated Association of Iron, Steel, and Tin Workers, called for organized labor to unite behind an independent political party. Resolution 31, introduced by J. J. Riley of the Pennsylvania State FOL, reported that body's endorsement of an independent political party of workers and farmers. Resolution 69, introduced by David McVey of the Chicago FOL, called for amendment of the AFL constitution so as to permit the Executive Council to take steps to create such a party. The first two resolutions were introduced on Oct. 1, 1923, and the other two on Oct. 2. On Oct. 9 the Committee on Resolutions recommended dismissing resolutions 9, 24, and 31 and non-concurrence with resolution 69; the convention adopted the committee's report on a roll call vote.

2. The official convention proceedings give the vote to endorse the recommendation of the Committee on Resolutions and reject the call for a labor party as 25,066 in favor, 1,895 opposed, and 1,628 not voting (AFL, *Proceedings*, 1923, pp. 290–91).

3. David A. McVey (b. 1878), who represented the Chicago FOL, was a member of

Wood, Wire, and Metal Lathers' International Union 74 of Chicago. He later served as president of the Illinois Farmer-Labor party.

4. Matthew Woll, an AFL vice-president, was a delegate for the International Photo-Engravers' Union of North America.

5. The telegram referred to, from Victor Olander to John Walker, Oct. 8, 1923 (AFL, *Proceedings*, 1923, pp. 285–86), reported the defeat of Foster's proposals at the recent convention of the Illinois State FOL and the Chicago FOL's endorsement of this action at its meeting on Sunday, Oct. 7, as being "in the best interests of the trade union movement" (ibid., p. 285).

6. Frank Duffy, an AFL vice-president, was a delegate for the United Brotherhood of Carpenters and Joiners of America.

Portland, Ore., October 10, 1923.

NINTH DAY—WEDNESDAY MORNING SESSION

. . .

Resolution No. 93—By Delegates Dan W. Stevens[1] of the Minneapolis Trades and Labor Assembly,[2] and James A. Duncan of the Seattle Central Labor Council:

. . .

Resolved, By the 43rd Annual Convention of the American Federation of Labor, in session assembled, that the Executive Council be, and hereby is, authorized and directed to use its good offices in an effort to have the lady barbers admitted to membership in the Journeymen Barbers' International Union of America; and, further, be it

Resolved, That in case of failure upon the part of the J.B.I.U. of A. to make provision for female workers in that organization within 60 days after the adoption of this resolution, the Executive Council is directed to grant Federal charters to such groups of lady barbers as may make application for same, subject to rules governing such applications and with the understanding that such groups shall be transferred to the J.B.I.U. of A. whenever such transfer can be arranged.

Your committee recommends non-concurrence in the foregoing resolution.

In this connection your committee desires to again point out clearly that each national and international organization affiliated with the American Federation of Labor has full and final control over its own internal affairs. The jurisdictional rights of each of the several national and international unions have been clearly and specifically outlined in their charters and such charters have been approved, first by the Executive Council and then by the convention of the American Federation of Labor, and in at least one instance the jurisdictional rights of a national union were approved by the convention of the American Federation of Labor before the charter was issued by the Executive Council.

No charter can be more exclusive in its nature than those granted by the American Federation of Labor to its affiliated organizations, and no charter is more sacred or will be more carefully respected than are these. It is not within the power or province of any affiliated organization to interfere with the discipline of management or control of its own affairs by another body so chartered from the American Federation of Labor. Therefore, it would be an unwarranted invasion on the part of this convention to undertake to prescribe, by resolution, to an affiliated organization the character or qualifications of its membership.

We earnestly hope that the several state and city central bodies which are chartered direct by the American Federation of Labor, and hold their powers and authority from the American Federation of Labor, give heed to the principle that the "creature cannot become greater than the creator," in this regard; that the restrictions placed upon the American Federation of Labor lie with added weight on the bodies subordinate to the American Federation of Labor, and that any invasion by a Central Labor Union or a State Federation of Labor of the jurisdictional rights of a national or international union is going far beyond the limit set for the subordinate bodies to control them in their action and relations to the American Federation of Labor.

A motion was made and seconded to adopt the report of the committee.

Delegate Duncan, Seattle Central Labor Council, spoke at length in opposition to the recommendation of the committee and in favor of the adoption of the resolution. He called attention to the fact that the Committee on Organization, in its report to the convention as recorded on page 226 of the fifth day's proceedings, had called attention to the necessity of the organization of women in industry, and that that report was unanimously adopted by the convention.[3] He told of the repeated efforts which had been made to secure a charter for the lady barbers of Seattle, both from the Journeymen Barbers' International Union and, following the refusal of that body to issue a charter, the American Federation of Labor itself, in the form of a Federal Labor Union charter. He made the statement that the splendid conditions enjoyed by the barbers of Seattle today were due in large measure to the fine support given them by the Seattle Central Labor Council and the affiliated unions.

. . .

Delegate Karston,[4] Atlanta Federation of Trades: A point of information—if a national organization disclaims jurisdiction over any branch of workers, has or has not the American Federation of Labor the right to issue a Federal charter?

President Gompers: Not in the same trade or industry. If the national union has jurisdiction over the industry, it has the right to prescribe the conditions under which that membership may be obtained.

Delegate Valentino,[5] Georgia Federation of Labor: I have been told that the American Federation of Labor either instructed or requested two international unions to strike out the word "white" in their qualifications for membership, where the international said that a man should be a white citizen in order to be eligible to membership. Is that true?

President Gompers: The only instance when that occurred was when an application for a charter was made and it was held up upon that condition.[6]

Delegate Fischer, Barbers: I want to explain to this convention a few of the circumstances in connection with this question. First of all, the body that seeks the passage of this resolution does not come in here with clean hands and a clean purpose. This matter has been before our International Convention on numerous occasions. We have made an investigation of the subject, and we have found that the greatest menace to our trade from the women engaged in it is their incompetency as tradesmen in our line. We have never found a man who goes to a barber shop who says that he goes there because he receives as good or better work in a female shop than he does by going into a male shop. Our organization has discouraged lady barbers in our industry because they don't usually stick at the trade long enough to become artists in this line.

The Central Labor Council of Seattle wants everybody organized, irrespective of who they are. We have in the city of Seattle not affiliated with us because of our laws a Japanese barbers' organization, and the Central body of Seattle is not so solicitous of their welfare, and we know why.

We stand by the right to work out our own problems in our own organization and trade. . . .

Many years ago, when this lady barber question came to the attention of our organization, they were in large numbers in the Central and Eastern States. Many of those towns and cities that had lady barbers then have none now. It is a fact that a few cities in the west, Spokane, Tacoma, Seattle and Portland, have a few of them at this time. There are probably a dozen in San Francisco, but they are becoming less in number every day, and we don't believe in encouraging them to come into the profession when they do not become artists in our line. We are trying to elevate our occupation and we have made some headway, and we expect to continue that work on lines that we deem best for the interests of our trade.

Delegate Hall,[7] United Mine Workers, moved that the subject matter contained in the resolution be referred to the Committee on Laws. . . .

· · ·

Delegate Walker[8] pointed out that if this convention assumed the right to appropriate to themselves the jurisdiction of the Barbers' Union and dispose of it as they saw fit for the barbers' organization, they would have the same right to do the same thing for every other organization. He felt that the adoption of the resolution would establish a very dangerous and far-reaching precedent.

· · ·

Delegate Hall's motion to refer the matter to the Committee on Laws was defeated, and the report of the committee was adopted by a very large majority.

· · ·

AFL, *Proceedings*, 1923, pp. 303, 328–31.

1. Daniel W. Stevens (b. 1878), a member of Brotherhood of Painters, Decorators, and Paperhangers of America 186 of Minneapolis, served as secretary of the Minneapolis Trades and Labor Assembly from 1922 to 1925 and represented that body at this convention.

2. The Minneapolis Trades and Labor Assembly was organized about 1888 and chartered by the AFL in 1903. It was reorganized in 1925 as the Minneapolis Central Labor Union.

3. The Report of the Committee on State Organizations recommended that women workers should be organized immediately in trade unions in order to safeguard their interests. The report was unanimously adopted on Oct. 5, 1923.

4. Carl Edward Karston (1875–1939), representing the Atlanta Federation of Trades, was secretary of American Federation of Musicians 148 of Atlanta from 1921 to 1927.

5. John Gabriel VALENTINO represented the Georgia State Federation of Labor.

6. That is, the International Association of Machinists, which affiliated with the AFL in 1895 after dropping "white" as a qualification for membership. (See *The Samuel Gompers Papers,* vol. 4, pp. 4, 130, 213.)

7. Harry Lee Hall (b. 1877), a delegate of the United Mine Workers of America, served as president of United Mine Workers District 6 (Ohio) from 1920 to 1933.

8. John Hunter Walker represented the Illinois State Federation of Labor.

Portland, Ore., Oct. 12 [1923]

GOMPERS, AT 73, AGAIN HEADS FEDERATION; SAYS OUSTING OF REDS AIDS CAUSE OF LABOR

Samuel Gompers, re-elected unanimously at the age of 73 as President of the American Federation of Labor just before the adjournment of the forty-third annual convention today, declared in his closing address that the gathering had given notice that a cleavage had been made between those loyal to organized labor and those who, boring from within, had sought to stab the labor movement in the back.

"The results of this convention," he said, "will make for solidarity in the ranks of labor."

The convention came to an exciting close in a sharp contest for the honor of entertaining the next convention in which El Paso won over Detroit by a vote of 14,588 to 12,884.[1]

All the present officers of the Federation were re-elected.[2]

President Gompers, in reviewing the convention's work, referred to the expulsion of William F. Dunne, delegate from Butte, Mont.

"This is a convention of organized labor," he said, "and any man who is hostile to labor has no right in this convention. I feel that the action taken has clarified the atmosphere. I think we have been entirely too lenient toward those who have been boring from within.

"Those men who meet at midnight in the forest,[3] plotting not only against the Government but against the labor movement, can go ahead as they please, but they must do so outside the ranks of organized labor."

. . .

New York Times, Oct. 13, 1923.

1. The official convention proceedings give the vote for El Paso, Tex., as 14,587 and the vote for Detroit as 12,885, with 1,116 not voting (AFL, *Proceedings*, 1923, pp. 373–74). The 1924 AFL convention met in El Paso, Nov. 17–25.

2. The officers elected by the convention to serve during the following year were SG, president; James Duncan, Joseph Valentine, Frank Duffy, William Green, Thomas Rickert, Jacob Fischer, Matthew Woll, and Martin Ryan, first through eighth vice-presidents; Frank Morrison, secretary; and Daniel Tobin, treasurer.

3. A reference to the August 1922 Communist party meeting at Bridgman, Mich. See "From George Perkins," Aug. 26, 1922, n. 3, above.

Charles Whiteley[1] and
Clem Burkard[2] to Frank Morrison

Butte Mont Oct 9 1923

Frank Morrison
Secy Amn Federation Labor
Multnomah Hotel Portland
The Silverbow Trades and Labor Council having learned through the press that our delegate to the convention of the AF of L has for some reason been unseated[3] hereby protest such a high handed outrage by

an officialdom that apparently cannot stand before an enlightened criticism We selected our delegate Brother W F Dunne not on account of his political views but because of his intense loyalty and devotion to the cause of the workers of this community and the state in all our struggles against the powers that derived pleasure from the act of the convention that deprives him of a seat as delegate and would if they could destroy every organization of labor in this state They have succeeded in laying some organizations of labor prostrate but happy to relate not one in Butte owing to this sincere efforts of Dunne and others We would like to suggest that the officials of the affiliated organizations get in closer touch with the rank and file before it is too late and efforts be put forth to prevent losses in membership instead of attacking persons that have put forth the best that is in them fighting the open shoppers.

> Chas Whiteley   President,
> Clem Burkhard   Secretary

TWSr, AFL Microfilm Convention File, reel 33, frame 1041, *AFL Records.*

1. Joshua Charles Whiteley (1874–1949) was a member of International Brotherhood of Firemen and Oilers 83 of Butte, Mont.

2. Clemens Daniel Burkard (1880–1937), a Butte electrician, served from 1922 to 1925 as secretary of the Silver Bow Trades and Labor Council and as financial secretary of International Brotherhood of Electrical Workers 65 of Butte.

3. See "Dunne Defies A.F. of L. to Expel Him," Oct. 8, 1923, in "Excerpts from Accounts of the 1923 Convention of the AFL in Portland, Ore.," Oct. 8–12, 1923, above.

An Excerpt from the Minutes
of a Meeting of the Executive Council of the AFL

Saturday, October 13, 1923.

. . .

It was decided that President Gompers investigate or cause to be investigated the situation, attitude and action of the central bodies of Detroit, Mich., Tacoma, Wash., and Butte, Mont., and make report to the next meeting of the Executive Council and that this investigation include an investigation of their minute books.[1]

. . .

TDc, Executive Council Records, Minutes, reel 7, frames 1390, 1399, *AFL Records.*

1. On Dec. 13, 1923, SG instructed AFL organizers William Collins and C. O. Young

to investigate the central bodies of Detroit, Tacoma, Wash., and Butte, Mont., and prepare reports on their findings for the next meeting of the AFL Executive Council in February 1924 (reel 296, vol. 309, pp. 280–82, SG Letterbooks, DLC). Collins submitted his report on the Detroit Federation of Labor on Jan. 23 (Executive Council Records, Vote Books, reel 18, frames 304–11, *AFL Records*), and Young reported on the Tacoma Central Labor Union on Jan. 28 (ibid., frames 297–303) and on the Silver Bow Trades and Labor Council of Butte on Feb. 9 (ibid., frames 191–296). The Executive Council discussed the issue at its May meeting, when it authorized SG to present terms to the three central bodies similar to those given to the Seattle Central Labor Council the previous October (see "To Charles Doyle," Oct. 1, 1923, above). Tacoma agreed to comply on June 11 and Detroit on June 20, and the two sent formal letters of acceptance on Sept. 10 and Sept. 13, respectively. On Sept. 20 SG forwarded copies of this correspondence to the members of the Executive Council and informed them that he had instructed AFL organizer Paul Smith to go to Butte (Executive Council Records, Vote Books, reel 18, frames 336–39, *AFL Records*).

To Gertrude Gompers

Southern Pacific Lines
Tuesday [October] 16. [19]23

My Beloved Wife

On The Train about an hour's run to S.F. & just want to send you a word of greeting.

To day, two & half years ago, we were married. May I ~~note~~ my hope for our future happiness and for all time?

I am awfully tired & on account of it so nerve-strung that sleep is difficult even when I get the chance.

I hope you are well & that I will see you soon

All my love & Kisses to you dearest.

Your devoted Husband—

Sam

N.B. I telegraphed for tickets for a Duse[1] performance & expect a reply at S.F.

ALS, NNAJHi.

1. Eleonora Duse (1858–1924), a renowned Italian actress. This was her first American tour in twenty years.

From Timothy Healy

Office of Timothy Healy, International President
International Brotherhood of Firemen and Oilers
Omaha, Nebr., November 5, 1923

Dear Sir and Brother:—

I beg to call your attention to the matter of federal charters that have been issued to colored machinists helpers, boiler makers helpers and other shop laborers at Raleigh, N.C.,[1] Spencer, N.C.,[2] Columbia, S.C.,[3] Savannah, Ga.,[4] Jacksonville, Fla.,[5] and other points in the South.[6]

I protested[7] to Secretary Morrison against these men being held by the A.F. of L. as our Brotherhood has organizations at these points. We claim that the helpers in question should be transferred to our Local Unions as our's is the organization that gets conditions for these men. The A.F. of L. is in no position to legislate for them. Any conditions they get, they get them through the efforts of our Brotherhood. Since the railroad strike occurred we have a hard time to keep men in the field and since the first of January last we have struggled to keep men in the South to organize Shop Laborers that come under the jurisdiction of our Brotherhood. There has been considerable correspondence between Secretary Morrison, President Johnston[8] of the International Association of Machinists and myself on this question. I am attaching herewith copies of letters that have passed on this matter and the letter of Secretary Morrison to Mr. Eugene Threat, financial Secretary, Machinists Helpers Union No. 17456 Columbia, S.C. has really been an injustice to our Organization in the South.[9] Our Organizer tells me that this letter has been circulated to show that he had no authority or right to organize helpers.

Secretary Morrison wrote me under date of August 22nd[10] inviting me to a conference in New York City on this question but at the time I was in the hospital and could not attend. However, at the close of the Metal Trades Convention[11] in Portland, Secretary Morrison, President Johnston of the Machinists, President Franklin[12] of the Boiler Makers and myself got together and talked the situation over. Brothers Johnston and Franklin pointed out to Secretary Morrison that the men in question should really come under the jurisdiction of our Organization at least until such time as the Machinists Organization and the Boiler Makers Organization may change their Constitution to take in colored helpers. Then of course the men would be turned over to them. At this conference it was agreed that I should write you on this matter at the close of the A.F. of L. Convention, therefore this letter, and I sincerely hope that you will agree to have these charters taken up and have the men transferred to our Brotherhood. We are to make a special effort as far as our means will permit this winter to organize these helpers in the South. We have got the backing of the Shop Crafts and I feel that we will be successful. I was down South myself last winter and hope to be in a position to spend some time there this coming winter also.

Hoping for a favorable reply,[13] I am

> Fraternally Yours,　　Timothy Healy
> International President.

Copies to
Frank Morrison,
Wm. Johnson,
Jos. P. Franklin.

TLS, AFL Microfilm National and International Union File, Brotherhood of Stationary Firemen, Firemen and Oilers Records, reel 37, frames 2341–42, *AFL Records.*

1. The AFL chartered Railroad Helpers' and Laborers' Union 15,900 of Raleigh, N.C., in 1917. In 1923 it was no longer an affiliate.

2. The AFL chartered Railroad Helpers' and Laborers' Union 15,842 of Spencer, N.C., in 1917. In 1923 it was no longer an affiliate.

3. The AFL chartered Boiler Makers' Helpers' Union 17,430 and Machinists' Helpers' Union 17,456, both of Columbia, S.C., in 1920. By February 1924 AFL 17,430 had been suspended, and AFL 17,456 had twenty members.

4. The AFL chartered Mechanics' Helpers' Union 17,597 of Savannah, Ga., in 1921. In February 1924 it had twenty members.

5. The AFL chartered Boiler Makers', Pipe Fitters', and Machinists' Helpers' Union 17,603 of Jacksonville, Fla., in 1921. In February 1924 it had thirty-two members.

6. The AFL chartered Railroad Shop Helpers' Union 17,300 of Fitzgerald, Ga., and Railroad Mechanics' Helpers' Union 17,362 of Americus, Ga., in 1920 and Railroad Laborers' Union 17,535 of Tampa, Fla., in 1921. In February 1924 AFL 17,300 and AFL 17,535 each had seven members, and AFL 17,362 had eight.

7. Timothy Healy, president of the International Brotherhood of Firemen and Oilers, discussed the issue with Frank Morrison in Portland, Ore., in October 1923 during the AFL convention, and the two agreed Healy should take up the matter with SG. (See Healy to Morrison, Nov. 5, 1923, AFL Microfilm National and International Union File, Brotherhood of Stationary Firemen, Firemen and Oilers Records, reel 37, frame 2341, *AFL Records.*)

8. William Hugh JOHNSTON, president of the International Association of Machinists from 1912 to 1926.

9. Eugene Threat had written Morrison on July 16, 1923, to say that a representative of the Firemen and Oilers was claiming jurisdiction over members of his local. Morrison replied on July 23 that the machinists' helpers in directly affiliated AFL locals did not come under jurisdiction of the Firemen and Oilers, and that their conditions and wages were actually more the concern of the Machinists' union. (AFL Microfilm National and International Union File, Brotherhood of Stationary Firemen, Firemen and Oilers Records, reel 37, frame 2342, *AFL Records.*)

10. In his letter to Healy of Aug. 22, 1923, Morrison stated that the AFL issued charters to the black machinists' helpers' locals as a temporary measure, at the request of

the Machinists, until the international could charter them directly (vol. 533, pp. 930–31, Frank Morrison Letterbooks, George Meany Memorial Archives, Silver Spring, Md.).

11. The 1923 AFL Metal Trades Department convention met in Portland, Sept. 26–28.

12. Joseph Anthony FRANKLIN served as president of the International Brotherhood of Boiler Makers, Iron Ship Builders, and Helpers of America from 1908 to 1944.

13. SG took the position that he had no authority to decide the question, and he suggested Healy, Franklin, and Johnston take up the matter with the AFL Executive Council at its next meeting. The Blacksmiths, Boiler Makers, Electrical Workers, Firemen and Oilers, Machinists, Railway Carmen, and Sheet Metal Workers subsequently agreed to allocate the black railroad shop craft mechanics' helpers to Healy's union. They were scheduled to present this agreement to the Council at its February 1924 meeting but withdrew it at the last minute and did not meet with the Council. The AFL shop craft helpers' locals did not affiliate with the Firemen and Oilers.

Excerpts from the Minutes of a Meeting of the Trade Union Legislative Conference Committee

Nov. 13, 1923.

. . .

President Gompers said that under the rules the Legislative Conference met the second Friday of each month unless extra meetings were called. He continued:

"Since the adjournment of congress on the fourth of March there was no necessity of a meeting of the Committee. The question of calling a meeting on the second Friday in November was out of the question. Owing to the absence of the officers and a number of members on the Pacific Coast attending the convention of the A.F. of L. I thought it unwise to postpone the meeting until the second Friday in December. As a number of congressmen were coming into the city I thought it advisable to call a meeting for tonight. Great subjects affecting the people must be considered. I sent for members of the A.F. of L. Legislative Committee who were out of the city lecturing and organizing so that they might be prepared to begin their duties at the proper time. During my absence from Washington I have been informed that I made more than 70 speeches. I gave particular attention to child labor legislation and always found a hearty response from my audiences whether of business men, a public mass meeting or representatives of central bodies or of unions. The A.F. of L. convention went on record emphatically that there must be some constitutional amendment so that child life will be protected in our nation.[1]

"The immigration question is also of great importance. People are coming here in hordes over the quota. I just had a communication[2] from Secretary of Labor Davis regarding the paroling of 4,000 immigrants in New York, October 1.[3] However, in his letter to me he makes a strong plea for the bill he is preparing for the registration of all aliens.[4] He says the object is to find out who are in this country illegally and then deport them. He said in his letter that such a law would make deportation easier. While this may be true it will also make easier the deportation of an alien engaged in a strike. It would be easier for an employer to swear he was a menace. This would intimidate other foreigners and they would thereafter sing their songs of protest in a minor key. Registration in peace times has been the policy of all tyrannical governments. We have lived without it all these years and we do not need it now.

"Then there is great propaganda for the sales tax which would relieve the well-to-do from taxation and place the burden upon those least able to bear it. In one of our play houses last week there was shown on the screen very insidious propaganda. Mrs. Income Tax was represented as wanting a husband. She advertised in a matrimonial paper and was answered by Mr. Public. They were married. When the couple returned to the home of the bride the husband discovered that she had several children labeled excess profits tax, sur-tax, etc. Mr. Public then said: 'You didn't tell me you had any children.' Just then a beautifully gowned willowy young woman passed by and made eyes at Mr. Public, who turned from Mrs. Income Tax and started for the beautiful girl, who was labeled sales tax. The title of the picture was 'Something to think Over.'

"Compulsory labor legislation is threatened. There will be legislation affecting railway employes. Legislation to encourage the development of power and super-power. I have had conferences on the giant power subject and when opportunity affords will inform you of the outcome."[5]

Mr. Forrester[6] said that Mr. Terrence Powderly[7] of the Department of Labor had distinctive views on the immigration question and wanted to meet the Trade Union Legislative Conference Committee at one of its meetings.

On motion of Mr. Morrison, Mr. Powderly was invited to attend the next meeting and give his views on immigration.[8]

Mr. Gompers then had read the letter addressed to him by Secretary Davis to which he had referred. He pointed out the following paragraph in the letter:

"In this connection I desire to call your attention to the fact that I have for some time advocated the annual enrollment of all aliens in the United States, so that, among other things, we may discover those who entered unlawfully, who are here for unlawful purposes, and whose presence in this country is a menace to the best interests of the wage-earner as well as the destiny of the nation."

Mr. Gompers then said: "I do not question Secretary Davis' sincerity but I believe he is honestly mistaken."

Vice President Ryan[9] said he had called at the office of the Secretary and had been given the same information as that written in the letter of the Secretary to President Gompers.

President Sheppard[10] of the Order of Railroad Conductors[11] said he had also discussed the matter with Secretary Davis.

Mr. Alifas said that the Secretary had also talked with him on the subject.

Mr. Gompers—Did you call the attention of the Secretary to the fact that Chinese are registered but that it has had no effect on the deportation of those who are not registered?

Mr. Alifas said "No."

Mr. Gompers—The law requires registration of Chinese. This bill provides for *annual* registration.

Mr. Furuseth[12]—If Secretary Davis wants registration for the purpose of deporting aliens why don't he deport the Chinese who are not registered?

Mr. Morrison said the American Federation of Labor wanted greater restriction than that provided in the present law.

Mr. Furuseth—Annual registration of aliens would be a joke, for the man or woman so registered would have to take his passport to a police station yearly and have it visaed. If he left New York for New Jersey he would have to register. Such registration could be used for no other purpose than intimidation.

Mr. Forrester said that if such a law was enacted unfair employers could more easily carry on their so-called open shop movement.

. . .

On motion of Mr. Doak the following committee was appointed to find out what program the immigration committees of the house and senate would follow and also to protest against the registration clause: Edgar Wallace, W. M. Doak, Andrew Furuseth, A. J. Berres[13] and R. H. Alcorn.[14]

In answer to a question of Mr. Furuseth, Mr. Sheppard said that no definite action had been taken on railroad legislation by the representatives of the 16 railroad organizations; that it was under consideration at a meeting being held in Washington and that an agreement would probably be reached the next day. He said that no legislation was being considered that would abridge the right of railroad employes to quit work.

Mr. Forrester asked what had been done about child labor legislation.

Mr. Gompers—The A.F. of L. convention at Portland again went on record for a constitutional amendment to permit congress to legislate on the subject. November 10, I issued a circular[15] calling a meeting of the Permanent Conference for the Abolition of Child Labor to be held November 19 at 2:30 p.m. in the Executive Council Chamber, A.F. of L. Building.[16] If any members of this conference can be present they can be helpful. The conference had previously agreed on the text of the proposed amendment but whether justified or not fault has been found with it. For that reason in the circular sent out I have asked the representatives to present anything that would be helpful in preparing a satisfactory amendment. We will have the best legal talent to deal with the subject. The joint resolution presented in the senate was reported favorably but with different wording. We are definitely committed to seeking constitutional power by congress to protect child life. The meeting of the Permanent Conference will prepare a new amendment to be submitted to the coming session of congress.

Mr. Alifas said that a number of bills would be presented in congress in the interest of the Metal Trades. One of them was known as the Hull bill[17] providing that all government work should be done in the government's own plants. When that had been introduced he would ask the support of the Conference Committee of Trade Union Legislative Representatives. He said that there was danger in the organization of the House in putting reactionaries at the head of committees and mentioned Representatives Anthony,[18] Madden[19] and Longworth.[20] He said that the progressives in the house should be consulted.

Mr. Gompers said that Mr. Alifas suggestion should be followed and members of the house interviewed.

Mr. Alcorn said that it would be helpful if Representative Lampert[21] could be made chairman of the District of Columbia Committee. The obstacle was that Representative Reed[22] of West Virginia, who was the ranking member, was insisting on appointment to that position.

Mr. Furuseth—There are sixty registered progressives in Congress. Representative Nelson[23] is chairman of the Progressive Committee. The committee appointed to interview members of the house had better step softly and first consult Chairman Nelson. The house cannot be reorganized or a speaker elected without the vote of the progressives. There should be enough progressives on the Committee on Rules to make it possible for the consideration of proper legislation. Care should be taken to find out who will be chairmen of the committees on interstate commerce, judiciary, labor and merchant marine and fisheries. The Rules Committee is most important of all.

On motion of Mr. Alifas the following committee was appointed to confer with the progressive members of congress; Mr. Frank Morrison, Mr. E. L. Tucker,[24] Mr. Edward F. McGrady, Mr. N. P. Alifas, Mr. N. C. Sprague,[25] Mr. Edgar Wallace, Mr. C. E. Rosemund and Miss Gertrude McNally.

Mr. Gompers suggested that it would be well to remember why the Conference Committee of Trade Union Legislative Representatives was organized. Before that Legislative Representatives frequently bored members of congress to death. Having no organizations individual legislative representatives would all call on the same men. This became irksome to members of congress and they protested. At other times men or women would appear alone before committees and suffer the grilling from the members. One of the objects of the Conference Committee was to see that no legislative representative should appear before a committee without having a number of other legislative representatives present to support his contentions. While committees are appointed to consider certain measures all are expected to help. Whenever any member hears of anything that will be helpful he should inform the Secretary who will pass it on to all members.

. . .

At the request of Mr. Rosemund Mr. Gompers reported the outcome of conferences held on the subject of power. He told of the tremendous development of giant power. He said there had been an increase of ten to one in horse power in industry in the last ten years and in the next decade it would be a full 1,000 per cent. He continued:

"What will be the status of labor during these marvelous changes? Sometime ago I learned that a conference was to be held in London in July next[26] to consider giant power in all its phases. The conference was to be composed of representatives of technical, financial and power associations. Labor would not have a seat at the table. I therefore got in touch with Chairman Miller[27] of the American Association for the Development of Super or Giant Power. I insisted that Labor should be represented. Mr. Miller said he would take it up with the Executive Committee. Later he told me that the Executive Committee had declined to include Labor in the organizations represented but said it was willing that Labor should be represented on the Executive Committee. A protest was made against this and Mr. Miller said another conference would be held in New York, November 14, and the matter again considered. Mr. Miller was informed that if Labor was not made a part of the organization he represented that it might join some other movement that would come into rivalry with it. This wonderful growth of power and its revolutionizing influence in industry is amazing."[28]

. . .

TDc, Files of the Office of the President, Conferences, reel 123, frames 155–61, *AFL Records*. Typed notation: "Minutes of Meeting of Conference Committee of Trade Union Legislative Representatives Held in the Executive Council Chamber, A.F. of L. Building, Tuesday, Nov. 13, 1923. at 8 P.M."

1. For the action on the child labor amendment by the 1923 AFL convention, see AFL, *Proceedings*, 1923, p. 244.

2. James Davis to SG, Nov. 9, 1923, reel 295, vol. 308, pp. 463–64, SG Letterbooks, DLC.

3. Davis approved the temporary admission "on parole" of some four thousand immigrants who were stranded on shipboard in New York harbor, pending assessment of whether their countries of origin had exhausted their quotas for the year.

4. Davis outlined his proposals for overhauling the laws dealing with aliens in the *Eleventh Annual Report of the Secretary of Labor*, released in late 1923, and in that document reiterated his call for the annual registration of unnaturalized immigrants and the prompt Americanization of those who could be naturalized. On Jan. 1, 1924, he sent a draft bill embodying his ideas to the Immigration Committees of the House and Senate, and on Jan. 29 Republican senator James Watson of Indiana introduced S. 2365 (68th Cong., 1st sess.), based on Davis's proposals. The bill died in committee.

5. SG met on Nov. 9, 1923, with Morris Cooke, director of the Pennsylvania Giant Power Survey, and on Nov. 12 with Oscar Merrill, executive secretary of the Federal Power Commission and general chairman of the American Committee, World Power Conference. For minutes of the meetings, see Files of the Office of the President, Conferences, reel 123, frames 143–46, *AFL Records*.

6. James Joseph FORRESTER, national legislative counsel of the Brotherhood of Railway and Steamship Clerks, Freight Handlers, Express and Station Employes from 1922 to 1925.

7. Terence Vincent POWDERLY, head of the KOL from 1879 to 1893, served as chief of the Division of Information in the Bureau of Immigration and Naturalization from 1907 until his death in 1924.

8. Powderly spoke on immigration at the Dec. 14, 1923, meeting of the Trade Union Legislative Conference Committee.

9. Martin Francis Ryan.

10. Lucius Elmer SHEPPARD served as president of the Order of Railway Conductors of America from 1919 to 1928.

11. The Order of RAILWAY Conductors of America.

12. Andrew FURUSETH, secretary of the Sailors' Union of the Pacific (1891–92, 1892–1936), president of the International Seamen's Union of America (1897–99, 1908–38), and legislative representative in Washington, D.C., for the Seamen.

13. Albert Julius BERRES, secretary-treasurer of the AFL Metal Trades Department from 1908 to 1927.

14. Robert H. Alcorn (1872?-1957), a member of International Molders' Union of North America 215 of Washington, D.C., was chairman of the Joint Conference Committee on Retirement for Civil Service (1919–44).

15. Reel 295, vol. 308, p. 29, SG Letterbooks, DLC.

16. The conference met Nov. 19–20, 1923. For minutes of the second day's session, see Files of the Office of the President, Conferences, reel 123, frames 185–89, *AFL Records*.

17. H.R. 2702 (68th Cong., 1st sess.), introduced on Dec. 6, 1923, by Republican congressman Harry Hull of Iowa, and S. 742 (ibid.), introduced on Dec. 10 by Republican senator Smith Brookhart of Iowa, called for the federal government to manufacture

all its munitions and as many non-military articles as possible in government-owned plants. Both bills died in committee.

18. Daniel Read Anthony, Jr. (1870–1931), served as a Republican congressman from Kansas from 1907 to 1929.

19. Martin Barnaby Madden (1855–1928) served as a Republican congressman from Illinois from 1905 until his death in 1928.

20. Nicholas Longworth (1869–1931) served as a Republican congressman from Ohio from 1903 to 1913 and again from 1915 until his death in 1931. He served as Speaker of the House from 1925 to 1931.

21. Florian Lampert (1863–1930) served as a Republican congressman from Wisconsin from 1918 until his death in 1930.

22. Stuart Felix Reed (1866–1935) served as a Republican congressman from West Virginia from 1917 to 1925.

23. John Mandt Nelson (1870–1955) served as a Republican congressman from Wisconsin from 1906 to 1919 and from 1921 to 1933. In 1924 he managed the Progressive campaign of Robert La Follette and Burton Wheeler.

24. Edward L. Tucker (1865–1943) was a member of International Association of Machinists 174 of Washington, D.C. He had served as president of the Washington Central Labor Union and as a member of the executive board of the international union.

25. Norman C. Sprague (1851–1944), a foreman at the Government Printing Office, was a member of International Printing Pressmen's and Assistants' Union of North America 1 of Washington, D.C.

26. The World Power Conference, attended by representatives from thirty-one nations, was held in London, June 30-July 12, 1924.

27. Actually Oscar Charles Merrill (1874–1951), the executive secretary of the Federal Power Commission from 1920 to 1929 (see also n. 5, above).

28. James Noonan, president of the International Brotherhood of Electrical Workers, represented American organized labor at the World Power Conference.

To William Johnston

November 14, 1923.

Mr. Wm. H. Johnston,
President, International Association of Machinists,
I.A. of M. Bldg., Washington, D.C.
Dear Sir and Brother:

This morning I received a letter from Frank Burch,[1] Secretary of the Central Labor Union of Philadelphia, in which he states:

"At a regular stated meeting of this Body, held Sunday November 11th, the undersigned was by motion instructed to convey to the American Federation of Labor, the following action:—

["]'That we request the American Federation of Labor to prevail on the International Association of Machinists that they request Mr.

Clinton S. Golden[2] of Philadelphia, a member of the International Association of Machinists, (formerly a Business Agent for the District Council of Machinists, now a General Organizer of the Amalgamated Clothing Workers of America)[3] to surrender his membership in the International Association of Machinists, or if Mr. Golden intends to continue as a member of the International Association of Machinists that he be directed by said International Association of Machinists to resign his position as General Organizer of the Amalgamated Clothing Workers of America.'

"In the debate on the motion it was pointed out that Mr. Golden's position is an untenable one, being a member of the American Federation of Labor through his affiliation with the International Association of Machinists, and acting in an official capacity for a seceding Organization, like the Amalgamated Clothing Workers of America.

"A number of serious allegations were made against Mr. Golden, and if they are true, he must be aligned with the groups of men against whom you directed your famous pronouncement in your closing address at the American Federation of Labor Convention at Portland, Oregon."[4]

I am bringing the above matter to your attention in compliance with the request of the Central Labor Union and I will appreciate your advice in regard to this so that I may be in a position to advise Secretary Burch what disposition you have made.

With kind regards and hoping to hear from you at your convenience, I am

> Fraternally yours,   Saml Gompers.
> President,   American Federation of Labor.

TLpS, reel 295, vol. 308, pp. 84–85, SG Letterbooks, DLC.

1. Frank Burch (1867–1946) served as secretary of the Philadelphia Central Labor Union from 1919 to 1944 and as secretary of United Hatters of North America 18 of Philadelphia from 1923 to 1937.

2. Clinton Strong Golden (1888–1961) joined the International Association of Machinists in 1917 and from 1920 until the summer of 1923 was business representative for Machinists' District 1 (Philadelphia). He began serving in 1923 as an organizer for the Amalgamated Clothing Workers of America but resigned in 1924 to take a position as field representative for the Brookwood Labor College. He was later a mediator for the Pennsylvania Department of Labor and Industry (1934), regional director for the National Labor Relations Board (1935), and director of the Steel Workers' Organizing Committee (1936) and from 1942 to 1946 was vice-president of the United Steelworkers of America. From 1952 to 1959 he was executive director of Harvard University's Trade Union program.

3. The Amalgamated CLOTHING Workers of America.

4. See "Gompers, at 73, Again Heads Federation; Says Ousting of Reds Aids Cause

of Labor," Oct. 12, 1923, in "Excerpts from Accounts of the 1923 Convention of the AFL in Portland, Ore.," Oct. 8–12, 1923, above. See also AFL, *Proceedings*, 1923, pp. 374–76.

To the Executive Council of the AFL

Washington, D.C., November 15, 1923

Document No. 121.

To the Executive Council American Federation of Labor.

Colleagues:

This is the birthday of the American Federation of Labor and I want to share my feeling of joy and gratification with my colleagues who are jointly with me responsible for shaping the policies and the destiny of our Federation.

Forty-three years ago we met in Turner Hall, Pittsburg to form a national organization of trade unions.[1] Although for years I had been working to bring about such a movement never in my wildest dreams did I foresee the splendid virile organization that has developed. It is beyond my power of words to describe how deeply the Federation is embedded in my heart. In the days of its infancy, my hopes, thoughts and ambitions centered in plans for the Federation. It was my child over which I yearned and worked, and laid awake at night to think of some plan for its growth. But the days of childhood are passed and now that the Federation is approaching the half-century mark, it is even more imperative that those of us entrusted with responsibility for directing the course of the Federation appreciate fully the tremendous possibilities of the future if we steer our course with wisdom. I am looking forward to our coming meeting[2] in eager anticipation of the important work before us with the hope that before the Federation shall have passed its first century of service changes shall have come in the life and work of industrial workers which we can only dimly foresee. It is given to us to build for future generations.

Enclosed is a statement[3] given to the papers today which will be of interest to you.

Fraternally yours, Saml Gompers.
President, American Federation of Labor.

TLcS, Executive Council Records, Vote Books, reel 18, frame 96, *AFL Records*.

1. See "A Series of News Accounts of the Founding Convention of the FOTLU in Pittsburgh," Nov. 15–19, 1881, *The Samuel Gompers Papers*, vol. 1, pp. 210–32.

2. The AFL Executive Council met Feb. 11–16, 1924, in Washington, D.C.

3. That is, SG's statement on the anniversary, contained in an AFL press release dated Nov. 15, 1923. See Executive Council Records, Vote Books, reel 18, frames 97–98, *AFL Records.*

To Frank Duffy

Nov. 16, 1923.

Mr. Frank Duffy,
Secretary, United Brotherhood of Carpenters & Joiners,
Carpenters' Bldg., 222 E. Michigan Street, Indianapolis,
    Indiana.
Dear Sir and Brother:

Your letter of November 13 enclosing clippings received and I thank you for them.

From information I have received the Ku Klux Klan issue is creating havoc in the trade unions in some parts of Indiana. It is a movement based on bigotry and cannot live. At the same time it may require a long period of time to wipe it out entirely. It is a renewal of the know-nothing and A.P.A.[1] organizations. The Ku Klux Klan will run its course but as certain as fate it will die like the know-nothing and A.P.A. organizations.

The firm attitude taken by the A.F. of L. convention[2] will hasten its death. However, it should be opposed at every turn.

Again thanking you for the clippings, I am

Fraternally yours,   Saml Gompers
President,   American Federation of Labor.

TLpS, reel 295, vol. 308, p. 188, SG Letterbooks, DLC.

1. The American Protective Association. See *The Samuel Gompers Papers,* vol. 3, p. 660, n. 30.

2. The AFL Executive Council's report to the 1923 AFL convention reiterated the 1922 convention's condemnation of the Ku Klux Klan (see "Aimed at Ku Klux Klan," June 20, 1922, in "Excerpts from News Accounts of the 1922 Convention of the AFL in Cincinnati," June 16–24, 1922, above). The convention endorsed the Council's report, as well as a denunciation of the Klan by the Committee on Resolutions, and it voted to have this portion of the *Proceedings* printed as a pamphlet for wide distribution. See *Declaration on the Ku Klux Klan Adopted by the Portland Convention of the A.F. of L.* (Washington, D.C., [1923]).

From Frank Kasten[1]

United Brick and Clay Workers of America[2]
Chicago, Ill., Nov. 16, 1923

Dear Sir and Brother:

When I was at Washington in September, we discussed the progress made by the workers organized under the banner of the American Federation of Labor. At that time I made certain statements in regard to the progress of the Brick and Clay Workers of Chicago. I thought that perhaps you would like an accurate statement of our progress, say since about 1914. Also a statement of what a few of our individual locals, surrounded by non-union clay factories, have accomplished.

In the spring of 1914, after a nineteen weeks' strike[3] in the Chicago District, we signed a compromise agreement as follows:

Common labor 34 cents an hour

Semi skilled labor 37 1/2 to 38 1/2 cents per hour

Skilled labor—day work 41 to 52 1/2 cents per hour

Piece work rates that would net our members about $6.00 per day.

After the signing of this agreement, we decided to pursue another course. Holding the right to strike, we decided to cooperate with the employers, if they in turn, would do the same with us. We arranged a conference and the employers agreed to go along.

The first step was the formation of the "Chicago Brick Exchange Insurance Department." We found the manufacturers paid exorbitant rates for liability insurance, and on the other hand, we had to fight for a just settlement of a claim. The Insurance Companies would always go the limit. Now if one of our members is injured our Business Agent meets the representative of the "Exchange," the agreement is searched for his earnings per hour, and the compensation is awarded according to the wording of the law without cost to our members. We selected the Doctor who makes final decisions for the "Exchange" by mutual agreement. After a few years of successful operation, the "Exchange" decided to employ an expert for the purpose of visiting all yards, make thorough inspections and then make recommendations. We felt that this department would help in the prevention of injury to our members.

The "expert" employed is one of our members, an engineer, who had reached that stage that so many of us may reach, ready to retire, because of ill health caused by too close an application to his work. Being a member of the Union and a capable man, we feel that he will be the means of safeguarding the lives and limbs of many of our members.

Later, we secured the so called "Check-off" so that we could discipline our members when necessary.

During the war period, we too reached a certain peak wage scale. The Manufacturers established a peak price for the finished product, and in the spring of 1921, the manufacturers reduced their price 25%. However, even though the manufacturer reduced his price 25% in the spring and our wage agreement expired May 1st, we maintained our peak to November 1st, when we accepted a 12 1/2% reduction. We signed up until May 1st, 1923 and when that day arrived, we succeeded in convincing the Chicago Brick Manufacturers that we were entitled to the reduction we accepted 18 months before. They agreed and we now once more enjoy the peak prices of a few years ago. The manufacturers, however, did not increase the price of the finished product and I think that because we have had practically no labor turnover and no strikes—wild cat—and good efficient service is the reason. We have not had a strike in Chicago since 1914.

Our wage scale now is as follows:

About four men on every plant, commonly called pensioners are paid 76¢ per hour.

The common labor scale is 80¢ per hour.

The semi-skilled 90 to 95¢ per hour and the skilled $1.05 per hour.

Those operating machines are allowed from 1 to 2 hours, according to the type of machine, per 8 hour day for oiling, and paid rate and one half for all work performed before or after regular hours. Piece workers $9.00 to $14.00 per day.

About 70% of our family men own or are paying for their homes.

About 60% of them own an automobile of some kind.

We negotiate a wage scale for twelve manufacturers and 16 Local Unions, and I believe that the above is convincing proof that the labor movement as organized by the American Federation of Labor is not a failure.

I might mention that at St. Louis, Mo., and in the Hudson River District that clayworkers far out number the Chicago brick makers, but they are not unionized and the wage scale is about one half that paid in Chicago. Some difference.

At Brazil, Ind., we have one plant organized, eight plants are not organized. Our members enjoy the eight hour day, a very good wage scale, a minimum of 50 cents an hour for common labor and rangeing from that on up to about 75 cents an hour. I was informed that 37 of our members out of 122 owned an auto; so you see we have a few luxuries.

The employees of the other eight plants are paid from 30 cents an hour up and work from 9 to 10 hours a day, and have no voice in the manner in which plants shall be operated. The same is true at Danville, Ill., where we have some 400 men employed. These men working as union men enjoy a real daily wage, have a voice in deciding how work shall be done and practically all of the family men own or are paying for their homes. This has been accomplished in spite of the fact that immediately across the State line are located about twelve factories within a radius of fifty miles, that we have been unable to organize and the wage scale ranges as low as 25 cents an hour. However, two of these companies have had their own troubles, one at Brazil and the other at Crawfordsville are in the hands of a receiver.

I think that we have made the most progress in the State of Ohio where we have about six locals. These locals were organized a few years ago and we managed to secure agreements including the "check-off." However, the agreements were not uniform, the 9 hour day prevailed. Last spring we met the manufacturers in a body and we secured the 8 hour day, wages same as paid for 9 hours and a uniform agreement. The minimum scale for 8 hours is $4.05, piece work in proportion. Surely a remarkable achievement for about 600 men surrounded by thousands of unorganized clayworkers working 10 to 12 hours a day for from 25 cents an hour up, and a highly organized group of employers spending thousands of dollars to prevent us from organizing the non-union plants.

Now, Sam, I have just touched a few spots, but what I have written is true and convinces me that the labor unions as guided by the American Federation of Labor, through you and your cabinet, are an honor and a credit to a great nation, and instead of a failure are a pronounced success.

I will compile a list of names of the several men employed in the several departments and ascertain their earnings for the year 1923 and shall forward that to you immediately after the first of the year.

With kind personal regards, I remain,

Fraternally yours,   Frank Kasten
General President.

TLS, AFL Microfilm National and International Union File, Brick and Clay Workers Records, reel 35, frame 1660, *AFL Records.*

1. Frank Morris KASTEN served as president of the United Brick and Clay Workers of America from 1916 until his death in 1946.

2. The United BRICK and Clay Workers of America.

3. On Mar. 9, 1914, some three thousand members of the Brick and Clay Workers in Chicago struck when employers rejected the union's demand for a pay increase. Because local teamsters' unions honored the strike and refused even to deliver bricks made before the strike began, the city's construction industry was also shut down. The

Chicago Building Trades Council tried to mediate a settlement based on an employer offer to raise wages a penny an hour for the lowest-paid workers, but strikers rejected the proposal when employers refused to grant them a voice in hiring and firing decisions. After employers announced they would resume work on an open-shop basis, however, the strikers voted on June 3 to accept the wage offer and went back to work the next day.

To the Executive Council of the AFL

Washington, D.C., November 19, 1923.

Document No. 128.
To the Executive Council, American Federation of Labor.
Colleagues:

I desire to bring to your attention a number of matters of particular interest and importance regarding the international relations of the American Federation of Labor on this continent.

In order that you may have sufficient information upon which to base judgment it will be necessary to furnish you a statement in considerable detail.

Before leaving Washington to attend the Portland convention I determined to return to Washington by way of California. This made it possible to stop at El Paso, Texas, also. It seemed advisable to have an interchange of opinion with representatives of the Mexican Federation of Labor and accordingly I invited[1] the Executive Council of the Mexican Federation of Labor to send representatives to El Paso for a meeting on October 25.[2] The Mexican Federation of Labor responded promptly, accepting the invitation. Three of the most capable and creditable representatives of the Mexican Federation of Labor Executive Council came to El Paso to participate in the conferences there.[3]

There were with me the members of the Executive Committee of the Pan-American Federation of Labor;[4] Mr. Santiago Iglesias, president of the Free Federation of Workers at Porto Rico and an organizer for the American Federation of Labor; and Mr. W. C. Roberts. Mr. J. W. Kelley,[5] an organizer for the American Federation of Labor who has spent many years in Mexico and who has an intimate knowledge of conditions in Mexico, was in El Paso during the conferences and, though not a participant, he gave us much valuable information as a result of his observation and experience.

I am attaching hereto for your information a summary of the proceedings[6] of the conferences which continued through three days. I believe you will find the proceedings of the conferences illuminating and interesting.

You will recall that during the convention at Portland Mr. J. W. Brown, one of the secretaries of the International Federation of Trade Unions, was present and upon invitation addressed the convention. Mr. Brown in his address did not inform the convention as to his entire purpose in being on this continent nor, so far as I am aware, did he make his full purpose known in any other manner at that time to the officers of the American Federation of Labor. After his address and prior to our adjournment, however, Mr. Brown proceeded to Mexico City.[7]

You will note in the proceedings of the El Paso conferences that a letter was brought from Mexico City addressed to me and signed by Mr. Brown. A copy of the letter is made a part of the proceedings of the conferences.[8]

We were informed during the conferences that a number of European labor officials are to be in Mexico in January.[9] These officials were invited to visit Mexico by the representatives of the Mexican Federation of Labor. They were invited to come to Mexico purely for purposes of observation and not for purposes of conference or for the reaching of any formal decisions or agreements while in Mexico.

The representatives of the Mexican Federation of Labor assured us in El Paso that it was their intention merely to entertain the European visitors as guests of the Mexican trade union movement and that they had no intention when issuing the invitations of holding any conferences or of arriving at any agreements with representatives of organizations to which the American Federation of Labor is not affiliated.

Among those from Europe who are expected to be in Mexico during January are representatives of the International Federation of Trade Unions, a representative from France, a representative from England, a representative from Spain and possibly representatives from Italy and one or two other countries.

It seems obvious that any occasion upon which so many representatives of European labor gather on the American continent must have a most unusual importance, regardless of whatever may be said or whatever may be intended to the contrary. It is not an everyday matter for a half dozen of the most important and busy officials of the European labor movement to gather on the American continent.

The position of the American Federation of Labor in relation to the labor movements of Europe and in relation to the International Federation of Trade Unions is clear and is well known in Europe.

Strong appeals have been made to the Mexican Federation of Labor and to other Latin-American labor movements to affiliate to the International Federation of Trade Unions and it is more than possible that such invitations may be renewed upon the occasion of such a gathering as that to be held in Mexico in January.

Representatives of the Mexican Federation of Labor assured us in El Paso that the Mexican Federation of Labor will enter into no agreement to affiliate with any European organization unless such affiliation meets with the approval of the American Federation of Labor.

I have every confidence in the intelligence, the understanding and the intentions of the Mexican Federation of Labor. Because of that and because of our own interest in the matter it seems to me extremely advisable that there should be in Mexico at the time of the visit of the European representatives a delegation representing the American Federation of Labor. Such a delegation would be able to advise with and furnish information to representatives of the Mexican Federation of Labor, with which we have affiliation through the Pan-American Federation of Labor. Such a delegation also would be able to keep at all times in the foreground the democratic, constructive viewpoint of the American Federation of Labor. This should be done even though no formal conferences are held.

I am sure that many other reasons will occur to you as they do to me for having capable representation in Mexico City while the European representatives are there. I believe that such representation can be had in Mexico City at a cost not to exceed five hundred dollars. I regard it as of paramount importance that we should be so represented.

I suggest that a delegation consisting of Santiago Iglesias, J. W. Kelley and C. N. Idar be instructed to proceed to Mexico City in January and to remain there during the period of the visit of the European representatives.

Mr. Iglesias has a thorough understanding of the viewpoint of the American Federation of Labor and an unusual ability in the presentation of that viewpoint through the medium of the Spanish language. He is also intimately familiar with the entire Latin-American situation and what is perhaps more important he is familiar with certain European movements having for their object the alienation of Spanish-American friendship from the United States, in order that there may be once more a Spanish domination of Latin-American thought and friendship.

Mr. Kelley has spent many years in Mexico, speaks the Spanish language fluently, has many close friendships in Mexico, understands the relations between Mexico and the United States both as to the labor movements of the two countries and otherwise, and at present is a volunteer organizer for the American Federation of Labor. Mr. Kelley at the present time is in Texas.

Mr. Idar, who also is in Texas, is an organizer for the American Federation of Labor, possessed of unusual ability and understanding and is of Mexican descent himself.

Each of the three men whom I have suggested has a command of both the English and Spanish languages, which is a matter of much more importance on a question like this than it would be if formal conferences were to be held. Where formal conferences are held it is possible to have translation of everything that transpires. The situation is different, however, where the mission is one purely of observation and personal interviews.

I have endeavored to set forth as fully as possible the facts in connection with the situation, though of course it would not be possible within the limits of any letter to set forth in detail everything that might be said and perhaps should be said in connection with a question so involved and so important. I trust, however, that I have been able to give you sufficiently detailed information to enable you to reach a decision.

May I urge that you apprise me as soon as conveniently possible of your views in this matter and may I hope to have your agreement in the suggestion that we send a delegation to represent us in Mexico during the extremely critical period to which I have called attention?[10]

> Fraternally yours, Saml Gompers.
> President, American Federation of Labor.

TLcS, Executive Council Records, Vote Books, reel 18, frames 123–25, *AFL Records*.

1. SG to Eduardo Moneda, Sept. 20, 1923, reel 294, vol. 307, pp. 41–42 (English text), 43–44 (Spanish translation), SG Letterbooks, DLC.

2. The meeting was held at El Paso, Tex., Oct. 25–27, 1923.

3. The representatives of the Confederación Regional Obrera Mexicana (Mexican Confederation of Labor) were Samuel O. Yúdico, Reynaldo Cervantes Torres, and Fernando Rodarte. Roberto Haberman served as their interpreter.

4. The Pan-American Federation of Labor representatives in addition to SG were Chester Wright and Canuto Vargas.

5. José W. Kelly (b. 1887?) was an organizer in Mexico for the International Association of Machinists. He attended the 1924 AFL convention as a fraternal delegate from the Confederación Regional Obrera Mexicana, and in the later 1920s he worked as an organizer among Mexican immigrants in the United States. Expelled from the Confederación in 1929, he apparently then served for several years as a labor agent in the United States for the Mexican government. Around 1929 he married Josephine Casey (b. 1878?), formerly organizer for the International Ladies' Garment Workers' Union, who was active in the National Woman's party.

6. Executive Council Records, Vote Books, reel 18, frames 125–31, *AFL Records*.

7. John William Brown (b. 1886) was a founder and vice-president of the National Federation of Professional, Technical, Administrative, and Supervisory Workers in Great Britain, head of the educational department of the International Federation of Trade Unions (IFTU), and a member of the executive committee of the British Institute of Adult Education. From 1924 to 1927 he served as the IFTU's English-language secretary. Brown's announced purpose for making the trip was to study educational aspects of the labor movement in the United States and Canada.

8. Brown to SG, Oct. 18, 1923, Executive Council Records, Vote Books, reel 18, frame 128, *AFL Records.* Brown inquired if SG and the AFL Executive Council could meet the party of European trade union leaders in Mexico City. SG replied on Nov. 7, inviting the European trade unionists to stop in Washington, D.C., in February 1924, on their return trip from Mexico, to meet with the Executive Council at that time (reel 294, vol. 307, pp. 892–93, SG Letterbooks, DLC). No further correspondence on the matter is to be found.

9. For discussion of this matter at the meeting, see the conference minutes, Executive Council Records, Vote Books, reel 18, frames 128–29, *AFL Records.* The Mexican delegates told SG that Luis Morones had invited European labor officials to visit Mexico while he was making a tour of various European countries, in hopes of broadening their understanding of American labor affairs.

10. The AFL Executive Council voted in favor of the proposal.

From Fannia Cohn

November 20, 1923

My dear President Gompers:

I wish at the outset to call your attention to the fact that this communication is not official. I am not presenting my arguments as an officer who speaks for her organization, but this is an appeal from a woman trade unionist to the head of the American labor movement.

I am impelled to write you after reading that part of the report of the Executive Council of the A.F. of L. to the Portland Convention dealing with working women.[1] I have been thinking about it for a long time—that not enough is done by the American labor movement to organize working women in this country. Whereas the A.F. of L. and its affiliated unions are carrying on their struggles for organization amongst working men on a strictly class basis, they are not following out the same when it comes to the organization of women. When the deplorable conditions of working women are to be considered, a conference is then called by many organizations, amongst them the Salvation Army, the Y.W.C.A., The Women's Temperance League. And they are the ones to decide "how to improve the conditions of the working woman."

By this time we all realize that women have come into industry for good; and this, whether it was done by choice or by necessity, points to the fact that women will more and more become a factor in our industrial society.

And what we need is organization amongst them. I realize the difficulties that we have to overcome in organizing working women into trade unions. But this should tend only to increase our efforts in this field. Many of us think that now is the time when we should begin to make an extensive study of the conditions of women engaged in the different industries, of women as trade unionists, the contribution they made to the labor movement and of conditions of women engaged in the various industries who are outside of the trade unions. It should not only be an economic and industrial study, but also a psychological one that will throw light on women's character and that will help us to employ the necessary means of reaching them.

It seems to me that it is the duty of the A.F. of L. to initiate such a study.[2] I do not intend to give you advice how this should be done. You may find it advisable to have a committee appointed or a conference of international unions which have women in their industries called.[3]

I, as a woman who has devoted her life to the labor movement, am eager that this be done by the trade union movement, instead of leaving it to other organizations that have different purposes in view. Therefore my appreciation of that part of the report of the Executive Council that deals with this question.

I took the liberty of writing you about this matter, because I am convinced that you, too, are interested in solving this problem,—the organization of women into trade unions.

With best wishes.

Fraternally yours,   Fannia M. Cohn.

TLS, AFL Microfilm Convention File, reel 33, frames 1164–65, *AFL Records.*

1. The Executive Council's report to the 1923 AFL convention recommended that the Federation give special emphasis to organizing women workers during the upcoming year and suggested that representatives of all affiliates directly involved meet in conference to plan and launch an organizing campaign for women (AFL, *Proceedings,* 1923, pp. 55, 76). The convention unanimously endorsed the proposal.

2. See "A Circular," Dec. 4, 1923, below.

3. SG invited representatives from unions in industries employing women to meet with him in Washington, D.C., on Feb. 14, 1924, to consider the problem and draw up a plan of action. What he hoped to create, SG said, was "a continuous permanent institution, for the organization of women wage earners," similar to the women's departments in the TUC and the German Federation of Trade Unions (Executive Council Records, Minutes, reel 7, frames 1422–23, 1427–29, *AFL Records;* quotation at frame 1422). Further meetings were held on Mar. 9 (see "An Excerpt from the Minutes of a Meeting on Organizing Women in Industry," Mar. 9, 1924, below), Apr. 12 (see Files of the Office of the President, Conferences, reel 123, frames 639–42, *AFL Records*),

and May 21 (see "Excerpts from the Minutes of a Meeting on Organizing Women in Industry," May 21, 1924, below). The effort stalled, however, when few unions proved willing to make financial contributions to the campaign and a number of them objected to naming a woman as executive secretary or to creating a women's department in the AFL. In August SG told the Executive Council the effort was at a standstill, and the Council concluded—in SG's absence—that the campaign was simply not feasible. The 1924 AFL convention endorsed the Council's decision to suspend the effort.

From Spurgeon Meadows[1]

Nov. 20 1923.

Dear Sir and Brother:—

I have been instructed to communicate to you certain facts concerning the Central Labor Union of this City so that you may be informed as to conditions existing in the labor situation and as a result thereof use your best efforts toward a solution of the difficulty.

One may as well be plain in stating these facts and begin by saying that the Ku Klux Klan have been very active in this City and that most of the Labor Organizations are honey combed with them.

In some of the Unions the Klan have been successful in electing to office the entire ticket from President down, this has been possible because of the fact that the membership did not know or believe that an "invisible government" was working in their midst.

As a result of the activities of the Klan many of the delegates of the Central Labor Union believed it advisable to force the issue and bring the fight out in the open so that they might know just what the situation realy was.

On July 9th—1923, the following resolution was introduced in the Central Labor Union.

Whereas:—the administration of the civil, State and Federal laws are vested soley in the duly elected and appointed officers and that those who are members of any seceret organizations assume to usurp the powers and functions properly belonging to legally constituted authorities, invite mob rule and create in the minds of our citizens disrespect and disregard for present laws, and

Whereas; it is not conducive to good government by law and the maintainance of peaceful and safe conditions in the community to have members of any organization to prade the streets so disguised that their idenitity can not be discovered, when such disguises are adopted for the purpose of inspiring the thought or belief that the disguised individual represents an invisible government,

Therefore be it Resolved; that the Indianapolis Central Labor Union do hereby condem that un-American and un-constitutional organization known as the Ku Klux Klan, as detrimental to organized labor.

President Kern ruled that the resolution had no place in the Central Body but on appeal he was over ruled and the resolution was referred to the Legislative Committee who recommended concurrence.
After some discussion the recommendation of the Committee was adopted. Immediately friends of the Klan got busy in an effort to have the resolution reconsidered at the next meeting of the Central body.

At the same time those who are opposed to the Klan got busy also so that there was a very large attendance at the next meeting of the Central Body.

At the meeting July 25th, the following resolution was introduced.

Whereas;—the daily presss have published accounts the past week of riots and lawlessness in our City in connection with the unlawful burning of firey crosses and when our City firemen and police attempted to put out these fires they were met with showers of rocks, and threats of bodily harm, and

Whereas; the organization of people responisble for these lawless demonstrations is in disrepute with all good law abiding American citizens, for their outlawery, therefore be it

Resolved; the Indianapolis Central Labor Union do hereby go on record as commending the action of Chief of Police Herman Rikoff[2] and other Public Official in their endeavor to forever end such displays as aforementioned and to keep our City free from such disgraces, be it fur ther resolved that a copy of these resolutions be sent to Mr Rikoff and the daily press of Indianapolis.

The resolution was reported favorably by the committee and put to a standing vote and carried. The Kluxers and their friends saw that they were defeated in geting control of the Central Body and scores of delegates immediate left the hall.

Then another campaign of activity was started by the friends of the Klan, this time in Local Unions affiliated with the C.L.U, with the result that Carpenters Local Union No 75 withdrew its affiliation. Painters No. 47, Typographical No. 1. Electrical Workers, No. 481. Garment Workers, No. 127. Letters Carriers No. 39, Electrotypers No. 30, Sheet Metal Workers,[3] and Hoisting Engineers[4] have withdrew their affiliation.

The Hod-Carriers and Building Laborers Local Union[5] had affiliated with the Central Body in July and voted in favor of the above mentioned resolutions. Later is seems that a movement of intimidation was started against members of the Building Laborers with the result that they have withdrawn from the C.L.u. This intimidation was started by an organization affiliated with the American Federation of Labor.

Members of the Labor movement in this City who believe more in Trade Unionism than they do in Klanism have instructed me to communicate these facts to you, and they are of the firm belief that an investigation of the labor situation in this City should be made by a representative of the A.F. OF. L so that you would have all the facts and both sides of the story.

All the activities of A. J. Allen,[6] Secretary of the Associated Employers against union labor has not done half the harm as has the activities of the Klan and its friends; all A. J. Allen need do now is sit back and laugh others are doing the work for him.

We respectfully request President Gompers, that you send a representative here at your earliest convenience.[7]

With best wishes,

> Fraternally yours,   S P Meadows
> Secretary.

TLS, United Brotherhood of Carpenters and Joiners of America Records, reel 1, frames 682–83, *AFL and the Unions.*

1. Spurgeon P. Meadows (b. 1870), an Indianapolis carpenter, served as secretary of the Indianapolis Central Labor Union in 1923 and 1924.

2. Herman Frederick Rikhoff (b. 1872).

3. Amalgamated Sheet Metal Workers' International Alliance 41.

4. International Union of Steam and Operating Engineers (Hoisting Engineers) 103.

5. International Hod Carriers', Building and Common Laborers' Union of America 120.

6. Andrew Jackson Allen (b. 1879) was executive secretary, business manager, and chief accountant of the Associated Employers of Indianapolis.

7. SG did not respond to this letter. When Meadows reiterated his request on Feb. 16, 1924, SG replied that the trade unionists in Indianapolis were simply "frittering away their time with the Ku Klux Klan and other incidents which tend to divide the workers, weaken their forces, destroy the morale and render them helpless to protect their rights and interests both as wage earners and citizens" and that the AFL could not "be of any material assistance" (SG to Meadows, Mar. 3, 1924, reel 297, vol. 311, p. 215, SG Letterbooks, DLC).

R. Lee Guard to John Macrae

Washington, D.C. November 21, 1923.

Mr. John Macrae,
E. P. Dutton & Company,
631 Fifth Avenue, New York, N.Y.
Dear Mr. Mcrae:

Your letter of the 19th instant received this morning together with enclosure. A few weeks before we left for the Pacific Coast, Mr. Gompers started a series of six articles for the Wheeler Syndicate. There are two more articles to follow the one enclosed. Last year, as you doubtless recall, also President Gompers also wrote a series of six articles for the Wheeler Syndicate.

Miss Thorne[1] is looking forward to seeing you in New York the latter part of the week. I am sorry that I, too, am not going over. She will tell you how near the manuscript is to completion ready to be placed in your hands. The great difficulty now is for President Gompers to give sufficient time to it. He is always so tremendously crowded. He has in mind always to give from an hour to two hours every day to this work. Yesterday that was all crowded out. It looks as though it will be crowded out again today. It is true we came to the office Sunday and worked steadily for several hours on the memoirs. He is as impatient as we are to get the matter into your hands. Even on the hard six weeks' trip to the West, he did a lot of work on it, giving an hour here and there as he could squeeze it in. Sometimes it was late at night that he and I worked for an hour. One day on the road down from Portland to San Francisco we worked nearly all day on it until we both were so tired we could hardly speak.

Sincerely yours,   R. Lee Guard
Secretary to President Gompers.

TLcSr, Files of the Office of the President, General Correspondence, reel 107, frame 470, *AFL Records.*

1. Florence Calvert THORNE, formerly a research assistant to SG and then an editor of the *American Federationist,* was helping SG with the preparation of his memoirs.

To Victor Olander

November 23, 1923.

Mr. Victor A. Olander,
Secretary-Treasurer, The Illinois State Federation of Labor,
164–166 W. Washington St., Chicago, Ill.
Dear Sir and Brother:

Your letter of November 14 received and contents noted.

In a previous letter to you[1] I discussed the election of Judges Sullivan[2] and Holden[3] and was certain their success came from the fact that they were at the head of their respective tickets especially Judge Sullivan. I can understand what odds you had to contend with but the results were that your work did much to cut down their votes. The organization of the anti-labor forces is practically perfect when it is necessary to elect an anti-labor judge. There are four organizations that have appeared in the last two or three years that have no respect for the constitution of the United States. They are the Ku Klux Klan, the Fascisti, the Minute Men[4] and the Communists, all of which are founded on bigotry and ignorance. They are ulcers on the body politic. They are composed of men in the streets who know nothing of what is going on in the world except what they read in the profit-making newspapers. The average citizen is only permitted to know what those who control publicity want them to know.

I feel that you and your associates are perfectly competent to deal with the communist forces in Chicago. If a daily paper is started in their interest there can be only one conclusion of where the money came from. It is quite a paradox that those who continually attack labor organizations and their members will give the greatest friendly publicity to those who are seeking the overthrow of our government. The efforts of the struggling wage earners for a better life are condemned while the insane utterances of the communists are heralded forth with the object of injuring the trade union movement. It is such publicity as that which has been fed the people and make them believe that all who work for wages are communists and desire to overthrow the government. I some times wonder how the brains of some of the labor-baiters are constructed. Sometimes I can see little difference between that of Mussolini Dawes[5] and his prototype in congress the bleating, blatant, Blanton.

What Mr. Dawes has said about me will be answered.[6] Such an attack on labor as that made by the banker Mussolini should be a warning to the wage earners of the country that they must organize more thoroughly than ever before in order to prepare for the struggle which the American fascisti threatens.

You must not think you burden me with the information you give. I am always glad to receive letters from you as you go thoroughly into the matter and give much that is important to know.

Fraternally yours,   Saml Gompers
President,   American Federation of Labor.

TLpS, reel 295, vol. 308, pp. 485–86, SG Letterbooks, DLC.

1. SG to Victor Olander, Nov. 15, 1923, reel 295, vol. 308, p. 145, SG Letterbooks, DLC.

2. Denis E. Sullivan (1869–1941), a Democrat and a former state legislator, served as a judge on the Superior Court of Cook County, Ill., from 1911 to 1934. He was re-elected in 1923.

3. Jesse Holdom (1851–1930), a Republican, served as a judge on the Superior Court of Cook County from 1898 to 1906 and again from 1923 to 1930.

4. The Minute Men of the Constitution was a group founded by Charles Dawes in the spring of 1923. It called for "the great patriotic majority" of Americans to support "law enforcement, the Constitution, and good government" and to demand action against "the criminal organizations of labor" and "lawless labor leaders" ("New Bill of Rights Due, Says Dawes," *Washington Post,* Feb. 23, 1923; "Dawes Attacks Political Leaders Who Bow to Aggressive Minorities," *Journal of Commerce,* Nov. 8, 1923; [Ralph Easley] to SG, Dec. 10, 1923, National Civic Federation Papers, NN).

5. Charles Gates Dawes (1865–1951), a brigadier general during World War I and the founder in 1923 of the Minute Men of the Constitution, served as vice-president of the United States from 1925 to 1929 and as U.S. ambassador to Great Britain from 1929 to 1932. He shared the 1925 Nobel Peace Prize for chairing the commission that drafted the Dawes Plan, which stabilized the German currency and rescheduled German reparations payments.

6. Dawes had condemned labor unions as "aggressive minority organizations" and censured union leaders who, he charged, "openly advocate the breaking of the law" ("Dawes Attacks Political Leaders Who Bow to Aggressive Minorities," *Journal of Commerce,* Nov. 8, 1923). Ralph Easley wrote SG that he and Rufus Bloodgood, a Milwaukee attorney who was a member of the National Civic Federation executive committee, had both replied to Dawes ([Easley] to SG, Dec. 10, 1923, National Civic Federation Papers, NN).

To the Executive Council of the AFL

Washington, D.C. November 27, 1923

Document No. 131.
Executive Council, American Federation of Labor.
Colleagues:
Information has reached me from several reliable sources that the

trade union movement of Germany is on the verge of disintegration by reason of the fact that the paper money (the mark) has depreciated so that it has become entirely and absolutely valueless. The contributions paid by unions to the German Federation of Trade Unions have, of course, depreciated in value to such an extent that officials have nearly all been laid off or resigned and what expenditures are made are so prodigious in marks that it baffles the imagination. As an instance I quote from official financial report that in July, 1923, the expenditures were 275,565,000 marks which have increased as follows:

August ——————— 6,364,900,000
September —— 270,636,000,000
October —— 36,358,907,000,000

and these expenditures were made for the same personnel and functioning.

The trade union movements of several countries have made contributions to the German Trade Union Federation in the sum of approximately thirty thousand ($30,000.00) dollars in the past two months which may help to tide over the movement for a few weeks and an appeal has been made to the American Federation of Labor by the officers of the national trade union movements of several countries. This information in full and more authentic official form[1] came to me during the latter part of last week and having in mind the declaration of the Executive Council of the A.F. of L. after the entrance of the United States into the World War:

"When victory is achieved none will be quicker to extend the fraternal hand of trade union fellowship to the organized workers in all countries now at war, or will do so more heartily than will the American Federation of Labor."

By word of mouth I had Organizer Hugh Frayne invite a number of representative trade union men whose offices are located in New York City and vicinity and on last Sunday, November 25th, a conference was held at the Aberdeen Hotel in New York at which twenty-five of them were present.[2]

The general situation was discussed and the sense of the meeting finally expressed that the American Federation of Labor should undertake, through its Executive Council, the organization of a national committee composed of trade unionists for the purpose of appealing to and receiving and forwarding such sums of money as can be raised for the purpose of the functioning of the trade unions in Germany as such; that the money raised and forwarded be utilized not for relief or what is known as charity or trade union benefits but for the exclusive administration of the affairs of the trade unions; that the A.F. of L. in carrying on this work will avoid groups or individuals here and there who raise money ostensibly for this purpose but in all probability to be used for ulterior objects.

We all know more or less the situation as it exists in Germany. There is the extreme Left or Soviets, Communists, who aim to sovietize Germany and bring additional misery and tyranny for all the people and on the other hand the extreme reaction which expresses itself in Kaiserdom, the Crown Prince—in fact the "man on Horseback Government" and that the trade union movement of Germany, even though it is not in exact accord with the American trade union movement, is the most stabilizing influence which Germany has to save it from ruin or military dictatorship.

Therefore, for the above reasons and more which could be supplied if necessary, I submit to the Executive Council of the American Federation of Labor, the following:

Resolved: That the American Federation of Labor undertake, by and with the advice and consent of its Executive Council, the formation of a national committee of trade unionists for the purpose of raising voluntary subscriptions from trade unions, trade unionists, and friends of the trade union movement to aid in maintaining the trade unions of Germany in the administration of trade union affairs.

Because of the extreme critical emergency, members of the Executive Council are urgently requested to transmit their votes to the undersigned by telegraph and if necessary confirm by mail.[3]

Fraternally yours,   Saml Gompers.
President,   American Federation of Labor.

TLcS, Executive Council Records, Vote Books, reel 18, frame 145, *AFL Records.* Typed notation: "*Copy.*"

1. That is, in a letter signed jointly by Léon Jouhaux, Theodor Leipart, Cornelius Mertens, Jan Oudegeest, and Johann Sassenbach.

2. For minutes of the meeting, which was chaired by SG, see Files of the Office of the President, Conferences, reel 123, frames 212–14, *AFL Records.*

3. The AFL Executive Council approved SG's proposal, and the appeal was issued Dec. 12, 1923 (SG to the Officers and Members of International Unions, National Unions, State Federations, City Central Bodies, Local Unions, Trade Unionists, and Friends; for a copy of the circular, see *American Federationist* 31 [Jan. 1924]:92–93). The effort raised just over $27,000.

A Circular

Washington, D.C. Dec. 4, 1923

To Presidents of National and International Unions.
Dear Sir and Brother:

As was reported by the Executive Council to the Portland Convention the necessity for systematic and carefully developed plans to organize women wage earners has been emphasized by the decision of the U.S. Supreme Court declaring certain legislative safeguards for women unconstitutional. In view of that decision there is no escape from the conclusion that the protection and the progressive development of better conditions and standards for women in industry depends upon the strength of their economic organization.

In order that the American Federation of Labor may deal with this problem comprehensively and intelligently I am enclosing an enumeration of points upon which data is most desirable. Will you please fill out the enclosed questionnaire and return to me at your earliest convenience together with any other data or information that you deem helpful in considering this problem?[1]

An early response will be most helpful cooperation.

Fraternally yours,
President   American Federation of Labor.

[ENCLOSURE]

WOMEN WAGE EARNERS

1. Are women wage-earners employed in your trade or industry?[2]
   What proportion to male workers do they constitute?
2. How many members of your organization are women?[3]
   Give approximation if exact figures not available.[4]
3. Are they organized in unions with men or in separate locals?[5]
   How many in each—or approximation?
4a. Are women in industry employed at skilled work?[6]
   Are they members of your unions?[7]
 b. Are some employed in unskilled work?
   Are they members of your unions?
5. What is the policy of your organization affecting membership and unemployment of women?[8]
6. Are the women wage earners in your industry increasing or decreasing?[9]
   Is the proportion of women members of your union increasing?[10]

7. What organizing efforts is your organization making to organize these women workers?[11]

8. Do you employ women organizers?[12]

Please enclose copy of constitution and by-laws and give us whatever other data will contribute to clearer understanding.

TLc and TDc, reel 295, vol. 308, pp. 967–68, SG Letterbooks, DLC.

1. SG received eighty-two replies to this and a follow-up circular that he sent on Jan. 14, 1924. For a summary of the information collected, see notes 2–12, below; for the AFL's compilation of the information, see AFL Microfilm Convention File, reel 33, frame 1175, *AFL Records.*

2. Forty-seven unions reported that women were employed in their industry; thirty-five said they were not (ibid.).

3. Forty-five unions reported women as members; thirty-seven said they were not (ibid.).

4. The AFL's tabulation of replies showed that some 140,000 women were union members. Among the unions with the most women were the Ladies' Garment Workers (41,000), the United Garment Workers (29,560), the Electrical Workers (12,000), the Railway Clerks (10,000), and the Federal Employees (9,000) (ibid.). The AFL subsequently raised its estimate of the number of women union members to 200,000 (AFL, *Proceedings*, 1924, p. 63).

5. Three unions reported women organized in their own separate locals, nine had them in both separate locals and mixed locals of men and women, and thirty-two organized them entirely in mixed locals (AFL Microfilm Convention File, reel 33, frame 1175, *AFL Records*).

6. Twenty-six unions reported women engaged in skilled work in their industries, six said they were in unskilled work, and eleven said they were in both skilled and unskilled work (ibid.).

7. Twenty-six unions reported that women members were engaged in skilled work, three said they were in unskilled work, and eleven said they were in both skilled and unskilled work (ibid.).

8. One union reported it was opposed to having women members, seven said they had special constitutional provisions for women, and thirty-nine said they had no special policy and that their men and women members were equal in all respects (ibid.).

9. Fifteen unions reported that women were increasing in their industries, thirteen said they were decreasing, and twelve said their numbers were not changing (ibid.).

10. Ten unions reported that the proportion of their women members was increasing, fifteen said it was decreasing, and fifteen said it was staying the same (ibid.).

11. Twenty-four unions said they were making no special effort; twenty-two reported that they made the same effort to organize men as women (ibid.).

12. Eight unions said they regularly employed women organizers; two reported that they only occasionally did so (ibid.).

To John Saylor[1]

December 7, 1923.

Mr. John C. Saylor,
Secretary, Central Labor Union,[2]
415 Shipley St., Wilmington, Delaware.
Dear Sir and Brother:

Your letter of December 5 received and contents noted.

The American Federation of Labor is opposed to the so-called equal rights amendment on the ground that its ratification would repeal all the laws for the protection of women in industry. Two years ago the National Woman's Party in order to have some issue that would attract attention to that organization began agitation in Washington for a constitutional amendment.[3] Representatives of the National Woman's Party called upon me to aid them. I emphatically refused. I told them that the A.F. of L. would oppose any such proposed amendment. Then representatives of that party went into the various states and introduced bills giving equal rights to women. I am pleased to say that wherever these bills were introduced they were defeated. The state federations of labor and central bodies were circularized by me calling attention to the dangers of the proposed equal rights bill.

This year the National Woman's Party has taken upon itself to renew its agitation for an equal rights amendment. A committee called upon the President[4] and in their speeches to him must have declared that the object was to free women from all laws that would handicap them in any way. These would include laws for the protection of women in industry.

I wrote a letter[5] to the President pointing out that the women who were urging the equal rights amendment were not women working in industry or their representatives but society women. That the President was not influenced by the National Woman's Party representatives was evidenced in his address today to members of the Senate and House of Representatives that a minimum wage law for women should be enacted for their protection.[6]

I hope the Central Labor Union of Wilmington and vicinity will use every endeavor to defeat any bill or proposed amendment to the constitution that is submitted to the Delaware Legislature on so-called equal rights for women. The women working in industry would lose all protection now given them by the law.

With best wishes and assuring you of my desire to be helpful in any way within my power, I am,

Fraternally yours,   Saml Gompers
President,   American Federation of Labor.

TLpS, reel 296, vol. 309, pp. 28–29, SG Letterbooks, DLC.

1. John Conrad Saylor (b. 1888) was a Wilmington, Del., printer. He served as secretary of the Wilmington Central Labor Union from 1917 to 1918 and again from 1922 to at least 1936.

2. The AFL chartered the United Labor League of Wilmington and Vicinity in March 1902 and then issued a new charter to the central body as the Wilmington Central Labor Union in September of that year.

3. See "To David Hanly," Mar. 1, 1922, n. 4, above.

4. The representatives of the National Woman's party met with President Calvin Coolidge at the White House on Nov. 17, 1923.

5. SG to Coolidge, Nov. 19, 1923, reel 295, vol. 308, pp. 245–46, SG Letterbooks, DLC.

6. Coolidge delivered his 1923 State of the Union address to a joint session of Congress on Dec. 6, 1923 (*Congressional Record,* 68th Cong., 1st sess., 1923, vol. 65, pt. 1, pp. 96–101).

To B. M. Jewell

Washington, D.C., Dec. 13, 1923

Mr. B. M. Jewell,
Riviera Bldg., 4750 Broadway, Chicago, Illinois.
Secretary Morrison and I have just concluded an interesting conference with Mr. Richberg. Mr. Richberg advises that the cost involved in the Michaelson case[1] up to and through the Supreme Court will not exceed two thousand dollars. For the American Federation of Labor I pledge the proportionate share of the expenditure as apportioned to each of the organizations.

Samuel Gompers

TWpSr, reel 296, vol. 309, p. 225, SG Letterbooks, DLC.

1. In July 1922 employees of the Chicago, St. Paul, Minneapolis, and Omaha Railway Co. went on strike. When they violated a temporary restraining order, they were charged with contempt under section 21 of the Clayton Act, found guilty, fined, and then jailed for failure to pay the fines. The strikers appealed their convictions, claiming they had been denied the right to trial by jury provided in section 22 of the Clayton Act. In July 1923 the Court of Appeals for the Seventh Circuit affirmed the convictions (*Michaelson et al. v. United States,* 291 F. 940 [1923]). On Oct. 20, 1924, however, the U.S. Supreme Court reversed the Court of Appeals, holding it had erred in ruling that because the

railroad strike was illegal, the strikers had ceased to be employees under the terms of the Clayton Act and thus no longer came under its protections. Moreover, the Supreme Court reversed the appellate court's decision that the Clayton Act's provision of jury trials in contempt proceedings was unconstitutional (*Michaelson et al. v. United States,* 266 U.S. 42 [1924]).

To F. Ernest Johnson[1]

December 14, 1923.

Rev. F. Earnest Johnson,
Research Secretary, Federal Council of the Churches of
    Christ in America,
105 East Twenty-second Street, New York City.
Dear Sir:

Your letter of November 30 received and contents noted.

I am very much interested in your criticism of the cartoon printed in the leaflet which is for the purpose of encouraging sentiment to secure the passage by congress of the proposed amendment to the constitution to protect children, and you say that "the conservative minded people whom we wish to win in support of the Child Labor Amendment will not be attracted but repelled, not to say angered, by this kind of publicity."

To my mind there is nothing more injurious for the children than to be sent to work in the factory or workshop before the age of sixteen years. I look with horror upon the exploiting of child life in the textile mills and in all other industries that are using them simply for the purpose of greed. I am also satisfied, from what I have learned in nearly sixty years of life in the United States, that the people as a rule look upon the employment of children with horror. It reminds me of a declaration of the convention of the American Federation of Labor in 1890[2] as follows:

"Of all the ills from which mankind suffers that which rises to horrible proportions is that of child labor. The children of the workers have none to raise a voice in their defense other than the organized workers."[3]

The 1893 convention[4] of the American Federation of Labor declared:

"The damnable system that permits young and innocent children to have their very lives worked out of them in factories, mills, workshops and stores is one of the very worst grievances of labor and in the reformation of which we never shall cease our agitation until we have rescued them and placed them where they should be, in the school room and playground."[5]

Every convention previous to that time declared most emphatically against child labor. In 1881 it was declared in the A.F. of L. convention that "there is no greater crime under the heavens than of employing children in factories."[6]

In 1884 the convention[7] condemned the pernicious system known as child labor.[8]

These are only a few of the declarations of labor against child labor. It may be that in all these years that labor has striven to emancipate the young we have grown to believe that there are no words sufficiently expressive of our detestation of such a practice, nor have we yet seen a cartoon criticising the greed of those who use child labor for their own profit that has been too strong. Therefore in all sincerity I must confess that I cannot agree with you. Milk and water cartoons will never save the children. The fight for their freedom cannot be successful if we go on the principles that it will not do to hurt the feelings of "conservative" people.

Yours very truly,   Saml Gompers
President,   American Federation of Labor.

TLpS, reel 296, vol. 309, pp. 267–68, SG Letterbooks, DLC.

1. Frederick Ernest Johnson (1884–1969) was secretary for research and education (1918–24) for the Federal Council of the Churches of Christ in America and subsequently executive secretary of the Council's Department of Research and Education (1924–50).

2. The 1890 AFL convention met in Detroit, Dec. 8–13.

3. The quotation is a paraphrase from SG's report to the 1890 AFL convention, which reads in part: "Of all the ills that mankind suffers from, the unjust and cruel tendencies of modern methods of wealth-producing, the one that seems to me to rise to horrible proportions is that of Child Labor. . . . The children of the workers have none to raise a voice in their defense other than the organized wage-workers" (AFL, *Proceedings,* 1890, pp. 15–16). The convention endorsed the statement.

4. The 1893 AFL convention met in Chicago, Dec. 11–19.

5. From SG's report to the 1893 AFL convention, which reads in part: "While it is true that through the efforts of our organizations the inhuman practice of allowing young children to be employed has been somewhat abated, the fact remains that the damnable system which permits young and innocent children to have their very lives worked out of them in factories, mills, workshops and stores, is one of the very worst of labor grievances, one which the Trade Unions have protested against for years, and in the reformation of which we shall never cease our agitation until we have rescued them, and placed them where they should be, in the schoolroom and the playground" (AFL, *Proceedings,* 1893, p. 15). The convention endorsed his statement.

6. A reference to a statement by Richard Powers to the 1881 FOTLU convention, which reads: "There is no crime greater under the heavens than that of employing child labor in mills, factories, and industrial establishments" (FOTLU, *Proceedings,* 1881, p. 18). See also *The Samuel Gompers Papers,* vol. 1, pp. 225–27.

7. The 1884 FOTLU convention met in Chicago, Oct. 7–10.

8. This statement is a paraphrase of a resolution presented by Robert Howard that was adopted by the 1884 FOTLU convention (FOTLU, *Proceedings,* 1884, p. 15).

To Fred Bramley[1]

Dec. 17, 1923.

Mr. Fred Bramley,
Secretary, British Trade Union Congress,
32 Eccleston Square, London, S.W. 1.
Dear Sir and Brother:

The American Federation of Labor has before it special consideration of the problem of organizing women wage earners in industry. In considering this problem we are anxious to have before us all the available data which the British trade union movement can give us. We are interested in having whatever statistical material you may have in your office and the benefit of your experiences with various methods of organizing. We should like to know of the work of your Women's Bureau, just what its relation is to the British trade union Congress and to the trade organizations.

My attention has been called to a report on British women in industry made by Gertrude Drake.[2] I am anxious to have a copy of this book which I understand was published under the auspices of the Labor Research Bureau. I shall appreciate it if you will help me to obtain copy of this report.

If you can suggest to me persons who can give me specific details and experiences I shall be very appreciative, or better still, if you will ask those whom you deem qualified to give this information to write me that will be a saving of considerable time as it is essential that our study and plans go forward.

I am enclosing an article[3] which embodies the result of my thinking on the power problem and I am very anxious to have your opinion on this matter. I hope that you can find time to read it carefully and give me the benefit of your judgment.

Fraternally yours,   Saml Gompers
President,   American Federation of Labor.

P.S. Please accept my best wishes for a happy yuletide.

S. G.

TLpS, reel 296, vol. 309, p. 365, SG Letterbooks, DLC.

1. Fred Bramley (1874–1925) served as assistant secretary (1917–23) and then secretary (1923–25) of the Parliamentary Committee of the TUC (from 1921, the General Council) and was also president of the Workers' Educational Association. A cabinet maker and a member of the National Amalgamated Furnishing Trades Association, he served as an organizer for that union from 1912 to 1917.

2. Actually Barbara Meinertzhagen Drake (1876–1963), the niece of Beatrice Webb. A leader of the Fabian Women's Group and a member of its Research Department, she was the author of *Women in the Engineering Trades* . . . (1917) and *Women in Trade Unions* (1920). She later served as a member of the London County Council (1934–46).

3. "Giant Power—Its Possibilities—Potentialities and Its Administration," *American Federationist* 30 (Dec. 1923): 973–82.

To John L. Lewis

Dec. 17, 1923.

Mr. John L. Lewis,
President, United Mine Workers of America,
Raleigh Hotel, Washington, D.C.
Dear Sir and Brother:

As per my conversation with you over the telephone enclosed you will please find copy of circular appeal for help for the German trade union movement.[1] Permit me again to thank you for your permission to use your name as member of the National Committee.

As you know as per the understanding between you and this office we send nothing to local unions of the Miners without your consent. In furtherance of the high purpose we have in mind in the endeavor to sustain the German trade union movement so that it may not be dismembered I am asking your consent to send the appeal to your local unions.[2] I am sending it to the locals of all affiliated organizations.

Looking forward to our conference tomorrow morning, I am

Fraternally yours,   Saml Gompers
President,   American Federation of Labor.

TLpS, reel 296, vol. 309, p. 385, SG Letterbooks, DLC.

1. SG to the Officers and Members of International Unions, National Unions, State Federations, City Central Bodies, Local Unions, Trade Unionists, and Friends, Dec. 12, 1923, United Brotherhood of Carpenters and Joiners of America Records, reel 2, frames 415–16, *AFL and the Unions*. The circular was later published in the *American Federationist* 31 (Jan. 1924): 92–93.

2. John L. Lewis gave his consent. See SG to Frank Morrison, Dec. 23, 1923, reel 296, vol. 309, p. 669, SG Letterbooks, DLC.

To Matthew Woll

Washington, D.C., December 17, 1923.

Matthew Woll,
Room 701, 166 West Washington Street, Chicago, Illinois.
Inasmuch as you will be in New York over this week-end, will you do me the kindness to meet me at Dutton Publishing Company at eleven o'clock Saturday morning when I shall turn over to Mr. Macrae the complete manuscript of my memoirs. Please telegraph answer.[1]

Samuel Gompers.

TWpSr, reel 296, vol. 309, p. 346, SG Letterbooks, DLC.

1. Matthew Woll wired a reply to SG the same day, to say he would meet him on Dec. 22, 1923, at the Dutton Publishing Co. offices in New York City (Files of the Office of the President, General Correspondence, reel 107, frame 539, *AFL Records*). R. Lee Guard and Florence Thorne also attended the meeting.

To Byron Patton Harrison[1]

Dec. 20, 1923.

Honorable Pat Harrison,
United States Senate Office Building,
Washington, D.C.
Dear Sir:

Last night I had the pleasure of listening to your address delivered over the radio and I am writing to you in response to the request made by the announcer, following your address, in which listeners in were asked to communicate with you.

I find myself in entire accord with your splendid presentation of thought on the subject of Americanization. Your remarks on the restriction of immigration were admirable.

I may say that I count the American Federation of Labor as one of the most potent agencies for Americanization in our country, just as it has been one of the most effective in securing the restriction of immigration. The American Federation of Labor has fought for restriction of immigration not from choice but from necessity. We have regarded it as imperative that our doors be not opened to hordes of immigrants who would neither understand our institutions nor maintain our standards of living.

With one portion of your address, however, I must disagree most emphatically. To my astonishment I heard you record your support of the proposal to register all aliens within our borders. I can only conclude that you have not given the matter sufficient thought, because I am sure that upon mature reflection you will agree that this proposal is essentially Prussian and un-American and that is in no wise either excusable or necessary.

In the January issue of the *American Federationist* I have dealt with this subject in the course of an editorial[2] discussing President Coolidge's message[3] to Congress in which he, also, approved the registration idea. I should be glad to have a copy of the magazine sent to you as soon as it comes from the press.

Registration of aliens would mean that we were to presume them potentially evil-doers and lawbreakers. This, as you will readily see, would be a reversal of our proper and long-established fundamental principle which is to believe every person innocent until proven guilty. We cannot reverse this principle in relation to any residents in our country without danger to its application to all others.

Registration furthermore would, whether or not it was so intended, constitute a weapon for the intimidation of alien non-citizens. It is not difficult to understand how registered alien residents would fear for example to join in a strike for the improvement of wages or working conditions under the belief that to do so might render them liable to deportation or other punishment. As a matter of fact they would doubtless even fear to become members of trade unions.

Registration, if it were to mean anything at all, would necessarily mean a continuous registration which would require renewal with every move made by each registered person. We should inevitably have a system of police permits and police surveillance, exactly on the order of systems which existed under the reactionary autocracies of Europe and which prevailed in practically every European nation during the war. Not only would such a system be repugnant to every idea and ideal of American freedom and to our American institutions, and not only would it result in wholesale intimidation of aliens, but it would no doubt result in weak, undesirable corruption among officials having to do with the registration system.

I can conceive of no argument of sufficient weight or validity to induce any real believer in American institutions to favor a proposal of this character.

As I have said, it was with great disappointment that I heard that portion of your address dealing with this subject. May I hope that upon further reflection you will join us in wholehearted opposition to the proposal?[4]

Assuring you of my highest regard and with the season's best wishes, I am,

Very truly yours,   Saml Gompers
President,   American Federation of Labor.

TLpS, reel 296, vol. 309, pp. 509–10, SG Letterbooks, DLC.

1. Byron Patton Harrison (1881–1941) served as a Democratic senator from Mississippi from 1919 until his death in 1941. He had previously served as a Democratic congressman from the state (1911–19).

2. "President Coolidge's Message," *American Federationist* 31 (Jan. 1924): 71–76.

3. See "To John Saylor," Dec. 7, 1923, n. 6, above.

4. Harrison replied that he continued to differ with SG on the issue but would be happy to discuss it with him (Harrison to SG, Dec. 22, 1923, Mississippi Collection, Pat Harrison Papers, MsU).

To Alfred E. Smith

Dec. 20, 1923.

Hon. Alfred E. Smith,
Governor of New York,
Executive Mansion, Albany.
Sir:

There is no public question of the age in which I am more deeply interested than that of power and probably there is no other one question in which so many different groups would be so [vit]ally affected by determination of policies than that of power. Both as a citizen of the state of New York and as president of the American Federation of Labor I feel keenly my responsibility for contributing as much as lies within my power to the determination of this program that looms so big today and promises to develop increasingly and rapidly in the months and years to come. The development of power projects came before the Portland convention and it was decided that labor do its utmost to see that decisions in this field would be of a nature to assure greater service and progress to industries and to society.[1] The social implications of power development are enormous. In no other industrial undertaking is the necessity of coordination so strikingly essential. We find coordination the basis of super-power and giant power projects and the tying together of power plants and transmission agencies into an almost unified cable along the Pacific coast. Coordination is essential to efficiency and the elimination of waste and to most effective service.

Although my time has been crowded since returning from Portland I have made opportunity to have conferences with a number of men directing plans that will have a determining influence in directing the solution of power undertakings for the future. One of the most important of these conferences was with the Secretary of Commerce, Herbert C. Hoover.[2] After discussing with him the problem as I saw it from the standpoint of labor he related to me his plan to confer with various state officials concerned with power undertakings in the hope that such conferences might result in the development of common problems with which all were concerned. Mr. Hoover understands so thoroughly the necessity of conserving individual initiative that he is not confusing the problem of power development and state regulation by proposing federal usurpation of state prerogatives. As I understand the undertaking it is a straight-forward proposal to investigate and find the facts. The states that enter the inquiry will do so only for the purpose of investigation. There will be no commitments. By participating in the inquiry each state through its representative will be in a position to contribute to the disclosure of all facts that ought to be taken into consideration in the development of power legislation that will bring about an absolutely free flow of power between the various states so that both our homes and our factories will be assured best service at minimum costs.

I have known Mr. Hoover for a number of years and have always had the pleasure of finding myself in accord with him upon the essentials of the various undertakings in which we have had common interests. Because of the personal friendship that has existed between you and me I am taking the liberty of writing you thus frankly, openly and fully upon the power problem because it has come to me from various sources that you are hesitating about cooperation in the committee proposed to study the legal questions necessary to carry into effect the super-power plan for the Boston-Washington region.

I am keenly interested in the super-power proposals and feel that such a development based upon proper principles will contribute more than any other single factor to the development of our future civilization, progress in industries, in transportation and the greater happiness and comforts in the homes of all. I am enclosing a reprint of an article[3] published in the December issue of the "American Federationist" which I urge you to read. May I repeat that the present proposal is simply for an investigation.[4]

With best wishes, I am

Respectfully yours, Saml Gompers.
President, American Federation of Labor.

TLpS, reel 296, vol. 309, pp. 551–52, SG Letterbooks, DLC.

1. Resolution 42, as amended and unanimously adopted by the 1923 AFL convention, called on states to control and develop the waters within their borders and provide water to their citizens at cost—for domestic use, irrigation, power, and navigation—to prevent the exploitation of this resource for profit.

2. SG met with Herbert Hoover in Hoover's office in Washington, D.C., on Dec. 3, 1923. For a transcript of the meeting, see Files of the Office of the President, Speeches and Writings, reel 123, frame 233, *AFL Records*.

3. See "To Fred Bramley," Dec. 17, 1923, n. 3, above.

4. Governor Smith replied to SG on Dec. 27, 1923, to say he had written Hoover suggesting the names of two New York representatives to participate in the study, state engineer and surveyor Dwight La Du and attorney George Van Kennen of Ogdensburg (AFL Microfilm Convention File, reel 32, frame 1736, *AFL Records*).

To B. M. Jewell

Dec. 21, 1923.

Mr. B. M. Jewell,
President, Railway Employes Department,
4750 Broadway, Chicago, Ill.
Dear Sir and Brother:

I have just learned with a great deal of interest of the cooperative arrangement with the Workers' Education Bureau to use the Pittsburgh experiment[1] as the basis for workers' education among groups of railway shopmen. That undertaking seems to me so essentially sound that I welcome it and hope to keep in touch with its progress. It is just that sort of development which I hope to see made the basis for control and development of the super-power undertakings which are coming so rapidly.

Comparatively few are aware of the revolutionizing changes and progress that are taking place through the substitution of white coal[2] for our other sources of power. This revolution is so compelling and so dynamic that it makes a powerful appeal to the imagination. Not only is there an intensely interesting scientific phase to the change but the industrial and social implications and problems following are of first order importance to those who desire to promote justice in industry and human welfare in living. The industrial and social consequences will be gigantic. Because I realized the significance to the labor movement of this change which is now in the making I sought to call attention to the situation in an article[3] published in the December issue of the "American Federationist" a copy of which is enclosed. As I want your help in meeting this problem in the best way to promote the interest and welfare of wage earners as well as of society I am sending you this article with the request that you read it carefully and let me have the benefit of any suggestions that may occur to your mind.

It is my purpose as soon as I return from Panama[4] to present this problem to such labor officials as are most directly concerned with the development of labor's attitude and program upon this matter and I want your advice and assistance in developing the best considered decisions.

I sincerely hope that you will find time to give this matter careful thought and will be ready to help in this undertaking.

With best wishes, I am

Fraternally yours,　Saml Gompers
President,　American Federation of Labor.

TLpS, reel 296, vol. 309, pp. 637–38, SG Letterbooks, DLC. Typed notation: "Dictated but not signed." The letter is stamped with SG's signature.

1. A reference to the labor-management cooperation plan launched in February 1923 at the Baltimore and Ohio Railroad Glenwood locomotive repair shop in Pittsburgh. Developed by International Association of Machinists' president William Johnston and representatives of the railroad and Baltimore and Ohio System Federation 30, it was designed to improve service, increase stockholder returns, and demonstrate that a union shop could work more efficiently than a nonunion shop. Under the Glenwood Plan, unions and management assumed joint responsibility for production, safety, and efficiency. Worker-management meetings were held biweekly to discuss operations, scheduling, performance, and morale, but wages, grievances, and work rules were outside their purview. In March 1924 management and unions agreed to extend the plan to all forty-five shop facilities on the line. In May 1924 delegates to System Federation 30's Philadelphia convention voted that their organization should join with the Workers' Education Bureau to develop courses in economics, railroads, and the science and art of their trades. In August 1925 the first Railroad Labor Institute was held at Brookwood Labor College.

2. That is, water as a source of energy, particularly hydroelectric power.

3. See "To Fred Bramley," Dec. 17, 1923, n. 3, above.

4. SG sailed from New York City on Dec. 24, 1923, and arrived in the Panama Canal Zone on Jan. 1, 1924, after a brief stopover in Haiti. Accompanied by William Spencer of the AFL Building Trades Department, Albert Berres of the AFL Metal Trades Department, G. M. Bugniazet of the Electrical Workers, George Hedrick of the Painters, W. C. Hushing, the Washington legislative representative of the Panama Canal employees, Luther Steward of the Federation of Federal Employees, and William Roberts, secretary for the group, SG made the trip pursuant to Resolution 1, adopted by the 1923 AFL convention, that called on him to investigate living and working conditions among American workers in Panama. SG visited Ancón, Balboa, Colón, Cristóbal, Naos Island, and Panama City, as well as the canal itself, before embarking on Jan. 9 for his return to the United States. He landed in New York on Jan. 17 after another stopover in Haiti. SG and the AFL commission presented the grievances of American workers to Canal Zone governor Jay Morrow on Jan. 8 and to Secretary of War John Weeks on Jan. 31, and SG met again with Weeks on Mar. 6. (For minutes of the meetings of Jan. 8 and Mar. 6, see Files of the Office of the President, Conferences, reel 123, frames 335–63,

528–30, *AFL Records.*) The grievances were still unresolved at the time of SG's death. For SG's account of the trip and other documentation, see his article "Conditions of Life and Labor on the Panama Canal Zone: Investigation, Reports, and Conferences," *American Federationist* 31 (Mar. 1924): 209–21.

To John Macrae

New York City December 24, 1923

Mr. John Macrae,
E. P. Dutton Co.,
681 Fifth Ave., New York City.
Dear Mr. Macrae:

The conference I had the pleasure of having with you last Saturday in your office when I handed to you the manuscript of my autobiography gave me a great deal of satisfaction as it did my associates who were with me.[1] Since then I have thought of the conference quite often and the thought has come to me which I desire to present to you for consideration.

In advance, let me say, that I do not pretend to have any "business sense," and yet a situation may arise in which the thought I want to present to you may interest you.

You know I have been frequently the object of attack and misrepresentation and that the press has not failed at times to exaggerate as well as to antagonize my position. In 1924 we shall have the nomination and election for president, vice-president of the United States, for a third of the members of the senate and all the membership of the house of representatives. I am quite sure that in the general election as well as the election for senators and representatives there may or will arise the necessity for my activity in the effort to defeat for re-election men who have proven themselves uncompromising antagonists to the cause of labor, freedom and justice. As a rule, these people have wealth and influence behind them and this wealth and influence are often expressed through newspapers or magazines. I have stated in the book that I give allegiance to no political party. I am wondering whether, if the book were published some time during the early part of June, or in May, if it might not be to the best advantage of its circulation before the campaign is really on its way to white heat. I have no predilection upon the subject.

As I have already stated my sense of business is not reliable, but it seemed to me I should convey this to you before sailing. I am dictat-

ing this on the steamer an hour before sailing of the steamer Panama
for the Canal Zone.

Wishing you a very Merry Christmas and a Happy New Year, I am,

Very sincerely yours,

President   American Federation of Labor.

TLc, Files of the Office of the President, General Correspondence, reel 107,
frame 544, *AFL Records.*

1. That is, R. Lee Guard, Florence Thorne, and Matthew Woll. See "To Matthew
Woll," Dec. 17, 1923, n. 1, above.

An Excerpt from the Minutes of a Meeting
with Representatives of
the Panama Federation of Labor[1]

Hotel Tivoli, Ancon, C.Z. January 1, 1924

. . .

When asked how he liked Panama, Mr. Gompers said:

"The country is most interesting. Some of the things which I have
seen are really wonderful. There are others again which do not appeal to me at all. From what I have been able to observe the economic
standard of the people is very low. Of course, insofar as housing conditions are concerned in the tropical climates they do not require the
homes such as we are accustomed to in the United States; but there are
great facilities for development—first, of your own initiative, and then
by the enterprise of the United States and the people of the United
States. I think one of the most fortunate things for your own people
of Panama is that the United States finally undertook the completion
and then completed the Panama Canal. We all learn by observing
the things that others do. You people can not help but learn from
the American people coming here their habits of life, their mode of
work, and to learn also their mode of thinking. In addition to what
the Panama Canal means [for] this Zone and for Panama, it means so
much for progress and civilization of the whole world. Probably, the
men who conceived and then carried into effect the Panama Canal
never dreamed it was going to be what it is now and what it is destined
to be."

Mr. Gompers was asked whether he believed a better feeling could
be brought about between the Panamanian laborites and the American laborites, and in reply he said:

"I hope always to bring about better understanding among workmen and peoples. You can't overturn a condition which has taken years and years to grow and develop. I think I know to what you refer, and that is the refusal to accept for membership men of your country into the unions of what they consider 'white men.'[2] They do not draw the color line in their organizations, or very few of them do, but the fact is—your home is here, you are here—these men are 2,000 miles away from their home and they were induced to come here for the purpose of constructing and maintaining this great public work. Now, when their standard of wages and hours and conditions are such that they must be maintained in order to give them their standard of life they can't, of course, very easily surrender the opportunities for such employment to men whose standards of wages and hours and conditions to which they are fortunate to obtain or achieve. Now, if these men were living here all the time and could just cross the street and be home, or take a street car or something like that, it might be different, but you are here permanently and they are simply sojourners, and you will find that the peoples of all countries protect themselves from peoples of others where lower standards obtain. Some of the Latin American countries—Chile, Argentina, and others—have rigid restrictions of immigration, and why? Because, if the standards of the others were higher they wouldn't object for that would help to lift their own standards, but they try to protect their standards against deterioration."

Replying to a question as to whether his presence here would enable them to get a square deal, Mr. Gompers said:

"There is one thing sure. If I can't better it I won't make it worse."

. . .

TDc, Files of the Office of the President, Conferences, reel 123, frames 298–99, *AFL Records*. Typed notation: "Canal Zone—Panama Federation of Labor. Conference held January 1, 1924 in the Hotel Tivoli, Ancon, C.Z. with a committee of the Panamanian Federation of Labor at 12 noon."

1. The Federación Obrera de la República de Panamá (Workers' Federation of the Republic of Panama), founded in 1921.

2. For discussion of discrimination in the Canal Zone by white, American-born trade unionists, see *The Samuel Gompers Papers*, vol. 11, pp. 391–93, 433–35.

To Frank Duffy

Washington, D.C. Jan. 21, 1924.

Mr. Frank Duffy,
Secretary, United Brotherhood of Carpenters and Joiners,
Carpenters' Bldg., Indianapolis, Indiana.
Dear Sir and Brother:

Your letter of January 17 and enclosed clipping have been read with a great deal of interest. I am glad you wrote me as you did for there is a great deal of misinformation being handed around in connection with workers' education. The writer of the article which you enclosed, Harry W. Laidler, is, as you probably know, the former secretary of the Inter-collegiate Socialist League and now Secretary of the League for Industrial Democracy which includes many of the same persons who belonged to the former and promotes the same general purposes.[1] In other words, it is the group to promote socialist propaganda. In his description of the Workers' Education Bureau he seizes upon such facts as appeal to a socialist mind and tries to emphasize them as the fundamentals of the Bureau. As the movement for workers' education is only now in the making its principles and methods have not been completely formulated and consequently there are about as many different ideas about workers' education as there are different people describing it. It is difficult for the uninitiated to point to any particular statement as that which is accepted as official.

Inasmuch as education has been all too often confused with propaganda it was seized upon by the socialist organizations as a method of promoting their ends and many active socialists became prominently identified with various educational undertakings. When, therefore, the American Federation of Labor undertook to organize educational work for trade unions and to direct activities in furtherance of true educational aims we found that our first and in some respects our most difficult problem was to coordinate existing forces in furtherance of a truly constructive program. Where there were those in the field who were not altogether in harmony with trade union policies and principles we first undertook to get them to go along with a re-organized undertaking. Of course if we found them not amenable to reason we substituted others in whom we had confidence. The movement as it is now going along is a pioneer undertaking that has to develop plans and methods in harmony with the principles of trade unionism. There are in the field people who have never worked together before but we hope that by the leavening process good judgment may be made to prevail throughout the general mass. This is something that cannot be done at once but in the end I feel confident that those not in harmony with our ultimate purposes will be ejected as that is demonstrated and that the result will be a new activity and development of the trade union movement.

When the Workers' Education Bureau was re-organized under the agreement between that Bureau and the A.F. of L. the Rand School was eliminated and also the Amalgamated Clothing Workers and all dual unions. The Federation has three representatives on the Executive Board one of whom, Matthew Woll, is chairman. James Maurer,[2] the first president of the Bureau, remains as president and he serves as presiding officer at conventions and has no executive duties. Miss Fannia Cohn, also mentioned in the Laidler article, is vice-president of the International Ladies Garment Workers. John Frey and George W. Perkins are the other Federation representatives on the Executive Board and their reputations are sufficient proof of the fact that the Bureau is trying to work out principles and methods in harmony with trade unionism. Mr. Laidler, the socialist propagandist, is not qualified to interpret the purposes of the educational work carried on under the Bureau. If he were qualified to understand what our trade union movement has in mind do you believe that the "Seattle Record" would care to publish his article?

The Workers Education Bureau which the American Federation of Labor has endorsed and with which some thirty-two of our national and international organizations are now affiliated ought to be so directed and managed that the purposes of trade unionism shall be furthered. The only way that this can be done is for bona fide, unchallenged trade unionists to give this work their active and constructive support. We know that the socialists have been interested in this field and that they are willing to be active so that they can control it for their own purposes. We know that it is an important field. Your own interest in education is so well known that your sympathetic cooperation would be of the greatest value in maintaining wise policies. The Field Secretary[3] of the Bureau has his headquarters in the Federation Building and is also commissioned as an organizer for the Federation. I am sure that such relations would not be maintained if not justified on the basis of performance and past record.

Sincerely and fraternally yours,　　Saml Gompers.

President,　　American Federation of Labor.

P.S. It will interest you to know that the pamphlet from which the "Record" quotes was offered to the W.E.B. and rejected by it.

S. G.

TLS, United Brotherhood of Carpenters and Joiners of America Records, reel 2, frame 404, *AFL and the Unions.*

1. Harry Wellington Laidler (1884–1970) was a founder of the Intercollegiate Socialist Society and served on its executive committee (1905–21), as its vice-president (1907–10), and as its organizing secretary (1910–21). When the Society was reorganized in 1921 to form the League for Industrial Democracy, he served as executive director of the new organization (1921–57) and then as executive director emeritus (1957–70). The group advocated the expansion of industrial democracy and encouraged the study of political, social, economic, and labor problems.

Laidler's article, "Recent Developments in the American Labor Movement," published in the *Seattle Union Record* of Jan. 11, 1924, discussed the aims and achievements of the workers' education movement. It portrayed the Workers' Education Bureau as a culmination of earlier efforts like the Rand School of Social Science and schools set up by the Amalgamated Clothing Workers and Ladies' Garment Workers, and it extolled the "energetic and progressive" leadership given to the Bureau by James Maurer and Fannia Cohn.

2. James Hudson MAURER served as president of the Pennsylvania State Federation of Labor from 1912 until 1928.

3. Hartwell Leonard Brunson (1875–1959?), an attorney, served as field secretary of the Workers' Education Bureau of America. During the summer of 1924 he went to Nicaragua at SG's request to investigate workers' conditions and offer advice to the Nicaraguan government on labor legislation. On his return, he directed the AFL's drive to raise money for the La Follette–Wheeler campaign.

From Albert Melville[1]

Central Labor Council[2]
San Pedro and Wilmington
San Pedro, California. Jan 22nd 1924

My dear Mr Gompers:

At the last meeting of our Council I was instructed to write you earnestly requesting that the A.F. of L. place an organizer in San Pedro to continue the work of re-organizing the water-front men of this district which was started by Bro Madson[3] of the I.L.A. who was forced to discontinue his work here on account of no finances. The Central Labor Council of San Pedro has been and is yet rendering all assistance humanely possible to the furtherance of this organizing campaign, and have arrived at the end of their resources consequently this appeal for aid.

We, who are here on the scene of activity know how very active the I.W.W. are and how they are at this very minute doing all in their power to tear down the good that Bro. Madson has done. They are sending men and organizers in here by the droves and seem to be making a concentrated move on this district. They are not confining their work against only the I.L.A. but are also attacking The Cullinary Alliance and the Building Trades in some cases to an alarming degree and are making their usual braggs about having all organized labor on the run by early spring. However even though they are active against all Labor Unions they are concentrating there main strength against the I.L.A. and are being given all consideration by the Fink Hall[4] operators. The I.L.A. boys cannot only in isolated instances procure a day's work on the front for all men are hired through the medium of the Fink Hall and all Ship-Owners have been instructed to hire only through this abominable organ of the Industrial Association. The Wobblies are given every cosideration at this Fink Hall and keep the jobs on the front continually filled with their scum while the good I.L.A. men who are 99 times out of 100 tax payers in the City Of Los Angeles (the Wobblies as you know only come and go) walk the streets while some of their families are in actual want.

While Bro. Madson was here he worked like a [. . .]an and got the I.L.A. organization fairly on its feet, and it was [. . .]ainly deplorable that he was forced to leave when he did, for a [. . .]f the good that he did is being wasted on account of not being [. . .]o follow up and hold the gains he had made. However it is the [. . .]us opinion of the Council that The American Federation of Labor [. . .] sit idly by when an opportunity such as we have before us to advance the interests of the Great American Federation of Labor and crush we hope forever the activities of The Industrial Workers of the World, in this locality.

We trust that it will be possible for The A.F. of L. to send in or defray the expenses of a man such as Bro. Madson or better still Bro. Madson as he is so familiar with the situation and pick up again the nearly broken threads of his former labor.

Trusting that you will give this your earnest and careful consideration and that we shall receive an agreeable and satisfactory reply soon,[5] for believe Mr Gompers that we are making this appeal at a time of dire necessity,

Fraternally yours,   San-Pedro Central Labor Council
A. L. Melville   Sec. Treas.

TLSr, AFL Microfilm National and International Union File, Longshoremen Records, reel 39, frame 1693, *AFL Records.*

1. Albert Loomis Melville (1886?-1944), a ship carpenter, was business agent for United Brotherhood of Carpenters and Joiners 1140 of San Pedro, Calif.

2. The AFL chartered the San Pedro and Wilmington Central Labor Council in 1914.

3. John Andrew "Andy" Madsen (1870–1927) served as a vice-president of the International Longshoremen's Association from 1922 to 1925.

4. That is, an employer-run hiring hall.

5. Melville's letter reiterated an appeal previously made to SG on Dec. 26, 1923, by Longshoremen's president Anthony Chlopek (AFL Microfilm National and International Union File, Longshoremen Records, reel 39, frame 1693, *AFL Records*). When SG did not reply to these letters, Chlopek renewed his request by wire on Feb. 19 and 29,

1924. SG replied to Chlopek on Feb. 29 to say the AFL lacked the funds to meet Madsen's salary and expenses (ibid., frame 1692). Chlopek appealed to the AFL Executive Council, which voted at its August meeting to pay Madsen's salary as an organizer for two months (Chlopek to the Members of the Executive Council, American Federation of Labor, July 30, 1924, Executive Council Records, Minutes, reel 7, frames 1550–52, *AFL Records*).

To Alvaro Obregón

January 29, 1924.

Honorable Alvaro Obregon,
President of Mexico,
Mexico City, Mexico.
Mr. President:

Within these past two weeks several telegrams were received from de la Huerta, Villareal,[1] Prieto Laurens,[2] appealing to Secretary Davison[3] of the International Association of Machinists, Santiago Iglesias, President of the Porto Rican Federation of Labor, myself and others imploring each and all of us to come to Vera Cruz, and offering to send money if either or all of us would consent to meet them.[4] These cringing solicitations show how desperate is the frame of mind and the situation of the rebels.[5]

I am authorized by the labor men whose names I have given above, and I speak also for myself and in the name of the American trade union movement, to state that so long as the leaders of the revolt continue their traitorous movement they can expect nothing but contempt from us. The duplicity of Adolfo de la Huerta and his followers is shown when they represent themselves to us as ultra-radicals saying that their movement has the support of the reds, while on the other hand they say to American investors that they stand for law and order and that Articles 27 and 123 of the Mexican Constitution will be made inoperative in so far as the labor and agrarian reforms are concerned.[6]

Proof of this duplicity is before me, and is undeniable. Jorge Prieto Laurenz in a telegram addressed to me, under date of December 27, 1923, stated that "*The object of this movement is the socialization of the land and of the instruments of production. The red workers support our movement.*"

On January 17, the rebel agent in Washington and New York, Enrique Seldner,[7] published a statement charging that "*The Obregon-Calles regime is so tainted with red tendencies that Mexico would be converted into a soviet state dominated by Moscow.*"

De la Huerta is evidently making every effort to deceive investors and employers of Mexico and the United States on the one hand, and to mislead the working people of Mexico on the other. But neither group nor the general public, will be so easily misled.

I refuse to communicate direct with Adolfo de la Huerta and his followers, despite the repeated attempts they have made to have me do so. The only thing they can do is to give up their unworthy movement and surrender to the democratic, constitutional government of Mexico.

Assuring you, Mr. President, of my personal consideration, I am

Respectfully yours,   (Signed) Samuel Gompers.
Chairman,   Pan-American Federation of Labor.

P.S. I am asking Dr. Frank Bohn to deliver this personally to you.

TLtcSr, RG 59, General Records of the Department of State, DNA.

1. Antonio I. Villarreal (1879–1944) supported Adolfo de la Huerta's 1923–24 rebellion against President Alvaro Obregón and went into exile when the uprising failed. He had served as secretary of the Junta Organizadora del Partido Liberal Mexicano (Organizing Committee of the Mexican Liberal Party; 1906), governor of Nuevo León (1914–15), and minister of the Secretariat of Agriculture (1920–21).

2. Jorge Prieto Laurens (b. 1895) served as president of the Mexican Chamber of Deputies (1923), governor of San Luis Potosí (1923), and president of the Cooperatist party (1923–24). When the Obregón government refused to recognize his election as governor of the state of San Luis Potosí, backing his rival Aurelio Manrique, Prieto Laurens joined de la Huerta's rebellion against Obregón and went into exile when it failed.

3. Emmett C. DAVISON served as secretary-treasurer of the International Association of Machinists from 1917 to 1944.

4. The telegrams are printed in "A Letter to Obregon," *American Federationist* 31 (Mar. 1924): 254–56. They include de la Huerta to SG, Jan. 12, 1924, quoting de la Huerta to Davison of the same date; Villarreal to SG, Jan. 12, 1924; Prieto Laurens to SG, Dec. 27, 1923; and Villarreal to Santiago Iglesias, Jan. 23, 1924, quoted in William Patterson to Iglesias, Jan. 26, 1924.

5. An uprising against Obregón began on Nov. 30, 1923. Triggered by opposition to Plutarco Elías Calles as Obregón's apparent successor, it was led by de la Huerta and involved much of the Mexican army and thousands of civilians. Peasant organizations and unions affiliated with the Confederación Regional Obrera Mexicana (Mexican Confederation of Labor) remained loyal to the government. By February 1924 the rebellion had been crushed. An estimated seven thousand Mexicans died in the fighting.

6. Article 27 of Mexico's 1917 constitution provided for the redistribution of land and the nationalization of natural resources. Article 123 outlined workers' rights, including an eight-hour day, the right to unionize and the right to strike, profit sharing and a minimum wage, equal pay for equal work regardless of sex or nationality, and a prohibition of child labor.

7. Enrique Seldner (b. 1880?) was de la Huerta's private secretary and had gone to New York City to act as his personal representative and commercial agent. He used the title Consul General of the Provisional Government of Mexico in New York.

From Louis Baer[1]

North Side Pittsburg, Pa. Feb. 1, 1924.

Dear friend Sam:

I received your welcome letter[2] and was very much pleased to hear from you and to know that you are well and happy and I hope you will continue that way for many years to come. Sam, you say you think of those days we worked together in Hirsh's shop. Yes Sam, take it all in all the boys that worked with us that time were above the average in intelligence, at least the majority were. Don't you think so? You remember our friend Ferdinand Laurell and Louis Berliner[3] and Dan Harris[4] and my brother Henry.[5] I can't think of the rest just now.

Yes Sam, I think of those days very often. You remember during that strike, I believe it was in the middle part of the seventies, when we paraded up the Bowery and it was raining pretty heavily. That was some time—do you remember that? Sam, I am sorry for one thing, that I joined that old bunch of radicals in the early part of the seventies, the so called internationals you know, to which F. Bolte[6] and Carl[7] and a lot of other radicals belonged to and listened to their radical foolishness, their good-for-nothing thoughts.

They never amounted to anything and I hope they never will here in this country. Of all the countries in the World, I regard this our country as God's country. If there are faults here it is the fault of us citizens and still Sam, it is the best government ever emanated from man. That is my opinion so far of what I know of the other governments on the other side.

Sam, I am always pleased when I read in the papers when you knock those radicals. This is confidential—had I known then what I know today I would be in better circumstances but it is too late to cry over the past.

Enclosed you will find a correct copy from your writing.[8] It is the same as when you wrote it for me. When you come here some day I will show it to you and we will sing it together. I sing it once in a while. It is a beautiful song. Well Sam, I hope you will have an opportunity to come to Pittsburgh soon so we can talk about olden times.

Fraternally yours,　Friend Louis Baer

Hoping these lines will reach You in good Health and spirits I am with good wishes

Your Friend　Louis Baer.

let me hear from You soon.[9]

T and ALS, Files of the Office of the President, General Correspondence, reel 107, frame 600, *AFL Records.*

1. Louis Baer (b. 1851), who came to the United States from Hamburg, Germany, in 1870, worked with SG in New York City during the mid-1870s at David Hirsch's cigar shop. He was a founder of the United Cigarmakers (1872) and Cigar Makers' International Union of America 144 (1875).

2. SG to Baer, Jan. 30, 1924, Files of the Office of the President, General Correspondence, reel 107, frame 592, *AFL Records.*

3. Louis Berliner (b. 1831), born in New York City, was another of SG's shopmates. He was a member of the United Cigarmakers, financial secretary (1877–79) and vice-president (1882) of Cigar Makers' local 144, and a founder of the Amalgamated Trades and Labor Union of New York and Vicinity. He was also a member of the American Section of the Workingmen's Party of the United States.

4. Daniel HARRIS, another shopmate, later served as president of Cigar Makers' local 144, president (1892–98) of the New York State Workingmen's Assembly, vice-president (1898) and president (1899, 1906–10) of the Workingmen's Federation of the State of New York, and president (1910–15) of the New York State Federation of Labor.

5. Henry Baer (b. 1852?), another immigrant from Hamburg, Germany, was a founder of Cigar Makers' local 144 and served variously as its recording secretary (1875), auditor (1878–79), and treasurer (1880).

6. Friedrich Bolte (b. 1833?), who was born in Hanover, Germany, worked in New York City during the 1870s as a cigar packer. He served as a member of the General Council of the International Workingmen's Association (1872–74) and as general secretary of the North American Federal Council of the International (1873), and he was a founder and served as German-language corresponding secretary of the Association of United Workers of America (1874).

7. Conrad Carl (1830?-90), born in Bavaria, came to the United States in 1854 and settled in New York City where he worked as a tailor. He served as a member of the North American Central Committee of the International (1871) and as a member of the International's General Council (1872–74), and he was an editor (1873–75) of the *Arbeiter-Zeitung* (New York), the International's organ in the United States.

8. That is, the lyrics for the song "The Nectar Cup May Yield Delight" (Files of the Office of the President, General Correspondence, reel 107, frame 603, *AFL Records*).

9. See "To Louis Baer," Feb. 11, 1924, below.

Frederick Suitor[1] to Frank Morrison

Headquarters
Quarry Workers International Union of North America
and office of the
Quarry Workers Journal
Barre, Vermont. Feb. 6, 1924.

Mr. Frank Morrison,
Sec'y., American Federation of Labor,
Washington, D.C.,
Dear Sir and Brother,

I wish to acknowledge your letters of January 15th 1924, and January 24th 1924, together with your telegram of January 24th.[2]

There are many and cogent reasons why the Quarry Workers' International Union of America has not complied with resolution number 55,[3] Portland Convention.

In the first place this resolution was founded upon the contract dated October 18th, 1921, which expired on October 18th, 1923, so that we do not see how we should act under a resolution that relates to an expired agreement. In the next place because of expiration of that agreement, the whole matter turns upon our original charter and the jurisdiction obtained thereunder. Our charter granted jurisdiction over "*quarry workers*." There can be no sane dispute about what the words "*quarry workers*" mean. Giving them their proper construction they include all persons that are actively engaged in the manual labor of a quarry. The man who handles a drill is no more a quarry worker than the man who handles a lever of a derrick hoist or turns on or off the steam power of an engine used on a quarry. If there is to be a subdivision by which engineers shall be separated from the quarry workers why not a subdivision that will separate the persons who run a steam drill from the persons who handle the derrick and so on ad infinitum until the workers are separated into such small groups that Unionism could not succeed.

Neither the workmen nor the employers should be required to deal with a multiplicity of contracts. One contract with a given firm should cover all quarry workers employed by that firm. To subdivide them into groups would be to multiply the occasions of friction to the worker and employer, to give to a small group, such as the engineers are as compared with the other numerous quarry workers, the power to disturb or to suspend business. If the representative principle is to govern in our Union management, certainly the majority of the workers on any particular job should have the right to control the agreement, to determine when there has been a breach, to insist upon suitable conditions and terms of employment, and to do any other matter or thing that is necessary in the interest of the business of quarrying.

If the comparatively few engineers are to make independent contracts they may do great injury to the majority of their fellow workmen. They should, therefore, submit to the discipline of the organization in which the greater number of workers belong. One small group should not control a much more numerous group. You realize that one of the serious causes of friction to Union labor today is a question of jurisdiction.

I would remind you of the results in the "Bedford, Ind. Limestone Belt." There we had 85% of all quarry workers organized in 1921 and because they had been put into the two separate unions—Engineers' Union and Quarry Workers' Union—by a local organizer of the A.F.

of L., as a result we could not get concerted action at the opportune time in a strike which followed.[4] They are today 100% disorganized. There are between three and five thousand non-union quarry workers in that district today, a striking monument to this distructive move on the part of the Engineers' Union.

The situation in the granite industry is critical, due to the fight to establish the so-called "American" plan which has been waged since 1921 and is still unsettled. We are 100% Union again in Concord, N.H., one of the places in which you are asked to interfere, yea, instructed to do so, and in Graniteville, Vt. three of the largest quarrying concerns have the stage set and are bending every effort to break the spirit of our men and put our Union out of business—every Union firm in this place but one have signed our new agreement to make their jobs 100% Union and to employ only members of our Union. One Union firm going along under old agreement and a very few engineers have not come under our new agreement. Are we to inject this division into our ranks and see the whole lost to organized labor? Graniteville, Vt. is ten miles from a main line railroad and no passenger trains go nearer than Barre, Vt., four miles from quarries. There is no other industry in Graniteville, Vt.—just the quarries. Our organization controls 95% of the Union men in Union quarries—why is this not sufficient for any Union man of experience?

The two Miners' Unions have same jurisdiction over miners as we have over quarry workers—why tear us apart and leave these as they are? Is it because their Might makes Right? We know the Miners' jurisdiction is right and their only practical jurisdiction and we of the Quarry Workers' International Union know by experience that our original jurisdiction is right and the only sensible and practical jurisdiction for quarry workers.

At the Portland Convention the following was unanimously adopted;—

" . . . [5] However, owing to the isolation of some few industries from thickly populated centers where the overwhelming number follow one branch thereof, and owing to the fact in some industries comparatively few workers are engaged over whom separate organizations claim jurisdiction, we believe that jurisdiction in such industries by the paramount organization would yield the best results to the workers therein, at least until the development of organization of each branch has reached a stage wherein these may be placed, *without material injury to all parties in interest,* in affiliation with their national trade unions. . . ."[6]

"2. We hold that the interests of the trade union movement will be promoted by closely allied and subdivided crafts giving consideration to amalgamation, and to the organization of District and National Trade Councils, to which should be referred questions in dispute, and which should be adjusted within allied crafts lines." Report of the Proceedings of the Forty-Third Annual Convention of the A.F. of L., page 268.

This resolution contains a great deal of wisdom. Amalgamation is certainly desired even though there may be enough employees to form a Union of some National trade organization. But the great body of men engaged in the quarry business are not engineers and their welfare should be considered as well as that of a minor group. One good strong Union is worth a dozen weak ones even though in the aggregate the weak ones may contain membership equal to the one strong Union.

It is considerations like these that have actuated the International Executive Board unanimously instructing me to say that we cannot give up our jurisdiction over quarry engineers; that we must maintain our original jurisdiction over all quarry workers.

We want to go along with the American Federation of Labor. We believe in a good strong bond of Unity between all departments of organized labor but we do not want our Union destroyed. If the only alternative left us is the destruction of our Union within the Federation of Labor or continued existence outside of the American Federation of Labor, we certainly must choose the latter. We should regret exceedingly to be compelled to take this alternative but we could not hesitate to do so if our Union is to be weakened by being deprived of the jurisdiction of all quarry workers, including engineers. To submit to the lessening of our jurisdiction would be to weaken us in the severe contests that we have sustained and that face us in the future.

We, therefore, earnestly appeal to you and through you to the executive council of A.F. of L. to take no action to carry out resolution 55. We deny that that resolution has any force at the present time because it is founded upon an expired agreement. I might write you more fully in regard to all the circumstances that led up the execution of the agreement of October 18th 1921. It was a purely temporary device and was urged upon us in view of pending contingencies that are now passed. It was not a bridge for permanent travel, but for temporary passage. It has effected its purpose and is no longer useful. The whole question now reverts to the situation as it existed before October 18th 1921. The very terms of that agreement suggest its temporary nature. It only had application in "new fields." Graniteville, Concord and other places are not "new fields" but were old land already tilled by the Quarry Workers' International Union of North America before the agreement.

Assuring you that we feel confident full justification for a stay of this distructive action is in the situation as it actually exists today, I am,

Fraternally yours,   Fred W. Suitor

Sec'y-Treas.[7]

TLS, AFL Microfilm Jurisdiction File, Operating Engineers Records, reel 49, frame 2426, *AFL Records.*

1. Frederick William Suitor served as secretary-treasurer of the Quarry Workers' International Union of North America from 1910 until his death in 1934.

2. Frank Morrison to Suitor, Jan. 15, 1924, AFL Microfilm Jurisdiction File, Operating Engineers Records, reel 49, frame 2424, *AFL Records;* Morrison to Suitor, Jan. 24, 1924, ibid.

3. Resolution 55, approved by the 1923 AFL convention, required the Quarry Workers to notify firms in Barre, Vt., and Concord, N.H., that the International Union of Steam and Operating Engineers had jurisdiction over engineers in local quarries. It called on the secretary of the AFL to contact the firms if the Quarry Workers failed to comply.

4. The Journeymen Stone Cutters' Association of North America had long had contracts with companies in Indiana's Bedford-Bloomington region that produced limestone blocks for use in building construction. But in 1921, after the union demanded an eight-hour day and discontinuance of use of the air hammer, the companies refused to renew these contracts and hired nonunion workers. After unsuccessful attempts to renew the contracts, the union in 1924 barred its members anywhere in the country from finishing Bedford-Bloomington limestone that had been worked on by nonunion labor, a ban that all but halted use of the stone in well-organized areas. The Bedford Cut Stone Co. and several other firms failed in their attempt to secure injunctions against the union, either in federal district court or the circuit court of appeals (*Bedford Cut Stone Company et al. v. Journeymen Stone Cutters' Association of North America et al.,* 9 F.2d 40 [1925]), but in 1927 the U.S. Supreme Court found for the companies, which were represented by Walter Gordon Merritt and Daniel Davenport, ruling the boycott was a conspiracy in restraint of interstate commerce (*Bedford Cut Stone Company et al. v. Journeymen Stone Cutters' Association of North America et al.,* 274 U.S. 37 [1927]).

5. Ellipses in original.

6. Ellipses in original.

7. As directed by action of the 1923 AFL convention (see n. 3, above), Morrison wrote eleven firms in Barre, Concord, and Graniteville, Vt., on Feb. 8, 1924, notifying them that engineers working in their quarries were now under jurisdiction of the Steam and Operating Engineers (AFL Microfilm Jurisdiction File, Operating Engineers Records, reel 49, frame 2425, *AFL Records*). He informed Suitor of his action the next day (ibid.). The Quarry Workers did not disaffiliate.

To Louis Baer

Washington, D.C. Feb. 11, 1924.

Mr. Louis Baer,
P.O. Box 227, No. Diamond Sta., Pittsburgh, Penna.
Dear friend:

Your letters have carried me back very vividly to the days when we were shop-mates and pals in Hirsch's shop. Do you suppose any outsider would ever know the meaning of that word, shop-mate? Those days when we talked and dreamed together were very happy ones.

Do you remember Amos Guerling[1] and the songs he used to sing and how he challenged us that he would sing two German songs to every English song we could sing? Those were surely happy days born of the camaraderie of the shop.

Then do you remember our special translation of the opening of the Communist Manifesto. "A red goose there was that ran around Europe, the ghost of communism" etc? I hope we shall have opportunity and time to talk over the old days.

Our dear friend Ferdinand Laurrell passed away last year. His last days were unhappy; for years he was a helpless invalid as a result of an accident. He was such a gentle big-minded friend to whom I feel that I owe much for his advice to me not to join the International.

Thanks for the words of the song.[2] I too hope we can sing it together.

Sincerely yours,
President,   American Federation of Labor.

TLc, Files of the Office of the President, General Correspondence, reel 107, frame 632, *AFL Records*.

1. Actually Asmus Gerling (b. 1841?), who was born in Prussia and emigrated to the United States in 1869, settling in New York City, where he worked as a cigarmaker.
2. See "From Louis Baer," Feb. 1, 1924, n. 8, above.

From John Donlin and William Spencer[1]

Building Trades Department.
Washington, February 16, 1924.

Dear Sir and Brother:

Your favor of the 15th instant[2] is at hand, in which you transmit the action of the Executive Council, A.F. of L., as taken on the complaint of the Brotherhood of Carpenters and Joiners that dual unions exist at Cincinnati and Dayton, Ohio, which alleged dual unions are affiliated with the local Building Trades Councils of these cities with the knowledge and consent of the Building Trades Department. The instructions of the Executive Council are to the effect that the Building Trades Department order the local Councils in Cincinnati and Dayton to unseat the alleged dual unions of Carpenters within ten days.[3]

Your letter fails to state, however, whether any corresponding action was taken by which the Brotherhood of Carpenters and Joiners is required, as provided in the law and the rules governing Departments, to affiliate with the Building Trades Department, or whether any steps have been taken by the Executive Council, A.F. of L. to put a stop to the pernicious practice of the Brotherhood of Carpenters and Joiners in obtaining injunctions either directly or indirectly for the purpose of thwarting the proper and rightful activities of the International Unions associated with the Building Trades Department. Surely the complaints of the Building Trades Department on both subjects herewith covered are of sufficient magnitude to call for at least some attention at the hands of the Executive Council, as well as an expression of opinion as to how the grievance of the Building Trades Department against the Brotherhood of Carpenters and Joiners might be redressed.

It cannot be assumed that the Building Trades Department shall extend cooperation, encouragement and assistance to an unaffiliated organization, more particularly when the said non-affiliation is the result of defiance and prejudice, for it must be perfectly obvious to the members of the Executive Council that the Brotherhood of Carpenters and Joiners is at liberty to commend the protection and cooperation of the Building Trades Department by a rightful resumption of relationship.

Aside from the allegation of the Brotherhood of Carpenters and Joiners that dual unions exist in the cities referred to, the Building Trades Department has no official knowledge of their existence, and your letter might well have contained the advice that the situation be investigated before presuming that the allegations of the Carpenters and Joiners are essentially correct.

It is most difficult to understand why the Executive Council should render so emphatic a decision on the grievance of the Carpenters while remaining profoundly silent on those of the Building Trades Department. From outward appearances it seems to be a case where the Building Trades Department is to be made the catspaw by the Executive Council in order that the chestnuts of the Brotherhood [of] Carpenters and Joiners might be pulled out of the fire, and you are informed that no action will or can be taken in so far as carrying out the instructions of the Executive Council is concerned in this case until the full correspondence covering the subject has been submitted to the Executive Council of the Building Trades Department for its consideration and action.

Fraternally yours,
(Signed) John Donlin   President.
Wm. J. Spencer,   Secretary-Treasurer
Building Trades Department A.F. of L.[4]

TLtcSr, Executive Council Records, Minutes, reel 7, frame 1446, *AFL Records.*

1. William J. SPENCER served as secretary-treasurer of the AFL Building Trades Department from 1908 to 1924 and again from 1927 to 1933.

2. SG to John Donlin, Feb. 15, 1924, AFL Microfilm National and International Union File, Carpenters Records, reel 35, frame 2633, *AFL Records.*

3. SG to Donlin, Feb. 16, 1924, AFL Microfilm National and International Union File, Carpenters Records, reel 35, frame 2633, *AFL Records.*

4. The controversy over the dual carpenters' unions in Cincinnati and Dayton, Ohio, arose out of the longstanding jurisdictional dispute between the United Brotherhood of Carpenters and Joiners of America and the Amalgamated Sheet Metal Workers' International Alliance (see *The Samuel Gompers Papers,* vol. 8, p. 151, n. 8). The AFL Building Trades Department had suspended the Carpenters in 1921 because of that dispute (see *The Samuel Gompers Papers,* vol. 11, p. 545, n. 1), and it subsequently encouraged the creation of dual carpenters' unions in several cities, including Cincinnati and Dayton. In February 1924 the AFL Executive Council directed the Department to order the Cincinnati and Dayton building trades councils to drop the dual carpenters' unions from membership, but the Department ignored the demand. When the independent carpenters opened a national headquarters in Cincinnati in January 1925 with the Department's approval, the AFL Executive Council again told the Department to drop them from membership. The dispute over the dual unions was finally resolved in late 1925, when the Carpenters admitted the independent Cincinnati and Dayton locals to membership. The Department readmitted the Carpenters in 1927, and the Carpenters-Sheet Metal Workers jurisdictional dispute was finally resolved in 1928.

To Reuben Lewis[1]

February 26, 1924.

Mr. Reuben A. Lewis,
Associate Editor, Journal of American Bankers Association.
110 East 42nd Street, New York City.
Dear Sir:

I am disinclined to write an article on the subject suggested in your letter of January 9th, but perhaps I may, in this letter, convey to you one or two thoughts in regard to the question of labor banks.

I am not in agreement with the suggestion that "labor will find the mobilization of savings and their strategic investment to be a more effective weapon than the strike as a means of advancing the workers' interest." I am convinced that such a suggestion misinterprets the functions of banking and the purpose of the strike. Of course, no one can foresee all that may come from such a development as that which has attended the establishment of labor banks, but I am confident that the functions of the economic organizations of the workers will never be replaced by any service which may be rendered by financial institutions.

Labor banks have, I think, fully justified their existence as banks, but I am not aware of any development which would justify the conclusion that their function will be anything more than good banking in the interest of their stockholders and depositors.

Of course, there are services which labor banks may render in behalf of wage earners which the ordinary bank would, at least, not be inclined to render. These services can not, however, go beyond the laws enacted for the control of banking, nor can [th]ey in any other way, go beyond the general rules and p[rinci]ples governing sound banking.

Labor banks must be, if anything, more carefully governed than other banks. The strike is in no way related to banking and I shall not discuss it in that connection. The thought that labor banks may become so potent in the control of industry that strikes will be unnecessary is equal to saying that the influence of labor banks may become such a controlling factor in industry that there will no longer be industrial disputes.

I like occasionally to look into the future and even to dream dreams but that thought has neither been among my dreams nor among my convictions concerning realities. Industrial disputes, which are, of course, nothing more than disputes concerning terms and conditions of employment and hours of work are likely to continue for a long period of time. The strike is resorted to by wage earners only when all efforts at negotiations fail and only when the wage earners feel that they cannot continue at work under the terms and conditions offered by the employers. The strike is merely a refusal to work under unacceptable conditions. If labor banks, through wise management, succeed in some measure in tempering here and there some of the extremes of financial opposition and employers' hostility, they will of course, be rendering a distinct service to the entire industrial world. I think I may say with safety, however, that such a service will be incidental.

These banks, like all others, are financial institutions which can not replace the economic organizations or take over any of their essential functions.

Very truly yours,   Saml Gompers
President,   American Federation of Labor.

TLpS, reel 297, vol. 311, pp. 97–98, SG Letterbooks, DLC.

1. Reuben Alexander Lewis, Jr. (1895–1948), was associate editor of the *American Bankers' Association Journal* from 1923 to 1928.

To Victor Gauthier[1]

March 5, 1924.

Mr. V. S. Gauthier,
Grand Lodge Representative, International Association of
    Machinists,
4114 Fairview Drive, Toledo, Ohio.
Dear Sir and Brother:

Your letter of March 1 received and contents noted.

In compliance with your request I am sending you copies of letters[2] sent out by William Z. Foster to different individuals in which instructions are given for the forming of branches of the Trade Union Educational League also the program for the guidance of the Workers Party presented to a convention of that party in December 1922.

The convention of the American Federation of Labor held in Portland, Oregon, October 1–12, 1923, expelled a member[3] of the Communist Party who held credentials from a central body. Enemies of the trade union movement should not be permitted to undermine or bore from within while members of trade unions.

With best wishes and assuring you of my desire to be helpful in any way within my power, I am,

Fraternally yours,   Saml Gompers.
President,   American Federation of Labor.

TLpS, reel 297, vol. 311, p. 325, SG Letterbooks, DLC.

1. Victor Sanford Gauthier (1879–1967), a member of International Association of Machinists 105 of Toledo, had served from 1918 to 1922 as a member of the international's general executive board.

2. SG enclosed three circulars written by William Z. Foster, dated Feb. 10, Feb. 17, and Feb. 25, 1922; "A Call to Action" and "The Principles and Program of the Trade Union Educational League" from the March 1922 issue of the *Labor Herald;* and a statement on trade unions presented by Charles Ruthenberg to the 1922 Workers' Party of

America convention in New York City (reel 297, vol. 311, pp. 326–48, SG Letterbooks, DLC).

3. William Dunne, representative of the Silver Bow Trades and Labor Council of Butte, Mont. See "Dunne Defies A.F. of L. to Expel Him," Oct. 8, 1923, in "Excerpts from Accounts of the 1923 Convention of the AFL in Portland, Ore.," Oct. 8–12, 1923, above.

An Excerpt from the Minutes of a Meeting on Organizing Women in Industry[1]

Hotel Aberdeen, New York, March 9, 1924

. . .

Mr. Gompers stated that the committee was acting to carry into effect the spirit of the conventions of the American Federation of Labor, to organize the women in industry as especially emphasised by the Portland Convention and further emphasised by the Washington conference[2] a few weeks ago. He expressed his disappointment at the replies received from the letters[3] sent out upon this matter and stated that the organizations seemed to lack an understanding of the move. Continuing he stated "the increased number of women in industry for either maintenance or independence is going to remain, unless by some means the whole human race is emancipated. There is a woeful waste of power and opportunity in failing to organize the women in industry. One of these obstacles is the Women's Trade Union League, and in saying that I mean no disparagement to that organization. I don't say that meaning harm. It appears though that it is the all sufficient organization which undertakes to organize all women in industry, and that being so, why go further? It seems to the unknowing that due to the existence of the Women's Trade Union League all bona fide trade unions of America have surrendered their jurisdiction."

Mrs. Conboy stated that the committee should show the outside organizations that the American Federation of Labor will organize women into trade unions and not into social clubs. The Textile Workers stood ready to do its share. She stressed three points: First, There should be a woman, a member of a bona fide trade union, in charge of the campaign under the direction and authority of the Executive Council of the American Federation of Labor. Second, No woman outside of the trade union movement should be on the committee. Third, Funds would have to be found.

Mr. Gompers hereupon requested that the following memorandum, previously sent out by him,[4] be read by Miss Thorne which was accordingly done:

Memorandum: Committee meeting to plan ways and means to promote continuous organization of women wage earners in industry.

1. *Organization.* What sort of committee composed of representatives of national trade organizations in whose industry women are employed can be devised so as to secure sustained effort and at the same time have that flexibility that is necessary to assure mutual confidence and cooperation?

2. Ought not this committee to have an executive secretary (or any other name deemed fitted for the work) located at Federation headquarters who shall act as the clearing agency for information as to the whole field and the work of each cooperating organization?

3. As a basis for sustained work what arrangements ought to be made for study of the distinctive problems in organizing women, also a study of how to develop within unions cohesive influences that will serve to retain members or in other words, make the union a vital force that women workers cannot afford to neglect?

4. *Educational Work.* Either under the direction or with the cooperation of the executive secretary, there should be arrangements for getting together data, statistics on the problem of women in industry as well as concrete information of how this problem has been handled both in foreign countries and by unions in the United States so that this material may be used to supplement organizing work.

5. All activity of this campaign for organization of women workers to be under the supervision of the President and the Executive Council of the A.F. of L.

6. *Finances.*

Mr. Sigman remarked that his organization has about twenty thousand organized women workers and there are forty thousand or more unorganized covering all branches of his industry. He remarked of the difficulties of organization at the present day as distinguished from those of the early period of his organization. The immigrants were not so hard to approach then as now. Coming as they do now from radical countries they are the hardest to approach. While making a very small salary they always compare it with its equal in marks, rubles or kronens. He suggested that joint efforts be made to tackle a certain market at a certain time. He expressed his approval of suggestion number two. He stated that the entire plan of the campaign in the United States should be conducted from Headquarters, under the supervision of the President and the Executive Council. It is essential that the committee consist of women connected with the trade union movement. He also expressed the opinion however, that a man experienced in organizing should be added to the committee as a representative of each International Union attempting to organize the women. He discoursed at length on the method of organization as conducted in his trade and said that the desire should not be to organize immediately but first to get acquainted with the workers and make their friendship. He further stated that his organization has spent One Hundred and Fifty Thousand Dollars in the past year in outside organization and expressed the hope that a pool might be made and the money applied to all unorganized trades instead of to one.

Mr. Gompers: "In several trades the girls all come from the same class of people. If each organization acts on its own as done in the past we don't get to the heart and the soul of it. If done jointly better and greater results can be obtained. In the shop let the girl who is the inside worker, be diffident and attract the rest of her workers. When the outside worker comes on, these inside workers become the leaders of the shop. There is no reason why we should not have these three million workers organized. The women must be organized into a trade union of the craft at which they are employed. There seems to be the idea prevalent among women that in belonging to a trade union they lose their femininity. This idea has to be overcome. Mr. Myrup's[5] time is all taken by the dispute of the Ward Baking Company.[6] Mr. Baine[7] had promised to attend but something unforeseen came up, and Mr. Rickert at the last minute was unable to be present but I am sure that if we who are gathered here apply some practical campaign they will come along with us."

Mrs. Conboy expressed the hope that in the selection of the executive committee the Executive Council and Mr. Gompers would not accept anyone who had tied her kite to the Women's Trade Union League. She told of Miss Rose Schneiderman[8] calling her and remarking that she had not been invited to attend this conference. Mrs. Conboy went into detail as to her former connection with the Women's Trade Union League and her reasons for severing it.[9]

Mr. Perkins stated that the women have been used to demoralize industry and that they have been misinformed by a predatory rich and privileged few. If we adopt the attitude that we believe in them, we think they can make good, and then tell them to go ahead and do it, much better results will be accomplished. We must not approach them patronizingly. We should appoint a committee to draw up a tentative plan. Every statement going out should bear the number of women employed in industry. The management should be in the hands of responsible officers of the unions who come in on this plan and then let them surrender the handling of it to the President of the A.F. of L. The management should not be in the hands of organizers.

President McMahon stated that his organization would start in immediately with two women[10] and two men organizers under the direction of the A.F. of L. It was suggested that a letter be sent to Central Labor Unions and State Branches asking the delegates how many women members of their family were working in industry and yet did not belong to the trade union of their craft.

Mr. Sigman expressed his approval of what Mrs. Conboy and Mr. Perkins had said relative to the President forming a committee of the women of the labor movement and when appointed each organization affiliated to the campaign should send in the name of a member of its council who should be added to the organization committee.

Mr. Gompers: "We dedicate our full endorsement of the movement for a thorough organization of all women wage earners into unions of their respective trades or callings in which they are employed. An officer or some named bona fide trade unionist should act as the representative of this movement and with headquarters in Washington, and all organizations interested in organizing women in industry be authorized to select a representative and these will constitute a sort of directing council with the executive secretary; that the organizing campaign be part of the secretarial work; that the entire movement for the organization of women wage earners together with activities of all persons entrusted with this work shall always be under the supervision and direction of the President and Executive Council of the American Federation of Labor."

Mrs. Conboy suggested that the organizations might agree to send to the American Federation of Labor a proportionate sum each month to cover the office expenses, and that each organization might bear the expenses and the salary of its organizers.

Mr. Gompers: "I suggest that the people invited here be constituted a committee to organize the women in industry and to set forth plans and activities, under the authority of the Portland and other conventions." It was agreed to. "Is the committee to draft these things to meet or by correspondence?" Mrs. Conboy suggested that President Gompers draw up a plan[11] and submit it to the organizations by mail. This was agreed to. Mr. Perkins remarked that each member of the committee state how far he can go in this matter and that if it were to have the direct force that it should be a woman who has had experience. If it is to be a woman is there a woman available who can fill the bill? He is not opposed to a woman but is of the opinion that women of the calibre required are not available, as they are working actively for their organizations.

Mr. Gompers: "The psychological effect in the labor movement would be great, if a woman were appointed it would be very helpful."

. . .

TDc, Files of the Office of the President, Conferences, reel 123, frames 532–36,

AFL Records. Typed notation: "Conference Hotel Aberdeen, New York, March 9, 1924, 11 A.M. Women In Industry."

1. Participants at the meeting included SG and Florence Thorne, Sara Conboy and Thomas McMahon of the United Textile Workers of America, George Perkins of the Cigar Makers' International Union of America, and Morris Sigman of the International Ladies' Garment Workers' Union. Invited but unable to attend were Charles Baine of the Boot and Shoe Workers' Union, Andrew Myrup of the Bakery and Confectionery Workers' International Union of America, and Thomas Rickert of the United Garment Workers of America.

2. That is, the conference held Feb. 14, 1924. (See "From Fannia Cohn," Nov. 20, 1923, n. 3, above.)

3. "A Circular," Dec. 4, 1923, above, and SG to Dear Sir and Brother, Jan. 14, 1924, AFL Microfilm Convention File, reel 33, frame 1162, *AFL Records.*

4. For copies of this undated memorandum, see AFL Microfilm Convention File, reel 33, frames 1161–62, *AFL Records.*

5. Andrew A. MYRUP served as secretary-treasurer of the Bakery Workers from 1923 to 1941.

6. The Ward Baking Co. was the largest baking concern in the country and had been unionized since 1917. In 1923 the company refused to renew its national agreement with the Bakery Workers and announced plans to cut wages, abandon the eight-hour day, and institute the open shop on May 1. Some five thousand workers struck the company's bakeries in many cities including Baltimore; Boston; Brooklyn, New York City, and Syracuse, N.Y.; Chicago; Cleveland, Columbus, and Youngstown, Ohio; Newark, N.J.; Philadelphia; Pittsburgh; Providence; and South Bend, Ind., but the company carried through with its plans to operate on an open-shop basis.

7. Charles L. BAINE, secretary-treasurer of the of Boot and Shoe Workers' Union from 1902 to 1931.

8. Rose SCHNEIDERMAN served as vice-president (1919–26) and president (1926–50) of the National Women's Trade Union League and was president (1918–49) of its New York branch.

9. See "From Sara Conboy," Apr. 3, 1924, below.

10. Conboy informed SG on Mar. 24, 1924, that the two women organizers would be Mary Kelleher and Melinda Scott (AFL Microfilm Convention File, reel 33, frame 1218, *AFL Records*).

11. SG's plan called for an executive board to give overall direction to the campaign, with representatives from all participating unions, and an executive secretary—a trade unionist, preferably a woman, to be named by SG—to see to day-to-day campaign activities and educational work. Unions involved in the campaign were to be asked to state how many organizers and how much money they could give to the effort. An early draft of the plan appears in Florence Thorne's account of the Mar. 9, 1924, meeting (AFL Microfilm Convention File, reel 33, frame 1174, *AFL Records*); for the plan itself, see "Excerpts from the Minutes of a Meeting on Organizing Women in Industry," May 21, 1924, n. 2, below. SG forwarded copies of the plan to participating unions on Mar. 29 and again on May 7 (AFL Microfilm Convention File, reel 33, frames 1215, 1185, *AFL Records*). For discussion of the plan at the conference on May 21, see "Excerpts from the Minutes of a Meeting on Organizing Women in Industry," May 21, 1924, below.

To John Walker

March 18, 1924.

Mr. John H. Walker,
President, Illinois State Federation of Labor,
728 Illinois Mine Workers Building, Springfield, Illinois.
Dear Sir and Brother:

Your undated letter received March 10.

You enclose two letters, one from Mr. A. W. Warinner[1] to you and your reply.

There have been many rumors of Senator LaFollette's candidacy on the third party ticket.[2] These always have been denied by the Senator. There are groups in Washington who, for obvious reasons, start presidential candidacies to attract publicity to their activities. The latest I have heard about the Illinois State Conference for Progressive Political Action is that it is friendly to Mr. McAdoo.[3]

The political situation is in a tangled state and it is impossible to forecast, but the American Federation of Labor has taken no part in any of the propaganda for a third party or for any individual candidate. You well know the policy of the American Federation of Labor which was endorsed and ordered continued by the Portland Convention of the American Federation of Labor held October 1–12, 1923.[4]

It is doubtful if any one knows what will be the outcome of the present investigations and which of the candidates for President will fall by the wayside because of the information gained. Until the atmosphere is cleared sufficiently to ascertain who is in the running nothing can be done, but I have been assured that there is no legitimate movement for a third party. The only movement along that line is by the Federated Farmer Labor Party, alias the Workers Party, alias the Communist Party and it has no following.

With best wishes, I am

Fraternally yours,   Saml Gompers.
President,   American Federation of Labor.

TLpS, reel 297, vol. 311, p. 565, SG Letterbooks, DLC.

1. Allen W. Warinner (b. 1881) served as educational director of the Central States Co-operative Wholesale Society from 1923 until the organization's demise in 1925. He was subsequently an officer of the Central States Co-operative League and, with John Walker, a director of the Co-operative League of the United States of America.

2. Wisconsin Republican senator Robert La Follette announced his candidacy for president of the United States as an Independent Republican on July 3, 1924. His running mate, Montana Democratic senator Burton Wheeler, ran as an Independent Democrat. The ticket was endorsed by both the Conference for Progressive Political

Action convention that met in Cleveland July 4–5 and the AFL Executive Council in August (see "Excerpts from the Minutes of a Meeting of the Executive Council of the AFL," Aug. 2, 1924, below).

3. The Illinois Conference for Progressive Political Action eventually supported La Follette for president.

4. The 1923 AFL convention rejected four resolutions relating to the creation of an independent political party (see "Third Party Turned Down by A.F. of L.," Oct. 9, 1923, in "Excerpts from Accounts of the 1923 Convention of the AFL in Portland, Ore.," Oct. 8–12, 1923, above). The convention did approve Resolution 102, which called on the leadership of the AFL and state federations of labor to publicize labor's positions and seek the achievement of labor's demands, particularly in the drafting of state and national political platforms.

To R. F. Noriega

March 21, 1924.

Hon. R. F. Noriego,
President, Panama Federation of Labor,
Panama City, Canal Zone.
Dear Sir and Brother:

Your letter of January 20[1] received and contents noted. An answer has been delayed because I have taken up the matter with Secretary of War Weeks and Governor Morrow[2] and until I receive a definite answer from them I could not give you any information.[3] I wish, however, to take up some of the matters you discuss.

You state that the interests of Panama and the United States are somewhat separated due to the discrimination toward the Panamanian workmen on the part of the American employes. This is a mistake. The discrimination if there be any is by the foremen or officials and not by the American employes.

I investigated the reason preference was given to West Indians over Panamanian workmen and have been told that the principal reason is that the West Indians speak English and therefore understand orders that are given. Panamanians on the other hand do not speak English. This causes confusion. It prevents American employes giving instructions to the Panamanians, a situation that not only retards the work but might result in accidents. I have been informed, however, that the Panamanians are studying English in order to be able to understand instructions given by foremen. I am glad to know this. If the Panamanians learn English there is no doubt but what there will be more chance of their being given preference over the West Indians or other aliens.

As to the claim that West Indians receive higher salaries than Panamanians this should not be the case. Any employee should be properly compensated regardless of his nationality.

There is no doubt that Panamanian workmen are inconvenienced by residing in the Canal Zone territory[4] but it also inconveniences Americans who live here and go to the Canal Zone. You ask that the Governor of the Canal Zone investigate why Panamanian workmen are not preferred. The Governor is thoroughly acquainted with the reason and therefore it is not necessary for him to make an investigation. He should be asked to remedy the situation.

In relation to the payment of house rent, etc. by the workers, this is being considered by the Secretary of War and refers to all employes on the Canal Zone. We have not yet had his answer.

You propose that the Governor shall appoint a committee of six to investigate the wages paid the silver roll employes.[5] The Governor now has a silver wage board composed of the department heads. He has declined heretofore to permit non-residents of the Canal Zone who are not employes to represent employes before him or any of the officials. The members of your federation employed on the Canal Zone should request permission to appear before the board on silver rates of pay.

In our letter[6] to Secretary of War Weeks we made the following request and recommendation:

"The employes object to the employing of aliens above the grade of laborers or messengers. We recommend all positions to be filled by American citizens or such labor as is covered by the agreement with the Republic of Panama."

You undoubtedly know that at the present time officials of the Republic of Panama and the United States are discussing the treaty between the two countries.

Let me assure you that everything possible will be done to protect the interests of the Panamanians. The American Federation of Labor always has come to the relief of any people suffering from injustices of any kind.

With best wishes and assuring you of my desire to be helpful in any way within my power, I am,

Fraternally yours,   Saml Gompers.
President,   American Federation of Labor.

TLpS, reel 297, vol. 311, pp. 759–60, SG Letterbooks, DLC.

1. R. F. Noriega to SG, Jan. 20, 1924, AFL Microfilm Convention File, reel 32, frame 1534, *AFL Records*.

2. Jay Johnson Morrow (1870–1937), governor of the Panama Canal Zone from 1921 to 1924.

3. SG passed Noriega's complaint on to Weeks and Morrow on Mar. 19, 1924 (reel 297, vol. 311, pp. 671–72, SG Letterbooks, DLC). On Mar. 27 Weeks acknowledged receipt and indicated that he had himself passed the matter on to Morrow (AFL Microfilm Convention File, reel 32, frame 1546, *AFL Records*). On Apr. 4 acting Canal Zone governor Meriwether Walker also acknowledged receipt of SG's letter, informing SG that the matter would be brought to Morrow's attention when he returned (AFL Microfilm Convention File, reel 32, frame 1546).

4. A reference to the requirement that Panamanian workers employed by the United States in the Canal Zone must live in the Canal Zone.

5. That is, non-white workers. See *The Samuel Gompers Papers,* vol. 11, pp. 392–93, n. 2.

6. SG et al. to Weeks, Jan. 31, 1924, AFL Microfilm Convention File, reel 32, frame 1520, *AFL Records*.

To Carl Norman[1]

March 25, 1924.

Dr. C. A. Norman,
Professor of Machine Design,
Ohio State University, Columbus, Ohio.
Dear Dr. Norman:

Thank [you] for your letter of March 20 which convinces me that there is much that you personally can do to promote the sort of relationship between labor and management (a term I prefer to "capital and labor"), which will make possible a constructive attitude toward production on the part of all concerned. To achieve this result it is just as necessary to educate management as it is to educate labor. In educating management I think it is evident the chief responsibility will fall upon engineers. If a constructive attitude toward this problem is stimulated by engineering schools a long step will have been made toward our goal.

The development on the Baltimore and Ohio is most encouraging.[2] It is not violating any confidence to tell you that for a number of years I was closely associated with Daniel Willard in public service which made it necessary for us to discuss fundamentals of industrial relations. As you will remember, we were members of the Advisory Commission to the Council of National Defense. Because of the relations that existed between us in that joint work Mr. Willard came to me with proposals in the recent strike of the men in the railroad shops which eventually resulted in an agreement between the shop crafts and the Baltimore and Ohio.[3] Out of this agreement came the proposal from labor that an attempt at constructive cooperation be made. A few weeks ago as perhaps you know, the plan under which the cooperative development at Glenwood was operated was extended to other shops on the B. & O. There is also the beginning of the same sort of arrangement on the C. & O. and the plans are under way for the relationship to be established on the Canadian National Railroad.

There were a number of conferences extending over a period of years that led to the formulation of the principles underlying this development. Many of these conferences were held in my office and others in which I participated elsewhere but the result has been mutual education of a group of considerable ability and influence. This is the sort of development that cannot be forced. The amount of educational work that has been necessary to bring this about can best be appreciated by those who have actively participated in the effort. We did not always secure immediate results. It would probably surprise you to know that in the conference called by the President to consider unemployment in 1921 I submitted to a committee of which I was a member the proposal that accepting the facts as developed in the Engineers' Committee on Waste in Industry, both labor and management assume their portion of responsibility allocated by that report and endeavor to work out methods and principles by which waste could be eliminated and constructive relations established. In a committee of five, of which I was the only labor member, this proposal received only one vote—my own.[4]

I think it was in 1919 that Herbert Hoover and Robert B. Wolf submitted to the Executive Council of the American Federation of Labor a somewhat less definitely stated proposal but with the same purpose in view.[5] It was agreed that we should attempt to work out some development in the building trades but it was not possible to find at that time a single construction company willing to take the initiative.

I am relating these incidents in order that you may see that the responsibility for achieving constructive relations does not rest solely upon labor and that we have not been unmindful of the possibilities of the field and our responsibility for achievement.

I am interested in what you say of the possibilities of a campaign to challenge profit beyond certain legitimate uses. That is the sort of a campaign of education to which it seems to me that engineers and economists could make most constructive contributions.

I agree with you that there are groups that could be helpful. I take it from your letter that you have some definite plans in mind. I shall be glad to consider anything that you may care to submit as I can assure you that there are many holding responsible places in the labor movement who feel deeply the responsibility for public service in addition to their responsibility to their organizations.

I am sending you another copy of the August issue of the "American Federationist" and am enclosing reprints from the "Machinists Monthly Journal" that will interest you.

Sincerely yours,   Saml Gompers
President,   American Federation of Labor.

TLpS, reel 297, vol. 311, pp. 809–10, SG Letterbooks, DLC.

1. Carl A. Norman (1879–1969) was a professor in the Engineering Department at Ohio State University in Columbus.

2. See "To B. M. Jewell," Dec. 21, 1923, n. 1, above.

3. For SG's negotiations with Daniel Willard in July 1922 to end the shopmen's strike, see Files of the Office of the President, Conferences, reel 122, frames 126–31, 145, *AFL Records.*

4. For additional discussion of the incident, see "Excerpts from the Minutes of a Meeting of the Executive Council of the AFL," Sept. 16, 1922, above.

5. See Herbert Hoover to SG, Oct. 23, 1920, reel 258, vol. 271, pp. 881–83, SG Letterbooks, DLC. See also *The Samuel Gompers Papers,* vol. 11, pp. 384–90.

To Abraham Baroff[1]

March 31, 1924.

Mr. Abraham Baroff,
Secretary-Treasurer, International Ladies Garment Workers
    Union,
3 West 16th St., New York, N.Y.
Dear Sir and Brother:

Your letter of March 28 received and given careful consideration.

You state that the International Ladies Garment Workers Union "cannot accept the penalizing of any race or nation as the principle for either regulation or restriction of immigration." You also say that your International Union "has always regarded regulation of immigration not merely as an economic question but as a problem of general humanity."

To carry this out you say you believe America "must not shut its doors to the oppressed of other nations." You, therefore, contend that you cannot support such a policy of extreme restriction as the Johnson bill[2] provides.

No citizen of another country has an inherent right to come to the United States. He has no more right to come to the United States without the consent of our people than you or I have to walk into a home in this country and say to the head of the family, "We intend to live here whether you want us or not."

You raise the issue that changing the census basis from 1910 to 1890 penalizes certain races. In that you are grievously mistaken. Among the races you claim will be penalized are the Jews, the Italians, the Slavs and the Magyars. The Jew is a citizen of every nation and under the 1890 census more of them could come to this country than under the census of 1910 because they would come within both the quota and non-quota clauses from countries in the northern and western part of Europe[3] and therefore in larger numbers than before.

There are few Jews in Italy. Mussolini, the fascisti dictator, also objects to the bill[4] because of "discrimination." He says it would prevent as many Italians immigrating to this country as he would wish. In the protest[5] made to the government of the United States Mussolini declared through the Italian Ambassador[6] that the economic restoration of Italy depends upon the money sent by immigrants from the United States to their families in Italy.

The Rumanian government makes the same protest.[7]

There is a clause in the Johnson bill which places in the non-quota class the fathers, mothers and children of foreign born citizens in this country. That would bring a great relief to the members of the Jewish race. The race issue raised by you so far as it affects the Jew is not well taken. We are having the same struggle against opponents of the exclusion of Japanese laborers. Following out your argument the American Federation of Labor should approve of the admission of exploited Chinese. It should permit the admission of the natives of India who are suffering from religious or political persecution.

You say that your International Union cannot accept the penalizing of any race or nation. Do you mean by this that you would admit the billion yellow and brown people living within the barred Asiatic zone from which no immigrant can come into this country? Do you see only the Jew, the Italian, the Slav and the Magyar?

There is a strong organization[8] in this country working for the admission of the Japanese under the quota system. It has managed to induce the Federal Council of Churches to endorse its position and the reason given for letting in the Japanese is that they are being discriminated against as a race.

The government of Hawaii for several years has endeavored to have Chinese coolies brought into Hawaii to take the place of Japanese who refuse to work for low wages. The reason given was that the Chinese were more docile and servile. It was also intended to deport these Chinese coolies within five years if they did not continue to remain docile and servile. The A.F. of L. through its influence defeated that proposition.

I am sorry that the International Ladies Garment Workers Union has failed to a[ppre]ciate the benefits to be gained by the Jew in the Johnson bill if enacted into law. Coming from every country as they do they are a privileged race and more of them can come to this country as immigrants than the citizens of any one country.

If as you say the policy of immigration should be controlled by the benefit that can be done humanity then we would have to have unrestricted immigration with no prescribed zone or no oppressed peoples that could not come to this country. I do not think you have studied this question as it should be. Therefore, I hope that you will consider the policy of the American Federation of Labor again, not in the light of securing benefits for any one race but what is best to be done for the people of the United States.

With best wishes and assuring you of my desire to be helpful in any way within my power, I am,

Fraternally yours,   Saml Gompers
President,   American Federation of Labor.

TLpS, reel 298, vol. 312, pp. 53–54, SG Letterbooks, DLC.

1. Abraham BAROFF served as secretary-treasurer of the International Ladies' Garment Workers' Union from 1915 until 1929.

2. H.R. 7995 (68th Cong., 1st sess.), introduced on Mar. 17, 1924, by Republican congressman Albert Johnson of Washington, was designed to replace the existing U.S. immigration law, passed in 1921 and extended in 1922, which was due to expire in June. The 1921 law established annual immigration quotas based on nationality, set at 3 percent of the number of foreign-born persons residing in the United States in 1910, as counted by the census. Immigrants from countries in the Western Hemisphere were not included under these quota provisions, and immigration of most Asians was already prohibited, so the vast majority of those admitted under the quotas were Europeans. The Johnson bill proposed to reduce the quotas from 3 to 2 percent and use the 1890 census, rather than the 1910 enumeration, as their basis, which had the effect of reducing the number of immigrants from eastern and southern Europe. The bill also barred any "alien ineligible to citizenship," thereby excluding Asians since Asians were not eligible for naturalization under U.S. laws. Consequently the Japanese, previously allowed to enter the country in limited numbers, were now excluded. The House and the Senate agreed to a revised version of the bill on May 15, and President Calvin Coolidge signed it into law on May 26 as the Immigration Act of 1924 (U.S. *Statutes at Large*, 43: 153–69; quotation at p. 162).

3. The Immigration Act of 1924 defined several categories of immigrants who could enter the United States outside the restrictions of the quota system. Categories applying to European immigrants included persons previously admitted who were returning from foreign travel; wives and unmarried children under eighteen years of age of resident U.S. citizens; religious ministers and university professors, along with their wives and unmarried children under eighteen, if they intended to continue in those professions; and students under fifteen who sought to immigrate to attend a school approved by the secretary of labor. The act provided that these categories of "nonquota" immigrants could be admitted on a discretionary basis.

4. On Dec. 5, 1923, Johnson introduced H.R. 101 (68th Cong., 1st sess.), an earlier version of the immigration bill he introduced in March 1924 (see n. 2, above). The

earlier bill also contained provisions restricting immigration by setting annual quotas at 2 percent of the number of foreign-born persons living in the U.S. in 1890. On Dec. 6 Republican senator Henry Cabot Lodge of Massachusetts introduced S. 35 (68th Cong., 1st sess.), a bill similar to H.R. 101.

5. The memorandum, which objected to H.R. 101 and S. 35, was presented to Secretary of State Charles Evans Hughes by the Italian ambassador to the United States on Dec. 15, 1923, and transmitted by Hughes to the House Immigration Committee on Dec. 31. See U.S. Congress, House, Committee on Immigration and Naturalization, *Restriction of Immigration*, 68th Cong., 1st sess., 1924, H. Rept. 350, pp. 15–16.

6. Gelasio Caetani (1877–1934), the Italian ambassador to the United States from 1922 to 1925.

7. The Romanian protest was presented to Hughes by the Romanian chargè d'affaires on Feb. 2, 1924, the day after Johnson's introduction of yet another version of his immigration bill (H.R. 6540, 68th Cong., 1st sess.). For a copy of the memorandum, see *Papers Relating to the Foreign Relations of the United States, 1924*, 2 vols. (Washington, D.C., 1939), 1: 213–14. Hughes subsequently passed the document on to the House Immigration Committee, and it is printed in *Restriction of Immigration*, pp. 14–15.

8. Probably either the National Committee for Constructive Immigration Legislation or the National Committee on American-Japanese Relations. Sidney Gulick (see *The Samuel Gompers Papers*, vol. 9, p. 515, n. 2), a leading opponent of Japanese exclusion legislation, was secretary of both organizations (the former from 1919 to 1934, and the latter from 1921 to 1934) as well as secretary of the Department of International Justice and Good-Will of the Federal Council of Churches of Christ in America (1914–34).

From Sara Conboy

Office of International Secretary Treasurer
United Textile Workers of America
New York, April 3, 1924

Dear Mr. Gompers:

Received your letter[1] yesterday and have carefully noted the contents. I wish it were possible for me to attend the conference in Chicago,[2] but owing to the various strikes in different parts of the country, I do not feel that we want to spend that money of the International Union, unless you deem it imperative that I be there.

I want, however, to express myself relative to the Womens Trade Union League, so that I may be placed clearly on record. First of all, the Womens Trade Union League was formed for the purpose of organizing the women workers. They have done everything else but that—they have organized all kinds of social things and socialistic things, but they have failed to perform the work for which they were organized.

I registered my objection to them at the meeting in New York,[3] and I am now registering my objection again to anyone holding the office of Secretary of our organizing campaign who is so closely allied to the Womens Trade Union League that they will be subservient to them.

I hope the conference at Chicago will assist in bringing about the work for which the committee was organized and that our organizing campaign may start as quickly as possible.

If you are passing through New York on your way to Chicago[4] and you have one minute or two to spare, I would be glad to talk with you relative to this campaign.

With kindest personal regards, I am

Fraternally yours,   Sara A Conboy
Secretary-Treasurer   United Textile Workers of America.

TLS, AFL Microfilm Convention File, reel 33, frame 1219, *AFL Records.*

1. SG to Sara Conboy, Mar. 31, 1924, reel 297, vol. 311, p. 1006, SG Letterbooks, DLC.

2. That is, an AFL conference on organizing women in industry, to include representatives of the National Women's Trade Union League (NWTUL), scheduled for Apr. 11, 1924. Conboy was unavailable on Apr. 11, so the meeting was held instead on Apr. 12, with a preliminary meeting on Apr. 10. Maude Schwartz, Elisabeth Christman, and Agnes Nestor, the NWTUL's president, secretary, and vice-president, attended the meeting on Apr. 12. For minutes of the two meetings, see Files of the Office of the President, Conferences, reel 123, frames 632–33, 639–42, *AFL Records.* A further meeting with NWTUL representatives was held on Apr. 22. For minutes of that meeting, see ibid., frames 662–65.

3. That is, the meeting of the AFL conference on organizing women in industry that was held in New York City on Mar. 9, 1924. See "An Excerpt from the Minutes of a Meeting on Organizing Women in Industry," Mar. 9, 1924, above.

4. SG's trip to Chicago was part of a larger trip that spanned two weeks and took him to several cities. He left Washington, D.C., on Apr. 3, 1924, for New York City, where he remained until Apr. 8, with the exception of a day trip to Bethlehem, Pa., on Apr. 6. On Apr. 8 he went to Harrisburg, Pa., spending the day there before going on to Chicago, where he arrived on the morning of Apr. 9. After holding a number of meetings with labor leaders and organizers, he left Chicago on the evening of Apr. 12, arriving back in New York on the morning of Apr. 13. SG's appointment records indicate he remained in New York until Apr. 16, and he arrived back in Washington that afternoon.

To Edna Truax[1]

April 5, 1924.

Miss Edna Truax,
1537 Crawford Avenue, Altoona, Pa.
Dear Madam:

Your letter of March 26 received and contents noted.

You ask for information to be used in a debate on the negro and chinese race problems in the United States.

Under separate cover, I am sending you a pamphlet entitled "Some Reasons for Chinese Exclusion."[2]

Slavery was abolished in the United States December 18, 1865, nearly fifty-nine years ago. Between three and four hundred years ago the bringing in of negroes from Africa began. They were barbarians. Their descendents now in this country were slaves up to fifty-nine years ago. It is not to be expected that they have advanced sufficiently to be able to solve their economic problems. You can imagine how many centuries it will take for them to advance to the stage now occupied by the white people. During the war many negroes served in the army. They learned a great many things they did not know. When the war was over they migrated from their old homes in the south to the north. Young men who secured employment in the north would write back home telling of the wages they were receiving and this encouraged more to migrate. In any discussion of the negro problem consideration should be given to their origination and the many years they were slaves.

Very truly yours,   Saml Gompers
President,   American Federation of Labor.

TLpS, reel 298, vol. 312, p. 188, SG Letterbooks, DLC.

1. Edna Truax, the daughter of an Altoona, Pa., carpenter, was about sixteen years old.

2. *Some Reasons for Chinese Exclusion. Meat vs. Rice: American Manhood against Asiatic Coolieism—Which Shall Survive?* (Washington, D.C., [1902?]).

To Frank Dickinson[1]

April 8, 1924.

Dr. F. G. Dickinson,
Economics Department,
University of Illinois,
305 Commerce Bldg., Urbana, Ill.
Dear Dr. Dickinson:

A few days ago I addressed a meeting of industrial physicians in New York.[2] In my remarks to them I pointed out the basis upon which industrial hygiene should be organized for service in the industry. A copy of my remarks is enclosed together with a copy of an article written sometime ago entitled "If I Were An Employer."[3]

Personnel administration as we use the term today originated with what is known as "scientific management." In looking over the records you will find that organized labor opposed the proposals of scientific management as first formulated. Our reasons for that position can readily be obtained and may be summed up in the statement that the earliest formulation of the policies of scientific management failed to recognize that workers were humans and also failed to appreciate the immense significance of the human factor in production. It was largely due to the protests of organized labor that management has revised its ideas of scientific management and has developed the more human program known as "personnel administration." Here again labor has been helpful in preventing personnel administration from degenerating into a welfare proposition.

We have consistently maintained that we must be treated as intelligent human beings and that our business relations must be determined upon principles of good business and free from the benevolent idea. It is an industrial waste as well as socially undesirable not to conserve the human producing agent. Personnel administration of course is an integral part of the field of management.

Of course you did not expect to find that organized labor has declared any specific attitude toward personnel administration as an abstract proposition. What we would take action upon is a specific policy for personnel administration. We have held that personnel administration should be based upon principles of industrial relations that guarantee to the workers their industrial rights and we have further held that industry is not organized which makes it necessary for all factors concerned in production to be organized as groups for functional purposes consequently organized labor has insisted that the trade union is the industrial unit in the formulation of industrial relations.

In order that you may get the background for your specific study I think it would be necessary for you to understand what organized labor thinks is the necessary and effective plan for organization of industry. I am therefore enclosing the following materials:

Industry's Manifest Duty[4]
From Politics to Industry[5]
A Worth While Revolution[6]

Should you need further material I shall be glad to assist you.

Sincerely yours,   Saml Gompers
President,   American Federation of Labor.

TLpS, reel 298, vol. 312, pp. 228–29, SG Letterbooks, DLC.

1. Frank Greene Dickinson (1899–1967) was a member of the faculty in the Economics Department at the University of Illinois, Urbana-Champaign.

2. On Apr. 4, 1924, SG spoke at a luncheon at the Hotel Astor in New York City opening the tenth annual meeting of the Conference Board of Physicians in Industry. For a copy of his address, see reel 298, vol. 312, pp. 24–27, SG Letterbooks, DLC.

3. Samuel Crowther, *If I Were an Employer: An Interview with Samuel Gompers* (n.p., [1920?]). The interview first appeared in *System: The Magazine of Business* 37 (Apr. 1920).

4. *Industry's Manifest Duty* (Washington, D.C., [1923?]) was excerpted from the report of the AFL Executive Council to the 1923 AFL convention.

5. *From Politics to Industry* (Washington, D.C., [1923?]) was an editorial by SG reprinted from *American Federationist* 30 (May 1923): 396–99.

6. "A Worth-While Revolution," *American Federationist* 31 (Apr. 1924): 318–21.

To D. C. Baker

April 17, 1924

Mr. D. C. Baker,
Organizer, American Federation of Labor,
P.O. Box 182, Redding, California.
Dear Sir and Brother:

Your letter of March 25th has been duly received and contents noted. You acknowledge receipt of the renewal of your commission as volunteer organizer of the American Federation of Labor dated March 14, 1924 and expiring March 14, 1925. Our records show that commission was issued to you on March 14, 1922 as organizer for Dunsmuir, California, upon the recommendation of the Federation of Shop Crafts. You now give your address as Redding, California.[1]

Then again you say: "However, I am working hard for an organization that stands for the same principles that the A.F. of L. stands for. It stands for (White Supremacy) Just Laws, and Liberty, the upholding of the Constitution of these United States, the Sovereignty of our State rights, the separation of Church and State, Freedom of Speech and Press, closer relationship between Capital and Labor, the limitation of foreign immigration all of which is good for the working man and the American citizens as well. I realize that the A.F. of L. cannot endorse the K.K.K. any more than it can oppose it. But with the united vote of organized labor and the vote of the Klansmen we can rid the capitol of the corrupt wealth which controls today every branch of our government.["]

In connection with this subject matter your attention is called to the report which the Executive Council of the A.F. of L. made to the Portland convention of the American Federation of Labor, October, 1923, under the heading "Klu Klux Klan" and the action of the convention thereon. Copy is enclosed herein. You will note that the Executive Council expressed the belief that:

"No trade unionist can consistently participate in the activities of the Klu Klux Klan or any similar organization and we unhesitatingly denounce its efforts to supplant organized government, to promote religious intolerance, racial antagonisms and bigotry."

This section of the E.C. report was referred to the committee on resolutions. You will note that the report of the committee fully supports the report of the Executive Council and that the committee's report was unanimously adopted by the convention and stands as the declaration of the A.F. of L.

Under these circumstances therefore I am constrained to advise you that until such time as you dissociate yourself from activities in the Klu Klux Klan, you are not eligible to hold commission as organizer for the American Federation of Labor. You will, therefore, please return to the undersigned the commission which you now hold as volunteer organizer for Dunsmuir and vicinity together with all documents which have been sent to you from time to time in connection therewith.

Fraternally yours,   Saml Gompers
President   American Federation of Labor.

TLpS, reel 298, vol. 312, pp. 389–90, SG Letterbooks, DLC.

1. Redding, Calif., the county seat of Shasta County, is located about forty miles south of Dunsmuir, Calif., a town in Siskiyou County.

To Bernard Baruch

April 18, 1924.

Mr. Bernard M. Baruch,
598 Madison Avenue, New York City.
Dear Mr. Baruch:

As I have just returned to the office from a two weeks business trip I have just had the opportunity of seeing your letter of April 5.[1] I am glad you wrote me immediately as to the rumor that reached you, for I had made no comment upon your suggestion for mobilizing industry.

You doubtless are aware that a number of those who have been making proposals to be incorporated in the War Department's plans have not had your sympathetic attitude toward labor. Several have made drastic suggestions as to how to bring workers to "a more flexible frame of mind." This propaganda has been pretty wide-spread.

An army officer in a statement that was broadcasted declared that if a worker were dissatisfied and inclined to make trouble he could be taken out of industry and put into the trenches which would adequately cure all truculency on the part of labor. It is this sort of thing against which I have protested. A representative of the American Federation of Labor appeared before the House Committee on Military Affairs and stated the Federation's opposition to war and declared for conscription of capital as well as all citizens equally if conscription is to be established.[2]

I must confess that I much prefer to give constructive thought and effort to the building up of international institutions for the maintenance of international peace rather than to developing plans for the next war, but I realize that until international agencies are developed it would be foolish to close our eyes to the possibility of another war.

As to the specific proposals you made to the Committee[3] I have not yet had an opportunity to see them in detail but from reports I have received I judge you presented to the committee the results of your experience with war production in the recent war. You will remember that Labor gave whole-hearted support in that war and that the basis of our cooperation was official recognition of our organizations which made it possible for us to participate in the determination of policies as well as in carrying them out. In organizing the War Industries Board you reco[gniz]ed [this] basic principle and provided that representation [b]e provided for all elements concerned in production including labor. Only decisions reached by a thoroughly representative group would have the confidence of the industry. Another significant factor in the success of the War Industries Board was that the Board functioned through the organized agencies of industry and enforced decisions by economic means. Your methods, your machinery, your decisions were essentially different from any results that could be secured through legislation or by political machinery. The complete collapse of political machinery during the war emergency has remained in my mind as a most significant feature. During the months of that intense activity we were scarcely aware of the existence of Congress. So I am inclined to feel that preparedness for national defense will be promoted most successfully by increasing development of economic organization and by making it possible for these organizations to develop the habit of basing their policies upon recorded experiences and organized facts.

It does not seem to me that it will ever be practicable to place military men in charge of war industries. In case of another war we shall have to mobilize in pretty much the same way that we did in the last war. Of course I have no objection to price-fixing in time of a war emergency provided all factors are given equal consideration. However, I think we ought not to forget the records in the Internal Revenue Bureau showing the number of firms that had to pay taxes on excess profits as well as other figures showing the number who grew rich during the war emergency.

There is one practice of the late war that caused much demoralization—the cost-plus practice. The principles would not have worked out so perniciously if cost estimates were submitted in advance. The idea is altogether too general that increases in wages resulted in higher prices. The order of occurrence was quite the other way round and it was not until early in 1921 that there was an increase in real wages. This was brought about by a steady decline in the cost of living. I shall be glad some time to talk over this important problem with you at a time mutually convenient.

Thank you for your inquiry as to my personal welfare. The report[4] that you saw in the paper following my address to the Conference of Industrial Physicians was wholly without basis. I had been suffering from bronchitis for some time and hence did not wish to read a prepared paper as I was conserving my voice for a mass meeting in Bethlehem.[5]

Sincerely yours,　Saml Gompers.

President,　American Federation of Labor.

TLpS, reel 298, vol. 312, pp. 445–46, SG Letterbooks, DLC.

1. Bernard Baruch to SG, Apr. 5, 1924, Files of the Office of the President, General Correspondence, reel 107, frames 748–49, *AFL Records*.

2. On Mar. 13, 1924, Edward McGrady, a member of the AFL Legislative Committee, testified before the House Committee on Military Affairs during its hearings on universal wartime mobilization.

3. On Mar. 28, 1924, Baruch appeared before the House Committee on Military Affairs to advocate legislation to mobilize all national resources in the event of war. His proposals, drawn from his experience as chairman of the War Industries Board during World War I, focused on the appointment of an industrial strategist or board to mobilize and allocate resources (including military and non-military manpower, money, materials, and food), fix prices and wages, and direct the activities of industry.

4. A reference to SG's participation in a luncheon marking the opening of the annual meeting of the Conference Board of Physicians in Industry (see "To Frank Dickinson," Apr. 8, 1924, n. 2, above). SG was ill at the time with a severe bronchial cold he had contracted in early February and that continued to trouble him until the end of April. When the time came for him to address the luncheon meeting, he announced he had been advised by his doctor not to speak in public and would therefore ask his traveling secretary, Edward Tracy, to read his remarks. (For the text of SG's announcement, see Files of the Office of the President, Speeches and Writings, reel 118, frames 829–30, *AFL Records*.) The incident led to news reports that SG had suddenly been taken ill, leaving him too weak to speak in public.

5. For SG's trip to Bethlehem, Pa., see "From Sara Conboy," Apr. 3, 1924, n. 4, above. For his remarks at a mass meeting there on the afternoon of Apr. 6, see Files of the Office of the President, Speeches and Writings, reel 118, frames 833–36, *AFL Records.*

To Edwin Lehman Johnson[1]

April 19, 1924

Mr. Lehman Johnson,
27 Vance Avenue, Memphis, Tennessee.
Dear Mr. Johnson:

That part of your letter of March 8th in which you wonder what the result would be if the "sleepy southern states" ever waked up to the fact of the inefficiency of the negro farmers interests me greatly. It seems to me that just that sort of waking up must precede constructive planning for the future. The first step in solving our problems is to find out the facts. The sooner any group makes a study of its problem in order to find out the facts, the sooner will bad situations be cleared up. If each community could make a survey of existing practices and compare these practices with the most efficient standards that science can suggest, the community would then be fully conscious of its deficiencies and in a position to make improvements, and importation of European farmers into the south would not solve the problem.

Negro farmers as well as white farmers who do not understand scientific farming and who do not bring to bear upon their problems all of the information that science affords would still be left in your community. It seems to me therefore that the point of attack is the education of those who are now tilling the soil.

In a conference I had a short time ago with an engineer I learned of a farm experiment that had been conducted in which the engineer who was operating the farm had thoroughly machinized all processes so that the laborers on his farm were practically all machinists.[2] As a result, the farm was bringing unusual profits to the farmer. This is the sort of thing that can be done if the farmer is given hope and information. I am here advocating principles that we have followed in the labor movement. The trade unions have not been able to choose their own personnel. That was, for the most part, selected by employers. In some cases the people we organized into unions were workers from low-standards countries who had been induced to come to America because employers wanted low-wage workers, yet the methods of the labor movement have been in every case the same. We sought to educate the workers to higher standards.

I have been in the labor movement for sixty years and my experience has taught me that educational work is the foundation of all real progress. I sincerely hope that you will take the initiative in an effort to induce the farmers of the south to organize to study their problems and work out better methods. Such an organization of farmers would have as its primary tool a fact-finding agency.

Sincerely yours,   Saml Gompers
President,   American Federation of Labor.

TLpS, reel 298, vol. 312, pp. 492–93, SG Letterbooks, DLC.

1. Edwin Lehman Johnson (1862–1929), a chemist and cotton seed specialist, was the owner of the Lehman Johnson Laboratory and School of Cotton Seed Manufacturing in Memphis.

2. A reference to SG's meeting at his office on Mar. 17, 1924, with engineer Morris Cooke. At the meeting, Cooke described the experimental agricultural work of Arthur Mason, who had mechanized many aspects of production on his farm. For minutes of the meeting, see Files of the Office of the President, Conferences, reel 123, frames 543–46, *AFL Records*.

A Statement by Samuel Gompers on Woman Suffrage

[April 19, 1924]

IS WOMAN SUFFRAGE FAILING? A SYMPOSIUM[1]

. . .

Samuel Gompers

The president of the American Federation of Labor says, "Woman suffrage does not need any justification.

"It cannot be said that woman suffrage is a failure because it has brought no drastic changes to society as a whole. I have from my early youth been an ardent advocate of woman suffrage because it is right and just, but I have never expected and do not now expect that giving women the vote would bring about the millennium.

"The most notable effect of the victory of suffrage, as evidenced in the past four years, was the removal of the question from the field of politics, once and for all. Settling the question, taking it beyond the possibility of political discussions and maneuvers, has had a salutary effect on national politics.

"I see no evidences that women have worked the miracles which some people seemed to expect from women suffrage. It is not a question of being disappointed in the results, because I looked for no startling results. I wanted women to have the ballot not for what they might accomplish with it, but because it was their inalienable right to have it. Viewed from this angle, there can be no question of whether or not woman suffrage has justified itself. It does not need any justification.

"I do not believe that the majority of women vote as their husbands vote, nor do I believe that they are any more interested or more capable than men to vote on certain kinds of public questions. They need education on economic and social questions, and so does the man voter. They are interested in social and welfare legislation just as men are interested. There is no fundamental difference between the man and the woman citizen, so it is fruitless to look for certain specific changes to be brought about by the woman voter.

"Woman suffrage is its own justification because it is right in principle."

. . .

Woman Citizen 8 (Apr. 19, 1924): 14, 16.

1. As published, the symposium included nine short articles. In addition to SG, the authors included war correspondent William Shepherd, novelist and playwright Zona Gale, labor organizer Mary Scully, Ohio Supreme Court justice Florence Allen, laboratory worker Edyth Rochelle, Hull-House founder Jane Addams, suffrage leader Alice Stone Blackwell, and Indiana Democratic senator Samuel Ralston.

A Memorandum by Paul Smith

[c. April 20, 1924]

In recalling an incident while in Chicago, Saturday, April 12, in which a reporter for the Daily Worker sought an interview with President Gompers. I remember that upon his entrance to President Gompers' room, substantially the following conversation:

Reporter (approaching Mr. Gompers)

"Mr Gompers I represent the Daily Worker and I have come to ask you some questions in regard to the Garment Workers' Strike,[1] and other things."

Mr. Gompers "Go ahead and ask your questions"

Reporter: "Do you intend to review the Strikers parade?"[2]

Mr. Gompers: "I would prefer that you ask all the questions you have to ask at once and then I will tell you what I want to"

Reporter: "Do you intend to review the Strikers parade?

["]Do you intend to address their meeting?[3]

["]Do you intend to speak on their injunction?[4]

["]What are you going to do to assist the Strikers while you are in Chicago?

["]And anything else you care to say?"

Mr. Gompers: "I don't know that I should tell you what I am going to do or that it should concern you and your paper, as to what I intend to do or that I will not do. I can't see that you have any interest in the matter, except to do everything you possibly can do to cause the strikers to lose their strike. It appears to me that that is what you have been doing and are trying to do now, and for what purpose or who is responsible for your actions I am unprepared to say, but nevertheless, all the harm you can do them is being done, whether it is intentional or otherwise, and therefore, I don't care to talk about what I am going to do."

Reporter: ["]Well, we are backing the Strikers in their fight and hope to see them win."

Mr. Gompers: ["]I don't care what you are backing, neither do I care who is behind you, or between you, or in front of you, and that's all there is to it."

Reporter: (approaching to shake hands) ["]Well, goodbye Mr. Gompers."

Mr. Gompers: "I don't know that I care to shake hands with you or any of those whom you represent."

The above is substantially, as well as I remember it, what transpired on the above occasion.

Paul J. Smith

Organizer.   A.F. of L.[5]

TDS, Files of the Office of the President, Speeches and Writings, reel 118, frame 846, *AFL Records.*

1. On Feb. 27, 1924, some 2,500 members of International Ladies' Garment Workers' Union 100 of Chicago (Dress and Waistmakers) struck for a 10-percent pay raise, a forty-hour workweek, and collective bargaining in the industry. Most of the strikers were women. Despite brutal police tactics and a sweeping injunction that prohibited picketing, the strike continued until July. Many of the smaller shops eventually settled with the union, but few of the larger downtown dress factories did so.

2. SG did not review a strikers' parade. Shortly after concluding this interview, he boarded a train for New York.

3. SG did not address a strikers' meeting.

4. Judge Denis Sullivan issued an injunction on Mar. 4, 1924, prohibiting picketing or interfering in any way with strikebreakers. There is no indication that SG spoke on the issue.

5. For R. Lee Guard's request for a statement about what happened at this meeting, see Guard to George Perkins, Apr. 20, 1924, reel 298, vol. 312, p. 520, SG Letterbooks,

DLC. For Perkins's statement, see Files of the Office of the President, Speeches and Writings, reel 118, frame 844, *AFL Records*.

To James Wood

April 25, 1924.

Mr. James E. Wood,
Member, Railway Mail Association of the A.F. of L.[1]
19 So. La Salle St., Chicago, Ill.
Dear Sir and Brother:

Your letter of April 22 received and contents noted.

You state that "the greatest blessing that has come to this great nation during the past twenty-five years has been the overthrow of 'King Booze.'["]

You are certainly an optimist. What authority have you for the statement that "King Booze" has been overthrown? In the city of Washington, the headquarters of the enforcement forces, there are more arrests for drunkenness than in pre-prohibition days. It is just such a condition that I am endeavoring to remedy. Before the Volstead Act went into effect 91 per cent of the so-called intoxicating drinks sold were beer. The other 9 per cent was of hard liquor and wines. Nowadays it is unlawful to brew beer that is more than half of one per cent alcoholic content. Therefore, 91 per cent of the liquor sold is whiskey and the various substitutes being manufactured. The homes have been turned into distilleries and breweries. Do you think that this condition should be continued?

I believe if the Volstead Act was amended to permit the manufacture of 2.75 per cent beer that instead of a nation of whiskey drinkers we would become a nation of beer drinkers and when I say 2.75 per cent beer, I mean beer that is non-intoxicating. This is admitted by the supreme court of the United States and also by the leaders of the Anti-Saloon League.[2] But the latter claim they will refuse to approve of a modification of the Volstead Act. Beer of 2.75 per cent alcoholic content is palatable and would be of great benefit to our people. I fear you have not studied this question or refuse to recognize facts.

With best wishes and assuring you of my desire to be helpful in any way within my power, I am,

Fraternally yours,   Saml Gompers
President,   American Federation of Labor.

TLpS, reel 298, vol. 312, p. 714, SG Letterbooks, DLC.

1. The Railway Mail Association.

2. The American Anti-Saloon League (later the Anti-Saloon League of America) was founded in 1895.

Excerpts from the Minutes of a Meeting[1] on the Farmer-Labor Progressive Convention[2] in St. Paul, Minn.

(April 28) [1924]

Mr. Gompers presided. He said:

"Circumstances were developing to such an extent particularly on the political field I felt the necessity for a conference of men who have been active in political life to bring about conservative and reformatory legislation. . . . This is a consulting conference. I ask you will you select a chairman. I have done my duty in inviting you and briefly stating why the conference was called."

Mr. Nelson nominated President Gompers and when put to a vote by Vice-President Duncan he was chosen unanimously. Mr. Gompers then said:

"May I then speaking freely among us call attention to what is obvious to all of you, that there is being maneuvered a movement that unless it is checked the political gains for the past two years will be lost. I speak of political gains which helped to bring about constructive legislation or at least to prevent legislation inimical to the interest of the people. Whether we like it or not or you agree or not a political labor party was formed and was called the Farmer-Labor Party. It made some progress and in a few states gained substantial success. Indeed around this board are some of the evidences. We found that after some degree of success that forces were at work, keen resourceful and with an organization that was masterful in every detail, so that when that group induced leaders of the Farmer-Labor Party to call a convention they ran away with it and called it the Federated Farmer Labor Party. With that name and the fervor it created the reaction that followed caused them to change the name of the Federated Farmer Labor Party to the Farmer-Labor Federated Party. Those acquainted with the Chicago meeting when the Federated Labor Party was stolen say that no gathering was so neatly turned from its purpose and that in comparison the burglar was an amateur. They are now calling their name the Farmer-Labor Progressive Party and are hiding behind this name to call a convention to meet at St. Paul June 17. All bona fide labor or-

ganizations, farmer, reformatory and political organizations are asked
to attend. They are also prevailed upon to select committees of five,
two of whom are trade unionists or farmers, and three communists in
good standing in the Workers' Party. People are being duped into the
movement. They do not know. A large part of these people are honest and do not suspect wrong doing. The danger is that some of you
gentlemen unless something is done to expose this convention your
senatorial togas will go and we will be set back a decade. Of course we
will get back but that will take another decade. The progress we have
all made is to be hazarded by those who have not the welfare of our
people at heart and who owe allegiance to some other power. These
thoughts have bothered me and I want your point of view. I therefore
lay the matter before you. If I have exaggerated or done any injustice
I would like to be rebuked."

Mr. Johnston—I heartily concur in what President Gompers has
said. The situation has given all of us some concern. . . .

. . .

Mr. Johnston—When the convention of June 17 was called I wrote
Mahoney.[3] I thought he was sincere. I told him that the Workers' Party
were coming to St. Paul in force to capture the convention like they
did in Chicago. I asked him to exclude the communists but he did
not. The Workers' party is making great efforts to see the meeting well
packed.

. . .

Mr. Smith—I do not question the sincerity or ability of either Mahoney or Tigan[4] but I do question their judgment. The June 17 convention was brought about by the refusal of the progressive convention in
Chicago to seat the Workers' Party. Foster and Mahoney looked about
so as to hide their real identity. Mahoney fell into a well laid trap laid
by Ruthenburg,[5] Foster and company in which Jos. Mandley[6] went to
Mahoney in order to get Mahoney into the trap. The trap was laid by
which Mahoney in his desire to unite all factions would fall. If they got
a big convention for June 17 it will aid in resurrecting the McKellogg[7]
machine which was so happily scattered in the 1922 convention. Out
of the committee that called the convention five are active communists.

Mr. Wright read several documents showing how the communists
controlled the Federated Labor Party and what their aims and objects
were. They were simply agents of Moscow.

Mr. Manley—Mahoney and Tigan have been dupes. . . .

. . .

Mr. Gompers—I concede a certain percent of mistakes, but when
mistakes have been made and repeated no defense can be made.

Mr. Wallace said he saw in the movement an intention of discrediting the Farmer-Labor Party in Wisconsin and Minnesota. That the forces of reaction were behind it and that it would be a setback for progressives.

. . .

Senator Johnson[8]—We can not afford to get into any group with which Foster, Ruthenberg, and Mandley are connected.

Mr. Wefald[9]—We do not want the reds.

Mr. Duncan—Are you prepared to repudiate the dictation of the proletariat?

Mr. Nelson—I wish to thank those present for the information I have received. I did not know what is going on. We have some concrete facts. It is very evident that the communists will do one of two things. If they do not get control they will be there and being there that fact will cause people everywhere to think. We have to do everything to purge ourselves to disavow any connection with communists. What shall we do? If reactionaries do not bring it about they will make use of it.

. . .

Representative Nelson—How can you, Mr. Gompers, save your group from getting into this convention?

Mr. Gompers—Every effort is being made by those who are calling the June 17 convention to obtain the names and addresses of officers and members of local unions in the United States. The appeals are being sent secretly and under cover. These communists are working every day and our people do not know the truth. It is the duty of the officers to know these things. A motion might be adopted that it is the sense of this meeting that the convention for June 17 should be disapproved.

Mr. Keating—We are up against a proposition. No doubt the elements anxious to discourage the progressive movement will flout the progressives at the St. Paul convention. It was the same in Chicago. Certain interests did not want a third party movement headed by Senator La Follette. I would like to get this movement out of this hole but I do not know how. It should be made clear that the June 17 convention does not represent the progressive movement. Some of them are crooks who are making reports to detective agencies.

Representative Nelson suggested that a committee of seven be appointed to consider carefully the best way to deal with the matter and report back.

Mr. Duncan opposed this proposition. He said that the Labor forces would take care of its forces and the farmers theirs. . . .

. . .

There was much further discussion on the matter. Mr. Wallace said that the conference should repudiate the June 17 convention. There was further discussion by Messrs. Furuseth, Morrison, Senator Johnson and Representative Keller.[10] The latter said that there was only one alternative, to send as many delegates as possible to the convention and then withdraw.

Mr. McGrady then offered the following motion: That each group here agree that it will handle its own group in its own way and meet again on the call of the chair. Senator Johnson thought it would be a good idea to bring Mahoney down to Washington. Mr. Manley said that while each group should carry out its own program all should work in harmony.[11]

Mr. Gompers—That is understood without any motion, it should either be unanimous or nothing.

The motion made by Mr. McGrady was carried unanimously.

. . .

TDc, Files of the Office of the President, Conferences, reel 123, frames 676–81, *AFL Records.* Typed notation: "St. Paul Communist Convention, June 17, 1924. Conference held in the Executive Council Chamber, American Federation of Labor Bldg., ~~April~~ May 8 (April 28), at 8:15 P.M., to consider conditions arising because of the communist convention to be held in St. Paul, June 17."

1. AFL participants at the meeting included SG, Frank Morrison, and James O'Connell representing the AFL National Non-Partisan Political Campaign Committee; James Duncan from the AFL Executive Council; Edward McGrady, W. C. Roberts, and Edgar Wallace of the AFL Legislative Committee; Chester Wright of the AFL Information and Publicity Service; AFL organizer Paul Smith; and R. Lee Guard, Florence Thorne, and Edward Tracy from SG's staff. Also participating were James Forrester of the Railway and Steamship Clerks, Minnesota senators Magnus Johnson and Henrik Shipstead, Minnesota congressmen Oscar Keller, O. J. Kvale, and Knud Wefald, Wisconsin congressmen Joseph Beck, John Nelson, Hubert Peavey, and George Schneider, and six representatives of the Conference for Progressive Political Action—former congressman John Baer, William Johnston of the Machinists, labor editor Edward Keating, Basil Manly of the People's Legislative Service, Benjamin Marsh of the Farmers' National Council, and James Noonan of the Electrical Workers.

2. The Farmer-Labor Progressive convention met in St. Paul, Minn., June 17–19, 1924. Although William Mahoney had called the convention in hopes of nominating Robert La Follette for president, La Follette repudiated the idea after learning that delegates from the Workers' Party of America, including William Z. Foster, would be seated. The convention then nominated Duncan McDonald for president, with the proviso that he would step aside if La Follette eventually agreed to accept the nomination together with the Farmer-Labor party's control of his election campaign and his campaign funds.

3. William Mahoney (1869–1952) was an organizer of the Farmer-Labor Progressive convention in St. Paul and in 1924 was a member of the general or national committee of the Conference for Progressive Political Action. A member of International Printing Pressmen's and Assistants' Union of North America 29 of St. Paul and editor of the

Minnesota Union Advocate (St. Paul; 1920–32), he served as president of the St. Paul Trades and Labor Assembly (1918), the Minnesota Working People's Non-Partisan Political League (1919–24), and the Minnesota Farmer-Labor Federation (1924). Mahoney later served for one term as mayor of St. Paul (1933–35).

4. Henry George Teigan (1881–1941), secretary to Minnesota senator Magnus Johnson (1923–25), had previously served as secretary of the National Non-Partisan League (1916–23). He later served as a Farmer-Labor party congressman from Minnesota (1937–39).

5. Charles Emil Ruthenberg (1882–1927) served as executive secretary of the Workers' Party of America from May 1922 until his death. As executive secretary, he was also a member of the party's central executive committee. Former secretary of the Socialist party organization in Cleveland (1909–19) and editor of the *Cleveland Socialist* (1911–13) and the *Socialist News* (1914–19), he was a founder of the Communist Party of America in September 1919 and served as the party's executive secretary until resigning in April 1920. He then served briefly on the central executive committee of the newly founded United Communist Party of America (May 1920) and edited the party's official organ, *The Communist*.

An author of the Socialist Party of America's 1917 declaration condemning the war and urging workers to oppose the war effort, Ruthenberg later served a one-year sentence in Ohio for abetting evasion of the draft (Feb. 1918-Jan. 1919). In October 1920 he was convicted of criminal anarchy in New York and imprisoned at Sing Sing; he was released in April 1922. He was arrested again in August 1922 in the Bridgman raid (see "From George Perkins," Aug. 26, 1922, n. 3, above) and convicted in May 1923 of advocating criminal syndicalism. His conviction was on appeal at the time of his death.

6. Joseph Manley (1887–1926), an Irish-born iron worker and an organizer for the International Association of Bridge, Structural, and Ornamental Iron Workers (1918–22), was secretary of the Federated Farmer-Labor party (1923–24). The son-in-law of William Z. Foster, he was active in the 1917 campaign to organize packinghouse workers in Chicago and the 1918–19 campaign to organize the steel industry. He served as secretary of the Trade Union National Committee for Russian Famine Relief (1922–23), as an organizer for the Trade Union Educational League (1923), and as campaign manager for the Workers' Party of America (1924). Manley was working as a member of Structural Iron Workers' local 40 in New York City when he fell to his death in August 1926.

7. That is, Minnesota senator Frank B. Kellogg.

8. Magnus Johnson (1871–1936) served as a Farmer-Labor party senator from Minnesota from 1923 to 1925 and as a Farmer-Labor party congressman from Minnesota from 1933 to 1935.

9. Knud Wefald (1869–1936) served as a Farmer-Labor party congressman from Minnesota from 1923 to 1927.

10. Oscar Edward Keller (1878–1927) served as an Independent Republican and then as a Republican congressman from Minnesota from 1919 to 1927.

11. For an AFL National Non-Partisan Political Campaign Committee circular condemning the forthcoming St. Paul conference, see "To All Organized Labor," May 28, 1924, Executive Council Records, Vote Books, reel 18, frame 322, *AFL Records*.

To Henry Allen[1]

April 29, 1924.

General Henry T. Allen,
National Chairman, American Committee for Relief of German
    Children,[2]
132 West 42nd St., New York City.
Dear Sir:

Your letter of April 26th received. I note your suggestion that I should serve as a member of the executive committee of the Jewish division of the American Committee for Relief of German Children.

Permit me to say in reply that in all of my activities throughout my entire life, I have consistently avoided associating my activities with any religious denomination or faith. Such service as I can render is given to my fellows without regard to their religious beliefs, faiths or affiliations. I must therefore respectfully decline your invitation.

Very truly yours,   Saml Gompers
President,   American Federation of Labor.

TLpS, reel 298, vol. 312, p. 753, SG Letterbooks, DLC.

1. Maj. Gen. Henry Tureman Allen (1859–1930) was the commander of U.S. occupation forces in Germany after World War I, serving in that post from 1919 to 1923.

2. The American Committee for Relief of German Children was founded in October 1923 to meet the desperate need for food in Germany; it operated through the American Friends Service Committee. The committee closed its operations in June 1924 because the increase of food stocks in Germany had reduced the need for outside assistance. During the nine months of its existence, it raised some $5,000,000 and was able to feed over a million children a day.

To Henry Pratt[1]

May 5, 1924.

Mr. H. W. Pratt,
553 E. 79th Street, Seattle, Washington.
Dear Sir:

Your letter of April 11 received and contents noted.

You say you are not satisfactorily informed of what was meant by the "non-partisan political action" of the American Federation of Labor.

You say that the non-partisan political action of the American Federation of Labor caused division in the State of Washington and nearly split labor into two warring factions. It was not the American Federation of Labor non-partisan movement that divided the Washington State Labor Movement. It was the partisan political movement of a certain few who refused to accept the advice of the American Federation of Labor and nearly prevented the defeat of one of labor's most bitter enemies.

You say that the non-partisan policy applied to politics is meaningless. Non-partisanship means that candidates for office are voted for according to the records they have made in political life. If they have violated their pledges to support legislation that would be a benefit to Labor and the people generally, then the American Federation of Labor will oppose them no matter on what ticket their names appear. If their record shows that they have been true to Labor and the people the American Federation of Labor will support them.

In the 1922 election the American Federation of Labor Non-Partisan Political Campaign Committee supported 23 candidates for the United States Senate who were elected. It opposed 11 Senators who were defeated. During that election the non-partisan committee supported 170 candidates who were elected to the United States Senate and House of Representatives. Of these 105 were Democrats, 63 Republicans 1 Farmer-Labor and 1 Independent.

In your State a candidate[2] for Senator was opposed because he had endeavored to pass legislation that would prohibit the normal activities of labor. I[n] fact that would provide for compulsory labor. By a trick he succeeded in having it pass the Senate when only 2 other Senators besides himself were present. Representatives of the American Federation of Labor had the vote re-considered and the bill died.[3] A certain portion of the Washington labor movement placed a candidate[4] in the field who if he had been supported would have defeated Senator Dill and re-elected Senator Poindexter. He was urged to withdraw but refused.[5] Nevertheless the non-partisan political policy was successful. Individual ambition should not be permitted to interfere with the election of the right kind of public officials.

By taking a leaf out of the history of Washington politics you can prove to your own satisfaction that independent political labor parties are failures. The American Federation of Labor does not take political parties into consideration. It simply realizes that generally either a Democrat or Republican will be elected to Congress or as President of the United States. It does not fool itself with the idea that a political labor party can be formed that will defeat both of the other political parties. None as yet have been able to do it in the history of the United States. The strongest third party ever formed was the progressive party organized by Theodore Roosevelt and hundreds of other progressive public men throughout the country. It had strong followers and plenty of money, still it carried only four states. Only six political parties have elected Presidents of the United States.

It is very easy to say that all wage earners whose interests are along the same line can organize politically and put themselves into our legislatures and make the laws. But events have proved that this is impossible at this time. There may be a day when some conditions may arise that will bring about such a situation, but it is not now.

The American Federation of Labor knows no creed, sex, race or color, and party politics has no place in any of its conventions. The strength o[f] the American Federation of Labor is that a member may worship where he pleases and vote the ticket he pleases. The American Federation of Labor simply gives the membership the record of the various candidates and leaves it to their conscience to vote for the best man or woman.

You say you are not a member of a labor organization. Therefore you can not appreciate that the American Federation of Labor has reached its present wonderful position through prohibiting partisan-politics or religious discussions in its meetings.

You are in no greater hurry than I am to have wage earners secure a just proportion of that which they produce. The experiences of the delegates [t]o the conventions of the American Federation of Labor have proved a non-partisan political policy to be the best for the interests of the organized wage earners as well as the unorganized. Some of those delegates have attended conventions for ten, twenty, thirty or more years. During that time they have been at the head of National or International Unions and traveled from one end of the country to the other many, many times in their long years of service. They are certainly in a position to know what is best for the labor movement.

Enclosed you will find three pamphlets entitled:

Should a Political Labor Party be Formed,

Non-Partisan Successes,[6]

Forty years of Action.

They may be helpful to you in learning why the American Federation of Labor insists on [a] non-partisan political policy.

Yours very truly,   Saml Gompers
President,   American Federation of Labor.

TLpS, reel 298, vol. 312, pp. 877–79, SG Letterbooks, DLC.

1. Henry W. Pratt (b. 1847) worked for many years as a carpenter and then as a janitor.

2. Miles Poindexter.

3. See *The Samuel Gompers Papers*, vol. 11, pp. 406–7.

4. James A. Duncan, the Farmer-Labor party candidate for senator.

5. SG to Duncan, Oct. 23, 1922, reel 284, vol. 297, pp. 619–21, SG Letterbooks, DLC.

6. *Non-Partisan Successes: Report of the Activities of the Non-Partisan Political Campaign Committee of the American Federation of Labor in the Primaries and Elections of 1922* ([Washington, D.C., 1922?]).

Excerpts from the Minutes of a Meeting of the Executive Council of the AFL[1]

Monday, May 12, 1924.

AFTERNOON SESSION.

. . .

President Moore, Secretary Draper[2] and Vice-President Foster[3] addressed the Council. They described the different phases of the movement which is causing concern to the Canadian Trades and Labor Congress. One of these is the continual diminishing of the membership of the organizations. President Moore referred to the fact that large numbers of workers who understand the trade union movement and its industrial policy are constantly migrating to the United States. Their places are being filled by green men who have entirely different conceptions. The representatives of trade unions in Canada find it very difficult to explain to them why they should affiliate with the American Federation of Labor. They are being organized into competitive and independent unions and if something is not done to meet the situation the international movement will be swamped with these independent unions. The purpose for which the Executive Officers particularly wanted the conference with the Executive Council was to find out what may be mutually arranged to overcome the situation in some degree.

Secretary Draper outlined the different forms of organization that are supported by the workers of the different sections of Canada. In the Western Provinces the "One Big Union" has wrought destruction by plundering the treasuries of the locals of international unions and left the Canadian movement with the sentiment created. East of the Great Lakes the Communist party is working in the large centers with their policy of boring from within. In the Province of Quebec there is the National Catholic Union[4] movement. In the Maritime Provinces the sentiment prevails that the trade union policy is too slow; they want social revolution. Secretary Draper stated that both the press and the government are always knocking the international labor movement.

The officers of the Canadian Congress wanted to know if there could not be a method by which the Canadian Congress could issue charters to this new element who take the places of the workers migrating to the United States, to educate them, organize them into Federal Labor Unions and later place them in affiliation with the American Federation of Labor.

Secretary Foster stated that the Canadian Trades and Labor Congress is not getting the support from the International Unions which they had been given to understand they might expect. He referred to the Canadian Brotherhood of Railway Clerks[5] with a membership of 10,000, that had been suspended from the Canadian Trades and Labor Congress. The Brotherhood of Railway Clerks has not cooperated to aid the situation.

Secretary Draper referred to the expense to maintain organizers and admitted that the International Unions were expending much more to help organization work in Canada than they are realizing in the way of revenue from the Canadian membership. He referred to the vast extent of the territory and the expense of covering it. He made the suggestion that the mobilizing of organizers with the advice of President Moore would be more effective.

They also made the request when sending out circulars from headquarters, to use the word "International" rather than "National."

President Gompers stated that he did not know that the word "National" was used and that it has been his purpose to avoid it.

The hour having arrived for the special order, it was decided that the conference with the representatives of the Canadian Trades and Labor Congress be adjourned until 2:30 tomorrow afternoon.

. . .

Tuesday, May 13, 1924.

AFTERNOON SESSION.

. . .

The conference with the officers of the Canadian Trades and Labor Congress was resumed with President Moore and Vice-President Foster present.

President Moore outlined the situation affecting the lumbermen in regard to the difficulty of organizing them. He wanted to know if the Executive Council would grant authority to the Canadian Trades and Labor Congress to issue a national charter which would authorize the organization[6] in existence to proceed with their effort to establish local unions and as soon as an international union is established among lumber workers with charter from the American Federation of

Labor, the Canadian Trades and Labor Congress would endeavor to bring about the amalgamation of the Canadian organization with the International. This proposition was made to meet the problem of the danger of the general sentiment that prevails for a Canadian national organization as well as to offset the development of the independent organization.

President Gompers: If we are willing to go along with the course proposed we should set forth in a written document an understanding of what is intended to be done. There exists between us a mutual confidence that can not be surpassed and [is] difficult to equal, but we are not always going to be in harness. Not all of us will be entrusted with the affairs of our movement as we are today and by nature, development, time, opportunity and years, changes must come, and whatever betide us in the future there ought to be some written document to which we will all subscribe, setting forth the real purpose. We do not want to do anything that will mar or place an obstacle in the way of our internationality. We should set it forth in definite language that there will be no misunderstanding.

President Moore then referred to the independent organization of the Longshoremen[7] with headquarters in Vancouver and wanted to know if the Executive Council of the Federation can find some opportunity of discussing the situation with the International Longshoremen's Association as to whether they would follow the course adopted by the United Mine Workers, which would allow the Congress to issue a charter for the purpose of educating these men and when the time would be ripe to turn them over to the International Union.

President Moore then referred to the proposition that the Canadian Trades and Labor Congress be permitted to issue charters to local Federal Unions, after investigation to determine that the locals do not come under the jurisdiction of international unions.

He then discussed the Canadian Brotherhood of Railway Employes which represents approximately 12,000 members, whereas the Brotherhood of Railway Clerks has about 2,000. He wanted to know if the Executive Council can not bring pressure on the Brotherhood of Railway Clerks to put in a real campaign to promote sentiment for the amalgamation of the Canadian organization with the Brotherhood.

The next proposition was for the International Unions with a small membership to pool amounts to put in one organizer, say for a period of a year, the organizer's activities to be supervised by the officers of the Canadian Trades and Labor Congress.

President Moore called attention to the fact that the time is opportune for reorganization work among the lumber workers, textile workers and other crafts in the maritime provinces, particularly New Brunswick.

A summary of the subjects which the officers of the Canadian Trades and Labor Congress brought to the attention of the Executive Council with suggestions are as follows:

1. The Lumber Workers on the Pacific Coast.

2. Longshoremen's organization, Vancouver.

3. The chartering by the Canadian Trades and Labor Congress of Federal Labor Unions.

4. Canadian Brotherhood of Railway Employes.

5. The small International Unions to pool amounts to place an organizer in the field.

. . .

Thursday, May 15, 1924.

MORNING SESSION.

. . .

The proposals submitted for the consideration of the Executive Council by the representatives of the Canadian Trades and Labor Congress were taken up and acted upon as follows:

1. The proposition that a national charter for Canada for Lumbermen be issued until such time as there are enough local unions in the United States to organize an international union when the effort will be made to bring about the amalgamation of the Canadian organization with the International Union.

In discussing the subject President Gompers said,—these men have a high purpose in mind but they can not accomplish it in that way. The seed of dissolution is in the very making of these various proposals they have submitted to us.

The following motion was seconded and adopted:

That the President of the American Federation of Labor be instructed to communicate with the officers of the Canadian Trades and Labor Congress, advising that the Council can not agree to this proposition and can not grant the request because it would strike at the very foundation of internationality.

2. The question of the International Longshoremen's Association permitting the Canadian Trades and Labor Congress to grant a separate charter to the Longshoremen's Union of Vancouver.

It was decided that a conference be arranged with President Chlopek for the purpose of devising ways and means for the purpose of bringing about the affiliation of the Longshoremen's Union of Vancouver with the International Longshoremen's Association.

3. The proposition that the Canadian Trades and Labor Congress be permitted to issue charters to Federal Labor Unions.

It was decided that the same action be taken as upon the proposition to issue a national charter for Canada for the Lumbermen.

4. The Canadian Brotherhood of Railway Clerks.

The following was adopted:

It is our earnest desire to be helpful in bringing about a reconciliation between the Canadian and American movements of Railway Clerks, and the Executive Council authorizes and directs that every effort be made for the purpose of bringing about a conference for the desired result of unity.

5. The proposition that smaller international unions pool amount to place an organizer in Canada.

It was decided that a general letter be sent to all the International Unions advising them in brief of the situation related to us by the officers of the Canadian Trades and Labor Congress, calling upon them to do all they possibly can to promote the organization of their respective crafts in Canada and in that letter make mention of the fact that these officers have made the suggestion that some of the smaller organizations might voluntarily join in providing an organizer by their own voluntary and joint agreement.

It was suggested that the communication be addressed to the secretaries of the International Unions.[8]

. . .

TDc, Executive Council Records, Minutes, reel 7, frames 1474–75, 1480–81, 1485–87, *AFL Records.*

1. The AFL Executive Council met in Montreal, May 9–15, 1924.

2. Patrick Martin DRAPER, secretary-treasurer (1900–1935) and later president (1935–39) of the Trades and Labor Congress of Canada.

3. John Thomas Foster (b. 1874), a member of International Association of Machinists 631 of Montreal and president of the Montreal Trades and Labor Council, served as vice-president of the Trades and Labor Congress of Canada from 1922 to 1931.

4. The Confédération canadienne et catholique du travail (Canadian and Catholic Confederation of Labor), founded in 1921.

5. That is, the Canadian Brotherhood of Railroad Employees.

6. The British Columbia Loggers' Union organized in January 1919 but changed its name to the Lumber Workers' Industrial Union that summer after affiliating with the One Big Union (OBU). It reorganized as the Lumber, Camp, and Agricultural Workers' Department of the OBU in July 1920, but by January 1921 had left the OBU and reorganized as the Lumber Workers' Union of Canada. In January 1924 the union applied to the Trades and Labor Congress of Canada for membership but was turned down.

7. The Vancouver and District Waterfront Workers' Association was established as a company union after the Shipping Federation of British Columbia defeated an International Longshoremen's Association strike in Vancouver late in 1923.

8. For one of these letters, see SG to Frank Duffy, May 29, 1924, United Brother-hood of Carpenters and Joiners of America Records, reel 1, frame 1293, *AFL and the Unions.*

Excerpts from the Minutes of a Meeting on Organizing Women in Industry[1]

Washington, D.C., Wednesday May 21, 1924.

. . .

A copy of the program[2] drafted for the work was passed to each representative in the conference, and upon Mr. Gompers' suggestion Mr. John Manning, (proxy for President Rickert of the United Garment Workers of America)[3] read the document.

. . .

Mr. Gompers then asked for an expression of opinion from the members of the conference upon the document which had been read. He said:

"This is the general plan; it places upon the president of the American Federation of Labor some responsibility and I am so constituted that I do not evade responsibility but I have experienced some perplexity in reaching a conclusion as to one whom I could appoint as executive secretary to carry out this job. I say it without the slightest reflection upon any one of our girls no matter who they may be. . . ."

Mr. Perkins suggested that the program be read section by section, with the object of bringing [out] just what is felt about it. This was adopted.

Mr. Perkins moved the adoption of the preamble. . . . This was adopted with the exception of the last sentence, as Mr. Manning expressed the belief that the preamble should end at the word "eligible." . . .

. . .

Paragraph No. 1 was adopted by unanimous vote.

On paragraph No. 2 there was some discussion as to leaving out the words "preferably a woman." Several of the representatives in the conference stated that in organizing the women in their particular trade greater success had been achieved by men organizers than the women organizers, the men having more aggressiveness and a wider experience than the women; that if it was finally decided to appoint a man as executive secretary that in itself would be an admission of failure to find a woman competent to fill the position. Mr. Gompers explained that the original program had limited the appointment to a woman, but had been changed so as to read "preferably a woman,"— that it should be a competent person, preferably a woman, it does not preclude the appointment of a man, but all things being equal, a woman should have the preference.

The requirements of the position of Executive Secretary, and the work to be undertaken, were discussed, and it was brought out that the executive secretary will have direction of the entire campaign work under the supervision of the President and Executive Council of the American Federation of Labor.

Mr. Gompers spoke of the work of the Secretary of the Union Label Trades Department, productive of good will and cooperation, winning the confidence and cooperation of all, as being the type of work required, combined with faithfulness and ability, aggressiveness and affability. Mr. Gompers also stated that it is not intended to provide a job for anybody, but rather to enlist a worker.

Mr. John Manning, of the United Garment Workers, stated that his executive board declines at this time to go along with the campaign if a woman is to be preferred, they want the field open; if there are better people for this work among the male sex, that is what they want. He said that no one would question the judgment of President Gompers in appointing somebody for this job, that it is to be a big one, and not to be accomplished in a short time. They think the proper selection would not be a woman because as indicated, the outstanding women are all tied up in their own organization work.

Mr. Perkins said that in view of President Gompers' intention to be guided by ability rather than any consideration of sex, he moved the adoption of Section No. 2. . . .

Section No. 2 was unanimously adopted.

Section No. 3 was unanimously adopted.

In connection with Section No. 4 Mr. Gompers suggested that each organization state how far they are prepared to go in financial contributions and assignment of organizers to this campaign work.

. . .

Mr. Manning then suggested that a committee be named to draw up a tentative budget so as to have something to work on.

A suggestion was made that the finances should be raised by an assessment by the Executive Council in convention. Mr. Gompers spoke on the difficulty of that course.

Mr. Baroff stated that the Ladies Garment Workers were prepared to assign two organizers to the work. He further suggested that the unions be asked to elect a member to the organizing council and thus see how many organizations are ready to act. Then it would be possible to work out a budget.

Mr. Gompers took up the suggestion of Mr. Manning, that a committee of three be appointed from this conference to sit for an hour and consider the question of a budget and make report as to the judgment and conclusions of the committee.

Mr. Baroff again asked that the organizations be requested to state if they will send representatives, before the budget is worked out.

Mr. Gompers suggested calling the roll to get an expression as to what the organizations might be prepared to do.

Mr. Perkins stated that a council was provided for and in his opinion the budget will be made up conforming to the number of unions going into this proposition. . . .

Mr. Stewart[4] expressed his opinion that it is necessary to have some outline of the target at which it is hoped to shoot before discussing the executive boards or urging the development of the plan. . . .

Mr. Manning moved that the chair appoint three national executives as a committee to prepare the budget for the initiation of this movement. This was seconded and carried unanimously, and Mr. Gompers appointed Mr. Baroff, Mr. McMahon and Mr. Burke.[5]

Mr. Baine declined to act on the committee to prepare a tentative budget because his executive board had taken definite action on the matter. They are prepared to furnish the services of two organizers and pay their expenses, but are opposed to contributing anything to a woman's department, opposed to contributing anything additional to what they are, to the A.F. of L. for organization purposes. . . .

Mr. Manning expressed the opinion that section No. 4 did not belong in the program at all, but was a matter for the executive committee.[6]

Mr. Gompers urged the impracticability of calling conferences so frequently, involving great expense and time.

Section 5 was read and adopted with the changing of the word "Entire" to "joint."

The last paragraph as a declaration of policy was read and unanimously adopted.

. . .[7]

TDc, Files of the Office of the President, Conferences, reel 123, frames 696, 698–703, *AFL Records*. Typed notation: "Conference on Women in Industry. Headquarters, American Federation of Labor. Washington, D.C., Wednesday May 21, 1924."

1. Participants at the meeting included SG, W. C. Roberts, and Florence Thorne; A. J. Berres of the AFL Metal Trades Department and John Manning of the AFL Union

Label Trades Department; Mary Anderson of the Women's Bureau, Department of Labor; and representatives of the Bookbinders; Boot and Shoe Workers; Brick and Clay Workers; Cigar Makers; Federal Employees; Firemen and Oilers; Glass Bottle Blowers; Garment Workers; Glove Workers; Hatters; Ladies' Garment Workers; Leather Workers; Molders; Piano Workers; Printing Pressmen; Pulp, Sulphite, and Paper Mill Workers; Railway and Steamship Clerks; and Textile Workers.

2. SG sent copies of this document to the unions involved in the women's organizing campaign on Mar. 29 and May 7, 1924 (AFL Microfilm Convention File, reel 33, frame 1175, *AFL Records;* see also frames 1215, 1185). It reads as follows:

["]The figures of the 1920 census show that there are now approximately 3,500,000 women in gainful pursuits engaged in industry and an estimate of the number of women belonging to unions totals approximately 200,000. Therefore, we declare our full endorsement of the movement initiated by the American Federation of Labor under the authorization of the Portland Convention for the more thorough organization of working women in unions to which they are eligible. We submit the following program for the effective carrying out of the above declaration:

["]1. That an organizing council composed of a representative designated from its Executive Board or other proper officials, by each national or international union concerned with the problem of organizing women in industry shall approve and initiate joint undertakings.

["]2. That an executive secretary who shall be a bona fide trade unionist, and preferably a woman, be designated by the President of the American Federation of Labor to act as the representative of the movement to organize women workers. The office of the executive secretary shall be in the A.F. of L. Building.

["]3. That the formulation of plans for the organization of women wage earners and the execution of these plans shall constitute the work to be carried on jointly through the secretarial office and the national and international unions cooperating. The secretary shall also have charge of the preparation of educational and informational matter on women in industry.

["]4. Each union to state what financial support it will contribute in a lump sum or monthly for this work. Each organization is also asked to state how many organizers can be assigned to this work.

["]5. That the entire movement for the organization of women wage earners together with the activities of all persons entrusted with this work shall always be under the supervision and direction of the President and the Executive Council of the American Federation of Labor.

["]It is believed that the best results will come from sustained activity to strengthen the work of national and international organizations and to provide for cooperative organizing campaigns between unions which have common problems in various localities. There is an advantage and an economy from central planning and execution of plans and from pooling of information. It will probably be necessary to make special arrangements for financing particular campaigns but this should not necessarily mean the expenditure of additional money but only the more effective expending of organizing funds in furtherance of common plans and interests.["]

3. The United GARMENT Workers of America.

4. Actually Luther Corwin STEWARD, president of the National Federation of Federal Employees from 1918 to 1955.

5. John P. BURKE, president-secretary of the International Brotherhood of Pulp, Sulphite, and Paper Mill Workers from 1917 to 1965.

6. The committee proposed a budget of $12,240. Its recommendation was approved unanimously.

7. Before closing the meeting it was decided to hold another conference in late June or early July. Those plans had to be cancelled, however, because of SG's sudden illness and hospitalization, and no further meetings were held. Also before closing the meeting SG asked for recommendations, in writing, on whom he should appoint as executive secretary. Only two unions responded with suggestions—the Cigar Makers naming R. S. Van Horn and the Federal Employees suggesting Elisabeth Christman.

Fannia Cohn to Florence Thorne

Fannia M. Cohn, Executive Secretary
Educational Department of the
International Ladies' Garment Workers' Union
New York May 22, 1924.

Miss Florence C. Thorne,
American Federation of Labor,
Washington, D.C.
My dear Miss Thorne:

By this time you probably know that I was re-elected vice president of the I.L.G.W.U.

I tried to keep well during the convention,[1] but now that it is all over I feel the effect of it. Some of the men say that it is due to my sensitiveness. Probably it is so. Men take everything easier; they never cherish their mistakes or worries. They make an effort to forget their mistakes soon after they are made.

The four and a half days' discussion on the report of the Credential Committee was enough to exhaust the strongest person.

From the discussions of the Credentials Committee's report an intelligent listener, who is not a "bitter-ender" on the left side or the right side, could learn of the two tendencies underlying the entire struggle within the trade unions. One is the tendency of those who hold that all the powers be in the economic organization and the function of politics is to serve it. The other is the tendency advanced by the Russian Bolsheviki, that every movement and institution be subordinated to the political organization. The Communist Parties demand from its members that the first allegiance be given to the political organization and that the purpose of their activities in the workers' economic organization is to advance the political organization. I belong to the first group, with the philosophy that the workers' economic organization is foremost.

I am not politically minded, and I do tolerate politics as much as it will assist me in advancing the economic interest of the workers. And this is because I hold the opinion that the future social organization will be the workers' industrial commonwealth.

It is to be expected that during such a controversy neither side will use good judgment and tact in defeating each other. I do hope that this internal strife will cease within the near future and that those of our members who believe that certain people be replaced appreciate that they will never succeed in realizing their aims through activities directed by outside organizations.

The honest and intelligent members of that group will sooner or later realize that to be effective in a trade union, as in any other organization, they will have to demonstrate their loyalty, their devotion to the trade union movement first, and they will have to give their first allegiance to the trade union and only then will they exercise a constructive influence.

I am anxious to hear from you about the conference[2] called by Mr. Gompers of the International presidents regarding the organization of women. From the few minutes' conversation I had this morning with Mr. Baroff, our General Secretary, who attended this conference, I understand that the planned advisory committee or council, which will work together with the executive secretary, will turn out to be a man's organization.

I am not one of those who believes in dividing the labor movement on sex lines. I do believe that the only salvation of the workers is that both men and women work side by side in solving its problems. I also believe that both have something of their own to contribute to the labor movement and they can learn much by working together. In my social activities I was seldom active in a purely woman's organization. You and I realize the necessity of women shouldering responsibility and acquiring self-confidence. There is a saying that if one wants to learn how to swim he must throw himself in the water. If women are to acquire experience in the labor movement they will have to be active in it. An opportunity will have to be given them to do so.

Women suffer more from lack of self-confidence than from lack of ability. Political organizations, to interest women in their campaigns, found it expedient to have women on their most important committees. Unfortunately, the labor movement has not come to this point. In the trade union movement men think that it is they who are to do the job not only for the men but also for the women, due to [their self-confidence that they are women's betters]. They do not realize that women will never be able to do their jobs unless they, too, will acquire this experience. Nothing encourages women to b[e] in the labor movement so [much] as the recognition that is accorded to some of them.

It seems to me that if the Committee for the Organization of Women will turn out to be a man's organization, the W.T.U.L. will have a just claim to its existence and full recognition. I hope that you will understand my intensity in this matter, knowing that my life was devoted to this movement, that all that is in me is placed at the disposal of the labor movement and realizing that more and more women will come into industry, and swell the ranks of the wage earners. Hence my great interest that these women be encouraged to take an interest in their economic organization.

What was on my chest I shared with you. Summoning my reasoning power and after deliberation with myself, I came to the conclusion that since my main interest in this, to my mind epoch-making movement on the part of the A.F. of L., is to see women organized, I will be the last person to bring in any element of controversy that will weaken this effort. Realizing as I do that the presence of the presidents or secretaries of the international unions on such a committee will enlist the interest of their organizations, I would let it stand as it is.

But I wish to make the following suggestion for your consideration and that is that in addition to this organization committee or council, whatever its name will be, an advisory educational committee composed of working women be appointed by President Gompers. The function of this committee should be to submit plans of an educational character to the organization committee. Women who can think and analyze their sex will, I am certain, prove helpful in devising ways and means of an educational character how to interest working women in organization.[3]

I am eager to have your opinion to my suggestion.

I hope to hear from you soon.

With best personal wishes.

Faithfully yours,   Fannia M. Cohn.

TLS, AFL Microfilm Convention File, reel 33, frames 1187, 1197, *AFL Records*.

1. The International Ladies' Garment Workers' Union convention met in Boston, May 5–17, 1924.

2. That is, the conference held May 21, 1924, to discuss SG's plan for organizing women workers (see "Excerpts from the Minutes of a Meeting on Organizing Women in Industry," May 21, 1924, above).

3. SG did not appoint such a committee. In its report on organizing women to the 1924 AFL convention, however, the Executive Council recommended ongoing educational work to bring about "better understanding of the problem of women in industry and the necessity for constructive action" (AFL, *Proceedings*, 1924, p. 64). The Council's recommendation was adopted unanimously.

From Mary Anderson

Women's Bureau
U.S. Department of Labor
Washington May 24, 1924.

My dear Mr. Gompers:

I want to thank you for inviting me to the various conferences which have been called for the purpose of organizing women workers. Apart from my official duties as a member of the trade union movement, I am very interested in this subject and deem it a privilege that you have given me the opportunity to attend the conferences.

I could not have attended and heard the discussions without observing the deep-rooted antagonism to the National Women's Trade Union League. While I knew of this antagonism before, it was more violent than I had anticipated. Mr. Manning's and Mr. McMann's[1] speeches in the last conference[2] were very uncalled for and very unjust to the women workers of the country and I know that no one appreciates that more than you do. I thought you might be interested to know that various men attending the conference representing their International Unions, took great pains to say that they did not concur in those expressions and some of them went so far as to say that they hated to be mixed up with anything like that. Some of them suggested that if these two organizations did not participate in this movement, that the movement could go on without them. They appreciated of course that both of these organizations had many women who ought to be organized in their trades but after all they had everything to gain through a movement like this and nothing much to give.

In regard to the appointment of the executive secretary, I think the American Federation of Labor would be open to a great deal of criticism and even ridicule if the opinion of those two organizations prevailed. I know that you appreciate that fact and I also have felt that you will do everything possible to appoint a woman in that position. Inasmuch as you asked for suggestions, and I know of course that applied particularly to the International Unions, I venture, nevertheless, to suggest Elisabeth Christman. I have known Elisabeth for a good many years, know of her sterling character, know of her unselfish motives and her genuine interest and work for the betterment of the women workers. She is a splendid secretary, knows that work as well as any other man or woman I can think of or have knowledge of. You will remember that during the war she was drafted by the War Labor Board to head up the women in industry section of that Board and her work there was of the best. Her work in the Glove Makers'

Union,[3] and from what I know of it I am sure there would not be an organization in that trade today—if it had not been for the work of Elisabeth holding on when everything seemed to fail. They have now paid their debts from their disastrous strike[4] in Chicago, which strike I know she opposed with all the vigor possible because she knew it was lost before it began, but radicals and private detectives put in there by the Manufacturers Association, took the people on strike against the plea of both Elisabeth Christman and Agnes Nestor.[5] They are now trying to reorganize with fair success. Her secretaryship in the Women's Trade Union League is said to be the best the League ever had. In other words she has been tried and not found wanting.

It is because of my genuine interest in the movement now undertaken by you that I am proposing Miss Christman as executive secretary.

Thanking you again for including me in this very important work, I am

Sincerely yours,   Mary Anderson

TLS, AFL Microfilm Convention File, reel 33, frame 1187, *AFL Records.*

1. Actually Thomas McMahon, president of the United Textile Workers of America.

2. That is, the conference held May 21, 1924, to discuss SG's plan for organizing women workers (see "Excerpts from the Minutes of a Meeting on Organizing Women in Industry," May 21, 1924, above).

3. The International GLOVE Workers' Union of America.

4. Glove Workers' locals 4 (Cutters) and 18 (Operators) of Chicago struck the C. D. Osborn Co., the Eisendrath Glove Co., and the Hickory Steel-Grip Glove Co. in early October 1920 after their contracts expired and the firms announced they would now operate on the open-shop "American Plan." By the end of the month, the union was claiming the strike had shut down all the organized shops in Chicago, but since the walkout coincided with the beginning of a sharp depression in the glove industry, employers blamed the lack of work, not the strike, for the shutdown. For a time the union was able to operate a cooperative glove factory to provide work for some of those who had left their jobs, but the five-month strike ended in failure, and the two locals suffered a significant loss of membership.

5. Agnes NESTOR was vice-president of the Glove Workers from 1903 to 1906 and from 1915 to 1938.

To Norman Thomas[1]

May 27, 1924.

Mr. Norman Thomas,
Director, The League for Industrial Democracy,
70 Fifth Avenue, New York City.
Dear Sir:—

The American Federation of Labor was represented in the All-American Conference held in Washington May 16th and 17th.[2] So far as I am informed the representatives of the American Federation of Labor supported every action taken, and as members of the committees, participated in the drafting of some of the reports and resolutions which were adopted.

The purpose of your inquiry is manifestly hostile but that is of no concern to me. To prate of industrial democracy and balk at its progress is a pink pastime. I may add that I am happy to know that so many organizations found it possible to agree upon measures and methods for the more complete unification of our citizenship in support of democratic American ideals and institutions.

Very truly yours,   (Signed) Samuel Gompers.
President,   American Federation of Labor.

TLtcSr, Files of the Office of the President, General Correspondence, reel 107, frame 855, *AFL Records.* Typed notation: "*Copy.*"

1. Norman Mattoon Thomas (1884–1968) was codirector of the League for Industrial Democracy from 1922 to 1937. He served as associate editor of *The Nation* from 1921 to 1922 and was the Socialist Party of America's candidate for governor of New York in 1924. In 1924 and 1925 he served as a member of the national committee of the Conference for Progressive Political Action. He subsequently ran as the Socialist candidate for president of the United States in all six presidential elections between 1928 and 1948.

2. The All-American Conference, sponsored by the American Legion, was held May 15–16, 1924, in Washington, D.C. It adopted resolutions condemning communist propaganda and opposing diplomatic recognition of the Soviet Union, congratulating the AFL for its stand against radicalism and SG for his promotion of Americanism, endorsing U.S. participation in World War I and condemning criticisms of U.S. involvement in the war by Victor Berger and others, demanding the teaching of "unadulterated and undiluted American history," as opposed to "emasculated history," in American schools, and demanding immigration restriction ("War on Radicals Aim of Conference," *New York Times,* May 17, 1924). Edward McGrady, a member of the AFL Legislative Committee, was an AFL delegate to the conference.

Labor's Political Demands[1]

Washington, D.C. June 9, 1924.

To the Chairman and Members of the Platform and
Resolutions Committee of the 1924 Republican National
Convention:

Out of our experiences as workers and citizens of this republic
American labor has reached carefully considered conclusions upon
proposals that should be embodied in our national policies. As your
political party is to make an appeal to the minds and consciences of
the voters for support of a national programme to be formulated in
your party platform, as representatives of America's workers we submit for your most earnest consideration proposals that labor deems
essential to continued national progress and maintenance of a genuine
patriotism that comes from confidence in guiding political ideals as
well as wisdom and integrity of administration.

With fully justified reasons our voters will scrutinize most critically
the declarations and decisions of party conventions held this year.
There is imperative need for revival of a feeling of high responsibility
for maintaining political activity on a plane compatible with those ideals for which we as a republic stand. The following proposals constitute
the legislative programme which labor urges as imperative and eminently constructive, and insists should be included in your platform:

To promote highest material progress which is the basis for national
effectiveness as well as an agency for national service, we urge that
industry and commerce be freed from legislative prohibitions that
restrict development in conformity to economic requirements. To
this end we propose the repeal of anti-trust legislation and the enactment of legislation that will provide regulation in public interest and
legalize economic organization as well as the constructive activities of
trade associations.

It is unescapable that an integral part of legislation establishing this
economic policy is full recognition of the right of workers to assist
themselves in unions for their protection and advancement both as
workers and citizens and collectively to carry on the legitimate functions of trade unions. Perversion of the injunctive process to apply
to personal relations in industrial disputes must be prohibited and
equity procedure returned to its beneficent service in protection of
property.

It is essential for the conservation of national virility that child life
be protected. We therefore urge the ratification by the states of the
joint resolution passed by the Congress,[2] to amend the Constitution

empowering the Congress to enact such legislation as will safeguard the future child life of our Republic.

Because the labor clauses of the transportation act of 1920 have proved ineffective, we ask their repeal and the enactment of legislation that will afford opportunity for the voluntary organizations of management and employes to deal with problems of industrial relations.

We demand the enactment of legislation providing that products of convict labor shipped from one state into another shall be subject to the laws of the latter state exactly as though they had been produced therein.

In order to mitigate unemployment attending business depressions, we urge the enactment of legislation authorizing that construction and repair of public works be initiated in periods of acute unemployment.

In appreciation we urge adequate provision for the full rehabilitation of all injured in the service during the World War.

We urge proper recognition of the work of those in the civilian service of the government with adequate compensation based upon equitable classification.

We favor the enactment of more comprehensive compensation laws to provide for all workers not covered by state compensation acts. We demand more liberal provisions for those incapacitated by industrial accidents or occupational diseases.

We maintain that the Volstead Act is contrary to the desire of the majority of our citizens as well as the spirit of the eighteenth amendment, and we demand that it be modified to permit the manufacture and sale of beer containing not more than 2.75 per cent alcohol.

We declare for the maintenance of freedom of speech, press, assemblage and association. We oppose any regulation to restrict these fundamental rights, believing that individuals and groups should be responsible for their acts and utterances.

We oppose conscription except as a military measure for defensive war and oppose all proposals to initiate compulsory labor under whatever guise.

In order to maintain representative government based upon the will of the people, we advocate a constitutional amendment enabling Congress to re-enact by two-thirds vote any measure declared unconstitutional by the supreme court of the United States.

Labor favors graduated income and inheritance taxes and opposes the sales tax as well as all other attempts to place excessive burdens on those least able to pay.

We demand that our nation identify itself with international agen-

cies and conferences to promote world peace. We urge membership
in the League of Nations and participation in the world court.

> Saml Gompers. President.
> Attest: Frank Morrison Secretary.
> James Duncan, First Vice-President.
> Joseph F. Valentine, Second Vice-President.
> Frank Duffy, Third Vice-President.
> William Green, Fourth Vice-President.
> T. A. Rickert, Fifth Vice-President.
> Jacob Fischer, Sixth Vice-President.
> Matthew Woll, Seventh Vice-President.
> Martin F. Ryan, Eighth Vice-President.
> Daniel J. Tobin, Treasurer.
> Executive Council American Federation of Labor.

Saml Gompers.
Frank Morrison
Jas. OConnell
Executive Committee
A.F. of L. National Non-Partisan Political Campaign Committee.

PLS and Sr, Executive Council Records, Vote Books, reel 18, frames 325–26,
AFL Records.

1. The AFL presented identical statements of labor's political demands to the Republican and Democratic platform and resolutions committees.

2. That is, H.J. Res. 184 (68th Cong., 1st sess.), approved by the House of Representatives on Apr. 26, 1924, and by the Senate on June 2. (See "To William Green," June 3, 1922, n. 5, above.)

To the Executive Council of the AFL

Lennox Hill Hopsital,
New York City Via Washington, D.C. June 10, 1924

No. 21
Executive Council, American Federation of Labor.
Colleagues:

In the last several months the duties I have been required to perform have been excruciatingly exacting and I have not spared myself in the slightest. Recently, I have been advised by personal friends as well as expert physocians that it is essential to take some rest and a rest cure. This advice I have rejected for many, many years, but within the past few weeks I have felt a reaction from the overstrain that was both painful and tending toward great depression.

Last week I was compelled to yield to the orders of my physician,[1] and I left Washington for New York[2] where, after a few days, I was ordered to go at once to the Lennox Hill hospital.[3] In this hospital I am receiving the expert advice and experience of the institution's physicians and surgeons and other specialists who have been called and are being called for consultation and further advice.[4]

Being under the impression that in a few days or a week I would be restored to something like a normal condition and resume my work and duties, I have succeeded in avoiding the dissemination of the idea that I am ill and in the hospital, even my office associates being uninformed, and they will be until they read this, of my whereabouts.

The members of the Executive Council will recall the instructions given given at our last meeting[5] for me to be the chair man of the committee to wait upon the major political party conventions and through their committees on platform present Labor(s dxmands.[6] You will, I am sure, appreciate the fact that I am greatly disappointed at being unable to fulfill that obligation, and this is really the main reason why I am dictating this letter on this date, June 10, 1924, when the national convention of the Republican Party begins its session at Cleveland, Ohio.[7]

So that the purpose of the Executive Council's action may not be entirely lost, I have asked the Executive Committee of the A.F. of L. National Non-partisan Campaign Committee to invite Vice-President Matthew Woll to act as my substitute in the performance of this duty,[8] and in addition to him Secretary Morrison, President O'Connell of the Metal Trades Department, Committee, consisting of Messrs. Roberts, Wallace and McGrady, and such other members of the Executive Council as may care to join in the one concentrated effort to present Labor's demands to the platform committee of the Cleveland Convention.

From the information available to me I feel confident that I shall be at my desk and perform the duties of my office within a week,[9] and for this reason, in addition to those already given, I am disclosing to the Executive Council the reason for my absence from the American Federation of Labor office for the past week.

Enclosed you will find a copy of the demands which the Executive Council in the name of the American Federation of Labor will present to the committee on platform of the republican national convention.

It is identical to the one which will be presented to the national democratic convention which meets at New York beginning June 24,[10] except, of course, the name of the party will be changed.[11]

In looking over the enclosed circular[12] you will notice a considerable number of changes which have been made in the one which was considered by the Executive Council and adopted by us at our meeting held last month. These changes were necessary to be made by reason of the new legislation passed by the Congress of the United States. These changes I made several days ago while in the hospital and am convinced that the Executive Council will approve them. In fact, the chamges were essential.

I am dictating this letter from my bed in Room 402, Lennox Hill Hospital, New York City, on June 10, 1924, the 61st anniversary of the date upon which, with my father and mother, brothers and sister, I sailed from London to New York.[13]

Good Luck.

> Fraternally yours,   Saml Gompers
> President   American Federation of Labor

P.S. For the time being please regard my whereabouts as confidential.

> S. G.

TLcS, Executive Council Records, Vote Books, reel 18, frame 324, *AFL Records*.

1. SG's personal physician at this time was Julius Auerbach (b. 1881) of New York City.

2. SG left Washington, D.C., for New York City on the evening of May 28, 1924.

3. In May 1924 SG's health, already weakened by a long siege of bronchitis that spring, began to break down. He found he could no longer walk without help, and although he continued to do routine work at the AFL office, he was forced to cancel important appointments. On May 28, after consulting with his son Samuel J. Gompers and Dr. William Mackay, the husband of his granddaughter Florence, he left Washington, D.C., for New York City to rest and recuperate. His health continued to decline, however, and on June 3 he was admitted to New York's Lenox Hill Hospital in grave condition. Although doctors initially feared for his life, by late June he was able to attend strategy sessions on the upcoming political campaign and to present labor's demands to the platform committee of the 1924 Democratic convention, which was meeting in New York. Released from the hospital on July 8, SG went first to the Shelburne Hotel at Brighton Beach on Coney Island and then on July 30 moved to the Ambassador Hotel in Atlantic City. During his convalescence he continued to meet from time to time with his aides, and he attended some of the AFL Executive Council's meetings in Atlantic City during the first week of August. In mid-August he suffered a setback, however, and on Sept. 11 he had to return to New York for further convalescence under the supervision of his doctors. It was not until mid-October that he was able to return to work at AFL headquarters.

4. SG's principal attending physician at Lenox Hill Hospital was Otto Hensel (1875–1935) of New York City. He served as a member of the hospital's consulting staff for some thirty-five years. Dr. DeWitt Stetten (b. 1881) of New York City also attended SG at Lenox Hill.

5. That is, the AFL Executive Council meeting held in Montreal in May 1924. For

minutes of the Council's discussion on May 12 regarding the presentation of labor's demands to the platform committees of the Republican and Democratic national conventions, see Executive Council Records, Minutes, reel 7, frames 1476–77, *AFL Records.*

6. AFL representatives presented identical lists of demands to the 1924 convention platform and resolutions committees of both the Republican and Democratic parties. For the document presented to the Republicans, see "Labor's Political Demands," June 9, 1924, above.

7. The Republican national convention met in Cleveland, June 10–12, 1924.

8. For SG's request that Matthew Woll take his place in appearing before the Republican platform committee, see R. Lee Guard to Woll, June 7, 1924, AFL Microfilm National and International Union File, Photo Engravers Records, reel 43, frame 2511, *AFL Records.*

9. On June 12, 1924, SG's doctors told R. Lee Guard that SG would not be leaving the hospital nearly this soon (Memo from Miss Guard, June 12, 1924, International Brotherhood of Teamsters, Chauffeurs, Stablemen and Helpers of America Records, reel 5, frame 958, *AFL and the Unions*).

10. The Democratic national convention met in New York City, June 24–July 10, 1924.

11. To the Chairman and Members of the Platform and Resolutions Committee of the 1924 Democratic National Convention, June 9, 1924, Files of the Office of the President, General Correspondence, reel 108, frames 11–12, *AFL Records.*

12. That is, the list of demands to be presented to the platform and resolutions committee of the Republican party's national convention.

13. See *The Samuel Gompers Papers,* vol. 1, pp. 4, 16.

Excerpts from the Minutes of a Meeting on the Presentation of Labor's Demands to the Democratic Platform Committee[1]

. . .

Astor Hotel, New York City, June 23, 1924.

. . .

President Gompers opened the conference. . . .

. . .

The American Federation of Labor in its conventions directed the Executive Council, and the Executive Council in turn has entrusted to a committee, national in scope, to bring to the respective conventions of the major political parties, the requests and demands which organized labor in the American labor movement has formulated for the purpose of prevailing upon these bodies to incorporate in their platforms. The Executive Council at its last meeting considered very carefully some of many of these demands and requests. They were formulated, discussed, then perfected and unanimously approved. Copies of these I think you have already seen. They were first presented to the national republican convention at Cleveland beginning June 10. . . .

I would say that the national convention of the democratic party will begin tomorrow in this city. The direction to us is that identical demands be presented to the committee on platform of that party. . . .

. . .

. . . Mr. Morrison made a brief report of the presentation of the demands to the republican platform committee, in Cleveland. He was allowed five minutes in which to read the declarations; vice-president Woll was given five minutes, and timed minute by minute in which to make the argument. The Federation committee was given scant time and little consideration, the whole proceeding showing clearly that it was all merely perfunctory, merely a form being observed with no intention of giving consideration to the matters presented. . . .

Mr. Woll briefly confirmed Mr. Morrison's statement of the Cleveland proceedings. In addition he stated that he felt very constrained to refuse to accept the five minutes given him, but that in the absence of President Gompers he hesitated to permit his personal feelings of indignation and resentment to cause him to withdraw.

Mr. O'Connell concurred in all said by Mr. Morrison and Mr. Woll. Further, that it was a foregone conclusion that nothing would have been gotten from the republican committee; that in all probability had Mr. Gompers been there, more time would have been given and the appearance of more consideration, but that nothing would have been secured.

Mr. Woll further states that the action of the committee in calling time on him—two minutes, one minute, half a minute—was to distract his thoughts and prevent the presentation of them; that he felt confident labor had few friends on the committee; that the treatment accorded them by the committee was anything but respectful to the great group of citizens which they represented. He concluded by saying: "We received no consideration at the hands of the committee nor by the convention itself."

Mr. Gompers then resumed:

At the republican national convention in 1908 Vice-President Duncan, O'Keefe[2] and I served as the committee of the Federation. We went before the platform committee. The committee undertook to do that same thing to us. I turned upon them and told them my associates and I would decline the courtesy extended if we could not have sufficient time and they could give the time to some one else. The fact of the matter was that I got more time. I too say, and without attempt at criticism—and probably other men might not be willing to assume the responsibility which I would have done, and did under similar circumstances, if the ten minutes had been spurned it might have had a jolting effect.

If any such arrangement should be attempted before the democratic committee on platform I would treat it in that way. The representatives of the American Federation of Labor represent more than a mere hobby—a pink parlor proposal. We represent four and a half million organized men and women of labor, and their wives and children and those not able to speak for themselves.

Mr. O'Connell gave as his opinion that because Mr. Gompers was not with the committee at Cleveland that the platform committee of the republican party looked upon the labor committee as a joke. "It impressed me that the republican platform committee is rather of the belief that the American Federation of Labor is inclined to or pledged to the democratic party, and the impression I got from the whole thing was that it was just going through the matter of form to get rid of it as rapidly as possible. Had you, President Gompers, been there undoubtedly we would have received greater courtesy and more time, but nothing would have been gotten from the committee."

. . .

There was some discussion as to what had been done and what should be done to secure favorable action by the platform committee upon labor's demands when presented. Mr. Gompers then stated:

During this year Secretary Morrison and I have had conferences with not less than half a dozen of the leading men having this convention in charge. In addition, Mr. Morrison has had conferences with them. I have had conferences with other men. Before you arrived here there have been several men high in the councils of this convention who have been here to talk with me and they are willing to go along with us and do everything they can to help.

There was some further discussion. The conference adjourned, the Federation committee with the members of the Executive Council present to seek an immediate conference with the platform committee. It was thought the labor group would not get before the committee before Wednesday. Mr. Gompers said he would know by then whether he would be able and would be permitted by his physicians to go with the Federation group before the committee.[3] He said he was there in the conference, with the promise to his physicians that he would hold himself in leash.

. . .

Mr. Gompers then left for the hospital, accompanied by his doctor, nurse, Mr. Monness[4] and Mr. Roberts.

TDc, Files of the Office of the President, Conferences, reel 123, frames 729–30, 732–38, *AFL Records*.

1. At this meeting were SG, Frank Morrison, and James O'Connell, the executive committee of the AFL National Non-Partisan Political Campaign Committee; Jacob Fischer, Martin Ryan, Daniel Tobin, Joseph Valentine, and Matthew Woll from the AFL Executive Council; Edward McGrady, W. C. Roberts, and Edgar Wallace of the AFL Legislative Committee; Chester Wright of the AFL Information and Publicity Service; AFL organizer Hugh Frayne; John Manning of the AFL Union Label Trades Department; John Sullivan of the Central Trades and Labor Council of New York and Vicinity; Peter Brady of the New York State Allied Printing Trades Council; and officers of several AFL affiliates.

2. That is, Daniel Joseph KEEFE, who served as an AFL vice-president from 1904 to 1908.

3. SG, accompanied by an AFL delegation, presented labor's demands to the platform committee of the Democratic national convention on June 25, 1924. For a transcript of his remarks, see Files of the Office of the President, Speeches and Writings, reel 118, frames 938–45, *AFL Records.*

4. Harry Maxwell Monness (1876–1946), a friend of SG's.

To the Executive Council of the AFL

Lenox Hill Hospital, New York City July 8, 1924

Document No. 22.
Executive Council American Federation of Labor.
Colleagues:

My physicians have agreed that I shall leave the hospital today. However, by their advice for the present I shall be located at a point convenient to the city so that I may still be under their daily supervision.[1] My nurse[2] goes with me. My physicians are gratified with the progress I am making. My steady daily gain in strength is very discernible to myself.

Miss Guard will continue the conduct of my office at the Continental Hotel[3] so that when it becomes necessary such important matters as require my personal decision or direction may be readily brought to my attention.

So far as concerns my office at headquarters, arrangements have been made whereby the routine work will be promptly disposed of there and such other matters, when necessary, immediately transferred to me to New York. I have worked with Miss Guard for the past two weeks as seemed necessary and expedient, and this has been with the approval of my physicians. It is easy to say: "Don't do any work; rest; dismiss work from your mind; relax; play." But to me that is not rest; that is punishment. And so my physicians decided that work in a reasonably moderate degree shall not be denied me; indeed, that it is good for me, and as they see me each day, they can very readily determine the effect of work upon me.

Through the radio, the newspapers and frequent conferences I have kept fully advised of the proceedings of both the Republican and the Democratic conventions. When the Democratic convention shall have adjourned I anticipate holding a conference at the Aberdeen Hotel with the members of the executive committee of the A.F. of L. National Non-Partisan Campaign Committee and the members of the A.F. of L. Legislative Committee to determine plans and procedure for conducting the A.F. of L. Non-Partisan Campaign work.[4]

I have had several conferences with the members of the executive committee of the A.F. of L. National Non-Partisan Campaign Committee, with the members of the Executive Council who have been in New York City, with the members of the Legislative Committee of the AF. of L., with other labor representatives and with representatives of nearly all shades of opinion in the political field.

I am looking forward to meeting the members of the E.C. at the Ambassador Hotel, Atlantic City, on August 1st.[5] In the meantime, when communicating with me please address me at headquarters.

Fraternally yours   Saml Gompers
President   American Federation of Labor

TLcS, Executive Council Records, Vote Books, reel 18, frame 326, *AFL Records*.

1. SG went from Lenox Hill Hospital to the Shelburne Hotel at Brighton Beach on Coney Island, N.Y. On July 30, 1924, he moved to Atlantic City for further convalescence, taking up residence at the Ambassador Hotel and remaining there for about six weeks. On his doctors' advice, he then returned to New York, going back to the Shelburne on Sept. 11.

2. By the time SG left Lenox Hill Hospital only one private nurse, a Miss Thompson, was attending him. She was with him at Brighton Beach throughout the month of July and then went on with him to Atlantic City, finally returning to New York City, by previous arrangement, in mid-August. Her replacement stayed with SG only a short time before being called away by a death in her family. A third nurse was then hired, Mathilde (often given as Mathilda or Hilda) H. May (b. 1873) of Atlantic City.

3. R. Lee Guard maintained an office at the Continental Hotel in New York City from June through July 1924. She then moved with SG to Atlantic City, setting up her office at the Ambassador Hotel, where he was located. With SG's return to New York on Sept. 11, she moved back to the Continental.

4. See "Excerpts from the Minutes of a Meeting on the 1924 Political Campaign," July 11, 1924, below.

5. The AFL Executive Council met in Atlantic City, Aug. 1–11, 1924.

Excerpts from the Minutes of a Meeting on the 1924 Political Campaign[1]

Continental Hotel, New York City, July 11, 1924.

Yesterday, Thursday July 10, 1924, President Gompers who is staying at the Shelburn Hotel, Brighten Beach, for a few days after leaving the hospital, called a conference to consider the political situation growing out of the declarations and candidates[2] of the two major political parties and the declaration and candidate of the Conference for Political Action[3] held at Cleveland, O.,[4] immediately following the Republican Convention.

. . .

[Mr. Gompers. "]I am greatly disappointed at the outcome of this convention. I expected nothing from the republican national convention in Cleveland, but I think we had the right to expect something from the democratic national convention. The platform adopted was disappointing from every standpoint and particularly that of labor. The only declaration containing a principle is the one which is enacted law of the country and not a demand for such a law—that is, that the labor of a human being is not a commodity. Almost in the same sentence, at any rate in the same paragraph, there is negation of that principle.

["]They have nominated a man for the presidency of the United States who is able, but as to his position upon questions affecting the rights, interests and the welfare of the people, economically, industrially and politically there is too little of a favorable character that I feel we can not come to his support.

["]The candidate for the vice-presidency, Governor Bryan[5] of Nebraska, he was originally a drug clerk. When William Jennings Bryan got into politics, he became his secretary and handled the Commoner branch of the business. He branched out into politics and became the mayor, ran for governor twice, and then got the nomination."

. . .

"Now the convention was held at Cleveland of the Conference for Progressive Political Action. At that convention they did rid themselves from the communists group and the communist party of this country. In so far as Senator La Follete knows he has presented some fundamental principles upon which we all agree. He knows nothing of economics. He thinks that political necessity and political reforms can cure the ills which result from modern industry. He does not know that it is an industrial not a political problem. He is faithfully for freedom, for justice, and for opportunity. The endorsement or nomination of him for his acceptance of nomination for the presidency of the United States upon this basis which he laid down and which was adopted by the Cleveland convention. He is now a candidate. I am not yet sure what our course should be toward him in this campaign.

"The LaFollette movement is not in itself technically what might be called a third party, and we are not committed to any party.

"The democratic party has no stronghold upon the American Federation of Labor. The seriousness of the situation is of another character in so far as the rights and the interests of labor of the United States are concerned; and that is, the decision of the Cleveland conference to enter into the congressional field and make the support of La Follette for the presidency the condition of support for nomination for the House of Representatives and Senate."[6]

Mr. Morrison. ["]I think they are not going to do this.["]

Mr. Gompers. ["]But they did do it. They have done it. I have not got the papers here. They decided in other words just as I have stated it. If that course is pursued it means that the success we have had in the 1922 campaign elections will not only be endangered but other members of the House of Representatives and other senators who have always been straight and true with us, with labor and the people generally, will be defeated by the nomination of candidates whose platform will be the support of Senator LaFollette for the presidency. That is the situation now, and the pity of it is, I must repeat it, that unless we support Davis and Bryan we will be charged with opposition to the ticket because Davis declined to interfere in the nomination of a running mate—not because we are against him and his record or that we are against Bryan and his record, but simply because we did not get the nomination or his promised support of the nomination for vice-presidency.[7] That is the charge that will laid against us."

. . .

["]The situation being as it is, it is not easy for us in the course we shall have to pursue. The Cleveland conference decided that its executive or national committee shall meet in Washington July 18, there place in nomination a candidate for vice-president on their ticket with Senator LaFollette,[8] and to take such necessary action as the conference at that meeting may determine in furtherance of their candidate and program.

["]I am wondering whether it would not be wise, and I want your thoughtful consideration of what I am about to say, to invite a few of the men, possibly located at Washington, to meet with a committee representing the American Federation of Labor, and to ascertain whether there can not be co-operation or co-ordination in this political situation and campaign.

. . .

"I do not know that this is definitely or finally my reaction upon this situation and the next step or the step which we are to take but it is a thought which has been pressing upon me and I have expressed it. The meeting of the national committee of the LaFollette movement will be July 18. This is July 10—in other words, more than a week from now. It ought not to be difficult to have a conference with some of the labor men and a few representatives of that movement in Washington with the Executive Committee of the National Non-Partisan Political Campaign Committee of the A.F. of L. myself excluded; that is, unless I am probably willing to make the last effort of my life, because I do not know what attendance at such a conference would be, probably no more than I know what the effects of this conference will be upon me. It may be impossible for me to attend such a conference at Washington. I might go anyway.

["]The conference should be held two or three days from now to go over this situation and see whether we can not get a fragment of comfort and help for labor out of this mess. There is no need for that national committee to decide finally all things on that date. Some things of great importance can well be left for decision to a later date, and that in the meantime the Executive Council of the American Federation of Labor will meet beginning August 1, and the whole situation will be presented to the Executive Council for their review and possible decision.["]

Mr. Woll: "We are in a most confusing and dangerous situation, there is no getting away from that. If we balance off the platforms of the various political conventions that have been held, there is no question that the LaFollette platform more nearly conforms to the aspirations of the American Federation of Labor. . . . I do not know how far platforms are going to count in this campaign but I am inclined to believe that personalities will be a great factor and if we balance off personalities I do not think there is any question that LaFollette more nearly conforms to our hopes and aspirations than any of those who have been mentioned.

"You brought out the point that the Cleveland conferences went further than was expected and that they have made the situation more confusing by entering the congressional field which places us in the position of defeating friends in the other parties. There is a still greater danger and that is the situation that we are going to be confronted with next November in our A.F. of L. convention. I do not know what the outcome of the campaign will be. The Cleveland conference decided that there shall be a further meeting early in January next year for the purpose of considering the formation of a permanent organization or a third party.[9] In connection with that the socialist party in following the Cleveland conference, made it very clear to their constituency that they see the hope of a third party similar to the English labor movement.

["]To make overtures of coming into the LaFollette conference unless it is safe-guarded, would place us in the position of being with that group. Whether we can disentangle ourselves from the other involved elements or not, is quite a difficult matter. We may get the national committee to modify its views on many things but whatever the outcome will be, we will be confronted at our own convention in November with being required to take part in this movement in January to form a third party.[10] That group will be at our convention. We are confronted not only with the present campaign but we are going to be confronted in November with the third party movement. I agree with Mr. Gompers that we have got to be extremely careful."

Mr. Morrison: "This is a situation we have got to meet. Within a few days after we return to Washington we should have a meeting with representative labor men for the purpose of finding out just what they have in mind and to see if arrangements cannot be made so the men who have been friendly to labor on the republican and democratic or progressive platforms will not be antagonized by that group and the support that they shall receive will not depend upon whom they shall support for president. . . . ["]

. . .

Mr. Gompers: "The officers of the unions affiliated with the A.F. of L. and probably one or two of the others, at the first conference, or take them into confidence later. I do not know just what; use good judgment and do not place us into a further bad hole."

. . .

Mr. Woll: "I think that whatever conferences are to be held ought to be of an informal nature because if the policies of this progressive group would not be expressed in keeping with the wishes of the A.F. of L. the fact that we had entered into negotiations and failed would make the situation even more embarrassing. So whatever is done at the beginning would have to be done in an informal way.

["]It strikes me that in order to protect ourselves in every possible way, if we are going to adopt any form of action with this group, it might be well that a careful study be made of the platforms of all of the political conventions and an analysis be prepared and a careful analysis made of the candidates for president, and that the sub-group get all the information they can regarding the possible procedure of all of these political parties. Our purpose would be to get in touch with the La Follette group. That would protect us that we were not negotiating with them but if something arises then it would be done in an official way."

Mr. Gompers: "The integrity of the American Federation of Labor, the American labor movement and its political policy must not be frittered or bartered away. We may, for the interest of our people and conforming to our own policy, seek the cooperation of all groups and all citizens in furtherance of the Non-Partisan policy of the A.F. of L., and even if we should say something or do some things to further the candidacy of Senator La Follette for president, why all right so long as we maintain our non-partisan policy clear."

. . .

TDc, Files of the Office of the President, Conferences, reel 123, frames 740, 749–55, 757–58, *AFL Records.*

1. Participants at the meeting on July 10, 1924, were SG, Frank Morrison, Matthew Woll, Chester Wright of the AFL Information and Publicity Service, and the members of the AFL Legislative Committee—Edward McGrady, W. C. Roberts, and Edgar Wallace.

2. The Republican candidates for president and vice-president in 1924 were Calvin Coolidge and Charles Dawes; the Democratic candidates were John Davis and Charles Bryan. The Republican convention renominated Coolidge by a wide margin and gave Robert La Follette, who also sought the Republican nomination, only thirty-four votes. Democrats chose Davis as a compromise candidate when their convention deadlocked between Alfred E. Smith and William McAdoo.

3. The Conference for Progressive Political Action (CPPA) was organized in Chicago, Feb. 20–21, 1922. The founding convention, attended by representatives from a broad range of progressive farmer, labor, and political organizations, was called by William Johnston of the Machinists, Timothy Healy of the Stationary Firemen, Edward Manion of the Railroad Telegraphers, Martin Ryan of the Railway Carmen, Lucius Sheppard of the Railway Conductors, and Warren Stone of the Locomotive Engineers. The CPPA's objective was to formulate a joint program of independent political action. It claimed substantial success in the 1922 congressional elections and in 1924 chose Robert La Follette and Burton Wheeler as its candidates for president and vice-president. Encouraged by the La Follette–Wheeler turnout that November (roughly 4.8 million votes or slightly less than 17 percent of the popular vote), the CPPA considered the creation of a third party, but the proposal split the organization, which dissolved in February 1925.

4. The CPPA Cleveland convention met July 4–5, 1924.

5. Charles Wayland Bryan (1867–1945), the Democratic nominee for vice-president in 1924, was mayor of Lincoln, Nebr., from 1915 to 1917 and 1935 to 1937 and governor of Nebraska from 1923 to 1925 and 1931 to 1935. In 1901 he was a founder, with his brother William Jennings Bryan, of *The Commoner,* a weekly, and he served as publisher and as an editor of the paper until it ceased publication in 1923.

6. The CPPA Cleveland convention directed the organization's national committee to take up "the task of securing the nomination and election of United States Senators, Representatives to Congress, members of State Legislatures and other State and local public officers who are pledged to the interests of the producing classes and to the principles of genuine Democracy in agriculture, industry and government" and "organize State and local campaign committees to conduct the campaign within their

respective territories under the supervision and direction of the National Committee" ("La Follette Named as Head of Ticket by the Progressives," *New York Times*, July 6, 1924). In the end, however, the CPPA did not nominate supporting tickets at the state level and chose instead to focus its energies on supporting its national ticket.

7. A reference to the Democratic vice-presidential candidacy of George Berry, president of the International Printing Pressmen's and Assistants' Union of North America. Berry declared his candidacy on Feb. 29, 1924, and opened his campaign headquarters at the Waldorf-Astoria in New York City on Mar. 31. He enjoyed considerable support from labor, and on July 9, shortly after the Democrats nominated John Davis for president, a delegation headed by Frank Morrison visited Davis to ask him to consider Berry as his running mate. Davis put them off, saying he did not wish to interfere in the matter, but he and other party leaders subsequently chose Bryan and the Democratic convention nominated him early on the morning of July 10.

8. The CPPA national committee nominated Burton Kendall Wheeler (1882–1975), Democratic senator from Montana (1923–47), as its candidate for vice-president.

9. The CPPA conference originally planned for January 1925 was held instead on Feb. 21, 1925, and the organization broke apart on the issue of creating a third party. After the CPPA dissolved, a number of its former delegates reconvened on the evening of Feb. 21 and met again on Feb. 22—without the representatives of the labor organizations that had been affiliated—to discuss preliminary steps toward the creation of a third party.

10. The 1924 AFL convention in El Paso, Tex., adopted a resolution endorsing the Federation's non-partisan political policy and rejected two resolutions calling for the creation of a third party.

From Matthew Woll

Raleigh Hotel Wash July 11, [19]24

My dear Mr Gompers

Chester Wright and I saw Senator La Follette early this afternoon— At suggestion of Wright and I La Follette immediately responded to a desire to see you—and will arrange to come to you— It is understood that you have not urged this— He was extremely well pleased with our call—anxious about you personally and expressed the kindest and warmest feelings for you— It would seem his views are entirely in accord with ours regarding the political program and he welcomes the opportunity of having a talk with you His visit will be entirely without solicitation and secret as well as confidential—[1]

Later Morrison, Wright, Wallace and I met with Bill Johnston[2] and Arthur Holder[3] No Vice Presidential Candidate has yet been selected— Johnston said he would urge Berry and thought he could have him named if [we] desired him. We declined to interfer—saying we were merely trying to get information and nothing more— It [is?] the purpose of selecting a progressive democrat. Stone[4] is not to be selected indeed they are inclined not to select a labor man because of the candidacy of several that had been urged. The platform adopted is to guide the Persidential and Vice Persidential Candidates alone— The candidates for Congress, Senators and Representatives, are in no way bound by the La Follette Platform— Support is to be given them strictly on a non-partisan basis—following practically the text heretofor followed by the A.F of L. and Johnston said we could work out the same standards and tests of judgement as their movement is strictly non-partisan even to the point of excluding La Follette's platform in making up the test.

They expect to be able to throw the election of President and Vice President out of the electoral college to Congress and believe that there substantial results will follow.

They are anxious for our support and co-operation and it would seem that they are willing to modify some of their arrangements to that end. We declined to make any statement—give any intimation whatever what we had in mind.

They are to enlarge their National Committee and would like A.F of L to be represented theren— We advised them we could not speak on the subject as the Executive Council must first consider entire situation and determine A.F of L's attitude after careful study of all platforms, candidates etc. It would seem their Nat'l Committee can even be enlarged after our Council meeting.

They are organizing groups throughout the states— Their is no thought of a third party movement at present and can't tell what the campaign may develop.

We are to be furnished with key note speech of Johnston, platform of La Follette[,] plan of organization, unions, Int'l, Local, Central Bodies and District organizations having participated in the Cleveland Conference. Int'l Brotherhood of Carpenters was not represented neither was the United Mine Workers though Lewis attitude has not been definitely expressed one way or other.

Just as soon as this documentary evidence is before us I will write you further or have Wright do so— On the other hand if any important suggestion occurs please telegraph me—as I expect to leave here tomorrow night for Chicago and return here Thursday of next week so as to be here when their National Committee meets to select a Vice Presidential Candidate and take care of other matters

Hope you are much better and with best of wishes

Fraternally   Matthew Woll[5]

ALS, Files of the Office of the President, General Correspondence, reel 108, frames 26–37, *AFL Records*.

1. SG eventually met with Robert La Follette on Sept. 19, 1924, in New York City. (See "An Account of a Meeting with Robert La Follette," Sept. 19, 1924, below.)

2. William Johnston served as chairman of the Conference for Progressive Political Action (CPPA) from the organization's founding in February 1922 until its dissolution in February 1925. He was also a member of the CPPA joint executive committee created to direct the La Follette–Wheeler campaign.

3. Arthur E. HOLDER, previously a member of the AFL Legislative Committee (1906–17) and chief of the legislative division of the People's Legislative Service (1921–23), served as secretary of the CPPA from December 1922 to February 1925.

4. Warren Sanford STONE, grand chief engineer (1903–24) and then president (1924–25) of the Brotherhood of Locomotive Engineers, served as treasurer of the CPPA from December 1922 to February 1925.

5. For Matthew Woll and Chester Wright's joint report on these meetings, dated July 12, 1924, see Files of the Office of the President, Conferences, reel 123, frames 763–66, *AFL Records;* for Frank Morrison's account of the meeting with Johnston and Holder, also dated July 12, see ibid., General Correspondence, reel 108, frames 38–42.

R. Lee Guard to Frank Duffy

Continental Hotel, New York City, July 15, 1924.

Mr. Frank Duffy,
Vice-President, American Federation of Labor,
Carpenters' Bldg., Indianapolis, Indiana.
My dear Mr. Duffy:

Your letter of July 10th[1] has been duly received. Yes, you are quite right; Mr. Gompers would not be satisfied to give up all work but what he is doing is of great value to the office and to the Federation. We are seeing to it that he does nothing that taxes him or tires him, or in any way will retard his progress towards recovery.

I was with him yesterday and he thoroughly enjoyed the work that he did and got through it without any fatigue or tax. I found him looking much improved, with his color almost normal and his voice nearly at its full vigor and timbre. He gets out every day and while, of course, he can walk but little as yet, each day he tries to walk a little more than he did the day before and he spends all of the time outside in the sea air. This has done him a world of good. His doctors are greatly pleased with the steady progress he is making.

I hope you will advise his friends whom you may see from time to time, as to his condition. I shall be very happy to write you occasionally as you suggest.

With all good wishes, I am,

Sincerely yours,
Secretary to President Gompers.

TLp, reel 299, vol. 314, p. 222, SG Letterbooks, DLC.

1. Not found. For two such letters that have survived, see Daniel Tobin to SG, June 14, 1924, Files of the Office of the President, General Correspondence, reel 108, frames 15–17, *AFL Records,* and George Perkins to SG, Sept. 30, 1924, ibid., frame 151.

The Minutes of a Meeting with Matthew Woll

Shelbrune Hotel, Coney Island, July 16, 1924

Mr. Woll came to the Shelburne hotel this evening from Chicago by the request[1] of President Gompers. Mr. Gompers desire was to have Mr. Woll go to Washington as his representative and confer confidentially with Senator LaFollette who had expressed the wish to have a conference with Mr. Gompers.

In addition to the report which Mr. Woll and Mr. Wright jointly made to Mr. Gompers of their previous conference confidential with the Senator,[2] Mr. Woll verbally went more into details of the conference, particularly the senator's deep solicitude regarding Mr. Gompers' health. Mr. Woll stated that the senator mentioned an incident where he and Mr. Gompers addressed the same meeting.[3] Mr. Gompers passed by the senator whose hand was hanging down from the chair. Mr. Gompers grasped his hand without saying anything, and the senator narrated how that touch thrilled him and how grateful he was.

Mr. Gompers stated in substance that he had asked Mr. Woll to come on to the Shelbrun so that he might briefly say to him just what he wanted him to convey to the senator and that he also wanted Chester Wright to go with Mr. Woll; that he had telegraphed[4] to Mr. Wright at Atlantic City to go on to Washington for a conference.

Mr. Gompers said to say to the senator that as far as possible the conference between him, Wright and Woll held previously should be regarded as confidential as well as the conference to be held tomorrow with the senator.

Mr. Gompers further said that in the conference with the senator Woll should take the same attitude as in the conference with the representatives of the Conference for Progressive Political Action, as set forth in the transcript already made of Mr. Gompers' statement to Mr. Woll.[5]

Mr. Woll: I can of course take up in a general way and see if I can secure his influence to see that the other group will follow that.

Mr. Gompers: If we can get any kind of an understanding or agreement with the representatives of the other group and the suggestions or proposals or recommendations by our group to our own Ex. Council we may be able to work together for the one common purpose.

Let the senator understand—evidently the fact that you come to him and the fact that you go to him again—he ought to understand that we are thoroughly unsatisfied and dissatisfied with the republican candidates and platform and that we are thoroughly disappointed and dissatisfied and unsatisfied with the democratic candidates and platform, and that we are willing as far as we can to do our best that there may be this co-ordination. We would not want our representatives on their national committee. We can not afford to lose our identity.

TDc, Files of the Office of the President, Conferences, reel 123, frame 770, *AFL Records.*

1. W. C. Roberts of the AFL Legislative Committee conveyed SG's request to Matthew Woll by telephone.

2. See "From Matthew Woll," July 11, 1924, n. 5, above.

3. The incident may have occurred during a two-day conference of progressives, sponsored by the People's Legislative Service and chaired by Robert La Follette, held in Washington, D.C., Dec. 1–2, 1922. SG addressed the meeting on Dec. 2. La Follette and SG were also brought together during the 1922 AFL convention, which La Follette addressed on June 14.

4. SG to Chester Wright, July 16, 1924, reel 299, vol. 314, p. 234, SG Letterbooks, DLC. SG also wired Frank Morrison on July 16, asking him to hold a conference the next day between representatives of the AFL and members of the Conference for Progressive Political Action (ibid., p. 230).

5. The document is dated July 16, 1924. SG gave Woll these instructions:

"You may say that the report which has been made—that I know the purport in full of the conference which is to be held and that we are thoroughly dissatisfied with the republican convention platform and candidates and with the democratic platform and candidates—unsatisfied and dissatisfied; that it may be possible for co-operation and co-ordination, but our co-operation and co-ordination must be independent of their movement. To give that co-operation and co-ordination from our viewpoint insofar as the candidates for president is concerned. As for the candidacy of any one for vice-president, the declaration made by the executive council of the nomination of an outstanding type of labor man for vice-president—that is our position, and that in principle was not confined to the democratic party.

"As for any particular individual, we felt that we are not justified in tying ourselves to any one particular man, for the reason that to propose any one man would be to discriminate against every other man, so that we would be free to stand by that declaration in any man in which we could be of service in the cause.

"I would like it to be made clear that there are parts of that platform and declaration with which we are not in accord; that the decision must finally rest with the Executive Council.

"As for the campaign for members of the House and of the Senate, that must be upon the test set by the American Federation of Labor Non-Partisan Committee that we can have their co-operation and co-ordination, but there must be no different test as to candidacy and fitness; that is our job. Inasmuch as they have gone into the presidency to deny this is to establish the whole political movement into a partisan channel; that the state tickets must be left to the local labor movement of the states letting the states take any course they will.

"If we can get any kind of an understanding or agreement with the representatives of the group and the suggestion or recommendations or proposals by our group to our own executive council, we may be able to work together for the one common purpose." (Files of the Office of the President, Conferences, reel 123, frames 768–69, *AFL Records*.)

From Matthew Woll

July [17, 1924]

My dear Mr Gompers:—

Saw Senator La Follette to-day and first conveyed to him your greetings. He was very anxious about your health and suggested that he thought that if you were to go to Atlantic City he could go there and quite accidentally meet you— I told him this was unnecessary as I just came from you.

I informed him of our dissatisfaction with both the democratic and republican platforms and candidates—that we disagreed with some of his pronouncements. He quite frankly admitted other friends of his also dissented from parts of his platform—but that he thought, in the main, he presented fundamental and progressive issues and he did not look for unanimous agreement upon any platform that might be drafted— He confirmed that the platform was only binding on himself and not anyone else.

I expressed the point of view that of the 3 presidential candidates, his candidacy more nearly conformed to our non-partisan standards and attitude of mind. He was pleased to receive this statement. However I advised him this was not an endorsement—or official expression as the Executive Council must utter the final expression. I also advised him our attitude would very largely—if not entirely—be governed by the form of organization and procedure followed in furthering the candidacy of Senators and Representatives; that if a strictly non-partisan basis was adopted and followed in keeping with that of the A.F of L., and if we were to be considered as leading the non-partisan campaign for Senators and Congressmen and the Conference for Progressive Political Action were to subordinate their support and co-operation to that of the A.F of L., there was a fair basis of our co-operating with the Conference for Progressive Political Action in the furtherance of his candidacy. He answered that he had really taken little interest in this phase of the movement; that he felt strongly however that friends of labor and of progressive pronouncements, tendencies and actions should be supported on a non-partisan basis and that he was in entire accord with the A.F of L. on this subject. He further stated that this subject had been left to the railroad organizations and that he would be glad to work out this procedure with us and the railroad organizations. He seemed in full agreement with our wishes and policies in this.

In speaking of the state tickets, after I had explained our wishes and fears of confusion and complications that might arise unless the A.F of L. policy was adhered to of leaving the State Federations handle these matters he emphatically declared himself—not only of his willingness but of the urgency of having the National Committee, which meets to-morrow, to make a pronouncement in this direction and in accord with our wishes.[1]

On the Vice Presidency I informed him of our general statement adopted at Montreal.[2] While we discussed Berry—it was in an informal way—but not as a possible candidate in any way as his running mate. Indeed I said very little on this subject.

Altogether my meeting with La Follette was one hundred pre cent agreeable and I believe wholly satisfactory— I alone saw him and the visit is confidential—

Later in the afternoon—Morrisn, Wright, Wallace McGrady and I met Keating,[3] Bert Jewell, and Basil Manly[4] in conference. Jonston was out of the city and Holder was engaged otherwise— We took up the propositions of Persidential preference, Vice Persidential candidate, congressional campaign and state tickets with this committee in practically the same way as I took them up with La Follette. I was the spokesman at the conference— We did not discuss the Persidential and Vice Persidential matters at length—but did devote considerable time to the non-partisan program for Representatives and Senators. We made it clear we could not leave others to assume leadership in this work but desired their co-operation and co-ordination. They assured us of all that and I immediately arranged for committee's of both the A.F of L. and their committee to get to-gether early next week to work out mutually satisfactory standards of Judgement and whereupon we will be ready to announce our decisions of preference and their group can then join and Co-operate with us under our leadership. Of course, you understand the present steps being taken are purely preliminary sort of preparatory and then the A.F of L will pass final Judgement and make its decision whenever it is deemed best. The conference also saw the importance of keeping out of state political affairs, leaving State Federations of Labor to work out this problem.

This conference was entirely successful and I later saw Bert Jewell personally to impress on him the desirability and necessity of working out this arrangement as you directed last night— He agreed to go along and help in this work

Of course all understand our conference was informal—shall I say a "conversation" using European terminology for diplomatic conferences? At any rate all understand the Executive Council is to be the final Judge of whatever will be done and that we are at present merely exchanging points of view and seeking enlightenment, while actual program is being made.

I am sure you will be pleased and satisfied with what has been accomplished and that you will have no cause for worry or disturbance of thought, feeling or quiete surroundings. If you have any thought, suggestion, advice or direction to offer in any way, I will be happy to receive and act upon same. Of course I shall do likewise, that is, first communicate to you any thought or suggestion that may occur to me and to keep you constantly informed.

Hoping that this letter will find you still further improved in health and spirit and that each succeeding day will mark a like or greater improvement I am with kindest personal regards and best of wishes

Yours   Matthew Woll

ALS, Files of the Office of the President, General Correspondence, reel 108, frames 70–87, *AFL Records.*

1. The national committee of the Conference for Progressive Political Action (CPPA) abandoned the idea of nominating state tickets to run alongside its presidential and vice-presidential candidates. See "Excerpts from the Minutes of a Meeting on the 1924 Political Campaign," July 11, 1924, n. 6, above. For a statement on the matter by the CPPA's joint executive committee, see "La Follette Fund by 'Cash and Carry,'" *New York Times,* July 27, 1924.

2. The AFL Executive Council's statement, approved May 15, 1924, expressed the "hope and insistence of the American wage earners that founded upon a platform of honor, honesty and progress, candidates will be nominated for president and vice-president of the United States who shall commend themselves to the favorable consideration of the great mass of the citizenship of our country, and that in the selection of these candidates the hopes, aspirations and claims of America's wage earners for favorable consideration shall be treated fairly and justly. Favorable consideration is strongly urged of the names of outstanding types of America's workers for the nominations to positions within the gift of these political party conventions, and all workers, all citizens are called upon in bringing to realization the high and lofty purpose of securing the selection of candidates capable of intelligently, fearlessly and justly promoting and protecting the human interest of our people and of restoring and safeguarding the principles of justice and freedom" (Executive Council Records, Minutes, reel 7, frame 1486, *AFL Records*).

3. Edward Keating, manager and editor of *Labor* (1919–53), the official journal of the railroad unions, was a member of the general or national committee of the CPPA (1922–24, 1924–25) and a member of the CPPA joint executive committee created to direct the La Follette–Wheeler campaign. (See also *The Samuel Gompers Papers,* vol. 10, p. 125, n. 5.)

4. Basil Manly was a member of both the CPPA general or national committee (1922–25) and the CPPA joint executive committee. He headed the Washington, D.C., office of the La Follette–Wheeler campaign.

To James Shanessy[1]

Continental Hotel, New York City July 19, 1924

Mr. J. C. Shannessy,
222 E. Michigan St., Indianapolis, Ind.
Dear Friend:

It does not now seem probable that I shall have the privilege and opportunity of accepting your invitation to be in attendance and address your convention[2] in September. It may be just barely possible, but as I say, it does not seem probable. And yet there are a few things that I should like to say to you, and I regret that I may not have the privilege of saying them to you orally, and because there may be no better opportunity, presuming upon the mutual friendship and confidence which have existed between us covering a long period of years, I feel impressed with the necessity of laying before you some information and thought which have come to me.

I know the attitude of yourself, brother Fischer and your organization upon the acceptance of women as members of your international union, and I approach this subject with considerable hesitancy; and yet, I repeat, I feel it my duty to lay the matter before you for your personal consideration. You may rely upon it that whatever your decision may be it will be regarded by me as absolutely confidential.

Due in large part to the change in women's hair dressing and arrangement, commonly known as "bobbed" hair, there has been a tremendous increase in those engaged in the barbering trade. There is no question but that a large part of this hair-cutting is done by men barbers in men's barber shops, but the information comes to me from various sources that women engaged in hair-dressing and hair-cutting are performing this work and are employed in what is generally regarded as women's hair establishments. A few days ago I came across an item published in the Washington Star bearing upon this subject.[3] Lest it has not come to your observation, I have had the item copied and enclose copy herein. More than likely, the item is exaggerated, but even if there is any appreciable foundation in fact it is worthy of consideration.

I am wondering whether it might be an advantageous position for you to take to rccommend and urge your associates and also the forth-coming convention the wisdom of the admission of women barbers and hair-dressers, even if under certain conditions and limitations. I know by observation and information as well as my own experience of a certain aversion to women barbers, and that is not founded alone upon the entrance of women into the industry. The sex question and the conditions in the lives of women enter into the question.

Years ago the labor movement objected to the entrance of women in industry. They held, and I was one of them who believed that the proper function of woman was the home and that the man was the natural bread-winner. In the early days I too opposed the acceptance of women to membership in our organization and hoped with other to prevent or at least to check the advent of women in industry. I soon realized that this position was futile, and then for the protection not only of the women themselves but of the standards of life and work of the men advocated the acceptance of the situation as we found it and to admit women to membership in our organization.

In my own organization we have no rules for the acceptance of women cigar makers which do not equally apply to men, and yet in some instances we recognize distinction in regard to our beneficial system.

I am wondering whether if your international union would declare for the acceptance of women as members of your international union with certain justified limitation and regulations, it could be brought about? For instance:

(a) No woman eligible to membership under the age of 18 years.

(b) No woman eligible to membership unless she is free from any chronic communicable disease.

(c) Women in advanced stage of pregnancy to be prohibited from working and for a proscribed limited period after confinement.

(d) Prohibition of women workers for a period of two or three days during periodical condition of women.[4]

I am impressed with the idea that if you and your organization were to take some action in respect to the above in principle there would result a great patronage of barber shops and hair-dressing establishments which would agree to and carry into effect these regulations and prohibitions not only upon grounds of sentiments but also of safety and sanitation.

I have unburdened myself of the thought; I felt that I owed it as a duty to you.

As I have said, this letter to you is, so far as I am concerned, absolutely confidential. You, however, may use your own judgment and use it as you may deem wise and best.

I know you will be glad to learn that I have pulled through a very serious situation and that I am improved in health? I hope and expect to participate in the E.C. meeting of the American Federation of Labor which begins its session August 1st.

With kindest regards and best wishes, I am,

Sincerely yours,   (Signed) Samuel Gompers

TLtcSr, Files of the Office of the President, Letterbooks, Miscellaneous Correspondence, reel 23, pp. 203–4, *AFL Records.* Typed notation: "*Confidential.*"

1. James Colmer SHANESSY served as president of the Journeymen Barbers' International Union of America from 1922 until his death in 1936.

2. The Barbers' convention met in Indianapolis, Sept. 9–17, 1924.

3. "Women Barbers Drive Out Men in Baltimore," *Washington Evening Star,* July 11, 1924. For a copy of the transcript of this article that SG sent to Shanessy, see Files of the Office of the President, Letterbooks, Miscellaneous Correspondence, reel 23, p. 205, *AFL Records.*

4. The Barbers' convention voted to admit women to the union, but with the proviso that they would not receive sick or death benefits for any illnesses other than those that men were subject to. For SG's wire to Shanessy of Sept. 14, 1924, congratulating the union "upon the forward step taken in accepting women barbers to membership," see reel 300, vol. 315, p. 237, SG Letterbooks, DLC.

From Chester Wright and Matthew Woll

Washington, D.C. July 25, 1924.

Mr. Samuel Gompers,
Hotel Shelburne, Brighton, N.Y.
Dear Mr. Gompers:

This afternoon at 2.30 we saw Senator LaFollette and were with him for about forty-five minutes. We called to his attention the newspaper stories which appeared this morning containing a black list of members of the House of Representatives.[1] We called to his attention the conference that had been held between representatives of the A.F. of L. on the one hand, and Mr. Johnston, Mr. Jewell and Mr. Manley on the other hand, and that it has been agreed in these conferences that the A.F. of L. should assume the leadership in the Congressional campaign, while cooperating in the Presidential campaign under the leadership of the C.P.P.A.

We submitted to him the thought that such action as that reported in this morning's newspapers was a violation of the agreement and that might endanger the success of the campaign and the materialization of hopes which we have in the direction of general unity in both the Presidential and Congressional campaigns. The Senator saw the point immediately and sensed the danger.

He brought to our attention several matters which showed lack of team work. For example he said that three weeks ago representatives of the sixteen railroad organizations called upon him and told him what they expected to do. He said they did not ask his opinion about what they ought to do or about what they could do in order to make their efforts most advantageous in every direction, but came merely to tell him their plans.

He said there had been no further visits to him from representatives of the railroad unions until this morning when Mr. Jewell and Mr. Keating called upon him to submit to him a list of Congressmen and Senators which was to be given out as a list of men to be opposed. They asked the Senator to immediately place his O.K. on the list. The Senator said they were unwilling to even give him time until later in the day so that he might study the list and not make mistakes in approval or disapproval of individuals.

The Senator indicated clearly that the railroad unions are not, at least thus far, giving him the support in the Presidential campaign which he had had reasons to expect. He had anticipated and desired that Mr. Jewell be assigned by the railroad unions to Chicago to join in the Presidential campaign from that point. This was not done, but on the contrary, Mr. Shepard, Grand Chief of the Order of Railroad Conductors, was assigned to Chicago to help in the Presidential campaign while Mr. Jewell was ordered to Washington to work in the Congressional campaign. Altogether there was made manifest a lack of coordination which ought to be remedied if possible, and as soon as possible.

It was suggested to the Senator that he consider the advisability of getting in touch with Mr. Jewell or Mr. Johnston asking that publication of any list of Senators and Congressmen be postponed and asking them whether the A.F. of L. has been consulted. It was suggested that he consider urging upon them the advisability of consulting the Federation in order that the interests of the general campaign be not placed in jeopardy through hasty or ill-considered action. The Senator said he was glad to have the suggestion and he expressed the thought that he might get quicker and better action by getting in touch with Mr. Johnston than he could get by approaching Mr. Jewell.

He appeared most anxious that nothing be done which was not in accord with agreement reached, or which might indicate a lack of unity or might prejudice this agreement. He expressed himself as in complete accord with the idea that the A.F. of L. should lead in the Congressional campaign and he seemed quite impatient with things that have been done out of accord with that idea. He seemed to want us to understand that his influence with the railroad unions was not strong and that they were not overly eager for his advice.

He spoke of forecasts which have been published regarding the action which the Executive Council might take in regard to his campaign. He said he could not understand where the leak was through which such stories had gotten into the papers. He said he was almost afraid to look at the newspapers each morning for fear of what he might see. He understands the delicacy of the situation and the complications which now exist and that may also arise when the Council meets. This summarizes the important points of the conversation. The Senator's desire for harmony is very keen and he is eager that as soon as the Council has acted there be created some definite interlocking of committees or some machinery of coordination that will prevent hasty or independent action by any singular subsequent groups.

Fraternally yours,   Chester Wright
Matthew Woll

P.S.—Mr. Morrison has arranged a meeting tomorrow with Mr. Johnston and Mr. Jewell. Mr. Morrison said today that Mr. Jewell had assured him today that he (Jewell) did not give out the list published and that no such list had been prepared. What may have happened is that somehow the minutes of the committees which are considering the records of Congressmen may have been given out or may have in some manner gotten out without the consent of the labor men or without their knowledge.

C. M. W. and M. W.

Wherever the word "agreement" has been used in the foregoing letter it does not imply a binding agreement, but means conversations held and suggestions made therein which have been accepted temporarily by those with whom our conferences have been held.

Our conference today with the Senator was unknown to Mr. Morrison.

TLS, Files of the Office of the President, General Correspondence, reel 108, frames 47–48, 88, *AFL Records*.

1. On July 25, 1924, the *Washington Post* reported that Progressive leaders had compiled a "blacklist" of forty Republican and Democratic congressmen and senators from seven states and now intended to review the records of the congressional delegations from all the other states ("40 Representatives Are Blacklisted by La Follette Chiefs," *Washington Post*, July 25, 1924).

Excerpts from the Minutes of a Meeting on the 1924 Political Campaign[1]

Shelburne Hotel, Coney Island, Sunday, July 27, 1924.

. . .

Mr. Woll and Mr. Morrison came over from Washington for the purpose of submitting to Mr. Gompers the draft of the report to be submitted to the Executive Council at its meeting August first, by the Executive Committee of the A.F. of L. Non-Partisan Campaign Committee, consisting of Messrs. Gompers, O'Connell and Morrison.[2] Owing to Mr. Gompers' illness, Mr. Woll acted for him on the Committee and attended both the Republican and the Democratic National Conventions.

. . .

Each paragraph was taken up line by line and such suggestions made by President Gompers as seemed pertinent to him, all of which were accepted by Mr. Morrison and Mr. Woll. Upon the conclusion of reading the entire report they both stated that Mr. Gompers additions to the report had rounded it out and greatly improved it.

Referring to newspaper reports of a black-list of members of Congress furnished by the Conference on Progressive Political Action, Mr. Morrison said:

"As soon as I saw the black-list in the papers I called up Jewell.[3] He said he did not give it out, that he was not responsible for it but he explained it in this way—the only explanation that could be made—that it resulted from the publication of the vote of the representatives from seven states, the primaries in these states to be held the first of August, the vote being on the Railway Labor Board. They evidently took that vote and used that as the foundation for their stories. . . ."

Mr. Woll: "Then we had a conference yesterday morning, of Johnston, Nelson,[4] Jewell and our people. They made practically the same statement. In addition, Johnston said he would give out a statement denying that they had made such a statement." (This denial appeared in the New York papers this morning.)[5]

Mr. Gompers: "It is an awful thing when you have to begin to deny. People will say, 'What, more denials.'"

Mr. Gompers continuing; I am unsatisfied with the relations, so far as I can gather from reports between representatives of the American Federation of Labor and those who are in control of the LaFollette campaign. I have great respect for Brother Jewell but in the position in which he now is, he is a novice. (This has reference to Mr. Jewell having been assigned by the railroad group to the Washington office instead of the office in Chicago as he had anticipated). Without flattery, our boys are experts. I cannot recall in all the period including 1906, that they have made a serious mistake. We have done no one an injustice. We have played the game squarely and cleanly and have come out of every campaign with our skirts clean and untainted. We may have been opposed and denounced but no one has a just cause for saying that we have done an injustice upon his record."

"Now, to submit ourselves and our position to a man of experience, and who is fighting in this campaign—but with us the American Federation of Labor must live. There were times when we could have taken advantage of certain situations which would have resulted in temporary success or attainments of certain things but it would have minimized its value and importance."

"The real strength of what support can be brought to the LaFollette candidacy will be the rank and file of the organizations of the American Federation of Labor. Our committee has been willing to urge that position and even to the Executive Council so that it may go forth to the world that we have proffered, in so far as we have had the right to proffer, our cooperation and coordination in the LaFollette campaign as a condition precedent that legislatively, in the matter of the members of Congress in either or both Houses, the American Federation of Labor must maintain its leadership and receive in return the cooperation and the coordination of this group."

Mr. Woll: "As I understand it, in our conferences which we held last week and this week, we made that very clear that we would never surrender the question of determining those whom we would support. The question then changed to eight years ago when in carrying on this same campaign, both groups had endeavored to avoid conflict, and quite successfully. They realized the necessity of no conflict. They understand that they would have to conform to us."

Mr. Morrison: "In our meeting we brought that out clearly to them, that we would cooperate with them in the election of LaFollette and Wheeler but that we would carry on our non-partisan political campaign just the same, that it was part of it and that we wanted their cooperation in electing Congressmen and Senators whose records entitled them to the support of labor. They agreed to that."

Mr. Gompers: "As to the test of records of the members of Congress, if we cannot agree our test goes and not theirs."

. . .

Mr. Woll: "They have no test in conflict with the American Federation of Labor."

Mr. Morrison: "They have accepted our test; they have other tests but they do not interfere."

Mr. Woll: "Mr. Wallace and Mr. McGrady met with them. I asked Mr. McGrady how their test conformed to ours. He said our test will govern. . . ."

After some further discussion Mr. Morrison stated: "I had a conference with Senator LaFollette on the position we want him to take in carrying on our campaign, that we want his group to cooperate with the American Federation of Labor in carrying on our campaign. He said, [']I told them I did not want to interfere in any way in the election of the men who were progressive in the support of labor, that is, to support the people which labor will support in the campaign.' He also sent his regards to you."

. . .

Mr. Gompers then said he had some valuable information to give and that if it would be of any addition to our cause he would disclose the means of his information but nothing of advantage could come and that he would therefore be indefinite as to the source of his information, but he said "I am fully convinced that Mr. LaFollette is in an unhappy frame of mind. He is the leader of that group. They do not so treat him. His voice is not the dominating one in regard to the campaign and what should be done. He is made to feel that he is their candidate and they lay down the law to him and he is in an unhappy frame of mind and his position does not permit him—at least, he feels that he must yield. Now, it is unfortunate. Senator LaFollette could understand direct from us what we want to do. We cannot give him at this time definite assurance that what we want to do will be the final act—whether that shall be approved by the Executive Council. Our course will be approved or disapproved but we want to play the game squarely with him and that in the last analysis, if that goes through he can count upon us 100 per cent and that in the presidential campaign he is the leader and we to help in carrying out his wishes. If we differ from him we will endeavor to get our point of view to him and when he decides, his decision goes."

. . .

TDc, Files of the Office of the President, Conferences, reel 123, frames 776–78, *AFL Records*.

1. Participants at the meeting included SG, Frank Morrison, Matthew Woll, W. C. Roberts, and R. Lee Guard.

2. See Executive Council Records, Minutes, reel 7, frames 1498–1502, *AFL Records*. The report was subsequently published as a circular (see "To William B. Wilson," Aug. 6, 1924, n. 8, below) and printed in the *American Federationist* ("Report and Action on Men and Platforms" 31 [Sept. 1924]: 705–11). For the report's conclusions and recommendations, and the Executive Council's discussion of the document, see "Excerpts from the Minutes of a Meeting of the Executive Council of the AFL," Aug. 2, 1924, below.

3. Press reports indicated that Bert Jewell was in charge of reviewing the records of members of Congress up for reelection in 1924 in terms of their positions on railroad labor legislation.

4. That is, John Mandt Nelson, the manager of the La Follette–Wheeler campaign and director of the campaign's Chicago office. He was also chairman of the Conference for Progressive Political Action joint executive committee.

5. For the denial, see "La Follette Fund by 'Cash and Carry,'" *New York Times,* July 27, 1924.

From William Z. Foster and Charles Ruthenberg

Chicago Ills July 31 1924

Saml Gompers
President Amn Fed of Labor
Atlantic City NJ

The Workers Party of America throws back in your teeth Mister Gompers your slanderous charges of political betrayal made against it yesterday[1] *Stop* Charges of political betrayal come with ill grace from you the arch betrayor of the American working class *Stop* In this particular crisis your Executive Counsel comes together to continue your old policy of quote victories for friends and great defeats for enemies unquote *Stop* This policy has resulted in low wages unspeakable [working][2] conditions in-junctions and general political help-lessness [*Stop*] [You] are a faithful ally of the capitalists class *Stop* The Republican convention gave you five minutes time to plead the cause of labor and then kicked you in the face *Stop* The Democratic convention showed equal contempt for your pleadings *Stop* The Republican answer was strike breaker Coolidge *Stop* The Democratic answer was Morgan Rockerfeller lawyer Davis *Stop* Now that the two parties of Big Business have thrown you overboard you are faced with the problem whether you will join the movement of Little Business in which LaFolette is attempting to lead us back to seventeen seventy six *Stop* If you were loyal to the interests of the working class [you] would flatly repudiate the Republican party the Democratic party and the backward looking LaFollette movement *Stop* You would call upon the workers to unite in the organizations of a Farmer Labor party and to fight for a workers and farmers government *Stop* But you and your socialists and LaFolette allies will not do this You will again betray the interests of the workers of this country *Stop* Over your head the Workers Party of America appeals to the broad masses of industrial workers and poor farmers *Stop* We will fight to mobolize them for independent political action on a platform representing their [class] interests We will stage the struggle against all the representatives of the employing class and the capitalists system itself *Stop* As against Coolidge Davis and LaFolette we call upon the workers to support the working class candidates Foster and Gitlow[3] and the communist program of the Workers Party of America *Stop*

Central Executive Committee,   Workers Party of America
William Z Foster   Natl Chairman
C E Ruthenberg   Executive Secy[4]

TWSr, Files of the Office of the President, General Correspondence, reel 108, frames 65–68, *AFL Records.*

1. For SG's statement of July 30, 1924, on the political campaign, see "Gompers Opposes Endorsing Parties," *New York Times,* July 31, 1924. Also see "Communists Drop Mask; Tricky Policy Has Failed," *AFL Weekly News Service,* July 26, 1924.

2. Text in brackets in this document is supplied from a transcribed copy of the telegram in the Files of the Office of the President, General Correspondence, reel 108, frame 69, *AFL Records.*

3. Benjamin Gitlow (1891–1965), a member of the central executive committee of the Workers' Party of America (1924–25), was running for vice-president of the United States on the party's ticket with William Z. Foster. Gitlow had joined the Socialist Party of America in 1909 and then had served for a time as president of the Retail Clerks' Union of New York, an independent body that later became Retail Clerks' International Protective Association 782. In 1918 he served for a term in the New York state assembly, representing the Bronx. The following year he was expelled from the Socialist party, helped organize the Communist Labor Party of America, and managed its paper, *Revolutionary Age.* Convicted of criminal anarchy in New York in 1919, he was imprisoned for three years before being released on appeal in 1922. His conviction was upheld by the U.S. Supreme Court in 1925, but Governor Al Smith subsequently pardoned him. In 1929 Gitlow was appointed to the secretariat of the Communist Party of the United States of America, but he was expelled from the party later that year. He next helped organize the Communist Party (Majority Group) with Jay Lovestone but in 1933 broke with them as well. Finally he rejoined the Socialist party, only to leave again, and by 1939 he had broken all his ties to the Left.

4. For SG's reply to this telegram, see "Labor Is Expected to Aid La Follette; Gompers Flays Foster," *New York Times,* Aug. 2, 1924.

Excerpts from the Minutes of a Meeting of the Executive Council of the AFL

Saturday, August 2, 1924.

MORNING SESSION.

. . .

LABOR'S NON-PARTISAN POLITICAL CAMPAIGN

Conclusions and Recommendations.

The Executive Committee of the American Federation of Labor National Non-Partisan Political Campaign Committee presented Labor's proposals to the Republican convention.

The Republican convention gave labor's representatives a brief and curt hearing. The Republican platform ignores entirely the injunction issue. It fails to deal with Labor's right to organize or the right of the workers even in self defense, collectively to cease work. That platform sustains the Railroad Labor Board, with all that it means in the direction of governmental coercion of wage earners. It fails to recommend the ratification by the States of the Child Labor constitutional amendment.

The Republican convention nominated candidates unacceptable to labor.

Its candidate for vice-president is one of the most outspoken enemies of Labor and is the founder of an organization dedicated to the task of writing into all political platforms planks calling for the anti-union shop—an organization which also encouraged and supported the Daugherty injunction against the railroad shopmen.

Labor's representatives submitted to the Democratic convention identical proposals to those submitted to the Republican convention. At this convention an extended hearing was granted. The Democratic platform pledges that party to legislation to regulate hours and conditions of all labor a proposal against which the American Federation of Labor has struggled throughout its whole history. It is silent as to the injunction. It does not meet the Railroad Labor Board issue. On that point it is so equivocal that the enemies of Labor may well feel that their desires will be met. It, too, fails to recommend the ratification by the States of the Child Labor constitutional amendment.

The Democratic convention nominated candidates unacceptable to Labor.

As to the candidates and platforms, both the Republican and the Democratic National Party conventions flaunted the desires of Labor, the Republican convention in an arrogant manner; the Democratic convention by that evasiveness which is the customary mark of insincerity.

There remains the candidacy of Robert M. La Follette and Burton K. Wheeler, the first an Independent Republican; the second an Independent Democrat, running as such.

These candidates have proffered a platform in which the economic issues of the day are met in a manner more nearly conforming to Labor's proposals than any other platform.

This platform pledges a remedy for the injunction evil.

It pledges the right to organize and collectively to cease work.

It pledges protection of the rights of free speech, free press and free assemblage.

It pledges abolishment of the Railroad Labor Board.

It pledges a measure to annul the power of the Supreme Court to declare laws permanently unconstitutional.

It declares for direct election of president and vice-president and election of federal judges.

It recommends prompt ratification by the States of the Child Labor constitutional amendment.

It pledges subsequent federal legislation to protect child life.

On international issues this platform does not conform to Labor's proposals but it does more fully than any other political platform meet Labor's views in relation to domestic economic issues.

We cannot do other than point out this fact, together with the further and perhaps more important fact that the candidates Mr. La Follette and Mr. Wheeler, have throughout their whole political careers, stood steadfast in defense of the rights and interests of the wage earners and the farmers.

We cannot fail to observe that both Republican and Democratic Parties through manipulated control are in a condition of moral bankruptcy which constitutes a menace and a peril to our country and its institutions. Machine politicians have brought upon our country moral obliquity and unashamed betrayal. We are judging on the basis of the condition which exists and this judgment will be reversed only when the conditions upon which it is based are changed.

Service to the people is a noble cause which demands consecration and the American labor movement demands that there be that consecration in candidates to whom it gives support.

Our course is clear. In pointing to the platform and records of the Independent candidates, we do so with the confidence that no other course can be pursued if we are to remain true to our convictions and our traditions. Those who are hostile to Labor and to the people generally and who devoted their energies to the service of re-action and special interests, must be opposed.

We call upon the wage earners and the great masses of the people everywhere who stand for freedom, justice, democracy and human progress, to rally in this campaign to the end that the representatives of reaction and special interests may be defeated and the faithful friends and servants of the masses elected.

Cooperation hereby urged is not a pledge of identification with an independent party movement or a third party, nor can it be construed as support for such a party, group or movement except as such action accords with our non-partisan political policy. We do not accept government as the solution of the problems of life. Major problems of life and labor must be dealt with by voluntary groups and organizations, of which trade unions are an essential and integral part. Neither can this co-operation imply our support, acceptance or endorsement of policies or principles advocated by any minority groups or organizations that may see fit to support the candidacies of Senator La Follette and Senator Wheeler.

In the campaign to elect men to Congress, regardless of their political group or party affiliation and deserving of Labor's support, there must be unity of purpose and method, therefore leadership must lie with the only organization having the right to speak for the entire labor movement. In this the American Federation of Labor yields to none but will maintain steadfast its leadership, guidance and direction.

In the selection and election of men to pubic office within the several states leadership must lie with our State Federations of Labor and in city or county elections this right must rest with central labor bodies.

Organized labor owes allegiance to no political party or group. It is not partisan to any political party or group. It is partisan to principles—the principles of freedom, of justice, of democracy.

It is the duty of trade unionists, their friends and sympathizers, and all lovers of freedom, justice and democratic ideals and institutions to unite in defeating those seeking public office who are indifferent or hostile to the people's rights and interests. It is the duty of all to support such candidates to public office who have been fair, just and outspoken in behalf of the welfare of the common people.

We shall analyze the record and attitude of every aspirant to public office and shall give our findings the widest possible publicity. Labor's enemies and friends must be clearly known and be definitely indicated.

In calling upon all affiliated and recognized national and international and brotherhood organizations, state federations of labor, central labor bodies, local unions, labor's friends and sympathizers, to give united, unrestricted, loyal and active support to the non-partisan campaign now set in motion, we emphasize the imperative need of an intensive educational campaign to enable all to act with discrimination and wisdom in this election, and to stand faithfully by our friends and elect them and to oppose our enemies and to defeat them.

> Samuel Gompers,
> Frank Morrison,
> James O'Connell,
> Matthew Woll
> Executive Committee,
> American Federation of Labor
> National Non-Partisan Political Campaign Committee.

It was moved and seconded that the report be adopted.

Treasurer Tobin moved as an amendment to the report to add in the last paragraph to the effect that we believe in the interests of our great movement and the principles we are striving for, that it is in the interests of the masses of the workers to support the candidacy of La Follette and Wheeler.

The proposal relative to naming candidates for whom the workers should vote and the relation of such a proposition to the non-partisan political policy of the American Federation of Labor was discussed by Treasurer Tobin and Vice-Presidents Duncan and Woll and was under discussion at the time of adjournment.

. . .

AFTERNOON SESSION.

. . .

President Gompers:—One of the reasons I ask to be heard now is I am taking a great risk in sitting in this Council meeting participating in discussions, even hearing discussions that I made up my mind if it is the last thing I do that I would be at this Council meeting.[1] There are other great questions coming before this Council but this is the most critical and I can not be neutral in a critical situation. I have been very seriously ill, critically ill and I am not out of the woods. I have been working some in the work, I cannot be idle, I cannot have my brain a vacuum. Some of the work came to me in which I was glad to indulge myself.

This document, a rough draft of it was prepared after discussion, I went over it line for line and word for word. It expresses in it what I think is the best thing to do, the right thing to do.

I have declined to discuss for publication anything of a political nature and the press has placed me in a wrong position. I have refused to correct or deny, reserving my statement for the Executive Council.

At one time I was a member of the Republican Party and left it and never joined any other political party. I owe allegiance to no political party. I am a trade unionist and try to be loyal to the American Federation of Labor. To me a Democrat does not look any better than a Republican, a Republican any better than a Democrat, or a C.P.P.A. does not look any better to me than either of the others. I judge organizations, I judge men by their deeds, by their acts, by the principles they espouse.

It may not be uninteresting to relate to you an incident that has great significance. You have not seen in the last few weeks much Communist propaganda, but from what I shall bring to your attention you will understand their activity.

Over a year ago in Chicago, I called a meeting[2] of the representatives of the labor movement of that city and predicated my request upon a resolution[3] adopted by the Chicago Federation of Labor calling upon the Executive Council to call a special convention for the purpose of amalgamation. At that meeting Foster was present and there was a long discussion and he called upon me for reference for his character and record. I gave him some *reference* and the result was that a change of sentiment set in. I put Fitzpatrick and Nelson on their guard as to what was up by Foster and his gang. When they held the convention[4] of the so-called Farmer Labor Party Foster and Ruthenberg stole the party and made it a Communist party, calling it the Federated Farmer Labor Party with Communism the avowed principle. It had a great influence with Fitzpatrick and the other men in repudiating the Fosterites and throwing them out and dissolving the Farmer Labor Party as such.

About three months ago a call was sent out for the St. Paul meeting by the Fosterites, getting some unions and union men in Minnesota to underwrite and subscribe to the whole thing. Thereupon I invited the representative labor men in Washington, officers of the American Federation of Labor who were in the city were present, Secretary Morrison among them, Brother O'Connell, President Johnston of the Machinists, representative men of the Metal Trades organizations in Washington, the progressive Senators and Members of the House of Representatives of both political parties. We had about thirty men there.[5] I related and disclosed the situation in their own states in regard to the Farmer Labor Party and that the progressive movement in these states would be undermined. The meeting to be held at St. Paul was for nothing more nor less than to capture the entire political effort of labor, farmer and progressives, for the Communist movement. There was only one Senator present who did not see it. I will not mention his name. His secretary was a member who issued the call with Foster and the others. He had been duped and did not know a thing that was going on. Senator Johnston,[6] Representative Nelson[7] and the others said—"That is a revelation, it has astounded me, if it is true!" My purpose was that those men should save themselves and that further Senator La Follette, who was to be the leader of the Progressive movement, if there is to be any Progressive movement, should not be crucified by the Communists.

After the discussion which lasted the whole evening I said: "The Senator must be made acquainted with this situation and save himself and save whatever there is of a Progressive movement, political, economic, industrial or agricultural. I will issue a circular letter[8] to organized labor of the country. I will assume the responsibility of advising them of the trap that has been laid for them by this St. Paul meeting. I will withhold the issuance of that circular letter if Senator La Follette will take a stand in repudiating this gang." I wanted him to have the opportunity to disentangle himself from that gang whoever they might be. That famous letter he wrote,[9] you remember. I had Secretary Morrison give him the information, go to him to save him,—not only his political career but the country and the movement of labor and the farmers.

They have put me in the class of opposing La Follette since the conventions. I say to you here and now that when those platforms were adopted by those two conventions and they nominated the men they did, I was against them and made up my mind if it takes the last bit of energy I have to put it in the La Follette campaign and for La Follette. The situation is entirely different from the previous campaigns. Here we have practically no choice, one is no nearer to us than the other. You look at the platforms of 1908, 1912 and 1916 and you will find nothing in either of them in the platforms of 1924. The Republican Convention, they have got hold of the boodle and where they cannot make excuses they have not said a thing. The Democrats say they want honesty. There must be something more than honesty—more than an indictment against crooks. Here is something where we may help. It is at least a protest and perhaps something better. . . .

. . .

If I thought the amendment offered by Treasurer Tobin would help our cause I would say yes let's do it. I think though that it would not. It is quite evident that the amendment offered would not receive the unanimous approval of this Executive Council. There is not anything that could hurt our cause so much as if there were division in the Executive Council upon such an endorsement. We have worked together so long, we talk among ourselves pretty frankly—Vice-presidents Duncan and Green would not feel that they could abide by any such decision as the endorsement of La Follette and Wheeler by name. Such a thing can not remain secret. It is not a matter that people can keep to themselves. This document follows the exact policy as we always carried it into effect. Quite apart from the first consideration I mentioned of the differences of the men upon the Executive Council on this subject—the newspapers. When we gave a bill of health to the Republican candidate the Democratic papers raised hell with us, the Republican papers were with us; when we gave a bill of health to the Democratic candidate the Republican papers raised hell with us and the Democratic papers were with us, but here we shall have none of that if we do not put the names in the document. There is no other construction that can be placed on that document than the feeling that La Follette and Wheeler deserve the support of the masses as between the others—Davis and Coolidge. Dawes and Bryan. There is no other construction can be placed upon that document than as against the other four candidates and that we are with these two.

I favor the adoption of this document not because I had a hand in its preparation and its revision, that has been a matter now of nearly three weeks and the final word was on last night to perfect it to do the right thing, and my opinion is its adoption in its form will bring about good results, open us less to attack and have unanimity in our course.

Treasurer Tobin spoke in support of the amendment which he offered at this morning's session.

A general discussion ensued in which the members stated their respective interpretations of the non-partisan political policy of the American Federation of Labor.

Treasurer Tobin asked President Gompers to answer the following question:

"If I received a letter from San Francisco, and I will be asked this question, asking if this Executive Council endorsed La Follette, would I be correct in answering yes?"

President Gompers. "Yes, that is what I would say."

It was argued that the Council is without any authority to name candidates.

Secretary Morrison made the statement in which he cited the fact that the Labor Representation Committee of the American Federation of Labor in the 1916 campaign had recommended the election of Mr. Wilson as against Mr. Hughes. As far as he knew there was no criticism of that recommendation.

President Gompers stated that he was going to do something that he did not often do and that was to ask Treasurer Tobin to withdraw the amendment to name La Follette and Wheeler. He stated his reason was that if an amendment was adopted with a division as was evidenced it would be from the discussion, it is going to hurt. If it is defeated it is a blow against La Follette and Wheeler, that either way it would hurt.

Vice-President Green made a statement in opposition to the proposition to name La Follette and Wheeler. He stated also that the demands would be challenged with reference to the statement of the candidates who are unacceptable and referred to the favorable record of Governor Bryan of Nebraska, the nominee of the Democratic party. Vice-President Green said if we name the men we should go all the way and form a third party and tell the workers all the men they should vote for.

Vice-President Rickert stated that he had received a long distance 'phone call from Mr. Keegan[10] at Washington, in which he stated that former Secretary of Labor Wilson, said he would like to have action on this subject delayed until he could get a statement here.

President Gompers again made his appeal that Treasurer Tobin withdraw his amendment.

Vice-President Duncan stated that in opposing the amendment to name La Follette and Wheeler, that it was not because of any opposition to La Follette. He knows of no man living who he considers better qualified to fill the office of President of the United States. His purpose in opposing the amendment is to preserve the history and tradition of the American Federation of Labor in its political activities.

Upon the request of Treasurer Tobin a recess was granted at five o'clock for fifteen or twenty minutes.

The meeting reconvened at 5:15.

Upon reconvening Treasurer Tobin stated that he had considered the statements made, particularly those of President Gompers and that no one could make the situation more clear than he had made it. One statement that impressed himself and those who supported the amendment more than any other is, that if this amendment is defeated it might be considered as a slap at the men we are trying to help. President Gompers' interpretation that the document is an endorsement of La Follette confirmed them in their understanding of the declaration and in order to go along and do the best we can, it is the consensus of opinion of the seconder of the amendment and myself and those supporting it that the amendment be withdrawn.

Vice-President Ryan stated that he consented to the withdrawal of the amendment. When the document was read he considered it a very clear and satisfactory statement and that if he is asked the conclusions of the Executive Council he would state that the Council has endorsed La Follette.

President Gompers then put the question for the withdrawal of the amendment. There being no objection the amendment was with-drawn.

The question was then put for the adoption of the report of the Executive Committee of the American Federation of Labor National Non-Partisan Political Campaign Committee as read at this morning's session.

Upon a viva voce vote, the report was adopted with one dissenting vote.[11]

. . .

TDc, Executive Council Records, Minutes, reel 7, frames 1498, 1500–1506, *AFL Records.*

1. SG attended meetings of the AFL Executive Council on Aug. 1–2 and Aug. 4–5 but was absent from the meetings held Aug. 6–11.

2. See "Excerpts from the Minutes of a Meeting with Chicago Trade Union Repre-sentatives," Apr. 12, 1922, above.

3. See "To John Frey," Apr. 5, 1922, n. 10, above.

4. See "To Frank Farrington," July 27, 1923, n. 1, above.

5. See "Excerpts from the Minutes of a Meeting on the Farmer-Labor Progressive Convention in St. Paul, Minn." Apr. 28, 1924, above.

6. That is, Magnus Johnson.

7. John Mandt Nelson.

8. See "Excerpts from the Minutes of a Meeting on the Farmer-Labor Progressive Convention in St. Paul, Minn." Apr. 28, 1924, n. 11, above.

9. La Follette wrote to Wisconsin attorney general Herman Ekern on May 25, 1924, stating his belief that "all Progressives should refuse to participate in any movement which makes common cause with any Communist organization." For the complete text of this letter, see "La Follette Ready to Lead New Party; Assails Communism," *New York Times,* May 29, 1924.

10. John J. Keegan (1872–1944?), previously a vice-president of the International Association of Machinists and a commissioner of conciliation for the U.S. Department of Labor, served as a member of the United States Employees' Compensation Com-mission from 1917 to 1944. (See also *The Samuel Gompers Papers,* vol. 6, p. 122, n. 3, and vol. 7, p. 378, n. 5.)

11. La Follette acknowledged the Executive Council's action in a telegram to SG dated Aug. 4, 1924 (Executive Council Records, Minutes, reel 7, frames 1513–14, *AFL Records*). For a National Non-Partisan Political Campaign Committee circular summa-rizing the AFL's position on the campaign, see "To All Organized Labor, Its Friends and Sympathizers," *American Federationist* 31 (Sept. 1924): 759.

From William B. Wilson

Democratic National Committee
Washington, D.C., August 2nd, 1924.

Honorable Samuel Gompers,
President, American Federation of Labor,
Ambassador Hotel, Atlantic City, N.J.
My dear Mr. Gompers:

I have accepted an invitation from the Democratic National Committee to assist in the campaign for the election of John W. Davis as President of the United States.

My close personal friendship with you and my life long association with the labor movement, prompts me to write you stating the reasons that have led me to this conclusion.

As you know, I was for a number of years a member of the Committee on President's report in the convention of the American Federation of Labor. As the president's report always dealt with the problems confronting labor, it became the duty of the committee to deal with the policies that should be pursued in solving the various problems present. Consequently it was my duty, as well as pleasure, to assist in the development of the policies expressed by the phrases, "The labor of a human being is not a commodity or article of commerce." "Labor is not partisan to a party, but is partisan to a principle"; "Labor will support its friends and oppose its enemies," and so on. These policies I thoroughly believe in, and for that reason have given my support in this campaign to John W. Davis.

I first came in contact with him when I was International Secretary of the United Mine Workers of America, and he was a young practicing attorney at Clarksburg, W.Va. Innumerable injunctions were being issued against us by Judge Jackson[1] at the instance of the Coal operators of the State; many of our organizers were cited to appear to show cause why they should not be held in contempt,—among them Mother Jones[2] and Thomas Haggerty,[3] a member of the International Executive Board from Central Pa. Our people were holding many meetings protesting against the action of the coal operators and the Courts. Large numbers of them were arrested and hailed before the local courts. John W. Davis volunteered his services to defend them. I did not see him again until he entered the Sixty Second Congress as Representative from West Virginia.

For a generation the Trades Union movement of the country had been seeking relief from the abuse of the writ of injunction. No headway had been made in securing federal legislation until Mr. Davis came to Congress. He was assigned to the Committee on Judiciary, and took an immediate interest in anti-injunction legislation.

During the year 1912, in consultation with Senator Hughes from New Jersey and Congressman Kitchen[4] of North Carolina, and myself, he wrote sections 6 and 20 of the Clayton Anti-Trust Law, approved October 15, 1914. They represent the most progressive and far reaching legislation enacted by any government in the history of the world. I am quoting the two sections in full, that you may have them before you for reference:

"Section 6. That the labor of a human being is not a commodity or article of commerce. Nothing contained in the anti-trust laws shall be construed to forbid the existence and operation of labor, agricultural, or horticultural organizations, instituted for the purpose[s][5] of mutual help, and not having capital stock or conducted for profit, or to forbid or restrain individual members of such organizations from lawfully carrying out the legitimate objects thereof; nor shall such organizations, or the members thereof, be held or construed to be illegal combinations or conspiracies in restraint of trade, under the anti-trust laws."

This is not the language of Mr. Davis. It is the language of the American Labor Movement, but it was adopted by him and through his influence, written into the law of the land. The first sentence of the section lays the foundation for abolishing the writ of injunction in labor disputes. The balance removes the taint of conspiracy from labor, agricultural and horticultural organizations, and has made possible the wonderful development of the farmers cooperative selling agencies. Without it they would have been conspiracies in restraint of trade.

Section 20 writes into the law what labor organizations had long been contending for. It is as follows:

"That no restraining order or injunction shall be granted by any court of the United States, or a judge o[r] the judges thereof, in any case between an employer and employee[s], or between employers and employees, or between employees, or between persons employed and persons seeking employment, involving, or growing out of, a dispute concerning terms or conditions of employment, unless necessary to prevent irreparable injury to property, or to a property right, of the party making the application, for which injury there is no adequate remedy at law, and such property or property right must be described with particular[ity] in the application, which must be in writing and sworn to by the applicant or by his agent or attorney.

"And no such restraining order or injunction shall prohibit any person or persons, whether singly or [in] concert, from terminating any relation of employment, or from ceasing to perform any work or labor, or from recommending, advising, or persuading others by peaceful means so to do; or from attending at any place where any such person or persons may lawfully be, for the purpose of peacefully obtaining or communicating information, or from peacefully persuading any person to work or to abstain from working; or from ceasing to patronize or to employ any party to such dispute, or from recommending, advising, or by persuading others by peaceful and lawful means so to do; or from paying or giving to, or withholding from, any person engaged in such dispute, any strike benefits or other moneys or things of value; or from peaceably assembling in a lawful manner, and for lawful purposes, or from doing any act or thing which might lawfully be done in the absence of any such dispute by any party thereto; nor shall any of the acts specified in this paragraph be considered or held to be violations of any law of the United States."

This work undertaken personally by Mr. Davis, without solicitation, clearly indicates his attitude of mind toward problems affecting the wage worker and farmer.

When the 8 hour law for railroad men was passed in 1916,[6] the officials of the railway organizations feared that it would not stand the test of the Supreme Court, that was made evident by the fact they had declared a strike on the members of the Brotherhood to take effect in the early part of 1917. The manner in which John W. Davis prepared and presented the case to the Supreme Court in behalf of the government, resulted in a favorable decision that came just in time to prevent the threatened strike.[7] This attitude of mind has been backed up by the action of the Democratic Party in federal legislation during the last 30 years. It has not enacted everything that the wage workers and farmers have demanded, but it has placed upon the statute books more well thought out constructive legislation that opened the doors of opportunity to wage workers and farmers, than all other parties, blocs, or groups combined. I shall not, at this time attempt to enumerate them, which would only be refreshing your memory on what your official records show.

I have no antagonism toward Senator LaFollette. He has done good service for the country in the way that he is best qualified to do it. He has ably called attention to existing wrongs; he has been "The voice crying in the wilderness."[8] He has attracted wide attention, but he does not seem to have the faculty of consolidating his contentions into concrete legislation for the relief of the people. In addition to that, he has allowed himself to be placed in the position in this campaign, where he is being used as the auger to bore the labor organizations of the country from within.

The records of all the candidates will not be complete until their letters of acceptance have been given to the public, and I take the liberty of suggesting that the Executive Council, or some person or persons representing the Council, attend the ceremonies for the notification of Mr. Davis, at Clarksburg, West Virginia, August 11, 1924, and listen to his letter of acceptance before taking definite political action.

Cordially yours,   (signed) W. B. Wilson.

TLtcSr, Files of the Office of the President, General Correspondence, reel 108, frames 90–94, *AFL Records.*

1. John Jay Jackson, Jr. (1824–1907), served as a U.S. district court judge for the Western District of Virginia (1861–64), the District of West Virginia (1864–1901), and the Northern District of West Virginia (1901–5).

2. Mary Harris "Mother" JONES, (1830–1930), a renowned labor organizer.

3. Thomas T. Haggerty (1865–1946), who immigrated to the United States from Scotland in 1881, played a key role in uniting the National Progressive Union of Miners and Mine Laborers and KOL National Trade Assembly 135 in 1890 to form the United Mine Workers of America. A prominent organizer for the Mine Workers, he served as a member of the union's executive board from 1903 to 1917. He was forced to resign when it became known that he had purchased an interest in a coal mine in West Virginia.

4. Claude Kitchin (1869–1923) served as a Democratic congressman from North Carolina from 1901 until his death in 1923.

5. Text in brackets in this document is supplied from U.S. *Statutes at Large,* 38: 731, 738.

6. The Adamson Act.

7. *Wilson* v. *New et al.,* 243 U.S. 332 (1917). See *The Samuel Gompers Papers,* vol. 9, p. 450, n. 2.

8. The quotation, a reference in the New Testament to John the Baptist, occurs in Matt. 3:3, Mark, 1:3, Luke 3:4, and John 1:23. See also Isa. 40:3.

To William B. Wilson

Ambassador Hotel, Atlantic City, New Jersey August 6, 1924.

Mr. W. B. Wilson,
323 Investment Building, Washington, D.C.
My dear Mr. Wilson:

Your letter of August 2nd,[1] requesting that the Executive Council of the American Federation of Labor should not consider and take definite action regarding the pending political situation until the Executive Council or some person or persons representing the Executive Council could attend the ceremonies for the notification of Mr. John W. Davis at Clarksburg, West Virginia August 11, 1924, was referred to the Executive Council of the American Federation of Labor following the receipt of your telegram of August 1st.

By and with the approval of the Executive Council I am submitting to you the following statement:

Three months ago the Executive Council of the American Federation of Labor directed that the E.C. next meet in Atlantic City, New Jersey, August 1st, to transact such business as required the attention of the Executive Council, including the defining of the attitude of the A.F. of L. in the furtherance of its Non-Partisan Political Campaign. On Friday August 1st, and before the receipt of your telegram, the question of determining our political course was made a special order of business for Saturday. The suggestion of a letter coming from you was mentioned during the discussion on Saturday, but the Executive Council deemed itself fully competent to deal with the problems entrusted into its keeping for consideration and action.

You know of course that the officers of the American Federation of Labor are fully informed of all that transpired in connection with the enactment of the Clayton law, especially Sections 6 and 20. We are likewise fully informed as to all who rendered valuable services in that legislation. We must dissent from the conclusions related by you. This dissent is borne out by records and facts readily available. At an opportune time these records and facts will be fully set forth, in none of which does Mr. John W. Davis appear.

Regarding your statement that it was the Supreme Court decision upholding the Adamson law which prevented a strike on the railroads of the country, and giving Mr. Davis credit for having won that decision and thus preventing the strike, let me recount facts with which you are familiar and which are in direct conflict with the statement in your letter.

President Wilson appointed a commission of four, President Daniel Willard of the Baltimore & Ohio, Secretary of the Interior Franklin K. Lane, you and myself, for the purpose of mediating and preventing a strike.

This commission brought about an agreement between the railroad brotherhoods and the representatives of the railroads and that agreement was signed in the presence of the commission, of which you and I were members, before the Supreme Court decision was handed down, and consequently before anyone had knowledge of what that decision would be. It was this agreement, and not the Supreme Court decision, which prevented the strike.[2] You may recall, as I do, the statement made by the late W. S. Carter,[3] then president of the Brotherhood of Locomotive Firemen and Enginemen. Mr. Carter said, as the agreement was signed by us all: "Gentlemen, this is the dawn of a new day," and those present generally felt that he voiced the conviction of all.

It was the machinery of the labor movement, and not the Supreme Court and Mr. Davis, which prevented the threatened strike.

The Executive Council appreciates your advice regarding the early struggle and career of Mr. Davis. It likewise has weighed in the balance his later utterances and courses, associations and training. We are confident that our judgment and action are well founded.

But quite apart from all this, your request that our Executive Council should adjourn to go to Clarksburg and there reconvene after considering his acceptance address, is utterly impossible and inconceivable. The suggestion could be made with equal propriety that we attend the acceptance ceremonies of President Coolidge so as to prevent being charged with party partisanship.

You know of course the practice of our organization in such matters as this, but a brief word may clarify the situation to you. The American Federation of Labor National Non-Partisan Political Campaign Committee, appointed by authority of the A.F. of L. convention and with the approval of the Executive Council, is charged with the duty of presenting labor's demands to the political conventions. It is then charged with the duty of considering the records of candidates and platforms adopted by the conventions. All of this proceeding has been carried out this year precisely as in every other campaign since 1906. Our committee held many meetings and considered all facts, records and platforms seriously and at length. The document adopted here was the report of that committee—the A.F. of L. National Non-Partisan Political Campaign Committee. Not only the matters to which you draw attention but all available information, were considered and weighed and our judgment then was expressed in the report submitted to and adopted by the Executive Council.

You may not know that John W. Davis, for whom you now speak, wrote me under date of July 17,[4] asking a conference at a time convenient to me at Brighton Beach where I was for a time recuperating from my illness. Mr. Davis asked me to fix a time when it would be convenient to see him, specifying only that I should not fix a time when he was on his vacation in Maine.

I replied by letter on July 22,[5] saying that I would be glad to see Mr. Davis at Brighton Beach, where I was then, in New York City prior to my coming here, or in this city after my arrival here for the Executive Council meeting.

To this letter Mr. Davis telegraphed a reply on July 24,[6] saying that it was impossible to finish the work he then had on hand and return to New York by July 29, the date which I suggested to conform to his wishes, that he was planning to leave Dark Harbor on August 1st and then suggested that I file with him "a statement of questions in which labor is chiefly interested at the moment."

On July 25[7] I replied to that telegram expressing my willingness that an interview take place "at the time designated by you." I further suggested that the several dates and places first proposed by me were still agreeable to me but that "I cannot submit questions to you which would not be equally submitted to other candidates for the presidency."

I have heard nothing further from Mr. Davis.

We have not overlooked your reference to Senator La Follette and we are glad, you may be sure, that you have "no antagonism toward" him. You will not fail to remember that among the many constructive legislative achievements of Senator La Follette the Seaman's Act stands out as a beacon light. It was this great piece of legislation which, in the language of our mutual friend Andrew Furuseth "made the last of the bondmen free." We recall no instance in which Senator La Follette has hesitated to give faithful service in furtherance of legislation supported by our movement.

We are sure that you did not fully comprehend the nature of your request or the impossibility of our compliance. You are aware, of course, that authorized representatives of the American Federation of Labor, including myself as chairman of the American Federation of Labor National Non-Partisan Political Campaign Committee, were in New York City during the entire period of the Democratic convention while the platform was being drafted and while candidates were being nominated and that there were laid before that convention, as well as before the Republican convention, the planks which the Executive Council formulated and which we believed should be incorporated in both platforms. It would have been better if these proposals had been considered when the time was opportune.

Inasmuch as you addressed us as an assistant to the Democratic National Committee and not as a trade unionist, will you kindly inform that committee of these conclusions?

For your full information there is enclosed herewith copy of the full and complete report[8] as made by the American Federation of Labor National Non-Partisan Political Campaign Committee and adopted and approved by the Executive Council on Saturday, August 2nd, 1924.

Very truly yours,

President, American Federation of Labor.[9]

TLc, reel 299, vol. 314, pp. 502–7, SG Letterbooks, DLC.

1. "From William B. Wilson," Aug. 2, 1924, above.
2. See *The Samuel Gompers Papers*, vol. 11, p. 259, n. 13.
3. William Samuel CARTER served as president of the Brotherhood of LOCOMOTIVE Firemen and Enginemen from 1909 to 1922, taking a leave of absence from 1918 to 1920 to direct the Division of Labor of the U.S. Railroad Administration.

4. John Davis to SG, July 17, 1924, Files of the Office of the President, General Correspondence, reel 108, frame 44, *AFL Records.*

5. SG to Davis, July 22, 1924, Files of the Office of the President, General Correspondence, reel 108, frame 43, *AFL Records.*

6. Davis to SG, July 24, 1924, Files of the Office of the President, General Correspondence, reel 108, frame 44, *AFL Records.*

7. SG to Davis, July 25, 1924, Files of the Office of the President, General Correspondence, reel 108, frame 45, *AFL Records.*

8. *Labor's Position in the 1924 Campaign. Report of the Executive Committee of the A.F. of L. National Non-Partisan Political Campaign Committee Which Was Adopted by the Executive Council of the American Federation of Labor at Atlantic City, New Jersey, August 2, 1924* ([Washington, D.C., 1924]).

9. For further correspondence, see SG to Wilson, Aug. 9, 1924, reel 299, vol. 314, pp. 564–67, SG Letterbooks, DLC.

A Memorandum by R. Lee Guard

Ambassador Hotel, Atlantic City, N.J. August 7, 1924.

This morning I went to President Gompers' room to take up with him the matter of a certain telegram to be sent. He asked for Mr. Wright. Mr. Wright came up and Mr. Gompers for five or ten minutes talked very forcefully on the letter from William B. Wilson to Mr. Gompers,[1] and Mr. Gompers' reply,[2] both of which were considered by the Executive Council at its meeting yesterday[3] and were given to the press last night.

After Mr. Wright left the room I protested to Mr. Gompers against the vehemence with which he had spoken and said that I hoped he would try to control himself and so save his nerve force and vitality and give himself greater opportunity for more speedy recovery.

He said he fully realized that he was "burning" himself up and then he told this story:

Paddy was drunk; he went to church; his intention was to put a penny into the collection plate; he had a five dollar gold piece with the penny. By mistake he put in the gold piece. After the church services were over Paddy wanted a drink and he put his hand in his pocket. He found he had only a penny; then he recalled that he by mistake had put the gold piece in for the penny, and he said, "It's for the church; to hell with it."

Mr. Gompers then said, "It is for the cause, the cause which is eating me up, that is burning me up. To hell with it."[4]

TDc, Files of the Office of the President, General Correspondence, reel 108, frame 104, *AFL Records.* Typed notation: "Dictated by Miss Guard."

1. "From William B. Wilson," Aug. 2, 1924, above.

2. "To William B. Wilson," Aug. 6, 1924, above.

3. At the AFL Executive Council meeting of Aug. 5, 1924, Wilson's Aug. 2 letter was read into the record and referred to SG, who was asked to draft a reply for the Council's consideration. At the Council's Aug. 6 meeting, SG submitted his draft reply, which the Council approved after voting to attach a copy of the statement of its position on the 1924 presidential campaign (see "To William B. Wilson," Aug. 6, 1924, n. 8, above).

4. On Aug. 15, 1924, R. Lee Guard notified Frank Morrison that SG's health had deteriorated: "He has been feeling so poorly for the last two days that I have not discussed anything with him and have not taken up any work with him except two or three telegrams and things of that nature which I knew would be no tax upon him, and which I knew would not worry him" (Files of the Office of the President, General Correspondence, reel 108, frame 109, *AFL Records*). On Sept. 10 SG admitted to Daniel Tobin that his doctors were so concerned by his condition that they had asked him to return to New York City for medical attention (reel 300, vol. 315, p. 194, SG Letterbooks, DLC). SG left Atlantic City for New York on Sept. 11.

To the Executive Council of the AFL

Ambassador Hotel Atlantic City N.J. August 28, 1924.

Executive Council American Federation of Labor.

Colleagues:

Since the adjournment of the Atlantic City Executive Council meeting from day to day I have continued to give such attention to the work of my office as the necessity and importance of the subjects seemed to demand. At my suggestion Secretary Morrison has been over for consultation with me and will come again the latter part of this week. In all matters where my advice and counsel seemed vital, I have been consulted; otherwise, both Secretary Morrison and my other associates in the office have been most kind and considerate, faithful and efficient, in their efforts to have the work of the office carried [on] expeditiously and at the same time to spare me every possible burden. I am deeply grateful to them.

I am still under the care of a nurse.[1] My physician in New York arranged for a physician here[2] to keep me under observation from day to day. I am trying to conform to the regime as advised by them, but it is a wearisome, discouraging process. No one except one who has passed through the ordeal can understand what it means to [wan]t to serve as one has served for more than fifty years and yet to find one's self so handicapped by physical weakness.

It causes me the keenest disappointment that my health will not permit my participating in any Labor Day celebration this year, and especially so by reason of the American Federation of Labor National Non-Partisan Campaign. I had so ardently hoped and looked forward to being able to take an active part in the campaign and to making a Labor Day address in whichever locality my presence would be productive of the greatest good. I would be very grateful if each member of the Executive Council would write me a summary of his opinion and judgment based upon his observation and experience of the Labor Day celebration in which he may have participated.

Secretary Morrison has of course kept you informed from time to time of any matters of especial importance.

With kindest regards and best wishes, and hoping to hear from you from time to time, I am

Fraternally yours,   Saml Gompers
President   American Federation of Labor.

TLcS, Executive Council Records, Vote Books, reel 18, frame 330, *AFL Records.*

1. That is, Mathilde May.
2. SG was under the care of Dr. William Wellington Fox of Atlantic City, N.J., who was collaborating on the case with Dr. Otto Hensel, SG's principal physician.

An Account of a Meeting with Robert La Follette

Waldorf-Astoria Hotel, New York City, September 19, 1924.

Arrangements were made for President Gompers to meet Senator LaFollette today at the Waldorf-Astoria. Mr. Woll and Mr. Wright came on from Washington to be with Mr. Gompers. Mr. Gompers also requested Mr. Frayne and Mr. Coughlin of the Central Body to accompany him. Mr. Wright arranged for the newspaper reports and the photographers both still and movie to be present.

The photographers posed the senator and Mr. Gompers together and took a number of views. Then the senator, Mr. Gompers and Mr. Woll went into another room for the conference. When that was over about twenty newspaper men gathered around Mr. Gompers for an interview. It is the first interview he has given personally since his illness except probably about two minutes in Atlantic City during the Executive Council meeting when it had been arranged that he should say a few words to the reports with the understanding that no questions should be asked. Mr. Gompers stated:

With a delegation of labor men I had a conference with Senator

LaFollette and discussed with him several features of the campaign in which we are engaged to bring the largest possible degree of success to the candidacy of Senators LaFollette and Wheeler for the presidency and vice-presidency of the United States. I have tried to be helpful and to give some service to this movement. I have been very ill and my service therefore has necessarily been limited. But I propose to enter into the campaign more actively and with full fervor and enthusiasm.

Question. Are you going to make speeches, Mr. Gompers?

Answer. As soon as I am permitted by my physician, but I have thus far been prohibited. I was asked to speak at the meeting last night (The LaFollette meeting at Madison Square Garden[1] at which Mr. Woll represented the Federation), but I felt of course the time should be the Senator's, and to attempt to speak five minutes is inconsequential and unimportant to any man who is accustomed to speak to great audiences; to speak longer might have given me a setback so that I would not have been able to do much after that. However, I feel that my health has been largely restored, though not completely, and I am going to serve.

The pretense of the candidates for the republican and the democratic parties is nauseating and wholly at variance even with their own party platform declarations. Insincerity, and because people have been aroused, American organized labor [is] deeply touched, and has made its position clear, that these late day utterances of both candidates have been made; that they are not binding upon the party—the platform is binding upon the party.

Look over the history of the political movement of our country and you will find there the platforms of each of the parties as they have come and gone, not any supplementary statements of the candidates running for office. I ask you whether the party is responsible or the candidates? In our opinion, as the parties are now constituted neither of them is responsible to the desires, the will, or the interests of the people.

We have never attempted to do what our critics and opponents say of us; that is, to deliver the labor vote. No man with an ounce of brains believes that we can deliver the vote of any one. Speaking for myself, the only vote I can deliver is my own, and that goes to LaFollette and Wheeler in this campaign, if I live to cast it, and I think I will. I know there are some who pray for us five minutes in the week and prey upon us the balance of the week.

Question, Mr. Gompers, do you see a parallel in the labor party in England with the LaFollette movement here?

Answer. There is no occasion—it comes from a different spirit and a different cause. There is no such cause, there is no such influence in British politics as there is in the politics of the United States in these last few years. There is no parallel.

There are several additional questions and answers which were not taken down. Then Mr. Gompers said:

In years of effort we have finally prevailed upon the representatives of the people of the United States to enact laws to safeguard the rights and interests, and welfare of the people, and in every instance within these past fifteen years, in spite of our success prevailing upon the congress of the United States the president of the United States to pass and to approve these laws, the courts of the country have annulled them and declared them void. No such attempt would dare to be made by any court in Great Britain. When the parliament of England enacts a law, it is the law, and the courts must interpret it in accordance with the hopes as expressed by the parliament.

I am keeping in close touch with our office at Washington and they with me, and my associates in the office such as the vice-presidents and organizers, the secretary of the Federation and my secretary, report to me daily, and I respond and help. The reports which come to us are positive to the effect that the large mass of the people—an overwhelming number of the wage-earners and business men, are enrolling in this movement for the election of LaFollette and Wheeler, for president and vice-president, and everything within honor we will do in furtherance of the success of this campaign.

Question. Mr. Gompers, do you care to make any prediction?

Answer. I am not a prophet, neither am I the son of a prophet.

Several other questions were asked by the reporters at this juncture. In response to the question of what proportion of the people would vote for LaFollette Mr. Gompers stated the vote would be overwhelming—"I mean of the intelligent, active people who understand something of the causes of this campaign.["]

Prompted by a question from Mr. Leary as to how the congressional campaign is going Mr. Gompers said:

It is a strange situation that there is the attempt being made to place the mark upon and belittle the congress of the U.S.—to defy the candidates for president on the republican and democratic tickets and to stigmatize the congress as if its members were great wrong-doers. As a matter of fact, the congress in the past year has been more responsive to the interests of the people of our country than any congress in a decade. In exposing corruption in high office, it seems that the candidates and some other influence are trying to besmirch the character of the members of congress for having exposed rather than condemn the corruptionists. As a matter of fact, of course, there has been defection from both parties, and they have worked to the interests of the masses of the people—to the true interests of the people.

I can say to your question Mr. Leary, that we contributed very considerably to the success of the change in the personnel of the members of both the house and the senate in 1922. We are carrying on the campaign so that the number of progressive men of any party or no party shall be returned to congress.

After ending the press interview, the senator and Mr. Gompers with some of the other gentlemen adjourned to the balcony on the fourth floor of the hotel where the moving picture men took a number of additional pictures as did a number of the still photographers.

Mr. Gompers accompanied by Mr. Roberts and his nurse (who had waited for him in the automobile) then returned to the Shelburne Hotel.

TDc, Files of the Office of the President, Conferences, reel 123, frames 791–95, *AFL Records.* Typed notation: "*Copy.*"

1. Matthew Woll made the opening speech at the La Follette campaign's mass meeting on Sept. 18, 1924, in New York City's Madison Square Garden. Some fourteen thousand people attended the event.

An Article by Samuel Gompers in the *New York Times*

[October 19, 1924]

GOMPERS ON WHY LABOR SUPPORTS LA FOLLETTE

The American Federation of Labor has two major concerns in the present political campaign. It is striving to increase the friendly and constructive membership in Congress and it is striving to bring about the election of Robert M. La Follette as President.

That Senator La Follette is already assured a place on the ballot in every one of the forty-eight States is largely due to the work of organized labor. I offer that statement for the benefit of those who doubt the effectiveness of labor in the political field. The Roosevelt Bull Moose undertaking was unsuccessful in eighteen States in this respect.

We are fighting this campaign on certain definite issues, which so far as we are concerned have mainly to do with the relation of government to industry and with the relation of government toward certain well-defined rights and liberties of the people.

It is a part of the campaign strategy of our opponents to make it appear that those who support Senator La Follette are unreasoning radicals and revolutionists. The revolutionists have their own ticket, headed by William Z. Foster. The Socialists, most of whom no longer know just what they want or where they are going, are to some extent giving Senator La Follette their support. Socialist political leaders believe it is wise to support La Follette, but that support cannot change Senator La Follette's platform nor his views. Neither can it alter ours. Many are, for their own reasons, supporting Mr. Davis and President Coolidge, but the fringe of support for these two candidates does not give to them the color of that fringe. The fact is, the frantic efforts of the opposition to brand Senator La Follette as a "radical" are the result of desperation and inability to find any more logical avenue of attack. Adjectives too often take the place of logic in American politics.

ATTITUDE OF FEDERATION DEFINED.

The American Federation of Labor will not be charged with radicalism, I think, provided the word is used as commonly accepted today. The American Federation of Labor is known for its sound and constructive principles and policies. It proceeds on the basis of facts. It is only for that reason that the American Federation of Labor can be non-partisan in politics.

"May the best man win," is an old slogan among Americans. That is Labor's motto in politics. We mean, "may the best man win" when we set about to help elect the friends of the people and to help defeat their enemies.

To find out who the best men are, we keep records. These records show the past performances of those who are candidates for office. These records also show the platforms of political parties. There is no other sound basis upon which judgment can be formed. Striving always to bring about the election of those most nearly satisfactory, we are at liberty always to support candidates regardless of their political party affiliations and we are at all times free from obligation to any political machine.

The legislative demands of labor are and always have been of such character that their satisfaction in law does not lay upon labor any obligation for further support of a party partisan character. Labor's demands involve measures of simple justice and those who in Congress give their support to such measures are entitled to have their services remembered, but such services do not lay upon labor any obligation to give its support to any party as a party or to any candidate that may be put forward by such a party.

PLATFORMS OLD AND NEW.

When the political parties met this year and drafted platforms they brought into being a new measure by which they were to be judged. The platforms written this year supersede all other platforms and must be accepted as the sole basis of judgment so far as parties are concerned. Platforms are not perpetual. Parties cannot be accepted on the basis of good platforms that have been written in the past if they replace those platforms with platforms that are unsatisfactory. The adoption of an unsatisfactory platform cancels every previous platform and becomes the pronouncement upon which the battle of the day is to be waged and upon which judgment must be formed.

Mr. Davis, for example, can claim none of the virtues of the platforms upon which Woodrow Wilson contested for the Presidency, because Mr. Davis's platform was written in New York this year.

Mr. Coolidge can make no claim to whatever may have been the good points of the platform upon which Theodore Roosevelt contested for the Presidency because Mr. Coolidge's platform was adopted in Cleveland this year.

It has been asserted repeatedly by those opposed to labor in this campaign that we should have taken into account the early career of Mr. Davis, that we should have considered the services rendered by the Democratic Party under President Wilson, and also that we should have considered the record of Calvin Coolidge as Governor of Massachusetts. It may be interesting to know that all of these things were considered but that whatever of constructive value was found in these earlier records was more than canceled—I think we may say repudiated—by subsequent performances and declarations.

Mr. Davis, for example, rendered some service as a member of the House of Representatives. Of course, his friends are trying to create for him the best possible record in this connection, and are not to be blamed for that. Mr. Davis, however, left public office to become a lawyer in private practice. He chose to become counsel for the House of Morgan. He associated himself with the biggest of Big Business and forgot entirely any inclination he might have had at an earlier day in the direction of protecting the rights and interests of the people. In one case, known as the Coronado case, which was a suit against the Miners' Union, Mr. Davis sought to establish through a court decision a condition which, had it been established, would have wrecked every national and international union in the country.

No man can erase such an effort by any protestation that he was merely doing his duty as a lawyer in behalf of his client. Beyond all that, Mr. Davis accepted the nomination for the Presidency on a platform that on its face is both insincere and inadequate. This platform meets none of the major demands of labor, but, on the other hand, in one most important particular, seeks to thrust upon labor a condition against which it has struggled throughout its organized existence. It does not recommend for adoption the Child Labor amendment.

Much the same state of affairs exists in regard to the Republican platform and the Republican candidates. The Republican platform is a repudiation almost in toto of the demands of labor and of the progressive demands of the time generally.

Mr. Coolidge, as President, has performed no act and initiated no measure or policy which could in the least impair the privileges of Big Business, or diminish the fatherly claim of Big Business upon the political organization under Mr. Coolidge's leadership.

This claim is acknowledged by the President not only in his record of activity and in the present platform upon which he is a candidate but in a selection from his book entitled, "The Price of Freedom,"[1] in which he says:

We justify the greater and greater accumulations of capital because we believe that therefrom flows the support of all science, art, learning and the charities which minister to the humanities of life, all carrying their beneficent effects to the people as a whole.

It will be noted Mr. Coolidge speaks of capital and not of industry and that he looks upon capital in great accumulations as something that has the character of a benevolent mastery or overlordship.

Praise for La Follette Platform.

Coming to the candidacy and platform of Senator La Follette, there is an entirely different story. Here we find none of the practices of stepping softly to avoid the displeasure of vested interests. There is in the La Follette platform no more hesitancy in striking out for righteous objectives than there was in Senator La Follette's conduct when, year after year, he faced the wrath of hostile Senators and powerful hostile interests outside the Senate in the great struggle to enact the Seamen's law.

Of the La Follette platform the American Federation of Labor National Non-Partisan Political Campaign Committee has said:[2]

This platform pledges a remedy for the injunction evil.

It pledges the right to organize and collectively to cease work.

It pledges protection of the rights of free speech, free press, and free assemblage.

It pledges abolishment of the Railroad Labor Board.

It pledges a measure to annul the power of the Supreme Court to declare laws permanently unconstitutional.

It declares for direct election of President and Vice President and election of Federal Judges.

It recommends prompt ratification by the States of the Child Labor Constitutional amendment.

It pledges subsequent Federal legislation to protect child life.

The La Follette platform goes beyond these extremely important and specific pledges and offers the only hope of relief from the results of the despotic control of commodities by great corporations and interests in practically all of the major necessaries of life. In a speech delivered by Senator La Follette on Labor Day[3] he pointed out this important fact, saying:

These monopolies, each having acquired economic control by combinations in his own field, were drawn together by common interest. They early saw the vital importance of the control of government.

They built up a perfect political system. The system controls the Government at Washington. It contributes the millions expended in the national campaigns by both political parties.

He reminded the Republicans of the teachings of Lincoln, Sherman, Garfield,[4] and McKinley, and the Democrats of the pledge of Woodrow Wilson in 1912 that he would free the Government from control of private monopoly. Both of these parties, as Senator La Follette pointed out, have been faithless to their trust, and have so far forgotten that trust as practically to acknowledge that they had no intention of making any effort to break the control over Government by great corporate interests or to break their autocratic control over the essential commodities of modern existence.

LABOR AND LA FOLLETTE.

Labor does not contend that political government can of itself bring relief from corporate autocracy. It believes that, to a large degree, control must be broken by the destruction within industry itself of that autocratic power. It does recognize, however, that a certain highly important degree of immediate relief can be had through governmental action and that it is unlikely to be had in any other way. Labor is satisfied that it is the purpose of the La Follette platform and of Senator La Follette himself to bring about that relief and to do so without plunging the Government into a program calculated to lead in the direction of Government bureaucracy and State socialism.

Senator La Follette said in his Labor Day speech that he was "not concerned by charges that the Progressive citizenship of this country is bent on radical and destructive ends, subversive of the Government and the Constitution under which we live." Labor is no more concerned than he by these charges, so frequently made by its reactionary opponents. The same accusation was made when Senator La Follette, supported by the trade-unionists of the country, began his fight for the enactment of direct primary laws. It has always been thus whenever there has been a struggle to wrest privilege and power from those who have sought to use them for their own ends.

Much has been said about "radicalism" in the campaign by those who lack a better and more intelligent argument of the proposal to curb the power of the United States Supreme Court. It is said that this proposal is destructive of the Constitution and is tainted with extreme radicalism. I am unable to see what there is of impropriety or of radicalism in a proposal to bring before the people of the United States for their approval or disapproval an amendment to the Constitution providing for the abrogation of the veto power of the Supreme Court. If the people want such a constitutional amendment they ought to have it, and if they do not want it they will, of course, reject it.

The Constitution itself provides a method whereby it may be amended. The Supreme Court has taken unto itself the power to declare unconstitutional acts passed by Congress. This power does not appear to be in the Constitution, but it is a power that the court exercises and which cannot be taken from the court except by placing in the Constitution a special provision denying such power to the court.

Meaning of the Pledge.

The La Follette platform pledges that such a proposed constitutional amendment shall be placed before the people for their action, and it does not pledge anything else. It has always been my opinion that the people of the United States could, with perfect propriety, and for that matter with perfect safety, vote upon any subject which might appeal to them and that this right and privilege constitute one of the most fundamental expressions of democracy.

When representatives of great political parties tell the people of the United States that it is dangerously radical and a menace to the Constitution for them to vote upon a constitutional amendment, or upon any other subject, then, in my opinion, the real danger to public welfare and public life is to be found in the ranks of the politicians who issue that warning. I think we may well beware of those who warn us against the use of our democratic right to exercise our judgment at the polls on any question, and we may take it for granted that they have some purpose to serve which they fear may not be served if an expression of the will of the people is permitted.

We have already made it clear that the logic of events has left open to us no course except the course we have adopted. Every argument of right and justice and every concept of duty makes it imperative that the wage earners, through their organized movement, throw their weight to the support of Senators La Follette and Wheeler.

There is involved in the campaign no commitment to a new political party, but there is involved a commitment to principles in harmony with the commitment by which labor has always been bound. What applies in the case of the Presidential candidates applies equally, and for similar reasons, in the cases of candidates for the United States Senate, the House of Representatives and for State and local offices.

Senator La Follette and Senator Wheeler are independent candidates for the Presidency and Vice Presidency. Their ticket does not include anything beyond their own candidacies. There are running with them on their tickets no candidates for the House and Senate and no candidates for State offices. They do, however, have the support and friendship of a great many candidates who are running on the Republican and Democratic tickets. Labor judges these candidates today, as in the past, on the basis of their records, and those records have already been sent broadcast through the country.

It is our hope that the next Congress may be even more progressive than the present Congress, and we are exerting every effort to materialize that hope. I hope that I have made clear the reasons for labor's action in this campaign.

New York Times, Oct. 19, 1924. For a typewritten draft of this article, see Files of the Office of the President, Speeches and Writings, reel 119, frames 54–64, *AFL Records*. The draft carries the typed notation: "Written for the New York Times. Sept. 23, 1924."

1. Calvin Coolidge, *The Price of Freedom: Speeches and Addresses* (New York, 1924).

2. The quotation is from *Labor's Position in the 1924 Campaign. Report of the Executive Committee of the A.F. of L. National Non-Partisan Political Campaign Committee Which Was Adopted by the Executive Council of the American Federation of Labor at Atlantic City, New Jersey, August 2, 1924* ([Washington, D.C., 1924]).

3. Robert La Follette delivered the speech by radio from Washington, D.C., on the afternoon of Sept. 1, 1924.

4. James Abram Garfield (1831–81), a Republican, served as president of the United States in 1881. He was shot in July of that year and died in September.

An Excerpt from the Minutes of a Meeting of the Executive Council of the AFL[1]

Saturday, October 25, 1924.

MORNING SESSION.

. . .

Vice-President Rickert explained his motion which was adopted at the Atlantic City meeting in regard to the allowance to be made to President Gompers on account of his illness. The stenographer was absent from the room when the action was taken and there was not a record of same. It was later submitted by Secretary Morrison to Vice-President Rickert for verification as to the correct wording of the motion. Vice-President Rickert explained that what he had had in mind was, that all expenses in connection with President Gompers' illness should be paid, including doctors, nurses, hospital, hotel, etc.

President Gompers explained his financial situation and said with his salary and an amount in his possession as a result of the sale of two lots which had been purchased some years ago, that he had been able to meet all obligations incurred in connection with his illness, that he was not in debt and that so long as this is the case he would not present any bills incurred for doctors, nurses, hospital, etc.

Several members of the Council expressed themselves emphatically that President Gompers should be reimbursed for all of these expenses, citing that he had been taken ill in the line of work. That everything should be done to conserve his health and to preserve to the labor movement the inestimable value of his services.

President Gompers persisted in his declination to accept reimbursement for expenses incurred on account of his illness, and stated that if the motion would be adopted they would have it upon the minutes for all time but he would not even then avail himself of it. He expressed his deep appreciation of the thoughtfulness and kindness of the members of the Executive Council throughout his illness as well as that of the office employes.

In view of President Gompers attitude on the subject and his request that the subject be dropped, no action was taken.

. . .

TDc, Executive Council Records, Minutes, reel 7, frames 1595, 1601, *AFL Records*.

1. The AFL Executive Council met Oct. 20–25, 1924, in Washington, D.C. SG attended all of the Council's sessions.

To Ricardo Treviño[1]

Nov. 5, 1924.

Mr. Ricardo Trevino,
General Secretary, Mexican Federation of Labor,
Mexico City, Mexico.
Dear Sir:

I am deeply appreciative of the invitation you extend to me to attend the Sixth Annual Convention[2] of the Mexican Federation of Labor during the week of November 17, and further to go to Mexico City to witness the ceremonies attending the inauguration of President-Elect Calles.[3]

It is with pleasure that I accept the invitation and have no doubt but that I shall be able to participate in the ceremonies.

With all good wishes and anticipating our meeting, I am,

Sincerely and fraternally yours,   Saml Gompers
President   American Federation of Labor.

TLpS, reel 300, vol. 315, p. 804, SG Letterbooks, DLC.

1. Ricardo Treviño (b. 1895), a native of Coahuila, Mexico, was general secretary in 1924 of the Confederación Regional Obrera Mexicana (Mexican Confederation of Labor). A former I.W.W. organizer in Tampico, he had edited the *Tribuna Roja*, the Tampico newspaper of the Casa del Obrero Mundial (1916), and had served as general secretary of the Casa in Tampico (1917) and general secretary of the Partido Laborista Mexicano (Mexican Labor party; 1923). Treviño was a member of the Mexican Chamber of Deputies from 1926 to 1928.

2. The 1924 convention of the Confederación Regional Obrera Mexicana met in Ciudad Juárez, Mexico, Nov. 17–23.

3. Plutarco Elías Calles was sworn in as president of Mexico on Nov. 30, 1924.

To H. Ben Humphrey

November 6, 1924.

Mr. H. Ben Humphrey,
The Euthalian Literary Society,
Mars Hill College, Mars Hill, N.C.
Dear Sir:

Your letter of November 3 received and contents noted.

You ask for information on the subject "that capital punishment should be abolished in the United States."

In 1895 the convention[1] of the American Federation of Labor declared capital punishment a barbarous and revolting practice and should be abolished.[2]

Personally I have always opposed capital punishment. A recent incident demonstrates most forcefully that if capital punishment was not enforced in Illinois the country would have been saved the horrors of a trial that shocked everyone. If the punishment for murder had been imprisonment for life, Leopold and Loeb would have been sent to the penitentiary without such a sensational trial.[3] I can conceive of no greater punishment than imprisonment for life. Death would be preferable. But the state should not be permitted to commit murder. The old Hebraic doctrine "An eye for an eye, and a tooth for a tooth" should not be followed in this stage of civilization. Whenever I have had an opportunity of expressing my opinion on capital punishment I have opposed it as strenuously as I could. All men who have been hanged have not been guilty. Some of them have been discovered innocent when it was too late. If sent to prison they could have been released when found innocent.

Yours very truly, Saml Gompers
President, American Federation of Labor.

TLpS, reel 300, vol. 315, p. 814, SG Letterbooks, DLC.

1. The 1895 AFL convention met in New York City, Dec. 9–17.

2. For the resolution opposing capital punishment adopted by the 1895 AFL convention, see AFL, *Proceedings*, 1895, p. 38. When delegate William Pomeroy of Chicago objected to the resolution on the grounds that some crimes warranted capital punishment, the *Proceedings* record that SG "denied the right of any man to take life, either legally or otherwise" (ibid.).

3. On May 21, 1924, fourteen-year-old Robert Franks was kidnapped and murdered in Chicago by nineteen-year-old Nathan Leopold, Jr., and his friend, eighteen-year-old Richard Loeb. The two confessed to the murder on May 31, were indicted by a grand jury on June 5, and entered guilty pleas on July 21. Their trial, held solely to determine the penalty to be imposed, took place from July 23 to Aug. 28; the two were represented by Clarence Darrow. On Sept. 10 Leopold and Loeb were sentenced to life in prison.

The Last Will and Testament of Samuel Gompers

[November 8, 1924]

I, *Samuel Gompers,* being of sound mind and memory, do hereby make, publish and declare this my last will and testament, hereby revoking, cancelling, and declaring for naught any prior wills or codicils by me made.

After the payment of my just debts and funeral expenses I give, devise and bequeath to my grand-daughters Henrietta and Ethel Mitchel, and to my sons Samuel J. Gompers,[1] Henry J. Gompers[2] and Alexander J. Gompers,[3] share and share alike of the residue of the estate to which I may die seized and possessed or in anywise entitled to, whether real, personal or mixed, after the minimum amount has been set aside and paid to my wife Gertrude A. Gompers, the minimum amount being that which the law provides, providing said Gertrude A. Gompers is my lawful, wedded wife at the time of my demise, but if said Gertrude A. Gompers shall not be my lawful wedded wife at the time of my demise, she shall not receive any part of my estate whether real, personal or mixed, and the whole amount of my estate whether real, personal or mixed shall be divided between my heirs whose names appear above in this will.

Excepting that there shall be given to the American Federation of Labor, the Cigarmakers' International Union, Cigarmakers' Local Union No. 144, New York City, Dawson Lodge No. 16 A.F. and A.M.,[4] Washington, D.C., Benevolent and Protective Order of Elks Lodge No. 15, Washington, D.C., Benevolent and Protective Order of Elks Lodge No. 1, New York City, the sum of $100.00 each to be devoted by these several organizations to the purchase of an American Flag for each of them, and these specific sums are to be devoted by these organizations to no other purpose.

I hereby make, constitute and appoint my eldest son Samuel J. Gompers executor of this my last will and testament to serve as such without being required to give bond.

Witness my hand and seal this 8th day of November, 1924.

Samuel Gompers. (*Seal*)

Made, published and declared by the said Samuel Gompers as his last will and testament, and signed by him in our presence, who in his presence and at his request, and in the presence of each of us, have hereto set our names as witnesses.

William C. Roberts   1012 12th st. N.W. Washington, D.C

Edward J. Tracy[5]   15 Girard St. NE, Wash, D.C.

TDS, District of Columbia Archives, Washington, D.C.

1. Samuel Julian GOMPERS.
2. Henry Julian GOMPERS.
3. Alexander Julian GOMPERS.
4. That is, Ancient Free and Accepted Masons.
5. Edward James Tracy (1893–1953), the son of SG's longtime associate Thomas F. Tracy, was employed as a clerk in the AFL office from 1911 to 1934. He was a member of AFL Stenographers', Typewriters', Bookkeepers', and Assistants' Union 11,773 of Washington, D.C.

Remarks by Samuel Gompers at a
Conference with Newspaper Reporters

Chicago, Illinois, November 10, 1924

We are on our way to attend the convention of the American Federa
tion of Labor and its departments at El Paso, Texas.[1] The convention
of the Federation opens a week from today. The Metal Trades Depart
ment, the Union Label Trades Department, The Building Trades De
partment and the Railway Employes Department have arranged the
dates of their conventions[2] so as to not overlap or prevent them from
being held as the hall facilities are not as good as in larger metropoli
tan centers. The American Federation of Labor convention lasts from
ten to fourteen days usually.

I do not want to anticipate what problems are likely to come before
our annual convention. Questions affecting the interests, the rights
and the wrongs of the wage earners and the people generally will re
quire the attention of the convention.

I have not much to say about the result of the election other than
I am not so disappointed as some people would try to put me in the
position of being. There never has been in the history of American
politics a movement begun and carried on for six months without any
organized effort in the beginning of the party that has made so splen
did a showing as was made in this campaign. It is not only recognized
but acknowledged by those who are leaders of the Republican Party
that it is reactionary or what they might call a conservative party, con
cerned with material things, business, property, wealth and to protect
its interests. About a year ago I had a conference with representatives
of the Democratic Party in my office.[3] I directed their attention to the
fact that the Republican Party was, as I have tried to indicate to you,
and said something in regard to the Democratic Party. I emphasized
the fact that two political parties, with the same general trend, differing
only in comparatively minor questions was an anomaly and that in the
frame of mind in which I believed the people were the necessity exists
for the Democratic Party to so change its course and policy that it shall
be a party representing the interests and welfare and progress of the
great masses of the people, a humanitarian liberty-loving, progressive
and constructive party, if they expected to have the confidence and
support of the people. In my judgment if they did not do that, the
Democratic Party had reached the point for its extinction and not only
this but I feel that it would be the duty of forward looking men and
women of America to defeat the party because it is no longer a party

contending upon high principles in the interests and welfare of the people and that so far as I was concerned I should help in seeing that the Democratic Party was so regenerated as to occupy that position in our American political life.

There are a number of people who mistakenly charge me with being a Democrat. I never was a member of the Democratic Party. I was at one time, in my early years, a member of the Republican Party, and cast my first vote for a Republican President—U. S. Grant as soon as I attained my majority. I never did belong to the Democratic Party. In the pursuit of the Nonpartisan policy of labor in which I thoroughly believe, I supported Republican or Democrat or publicist as in the varying parties I believed that they would best serve the people without regard to party. In the last twelve years and up to 1924 the Democratic Party, a large number of them represented these principles in advocacy of the peoples rights—that there were a larger number of them in Congress than Republicans—it was not because of partisanship that we supported a larger number of Democrats than Republicans but because, as I say, there was a larger number of Democrats favorably inclined toward the pressing interests and rights of the masses of the people. When therefore the Republicans, true to form, in their convention in Cleveland flouted the support of labor, made short shrift of the committee of the American Federation of Labor which appeared before the Committee on Resolutions, and adopted a platform running true to form as in the past thirty years; I was quite ill and unable to go to Cleveland and I was not recovered fully but I went with the committee of the American Federation of Labor to the Democratic convention and went before the committee on Platform and while we were heard respectfully and apparently with interest, the platform adopted by that convention was threadbare, impotent, and failed to grasp the industrial, political, sociological situation with any material difference from the Republican platform.

So we had no alternative but to enter a protest, a protest vote. Although the vote did not reach the hopes of many of us I am not disappointed with the result. I never build my castles so high nor my foundations so weak as to be greatly disappointed. I realize the power of the vested interests and that they are not easily dislodged. They have the power of the press, the telegraph, the wireless, the radio, the newspaper as a rule and to have made the showing to make that protest as emphatic as it has been made, which must be reckoned with, no one can laugh at that. Those who laugh will probably have cause for regret.

That the pendulum in Great Britain has swung the other way there is no question, insofar as seats in the House of Commons are concerned but in the popular vote there was an increase by several millions over the last election when they secured the so-called labor government by the grace of the Liberal Party.

Answering your question if I think there is a widespread movement of reaction over the world, I think the reaction is here and the evidence of the protest is here. What the future may hold is not a question I wish to discuss now except that it may be longer delayed than is generally hoped but the future is ours, politically and industrially.

TDc, Files of the Office of the President, Speeches and Writings, reel 119, frames 92–93, *AFL Records*. Typed notation: "Statement by Samuel Gompers, President, American Federation of Labor, Chicago, Illinois, November 10, 1924."

1. On Nov. 9, 1924, SG left Washington, D.C., for El Paso, Tex., where he arrived Nov. 12. He attended the AFL convention held there Nov. 17–25 and on Nov. 18 addressed a convention of the Confederación Regional Obrera Mexicana in Ciudad Juárez. On Nov. 27 SG left El Paso for Mexico City.

2. The 1924 AFL Metal Trades Department convention met in El Paso, Tex., Nov. 12–14, the AFL Union Label Trades Department convention met there Nov. 13–14, and the AFL Building Trades Department convention met there Nov. 10–13. The AFL Railway Employes' Department held no convention in 1924.

3. See "An Excerpt from the Minutes of a Meeting between Representatives of the AFL and Officers of the Democratic National Committee," Jan. 6, 1923, above.

Excerpts from Accounts of the 1924 Convention of the AFL in El Paso, Texas

El Paso, Texas, Nov. 17, 1924.

FIRST DAY—MONDAY MORNING SESSION

. . .

Vice-President Green[1] read the following statement prepared by President Gompers:

Forty-four years ago in the city of Pittsburgh a group of labor men met to bring to fruition an effort extending over a period of years—to organize a national labor movement.[2] We were a group of labor men with little experience in a national labor movement. We had to find our problems and devise ways of meeting them. There was little to guide us. The majority of us had a standing in our local trade unions and in our national trade organizations, but we had not joined hands with the representatives of other trade organizations in an effort to make the labor movement a force in the determination of national policies.

The National Labor Union, like previous similar labor efforts, had organized a labor party and then passed out of existence. Industrialism growing out of constantly increasing invention of machinery, application of mechanical power which necessitated the factory system and the substitution of new materials for old, was making the need of economic protection for the workers increasingly imperative. Those of us who had opportunity to observe tendencies felt the responsibility to our fellow workers to make the effort for protection and for future progress.

There were but few paid trade union officials in those days, but after the day's work was done, those with the vision and spirit of service gave the evening hours and holidays to the cause of betterment of their fellow workers. More frequently than not the office of trade union official was carried in his pocket and its code of laws in his heart and mind; benefits, even strike assistance, were irregular and undependable if provided at all; union dues and union rules varied from city to city, if not from shop to shop. The present trade union movement was then in the making—aye, had hardly begun.

But the men who constituted that Pittsburgh labor congress in 1881 were as brainy and resourceful a group as ever gathered; they were men who knew the joy and inspiration of service that entailed sacrifice. Service in the early trade union movement meant to become a marked man whom employers were reluctant to hire and who was discharged first; whose family must forego the comforts and often the necessaries of life; upon whose children the handicap attaching to the name of a "labor agitator" fell.

These very conditions of service in the labor movement assured the cause selected men of unusual qualities. They were men of self respect and character.

When the Pittsburgh labor congress set itself to the task of planning an organization, it studied the British Trades Union Congress, drafted a similar plan and organized the Federation of Trades and Labor Unions of the United States and Canada. In our optimism we thought that we had settled our economic problems and that we needed only to consider the field of labor legislation. We elected as our executive, a legislative committee, but provided no salaries, no permanent office, no full-time representatives. From year to year we met, accomplishing a little but keeping alive the thought of national organization and calling attention to the needs of the workers, until there came a crucial contest in which the existence of trade unions was threatened. Then the trade unions sent out the warning of danger and sent a small group to carry by word of mouth a message to rouse labor. Again in 1886 a national labor conference was called.[3] This time it was designated a trade union conference to be composed of representatives of trade unions and to consider trade union problems. The deliberations of that conference resulted in the formation of our present American Federation of Labor with which the old Federation of Trades and Labor Unions was merged. This new federation recognized only the trade union card as a credential and proposed to deal primarily with economic problems. It was an organization that had no power and no authority except of a voluntary character. It was a voluntary coming together of unions with common needs and common aims. That feeling of mutuality has been a stronger bond of union than could be welded by any autocratic authority. Guided by voluntary principles our Federation has grown from a weakling into the strongest, best organized labor movement of all the world.

So long as we have held fast to voluntary principles and have been actuated and inspired by the spirit of service, we have sustained our forward progress and we have made our labor movement something to be respected and accorded a place in the councils of our Republic. Where we have blundered into trying to force a policy or a decision, even though wise and right, we have impeded, if not interrupted, the realization of our own aims.

But the very success of our organization has brought additional and serious dangers. Office in the labor movement now offers opportunity for something in addition to service—it offers opportunity for the self-seeker who sees an instrumentality for personal advancement both in the economic and in the political field. There are serious problems confronting us. Wisdom and conviction are necessary to wise decisions.

Men and women of our American trade union movement, I feel that I have earned the right to talk plainly with you. As the only delegate to that first Pittsburgh convention who has stayed with the problems of our movement through to the present hour, as one who with clean hands and with singleness of purpose has tried to serve the labor movement honorably and in a spirit of consecration to the cause of humanity, I want to urge devotion to the fundamentals of human liberty—the principles of voluntarism. No lasting gain has ever come from compulsion. If we seek to force, we but tear apart that which, united, is invincible. There is no way whereby our labor movement may be assured sustained progress in determining its policies and its plans other than sincere democratic deliberation until a unanimous decision is reached. This may seem a cumbrous, slow method to the impatient, but the impatient are more concerned for immediate triumph than for the education of constructive development.

Our movement has found these voluntary principles the secure foundation upon which the workers of all America make united effort, or our voluntary co-operation has ignored lines of political division separating the United States and Canada, because economically we are a unit. Because we refused to be bound by arbitrary restrictions or expedients we have fostered cohesive forces which give play to the finer and more constructive faculties of the peoples of both countries. We are eager to join in an international labor movement based upon the same principles of voluntarism. We are willing to co-operate if we can be assured a basis that will enable us to maintain our integrity—a condition necessary for our own virility and continued progress.

Understanding, patience, high-minded service, the compelling power of voluntarism have in America made what was but a rope of sand, a united, purposeful, integrated organization, potent for human welfare, material and spiritual. I have been with this movement since the beginning, for I have been given the privilege of service that has been accorded but few. Nor would that privilege have continued open to me had not service to the cause been my guiding purpose.

Events of recent months made me keenly aware that the time is not far distant when I must lay down my trust for others to carry forward. When one comes to close grips with the eternal things, there comes a new sense of relative values and the less worthy things lose significance. As I review the events of my sixty years of contact with the labor movement and as I survey the problems of today and study the opportunities of the future, I want to say to you, men and women of the American labor movement, do not reject the cornerstone upon which labor's structure has been builded—but base your all upon voluntary principles and illumine your every problem by consecrated devotion to that highest of all purposes—human well being in the fullest, widest, deepest sense.

We have tried and proved these principles in economic, political, social and international relations. They have been tried and not found wanting. Where we have tried other ways, we have failed.

A very striking illustration is emphasized by circumstances connected with the present location of our convention. For years force and selfish interests dominated relations across this international border, but the labor movement brought to an acute and difficult situation the spirit of patience and the desire of service and a transformation has been brought which gives us courage and conviction for wider application of the same principles. As we move upward to higher levels, a wider vision of service and responsibility will unfold itself. Let us keep the faith. There is no other way.[4]

. . .

AFL, *Proceedings*, 1924, pp. 1, 4–6.

1. AFL vice-president William Green was a delegate of the United Mine Workers of America.

2. See *The Samuel Gompers Papers*, vol. 1, pp. 210–32.

3. See *ibid.*, pp. 453–71.

4. SG's statement was subsequently published as "The Voluntary Nature of the Labor Movement: A Trade Union Creed," in *In Memoriam. Samuel Gompers . . . President and Builder of the American Federation of Labor* ([Washington, D.C., 1924]).

El Paso, Texas, Nov. 17. [1924]

FIVE NATIONS JOIN IN LABOR COUNCIL

Representatives of 14,000,000 wage earners of the United States, Mexico, Canada, England and Germany gripped hands today at the conclusion of the first joint session of the American Federation of Labor and the Mexican Confederation of Labor, and, amid the cheers of American delegates and the repeated "vivas" of Mexicans, pledged the forces of organized labor to preserve the peace of the world.

One thousand delegates of the Mexican Confederation of Labor, in sixth annual convention at Juarez, across the Rio Grande, marched over the International Bridge late this afternoon and joined forces at Liberty Hall with the 400 delegates to the forty-fourth annual convention of the American Federation of Labor.

Addresses were made by Samuel Gompers, President of the American Federation; Ricardo Trevino, General Secretary of the Mexican Confederation; Juan Rico, President of the American Confederation;[1] and Joseph Kelly of the International Association of Machinists.

John Sullivan,[2] President of the Central Trades and Labor Councils of New York, and a committee welcomed the Mexican delegates halfway across the International Bridge. There was a short delay because of the presence of one Chinese and a Mexican without credentials among the Mexican delegates, but after this was straightened out the Mexicans, with a uniformed band at their head, marched to the hall half a mile away.

Mexicans Cheered in Hall.

Entrance of the Mexicans brought the American delegates to their feet. Trevino and Rico were escorted to the platform, where they embraced Mr. Gompers. Trevino gripped a standard with the Mexican flag. As column after column of the Mexican delegates swept into the hall the American delegates cheered and applauded.

The agrarian delegates, sent to the convention direct from the farm, were clad in white cotton suits, broad straw sombreros, sandals and pink and orange scarfs. The industrial delegates, from machine shops and railroads, wore overalls, and the representatives of the clerical and intellectual workers were attired in the conventional business suits and white collars.

Orange and white blouses mingled with white costumes and the black shawls of the Mexican women to make a colorful spectacle.

Mr. Gompers, whose remarks were translated by C. N. Idar, was applauded enthusiastically by the Mexican contingent when he said that ten years ago no such gathering of the working men of the two countries could have taken place. He declared that the bullet "which found lodgment in the body of that great Mexican leader, Luis N. Morones,[3] was a blow aimed at the democratic Republic of Mexico."

Welcomed by Gompers.

"I bid you thrice welcome to the American Federation of Labor," said Mr. Gompers, who spoke of the time when "adventurers and profit-mongers took advantage of the situation in Mexico to stir up ill feeling on both sides of the line," and predicted that the good will existing in the organized labor movements on both sides of the line would always result in peace between the two nations. He praised the work of President Obregon, President-elect Calles, Morones, Trevino and Rico.

For the Mexican delegates Mr. Rico spoke with regret of the "tragic accident" which had resulted in the attack on Morones. He said organized labor in Mexico was proud of its strength, and added that its strength was due to the cooperation and advice of Mr. Gompers.

Mr. Trevino, whose speech, as well as that of Mr. Rico, was translated by C. N. Vargas of the Pan-American Federation of Labor, declared that the struggles of the American and Mexican labor movements both were directed "against a group of capitalists who reside in the United States and who are now the strongest financial force in the world." The struggle against those forces, he said, was not a struggle of Mexico or of the United States, but of the working people of the world.

"Even if this group of men is again attempting to arm traitors, as it armed those who attacked Morones, even if Morones should fall by the wayside, behind him will be all the members of organized labor who will take up the fight," he declared.

Mr. Trevino warned all enemies of the labor movement in Mexico "that the men in the labor ranks would be happy to lose their lives in the struggle for liberty." Only one thing could make the Mexican labor movement fearful of its future, he said, and that would be if it were to lose the friendship of the American labor movement.

Grasps Hands for Peace.

After a short address by Mr. Kelly, President Gompers called on the Mexican leaders and on the fraternal delegates from England, Germany and Canada to grasp hands as a demonstration that the labor organizations of the five countries were determined to maintain the peace of the world.

The spectacle of Mr. Gompers, Mr. Trevino, Mr. Rico, A. B. Swales,[4] President of the British Trades Union Congress; John Colbert[5] of the same congress, C. T. Cramp[6] of the Canadian Trades and Labor Congress, and Peter Grassman,[7] Vice President of the German Federation of Trades Unions, standing on the platform with firmly gripped hands evoked an enthusiastic demonstration. Tears were rolling down the cheeks of Mr. Gompers when he announced the adjournment.

Tomorrow the American delegation will visit Juarez, and a joint session of both organizations will be held there.

. . .

New York Times, Nov. 18, 1924.

1. Juan Rico (b. 1889), a native of Mexico City, was actually president in 1924 of the Confederación Regional Obrera Mexicana (Mexican Confederation of Labor). A linotype operator by trade, he also served as general secretary of the Unión de Linotipistas (1924) and was editor of its newspaper, *La Lucha* (1921–25).

2. John SULLIVAN served as president of the Central Trades and Labor Council of Greater New York and Vicinity from 1920 to 1927.

3. Luis N. MORONES Negrete, a founder of the Confederación Regional Obrera Mexicana and the Partido Laborista Mexicano (the Mexican Labor party), served from 1924 to 1928 as minister of the department of industry and commerce in the Mexican government. On Nov. 12, 1924, a gunfight broke out at a meeting of the Chamber of Deputies in Mexico City during which, according to press accounts, more than two hundred shots were fired. Morones, whose dispute with agrarian leader José Maria Sanchez led to the incident, was wounded in the fracas.

4. Alonzo Beaumont SWALES, a member of the executive council of the Amalgamated Engineering Union (1920–35) and the Parliamentary Committee (from 1921, the General Council) of the TUC (1919–35), was a fraternal delegate to the 1924 AFL convention from the TUC.

5. John Colbert, a member of Amalgamated Association of Street and Electric Railway Employes of America 741 of London, Ont., was the fraternal delegate to the 1924 AFL convention from the Trades and Labor Congress of Canada.

6. Concemore Thomas Thwaites CRAMP, industrial secretary of the National Union of Railwaymen from 1920 to 1931, was a fraternal delegate to the 1924 AFL convention from the TUC.

7. Peter Ottmar GRASSMANN, vice-chairman of the Allgemeiner Deutscher Gewerkschaftsbund (General German Federation of Trade Unions) from 1919 to 1933, was the fraternal delegate from that body to the 1924 AFL convention.

El Paso, Texas, Nov. 24, 1924.

SEVENTH DAY—MONDAY MORNING SESSION

. . .

Delegate Sigman, Ladies' Garment Workers: I rise to ask the privilege of the floor of this convention to address it on a special matter. I ask you to bear with me just a few minutes and give me the opportunity to share with you some of the joy and happiness of my organization, the International Ladies' Garment Workers' Union. My organization, which is a part of the great American labor movement, is celebrating its twenty-fifth anniversary. I am sure that a great many of the delegates here know something about the organization I represent, but it seems to me there is much more connected with the efforts of the Ladies' Garment Workers that the delegates here may not be acquainted with.

Many of the delegates coming from New York, Cleveland or Chicago still remember the record of the ladies' garment industry of about twenty-five or thirty years ago, when it was recognized as the sweatshop industry. The ladies' garment industry was always one of the most prosperous industries, but not for those who were working to produce these fine, artistic garments for the women of our country. It has been a good and prosperous industry for the employers engaged in it. The workers in the industry had been working unlimited hours for the smallest wages one might imagine, and under circumstances which had caused them to contract occupational diseases in large proportions, compared to other industries.

About forty or more years ago, individuals engaged in our industry undertook the pioneering work of organizing these men and women, but the task was very difficult—difficult because of the fact that in this industry of ours we had to educate the workers in many languages. We had the Jewish worker, we had the Italian worker, with his temperamental attitude, we had some Polish workers, and we had some who came from Ireland; they occupied the more aristocratic positions in the industry; they were the cutters and the graders.

The work was undertaken, as I said before, by a few pioneers, and from time to time spontaneous outbreaks and spasmodic strikes were called in the various existing markets, but with no result as far as establishing a permanent organization in the industry was concerned.

Twenty-five years ago some of the pioneers in this industry decided to ask the American Federation of Labor to issue them a charter for an international union. This was granted, and efforts were again made, with the aid and assistance of the organized labor movement of the country, to organize the workers. The struggle was hard, the task was difficult. Some organization developed, but not strong enough to demonstrate any influence in the trades. As late as 1905 or 1906, I am told, after the very many efforts, the then officials of my international union were obliged to appeal to the President of the American Federation of Labor and the Executive Council, and asked assistance because they had lost faith in the possibility of ever organizing the ladies' garment workers.

It was then that the American Federation of Labor, through its officers, undertook to not only supply the necessary courage and imbue our officials with the desired spirit to continue in their organizing efforts, but also to supply the financial needs to pay rentals and other expenses.[1] With that aid, financial, moral and spiritual the work was undertaken again, and when we reached the year 1908, we had again reached the stage where most of our leaders and some who had taken a very prominent part in the life of this struggling international felt that the time had come again when we had to give it up.

Again, I remember, Brother Abe Rosenberg[2] and John Dyche,[3] president and secretary of the International Union, immediately communicated with President Gompers,[4] and when they returned from Washington we saw the two high officials of our International Union in a new mood, a new spirit, with a new desire to again take up the task of building up an organization within our ranks.

I am relating this to you delegates because to me it is of great significance. I recall that after a session of our Executive Board we decided to start a movement for a general strike in the cloak and suit industry in the city of New York. After reaching a decision—not having the necessary confidence in ourselves—we communicated with a good many who had been active in former years in our International Union, and when we presented to them the thought that we wanted to call upon the fifty or sixty thousand cloak makers in the city of New York to cease work and once more make a fight for humane conditions in the industry, some of them went so far as to tell us that if we dared take such a position they, on their own initiative, would go out and advise the cloak workers of New York not to respond to a general strike call, because in their judgment they felt we were going to bring more sacrifices and more misery upon these already exploited workers.

Again our Executive Board instructed its officers to communicate with the chief of the American labor movement, and again they were advised never to give up, but to keep on fighting, that the day must come when the oppressed workers in the ladies' garment industry would arise against these miserable sweatshop conditions under which they had been working.

In 1910 a great event took place. The cloak makers were called to a mass meeting in Madison Square Garden. To that meeting President Gompers was invited as the chief speaker. It was a wonderful scene when he saw the cloak makers, faces pale from overwork, with their coats off and their sleeves rolled up, soiled of the cloths they had handled, while producing clothing for the women of our country.[5]

When the time came President Gompers had his say. I, as an ordinary worker, active in the campaign, felt that the inspiration given to the workers by the address delivered by President Gompers, was sufficient to cause the ladies' garment workers to again take up the battle. Most of you probably know that our international union with about two or three thousand members conducted a strike of 60,000 men and women for twelve long weeks,[6] with the result that we obtained many improvements for the workers in the industry, and a ray of hope and sunshine at last started to come into the ranks of the garment workers.

During that strike we accomplished a protocol of peace[7] which was discussed throughout the world of labor, as well as the community in general, and from that day we began working under American standards, living under American standards and thinking in an American way. From that day our organization has continued to make progress.

You have probably learned of our effort to renew our recent unexpired agreements in the city of New York, and now, too, we have accomplished something new in our industry. A commission selected by Governor Al Smith for the purpose of bringing peace and harmony in our industry in the great city of New York has established an unemployment insurance system to which the employers are contributing two per cent of their total payroll and the workers are contributing one per cent of their earned pay. This will bring in about $1,600,000 per year, to be divided among such cloak workers as may be unemployed.

Another recent accomplishment is the adoption of a sanitary label that each garment manufactured under the present contract in the City of New York must bear. That label signifies that the garment bearing it has been produced in a sanitary shop and under union conditions. That label represents three different parties—the union, on the one hand, the employers on the other, and the public. The public is represented by Dr. Schefelin,[8] Dr. Henry Moskowitz[9] and Lillian De-Wald.[10] Under the supervision of these three factors, the public, the employers and the union, this label of sanitary union conditions must be on every garment, and it has been made obligatory on the part of the employers' associations as well as on the part of individuals.

You will therefore realize, delegates, when you consider that we are comparatively youngsters in the movement, that we certainly feel proud of the fact that the garment workers have succeeded in establishing such a wonderful organization as we have. We felt that we would not have completed the performance of our duties as men and women of organized labor if we did not come before this convention and express our joy, and at the same time express our thanks to all those who have been helpful in building up our organization in the face of these conditions, and particularly have we felt it our duty to express our appreciation to the Grand Old Chief of the American labor movement, Brother Samuel Gompers, because it was due very much to the courage with which he imbued our leaders that we have been able to build up this wonderful organization of ours.

(At this point in Delegate Sigman's address, two of his co-delegates, Louis E. Langer[11] and Louis Pinkofsky,[12] unveiled a beautiful bust of President Gompers, done in Italian marble.[13] The delegates and visitors arose and applauded for several minutes.)

Delegate Sigman: We could not find a better way of expressing our deep and sincere appreciation to President Gompers than by presenting what you delegates see here before you this moment. We want President Gompers to see himself in the way we see him. This bust represents, in the judgment of the members of the International Ladies' Garment Workers' Union, one of the greatest men that the labor movement has ever known, and it is because of this feeling that we have toward President Gompers that we came to the conclusion to avail ourselves of the genius of a young, but recognized artist—recognized as the best artist in the sculptural world—Moses Dykaar,[14] to build up this bust of President Gompers, with his fighting features in his face, but with a broad human heart of sympathy and love for all those who suffer in the labor world and in the community in general.

President Gompers, with this gift here my organization extends to you the wish, from the depths of its heart, for further work, for further activities for many years to come for this great cause of organized labor in the United States and the world over.

President Gompers: It is difficult for me to express that which wells up in my soul. How can words convey what you know one must feel under such circumstances as this? Earlier in the convention a great tribute was paid me.[15] I was then unable to say anything with respect to it. I am not in a much better condition to express myself now.

Brother Sigman came to me this morning with Brother Langer, one of his associates, and said that he would like to say something to the convention, the nature of which he did not care to disclose to me, but wanted to have that privilege because he had no proposition to make; he simply wanted to say something in regard to his international union which would interest the delegates and the labor movement generally.

This American Federation of Labor of ours is, I believe, the freest forum of any legislative or organized body of which I have any knowledge; recognizing the intense desire of the convention to proceed with our business, I hesitated for a moment, but said that at some appropriate time during the afternoon I would recognize Brother Sigman for the purpose he indicated.

You have heard what he has said. Somehow or other opportunities have been given to me which have been given to few men of my time.

Whatever I am, whatever I have tried to do, I owe to you, my fellow trade unionists, I owe to the great rank and file of our movement, the men and women who are yearning for a better life and who, many of them, did not know how to accomplish it. They believed in one thing in so far as I was concerned—if I could not help them, by all that is holy I would not hurt them. There is nothing in life that I value so much as to be of some service to my fellows. Station in life, in public affairs, or private advantage had no allurements. Nothing in the whole world so glorifies the soul as service to our fellows.

These men and women to whom Brother Sigman referred and whom he so ably and faithfully represents, were struggling and yearning and striving—demoralized, impoverished, and scarcely even hoping. They knew me and believed in me and trusted me. I gave whatever help I could, and upon occasions when they were in a quandary as to what to do they came to me and asked my counsel, and I gave it, I gave my support to the full extent of whatever ability I possessed.

I remember that tremendous mass gathering in Madison Square Garden, and no one can understand their situation unless they had seen the gaunt figures and pinched faces and sunken eyes of the tattered men and women in that assemblage. Thousands were unable to gain admission to that great hall. And it was really left for me to give the battle cry or to advise the men and women to go back into their bondage.

The utterance that I then gave that night was in a sentence: "This is not to be a general strike, it is to be an industrial revolution, and it is better to die in a struggle for freedom than to end a mass gathering in slavery."

I didn't know at the time, but it was evident that at least one time in my life my audience was electrified and transformed into action, with the result that has been only too indefinitely described by Brother Sigman.

The incident which has just transpired is momentous and some lesson to us. It is quite true that our American labor movement has not ventured upon some courses which appeal to the uninitiated and uninformed and inexperienced. I would rather that the American labor movement put a dollar in the pay envelope at the end of the week and cut down an hour a day of the burdensome toil than to cast votes once in every four years. I don't underestimate the value or the importance of that duty and that function, but, after all, the great aim of labor is progress economically, more than politically.

There are some people who imagine that poverty and misery will drive men to revolution and the attainment of right. Hungry stomachs may create a riot, but never a successful revolution. People become accustomed to hunger and misery. The path of liberty is always enlivening and a spur to still greater progress.

I do wish that the students of the labor movement—and I mean you and me, also—would undertake to know and learn what the Ladies' Garment Workers' International Union has done. It is a revelation to those who have not yet known. When the Ladies' Garment Workers' International Union completed their new home they informed me, through their officers, that they had a few niches in their great assembly hall in which they desired to place pictures or busts of some of the men who had given service in the labor movement, and asked me whether I would not pose for a great sculptural artist for a bust of myself to occupy one of those niches. I consented. I never dreamed—my credulity was imposed upon—I never thought that the bust, when completed, was really intended as presented by Brother Sigman.

I don't know what to say in expression of my appreciation. No word can convey to you what I feel in regard to the presentation of this bust or to the fellowship which you have instituted. What can I say other than that I am profoundly grateful? I would like you to understand what I would like to say. Let me sum it up, then, just in this: I know of no other or no better way to show my appreciation and gratitude than by giving you and the cause of Labor and all of that for which our movement stands the best service that I can without sparing myself, no matter what the cost or the result.

I want to live for one thing alone—to leave a better labor movement in America and in the world than I found in it when I entered, as a boy, the field of industrial and humane struggle for right.

. . .

AFL, *Proceedings,* 1924, pp. 251, 277–81.

1. According to SG, the AFL spent $782.90 between 1904 and 1906 to assist the International Ladies' Garment Workers' Union in its organizing efforts. See *The Samuel Gompers Papers,* vol. 7, p. 165.

2. Abraham Rosenberg served as vice-president (1907–8) and then president (1908–14) of the Ladies' Garment Workers.

3. John Alexander Dyche served as secretary-treasurer of the Ladies' Garment Workers from 1904 to 1914.

4. SG met with Dyche on July 28, 1908, and agreed to Dyche's proposal to have Rosenberg appointed as an AFL salaried organizer for a period of five weeks.

5. See *The Samuel Gompers Papers,* vol. 8, p. 109 and p. 114, n. 7.

6. See *The Samuel Gompers Papers,* vol. 8, p. 114, n. 3.

7. Ibid.

8. William Jay Schieffelin (1866–1955), chairman of the board of Schieffelin and Co., a wholesale drug firm, was a member of the Joint Board of Sanitary Control, created in 1910 under the Protocol of Peace between the Ladies' Garment Workers and the New York City garment manufacturers to fix sanitary standards in the garment industry. He had served on the board since its founding.

9. Henry Moskowitz (1878–1936), a civic leader and reformer, was a member of the Joint Board of Sanitary Control from its founding in 1910. He was a founder of the Down Town Ethical Society, later renamed the Madison House, a settlement house on New York's Lower East Side.

10. Lillian D. Wald (1867–1940), a nurse and social worker, was a member of the Joint Board of Sanitary Control from its founding in 1910. She was a founder in New York City of the Visiting Nurse Service (1893) and the Nurses' Settlement (1895), which was renamed the Henry Street Settlement in 1903. Also a founder of the National Child Labor Committee (1904) and the National Organization for Public Health Nursing (1912), which she served as president, her work led to creation by Congress of the U.S. Children's Bureau (1912).

11. Louis Elias Langer (born Elias Langer; 1885–1957), an Austrian immigrant and member of Ladies' Garment Workers' local 35 (Cloak Pressers) of New York City, served as secretary of the New York Joint Board of Cloak Makers' Unions (renamed the New York Joint Board of Cloak, Skirt, Dress, and Reefer Makers' Unions around 1923) from 1916 to 1925.

12. Louis Pinkofsky (variously Pinkowsky or Pinkovsky; b. 1888), a Russian immigrant, was the manager of Ladies' Garment Workers' local 23 (Skirt and Cloth Dress Makers) of New York City. He served as chairman of the New York Joint Board of Cloak Makers' Unions from 1921 to 1924.

13. SG posed for the bust during the summer of 1923. For a photograph of the bust, see *American Federationist* 32 (Jan. 1925): 44.

14. Moses Wainer (variously Weiner) Dykaar (1885?-1933), a Lithuanian-born sculptor, emigrated to the United States in 1916. He executed busts of a number of notable Americans in addition to SG, including Alexander Graham Bell, Calvin Coolidge, Warren Harding, Charles Evans Hughes, and John Pershing.

15. On the afternoon of Nov. 22, 1924, the convention had voted unanimously to establish an annual scholarship, to be called the Samuel Gompers Fellowship, to celebrate the ties of amity between the Confederación Regional Obrera Mexicana (Mexican Confederation of Labor) and the AFL.

R. Lee Guard to John Macrae

Hotel Paso del Norte, El Paso, Tex., Nov. 26, 1924.

Mr. John Macrae,
President, E. P. Dutton and Company,
681 Fifth Avenue, New York, N.Y.
Dear Mr. Macrae:—

Your several telegrams[1] and your letter[2] have been duly received. I am sure the telegram[3] which Mr. Woll sent you yesterday advising you of the action of the convention as regards President Gompers' Memoirs[4] must have been exceedingly gratifying to you as it was to us.

I have heard nothing but words of the highest commendation of the style of the book, the circular and the poster. Needless to say I am delighted with it. I am looking forward with the greatest eagerness to the final publication.

I wish you could have been with us on several days during the convention. I[n] all the many years I have attended the conventions I have never known so many dramatic happenings as in this. Mr. Gompers' address[5] upon the opening day of the convention made a profound impression,—not only the address itself but its high, lofty tone, coming as it did from him, his first address since his months of illness.

Then again the afternoon of the opening day the convention of the Mexican Federation of Labor marched in a body across the international bridge from Juarez and met with our convention.[6] There were delegates there also from the labor movement of England, the German labor movement, of Canada, of Santo Domingo and of Porto Rico. Mr. Gompers made the occasion one of the most dramatic incidents I have ever witnessed. That vast audience of delegates from the labor movements all over the United States, Mexico and the many visitors were thrilled to their very souls and there were many whose emotions became so overwhelming as to be visibly manifested.

Then on the second day our convention, in turn, went across the international bridge to Juarez and met with the Mexican Federation of Labor. During the long years which I have been associated with President Gompers, I have heard him deliver many addresses but never have I heard anything from him equal to what he said at the joint meeting of the two conventions in Juarez, Mexico.[7] He was a man inspired. He reached the greatest heights of idealism, of statesmanship, of prophetic vision, of wise leadership and with it all his voice had regained all of its wonderful volume and music which so played upon the human emotions.

Another dramatic incident was when the President of one of the affiliated organizations, during one of the regular sessions of the convention, asked for the privilege of the floor and presented the marble bust made by Mr. Moses Dykaar.[8] No one in the convention except one or two of us had any idea that this was to be done and least of all did Mr. Gompers. I am anxious that you should see the bust. It is the highest expression of art.

Thinking you would be interested in all of these matters I have clipped the record of them from our official proceedings and enclose them herein, including the address made by one of the delegates upon President Gompers' reelection.[9] Mr. Gompers has never more forcefully demonstrated his absolute leadership and guidance of the labor movement than he has done at this convention.

Tomorrow the whole party leaves for Mexico City to be the guests of the Mexican Government at the inauguration of President-Elect Calles.[10] Everything that can possibly be done by the Mexican Government will be done on this occasion to demonstrate to Mr. Gompers the profound appreciation of the Mexican Government and the Mexican people for the tremendous service which he has rendered Mexico during all of her struggle to become a free people and to establish a democratic form of government.

The representative of the Mexican Government who is acting as the liason officer told me that something very unusual is in contemplation to show honor to President Gompers and something that has never before been done by any government.[11] He wouldn't tell me what it was but said it should come as a complete surprise.

If President Gompers should, sometime in the future, add to his Memoirs as indicated that he might possibly do, the happenings here and in Mexico would make a most interesting and impressive chapter.

I am leaving El Paso Friday, the 28th for Washington as I am not making the Mexican trip. So far as I now know I will remain in Washington. I am due to reach there on Monday morning, November 30th.

With all good wishes, I am,

Sincerely yours,   R. Lee Guard
Sec'y.

TLcS, reel 301, vol. 316, pp. 29–30, SG Letterbooks, DLC.

1. John Macrae to R. Lee Guard, Nov. 21 and Nov. 25, 1924, Files of the Office of the President, General Correspondence, reel 108, frames 200, 209, *AFL Records.*

2. Macrae to Guard, Nov. 21, 1924, Files of the Office of the President, General Correspondence, reel 108, frames 201–2, *AFL Records.* See also Macrae to Guard, Nov. 25, 1924, frame 210, ibid.

3. Matthew Woll to Macrae, Nov. 25, 1924, Files of the Office of the President, General Correspondence, reel 108, frame 211, *AFL Records.*

4. On Nov. 25, 1924, the convention unanimously adopted Resolution 79, presented by Woll, endorsing SG's autobiography "as the official expression of the life and work of the President of the American Federation of Labor and of the American trade union movement" and pledging to "do everything within our power and ability to bring this expression into the homes of the members of our trade union movement" (AFL, *Proceedings,* 1924, p. 313).

5. See "First Day—Monday Morning Session," Nov. 17, 1924, in "Excerpts from Accounts of the 1924 Convention of the AFL in El Paso, Texas," Nov. 17–24, 1924, above.

6. See "Five Nations Join in Labor Council," Nov. 17, 1924, in "Excerpts from Accounts of the 1924 Convention of the AFL in El Paso, Texas," Nov. 17–24, 1924, above.

7. See AFL, *Proceedings,* 1924, pp. 124–25.

8. See "Seventh Day—Monday Morning Session," Nov. 24, 1924, in "Excerpts from Accounts of the 1924 Convention of the AFL in El Paso, Texas," Nov. 17–24, 1924, above.

9. A reference to the remarks of James FitzPatrick, the delegate representing the Waterbury (Conn.) Central Labor Union. (See AFL, *Proceedings,* 1924, pp. 307–8.)

10. Late on the afternoon of Nov. 27, 1924, SG left El Paso, Tex., for Mexico City, where he arrived early on the morning of Nov. 30. He attended the inauguration of Plutarco Elías Calles later that day and presided over the convention of the Pan-American Federation of Labor Dec. 3–6. His health then gave way, and apart from attending a performance of the opera "Rigoletto" he was confined to his hotel room from Dec. 7 until Dec. 10, when he was put aboard a train for the United States. He arrived in San Antonio, Tex., on Dec. 12 and died there Dec. 13.

11. Possibly a reference to the celebration of Dec. 2, 1924, as "Gompers Day" in Mexico City.

An Address before the Fourth Congress of the Pan-American Federation of Labor in Mexico City[1]

Mexico City, December 3, 1924.

. . .

FIRST DAY—WEDNESDAY SESSION

. . .

REMARKS OF PRESIDENT GOMPERS

"I have just a word of welcome to add to the cheering words of welcome expressed to us by the representatives of labor this afternoon. This, for the present at least, is not a mass movement, it is true, but we are still in the infancy of the movement of the organized workers, or to organize the workers of the Pan-American countries. It was more than ten years ago when the Mexican Federation of Labor was formed. Today it has a million and a quarter of organized working men in the Republic. It is not more than twenty-five or thirty years ago when the American Federation of Labor had less than a million organized workers, and now, counting the men who are unemployed and who can not pay their dues, (men who are engaged in strikes and lock-outs who can not pay dues) there are over five millions of organized trade unionists in the United States and Canada.

"Last December I had a commission from the American Federation of Labor to go to Panama[2] and there I saw the Panama Federation of Labor in convention[3] for the second time[4] and I had great pleasure in the opportunity of addressing that convention.[5] I understand that there are now several thousand organized workers in that agricultural country. And so on, in the other smaller Pan-American countries, largely, yes, almost entirely primitive in their agricultural pursuits, and these men of labor are not given the right to organize; on the contrary any attempt on their part to organize simply sends them either to prison or to death. Therefore, when in any one of these countries we can help them to plant the seed of organization and bring about a feeling and a consciousness among the working people of these countries that they must strive and strive, and if necessary sacrifice, to organize, we are doing a duty to ourselves as well as to them. To help them so that they can help themselves is a service which no one can now calculate as to its advantages.

"So far as we possibly can we want to be upon an equality in our congress but we must understand this—that the labor movements which are now in the beginning, and those of the labor movements which have had an existence and greater responsibility, can not permit that those who have less experience shall have fullest opportunity of determining the policy of all. You may rest assured of absolute freedom of discussion within the limits of reason and fair dealing, one with another.

"Truly we are grateful to Mr. Grassman, the representative of the German trade union movement, for his words of good cheer and fraternity.[6] With us, I may say, with the labor movement of America including the labor movement of Pan-America, the world war is over and we are going to try and bring about a lasting peace and brotherhood the world over.

"Bro. Juan Rico, as the delegate to this convention representing with his comrades the Mexican Federation of Labor, in his welcome on behalf of the Mexican labor movement to this congress,[7] his wholeheartedness and his splendid vision of the fundamental principles of trade unionism, has cheered every man who loves liberty and aims to help the labor movement.

"It is not necessary for the Mexican Federation of Labor and the American Federation of Labor to pledge to each other assistance, unity and brotherhood; that pledge has been given long ago. That pledge is now more firmly established than at any other time in the history of our movement. To the representatives of the other labor movements and movements groping toward the labor movement in your respective countries, let me say you may rest assured that if we can not help you, we will not harm you, and at least we will make the effort to help you in every way within our power so that you may attain the proud position now enjoyed by the men and women in the labor movement of Mexico and of the United States and Canada.

"The mission of the labor movement is to bring about peace and good will, to uplift the conditions of the masses of our wealth producers, to bring about human brotherhood, not for a day, not for a decade, but for all time, that we may live in peace, in happiness and prosperity, raising a generation and generations yet to come of great men and women, beautiful children to take our places when our time shall come, and generations yet unborn shall call us blessed for the work and service we have in our time performed.["]

. . .

Report of the Proceedings of the Fourth Congress of the Pan-American Federation of Labor, Held in Mexico City, Mexico, December 3rd to 9th, Inclusive, 1924 ([Washington, D.C.], n.d.), pp. 3–6.

1. The Pan-American Federation of Labor met in Mexico City, Dec. 3–9, 1924.
2. See "To B. M. Jewell," Dec. 21, 1923, n. 4, above.
3. The Federación Obrera de la República de Panamá (Workers' Federation of the Republic of Panama) met in Panama City, Jan. 1–6, 1924.
4. The founding convention of the Federación Obrera de la República de Panamá was held in Panama City in the summer of 1921.
5. For SG's address to the convention, delivered on Jan. 6, 1924, see Files of the Office of the President, Speeches and Writings, reel 118, frames 729–34, *AFL Records.*
6. Peter Grassmann's remarks are summarized in *Report of the Proceedings of the Fourth Congress of the Pan-American Federation of Labor, Held in Mexico City, Mexico, December 3rd to 9th, Inclusive, 1924* ([Washington, D.C.], n.d.), p. 3.
7. For Juan Rico's address, see ibid., pp. 3–4.

R. Lee Guard to the Executive Council of the AFL

Washington, D.C., December 12, 1924.

Executive Council, American Federation of Labor.
Gentlemen:

When the sensational reports were published yesterday by the International News Service and the Hearst papers,[1] I appreciated of course that you gentlemen of the Executive Council would be greatly disturbed, and I was very desirous of sending you some reassuring word. However, while feeling perfectly satisfied in my own mind that the reports were erroneous, yet as I had no direct message from any member of Mr. Gompers party, I hesitated to send you a telegram based upon the frequent reports given me during the day by the Associated Press representative who was stationed in my office all day.

For the entire time of Mr. Gompers stay in Mexico I received daily telegrams. Monday, the eighth, was the first message I had that Mr. Gompers was not well. The message stated that he was not well but that he had excellent medical attention. On Tuesday afternoon the message stated President Gompers was better, that the party would leave on Wednesday evening for San Antonio with headquarters at the St. Anthony Hotel. On Wednesday at 5:25 the message stated Mr. Gompers was improved and that they would leave at seven o'clock that night.

I was called up by the United Press at one o'clock on Wednesday night and informed that they had a rumor to the effect that Mr. Gompers had passed out. I refused to accept the message as true and asked that they make every effort to confirm it.

From time to time all during the day Thursday conflicting reports were given me by the Associated Press, the United Press and the International News Service. The International Service repeatedly reported Mr. Gompers death. The Associated Press from time to time gave encouraging reports as to his condition.

I sent several telegrams[2] hoping to intercept Mr. Gompers train somewhere enroute but evidently none of my messages were received except the one addressed to Laredo.[3]

Upon the arrival of the party at Laredo this morning I received direct messages[4] from them and immediately telegraphed to the Executive Council, which for confirmation I quote as follows:

"Telegram received this morning from President Gompers party Laredo that 'President Gompers passed through night better than expected. Condition slightly improved. Temperature normal.'"[5]

"Telegram from Secretary Morrison ten forty four this morning Laredo that President Gompers condition good and improving. They are on way to San Antonio. Mr. Gompers will be taken to St. Anthony Hotel."[6]

Later, I received another telegram[7] from Laredo stating that telegrams had been sent to me all the way from Mexico City to Laredo and that they could not understand why I had not received them and why I should not have received any direct message for thirty six hours.

No doubt Secretary Morrison upon his arrival at the St. Anthony Hotel, San Antonio, Texas, this afternoon, will communicate direct with you.

Very truly yours,   R. Lee Guard
Secretary to President Gompers.

TLcS, Executive Council Records, Vote Books, reel 18, frames 362–63, *AFL Records.*

1. See, for example, "Gompers Expires on Train Speeding to U.S., Is Report," *Washington Evening Star,* Dec. 11, 1924.

2. See, for example, R. Lee Guard to Florence Thorne, Dec. 11, 1924, Files of the Office of the President, General Correspondence, reel 108, frame 230, *AFL Records.*

3. Guard to Thorne, Dec. 11, 1924, ibid., frame 229.

4. J. E. Giles to Guard, Dec. 12, 1924, and Frank Morrison to Guard, Dec. 12, 1924, ibid., frames 240, 258.

5. Guard to the AFL Executive Council, Dec. 12, 1924, ibid., frame 252.

6. Guard to the AFL Executive Council, Dec. 12, 1924, ibid., frame 251.

7. E. J. Tracy to Guard, Dec. 12, 1924, ibid., frame 260.

An Excerpt from an Article in the *New York Times*

San Antonio, Texas, Dec. 12. [1924]

GOMPERS IS BETTER, BUT STILL VERY LOW.

Samuel Gompers's condition was pronounced unfavorable in a bulletin issued tonight by Dr. Lee Rice[1] of San Antonio, who was called into consultation. Mr. Gompers arrived here this afternoon soon after 5 o'clock after a forty-six-hour ride from Mexico City.

The following bulletin was issued at 9:35 o'clock tonight on the condition of Mr. Gompers:

President Gompers's condition is practically unchanged, but the lower altitude may have a favorable influence, and it is hoped he will have a comfortable night. The condition is still grave.

Dr. Lee Rice,
Dr. W. B. Russ,[2]
Dr. W. S. Hanson.[3]

. . .

New York Times, Dec. 13, 1924.

1. Estill Lee Rice (b. 1892).
2. Witten Booth Russ (1874–1964).
3. William Samuel Hanson (1891–1945).

A News Bulletin Issued by the AFL Information and Publicity Service

San Antonio, Texas, December 13, 1924.

The following statement was issued by Frank Morrison, Secretary of the American Federation of Labor and members of the Executive Council present at six o'clock this morning:

"President Gompers died at 4:05 o'clock this morning after heroic efforts to save his life. Dr. Lee Rice and Dr. W. S. Hanson of San Antonio were in attendance.

"Dr. Rice stated that Mr. Gompers' heart failed to respond to restoratives. There had been an acute condition of the heart and kidneys for fully a year and a half past. It was impossible to overcome the weakness of the heart.

"Every possible measure was taken to prolong Mr. Gompers' life but to no avail. At 2:30 this morning he uttered his last words. 'Nurse, this is the end,' he said, 'God bless our American institutions. May they grow better day by day.'

"From that time until the end Mr. Gompers was unconscious. His breathing was heavy until just a few moments before the end. As death approached his face became calm and he sank peacefully and quietly into his last slumber. In accordance with a wish expressed in Mexico City when he believed the end to be near, Vice-President James Duncan held Mr. Gompers' hand and he passed away.

"Members of the Executive Council present in San Antonio are discussing arrangements for the funeral and an announcement in that respect will be made later. Mr. Gompers, during his last moments, was surrounded by a group the members of which have for years been his intimate associates and co-workers. They were Dr. Lee Rice and Dr. W. S. Hanson of San Antonio; Frank Morrison, Secretary of the American Federation of Labor; Vice-Presidents James Duncan, Matthew Woll and Martin F. Ryan; W. D. Mahon, President of the Amalgamated Association of Street and Electric Railway Employes; John P. Frey, Editor of the Molders Journal and President of the Ohio State Federation of Labor; Florence C. Thorne, Member of the A.F. of L. Research Staff; William C. Roberts, Chairman of the A.F. of L. Legislative Committee; Chester M. Wright, Director A.F. of L. Information and Publicity Service; J. E. Giles[1] and E. J. Tracy, Members of the A.F. of L. office force; T. J. McQuade,[2] Plate Printers Union, Washington, D.C.; C. N. Idar, A.F. of L., Organizer in San Antonio; Joseph L. Lynch,[3] Member of the Amalgamated Association of Street and Railway Employes and A. L. Bytal, U.S. Immigration Officer. The two nurses present were M. H. May, R.N., of New York and Miss Marie Jameton,[4] R.N., of San Antonio."

TDc, Files of the Office of the President, Speeches and Writings, reel 119, frame 138, *AFL Records.*

1. John Edwin Giles (1888–1927) worked in various capacities in the AFL office. At the time of his death he was serving in the post of chief auditor. (See also *The Samuel Gompers Papers*, vol. 10, p. 471, n. 9.)

2. Thomas Joseph McQuade (b. 1873), a plate printer at the Bureau of Engraving

and Printing, was chairman of the executive committee of International Plate Printers' and Die Stampers' Union of North America 2 of Washington, D.C.

3. Joseph L. Lynch (1876–1946), a former motorman and member of Amalgamated Association of Street and Electric Railway Employes of America 241 of Chicago, manufactured union buttons, badges, banners, and flags.

4. Marie S. Jameton (1885–1981).

A Memorandum by Lee Rice

San Antonio, Texas 13 December 1924

Mr. Gompers condition was very critical when he arrived from Mexico City yesterday. His heart was in a state of fibrillation with a rate at the apex of 160, and the lungs were oedematous; that is the bronchial tubes were partially filled with frothy material which interfered with respiration. His liver was enlarged and tender, and the feet and legs were oedematous. A mild uremia existed, and the urine showed a small amount of albumen with casts, but it was free of sugar, and an intermittent diabetes did not participate in the termination of his life.

For a few hours he responded to digitalis and other stimulation, but the heart muscle was so nearly exhausted from his long labors, that its strength could not be recovered, and toward the depressing hours of morning it slowly failed. The fluid recollected in his lungs in spite of the atropine administered, and although epinephrin was administered and the patient was bled 700 c.c. to relieve some of the strain on his heart, all efforts were futile.

Mr. Gompers nurse, Miss Mae, and the other members of his staff were able to give me an accurate history of his condition during the past few months, and I also talked to Dr. Julius Auerbach, his personal physician in New York City, who helped to guide his treatment, along with the advice of Dr. W. B. Russ and Dr. W. S. Hansen.

His last illness was a recurrence of several similar attacks of heart failure accompanied by uremia, and the acute onset was brought about by exposure and activity beyond his limit of tolerance in the high altitude of Mexico City. He had the constant attention of two nurses, and every attention required to meet the emergencies of his last night's illness.

Lee Rice

TDS, Files of the Office of the President, General Correspondence, reel 108, frame 330, *AFL Records.*

A Memorandum by R. Lee Guard

Washington, D.C., Saturday, December 13, 1924.

The Associated Press called me up this morning at my house at 5:15 and read me three bulletins that they had had from San Antonio showing Mr. Gompers was rapidly sinking. The members of the Executive Council had been called into his room.

A few minutes later Mr. Weikel,[1] one of the young men at the office, called me up from Clarendon, Virginia, and said that he had a flash from the Press Association that Mr. Gompers had passed out.

Five minutes later the Associated Press again called and in the most feeling, sympathetic manner, read me the bulletin announcing Mr. Gompers' death at five minutes after four. They said they had the bulletin when they read me the previous ones but they did not have the heart to read it to me at that time.

I then tried to get Mr. Gompers' son but did not succeed in reaching him until after half past six o'clock.

I called up Harry Monness in New York and told him. He was so overcome he could hardly speak.

I then telegraphed[2] over the telephone to Miss Thorne in San Antonio.

I again called up Mr. Gompers' son and suggested that it would be well if he would agree to my sending a telegram in his name to Mr. Morrison. I outlined what the telegram should say—he agreed and consented. I then prepared the telegram in his name, read it to him over the telephone and he fully agreed to its being sent. Copies of this telegram are attached hereto.[3]

Between half past five and six Mr. Roberts and Mr. Giles called me over long distance telephone from San Antonio and told me that they were all two-thirds sick and asked if there was anything special I wanted them to do.

At eight o'clock Mr. Weikel came and took me from my home down to the office. Shortly after reaching here I received a telegram from Mr. Morrison announcing the death of President Gompers. The telegram is attached hereto.[4]

Mr. Weikel came to the office at seven o'clock and at my request arranged for the flag to be put at half mast and the flag on the machinists' building. Mr. Howlin[5] and he arranged for the building to be draped in black.

I got to the office at eight o'clock and shortly after Mr. Manning, Mr. Berres, Mr. Wallace and Mr. Egan[6] all came. Upon suggestion of Mr. Manning and Mr. Berres I telegraphed[7] Mr. Morrison suggesting that the members of the Executive Council who were not in San Antonio and the officers of the several departments meet the funeral cortege somewhere on route and escort it to Washington.

One by one the young men representing the Press Associations who have been coming to headquarters came personally to me and expressed their very profound grief and to offer their services in any way within their power. I told them all that the gentlemen of the press had been beautifully kind and courteous and that I appreciated it so deeply. The Associated Press called me at several different times during the morning. I expressed to them my great appreciation of their courtesy and they all put their services at my disposal in any way I might designate.

TDc, Files of the Office of the President, Reference Material, reel 134, frames 107–8, *AFL Records.* Typed notation: "*Dictated by Miss Guard.*"

1. Frank Weikel (1902–87), a clerk in the AFL office, later served on the staff of AFL president William Green. In 1937 he was named to head the AFL's newly created Office Employees' International Council, and from at least 1947 through 1960 he was director of labor relations for the Reynolds Metals Co.

2. R. Lee Guard to Florence Thorne, Dec. 13, 1924, Files of the Office of the President, General Correspondence, reel 108, frame 285, *AFL Records.*

3. Samuel Gompers, Jr., to Frank Morrison, Dec. 13, 1924, ibid., frames 273–74.

4. Morrison to Guard, Dec. 13, 1924, ibid., frame 300.

5. William Henry Howlin (1882–1953) was a clerk in the AFL office.

6. James P. Egan (1866–1931), editor of the *AFL Weekly News Service* (to 1921, the *AFL Weekly News Letter*) from about 1915 until his death. In 1914 he served as a member of the AFL Legislative Committee. (See also *The Samuel Gompers Papers,* vol. 8, p. 409, n. 9.)

7. Guard to Morrison, Dec. 13, 1924, Files of the Office of the President, General Correspondence, reel 108, frame 284, *AFL Records.*

George Perkins to Frank Morrison

Headquarters
Cigar Makers' International Union of America
Chicago, Ill., December 15, 1924.

Mr. Frank Morrison,
Sec'y. and Acting President, American Federation of Labor,
Washington, D.C.
Dear Sir:

Samuel Gompers is dead; his spirit goes marching on. We have all lost a worth while friend. We shall miss his keen judgment, his sound counsel, and his genial companionship.

The American Federation of Labor, for which he did so much and which he loved with all his passionate soul, has lost a strong, sustaining force.

Humanity, justice, freedom, democracy, America, and the whole world will miss him and now mourns with us.

We are plunged into heartfelt regret and deep grief by his passing into the ages. We are consoled by the fact that under his constructive genius and powerful leadership the American Federation of Labor finds itself upon a solid foundation prepared and ready to go forward under new leadership in the future just as safely and surely as in the past. Always inspired by his memory indelibly impressed upon our minds and hearts we shall keep the faith which he kept and held aloft even as he passed through the gates to eternity.

Yours fraternally,   G. W. Perkins,
President,   Cigar Makers' Int'l. Union.

TLS, AFL Microfilm National and International Union File, Cigar Makers Records, reel 36, frame 2045, *AFL Records.*

An Article in the *New York Times*

[December 19, 1924]

THOUSANDS PAY LAST TRIBUTE TO GOMPERS

Under leaden skies that poured a cold drizzle on Tarrytown's storied Sleepy Hollow Cemetery yesterday afternoon, the stricken relatives of Samuel Gompers turned their reluctant footsteps from a newly made grave and returned to the city which in the forenoon had witnessed a tribute seldom if ever accorded to a private citizen.

They had heard Rabbi Stephen S. Wise, in vibrant voice, describe the late President of the American Federation of Labor, as "a frontiersman of industrial freedom" whose love for the flag was a religion and whose life was "an American epic." Almost as from the mute lips of the beloved one before them they had heard his last message to those millions in whose cause he had labored for sixty years.

James Duncan, co-worker of Mr. Gompers in upbuilding the American Federation, in sentences broken with emotion, had described how his old friend, fearing death was not far off, had sent for him and had given him this message to the toiling millions:

"I have kept the faith; I expect them to keep the faith."

Many Nations Pay Tribute.

Representatives of the city, State and nation and representatives of many foreign countries paid tribute and gave reverence yesterday to the passing labor leader. Tens of thousands lined the streets here as the funeral cortège passed. Waves of invisible ether carried the solemn funeral service from the Elks Club on West Forty-third Street to hundreds of thousands of homes within a radius of several thousand miles.

In the United States Senate a eulogy was spoken on the life of "the industrial pioneer." In innumerable workshops in all parts of the land heads were bowed in silence for two minutes when the clock pointed to eleven. In Mexico, Nicaragua and the countries of Central America, South America and Canada exercises were held in honor of Mr. Gompers. Trades unionists in far-off Manila united in sentiment with European workmen to do reverence. Street traffic in Havana was halted five minutes during the funeral.

The crowds that streamed past the bier in the lodge rooms of the Elks Club, where the body lay in state all day Wednesday, thinned out toward midnight, but in the following early morning hours printers from newspaper offices and other night workers filed past the casket.

Officials of international unions, State federations, local unions and other organizations began to gather at 7 A.M. for the services. Fifteen hundred seats in the lodge room were reserved for the honorary pallbearers, comprising Governor Smith, Mayor Hylan, Acting Secretary of Labor E. J. Henning,[1] Rear Admiral Charles P. Plunkett,[2] Major Gen. Robert Lee Bullard[3] and distinguished men from all fields of the nation's activity.

Thousands Gather for Service.

The seats on the right were occupied by members of the Gompers family, the widow, children and grandchildren. The seats on the main floor and in the two tiers of boxes were occupied before 9 o'clock. Fully one-fourth of the floor space on the south side of the room was filled with floral offerings.

As the hour for the funeral service approached a great crowd gathered and a thousand got into Town Hall, opposite the club, where the service was heard by radio. Many more thousands gathered at Sixth Avenue and Broadway to await the end of the services.

Mayor Hylan and Murray Hulbert,[4] President of the Board of Aldermen, entered at 9:10 and were followed in a few minutes by Governor Smith and his naval and military aids. The Governor shook hands with the Mayor and sat on a near-by bench.

Rabbi Wise opened the services by reciting the Twenty-third psalm in Hebrew and then in English. He unfolded an impressive eulogy.

"Some one has said of Gompers that he was a frontiersman," he said. "What a perfect characterization, for he had all the virtues and some of the defects of the frontiersman."

SOBS PUNCTUATE EULOGY.

Dr. Wise spoke slowly. Many eyes were moist. Occasionally a sob was heard. Toward the end the notes of the organ were heard faintly in Chopin's Funeral March.

"Among all the characterizations of Samuel Gompers I have come upon," said Dr. Wise, "none is more fitting than 'frontiersman.' For Samuel Gompers was a pioneer, rugged rather than suave, firm rather than conventional. Pioneer was he in the military sense, for his was the militant mood and throughout his life he was a battler. As a pioneer Gompers fought for a great cause, not for larger wage or added comfort, but for a freer and fuller life for the toilers of the nation—which could not be without these instrumentalities of life and freedom.

"He had all the ruggedness and courage, but he had more than the moderation of the pioneer. His was the moderation of the highest courage, rather than the immoderateness of the lower daring. Iconoclast, he seemed to those Bourbons who in every generation contest the forward march of the workers to the larger life. Not immoderate he, whose was the moderation of statesmanship, which is not irreconcilable with the finest courage and the noblest daring.["]

A MAN OF MANY IDEALS.

"Concentrating upon and consecrated to his purpose, he was unlike the pioneer in that he was a man of more than one ideal and more than one loyalty. Long will men remember the ardor with which he espoused the cause of international peace, seeking it on high ground and for the highest ends. In his quest of international understanding he gave generous support and ardent loyalty to the greatest of the friends of man in our day, Woodrow Wilson.

"His was the unselfishness of the pioneer, the man who plans and builds for others, who deems himself the instrument and servant of that higher purpose in which he unswervingly believes. His was the integrity of the pioneer, unstained and unchallengeable, the integrity of the man who puts his cause first and himself last, the man who counts nothing worth while save the triumph of the issue to which he has dedicated himself.

"Dedicated—for here was truly a high priest at the shrine of men's yearnings for freedom and justice. Samuel heard the voice and beheld the vision of God. Truly did this Samuel, too, hear the voice of God, who ever lays the command, 'Let my people go that they may serve me,'[5] upon the heart of his servant, whether Moses or Samuel or Jesus or Savanarola,[6] or Cromwell[7] or Lincoln or Wilson.

"Considering that he was a pioneer, he must be judged by his achievements, not his failures, though these, too, were significant. The life of this frontiersman of industrial freedom seems one of marvelous, even incredible achievement when it is borne in mind that from the beginning to the end of his years of leadership he stood like a man unafraid against outlawry, attempted always and effective sometimes, against organized labor.["]

Serving Labor He Served America.

"Withal, he was lawful and honorable, yea, more truly lawful and honorable in his dealings than the technically lawful oppressors of organized labor.

"Serving most the cause of organized labor, he best served America. For the organization of the workers of America is no less truly a democratic and even spiritual achievement than the founding of a mighty industry or the leadership of a successful financial institution.

"Patriot was he in battling for the freedom and self-determination for the workers, that they might be not 'least of men' in the fellowship of our American democracy.

"To this once immigrant lad America was not a habit but an ideal, not a birthright possession but a religion. America remade this youthful and unafraid immigrant. The stuff was there, for he was of sturdy and honorable parentage. His English birth had endowed him with, or in any event had deepened, his native passion for freedom.

"Knowing Gompers as I did, I felt, and feel, that his idealism, his unfaltering courage, his life for his fellow-men, were nurtured by his Jewish past, emerged out of that background of centuries of high moral purpose and unwithstandable spiritual resolve, to which heritage he gave conscious loyalty.

"Who knows but that he might have been a steadfast worshiper within the walls of the synagogue had he found within church alike less of social timidities and more of the unquailing courage in dealing with industrial iniquity and social oppression?["]

A Man That America Remade.

"Of Lincoln it was said that he was such a man as freedom knows how to make. We name Samuel Gompers such a man as America knew how to remake; how to refashion to its lofty uses. America remade this immigrant lad, even as America has taken multitudes of immigrant sons and daughters and won by virtue of its kindling genius and their eager hearts to the uttermost devotion of service to American purposes.

"What romance and wonder in his story! It is in truth an American career, an American epic. Born in England, he got little more than the rudiments of education in his native land; he came to this country as a poor boy and quickly found his way to the cigar maker's bench.

"This protagonist of a great cause became one of the trusted counselors and leaders of the nation in the time of the crisis, evoking and strengthening the faith of millions, who looked for him for leadership and found it in their hour of doubt and in their country's hour of need. Chosen was he some weeks ago for the fortieth time or more as President of the Federation. His last public appearance was in connection with the inaugural of a worker at the head of the neighbor republic of Mexico, relations of understanding and amity with which he had done much to foster.

"And in the last moments he hastened back to his native country that here he might die, almost his [last] words being[8] 'God bless our American institutions; may they grow better day by day.' Hither he came to live and hither he came to die.

"His last word was a prayer for and a benediction upon the country of his choice, the country he served and blessed. Gompers died a poor man. You, his nearest, will have no inheritance tax to pay. But he has left you, his very own, and you, his comrades of the cause, rich indeed. His work is done, neither to be done over, nor to be undone.["]

DUNCAN DELIVERS LABOR'S FAREWELL.

Labor's farewell was delivered by James Duncan, First Vice President of the Federation. He told of his forty years of friendship with Mr. Gompers and of his thirty years of association with him on the Executive Council.

Some years ago Mr. Gompers told the speaker, "If you are alive when it comes my time to go and are near to me, come to me. I have a message to leave to our people."

"He sent for me in Mexico City, for he had a premonition of his death," continued Mr. Duncan, "and this is the message he gave, not only for those in the Federation, but for all others in labor:

"'Say to them that as I kept the faith I expect they will keep the faith. They must carry on. Say to them that a union man carrying a card cannot be a good citizen unless he upholds American institutions, and he is a poor citizen if he upholds American institutions and forgets his obligations to his trade association.[']"

Mr. Duncan told of his friend's early years as a cigarmaker, and spoke feelingly of Mr. Gompers's long war against the idea of compulsory arbitration and the illegal use of injunctions by the courts. He closed with the verses of James Whitcomb Riley, "I cannot say and will not say he's dead; he's just away."[9]

The Elks ritual was then conducted by Exalted Ruler Solomon Tekulsky,[10] who organized a "Lodge of Sorrow." A choir sang "Absent," "Going Home" and "The Vacant Chair" as part of the ritual.

PROMINENT MEN AT SERVICE.

Mrs. Gompers, the widow, viewed the dead face for the last time. The other relatives followed. The lid of the casket was locked at 10:45. Slowly there filed from the room the members of the Executive Council, Governor Smith, Mayor Hylan, Aldermanic President Hulbert, Mr. Henning, Rear Admiral Plunkett, Major Gen. Bullard, distinguished citizens and union officials. These included Bernard M. Baruch, Gerard Swope,[11] Owen D. Young,[12] Ralph M. Easley, Alton B. Parker, Peter J. Brady, John L. Lewis, Philip Murray, J. C. Lewis, Thomas Kennedy,[13] Lee Hall,[14] Michael Breen, Martin Lawlor,[15] Michael F. Tighe, Neil J. Ferry,[16] William J. Bowen,[17] William Dobson,[18] Thomas Preece,[19] Bird S. Coler,[20] Commissioner of Public Welfare; William H. Johnston, Frank Gillmore,[21] A. J. Flores, Emanuel Kovaleski,[22] Michael J. Keough,[23] John P. Frey, Charles L. Bain, Albert Adamski, Edward L. McGrady, John J. Connolly,[24] Michael Green,[25] James M. Lynch,[26] Morris Sigman, Louis E. Langer, Luigi Antonelli,[27] Max Feinstone,[28] Peter J. Doyle,[29] City Judge Shientag,[30] Arthur M. Huddell,[31] Thomas F. McMahon, John R. Alpine,[32] William L. Hutcheson,[33] James P. Holland,[34] J. P. Noonan, J. Coefield,[35] Richard H. Curran,[36] Harry Monness, Louis Wiley[37] and George W. Perkins. They were escorted by Hugh Frayne, General Organizer in New York of the A.F. of L., and his assistants.

Hats came off as the casket was borne to the waiting hearse. The crowd remained silent. The ten members of the Executive Council entered automobiles. They were followed by members of St. Cecile Lodge 568, F. and A.M.,[38] who conducted the services at the cemetery.

THOUSANDS CROWD THE STREETS.

As the cortège began to move a fine drizzle began. Thousands lined the streets, but nowhere was the crowd so great as at Times Square, where the police estimated the number at 15,000. The people were wedged in tightly in the open space opposite the Times Building and stood ten deep on the sidewalks. Traffic in the Times Square section was at a standstill until the police made a lane for the cortège to pass. Hats were doffed as the hearse passed and the crowd surged forward eagerly for a view of the flag-draped casket.

Police Inspector Edwin H. West[39] of the Second Division, Deputy

Inspector William V. McGrath[40] and Captains John J. Noonan[41] and William Kelleher directed the 125 patrolmen who made Broadway passable. Mounted patrolmen and motorcycle patrolmen assisted in keeping police lines.

The procession proceeded north at a snail's pace. Following the hearse came the automobiles containing the members of the Gompers family and then more than 100 automobiles filled with labor union officials from every part of the United States.

The automobiles proceeded more rapidly after passing Columbus Circle. Up to Seventy-second Street a crowd lined the streets, although it was drizzling. Led by two motorcycle patrolmen, the procession went west in Seventy-second Street to Riverside Drive and north to 155th Street, where it turned into Broadway, which was followed to the city line. There the New York policemen turned back and mounted patrolmen and motorcycle patrolmen of the Yonkers Department took up the guidance of the party.

YONKERS DELEGATION MEETS CORTEGE.

Mayor Weisendanger[42] of Yonkers, city officials and members of the Yonkers Federation of Labor and Yonkers building trades met the cortège at the city line and the slow procession filed to Getty Square. There 5,000 persons stood with bared heads as the hearse passed.

The Yonkers mourners escorted the body to the Hastings line. Through Hastings, Dobbs Ferry and Tarrytown, mechanics, laborers on the streets, school children, teachers, priests, nuns, housewives, shopkeepers and citizens in every walk of life turned out to see the procession.

It was 1:20 when the funeral party reached the cemetery. The chimes in the chapel played "Nearer, My God, to Thee" as the party made its way to the Gompers plot, 200 feet from the entrance. Mrs. Gompers, her brother, Walter Gleaves;[43] Samuel, Henry and Al Gompers, sons of the decedent, and other relatives took places under a canvas marquee a few feet from the driveway. Two thousand persons gathered as close to the grave as it was possible to get without stepping on the flowers spread on the ground.

When the coffin was lowered to the asphalt vault the Masonic commitment service was delivered by the Very Rev. Oscar F. R. Treder,[44] Dean of the Cathedral of the Incarnation, Garden City, and Chaplain of the New York Grand Lodge of Masons, assisted by Archie Ralph Kerr,[45] Past Master of St. Cecile Lodge and Grand Junior Deacon, and Winfield C. Terry,[46] Master of St. Cecile Lodge. Mr. Kerr and a committee represented Dawson Lodge of Masons in Washington, in which Mr. Gompers had membership. Grand Secretary Robert Judson

Kenworthy[47] assisted in the ceremony. The Masons wore their Masonic aprons.

The St. Cecile Quartet—Homer Burress,[48] De Los Becker,[49] Alvah E. Nichols[50] and James D. Thomas—sang the Twenty-third Psalm, "Beautiful Isle of Somewhere," the Lord's Prayer and "The Long Day Closes."

Mrs. Gompers was weeping as the services ended. She and the Gompers family took one last look into the grave and were then escorted to automobiles, and the party left the cemetery.

Mrs. Gompers looked back so long as a glimpse of the grave on the knoll was possible. The last object she saw was the giant poplar that stands like a sentinel at the foot of the knoll.

New York Times, Dec. 19, 1924.

1. Edward J. Henning (1868–1935) served as assistant secretary of labor from 1921 to 1925 and as a U.S. district court judge from 1925 to 1929.

2. Charles Peshall Plunkett (1864–1931) served as chief of staff at the Naval War College from 1920 to 1921 and as commander of the Third Naval District and Brooklyn Navy Yard from 1922 until his retirement in 1928.

3. Robert Lee Bullard (1861–1947) served as commanding officer of the Second Corps at Fort Jay, Governors Island, N.Y., from 1919 until his retirement in 1925.

4. George Murray Hulbert (1881–1950) served as president of the New York City Board of Aldermen from 1921 to 1925. He had previously served as a Democratic congressman from New York (1915–18), and he was later a U.S. district court judge (1934–50).

5. The passage occurs repeatedly in the book of Exodus (7:16, 8:1, 8:20, 9:1, 9:13, 10:3).

6. Girolamo Savonarola (1452–98), a Dominican preacher and religious zealot, dominated Florence, Italy, after the overthrow of the Medici in 1494. He was excommunicated by the pope in 1497 and executed in 1498.

7. Oliver Cromwell (1599–1658) was the leader of the Parliamentary forces that overthrew the Stuart monarchy in the English Civil War and then from 1653 until his death served as Lord Protector of England, Scotland, and Ireland.

8. In the transcript of the eulogy in the AFL's files, this passage reads, "the last words on his lips being" (Files of the Office of the President, Reference Material, reel 134, frame 217, *AFL Records*).

9. The opening lines of the poem "Away" by James Whitcomb Riley (1849–1916), which reads, "I can not say, and I will not say / That he is dead.—He is just away!"

10. Solomon Tekulsky (1882–1969) was a New York City attorney.

11. Gerard Swope (1872–1957) served as president of General Electric from 1922 to 1939 and again from 1942 to 1944.

12. Owen D. Young (1874–1962) served as chairman of the board of General Electric from 1922 to 1939 and again from 1942 to 1944. He was an author of the Dawes Plan of 1924 and the Young Plan of 1929, which reduced German reparations payments and established the Bank for International Settlements.

13. Thomas KENNEDY served as president of United Mine Workers of America District 7 (Pennsylvania) from 1910 to 1924.

14. Harry Lee Hall (1877–1950) of Columbus, Ohio, served as president of United Mine Workers District 6 (Ohio) from 1920 to 1933.

15. Martin LAWLOR served as secretary-treasurer of the United Hatters of North America from 1911 to 1934.

16. Neal (variously Neil) J. Ferry (1874–1932), an anthracite miner from McAdoo, Pa., represented District 7 (Pennsylvania) on the executive board of the United Mine Workers from 1908 until his death.

17. William J. BOWEN was president of the Bricklayers', Masons', and Plasterers' International Union of America from 1904 to 1928.

18. William DOBSON served as secretary of the Bricklayers from 1900 to 1925.

19. Thomas R. Preece (1860–1940), a member of Bricklayers' local 21 of Chicago, served as a vice-president of the international union from 1904 to 1925.

20. Bird Sim Coler (1867–1941) served from 1918 to 1920 as New York City's commissioner of public charities and then from 1920, when the post was renamed, until 1929 as the city's commissioner of public welfare.

21. Frank P. GILLMORE served as secretary of the Actors' Equity Association from 1918 to 1928.

22. Emanuel KOVELESKI, secretary and business agent (1910–48) of Hotel and Restaurant Employees' International Alliance and Bartenders' International League of America 171 of Rochester, N.Y., was a vice-president (1913–33) of the New York State Federation of Labor.

23. Michael J. KEOUGH served as president of the International Molders' Union of North America from 1924 to 1932.

24. John Joseph Connolly (b. 1867), a member of International Association of Machinists 264 of Boston, served as a vice-president of the international union from 1921 to 1925.

25. Michael F. GREENE was president of the United Hatters of North America.

26. James Matthew LYNCH served as president of the International Typographical Union from 1900 to 1914 and from 1924 to 1926.

27. Actually Luigi Antonini (1883–1968), the founder and secretary of International Ladies' Garment Workers' Union 89 (Italian Dressmakers). In 1922 he was a founder of the Anti-Fascist Alliance, and from 1934 to 1968 he served as a vice-president of the Ladies' Garment Workers.

28. Actually Morris C. Feinstone (1878–1943), secretary of AFL Umbrella Handle and Stick Makers' Union 14,581 of New York City and assistant secretary (later secretary) of the United Hebrew Trades.

29. Peter Aloysius Doyle (1887–1963), a member of Bricklayers' local 34 of New York City, was a mediator for the New York State Department of Labor.

30. Bernard Lloyd Shientag (1887–1952) served as a New York city court judge from 1924 to 1930 and as a justice of the New York Supreme Court from 1930 until his death in 1952.

31. Arthur McIntire HUDDELL served as president of the International Union of Steam and Operating Engineers from 1921 to 1931.

32. John R. ALPINE had served from 1906 to 1919 as president of the United Association of Journeymen Plumbers, Gas Fitters, Steam Fitters, and Steam Fitters' Helpers of the United States and Canada (from 1913, the United Association of Plumbers and Steam Fitters of the United States and Canada) and from 1909 to 1919 as an AFL vice-president.

33. William Levi HUTCHESON was president of the United Brotherhood of Carpenters and Joiners of America from 1915 to 1952.

34. James P. HOLLAND was president (1915–26) of the New York State Federation of Labor (to 1910, the Workingmen's Federation of the State of New York).

35. John COEFIELD served as president of the Plumbers from 1919 to 1940. He was also a vice-president of the AFL Metal Trades Department.

36. Richard H. Curran (1864–1932), secretary of Molders' local 11 of Rochester, N.Y., served as a member of the New York State Industrial Commission from 1915 to 1926.

37. Louis Wiley (1869–1935) served as business manager of the *New York Times* from 1906 to 1935.

38. That is, Free and Accepted Masons.

39. Edwin Haskin West (b. 1874).

40. William J. McGrath (1867–1929).

41. John Joseph Noonan (b. 1877).

42. Ulrich Weisendanger (b. 1872) served as the Republican mayor of Yonkers, N.Y., from 1924 to 1925.

43. According to other news accounts, Gertrude Gompers was accompanied at the funeral by her father William Thomas Gleaves (b. 1854), her brothers William Henry Gleaves (b. 1885) and Albert Edgar Gleaves (b. 1888), her sister Mabel Brown (b. 1889), and a number of friends.

44. Oscar Frederick Rudolph Treder (1877–1952) served as dean of the Cathedral of the Incarnation, Garden City, N.Y., from 1916 to 1926.

45. Archie Ralph Kerr (b. 1882) was a New York City salesman.

46. Winfield Clinton Terry (1888–1949) was a New York City dentist.

47. Robert Judson Kenworthy (1861–1931), an advertising agent, was secretary of the New York Grand Lodge of Masons.

48. James Homer Burress (b. 1876) was a professional singer in New York City.

49. De Los Isaac Becker (1883–1965) was a professional singer in New York City.

50. Alvah Edgar Nichols (b. 1882) was a voice teacher in New York City.

Excerpts from the Minutes of a Meeting of the Executive Council of the AFL[1]

Friday, December 19, 1924.

Meeting called to order at 10:45 A.M. Secretary Morrison in the chair.

Secretary Morrison: Members of the Executive Council—We are here this morning after having paid the last tribute of affection and homage to the mortal remains of Samuel Gompers. His sound philosophy, high ideals and integrity have guided the American Federation of Labor for over forty years. The American Federation of Labor is a monument to his genius. His championship of the cause of labor and human rights endeared him to the peoples of all Nations. We have a pride in his accomplishments, they reflect glory upon the labor movement and its ideals.

It was my good fortune to have worked in harness with him for over twenty-seven years. The great movement has grown in power and influence. We had that influence and power demonstrated in the wonderful triumphal trip across the continent. In the expressions of good will, affection and love in every city and hamlet, in Washington, and the wonderful demonstration in this building yesterday and at the grave. I do not believe that any member of the Council will live to witness such another demonstration and expression of good will, affection and love which the people gave to Samuel Gompers. The reflected glory rests also upon this great movement for which we stand.

It devolves upon the members of the Council called here today to make the selection of the successor to this illustrious leader. We recessed from Washington to New York for this purpose. It devolves upon me, as Secretary, to call this meeting for the purpose outlined in the constitution. I, therefore, declare this Executive Council meeting open for the transaction of business and with your permission I request Vice-President Duffy to call the roll.

The following responded to the roll call: Duncan, Duffy, Green, Rickert, Fischer, Woll, Ryan, Wilson,[2] Tobin and Morrison.

. . .

Secretary Morrison: The procedure will be to fill the vacancy in the unexpired term of President which expires on the first of January, and then to proceed to elect the President for the ensuing term, beginning January 1, 1925.

Vice-President Duncan: I desire to make a statement about myself. I know that the laws of the American Federation of Labor do not contemplate the succession of Vice-President to the Presidency and so on. It is the customary thing to do, however. It is the popular way in most associations.

I have for a long time been a Vice-President of the American Federation of Labor and have given it a great deal of work. I feel that I am justified in having your support at least until the next convention.[3] I am, of course, much older than I was a long time ago and I would not remain in office to harass my life simply to be in office, but for the time I have been a Vice-President of the American Federation of Labor, I think it is an honor that is due to me from this Council to make me the successor of President Gompers until the next convention.

I have made no arrangements about nominations, nor have I asked any one about their votes. I simply want to make that statement because I think I am entitled to it. I think I should have your support and assistance at least until the next convention of the American Federation of Labor.

Secretary Morrison: Nominations are in order.

Vice-President Rickert: For the office of President for the unexpired term, since you have declared that the proper procedure, I desire to place in nomination one of our colleagues on this Council whom you all know, with whose ability you are familiar, so it is not necessary to eulogize him, but I do want to say this, that I think it becomes the duty of every member of this Council not to consider self, not to consider his organization but to consider the labor movement as a whole from all its aspects and angles, not for today, not for tomorrow but for all time,—not for giving one man honor. It is not a question of giving to one man what he may feel his right to is due him. It is a question of filling this position with a man who can hold the office, not for a short period, but let us hope for as many or more years than our departed leader held it.

The labor movement in my limited experience and in my judgment is waiting everywhere in this land—waiting to hear who the men, who are the chosen leaders of this movement, are going to select for this position. The labor movement is going to be the judge and perhaps the business world as well as the labor world is waiting to hear who is going to lead this movement since Samuel Gompers is gone. They are not interested in paying honor to any one man how ever much it may be his due. From the humblest member in the ranks to the international officers, the question is on every lip and the thought in every mind, who is going to lead this movement from now on? Explanations, whatever they might be for a temporary selection, might meet with approval of some, but surely would meet with a great deal of criticism, all of which can be obviated by the selection of some one man not for a little while but permanently.

I know this that for myself I would not feel as a member in the ranks, that he whom my organization had selected or helped to select as a member of this Council would have done his duty if he had selected some one to fill this vacancy temporarily. It is my opinion that the labor movement is like many other movements. If you can say to them—here we present to you a new leader, we present a new leader to whom you should give the same allegiance, the same support even to a greater extent perhaps than was given to President Gompers, that the labor movement will unite and give that loyal support.

There is so much needed now more than ever in this movement that Samuel Gompers served for so many years, if such a man can be found to take his place. I think the whole movement realizes that Samuel Gompers developed with the passage of years and he became the Samuel Gompers whom we all honored and respected. We know the movement will do for its new leader what it did for him when he became its leader—loyally rally to his support. That is my firm conviction if we can now present to the world a new leader, whom the members have decided that in the interest of the movement it is best to select now permanently, and in the selection of that man present to them a leader who can surround himself and secure to himself the loyal support, first of the international officers in the labor movement, the delegates who come to conventions and through them from the very beginning the loyal support of the trade union movement.

In addition to that the man I have in mind will be able to secure the favorable press comment of the country. By selecting him the consensus of opinion from all angles will be that we have made a good choice. You will obviate the necessity of selecting some one at the next convention, because I believe that the delegates have always demonstrated that the movement is fair by deciding that the man selected shall be given a chance not for one year or two years, but will rally to his support year after year, and by his ability he will demonstrate that he merits their support for the years to come, and in time we will have another Samuel Gompers. With that in mind I present the name of William Green.

Vice-President Wilson seconded the nomination.

Vice-President Ryan: I have listened with attention to the remarks of Brother Rickert and the nomination he has made. I will not yield to any man for having a greater admiration for the man he has named than I have because I think I know William Green, I know his qualifications, his ability and believe he will be an ideal man. At the same time you must take into consideration through the order of common courtesy, decency and respect, the remarks made by our honored First Vice-President of the Federation. It is perfectly apparent to me, as it must be to every member of this Council,—I would not have you misunderstand me in making that statement—that Vice-President Duncan can not be elected. This is my opinion. I am making these remarks with the thought in mind of not doing anything possible that would humiliate him or cast reflections upon the great service he has rendered for thirty or thirty-five years. If I thought that Brother Duncan could be elected here, I would place his name in nomination, in order that he would have the great honor which it is natural that he or any other man would like to have after serving this great movement as First Vice-President for so many long years. But knowing Duncan as I do and having the love and admiration I have for him, and having learned to respect men who have rendered service, I want to stand here and say that I do not want to see anything done that will humiliate a man who has served us for so many years.

I have not arisen at this time for the purpose of nominating Brother Duncan, for I believe it would be a humiliation to you my friend. I say that in all honesty, sincerity and candor. I do not care to have it said that there was a contest here and a man who served the labor movement for thirty-five years was defeated.

I surrender to no man on this Council the right of greater confidence or greater respect to the man who has been nominated by Mr. Rickert, and if elected I pledge to him my whole hearted cooperation 100 per cent, but in doing so let us not humiliate a man who has served us so long.

Treasurer Tobin:—I desire to second the nomination of Brother Green. There is no more unpleasant position to place a human being, especially men of our type who are thoroughly sentimental and human than to place us between two friends and ask us to choose between the two. As leaders in this movement we have been chosen because we have been found by our membership capable of setting aside sentiment and of exercising our judgment in the interest of those we represent. If we did not possess these qualifications we would not be successful as leaders. In all my years as an officer of my organization I have never been confronted with a more unpleasant position than confronts me this morning. I am asked to choose between love and duty and in seconding the nomination of Brother Green I feel it is a duty because I feel that the labor movement desires a man for the Presidency of the Federation other than my friend Jim Duncan. In the first place it is an unwritten law in the Federation—a declaration was made by John Mitchell that a man who is not in a representative capacity in his own organization should not be continued as a member of the Council. That is not written into the law but the declaration made by Mitchell was almost unanimously applauded in the convention. We have continued men in our Council through love of their service after they have ceased to be active in their own organization.

The man who has been nominated represents the most powerful organization in America and of any other country. In saying his record is clean, open and above board both in political life in which he has held office and in the economic field, it is not a reflection upon the aspirations of any other member of this Council, but I know no man and I know Brother Green since he first became an officer, that holds a higher place in the hearts of men and in the eyes of the public than the individual who has been nominated by Brother Rickert. In fellowship, in palship, perhaps I have been nearer to Duncan than to Green. I think you men and he himself understand my feeling, but I say to you in all sincerity according to my analysis of the movement, it insists that we nominate the representative of the Miners, who has been named here. I wish perhaps that we could divide the honor. I say that in all sincerity but it can not be done. This movement of ours needs closer attention today than ever in its history or at least in my knowledge of its history. We need to build it up with men who are representatives of strong organizations. You might say that has not prevailed, but there was never a time when the workers demand more from you as a Council than they demand at this time.

I do not agree that we are going to elect a President for an indefinite number of years. I say that if Brother Green does not fill the bill, and I am confident that he will, I will be as strongly opposed to him for re-election as I am in sustaining his nomination. I think we ought to put our personal feelings aside; it is hard to do it but we are rugged men and have gone through persecutions innumerable and sometimes indescribable. Men have suggested other men for this honor. There has been more than one mentioned. You men who understand me know that I am not an egoist. Rickert's name has been mentioned, Brother Woll has been mentioned, I have been mentioned. It is not a question of self. I have talked with Rickert and Woll and they have talked with me. It is a great honor, few could refuse to consider it but there is not one of us here who is not big enough to forget himself when he believes the greater good can be accomplished, or he does not come within the high appraisal I have always held for the members of the Council.

I feel that we owe honor and respect to James Duncan who in my opinion has the greatest fund of knowledge and those on this Council have benefited by it for twenty-five years. I also feel that the man coming from the Miners whose name has been suggested, is the man we must consider as the man for this office. I would go perhaps anywhere if it was say between two men, Duncan and myself, to help him, but there are things which I can not always do, things I would like to do. There is a greater power and interest involved than my personal feelings, and those are my reasons for seconding the nomination of Brother Green.

Vice-President Woll: I wish to second the nomination of Mr. Green. I think we are facing a crisis and we have to meet the situation as men and there can be only one way to meet it and that is by selecting a man who can command the confidence and support of the organizations. I take great pleasure in seconding the nomination of Brother Green.

Upon roll call upon the nomination of Vice-President Green the members responded as follows:

Morrison—Green
Duncan—Not voting
Duffy—Green
Green—I ask to be passed.
Rickert—Green
Fischer—Green
Woll—Green
Ryan—Green

Wilson—Green

Tobin—Green

Secretary Morrison: I declare Wm. Green elected to the office of President of the American Federation of Labor for the unexpired term of 1924.

Vice-President Rickert: I desire to place the name of William Green in nomination to fill the ensuing term upon the expiration of the present term, the new term to begin January 1, 1925.

There being no other nominations, the Chair declared them closed.

Vice-President Duffy called the roll:

Morrison—Green

Duncan—Not voting

Duffy—Green

Green—Not voting

Rickert—Green

Fischer—Green

Woll—Green

Ryan—Green

Wilson—Green

Tobin—Green

Secretary Morrison: I herewith declare William Green elected President of the American Federation of Labor for the ensuing term beginning January 1, 1925, and will request the newly elected president to take the chair. In doing so I want to say to President Green that as Secretary of the American Federation of Labor I shall give to him every assistance within my power to carry the great labor movement to a successful issue during the term of office. I feel that there is some splendid and constructive work that can be accomplished during the coming year. I welcome you as President of the American Federation of Labor.

. . .

Resolutions Drafted Pursuant to the Directions of the Executive Council

Whereas, the death of our beloved chief, Samuel Gompers, has ended a leadership of the American labor movement that guided our Federation from its organization through the difficult stages of establishing an authoritative, competent, economic organization truly representative of the wage earners of the United States and Canada; and

Whereas, that leadership has developed in our American Federation of Labor a discipline necessary to the maintenance of voluntary associated effort, an understanding of the principles of voluntarism, an appreciation of the nature of economic power and its competence as a force for human welfare when organized and utilized in furtherance of constructive purposes; and

Whereas, our revered president has for years been the public spokesman for Labor who under all circumstances spoke fearlessly and compelling against exploiting interests, materialistic forces, and existing conventions that sought to subordinate human welfare and the advancement of the common people to special privilege and material progress, and whose personal integrity, great mental ability, magnetic personality and immovable insistence upon rights and opportunities of Labor have secured for our movement an accepted position as a constructive agency; and

Whereas, through his work the standards of working conditions, wages, and labor legislation have been permanently raised and there is now more adequate recognition of the constructive service that can be rendered through the development of collective bargaining with trade unions, and society has come to recognize the far-reaching significance of the implications of human welfare as furthered through trade union organization; and

Whereas, Samuel Gompers devoted his life to advocacy of the gospel of human welfare, and has left Labor as a heritage an appreciation of the permanent results gained through educational methods; a labor philosophy implied in the phrase he coined, "The labor of a human being is not a commodity"; a trade union creed embodied in his conception of voluntary principles as the corner-stone upon which Labor must rest its building; an ideal of national service in his parting prayer for American institutions and a realization of the potent influence of Labor internationally as manifest in the constructive purposes and beneficent achievements of the Pan-American Federation of Labor and in the International Labor Charter of the Versailles Treaty which he helped to formulate and which authorized an international agency to advance and unify standards of labor welfare the world over; therefore, be it

Resolved, that speaking for the wage earners of America we declare our deep and lasting obligation to him who in the early years of our movement suffered personal privations that he might render service to humanity and who because of his faith in the high cause of Labor has given his life as a crusader against injustice and wrongs to humanity and as a prophet declaring the transcendent value of human life and the possibilities of human development. We realize that his leadership was based upon an understanding of permanent values and that his death has revealed the spiritual forces which directed his work and which he fostered and developed in the labor movement. In the great cause of human emancipation the work of Samuel Gompers supplemented that of Abraham Lincoln and established new goals and new ideals of democracy in our common life. The spirit of Samuel Gompers is permanently a part of the world's constructive ideals and forces for human welfare.

William Green
Frank Morrison
Daniel J. Tobin
James Duncan
Frank Duffy
T. A. Rickert
Jacob Fischer
Matthew Woll
Martin F. Ryan
James Wilson
James P. Noonan.
Executive Council   American Federation of Labor.

TDc, Executive Council Records, Minutes, reel 7, frames 1628–33, 1638, *AFL Records.*

1. The AFL Executive Council met in New York City, Dec. 19, 1924.
2. James Adair WILSON was president of the Pattern Makers' League of North America from 1902 to 1934 and an AFL vice-president from 1924 to 1934.
3. The 1925 AFL convention met in Atlantic City, Oct. 5–16.

GLOSSARY

ALPINE, John R. (1863–1947), was born in Maine and worked as a gas fitter in Everett, Mass., and then in Boston, where he was president of United Association of Journeymen Plumbers, Gas Fitters, Steam Fitters, and Steam Fitters' Helpers of the United States and Canada 175 (1904–5) and of the Boston Building Trades Council (1905). Alpine served as special organizer, vice-president (1904–6), and president (1906–19) of the international (in 1913 renamed the United Association of Plumbers and Steam Fitters of the United States and Canada) and as an AFL vice-president (1909–19). During World War I he was appointed to the Cantonment Adjustment Commission that supervised labor relations on military construction jobs. He lived in Chicago from 1906 until 1920, when he moved to New York City, where he was employed by the Grinnell Co. as assistant to the president for labor relations. In 1931 President Herbert Hoover appointed him assistant secretary of labor in charge of the Federal Unemployment Service.

BAINE, Charles L. (b. 1870), was born in Canada and immigrated to the United States with his family in 1880. He settled in Chicago where he worked as a shoe cutter and served as business agent of Boot and Shoe Workers' Union 133. He was elected to the executive board of the Boot and Shoe Workers in 1899 and served as the union's secretary-treasurer from 1902 to 1931.

BAROFF, Abraham (1870–1932), was born in Russia and immigrated to the United States around 1890, obtaining work in the women's garment industry in New York City. He was a leader of the 1909–10 shirtwaist and dressmakers' strike in New York City and was a founder of International Ladies' Garment Workers' Union 25 (Ladies' Waist and Dress Makers) of New York City, serving for several years as its manager. Baroff became a vice-president of the Ladies' Garment Workers and a member of the union's general executive board in 1914, and he served as the union's secretary-treasurer from 1915 until 1929.

BARRETT, James Festus (1882–1959), was born in North Carolina and in 1900 graduated from Washington College in Tennessee. A resident of Asheville, N.C., he served as an AFL volunteer organizer and as president of the Asheville Central Labor Union (1909), president of International Typographical Union 263 of Asheville (1918–19), and president of the North Carolina State Federation of Labor (1921–22). Barrett worked for the *Asheville Citizen* from about 1912 to 1917, when he launched the *Asheville Labor Advocate*. In 1922 he sold his interest in that paper and moved to Charlotte, N.C., where he joined Typographical local 338 and served as managing editor of the *Charlotte Herald* from 1923 until 1925. In the 1930s he edited a county paper in Brevard, N.C., and he subsequently served again as an AFL organizer and as AFL publicity director in the South. He retired in 1949.

BERGER, Victor Luitpold (1860–1929), was born in Nieder-Rehbach, Austria, and attended the universities of Vienna and Budapest before immigrating to the United States in 1878. He lived in Bridgeport, Conn., for two years, working as a boiler mender, metal polisher, and salesman, and then moved to Milwaukee where he taught German in the public school system. In 1892 he resigned and bought the *Milwaukee Volkszeitung*. He changed its name to *Wisconsin Vorwärts* in 1893 and edited the paper (later renamed the *Vorwärts*) until 1911. In 1897 he helped form the Social Democracy of America and in 1898 the Social Democratic Party of the United States, which became the Socialist Party of America in 1901. He served on the party's national executive committee from 1901 until 1923. He edited the weekly *Social Democratic Herald* from 1901 to 1913 and the daily *Milwaukee Leader* from 1911 until his death. In 1910 he was elected alderman-at-large for Milwaukee and later that year was elected a congressman on the Socialist ticket, serving from 1911 to 1913. After his reelection to Congress as a Socialist in 1918, he was found guilty of conspiracy to violate the Espionage Act and sentenced to twenty years imprisonment in early 1919 by Judge Kenesaw Mountain Landis. He was released on bail pending review of the case, but the House of Representatives refused to seat him. Reelected in late 1919, he was again denied his congressional seat. The U.S. Supreme Court overturned Berger's conviction in 1921, and he was elected to Congress on the Socialist ticket again the following year, serving from 1923 to 1929.

BERRES, Albert Julius (1873–1940), a longtime resident of Washington, D.C., served as chairman of the executive council of the District of Columbia branch of the Pattern Makers' League of North America (1906–10) and as a member of the union's executive board (1909–14).

Berres also served as secretary-treasurer of the AFL Metal Trades Department (1908–27), resigning that position to become secretary in charge of industrial affairs for the Motion Picture Producers' Association in Hollywood, Calif.

BERRY, George Leonard (1882–1948), was born in Tennessee. After serving in the Spanish-American War, he took a job as a press feeder for the *St. Louis Globe-Democrat* and joined the International Printing Pressmen's and Assistants' Union of North America in 1899. About 1902 he earned his pressman's card and moved to San Francisco, where he was an active member of Printing Pressmen's local 24, serving as its president (1906) and then as business agent. Berry was president of the international from 1907 until his death, moving to union headquarters in Cincinnati in 1907 and then to Rogersville, Tenn., in 1911. He served in the army during World War I, taking a leave of absence from his union responsibilities, and in 1921 helped organize the American Legion. He later served as an AFL vice-president (1935) and as a Democratic U.S. senator from Tennessee (1937–38).

BOWEN, William J. (1868–1948), was born and attended grammar school in Albany, N.Y., and at the age of thirteen apprenticed there as a bricklayer. In 1890 he joined Bricklayers' and Masons' International Union of America 6 of Albany, serving over the following years as its business manager and president. Bowen also served as a vice-president (1901–4) and president (1904–28) of the international (in 1910 renamed the Bricklayers', Masons', and Plasterers' International Union of America).

BURKE, John P. (1884–1966), was born on a farm near North Duxbury, Vt., moved with his family to Franklin, N.H., when he was twelve, and went to work in a hosiery mill there at the age of thirteen. Within a few years he began working at the Franklin plant of the International Paper Co., and in 1905 he joined the pulp and sulphite workers' local of the International Brotherhood of Paper Makers, Pulp, Sulphite, and Paper Mill Workers at Franklin. The next year, when pulp and sulphite workers seceded from the Paper Makers to form the International Brotherhood of Pulp, Sulphite, and Paper Mill Workers, he became a member of that union's local 9 in Franklin. Burke was a vice-president of the New Hampshire State Federation of Labor (1914–16?), was the Socialist candidate for governor of New Hampshire in 1914, and served as a vice-president (1914–17) and president-secretary (1917–65) of the Pulp and Sulphite Workers, moving to the union's headquarters at Ft. Edward, N.Y., upon becoming its president.

CARTER, William Samuel (1859–1923), a native of Austin, Tex., worked as a railroad baggageman, fireman, and engineer from 1879 to 1894. He edited the official journal of the Brotherhood of Locomotive Firemen (1894–1904) and later served the union (in 1906 renamed the Brotherhood of Locomotive Firemen and Enginemen) as secretary and treasurer (1904–9) and president (1909–22). From 1918 to 1920, he took a leave of absence from the union's presidency to direct the Division of Labor of the U.S. Railroad Administration.

CHLOPEK, Anthony John (1880–1937), was born in Toledo, Ohio, where he began working as a longshoreman at the age of fifteen and joined International Longshoremen's Association 151 of Toledo at the age of nineteen. He also worked as a conductor, as an inspector for the city's Bureau of Public Service, as a food inspector, and as an assistant state fire marshal before becoming a union officer. Chlopek served the international as vice-president (1909–21), president (1921–27), and legislative representative (1927–31).

COEFIELD, John (1869–1940), was born in Franklin, Pa., and apprenticed as a plumber after attending high school. He worked in a number of cities and then settled in San Francisco, where he joined the Plumbers', Gas Fitters', and Steam Fitters' Association, an independent union that in 1903 affiliated with the United Association of Journeymen Plumbers, Gas Fitters, Steam Fitters, and Steam Fitters' Helpers of the United States and Canada as local 442. From about 1907 to 1919 he was the business agent for the San Francisco Building Trades Council and a vice-president of the California Building Trades Council. Coefield served as vice-president (1911–19) and president (1919–40) of the international (in 1913 renamed the United Association of Plumbers and Steam Fitters of the United States and Canada, and in 1921 renamed the United Association of Journeymen Plumbers and Steam Fitters of the United States and Canada). He also served as vice-president of the AFL Metal Trades Department (1920–39) and as an AFL vice-president (1929–40). He moved in 1920 to Chicago, where the international's headquarters were located, and then in 1929 to Washington, D.C., when the union's headquarters were relocated to that city.

CONBOY, Sara Agnes McLaughlin (1870–1928), was born in Boston. A candy worker by age eleven, she later worked in a button mill and then in a carpet mill, where she became a highly skilled weaver. Conboy was a young widow working in Roxbury, Mass., in 1909 when she successfully led a strike that resulted in the organization of the carpet weavers in that city and her appointment as a United Textile Workers of America organizer (1910–15?). She subsequently served the Textile Workers as acting secretary (1915) and secretary-treasurer (1915–28), moving to Brooklyn where the union's offices were located. She was also a vice-president of the National Women's Trade Union League (1911–13) and an AFL salaried organizer for women (1914–15). During World War I she served on the subcommittee on Women in Industry of the Committee on Labor of the Advisory Commission of the Council of National Defense.

COULTER, Clarence Castrow (1882–1948), was born in Venango County, Pa., and by 1900 had moved to Washington, D.C., where he worked as a shoe salesman and joined Retail Clerks' International Protective Association 262. He was business representative of the local (1916–25) and a vice-president of the Maryland State and District of Columbia Federation of Labor (1916–26), and he served the international as vice-president (1916–25), president (1925–26), and secretary-treasurer (1926–47). After he was elected union president in 1925, he moved to Lafayette, Ind., where the international had its headquarters.

CRAMP, Concemore Thomas Thwaites "Charlie" (1876–1933), was born at Staplehurst, Kent, England. He left school at the age of twelve and when he was twenty moved to the West Riding to work for the Midland Railway. Employed first as a platform porter and then as a passenger guard, Cramp joined the Amalgamated Society of Railway Servants and served on its executive council (1911–13). Active as well in the National Union of Railwaymen, successor to the Amalgamated, he served on its executive council (1913–16) and as its president (1917–19), industrial general secretary (1920–31), and general secretary (1931–33). Cramp was also a member of the national executive board of the Labour party (1919–29) and the general council of the TUC (1929–33).

DAVISON, Emmett C. (1878–1944), was born in Chesterfield County, Va., attended school in Richmond, and served in the Spanish-American War. After completing his apprenticeship, he joined International Association of Machinists 10 of Richmond, becoming its business agent around 1910. Davison served as secretary-treasurer (1911–12) and president (1912–15) of the Virginia State Federation of Labor and as organizer (1913–17) and secretary-treasurer (1917–44) of the Machinists. Around 1923 he moved to Alexandria, where he served as a member of the city council (1932–34) and mayor (1934–37).

DOBSON, William (1864?–1953?), was born in England where he became a bricklayer. He emigrated in the 1880s, living first in Toronto and then in Buffalo, where he was secretary (1893) of Bricklayers' and Masons' International Union of America 36. In 1895 he moved to North Adams, Mass., where he served as corresponding secretary (1896–1901) of Bricklayers' and Masons' local 18. Dobson served as secretary (1900–1925) of the international (in 1910 renamed the Bricklayers', Masons', and Plasterers' International Union of America), moving with the union headquarters to Indianapolis in 1905. After leaving union office, he remained in Indianapolis, working as vice-president of the United Labor Bank and Trust Co. until 1934.

DONLIN, John H. (1868–1952), was born in Illinois. He worked as a plasterer in Chicago and was a founding member of Operative Plasterers' International Association of the United States and Canada 5 of Chicago. In 1908 he became president of the international, serving until 1912. Donlin was president of the AFL Building Trades Department (1916–24) and served on the Committee on Emergency Construction of the War Industries Board during World War I. From 1927 until his death he was editor of *The Plasterer,* the international union's official publication.

DRAPER, Patrick Martin (1867?–1943), was born in Aylmer, Que. At the age of fifteen he began working at the Government Printing Bureau in Ottawa, where he joined International Typographical Union 102 in 1887; when he retired in 1933 he was superintendent of the bureau. He served his local as president (intermittently between 1893 and 1942) and was an organizer for the international in 1900 and 1901. Draper also served as secretary-treasurer (1900–1935) and president (1935–39) of the Trades and Labor Congress of Canada.

DUFFY, Frank (1861–1955), was born in County Monaghan, Ireland. At the age of two he immigrated with his family to England, and in 1881 he came to the United States, settling in New York City. There he joined United Order of American Carpenters and Joiners 2 and served as the first president of the order's executive council for Greater New York. In 1888, when the order merged with the Brotherhood of Carpenters and Joiners of America to form the United Brotherhood of Carpenters and Joiners of America, Duffy became a member of Carpenters' local 478. He served as president of the local's executive council (1888–1901) and as its business agent (1896–98), and for four terms he was financial secretary of the brotherhood's New York district council. He was an organizer for the Carpenters in 1896 and four years later was elected to the union's executive board. Duffy served the brotherhood as secretary-treasurer (1901–2), secretary (1903–48), and editor of the union's official journal (1901–41). He moved to Philadelphia in 1901 and then to Indianapolis in 1902 when the union changed the location of its headquarters. Duffy served as an AFL vice-president from 1914 to 1939. He was also a board member of the National Society for the Promotion of Industrial Education (1912–20), served on the Indiana State Board of Education (1915–19), and was a member of the American labor mission to the 1919 Paris peace conference.

DUNCAN, James (1857–1928), was born in Scotland and immigrated to the United States in 1880. He joined the Granite Cutters' National Union of the United States of America in 1881 and during the early 1880s served as an officer of the union's locals in New York, Philadelphia, Richmond, and, finally, Baltimore, where he settled in 1884. He was Maryland state organizer for the Granite Cutters, organizer for the AFL, and president of the Baltimore Federation of Labor (1890–92, 1897). Duncan served the Granite Cutters (in 1905 renamed the Granite Cutters' International Association of America) as secretary (1895–1905), secretary-treasurer (1905–12), and president (1912–23) and edited the union's official journal from 1895 to 1928. He was an AFL vice-president (1895–1928) and acting president of the Federation during President John McBride's illness in 1895. He was also a member of the National Civic Federation Industrial Department (1901–2) and executive committee (1903 to at least 1923). President Woodrow Wilson appointed him a member of the Root mission to Russia in 1917, and he also served as a member of the American labor mission to the 1919 Paris peace conference.

DYCHE, John Alexander (1867–1938), was born in Kovno, Lithuania; he immigrated to England in 1887 and then to the United States in 1901. He worked as a skirt maker in New York City and joined the International Ladies' Garment Workers' Union first as a member of a sub-local of local 1 (Cloak Operators) and then local 23 (Skirt Makers). Dyche was appointed secretary-treasurer of the international in 1904, retaining that position until 1914 when he retired, and he edited its official journal from 1910 to 1914. He later opened a small business in the industry, and in 1926 published *Bolshevism in American Labor Unions,* an anticommunist tract.

EASLEY, Ralph Montgomery (1856–1939), was born in Browning, Pa., founded a daily newspaper in Hutchinson, Kans., and then moved to Chicago to work as a reporter and columnist for the *Chicago Inter*

Ocean. In 1893 he helped organize the Chicago Civic Federation, leaving the *Inter Ocean* to serve as the federation's secretary. He resigned from that position in 1900 and moved to New York City to organize the National Civic Federation, bringing together prominent representatives of business, labor, and the public in cooperative reform efforts and in the settlement of labor disputes. Easley served as secretary of the National Civic Federation (1900–1903) and as chairman of its executive council (1904–39). In his later years he increasingly devoted himself to opposing radical labor organizations and social movements.

FISCHER, Jacob (1871–1936), was born in Osborne, Ohio, and at the age of sixteen moved to Indianapolis. He served the Journeymen Barbers' International Union of America as a vice-president (1894–98), president (1898–1902), organizer (1902–4), and secretary-treasurer (1904–29). Fischer was also an AFL vice-president (1918–29) and a vice-president of the AFL Union Label Trades Department.

FITZGERALD, Edward H. (1877–1961), was born in Rochester, Minn., began working as a railroad clerk around 1898, and in 1912 moved to Los Angeles. In 1918 he organized Brotherhood of Railway Clerks 602 there, and he served as the local's first president (1918–19). In 1919 FitzGerald was elected grand vice-president of the Brotherhood (renamed that year as the Brotherhood of Railway and Steamship Clerks, Freight Handlers, Express and Station Employes), and in 1920 he became president of the brotherhood and moved to union headquarters in Cincinnati. In 1924 and 1925 he served as a member of the national committee of the Conference for Progressive Political Action. After retiring from union office in 1928, he returned to California, settling in Glendale. In 1931 he was appointed a commissioner of the Conciliation Service of the U.S. Department of Labor, a position he held until 1948.

FITZPATRICK, John J. (1871?–1946), was born in Athlone, Ireland, and was brought to Chicago by his uncle after the death of his parents. He worked in the Chicago stockyards and in a brass foundry and then took up horseshoeing and blacksmithing. In 1886 he joined Journeymen Horseshoers' National Union of the United States 4 and over the years served as the local's vice-president, treasurer, business agent, and president. Around 1921, after the local broke with the Chicago Federation of Labor (FOL), he joined International Brotherhood of Blacksmiths, Drop Forgers, and Helpers 122. Fitzpatrick served as an executive committee member (1899–1900), organizer (1902–4?), and president (1900–1901, 1906–46) of the Chicago FOL and as an AFL salaried organizer (1903–23). He played a major role in the 1917 meatpackers' organizing campaign and the steelworkers' organizing campaign of 1918–20, ran unsuccessfully for mayor of Chicago on the Labor party ticket in 1919, and served on the National Recovery Administration Regional Labor Board (1933–35).

FLOOD, Emmet T. (1874–1942), was born in Illinois and worked as a teamster in Chicago, where he joined International Brotherhood of Teamsters 715 (Department Store Drivers). He served as an AFL salaried organizer from 1904 to 1925, organizing, among others, a nurses' and attendants' union in Illinois state hospitals. Flood retired from the labor movement after SG's death and worked in the trucking business.

FORRESTER, James Joseph (1867–1939), was born in Ohio. The son of a farmer, he taught school to put himself through college and was admitted to the bar in 1888. He was employed as a letter carrier in the 1890s and then took a job as a railway clerk. Forrester served the Brotherhood of Railway Clerks (in 1919 renamed the Brotherhood of Railway and Steamship Clerks, Freight Handlers, Express and Station Employes) as organizer (1907–8), deputy grand president (1908–10), vice-grand president (1910–15), and grand president (1915–20). He was later a member of the U.S. Railroad Labor Board (1920–21), the brotherhood's vice-grand president for legislative matters (1921), and its national legislative counsel (1922–25). From 1925 to 1928 he served as president of the rival American Federation of Express Workers. A resident of Washington, D.C., he later worked as a special investigator for the immigration bureau of the U.S. Department of Labor (1931–33) and as a researcher and statistical expert for various government agencies until he retired in 1937.

FOSTER, William Z. (1881–1961), born in Taunton, Mass., was a member of the Socialist Party of America from 1901 to 1909, joined the United Wage Workers' Party of Washington in 1909, and became a member of the IWW in 1910, participating in the Spokane free-speech campaign. He then traveled to Europe, where he became a convert to the strategy of "boring from within" existing trade unions. After unsuccessfully contesting the AFL's right to represent the American labor movement at the 1911 meeting of the International Secretariat in Budapest, he returned to the United States and settled in Chicago. He left the IWW in 1912, joined the Brotherhood of Railway Carmen of America, and subsequently organized the Syndicalist League of North America and the International Trade Union Educational League. Between 1917 and 1919 he led AFL organizing campaigns in the packinghouse and steel industries, and in 1920 he founded the Trade Union Educational League. The following year he went to Moscow and, upon his return, joined the American Communist party. He was the party's candidate for president in 1924, 1928, and 1932 and served as the party's longtime chairman (1930?–44, 1945–57) and chairman emeritus (1957–61). He died in Moscow, where he had gone for medical care.

FRANKLIN, Joseph Anthony (1868–1948), was born in Sedalia, Mo., and took up the boilermaking trade in 1892. A charter member of Brotherhood of Boiler Makers and Iron Ship Builders of America 221 of Pittsburg, Kans., he served the Boiler Makers (in 1906 renamed the International Brotherhood of Boiler Makers, Iron Ship Builders, and Helpers of America) as vice-president (1906–8) and president (1908–44). From 1922 to 1925 he was a member of the general or national committee of the Conference for Progressive Political Action.

FRAYNE, Hugh (1869–1934), was born in Scranton, Pa., and began working as a breaker boy in the mines when he was eight. He later became a sheet metal worker and was a charter member of Amalgamated Sheet Metal Workers' International Association 86 of Scranton. From 1901 to 1902 and again from 1904 to 1905 he served as a vice-president of the international (in 1903 renamed the Amalgamated Sheet Metal Workers' International Alliance). Frayne was an AFL salaried organizer from 1902 until his death, and beginning in 1910 he was in charge of the AFL's New York City office. During World War I, he chaired the labor division of the War Industries Board.

FREY, John Philip (1871–1957), was born in Mankato, Minn., and moved to Montreal in 1878, where he lived until the age of fourteen. He worked in a Montreal printing shop and on a farm and lumber camp in Upper Ontario before moving with his family to Worcester, Mass., in 1887. After finding work first as an errand boy and then in a grocery, he apprenticed as a molder. In 1896 he helped organize Iron Molders' Union of North America 5, serving as the local's president until 1900 and as vice-president of the Molders from 1900 to 1903. Frey moved to Bellevue, Ky., in 1903 after he was appointed editor of the union's official journal, which was published in Cincinnati, and about 1909 moved to Norwood, Ohio. He served as editor of the journal until 1927 and was president of the Ohio State Federation of Labor from 1924 to 1928. Frey moved to Washington, D.C., to serve as secretary-treasurer (1927–34) and president (1934–50) of the AFL Metal Trades Department.

FURUSETH, Andrew (1854–1938), was born in Furuseth, Norway, and went to sea in 1873. He immigrated to California in 1880, making his home in San Francisco, and in 1885 he joined the Coast Seamen's Union, serving as secretary from 1887 to 1889. He later served as secretary of the Sailors' Union of the Pacific (1891–92, 1892–1936) and president of the International Seamen's Union of America (1897–99, 1908–38) and was a legislative representative in Washington, D.C., for the AFL (1895–1902) and for the Seamen.

GILLMORE, Frank P. (1867–1943), was born in New York City and educated in England before launching a career as an actor. A founder of the Actors' Equity Association in 1913, he served as its executive secretary (1918–28) and president (1929–37). Gillmore was also a founder of the Associated Actors and Artistes of America, an umbrella organization for performing arts unions, serving as its president from 1928 until his death.

GOMPERS, Alexander Julian (1878–1947), was a son of SG and Sophia Julian Gompers. He was a cigarmaker and cigar manufacturer in New York City and in Washington, D.C. From 1914 to 1947 he served as an official of the New York State Department of Labor. He and his wife, Ella Appelbaum Gompers, had three children: Esther, Sophia, and May.

GOMPERS, Gertrude Annersly Gleaves (1881–1953), SG's second wife, was born in Staffordshire, England, immigrated with her family to Trenton, N.J., in 1895, and by 1905 was working as a piano teacher in Philadelphia. She married Louis Neuscheler (b. 1868), a furniture dealer, and by 1920 the two were living in New York City. After divorcing Neuscheler in 1921, she married SG and moved to Washington, D.C. She returned to New York City in 1925 after SG's death and resumed teaching piano. She was later employed by the Works Progress Administration and, in 1940, worked as an organizer for the Five and Ten Cent Store Committee of the United Retail and Wholesale Employes.

GOMPERS, Henry Julian (1874–1938), a son of SG and Sophia Julian Gompers, was the AFL's first office boy (1887) and later became a granite cutter. About 1914 he moved from New York City to Washington, D.C., where he ran Gompers' Monumental Works. He and his wife, Bessie Phillips Gompers, had four children: Sophia, Samuel, Alexander, and Louis.

GOMPERS, Sadie Julian (variously Julia; 1883–1918), the youngest child of SG and Sophia Julian Gompers, was born in New York City. After the family's move to Washington, D.C., she studied voice and then for a time sang in vaudeville and on the concert stage. She died in the World War I influenza epidemic.

GOMPERS, Samuel Julian (1868–1946), was a son of SG and Sophia Julian Gompers. Born in New York City, he left school at the age of fourteen to work in a New York City print shop. He moved to Washington, D.C., about 1887 and worked as a printer in the Government Printing Office, a compositor in the U.S. Department of Commerce and Labor, and a clerk in the U.S. Census Office. He was a member of the Association of Union Printers and the Columbia Typographical Union (International Typographical Union 101). In 1913 he became chief of the Division of Publications and Supplies of the U.S. Department of Labor, and in 1918 he became chief clerk of the Department of Labor, a position he held until 1941. Gompers and his wife, Sophia Dampf Gompers, had one child, Florence.

GOMPERS, Samuel Moses (Salomon Mozes; 1803?–81), SG's paternal grandfather, was born in Amsterdam. Originally a calico printer, he later became an import-export merchant. He married Henrietta Haring, and they had six children: Solomon, Fannie, Clara, Kate, Sarah, and Simon. In 1845 he immigrated to London, and about 1869 came to the United States, returning to London in 1876.

GOMPERS, Sophia Julian (1850–1920), SG's first wife, was born in London and immigrated to the United States about 1855. She was living with her father and stepmother in Brooklyn and working as a tobacco stripper in a cigar factory when she married SG in 1867. Between 1868 and 1885 she and SG had at least nine children, six of whom lived past infancy: Samuel, Rose, Henry, Abraham, Alexander, and Sadie.

GRASSMANN, Peter Ottmar (1873–1939), was born in Munich and at age thirteen went to work as a typesetter. He joined the printers' union in 1891, and from 1908 to 1919 served as its vice-president. From 1919 to 1933 he served as vice-chairman of the Allgemeiner Deutscher Gewerkschaftsbund (General German Federation of Trade Unions), and from 1920 he was a member of the general council of the International Federation of Trade Unions. From 1924 to 1933 Grassmann was a delegate to the Reichstag (Sozialdemokratische Partei Deutschlands [Social Democratic Party of Germany]). He was arrested and imprisoned in May 1933 following the Nazi suppression of the Gewerkschaftsbund.

GREEN, William (1870–1952), was born in Coshocton, Ohio. He left school after the eighth grade and at the age of fourteen became a water boy for track layers on the Wheeling Railroad. At sixteen he joined his father in the coal mines. In 1888 he joined the local chapter of the National Progressive Union of Miners and Mine Laborers, which later became local 379 of the United Mine Workers of America. Green held various offices in his local including secretary, business agent, vice-president, and president, and he served as president of subdistrict 6 of United Mine Workers' District 6 (Ohio; 1900–1906), as president of District 6 (1906–10), and as statistician (1911–13) and secretary-treasurer (1913–24) of the international union. In 1910 and again in 1912 he was elected as a Democrat to the Ohio senate. In 1914 Green became a member of the AFL Executive Council and, after SG's death in December 1924, became AFL president, an office he held until his death.

GREENE, Michael F. (1884–1951), was born in County Clare, Ireland, and immigrated to Connecticut in 1887. After leaving school at the age of thirteen, he worked at various jobs before apprenticing in 1901 as a hatter in Danbury, Conn., and then joining United Hatters of North America 17 of Danbury in 1904. He then worked as an itinerant hatter in Wabash, Ind., Orange, N.J., St. Louis, and Norwalk, Conn., among other places, but by 1907 had returned to Danbury, where he served as president (1910–12) and secretary-treasurer (1912–18) of local 17. Greene was president of the Hatters from 1918 to 1934, and then served as president (1934–36) and secretary (1936–49) of the United Hatters, Cap, and Millinery Workers' International Union, which was formed in 1934 by the merger of the Hatters and the Cloth Hat, Cap, and Millinery Workers' International Union.

GREENSTEIN, Abraham (b. 1878), was born in Russia and immigrated to the United States in 1908. A charter member of the International Jewelry Workers' Union, he served as the union's secretary-treasurer from 1916 to 1923 as well as editor of its official journal, the *Jewelry Workers' Monthly Bulletin*. After dissatisfaction with his leadership forced Greenstein out of office, he made his living as a diamond merchant in New York City.

GUARD, Rosa Lee (1863?–1937), was born near Charlottesville, Va., and began working as a schoolteacher at the age of fifteen. She moved to Washington, D.C., around 1897 and the next year began working as a typist at AFL headquarters, where she became chief clerk and SG's private secretary. After SG died she served until her own death as chief clerk to his successor, William Green.

HARRIS, Daniel (1846–1915), a Civil War veteran and cigarmaker, was born in England and immigrated to the United States in the early 1860s. During the 1877–78 cigarmakers' strike the Central Organization of the Cigarmakers of New York appointed Harris to its Committee on Organization for Pennsylvania. In the late 1880s Harris was president of Cigar Makers' International Union of America 144 of New York City. He served as president (1892–98) of the New York State Workingmen's Assembly, vice-president (1898) and president (1899, 1906–10) of the Workingmen's Federation of the State of New York, and president (1910–15) of the New York State Federation of Labor.

HAYES, Max Sebastian (1866–1945), was born near Havana, Ohio, and apprenticed as a printer at the age of thirteen. Moving to Cleveland in 1883, he joined International Typographical Union 53 in 1884 and served as an organizer for the international for the next fifteen years. A founder of the *Cleveland Citizen* in 1891, Hayes worked as the paper's associate editor (1892–94) and editor (1894–1939). He was active in the Cleveland labor movement as corresponding secretary (1896–97) and recording secretary (1898–1901) of the Cleveland Central Labor Union, recording secretary (1902–3) of the United Trades and Labor Council, and recording secretary (1910) of the Cleveland Federation of Labor. Politically, Hayes worked in the People's party campaign in 1896, was active in the Socialist Labor party from 1896 to 1899, and was a founder of the Socialist Party of America in 1901. In 1919 he chaired the executive committee of the National Labor party (in 1920 renamed the Farmer-Labor party), and in 1920 he was the party's vice-presidential candidate. Hayes was a charter member of the Cleveland Metropolitan Housing Authority in 1933, and from 1933 to 1935 he served on the Ohio State Adjustment Board of the National Recovery Administration.

HAYS, John W. (1860–1931), was born in Canada and immigrated to the United States in 1863. He entered the printers' trade in 1878 and joined International Typographical Union 186 of Fargo, N.Dak., in 1882. By 1884 he was living in Minneapolis, where he joined Typographical local 42; he served as its president intermittently between

1897 and 1904. He served the international as district organizer (1898–1904), vice-president (1904–9), and secretary-treasurer (1909–28), and was president of the AFL Union Label Trades Department (1916–28). After his retirement, Hays moved to the state of Washington for a short time but then returned to Minneapolis, where he remained active in the trade union movement.

HEALY, Timothy (1863–1930), was born in County Cork, Ireland, and immigrated to New York City in 1888. A leader of the Eccentric Firemen of New York City, Healy brought that independent union into the International Brotherhood of Stationary Firemen in 1900 as local 56 and remained its longtime leader. He served the Stationary Firemen as vice-president (1902–3) and president (1903–27). Healy organized the engineering department of the New York naval militia during the Spanish-American War and served as deputy sheriff of New York County (1903–4) and as coroner for the Borough of Manhattan (1913–18). He was a member of the National Civic Federation executive committee from 1907 to at least 1923.

HESKETH, Robert Bruce (1870–1939), was born in Lancashire, England, where his father was a mine engineer. After working as a miner and then as a compositor, Hesketh immigrated to the United States in 1888 or 1889 and settled in Seattle, where he worked as a cook. He joined Cooks' and Waiters' Union 1 in 1889, and from 1901 to 1904 and again from 1905 to 1907 he served as secretary and business agent of Hotel and Restaurant Employees' International Alliance and Bartenders' International League of America 239 (Cooks and Waiters). He transferred his membership in 1907 to Hotel and Restaurant Employees 33 (Cooks and Assistants), when that union was chartered, and he served as the local's business agent from 1907 to 1911. He was president of the Western Central Labor Union of Seattle in 1902 and 1903 and in 1904 was elected vice-president of the international, a position he held until 1928. Active in state and local politics, Hesketh served on the Seattle city council from 1911 to 1928, when he resigned to become secretary-treasurer of the Hotel and Restaurant Employees, a position he held for the rest of his life. After moving to union headquarters in Cincinnati, he also served as editor of the *Mixer and Server* (after October 1929, the *Catering Industry Employee*).

HILFERS, Henry F. (1862–1932), was born in Germany and immigrated to the United States in 1865. He became a cigarmaker in Newark, N.J., during the late 1880s and served as secretary of Cigar Makers' International Union of America 138 of Newark from 1897 to 1927.

Hilfers also served as secretary of the Essex Trades Council (1907–29) and the New Jersey State Federation of Labor (1909–26) and was an AFL salaried organizer (1912, 1917 to at least 1924). He was later president of the Labor National Bank of Newark (1927–29) and the Union National Bank of Newark (1930–31).

HILLQUIT, Morris (1869–1933), was born in Riga, Latvia, and immigrated to the United States with his family in 1886, settling in New York City. He joined the Socialist Labor party and was a member of the faction that broke with Daniel DeLeon's leadership in 1899. Two years later he participated in the formation of the Socialist Party of America. Hillquit emerged as a leading figure in the Socialist party and served as a member of its national executive committee (1907–12, 1916–19, 1922–33) and as party chairman (1929–33).

In 1888 Hillquit helped found the United Hebrew Trades and was its first corresponding secretary. He graduated from the law school of the University of the City of New York (now New York University) in 1893 and subsequently developed a successful law practice that included serving as counsel to the International Ladies' Garment Workers' Union from 1914 to 1933. He was also a director, trustee, and lecturer at the Rand School and the author of a number of works on socialism. Hillquit twice ran unsuccessfully on the Socialist party ticket for mayor of New York City (1917, 1932) and was five times a candidate for the U.S. House of Representatives (1906, 1908, 1916, 1918, 1920). From 1922 to 1925 he was a member of the general or national committee of the Conference for Progressive Political Action.

HOLDER, Arthur E. (1860–1937), was born in Wales and apprenticed as a machinist in England, where he joined the Amalgamated Society of Engineers in 1875. After immigrating to the United States, he settled in Sioux City, Iowa, where he joined KOL Local Assembly 212 in 1883 and International Association of Machinists 178 in 1894. Employed in the railroad shops and as an organizer, Holder moved to Des Moines in 1900 after he was appointed deputy commissioner of the Iowa Bureau of Labor Statistics, serving from 1900 to 1903. He was elected president of the Iowa State Federation of Labor in 1901 and served until 1903. In 1904 Holder moved to Washington, D.C., where he was associate editor of the *Machinists' Monthly Journal* until 1906 and served on the AFL Legislative Committee from 1906 to 1917. He also served as an AFL salaried organizer (1902–3, 1907–9, 1912). From 1917 to 1921 Holder was labor representative on the Federal Board for Vocational Education, from 1921 to 1923 he was chief of the legislative division of the People's Legislative Service, and from

1922 to 1925 he served as secretary of the Conference for Progressive Political Action. After working for a time for the U.S. Department of Labor, he retired to Florida in 1931.

HOLLAND, James P. (1865–1941), was born in New Jersey and grew up in New York City. The longtime business agent of local 56 (Eccentric Firemen) of the International Brotherhood of Stationary Firemen, he also served as vice-president (1907–15) and president (1915–26) of the New York State Federation of Labor (to 1910, the Workingmen's Federation of the State of New York) and was a member of the New York City Board of Standards and Appeals (1918–25, 1926–34).

HUDDELL, Arthur McIntire (1869–1931), was born in Danvers, Mass., and worked as a coal-hoisting engineer before going into the building trades. A resident of Chelsea, Mass., and, from 1898, a member of International Union of Steam Engineers 4 (Hoisting and Portable Engineers) of Boston, he served his local as president and business agent and also served as president of the Boston Central Labor Union (1906–7) and business agent for its building trades section (1909–14). Huddell also played an active role in the international (in 1912 renamed the International Union of Steam and Operating Engineers), serving as its vice-president (1905–10, 1916–21) and president (1921–31). He was a vice-president of the AFL Building Trades Department from 1921 to 1931.

HUTCHESON, William Levi (1874–1953), was born near Saginaw, Mich., and became a shipyard carpenter's apprentice at age fourteen. He subsequently worked as a dairy farmer, a farm laborer, a well digger, and a miner before finding employment as a carpenter in Midland, Mich., where he helped organize and served as president of United Brotherhood of Carpenters and Joiners of America 1164. Soon fired for his union activities, Hutcheson returned to Saginaw, becoming a member of Carpenters' local 334 and serving as its business agent for several years. He was vice-president (1913–15) and president (1915–52) of the Carpenters and a member of the War Labor Conference Board (1918) and the National War Labor Board (1918–19). Hutcheson became an AFL vice-president in 1935 but resigned the following year; reelected vice-president in 1939, he held that position from 1940 until 1953.

IGLESIAS Pantín, Santiago (1872–1939), was born in La Coruña, Spain, where he attended local schools and in 1884 apprenticed as a cabinetmaker. After working briefly in Cuba he returned to Spain in 1886. In 1888 he moved to Havana, where he took part in the independence movement led by José Martí, served as secretary of the Círculo de Trabajadores (Workmen's Circle) from 1888 to 1895, and edited the newspaper *La Alarma* in 1895. He fled to Puerto Rico in 1896 following the suppression of the Cuban labor movement and Gen. Valeriano Weyler's order for his arrest. In Puerto Rico he was a founder and editor of several labor journals including *Ensayo Obrero* (1897–98), *El Porvenir Social* (1898–1900), *Unión Obrera* (1902–6), and *Justicia* (1914–25). In 1899 he helped organize the Federación Libre de los Trabajadores de Puerto Rico (Free Federation of the Workers of Puerto Rico), serving as its president from 1900 to 1933. He was also a founder in 1899 of the Partido Obrero Socialista de Puerto Rico (Socialist Labor Party of Puerto Rico), reorganized in 1915 as the Partido Socialista de Puerto Rico (Socialist Party of Puerto Rico). Iglesias moved to Brooklyn in 1900 and joined United Brotherhood of Carpenters and Joiners of America 309. He returned to Puerto Rico the next year as an AFL salaried organizer for Puerto Rico and Cuba, a post he held until 1933. He also served as a Partido Socialista member of the Puerto Rican senate (1917–33), secretary of the Pan-American Federation of Labor (1925–33), and Coalitionist resident commissioner from Puerto Rico in the U.S. House of Representatives (1933–39).

JAMES, Newton A. (1874–1933), was born in Sharpsburg, Md., and moved to the Maryland suburbs of Washington, D.C., as a young man. Joining local 63 (Washington, D.C.) of the International Brotherhood of Stationary Firemen, he served for many years as the local's secretary and business agent. From 1907 to 1919 and again from 1930 to 1933 he served as a vice-president of the international (in 1917 renamed the International Brotherhood of Stationary Firemen and Oilers, and in 1919 renamed the International Brotherhood of Firemen and Oilers). James was also financial secretary (1912?–13, 1925–33), secretary (1917–19, 1923), and president (1914–15, 1916, 1921) of the Washington, D.C., Central Labor Union and secretary (1917–21) and a vice-president (1922–33) of the Maryland State and District of Columbia Federation of Labor.

JEWELL, Bert Mark (1881–1968), was born in Brock, Nebr., and attended school in Omaha and Ocala, Fla. He worked at a variety of jobs on farms and in sawmills, phosphate mines, and machine shops before becoming an apprentice boilermaker in 1900 in High Springs, Fla. In 1905 he joined the Brotherhood of Boiler Makers and Iron Ship Builders of America, and he served the brotherhood (in 1906 renamed the International Brotherhood of Boiler Makers, Iron Ship Builders, and Helpers of America) as general chair of the Seaboard

Air Line Railroad (1912–16) and as an organizer (1916–18). He was president of the Jacksonville Central Trades and Labor Council in 1914. Appointed acting president of the AFL Railway Employes' Department in 1918, Jewell became president in his own right in 1922, serving until 1946. From 1948 to 1952 he was a labor adviser to the U.S. Economic Cooperation Administration, which administered the Marshall Plan, and in 1955 he moved to Kansas City, Kans., to become an adviser to the Boiler Makers. He held that post until his death.

JOHNSTON, William Hugh (1874–1937), was born in Nova Scotia and immigrated to the United States in 1885. He settled in Rhode Island, where he apprenticed at a locomotive works, joined the KOL, and, in 1895, helped organize International Association of Machinists 379 in Pawtucket. He later moved to Providence, where he served as president (1901) and business agent (1906–8) of Machinists' local 147. He was also president of Machinists' District 19 (New England; 1905) and president and general organizer of Machinists' District 44 (Navy Yards and Arsenals; 1909–11). He moved to Washington, D.C., around 1910, where he joined Machinists' local 174. Johnston served as president of the international from 1912 to 1926 and as a member of the National War Labor Board from 1918 to 1919. In February 1922 he helped organize the Conference for Progressive Political Action (CPPA), and he served as the organization's chairman until its dissolution in February 1925. He was also a member of the CPPA joint executive committee created to direct the La Follette-Wheeler campaign in 1924. He resigned his union office following a stroke but later served as vice-president of the Mount Vernon Savings Bank and then returned to work at Machinists' headquarters in Washington, D.C.

JONES, Jerome (1855–1940), was born in Nashville, where he worked as a reporter, printer, and editor for several newspapers, including the *Nashville Herald*, the *Nashville Sun*, and the *Journal of Labor*. He joined the International Typographical Union in 1876 and later served as president of the Nashville Federation of Trades and, from the early 1890s, as an AFL organizer. In 1898 he established the *Journal of Labor* in Atlanta, serving as its editor until 1940. He was active in Typographical local 48 in Atlanta and helped organize the Georgia Federation of Labor in 1899, serving two terms (1904–5, 1911–12) as its president. He was also a founder of the Southern Labor Congress in 1912 and its president until its demise in 1919.

JONES, Mary Harris "Mother" (1830–1930), was born in County Cork, Ireland, and grew up in Toronto, where her father worked as a railroad construction laborer. She was employed as a teacher in Monroe, Mich., as a dressmaker in Chicago, and then again as a teacher in Memphis, where she was married in 1861. Jones lost her husband and four children to a yellow fever epidemic in 1867 and soon after moved to Chicago, where she took up dressmaking again. Losing her business in the great Chicago fire of 1871, she became active in the KOL and, during the railroad strike of 1877, went to Pittsburgh to assist the strikers. From that time on she labored as an organizer, working particularly with miners but also on behalf of child laborers and a wide range of others, including textile, streetcar, and steel workers. She remained active in labor affairs into her nineties.

KASTEN, Frank Morris (1878–1946), was born in Dolton, Ill., and left school at the age of fifteen to become a brickmaker. He subsequently joined International Brick, Tile, and Terra Cotta Workers' Alliance 3 of Blue Island, Ill., and served as president of the local from 1907 to 1912. In 1916 Kasten was elected president of the United Brick and Clay Workers of America, a seceding faction of the Brick and Terra Cotta Workers, and he continued to hold that position to the end of his life. In 1929 he was elected mayor of Blue Island on the Republican ticket, and he served in that office until 1935.

KEEFE, Daniel Joseph (1852–1929), was born in Willow Springs, Ill., and worked as a longshoreman and tugboatman in Chicago. In 1877 he organized the Lumber Unloaders' Association and for a few years simultaneously headed that organization and the Lake Seamen's Benevolent Association. Through the mid-1890s he was a leader on the Chicago docks, serving as president of the stevedores' union (1892) and the lumber shovers' union (1893–96). In 1892 he founded the Lumber Handlers of the Great Lakes, which in 1893 became the National Longshoremen's Association of the United States and, in 1895, the International Longshoremen's Association. He was president of the Longshoremen from 1893 to about 1896 and from 1899 to 1908. He served as a member of the Illinois State Board of Arbitration (1897–1901) and as an AFL vice-president (1904–8). Keefe was active in the National Civic Federation from 1901 until 1908, serving on its executive committee (1901, 1903–8) and in its Industrial Department (1901–2). He served as commissioner general of immigration (1908–13) and later worked with the U.S. Shipping Board Merchant Fleet Corporation (1921–25).

KELLEY, Florence (1859–1932), was a prominent reformer in the areas of tenement-house manufacturing conditions and child labor and the translator of a number of works by socialist authors, among them *The Condition of the Working Class in England in 1844* by Friedrich Engels. In 1884 Kelley married Lazare Wischnewetzky, himself also a student and a fellow socialist. In 1891, after separating from Wischnewetzky, she reassumed her maiden name and moved to Chicago, residing at Hull-House until 1899 and serving as chief state inspector of factories for Illinois from 1893 to 1897. Moving to New York City in 1899 she became secretary of the National Consumers' League, a position she held until her death. She also served on the boards of directors of the New York State and the National Child Labor Committees, was a founder and board member of the National Association for the Advancement of Colored People, and was vice-president of the National American Woman Suffrage Association.

Kennedy, Thomas (1887–1963), was born in Lansford, Pa., left school at age eleven to work as a breaker boy, and joined the United Mine Workers of America in 1900. He served as secretary of United Mine Workers' local 1738 of Lansford (1903–10) and as an executive board member (1908–10) and president (1910–24) of United Mine Workers' District 7 (Pennsylvania). After William Green became AFL president in 1924, Kennedy replaced him as secretary-treasurer of the United Mine Workers, serving in that post until 1947, when he was appointed vice-president of the union. He served as vice-president until 1960, when he became president of the union; he held that position until his death. A longtime resident of Hazleton, Pa., Kennedy was active in Democratic state politics and served one term as lieutenant governor of the state (1935–39).

Keough, Michael J. (1859–1932), was born in Troy, N.Y., apprenticed as an iron molder in nearby Green Island, and in 1882 joined Iron Molders' Union of North America 2 of Troy. He served the international (in 1907 renamed the International Molders' Union of North America) as vice-president (1895–1924) and president (1924–32). He was also a vice-president of the AFL Metal Trades Department (1924–31).

Kline, James Waller (1860–1937), was born in Luzerne County, Pa., and subsequently moved to Kansas City, Kans. A railroad and machine smith, he joined KOL Local Assembly 3694 of Kansas City and, later, International Brotherhood of Blacksmiths 66. He served the international (in 1903 renamed the International Brotherhood of Blacksmiths and Helpers; and in 1919 renamed the International Brotherhood of Blacksmiths, Drop Forgers, and Helpers) as a trustee (1901–3), vice-president (1904–5), and president (1905–26).

KOVELESKI, Emanuel (1876–1950), was born in England, immigrated with his family to the United States, and settled in Rochester, N.Y., where he became a bartender. He served as an organizer for the Hotel and Restaurant Employees' International Alliance and Bartenders' International League of America (1906–10) and as secretary and business agent of Hotel and Restaurant Employees' local 171 of Rochester (1910–48). Koveleski was president (1912–13, 1914–17) of the Rochester Central Trades and Labor Council and served as a vice-president (1913–33) and president (1933–34) of the New York State Federation of Labor. From 1922 until the repeal of Prohibition, he worked as an examiner for the U.S. Employment Bureau. Koveleski also served for many years as president of the New York State Culinary Alliance and secretary of the Rochester Brewers' Exchange.

LAURELL, Carl Malcolm Ferdinand (1843–1922), was born in Sweden, where he completed a cigarmaker's apprenticeship in 1862. Joining a cigarmakers' union in 1863, he worked at his trade in Stockholm, in Copenhagen, and in Hamburg before immigrating to the United States in 1871 or 1872 and settling in Jersey City, N.J. Laurell was elected in July 1872 to the North American Federal Council of the International Workingmen's Association (IWA) and in September 1872 to the IWA's General Council to represent Scandinavian workers; he served on the Council into 1874. With David Kronburg and J. P. McDonnell he was a founder in 1874 of the Association of United Workers of America. SG's shopmate during the 1870s, Laurell played a decisive role in shaping the younger man's thinking on trade unionism and the labor movement, and SG dedicated his autobiography to Laurell's memory.

LAWLOR, Martin (1868–1959), was born in Ireland and immigrated to the United States in 1885 or 1886. After working briefly in New York City, he moved to Bethel, Conn., where he became an apprentice hatmaker and, in 1890, secretary of the Bethel Hat Makers' Union (from 1896, United Hatters of North America 1). In 1892 Lawlor was named to the board of directors of the National Hat Makers' Association of the United States. When that organization merged with the International Trade Association of Hat Finishers of America in 1896 to form the United Hatters of North America, Lawlor continued as a board member. He served the United Hatters as vice-president (1898–1904), secretary (1904–11), and secretary-treasurer (1911–34). After 1934, when the United Hatters merged with the Cloth Hat, Cap, and Millinery Workers' International Union, forming the United Hatters', Cap, and Millinery Workers' International Union, Lawlor served as the new union's vice-president (1934–36), secretary-treasurer of its Men's Hat Department (1934–36), and label secretary (1936–59).

LEWIS, John Llewellyn (1880–1969), born in Cleveland, Iowa, was a founding member and in 1901 secretary of United Mine Workers of America 1933 of Chariton, Iowa. After traveling in the West, where he worked as a coal and hardrock miner, he returned to Iowa in 1905, resuming work in the mines and starting an unsuccessful grain and feed distribution business. In 1908 Lewis moved to Illinois, where he served as president of United Mine Workers' local 1475 of Panama (1909?–11?) and as legislative agent for United Mine Workers' District 12 (Illinois; 1909–11). He was a salaried organizer for the AFL from 1911 to 1917, when he was named chief statistician for the United Mine Workers. He was appointed acting vice-president of the union in 1917 and was elected to that post in 1918. Named acting president of the union in 1919, he was elected president in 1920 and held the position until he retired in 1960. Lewis was briefly a member of the AFL Executive Council in 1935 but resigned his position. He was a founder of the Committee for Industrial Organization that year, serving as its chairman until 1938, when it became the Congress of Industrial Organizations; he was president of that body from 1938 to 1940.

LORD, James (b. 1879), was born in England, immigrated to the United States in 1890, and became a member of United Mine Workers of America 1213 of Farmington, Ill. He served as vice-president (1912–14) of United Mine Workers' District 12 (Illinois), president of the AFL Mining Department (1914–22), treasurer of the Pan-American Federation of Labor (1918–24), and as an AFL salaried organizer in California (1922). During World War I he was a member of the Committee on Labor of the Advisory Commission of the Council of National Defense.

LYNCH, James Matthew (1867–1930), was born in Manlius, N.Y., where he attended local public schools. He apprenticed as a printer at a Syracuse, N.Y., newspaper at the age of seventeen and in 1887 became a journeyman and joined International Typographical Union 55, serving as its vice-president (1890) and president (1891–92). He was also president of the Syracuse Central Trades and Labor Assembly (1894, 1896–98). In 1898 he was elected a vice-president of the Typographical Union, and he later served as its president (1900–1914, 1924–26). He was a member of the National Civic Federation Industrial Department (1901–2) and executive committee (1901, 1903–18). From 1901 to 1912 he resided in Indianapolis. Returning to Syracuse, he was New York State commissioner of labor (1913–14) and a member of the New York State Industrial Commission (1915–21). He served as president of the Labor Temple Association in Syracuse (1923–24) and was intermittently in the insurance business during his last decade.

McCarthy, Frank H. (1864?–1932), was born in England, immigrated as a child to the United States, and lived in Bangor, Maine, until 1876 when he moved to Boston. He joined Cigar Makers' International Union of America 97 of Boston in 1883 and was its president in 1890. McCarthy served as president of the Boston Central Labor Union (1891–92), as president of the Massachusetts State Federation of Labor (1900?–1902), and as an AFL salaried organizer from 1903 until his death.

McMahon, Thomas F. (1870?–1944), was born in County Monaghan, Ireland, and attended school until 1885 when he immigrated with his family to the United States. First employed as a harness boy in a textile mill in Westerly, R.I., and then trained as a woolen weaver and finisher, McMahon had joined the KOL by 1887. By 1901 he was a member of United Textile Workers of America 505 (Cloth Folders) of Providence, R.I., and he served the local as business agent from 1904 until 1912. McMahon served as an organizer for the Textile Workers from 1912 to 1917, and as an AFL salaried organizer from 1914 to 1915. Elected international vice-president in 1917, McMahon assumed the presidency in 1921 after John Golden's death, and served until 1937 when he was appointed chief of the Rhode Island Department of Labor, a position he held until 1939. He subsequently served as a national representative for the Textile Workers' Organizing Committee.

McNally, Gertrude Marie (1887–1968), was born in Baltimore and by 1906 was living in Washington, D.C., where she worked for the U.S. Bureau of Engraving and Printing. In 1909 she was elected secretary of AFL Federal Labor Union 12,776 (the Women's Union of the Bureau of Engraving and Printing), which joined the National Federation of Federal Employees in 1918 as local 105; she served in that post for many years. She served the Federal Employees as organizer (1918–19), vice-president (1919–25), and secretary-treasurer (1925–55). After retiring in 1955, McNally married Luther Steward, longtime president of the union, who also retired that year.

Mahon, William D. (1861–1949), was born in Athens, Ohio, and worked as a coal miner in the Hocking Valley district. In the late 1880s he moved to Columbus, Ohio, where he worked as a mule car driver and helped to organize street railway workers in the early 1890s. In 1893 he was elected president of the Amalgamated Association of Street Railway Employes of America and shortly thereafter moved to Detroit. He served as president of the union (in 1903 renamed the Amalgamated Association of Street and Electric Railway Employes of America) until retiring in 1946. Mahon was presiding judge of the Michigan State Court of Mediation and Arbitration (1898–1900), a member of the executive committee of the National Civic Federation (1903 to at least 1923), and an AFL vice-president (1917–23, 1936–49).

MANNING, John J. (1868–1934), was born in Troy, N.Y., where he became a member of AFL Shirt Ironers' Union 7551 and in 1900 helped organize the Shirt, Waist, and Laundry Workers' International Union. He served the international (in 1909 renamed the Laundry Workers' International Union) as president (1900–1902), eastern organizer (1904–5), and secretary-treasurer (1905–10). After jurisdiction over shirt workers was transferred to the United Garment Workers of America, Manning became associated with that union, serving as an organizer and as associate editor of its official journal, the *Garment Worker*, until 1917. He served as a vice-president of the AFL Union Label Trades Department from 1909 to 1910 and as its secretary-treasurer from 1917 to 1934.

MAURER, James Hudson (1864–1944), was born in Reading, Pa., and at an early age worked variously as a newsboy, hat maker, and machinist. He joined KOL Washington Assembly 72 of Reading in 1880 and served as an officer of that local assembly, as a KOL organizer, as master workman of KOL Iron Workers' Assembly 7975, and as a KOL district master workman. During the 1890s he found employment as a steamfitter, newspaper publisher, and cigarmaker, and by 1901 he was working as a plumber and was a member of United Association of Journeymen Plumbers, Gas Fitters, Steam Fitters, and Steam Fitters' Helpers of the United States and Canada 42 of Reading. He served as president of the Pennsylvania State Federation of Labor from 1912 until 1928.

Maurer joined the Socialist Labor party in the late 1890s and, after 1902, was a member of the Socialist Party of America (SPA), serving on the party's state and national executive committees. He ran unsuccessfully as the SPA candidate for governor of Pennsylvania in 1906 and then served as a Socialist member of the Pennsylvania House of Representatives (1911–13, 1915–19). From 1922 to 1925 he was a member of the general or national committee of the Conference for Progressive Political Action. Maurer ran unsuccessfully on the SPA ticket for vice-president of the United States in 1928 and 1932, for governor of Pennsylvania in 1930, and for the U.S. Senate in 1934. In 1936 he left the Socialist party and joined the newly organized Social Democratic Federation.

MOFFITT, John A. (1865–1942), was born in Newark, N.J., and moved to Orange, N.J., at the age of twenty-one. There he worked as a hatter and served as business agent of the Orange local of the National Hat Makers' Association of the United States. He was a cofounder in 1896 of the United Hatters of North America and served as its vice-president (1896–98), president (1898–1911), and editor of its official journal (1898–1911). Moffitt was a member of the AFL Legislative Committee (1903, 1912–13) and helped draft the law establishing the U.S. Department of Labor in 1913. From that year until his death he served as a commissioner of conciliation for the department; he worked briefly during World War I as a conciliator in railroad disputes for the U.S. Treasury Department. He practiced law in Washington, D.C., beginning in the mid-1920s.

MOORE, Tom (1878–1946), was born in Leeds, England, and at the age of twelve took up work as a carpenter. After immigrating to Canada in 1906, he joined United Brotherhood of Carpenters and Joiners of America 713 of Niagara Falls, Ont., and served as business agent for the local (1910–12) and as general organizer for the international (1912–18). In 1918 Moore was elected president of the Trades and Labor Congress of Canada. He moved to Ottawa and transferred his union membership to Carpenters' local 93 of that city. He served as president of the Trades and Labor Congress until 1935, when he was appointed to the National Employment and Social Insurance Commission, and he was reelected president of the Congress in 1939 after the commission disbanded. Moore also edited the *Canadian Congress Journal* (1924–35), and he served on the board of directors of the Canadian National Railways (1922–33) and on the governing board of the International Labor Organization (1922–35?). After suffering a stroke, he resigned as president of the Trades and Labor Congress in 1943.

MORONES Negrete, Luis N. (1890–1964), was born in San Fernando de Tlalpan near Mexico City, began working as an electrician around the age of sixteen, and joined the Casa del Obrero (House of the Worker) in 1912. He organized an electricians' union in Mexico City around 1915 and was a founder of the short-lived Confederación del Trabajo de la Región Mexicana (Confederation of Labor of the Mexican Region) in 1916. In 1918 he participated in organizing the Confederación Regional Obrera Mexicana (Mexican Confederation of Labor), serving as its secretary and head of its policy-making board, Grupo Acción, and in 1919 he was a founder of the Partido Laborista Mexicano (the Mexican Labor party). He later served as director of factories in the department of war and navy (1920–23) and as minister of the department of industry and commerce (1924–28).

MORRISON, Frank (1859–1949), was born in Frankton, Ont. In 1865 his family moved to Walkerton, Ont., where he became a printer. Beginning about 1883, he worked at his trade in Madison, Wis. In 1886 he moved to Chicago, where he joined International Typographical Union 16. From 1893 to 1894 he studied law at Lake Forest University, becoming a member of the Illinois bar in 1895. The following year he was elected secretary of the AFL, serving in that post from 1897 to 1935 and as AFL secretary-treasurer from 1936 until his retirement in 1939. During World War I Morrison was a member of the Committee on Labor of the Advisory Commission of the Council of National Defense.

MOSHER, Aaron Alexander Roland (1881–1959), was born in Cow Bay, Nova Scotia. Leaving school at the age of fifteen, he worked as a farm laborer, gold miner, and storekeeper before taking a job as a freight handler in 1902. In 1907 he was elected treasurer of the Halifax local of the newly organized International Brotherhood of Railroad Employees, and in 1908 he helped organize the Canadian Brotherhood of Railroad Employees. Moving to Ottawa, he served as president of that union from 1908 until he retired in 1952. He also served as a member of the Canada Labour Relations Board (1916–59) and as president of the All-Canadian Congress of Labour (1927–40) and its successor, the Canadian Congress of Labour (1940–56).

MURRAY, Philip (1886–1952), was born in Scotland, began working as a miner at the age of ten, and immigrated with his family to the United States in 1902. Settling in western Pennsylvania, he worked in the mines near Pittsburgh and joined the United Mine Workers of America. He served as the representative to the national executive board from United Mine Workers' District 5 (Western Pennsylvania; 1913–16) and as the district's president (1916–20), and he was a vice-president of the United Mine Workers from 1920 to 1942. Murray served as head of the Steel Workers' Organizing Committee (1936–42) and then as president of the United Steelworkers of America, its successor organization (1942–52). He was a vice-president of the CIO from 1938 to 1940 and served as its president from 1940 until his death.

Myrup, Andrew A. (1880–1943), was born in Copenhagen and immigrated with his family to Racine, Wis., in 1893. After apprenticing as a baker and then traveling as a journeyman between 1897 and 1901, Myrup settled in Illinois and joined Bakery and Confectionery Workers' International Union of America 62 of Chicago. He was elected business agent of the local in 1904. Myrup served the international as treasurer (1907–23), secretary-treasurer (1923–41), and president and secretary-treasurer (1941–43). He also served as a vice-president of the AFL Union Label Trades Department (1928–43).

Nelson, Oscar Fred (1884–1943), was a lifelong resident of Chicago. He began working as a newsboy when he was nine, left school at thirteen to work in a department store, and became a post office clerk at eighteen, joining AFL Post Office Clerks' Union 8703. In 1906 the union became local 1 of the National Federation of Post Office Clerks. He served as president of the local from 1907 to 1910, as president of the international from 1910 to 1913, as editor of the *Union Postal Clerk*, the union's official journal, from 1913 to 1917, and as vice-president of the Chicago Federation of Labor from 1910 to 1935. From 1913 to 1917 Nelson was chief factory inspector for the state of Illinois and from 1917 to 1922 a commissioner of conciliation for the U.S. Department of Labor. In 1927 and 1928 he served as interim president of the Building Service Employees' International Union. He was admitted to the Illinois bar in 1922, served as a member of the Chicago City Council from 1923 to 1935, and was a Cook County Superior Court judge from 1935 until his death.

Nestor, Agnes (1880–1948), was born in Grand Rapids, Mich., and in 1897 moved to Chicago, where she worked in a glove factory. She joined a local glove workers' union in 1901 and was a founder of International Glove Workers' Union of America 18 in 1902, serving as its president from 1902 until 1906. She served the international as vice-president (1903–6, 1915–38), secretary-treasurer (1906–13), president (1913–15), and director of research and education (1939–48). During World War I Nestor served on the Committee on Women's Defense Work of the Council of National Defense and on the subcommittee on Women in Industry of the Committee on Labor of the Advisory Commission of the Council of National Defense. She was also a member (1907–48) of the National Women's Trade Union League and president (1913–48) of its Chicago branch, and from 1922 to 1924 she served as a member of the general committee of the Conference for Progressive Political Action.

NOONAN, James Patrick (1877–1929), was born in St. Louis, attended grammar school until he was fourteen, and then went to work in a mill. A veteran of the Spanish-American War, he joined International Brotherhood of Electrical Workers 2 of St. Louis around 1900 and served as its recording secretary (1903–4) and president (1904–5). In 1905 he was elected vice-president of the international and moved to Springfield, Ill., where the union had its headquarters. Noonan remained vice-president until 1918, when he was appointed acting president of the union. Elected in his own right in 1919, he moved with the union's headquarters to Washington, D.C., and he served as president until his death. Noonan also served as a vice-president of the AFL Building Trades Department (1922–29) and as an AFL vice-president (1924–29). In 1924 and 1925 he served as a member of the general or national committee of the Conference for Progressive Political Action.

O'CONNELL, James (1858–1936), was born in Minersville, Pa., learned his trade as a machinist's apprentice, and began working as a railroad machinist. He served as a lobbyist for the KOL in Harrisburg, Pa., in 1889 and 1891. Joining National (from 1891, International) Association of Machinists 113 of Oil City, Pa., around 1890, he became a member of the Machinists' executive board in 1891 and later served the international as grand master machinist (1893–99) and president (1899–1911). He moved to Chicago in 1896 and to Washington, D.C., in 1900. O'Connell served as an AFL vice-president (1896–1918) and as president of the AFL Metal Trades Department (1911–34). He was also a member of the National Civic Federation executive committee (1901, 1903–10) and Industrial Department (1901–2), the U.S. Commission on Industrial Relations (1913–15), and, during World War I, the Committee on Labor of the Advisory Commission of the Council of National Defense.

OLANDER, Victor A. (1873–1949), was born in Chicago and at the age of fourteen began working as a sailor on the Great Lakes. He served as business agent (1901–3), assistant secretary (1903–9), and secretary (1909–20) of the Lake Seamen's Union (in 1919 renamed the Sailors' Union of the Great Lakes) and as vice-president (1902–25), secretary-treasurer (1925–36), and member of the legislative committee of the International Seamen's Union of America. Olander was also active in the Chicago Federation of Labor (FOL) and served as secretary-treasurer of the Illinois State FOL from 1914 until his death. During World War I he was a member of the National War Labor Board (1918–19) and the Illinois State Council of Defense, and he later served on the National Recovery Administration district board for Illinois and Wisconsin, the Illinois Department of Labor Unemployment Compensation Advisory Board, and the board of directors of WCFL, the radio station of the Chicago FOL. He was a lifelong resident of Chicago.

OUDEGEEST, Jan (1870–1951), was born in Utrecht, Netherlands. A railroad worker, he was a founder in 1898 and the first president of the Nederlandsche vereeniging van spoor- en tramwegpersoneel (Netherlands Association of Railway and Tramway Employees); he continued as an officer of that organization until 1942. He was elected secretary of the Nederlandsch verbond van vakvereenigingen (Netherlands League of Trade Unions) in 1905 and served as its president from 1908 to 1918. During World War I Oudegeest was head of the auxiliary office of the International Federation of Trade Unions in Amsterdam, and from 1919 to 1927 he was secretary of the organization. Also active in local and national politics, he served as a member of the lower (1918–22) and upper (1928–36) chambers of the Dutch parliament and from 1927 to 1934 was chairman of the Sociaal-democratische arbeiderspartij (Social Democratic Workers' party).

PERKINS, George William (1856–1934), was born in Massachusetts and joined Cigar Makers' International Union of America 68 of Albany, N.Y., in 1880. He served as a vice-president of the Cigar Makers from 1885 to 1891 and as acting president for six months in 1888 and 1889. In 1891 he was elected president, an office he held for the next thirty-five years. By early 1892 he had moved to Buffalo, and later in the year he moved to Chicago. He became the president of the AFL Union Label Trades Department in 1928, serving until his death.

POWDERLY, Terence Vincent (1849–1924), was born in Carbondale, Pa., apprenticed as a machinist, and moved to Scranton, where he joined the International Machinists and Blacksmiths of North America in 1871, becoming president of his local and an organizer in Pennsylvania. After being dismissed and blacklisted for his labor activities, Powderly joined the KOL in Philadelphia in 1876 and shortly afterward founded a local assembly of machinists and was elected its master workman. In 1877 he helped organize KOL District Assembly 5 (number changed to 16 in 1878) and was elected corresponding secretary. He was elected mayor of Scranton on the Greenback-Labor ticket in 1878 and served three consecutive two-year terms. He played an important role in calling the first General Assembly of the KOL in 1878, where he was chosen grand worthy foreman, the KOL's second highest office. The September 1879 General Assembly elected him grand master workman, and he continued to hold the Order's leading position (title changed to general master workman in 1883) until 1893. Active in the secret Irish nationalist society *Clan na Gael,* Powderly was elected to the Central Council of the American Land League in 1880 and was its vice-president in 1881. He became an ardent advocate of land reform and temperance and, as master workman, favored the organization of workers into mixed locals rather than craft unions, recommended that they avoid strikes, encouraged producers' cooperatives, and espoused political reform.

In 1894 Powderly was admitted to the Pennsylvania bar, and in 1897 President William McKinley, for whom he had campaigned, appointed him U.S. commissioner general of immigration. President Theodore Roosevelt removed him from this position in 1902 but in 1906 appointed him special representative of the Department of Commerce and Labor to study European immigration problems. Powderly was chief of the Division of Information in the Bureau of Immigration and Naturalization from 1907 until his death.

PRESCOTT, William Blair (1863–1916), was born in Ontario, Canada, and in 1883 joined International Typographical Union 91 of Toronto. He served as president of the international from 1891 to 1898 and then worked as a proofreader for newspapers in Indianapolis and Baltimore.

RANDOLPH, Asa Philip (1889–1979), Socialist, trade unionist, and civil rights leader, was born in Crescent City, Fla., and moved to New York City in 1911. He was a founder of the United Brotherhood of Elevator and Switchboard Operators (1917), the National Brotherhood Workers of America (1919), the National Association for the Promotion of Labor Unionism (1919), the Friends of Negro Freedom (1920), and the United Negro Trades (1923). He was also coeditor of the *Messenger,* a Socialist monthly (1917–28), and ran for New York state comptroller (1920) and secretary of state (1922) on the Socialist ticket. He subsequently served as organizer (1925–29) and president (1929–68) of the Brotherhood of Sleeping Car Porters, president of the National Negro Congress (1936–40), and head of the March on Washington Movement (1941–46), the Committee against Jim Crow in Military Service and Training (1947), and the League for Non-Violent Civil Disobedience against Military Segregation (1948). Randolph also served as a vice-president of the AFL-CIO (1955–74), president of the Negro American Labor Council (1960–64), and national director for the March on Washington for Jobs and Freedom (1963).

RICHARDSON, George James (1893–1980), was born in Winchester, Mass., and attended high school there. In 1913 moved to Vancouver, B.C., and began working as a fire fighter. He helped organize the first fire fighters' union in Canada (from 1918, International Association of Fire Fighters 18 of Vancouver) and served as its secretary (1916–17, 1918–20) and president (1917–18). Richardson was a delegate to the international union's founding convention in 1918 and subsequently served as vice-president (1918–20) and secretary-treasurer (1920–56) of the organization. He moved to the Washington, D.C., area in 1920, eventually making his home in Silver Spring, Md. After retiring from the Fire Fighters, Richardson served as a special assistant to AFL-CIO president George Meany (1957–62) and then, until 1972, as a consultant on civil defense to the Defense Department.

RICKERT, Thomas Alfred (1876–1941), was born in Chicago and attended business college before becoming a garment cutter and joining United Garment Workers of America 21 of Chicago at the age of nineteen. He served as president (1904–41) and acting secretary-treasurer (1934–41) of the international and was an AFL vice-president (1918–41). During World War I he served on the National War Labor Board (1918–19).

ROSEMUND, Charles L. (1879–1963), was born in Missouri. He served in the navy during the Spanish-American War and the Boxer Rebellion and then worked as an engineer and designer in various locations in the Midwest and South. By about 1912 he was living in Portsmouth, Va., where he worked as a draftsman in the navy yard. In 1916 he was a founding member of AFL Draftsmen's Union 15,327 of Portsmouth, and he subsequently served as the union's president. He served as president (1920–42) and then vice-president (1946–47) of the International Federation of Technical Engineers', Architects', and Draftsmen's Unions and was a labor advisor for the National War Labor Board during World War II.

ROSENBERG, Abraham (1870–1935), was born in Russia and immigrated to New York City in 1883, where he worked as a cloakmaker. A member first of the KOL and then of International Ladies' Garment Workers' Union 1 (Cloak Operators), he served the international as vice-president (1907–8), president (1908–14), and organizer.

RYAN, Joseph Patrick (1884–1963), was born in Babylon, N.Y., and grew up near the North River docks where he began working when he was twelve. In 1912 he joined International Longshoremen's Association 791 of New York City, and he was elected its financial secretary the following year. By 1918 Ryan was president of the Longshoremen's Atlantic Coast District, and in 1919 he was elected an international vice-president, a position he held until 1927 when he was elected president of the Longshoremen. He also served as president of the Central Trades and Labor Council of Greater New York and Vicinity (1926–37) and as a vice-president of the New York State Federation of Labor (1923–53). A controversial figure, Ryan was elected the Longshoremen's president "for life" in 1943, but he retired in 1953 after he was indicted for misusing union funds and the AFL suspended the union for corruption.

RYAN, Martin Francis (1874–1935), was born in West Virginia and moved to Texas at the age of eighteen. He joined the Brotherhood of Railway Carmen of America as a charter member of Fort Worth Lodge 23 in 1899, and he was a member of Pine Tree Lodge 81 of Beaumont, Tex., when he was elected to the executive board of the Railway Carmen in 1903. He subsequently served as vice-grand chief carman (1905–9) and president (1909–35) of the brotherhood. Ryan also served as an AFL vice-president (1923–28) and treasurer (1929–35), and he was a founder and treasurer (1927–35) of the Union Labor Life Insurance Co. At the time of his death, he was living in Washington, D.C.

SCHNEIDERMAN, Rose (1882–1972), was born in Russian Poland, immigrated with her family to the United States in 1890, and settled on Manhattan's Lower East Side, where she began working at the age of thirteen. In 1903 she organized United Cloth Hat and Cap Makers of North America 23 at the cap factory where she was working, and in 1904 she was elected vice-president of the international and a member of its general executive board. Schneiderman joined the New York branch of the Woman's Trade Union League in 1905 and became its vice-president the next year, an organizer in 1908, and a member of its executive board in 1911. Under the league's auspices she helped organize locals 25 (Shirtwaist Makers) and 62 (White Goods' Workers) of the International Ladies' Garment Workers' Union and was a leader of the New York City garment workers' strikes in 1909–10 and 1913. She subsequently took a post as national organizer for the Ladies' Garment Workers. Schneiderman resumed organizing work for the New York branch of the National Women's Trade Union League of America in 1917, and in 1918 she became its president, a position she held until 1949. She served the Women's Trade Union League as vice-president from 1919 to 1926 and as president from 1926 until it disbanded in 1950. In 1924 and 1925 she served as a member of the national committee of the Conference for Progressive Political Action.

SCOTT, John (1867–1930), was born in Scotland, worked for a time as a sailor, and then settled in San Luis Obispo, Calif., where he was a car inspector for the Southern Pacific Railroad. He became a member of Brotherhood of Railway Carmen 327 of San Luis Obispo, serving as its president (1911–12) and as secretary of the system federation for the Harriman railroad lines (1911). Scott was secretary-treasurer of the AFL Railway Employes' Department from 1912 to 1926.

SHANESSY, James Colmer (1870–1936), was born in Watertown, N.Y., and grew up in Cleveland. Self-educated after leaving school at the age of eight, Shanessy began working as a barber at fourteen. A member first of Journeymen Barbers' International Union of America 141 of Buffalo, he later moved to St. Louis, where he served as deputy inspector of the Barbers' examining board (1903) and then as business agent of Barbers' local 102 (1902–9). In 1909 Shanessy was elected general organizer for the international, serving in that position until 1922, when he was appointed president of the Barbers, a position he held for the rest of his life. He died in Indianapolis.

SHEPPARD, Lucius Elmer (1863–1934), was born in Bridgeton, N.J., and worked variously as a railroad brakeman, conductor, baggage master, and yardmaster. He joined Order of Railway Conductors of America division 170 of Camden, N.J., in 1885 and later moved to Cedar Rapids, Iowa. He served the Order as grand junior conductor (1901–6), assistant grand chief conductor (1906–7), senior vice-president (1907–19), and president (1919–28).

SHORT, William Mackie (1887–1947), was born in Dailly, Scotland, immigrated to the United States in 1905, and subsequently worked as a miner in Washington state and British Columbia. Short served as secretary of United Mine Workers of America District 10 (Washington; 1914–18), vice-president (1915–18) and president (1918–27) of the Washington State Federation of Labor, and editor of the *Washington State Labor News* (1924–28). He left union office to go into banking, serving as vice-president (1927–30), president (1931), and liquidator (1933) of the Brotherhood Bank and Trust Co. (from 1929, the North Coast Bank and Trust Co.). In 1932 he entered the laundry business, serving as manager of the Mutual Laundry Co., administrator of industrial agreements for the Seattle Associated Laundries, and then as administrator of the Laundries and Dry Cleaners Association.

SIGMAN, Morris Solomon (1881–1931), was born in Russia. In 1901 he immigrated to London, where he worked in a men's clothing shop, and in 1903 he emigrated to New York City, where he worked as a presser and organized the Independent Cloak Pressers' Union, which affiliated in 1904 with the Socialist Trades and Labor Alliance. When the union joined the IWW in 1905 as a branch of local 59, Sigman served as an organizer. By 1908 he had joined the International Ladies' Garment Workers' Union, and he helped organize the New York City Joint Board of Cloak Makers, serving as its general manager from 1910 to 1913. He served the international as vice-president (1910–13) and secretary-treasurer (1914–15) but resigned after being indicted and jailed for strike activity. Found not guilty and released in 1915, he again served as manager of the Joint Board (1917–21) and as vice-president of the international (1920–22). He retired in 1922 but then served as president of the Ladies' Garment Workers from 1923 to 1928. In 1924 and 1925 he served as a member of the national committee of the Conference for Progressive Political Action.

SPENCER, William J. (1867–1933), was born in Hamilton, Ont., where he apprenticed as a plumber. He immigrated to New York state about 1894 and joined United Association of Journeymen Plumbers, Gas Fitters, Steam Fitters, and Steam Fitters' Helpers of the United States and Canada 36 of Buffalo. Spencer served as secretary-treasurer (1897–1900) and general organizer (1900–1904) of the Plumbers, was a vice-president of the AFL (1904–5), secretary-treasurer of the Structural Building Trades Alliance (1903–8), and secretary-treasurer of the AFL Building Trades Department (1908–24, 1927–33). He lived in Dayton, Ohio, from about 1902 until 1912, when he moved to Washington, D.C.

STEWARD, Luther Corwin (1877–1966), was born in Chattanooga, attended schools in Nashville, Columbus, Ohio, and Washington, D.C., and graduated with a law degree from Fordham in New York City. He began working for the federal government at the age of eighteen, and over the next two decades worked in a variety of positions, including the railway mail service, the Civil Service Commission, the Department of Labor, and the Bureau of Immigration. Steward served as vice-president (1917–18) and president (1918–55) of the National Federation of Federal Employees, and he was also a founder and board chairman of the Prudential Building Association.

STONE, Warren Sanford (1860–1925), was born in Ainsworth, Iowa, and became a locomotive fireman on the Chicago, Rock Island, and Pacific Railroad in 1879. He was promoted to engineer in 1884 and subsequently joined Brotherhood of Locomotive Engineers' lodge 181 of Eldon, Iowa, which he served as first assistant engineer (1896–97) and grand chief engineer (1897–1903). Stone served as grand chief engineer of the Locomotive Engineers from 1903 to 1924 and as president of the union from 1924 until his death. During World War I he was a member of the Committee on Labor of the Advisory Commission of the Council of National Defense, and from 1922 to 1925 he served as treasurer of the Conference for Progressive Political Action.

SUITOR, Frederick William (1879–1934), was born in Quebec and immigrated to Vermont in 1890. Initially employed as a breaker boy, tool boy, and tool sharpener in a granite quarry in Graniteville, Vt., he later worked as a quarryman and as a quarry blacksmith. Suitor served as president (1907) and financial secretary (1908–10) of Quarry Workers' International Union of North America 12 of Graniteville and was subsequently secretary-treasurer of the international (1910–34). He served the Vermont State Federation of Labor as organizer (1911–14), president (1914–20), secretary (1922–29), and secretary-treasurer (1930–34). Also active in the Socialist party, he was its nominee for governor of Vermont in 1912 and 1932.

SULLIVAN, Jere L. (1863–1928), was born in Willimansett, Mass., worked as a waiter in New England, Chicago, and St. Louis, and founded St. Louis KOL Local Assembly 9124 (Waiters), which later became local 20 of the Hotel and Restaurant Employees' International Alliance and Bartenders' International League of America. He was active in Hotel and Restaurant Employees' local 6 of Salt Lake City in the 1890s, returned briefly to St. Louis in 1899, and then moved to Cincinnati, where he joined local 161. Sullivan served as vice-president (1899) and secretary-treasurer (1899–1928) of the Hotel and Restaurant Employees and edited the union's official journal, *Mixer and Server*, from 1900 until his death.

SULLIVAN, John (1869–1943), was born in Ireland and immigrated to New York City in 1890. In 1897 he became a member of National Union of the United Brewery Workmen of the United States 59 of New York, and he subsequently served the local for many years as financial secretary. From 1909 to 1935 he was a member of the executive board of the international (in 1902 renamed the International Union of the United Brewery Workmen of America; in 1917 renamed the International Union of United Brewery and Soft Drink Workers of America; and in 1918 renamed the International Union of United Brewery, Flour, Cereal, and Soft Drink Workers of America). Sullivan also served as president of the Central Trades and Labor Council of Greater New York and Vicinity (1920–27) and as vice-president (1920–26, 1933–42) and president (1926–33) of the New York State Federation of Labor. In 1933 he was appointed to the New York State Alcoholic Beverage Control Board, a position he retained until 1942.

SWALES, Alonzo Beaumont (1870–1952), was born in Middleborough, Yorkshire, England. He apprenticed as a blacksmith and by 1890 had joined the Stockton-on-Tees branch of the Amalgamated Society of Engineers. An active union member and a Socialist, he had to leave Stockton-on-Tees in 1904 and moved to London, where he served on the union's London district committee and as a district organizer (1912–17). Swales also served on the executive council of the Amalgamated Society of Engineers (1917–19) and its successor, the Amalgamated Engineering Union (1920–35). In 1919 he was elected to the Parliamentary Committee (from 1921, the General Council) of the TUC, and he served in that post until he retired in 1935.

TANSEY, James (1867–1953), was born in England and immigrated to the United States in 1893. He became a textile mill carder in Fall River, Mass., serving as secretary (1896–1904) of the Fall River carders' union and vice-president (1897–98) and president (1898) of the Fall River Central Labor Union, president (1899, 1901–30) of the Fall River Textile Council, and president (1905–20) and secretary (1921–51) of the Fall River Card Room Protective Association. A founder in 1900 of the American Federation of Textile Operatives, he served as the union's president from 1900 to 1901. He took part in the founding convention of the United Textile Workers of America in 1901 and served that union as president (1901–3) and vice-president (1903–15). Tansey was subsequently president (1915–32) of the National Amalgamation of Textile Operatives (in 1920 renamed the American Federation of Textile Operatives), established by a seceding faction of the Textile Workers.

THOMAS, Albert Aristide (1878–1932), was born in Champigny-sur-Marne, France. He joined the Parti Socialist Française (French Socialist party) in 1902 and wrote for *L'Humanité* and *La Petite République* before starting his own publication, *La Revue Syndicaliste*, in 1905. He was elected to the Chamber of Deputies in 1910, serving until 1921, and was mayor of Champigny from 1912 to 1925. Thomas was appointed under-secretary of state for artillery and military equipment in 1915 and minister for munitions in 1916, holding the latter post until the Socialists resigned from the government the next year. In 1919 he attended the peace treaty negotiations in Paris and helped draft the treaty's labor provisions, including the creation of the International Labor Organization. When the organization's structure was formalized in late 1919, Thomas became its director-general, serving until his death.

THORNE, Florence Calvert (1877–1973), was born in Hannibal, Mo., and was educated at Oberlin College and the University of Chicago. Between 1912 and 1918 she worked as a research assistant to SG and as an editor of the *American Federationist.* She left the AFL in 1918 to take a position with the U.S. Department of Labor, and she served as a member of the Committee on Women in Industry of the Advisory Commission of the Council of National Defense. Beginning in 1919 Thorne assisted SG in preparing his memoirs, *Seventy Years of Life and Labor,* and from 1925 she was an administrative assistant to William Green and Matthew Woll. Between 1933 and 1953 Thorne served as the director of the AFL Research Department.

TIGHE, Michael Francis (1858–1940), was born in Boonton, N.J., moved with his family to West Virginia a few years later, and was working for the Wheeling (W.Va.) Iron and Nail Co. by the time he was ten. In 1877 he joined lodge 5 of the Amalgamated Association of Iron and Steel Workers of the United States, and he held various offices in this and other Wheeling-area lodges before becoming an officer of the international (in 1907 renamed the Amalgamated Association of Iron, Steel, and Tin Workers). Tighe served the Iron and Steel Workers as assistant secretary (1899–1911), secretary-treasurer (1911–18), and president (1918–36). He also served as secretary of the Ohio Valley Trades and Labor Assembly (1896–99).

TOBIN, Daniel Joseph (1875?–1955), was born in Ireland and immigrated to the United States about 1889, settling in East Cambridge, Mass., in 1890. He worked in a sheet metal factory, then as a Boston street railway motorman, and by the end of the decade was working as a teamster and had joined Boston local 25 of the Team Drivers' International Union, a union he later served as business agent. In 1907 Tobin was elected president of the International Brotherhood of Teamsters and moved to Indianapolis. He served the international (in 1910 renamed the International Brotherhood of Teamsters, Chauffeurs, Stablemen, and Helpers of America) as president until 1952. He was also a member of the National Civic Federation executive committee

(1911–14) and served as AFL treasurer (1918–28) and as an AFL vice-president (1935–55). In 1932, 1936, 1940, and 1944 he chaired the Labor Division of the Democratic National Committee and in 1940 served briefly as administrative assistant to President Franklin Delano Roosevelt.

VALENTINE, Joseph F. (1857–1930), was born in Baltimore, where he apprenticed as an iron molder. After moving to San Francisco, he joined Iron Molders' Union of North America 164 and served as the local's president from 1880 to 1890. He was elected vice-president of the Molders in 1890 and moved to Cincinnati. He held that office until 1903 and then served as president of the international (in 1907 renamed the International Molders' Union of North America) until he retired in 1924. He was also a member of the National Civic Federation executive committee (1904 to at least 1923), a vice-president of the AFL (1906–24), and a vice-president of the AFL Metal Trades Department (1908–24). In 1927 he returned to San Francisco.

VALENTINO, John Gabriel (1888–1986), was born in Brunswick, Ga., and later moved to Savannah, where he worked for the Seaboard Air Line Railway. From 1921 to 1922 he represented Chatham County in the Georgia state legislature. He served as vice-president (1920) and president (1921–23) of the Georgia State Federation of Labor, as secretary-treasurer of International Association of Machinists' District 16 (1921–22), and as secretary of Machinists' local 23 (Forest City Lodge; 1922). He later worked as the superintendent of the Savannah water department (1923–24), as an officer of the Citizens' Loan and Investment Co. of Savannah (1928–30), and as a salesman.

WALKER, John Hunter (1872–1955), was born in Scotland, immigrated to the United States in 1882, and began working in the mines in Coal City, Ill. He returned briefly to Scotland and then settled permanently in the United States in the 1890s. Walker served the United Mine Workers of America as an organizer for West Virginia, president of the Danville, Ill., subdistrict of District 12 (Illinois), and then as executive board member (1905–6) and president (1906–9, 1910–13, 1931–33) of District 12. He was president of the Illinois State Federation of Labor (1913–19, 1920–30), and in 1915 helped organize the Illinois State Cooperative Society, serving as its first president (1915–21). In 1906 Walker ran unsuccessfully on the Socialist Party of America ticket for a seat in the U.S. House of Representatives. He was expelled from the party in 1916. In 1917 he served on the President's Mediation Commission. In 1919 he joined the National Labor party (in 1920 renamed the Farmer-Labor party) and was its unsuccessful candidate for governor of Illinois in 1920. In 1930 he and other opponents of United Mine Workers' president John L. Lewis launched the Reorganized United Mine Workers of America in Springfield, Ill., and he served as secretary-treasurer of this short-lived union. Around 1952 he moved to Denver.

WILSON, James Adair (1876–1945), was born in Erie, Pa., where he joined a local of the Pattern Makers' League of North America in 1898. He served as president of the Pattern Makers (1902–34), moving to New York City and then, in 1906, to Cincinnati. Wilson also served as an AFL vice-president (1924–34) and, later, as a labor counselor for the International Labor Organization in Geneva.

WILSON, William Bauchop (1862–1934), was born in Blantyre, Scotland, and immigrated to Arnot, Pa., in 1870. The son of a coal miner, he began working in the mines at the age of nine, became a member of a local miners' union, and was later elected its secretary. Blacklisted in 1880, he worked briefly in sawmills and lumber yards in the West and then as a fireman on the Illinois Central Railroad before returning to Pennsylvania. He settled in Blossburg, where he worked in the 1880s and 1890s as a miner and check weighman in the Tioga County mines and, for a time, as a typesetter for the *Blossburg Advertiser*. Wilson was master workman of District 3 of KOL National Trade Assembly 135 from 1888 to 1894 and headed the Independent Order of the KOL, organized by the United Mine Workers of America, from 1894 to 1897. In 1890 he was a founder of the United Mine Workers, serving on its executive board and, during the 1890s, as president of District 2 (Central Pennsylvania). He was secretary-treasurer of the United Mine Workers from 1900 to 1908. Wilson was elected to Congress as a Democrat from Pennsylvania in 1906, serving from 1907 to 1913 and chairing the House Committee on Labor between 1911 and 1913. He was the first U.S. secretary of labor, serving from 1913 to 1921, and a member of the Council of National Defense.

WOLL, Matthew (1880–1956), was born in Luxembourg and immigrated to the United States in 1891. He grew up in Chicago, where he apprenticed as a photoengraver in 1895, and around 1900 he joined International Photo-Engravers' Union of North America 5 of that city. In 1901 he began studying law at Lake Forest University, and he became a member of the Illinois bar in 1904. Woll served as president of the Photo-Engravers (1906–29), as an alternate for Victor Olander on the National War Labor Board (1918–19), and as a vice-president of the

AFL (1919–55) and AFL-CIO (1955–56). He was also a founder and president (1929–56) of the Union Labor Life Insurance Co.

WRIGHT, Chester Maynard (1883–1964), was born in Milwaukee, worked for the *Milwaukee Journal,* and was later editor of the *New York Call* (1914–16) and was then connected with the Newspaper Enterprise Association of Cleveland (1917). Wright broke with the Socialist Party of America over its opposition to the entry of the United States into World War I, and during the war he served as director of the news department of the American Alliance for Labor and Democracy. He was a member of the first American labor mission to Europe in 1918 and then worked as a reporter for the *New York Tribune*'s European bureau (1918–19), as English-language secretary of the Pan-American Federation of Labor (1919–27), as director of the AFL Information and Publicity Service (1920 to at least 1925), and as assistant editor of the *American Federationist* (1922 to at least 1925). Wright was subsequently the editor of the International Labor News Service, and around 1933 he founded Chester M. Wright and Associates, a Washington, D.C., news service and research firm that published *Chester Wright's Labor Letter.* After he retired in 1948, his colleague John Herling took charge of the publication, which was renamed *John Herling's Labor Letter.*

YOUNG, Charles O. (1858–1944), was born in Carthage, Mo., and moved to Seattle in 1883, where he worked as an operating engineer, joined the KOL for a time, became active in the anti-Chinese movement, and helped organize the Western Central Labor Union in 1888. By 1894 he was living in Olympia, Wash., where he was engineer in charge of the water works, and by the latter part of the decade he had moved to Tacoma, where he joined International Union of Steam Engineers 2. In 1898 Young helped organize the Washington State Labor Congress, predecessor of the Washington State Federation of Labor, and in 1899 he was an organizer of the Tacoma Central Labor Council. In 1904 he became a salaried organizer for the AFL, and he served in that capacity until his retirement around 1933.

ORGANIZATIONS

The Journeymen Barbers' National Union, founded in 1887 by unions formerly affiliated with the KOL, affiliated with the AFL in 1888 as the Journeymen BARBERS' International Union of America.

The International Brotherhood of Blacksmiths organized in 1889 and affiliated with the AFL in 1897. In 1903 it absorbed the AFL's federal labor unions of blacksmiths' helpers and changed its name to the International Brotherhood of Blacksmiths and Helpers. In 1919 it amalgamated with the Brotherhood of Drop Forgers, Die Sinkers, and Trimming Die Makers to become the International Brotherhood of BLACKSMITHS, Drop Forgers, and Helpers.

The National Boiler Makers' and Helpers' Protective and Benevolent Union organized in 1881 and in 1884 changed its name to the International Brotherhood of Boiler Makers' and Iron Ship Builders' Protective and Benevolent Union of the United States and Canada. In 1887 it affiliated with the AFL as the International Brotherhood of Boiler Makers. It withdrew in 1893 and merged with the National Brotherhood of Boiler Makers to form the Brotherhood of Boiler Makers and Iron Ship Builders of America, which affiliated with the AFL in 1896. In 1906 the union adopted the name International Brotherhood of BOILER Makers, Iron Ship Builders, and Helpers of America.

The National Union of Brewers of the United States organized in 1886 and affiliated with the AFL as the Brewers' National Union in March 1887. Later that year it changed its name to the National Union of the United Brewery Workmen of the United States; it became the International Union of the United Brewery Workmen of America in 1902. After a prolonged series of jurisdictional disputes the AFL revoked the union's charter in 1907 but reinstated the Brewery Workmen in 1908. In 1917 the union became the International Union of United Brewery and Soft Drink Workers of America and, in 1918, the International Union of United BREWERY, Flour, Cereal, and Soft Drink Workers of America.

A group of AFL federal labor unions organized the National Brickmakers' Alliance in 1896 and affiliated with the AFL the same year. In 1901 the union absorbed several local unions and changed its name to the International Brick, Tile, and Terra Cotta Workers' Alliance. In 1913 seceding members formed the United BRICK and Clay Workers of America, and the two groups merged under that name in 1917.

The Bricklayers' and Masons' International Union of America was organized in 1865 and changed its name to the BRICKLAYERS', Masons', and Plasterers' International Union of America in 1910. It did not affiliate with the AFL until 1916.

The International Association of Bridge and Structural Iron Workers (in 1915 renamed the International Association of Bridge, Structural, and Ornamental Iron Workers and Pile Drivers; and in 1917 renamed the International Association of BRIDGE, Structural, and Ornamental Iron Workers) was organized in 1896 and affiliated with the AFL in 1901. It soon became involved in jurisdictional conflicts with several metal trades unions and was suspended from the AFL in 1902 for non-payment of dues. After the conflict was resolved in 1903, it rejoined the Federation. It was briefly suspended again in 1917 during a conflict with the United Brotherhood of Carpenters and Joiners of America.

The Brotherhood of Carpenters and Joiners of America was organized in 1881 and chartered by the AFL in 1887. In 1888 the Brotherhood and the United Order of American Carpenters and Joiners merged, forming the United Brotherhood of CARPENTERS and Joiners of America.

The Cigar Makers' National Union of America was organized in 1864 and changed its name to the CIGAR Makers' International Union of America in 1867. The union received an AFL charter in 1887.

The Retail Clerks' National Protective Association of America was organized in 1890 as an AFL affiliate. It changed its name to the Retail CLERKS' International Protective Association in 1899.

The Amalgamated CLOTHING Workers of America was organized in New York City in 1914 by a seceding faction of the United Garment Workers of America.

The National Brotherhood of Electrical Workers of America was organized in 1891 and affiliated with the AFL the same year. In 1899 it became the International Brotherhood of ELECTRICAL Workers.

The International Brotherhood of Stationary Firemen was organized in 1898 and received an AFL charter the next year. In 1917 it became the International Brotherhood of Stationary Firemen and Oilers, and in 1919, the International Brotherhood of FIREMEN and Oilers.

The United GARMENT Workers of America was organized in 1891 and affiliated with the AFL the same year.

The International GLOVE Workers' Union of America was organized in 1902 and chartered that year by the AFL.

The Granite Cutters' International Union of the United States and the British Provinces of America was formed in 1877 and in 1880 changed its name to the Granite Cutters' National Union of the United States of America. It joined the AFL in 1888, left the Federation in 1890, and then rejoined it in 1895. In 1905 it adopted the name GRANITE Cutters' International Association of America.

The International Hod Carriers' and Building Laborers' Union of America was organized and affiliated with the AFL in 1903. It became the International Hod Carriers' and Common Laborers' Union of America in September 1912 and the International HOD Carriers', Building and Common Laborers' Union of America in December of that year.

The Waiters' and Bartenders' National Union was organized and affiliated with the AFL in 1891. The following year it changed its name to the Hotel and Restaurant Employees' National Alliance and, in 1898, to the HOTEL and Restaurant Employees' International Alliance and Bartenders' International League of America.

The Amalgamated Association of Iron and Steel Workers of the United States was organized in 1876 and in 1887 was chartered by the AFL. In 1897 it changed its name to the Amalgamated Association of IRON, Steel, and Tin Workers.

The International JEWELRY Workers' Union was organized and affiliated with the AFL in 1916. It was suspended in 1920 because of jurisdictional conflicts with the Metal Polishers' International Union and was reinstated in 1922 after these conflicts were resolved.

The International LADIES' Garment Workers' Union was organized and affiliated with the AFL in 1900.

The Brotherhood of Locomotive Firemen was organized in 1873. In 1906 it adopted the name Brotherhood of LOCOMOTIVE Firemen and Enginemen.

The Lumber Handlers of the Great Lakes was founded in 1892 and received its AFL charter in 1893 as the National Longshoremen's Association of the United States. In 1895 it was renamed the International Longshoremen's Association. It became the International Longshoremen, Marine, and Transport Workers' Association in 1901 but changed its name back to the International LONGSHOREMEN's Association in 1908.

The Order of United Machinists and Mechanical Engineers of America was organized in 1888 and the following year changed its name to the National Association of Machinists. It changed its name again, in 1891, to the International Association of MACHINISTS, affiliating with the AFL in 1895.

The United MINE Workers of America was established in 1890 with the merger of the National Progressive Union of Miners and Mine Laborers and KOL National Trade Assembly 135 (miners). The new union affiliated with the AFL the same year.

Locals of the Paving Cutters' Union of the United States and Canada, which was organized in Baltimore in 1887, reorganized in 1901 as the Paving Cutters' Union of the United States of America and received an AFL charter. In 1904 the union changed its name to the International PAVING Cutters' Union of the United States of America and Canada.

. The International PHOTO-ENGRAVERS' Union of North America was organized in 1900 by seceding locals of the International Typographical Union, which recognized its jurisdiction by a referendum vote in 1903. The AFL chartered the union in 1904.

In 1889 representatives of KOL District Assembly 85 and the moribund International Association of Journeymen Plumbers, Steamfitters, and Gasfitters founded the United Association of Journeymen Plumbers, Gas Fitters, Steam Fitters, and Steam Fitters' Helpers of the United States and Canada, which affiliated with the AFL in 1897. It changed its name to the United Association of Plumbers and Steam Fitters of the United States and Canada in 1913 and to the United Association of Journeymen PLUMBERS and Steam Fitters of the United States and Canada in 1921.

The International Printing Pressmen's Union of North America was founded in 1889 and affiliated with the AFL in 1895. In 1897 it changed its name to the International Printing PRESSMEN's and Assistants' Union of North America.

The QUARRY Workers' International Union of North America was organized in 1903 and chartered by the AFL the same year.

The Canadian Brotherhood of RAILROAD Employees, a national industrial union, was organized in 1908. In 1917 it affiliated with the Trades and Labor Congress of Canada. That year it also assumed authority to grant charters in the United States, which led to jurisdictional conflict with the Brotherhood of Railway and Steamship Clerks, Freight Handlers, Express and Station Employes. The Trades and Labor Congress tried to amalgamate the two unions, but when that effort failed it revoked the Railroad Employees' charter in 1920. The revocation was reversed by the courts but was reinstated by the Congress in 1921.

The Order of Railway Clerks of America was organized in 1899 and affiliated with the AFL in 1900; it withdrew from the Federation in 1901. The organization adopted the name Brotherhood of Railway Clerks in 1904 and reaffiliated with the AFL in 1908. It adopted the name Brotherhood of RAILWAY and Steamship Clerks, Freight Handlers, Express and Station Employes in 1919.

The Brotherhood of RAILWAY Carmen of America was organized in 1890 through the merger of the Brotherhood of Railway Car Repairers of North America, the Carmen's Mutual Aid Association, the Car Inspectors', Repairers', and Oilers' Protective Association, and the Brotherhood of Railway Carmen of Canada. It received an AFL charter in 1910.

The Conductors' Union was organized in 1868, changed its name to the Conductors' Brotherhood in 1869, and was renamed the Order of RAILWAY Conductors of America in 1878.

The National Association of Railway Postal Clerks was organized in 1891. In 1904 it was renamed the RAILWAY Mail Association, and in 1917 it affiliated with the AFL.

The Tin, Sheet Iron, and Cornice Workers' International Association was organized in 1888 and affiliated with the AFL the following year. Its charter was recalled in 1896. The union reorganized in 1897 as the Amalgamated Sheet Metal Workers' International Association, which was chartered by the AFL in 1899. In 1903 it merged with the Sheet Metal Workers' National Alliance, a secessionist group that had broken away from the union in 1902, to form the Amalgamated SHEET Metal Workers' International Alliance. In 1907 the international amalgamated with the Coppersmiths' International Union and, in 1924, absorbed the chandelier, brass, and metal workers, adopting the name Sheet Metal Workers' International Association.

The International SHINGLE Weavers' Union of America was organized and affiliated with the AFL in 1903. In 1913 the union changed its name to the International Union of Shingle Weavers, Sawmill Workers, and Woodsmen, and in 1914 to the International Union of Timberworkers. It reorganized in 1916 under its original name and in 1918 amalgamated with a newly organized International Union of Timberworkers and adopted that name. The union disbanded in 1923.

The Amalgamated Association of Street Railway Employes of America was established in 1892 and affiliated with the AFL in 1893. It absorbed the Brotherhood of Surface Car Employes in 1894. In 1903 it changed its name to the Amalgamated Association of STREET and Electric Railway Employes of America.

The Journeymen Tailors' National Union of the United States was organized in 1883 and chartered by the AFL in 1887. It changed its name in 1889 to the Journeymen Tailors' Union of America and in January 1914 to the Tailors' Industrial Union. It merged that year with the Amalgamated Clothing Workers of America but in 1915 seceded from the Clothing Workers and reassumed the name Journeymen TAILORS' Union of America.

In 1898 several team drivers' locals combined to form the Team Drivers' International Union, which received an AFL charter in 1899. Seceding Chicago locals organized the Teamsters' National Union in 1901, and in 1903 the two unions merged to form the International Brotherhood of Teamsters. In 1910 the union changed its name to the International Brotherhood of TEAMSTERS, Chauffeurs, Stablemen, and Helpers of America.

The National Union of Textile Workers of America was organized in 1891, affiliated with the AFL in 1896, and changed its name to the International Union of Textile Workers in 1900. The following year it merged with the American Federation of Textile Operatives and several AFL federal labor unions to form the United TEXTILE Workers of America.

Sawmill and logging camp workers in the Pacific Northwest formed the International Union of TIMBERWORKERS in January 1917 and received an AFL charter in August of that year. The Timberworkers absorbed the International Shingle Weavers' Union of America in April 1918. The union disbanded in 1923.

The National Typographical Union was organized in 1852 by a group of locals that had held national conventions in 1850 and 1851 under the name Journeymen Printers of the United States. In 1869 it adopted the name International TYPOGRAPHICAL Union. The AFL chartered the union in 1888.

INDEX

Names of persons or organizations for whom there are glossary entries are followed by an asterisk.

An italicized page number indicates the location of a substantive annotation in the notes following a document. While this index is not cumulative, it includes references to substantive annotations or glossary entries in earlier volumes that are relevant to this one but that are not repeated here; these appear first in the index entry. For example, reference to the substantive annotation of Albert Adamski in volume 9 appears in this index as *9:406n;* the glossary entry for Henry Abrahams in volume 2 is referenced in this index as *2:**.

Abern, Martin, 275–77, 277–*78n*
Abrahams, Henry, *2:**, 91n
Accidents, industrial, benefits for, 6
The Acquisitive Society (Tawney), 191, *192n*
Adamski, Albert, *9:406n,* 550
Addams, Jane, *9:231–32n,* 427n
Adkins et al. v. *Children's Hospital of D.C.,* 227, *228n,* 230, 244, 246, 248–50, 370
Adolescents, 52–53
AFL. *See* American Federation of Labor
Albright, Albion D., 276, *278n*
Alcorn, Robert H., 345, *348n*
Alger, George W., *8:493n,* 74n
Alifas, Nels P., *10:21n,* 345–47
All-American Conference (1924, Washington, D.C.), 452, *452n*
Allen, Andrew J., 364, *364n*
Allen, Florence, 427n
Allen, Henry J., *11:290n,* 169
Allen, Henry T., *435n;* letter to, 435
All-Russian Congress of the Russian Communist Youth League, Fifth (1922, Moscow), 293, *294n*
Alpine, John R.,* 550, *553n*
Alschuler, Samuel B., *10:304n,* 154

American Anti-Saloon League, 429, *430n*
American Association for Labor Legislation, *9:277n;* and AFL Permanent Conference for Abolition of Child Labor, 82n
American Association of University Women, and AFL Permanent Conference for Abolition of Child Labor, 82n
American Civil Liberties Union, *10:485n,* 263–64, 265n, 309, 311n
American Committee for Relief of German Children, 435, *435n*
American Federationist, 277
American Federation of Labor (AFL): affiliates, autonomy of, 87n, 88, 89n; as bulwark against communism in U.S., 12, 172–73; financial resources of, 242–43; and local unions, affiliation with central bodies, 88, 89n; and local unions, affiliation with state federations of labor, 88; membership, 276; Scranton Declaration, *8:106n,* 102, 102n, 126; and transfer of union membership, 86, 87n
—Building Trades Department,

611

University of Illinois Press
1325 South Oak Street   Champaign, IL 61820-6903
www.press.uillinois.edu